JOYNSON-HICKS

ON

UK COPYRIGHT LAW

AUSTRALIA AND NEW ZEALAND
The Law Book Company Ltd.
Sydney : Melbourne : Perth

CANADA AND U.S.A.
The Carswell Company Ltd.
Agincourt, Ontario

INDIA
N.M. Tripathi Private Ltd.
Bombay
and
Eastern Law House Private Ltd.
Calcutta and Delhi
M.P.P. House
Bangalore

ISRAEL
Steimatzky's Agency Ltd.
Jerusalem : Tel Aviv : Haifa

MALAYSIA : SINGAPORE : BRUNEI
Malayan Law Journal (Pte.) Ltd.
Singapore and Kuala Lumpur

JOYNSON-HICKS

ON

UK COPYRIGHT LAW

by

David Lester

and

Paul Mitchell

London
Sweet & Maxwell
1989

Published in 1989 by
Sweet and Maxwell Limited of
South Quay Plaza
183 Marsh Wall
London E14 9FT

Computerset by CCI Technical Services Limited
Printed by Butler and Tanner, Frome, Somerset

British Library Cataloguing in Publication Data
Lester, David
   Joynson-Hicks on U.K. copyright law after the 1988
act.
   1. Great Britain. Copyright. Law
   I. Title   II. Mitchell, Paul
   344.1064'82

   ISBN 0–421–40960–6

This book
is dedicated
to
ROSINA HARRIS
Senior Partner, Joynson-Hicks 1977–1987
Member of the Whitford Committee
on Copyright Reform
and
COLIN FRASER
Partner, Taylor Joynson Garrett
Member of the Committee of the Music Copyright
Reform Group

PREFACE

We owe a great debt to many people both within and outside Joynson-Hicks who helped with the preparation of this book.

From within the firm, we should like to thank for help in relation to particular subjects Christopher Belk (on UK Competition Law), Emma Chamberlain (on domicile and residence), Peter Kempe (on insolvency), Richard Marsh (on employment), Deborah Stones (on damages) and Jean Woodhead (on probate). Deborah Stones also prepared the comparative table which appears as Appendix 1. Sarah Faulder and Charles Lloyd both read sections of the book and gave us much help. Particular thanks, however, are due first to Alison Sarsfield-Hall and Nainan Shah who both covered a wide variety of specific subjects in the research carried out for us as well as preparing the table in Appendix 3, and secondly to our secretaries Julie Taylor and Carla Farrell who cheerfully bore the burden of additional work and our frequent re-drafting.

From outside the firm, we had the benefit of advice from several sources. Jean-Francois Bellis of Messrs. Van Bael & Bellis in Brussels very kindly offered to read the sections on the Treaty of Rome, and we benefited greatly from his expertise in relation to the effect of EEC law on intellectual property rights. Richard Spearman of Counsel gave us considerable help on the complicated provisions on qualifying for copyright protection, and Robert Abrahams, Director of External Affairs for the Performing Right Society Limited on broadcasts and cable programmes. Michael Wisher of Urquhart-Dykes & Lord and John Cheyne of Haseltine Lake & Co. both gave valuable comments and advice on the sections dealing with the new design right. Robert Englehart Q.C. to our great good fortune agreed to read the whole book through, and his invaluable suggestions and comments helped throw much light on many of the murkier provisions of the 1988 Act.

To our publishers we are most grateful for being patient with us when it must on occasions have felt as if we were carrying out the writers' equivalent of what the Opposition in the Standing Committee on the Bill called "legislating on the hoof."

To the dedicatees of this book we owe a particular debt which it is impossible to repay. Not only did they offer us much advice in the writing of this book, but their enormous experience as well as their encouragement gave us the inspiration to write it in the first place.

We owe it to all these parties not just to thank them but also to emphasise that they are not responsible for any errors or omissions which may appear.

The division of labour in the writing of the book was that David Lester was responsible for Chapters 1 to 10 and 14, and Paul Mitchell for Chapters 11 to 13.

vii

Preface

We have tried to explain the law as we understood it to be on January 1, 1989. However, due to the kindness of our publisher, we have been able to incorporate the most important developments up to April 30, 1989 and in some cases beyond.

Since writing this book, Joynson-Hicks has merged with Taylor Garrett to form the new firm of Taylor Joynson Garrett.

CONTENTS

Contents

Contents

INTRODUCTION

The Copyright Designs and Patents Act 1988 received Royal Assent on November 15, 1988. The provisions relating to "Peter Pan" (see Chapter 14) came into effect immediately. The remainder of the provisions dealt with in this book will come into effect on August 1, 1989.

The 1988 Act is the first major overhaul of copyright legislation for over 30 years, and is the culmination of a 15 year process of re-examination of copyright law in the United Kingdom. There is little point at this stage in reporting the history of this process. However, the Report of the Whitford Committee (Cmnd. 6732), the two Green Papers (Cmnd. 8302 and 9445) and the White Paper on Intellectual Property and Innovation (Cmnd. 9712) still make interesting reading, not only as a record of how new technology and copyright issues can develop and change over a period of years. Equally fascinating are the various versions of the Bill from its first draft to its final form, and many of the debates which took place in both Houses.

It is perhaps useful to record briefly those proposals for change in the White Paper which failed to reach the Act. First and foremost, the levy on audio-only blank tape proposed as compensation for copyright owners in return for entitling domestic users to make private recordings. With the arrival of Lord Young and Kenneth Clarke at the Department of Trade and Industry, the proposal disappeared even before the Bill was first published, and the Government thereafter resisted all attempts to incorporate enabling powers in the Bill with the same commitment as it had previously demonstrated in favour of a levy. Secondly, the proposal that copying for the purposes of commercial research be excluded from the scope of the fair dealing exception for research and private study was abandoned during the passage of the Bill. Lastly, proposals to strengthen the general presumptions on subsistence and ownership of copyright in infringement proceedings were not fulfilled. These of course are not the only differences between the proposals in the White Paper and the provisions of the Act, and in many other cases, initial proposals were modified as a result of representations made to the Government.

The "layman's guide" to the Bill published by the Department of Trade and Industry at the same time as the Bill was introduced claimed that the Bill was a "fresh statement of the law on a more logical and consistent basis, taking account of the technological changes of the last 30 years." There is no doubt that the Act itself is easier to find one's way about. In particular, the old distinction between Part I works (literary, dramatic, musical and artistic works) and Part II subject-matter (sound recordings, films and so on) has been removed. Particular topics such as ownership and duration are now dealt with in one place for all works. Generally, the new Act is not "labrynthine" as the 1956 Act has been described, and where one is reminded of that damning description by Lord Wilberforce

(*Infabrics* v. *Jaytex* [1981] 1 All E.R. 1057 at p. 1060), this is not so much due to the lay-out or drafting of the Act as the nature of the subject itself.

Of course, there are specific problems with the provisions of the 1988 Act, and many of these are highlighted in the text of this book. Strangely perhaps, the general criticism which might be made lies in its professed aim to make the law more logical and consistent. Leaving aside those provisions which many would say are neither logical nor consistent, it could be argued in any event that in copyright law logic and consistency are laudable aims, but in practice can create difficulties where concepts which make sense in relation to one area cause confusion when applied to others.

Anyone who reads just the body of the 1988 Act will get a very distorted veiw of copyright law in this country. This is because the main provisions of the 1988 Act are modified, in many cases quite drastically, in relation to works created prior to commencement of the 1988 Act, and many of these works will remain in copyright well into and perhaps even throughout the next century. These modifications are tucked away in Schedule 1 to the Act, which for the most part failed to provoke debate during the passage of the Bill — not surprisingly perhaps, since the "tortuous and labrynthine" description almost seems understated here. These modifications preserve for existing works much of the law which subsisted under legislation in force at the time such works qualified for copyright protection — even in some cases pre-1911 Act legislation. One of the aims of this book has been to integrate the rules in Schedule 1 with those in the body of the Act, so that it is (hopefully) clearer which rules apply to which works.

The principal aim of this book is to provide a concise summary of copyright law following the commencement of the 1988 Act. In each chapter, a summary of the relevant provisions of the new Act is provided, together, where relevant, with a comparison of the 1988 Act with the 1956 Act. It is necessary to emphasise that the book is a summary of the law only, and copyright law is impossible to explain concisely without sacrificing some of the detail which could be relevant to individual cases. The book is not therefore a substitute for legal advice where difficult or unusual problems arise.

This book is intended as a practical guide to the law both for lawyers and those who work in areas where copyright law is a vital aspect of the relevant business, either in terms of copyright owner or user. By and large, it deals with the various aspects of the law in the same order as the 1988 Act covers them, although in some cases we felt that it would be better to consider specific provisions in a different place.

Finally, it may help to provide a very basic outline of this book in order to indicate where particular aspects are dealt with:-

(1)   Copyright is a species of property which subsists in certain works. These works are referred to in Chapter 1. Copyright subsists in works, not in articles which embody those works. Only original works are protected in the sense that the work must not simply be a copy of a previous work.

(2)   No United Kingdom copyright subsists in a work unless it qualifies for copyright protection under the rules referred to in Chapter 2, either because of its connection with the United Kingdom or some other country. There is no system requiring registration of a work for copyright to subsist in the United Kingdom.

(3)   The first owner of the copyright in a work depends on the category of work. This is dealt with in Chapter 3. Ownership may be transferred either by the first or a subsequent owner or in some cases by operation of law: this subsequent ownership is dealt with in Chapter 8.

(4)   Copyright is not perpetual, but subsists only for a limited period of time, after which the work falls into the public domain. The duration of copyright depends on the category of work. This is dealt with in Chapter 4.

(5)   Copyright is in essence a negative right which gives the owner the right to prevent others doing certain acts in relation to the relevant works. These acts are divided into primary restricted acts (where generally absence of knowledge is no defence) and secondary acts (where knowledge to some degree is generally a pre-requisite for the provision to apply). Primary acts are dealt with in Chapter 5 and secondary acts in Chapter 6.

(6)   In some cases, acts which the copyright owner would normally be able to prevent are permitted without infringing copyright. These permitted acts are dealt with in Chapter 7. The licensing and exploitation of copyright works are also subject to control in certain cases, the two main examples being the jurisdiction of the Copyright Tribunal and the effect of competition law: these aspects are dealt with in Chapter 9.

(7)   If copyright is infringed, both the owner of the copyright and an exclusive licensee are given remedies not only against a person doing the relevant act but, in the case of primary acts of infringement, a person authorising the act to be done. Remedies include injunctions to prevent further infringement, damages, an account of profits and delivery-up, destruction or forfeiture of infringing copies. Criminal proceedings will also lie against an infringer in many cases. Remedies for infringement are dealt with in Chapter 10.

(8)   The 1988 Act creates a new unregistered design right which will exist in original designs. The purpose of this new design right is to replace the copyright protection previously given to industrial designs, which was considered to be unjustifiably great. The new design right and its relationship with copyright are discussed in Chapter 13.

(9)   Some new Moral Rights are expressly protected for the first time in United Kingdom law by the 1988 Act. Four specific moral rights are created, one of which, the false attribution right was dealt with in the 1956 Act. The other three are entirely new, and

are the right to be identified as author or director, the right to object to derogatory treatment of a work and the right to privacy in relation to certain photographs and films. All these rights are dealt with in Chapter 11.

(10) The law relating to rights in performances is substantially changed. The Performers' Protection Acts 1958 to 1972 are repealed and replaced by a much more comprehensive set of rules. Civil remedies for infringement of those rights are introduced expressly for the first time. Rights are conferred not only on performers, but also on those "having recording rights." The new provisions and the Performers' Protection Acts, which continue to apply to acts done prior to August 1, 1989, are covered in Chapter 12.

TABLE OF CASES

TABLE OF STATUTES

1 THE WORKS PROTECTED BY COPYRIGHT

I INTRODUCTION

Copyright only subsists in certain works, and this Chapter deals with those works and their definitions.   **1.01**

1. Summary of the 1988 Act

Under the 1988 Act, copyright subsists in the following: **1.02**
(a) Original literary works
(b) Original dramatic works
(c) Original musical works
(d) Original artistic works
(e) The typographical arrangement of published editions
(f) Sound recordings
(g) Films
(h) Broadcasts
(i) Cable programmes

2. Subsistence in works not articles

Copyright subsists in works and not articles which embody or reproduce those works. For example, a record may not only contain a copyright in the sound recording reproduced on that record, but also copyrights in one or more musical and literary works (for example, the music and lyrics of a song), and perhaps a copyright in a drawing reproduced on the label. The record itself is not a copyright work.   **1.03**

3. Comparison between the 1956 Act and the 1988 Act

The 1988 Act has made some changes as regards the definitions of works in which copyright subsists, as follows: **1.04**

(a) It is no longer a special condition of protection for choreographic works such as ballets or works of mime that they be reduced to writing although they are still subject to the general requirements on fixation. (See paragraphs 1.12 and 1.18.)

(b) As regards works of architecture, a part of a building (such as one room) or of a fixed structure is now protected in its own right. (See paragraph 1.28.)

(c) The typographical arrangement copyright now covers any part of a literary, dramatic or musical work, as well as the whole of such a work or one or more such works. (See paragraph 1.41.)

(d) The sound-track of a film is no longer protected as a part of a film, but as a sound recording. (See paragraph 1.45.)

(e) The definition of broadcast has been amended, so that it now covers so-called Fixed-Satellite Service transmissions, and it is no longer necessary that the broadcast be made by the BBC, IBA or certain foreign organisations. (See paragraph 1.51.)

(f) Cable programme services where the apparatus is situated in premises in single occuption are no longer excluded from the definition of those to which the copyright provisions apply if they are operated as part of the amenities provided for residents or inmates of premises run as a business. (See paragraph 1.59.)

(g) A collage is now protected as an artistic work. (See paragraph 1.26.)

(h) The definitions of literary, dramatic and musical works, photographs, sound recordings and films have been revised, and a new term introduced in the context of artistic works, namely that of a graphic work.

4. The effect of the 1988 Act on existing works

1.05 If under the new Act works are protected which would not have been under the 1956 Act, this does not mean that an existing work unprotected in 1987 will be given protection after the 1988 Act comes into force. The transitional provisions state that copyright subsists in an existing work after commencement of the new Act only if it was protected immediately before commencement. (See schedule 1 paragraph 5(1).)

II LITERARY, DRAMATIC, MUSICAL AND ARTISTIC WORKS

1.06 This section deals first with literary, dramatic and musical works, and the requirement that they be recorded as a condition of protection. It then considers artistic works. No literary, dramatic, musical or artistic work is protected by copyright unless it is original, and therefore the law on this is subsequently summarised. Finally the possibility of protection being refused on grounds of public policy is considered.

A. LITERARY, DRAMATIC AND MUSICAL WORKS

1. Literary works (s.3(1))

1.07 Neither the 1911 nor the 1956 Acts contained a comprehensive definition of a literary work. The 1988 Act includes this for the first time. It means any work (other than a dramatic or musical work) which is written, spoken or sung. This is expressly stated to include a table or compilation, and a computer program.

"Written" is very widely defined. It includes any form of notation or code, and it does not matter whether this is done by hand or otherwise. Neither does it matter by what method it is recorded, nor the medium on which it is recorded.

Thus, in considering what is protected as literary works, it is necessary first of all to forget any requirement of aesthetic merit, and secondly any need for writing in the conventional sense of that word. Neither does it matter whether the work consists of words or numbers, or a combination of the two.

Examples of works which were held to be protected as literary works **1.08** under pre-1988 Act legislation are as follows:

—calendars

—catalogues and directories

—letters and telegrams, even if of a business nature

—forms

—timetables

—lists of information, such as football fixtures or television and radio programmes

—football coupons

—reports, such as those of speeches

—statistical or mathematical tables

—rules of games

—examination papers

—the lyrics of a song

—a written work in code

In our view, each of the above would be protected under the new Act subject to the requirements of fixation and originality. Indeed, the new definition may be even wider than the old one. In a case under the 1956 Act, *Exxon Corporation* v. *Exxon Insurance Consultant International Limited* ([1982] Ch. 119), Stephenson L.J. said as follows:

"I would have thought, unaided or unhampered by authority, that unless there is something in the context of the Act which forbids it, a literary work will be something which was intended to afford either information and instruction, or pleasure in the form of literary enjoyment . . . "

Under the 1988 Act, a literary work need not have been created with

3

any such intention. If the work is written, spoken or sung, it is protected, provided that it is not a dramatic or musical work, and that it is also an original work as referred to in paragraph 1.30 below.

1.09   The point at issue in the *Exxon* case was whether the word "Exxon" was a literary work. Submissions were made to the court that a great deal of effort had been put in to composing a suitable word for the plaintiff's business. It was argued therefore that the word was original, as well as both literary and a work. The judges of the Court of Appeal did not say whether they accepted that each of these three constituents of the phrase "original literary work" was fulfilled, but simply said that in their view the word "Exxon" did not come within the definition.

Whether or not the *Exxon* case would be decided differently today depends upon whether one word can be said to be a work. As referred to in the judgment of Stephenson L.J. in the *Exxon* case, one definition of a work (in Webster's Dictionary) is " ... something produced or accomplished by effort, exertion, or exercise of skill ... something produced by the exercise of creative talent or expenditure of creative effort." Certainly it is arguable that in the *Exxon* case, this was fulfilled. However, we still believe it unlikely that the courts will wish to grant copyright protection to a single word if only on policy grounds.

(a) *Tables and compilations*

1.10   As stated, the definition of literary work in the 1988 Act expressly refers to tables and compilations. Examples of tables which were held to be protected under the 1956 Act are included in paragraph 1.08.

A compilation could be of information gathered from different sources, or of poems or short stories. As collections of information, databases for computer programs will in most cases be protected as compilations, and therefore as literary works.

Particularly in the case of works such as anthologies of poems or short stories, the individual constituents of compilations may be protected as well as the selection and arrangement of those constituents.

(b) *Computer programs*

1.11   Until 1985, it was unclear to what extent computer programs were protected under the 1956 Act. It was generally accepted that they were protected as a species of literary work, although there was more doubt about whether object codes were protected than source codes. The Copyright (Computer Software) Amendment Act 1985 clarified the position by stating that the Copyright Act 1956 applied to computer programs as it applied in relation to literary works, and this applied to pre-1985 computer programs as well as ones made after the commencement of the 1985 Act.

The 1988 Act follows the 1985 Act in not defining what a computer program is, and it is clear from the debates in the Standing Committee that this was deliberate policy, because the advances in technology were such that any definition might have the effect of limiting the scope of what could be protected in the future. One judicial definition, which appears in the judgment of Gibbs C.J. in the High Court of Australia case *Computer Edge Pty. Ltd.* v. *Apple Computer Inc.* ([1986] F.S.C. 537), is that "a computer program is a set of instructions designed to cause a computer to perform a particular function or to produce a particular result."

A computer program as with any other literary work can be recorded in many ways. So, copyright can subsist in a computer program whether it is handwritten or printed out, stored on a floppy disk, tape cassette or Random Access Memory (RAM) semi-conductor chip or more permanently embodied in a Read Only Memory (ROM) semi-conductor chip. Some computer programs are an essential part of the operation of the computer but may not have any other function. Such programs enable the computer to do its job and are capable of protection in the same way as those programs with external functions which they help to run.

Computer programs are also used in the operation of databases. As referred to above, the information stored in a database might well be protected as a literary work. The information stored in the database should be distinguished from the computer program used to operate and update it: the distinction could be important in relation to rental rights. (See paragraph 5.26.) However, it should be appreciated that using the computer program will often involve using the relevant database, and vice versa.

2. Dramatic works (s.3(1))

Under the 1988 Act, as the 1956 Act, there is no exhaustive definition of   **1.12**
such a work. The 1988 Act simply states that it includes a work of dance or mime. Under the 1956 Act, works of dance or mime were protected only if they were reduced to writing in the form in which they were to be presented. This meant for example that if a ballet was filmed, but not notated in any form, the work would not have been protected. This would not be the same now although these works like all dramatic works are subject to the general requirement of fixation referred to in paragraph 1.18 below.

The 1956 Act also stated that a post-1956 Act film was not a dramatic work. The 1988 Act omits this, and the question arises whether in certain cases a film could be protected both itself as a work in its own right, and as a dramatic work. We doubt whether the Courts would hold that a film itself, as opposed to the content of a film in certain cases, could be a dramatic work, but the point is not free from doubt.

Examples of dramatic works otherwise are as follows: **1.13**

—plays

—operas

—ballets

—musicals

—revues

5

(a) *Works contrasted with performances*

A work such as a literary work or musical work does not become a dramatic work simply because it is presented in a dramatic manner. Thus, in *Fuller* v. *Blackpool Winter Gardens and Pavilion Company* ([1895] 2 Q.B. 429), it was held by the Court of Appeal that a song performed by someone in costume and accompanied by dramatic action would not in itself be a dramatic piece. The case was decided under an earlier statute, but would probably be decided in the same way now. Of course, if the song was an individual number from a musical or opera, then it would probably be protected as a substantial part of the whole work and the lyrics and the music of a song would also be protected separately.

A dramatic work is something the performance of which requires acting, or, at least, dancing. However, one must be careful here to distinguish between the work itself, and how the work is performed. If the stage directions in a play state that a character must behave in a certain way at a crucial point in the plot, that is part of the dramatic work. If it does not appear in the stage directions, but is simply part of one actor's interpretation, it is not part of the work.

(b) *Pre-1956 Act films* (schedule 1, para. 7)

1.14   Pre-1956 Act films are not protected as films in their own right, but only either as dramatic works, or as a series of photographs or (in the case of cartoons), drawings. However, it is not every pre-1956 Act film which is protected as a dramatic work. Under the 1911 Act, a film was protected as a dramatic work only where the arrangement or acting form or the combination of incidents represented gave the work an original character, and it is only these pre-1956 Act films which will still be protected as dramatic works under the 1988 Act.

This means that a pre-1956 Act film must be original in two ways. First, it must be original in the general sense used in paragraph 1.30, and secondly it must have an original character drawn from the arrangement or acting form or the combination of incidents. This does not in our view limit the expression to theatrical motion pictures, because films such as documentaries may be given an original character by the combination of incidents included in the film. The expression is however unlikely to apply to simple newsreel, although even there, a film which takes individual parts from several newsreels and combines them to make a documentary would probably come within the definition.

3. Musical works (s.3(1))

1.15   Neither the 1911 nor the 1956 Acts contained a definition of a musical work, and it seems that no judge in this century at least has been prepared to define its parameters under United Kingdom law. The 1988 Act gives an exhaustive definition, and states that a musical work is a work consisting of music, exclusive of any words or action intended to be sung, spoken or performed with the music.

This definition does not really take the position any further, and it is beyond the scope of this work to define what music is. The practical difficulty perhaps comes with sound effects, where there may be a thin dividing line between what is a musical work and what is simply sound but not music.

(a) *Lyrics*

It has already been stated that the lyrics of a song are protected as a   **1.16**
literary work, so the words and music of a song are protected separately. In *Williamson Music Ltd.* v. *The Pearson Partnership Ltd.* ([1987] F.S.R. 97), Deputy Judge Paul Baker Q.C. held that it was misleading to think of the words and music in mutually exclusive compartments, because when the words are sung they are part of the music. In our view, it is certainly misleading to separate out the vocal line or lines from instrumental lines in the music, but one must still ignore the actual words for the purposes of defining the parameters of the musical work. If a voice is singing a vocal line without any words (a vocalise), that is part of the music. If the voice part has words to it, one should ignore the actual words and treat the vocal line as part of the music in the same way as an instrumental line is part of the music.

(b) *Works contrasted with performances*

Again, one must distinguish between the musical work itself, and the   **1.17**
interpretation of that musical work. However, the dividing line in music is difficult to draw. This is particularly so in some modern classical music where on occasions the directions given to the performers are of the nature of general instructions to the performer as to what to do at a given point rather than precisely defining the actual notes or the way in which the notes are sung or played. A similar difficulty arises with much modern popular music which is frequently not written down. Where a performer writes and performs his own music, and records it first without writing it down this interpretation of it must be taken into account as part of the musical work which is protected. (See further paragraph 1.18.)

4. The requirement of fixation (s.3(2))

There is no copyright in a literary, dramatic or musical work, unless and   **1.18**
until it is recorded, whether in writing or otherwise. In the 1956 Act, the equivalent section (s.49(4)) stated that the work must first be reduced to writing or some other material form. Although there was some argument about the meaning of this, it was generally accepted that this applied where a work was recorded on to tape, but the new definition now makes this clear.

The effect of the provision is to define the time from when copyright subsists. If a restricted act (see Chapter 5) is done in relation to a work prior to that time, no infringement takes place, because there is at that stage no copyright to infringe. This can be best demonstrated by an example. A composer composes at the piano a new song. Someone overhears the song, thinks that the melody is wonderful, and writes it down. The composer then records the work on to tape. The second person subsequently gets a record company to make a recording including the melody. Although the writing down of the melody by the second person would not have infringed copyright, because the copyright did not yet subsist, the subsequent recording of the melody after it had been recorded on to tape by the composer would be an infringement.

Copyright subsists as soon as the relevant work is recorded by anyone. It does not matter whether this was done by the author, or even whether he knew or agreed to the work being recorded. (See s.3(3).)

1.19   Nowadays, recording is used as much in the process of creating a literary, dramatic or musical work as in providing a vehicle for expressing such a work in permanent form. This gives rise to copyright problems which the Courts have not yet faced. For example, it is now common for popular music to be created with the aid of a computer-aided device known as a "Fairlight". Individual elements of a musical work are created and stored separately, and can be changed both individually and in combination ad infinitum to create ultimately what the writers believe to be the perfect work. The difficult question is not only whether the individual elements are works in their own right, but also whether each earlier version of the musical work is itself the subject of copyright. There is no requirement that a work be recorded permanently or be in final form for it to be the subject of copyright.

Similar conceptual problems arise in relation to works which are constantly being altered. The example commonly used is that of a database containing facts and figures which are regularly up-dated. The question which arises there is whether each time some of the information contained in the database is altered a fresh work is created.

These are complex problems, which fortunately have not yet seemed to have caused insuperable difficulties in practice. Our view is that, however transient it makes the definition of work, the Courts would be likely to accept generally that separate copyrights subsist in earlier versions of works and in altered versions. But it must be remembered that there must be a work (see the *Exxon* case paragraph 1.09) and there must still be originality. (See the *Interlego* case, paragraph 1.32.)

B. ARTISTIC WORKS (s.4)

1.20   Artistic works are defined as:

(a) Graphic works, photographs, sculptures or collages, irrespective of artistic quality.

(b) Works of architecture.

(c) Works of artistic craftsmanship.

The meaning of each of these is dealt with in turn.

Although there is no provision as regards artistic works that copyright does not subsist until it is fixed in some form or other, the above definitions are such that copyright cannot exist unless the work is in physical form.

1. Graphic works (s.4(2))

This word did not appear in the 1911 or 1956 Acts, but includes in its   **1.21**
definition under the 1988 Act many of the works which were mentioned separately as being protected under former legislation. The definition is not exhaustive, but is said to include any painting, drawing, diagram, map, chart or plan. It also includes any engraving, etching, lithograph, woodcut or similar work.

Most of the reported cases on artistic works over the last 10 years or so have concerned drawings, and in particular designs for products to be manufactured commercially. Under the 1988 Act, such drawings will still be protected as artistic works, but in many cases, the ability to use this copyright to prevent the manufacture of articles which are copies of the design will in future be much restricted, by reason of what is set out in Chapter 13 below.

The natural meaning of such works as engravings, woodcuts and so on   **1.22**
is the print which is produced by applying paper or some other material to the surface of the relevant block. In *James Arnold and Co. Ltd.* v. *Miafern Ltd.* ([1980] R.P.C. 397), it was held that the block itself was protected, and also that the word engraving covered not only those made by the process of cutting into metal or wood or other material, but also where the block was made in the form of a mould.

2. Photographs (s.4(2))

The definition of a photograph in the 1911 and 1956 Acts was broadly   **1.23**
similar. Under the 1911 Act (s.35) it included any work produced by any process analogous to photography, and under the 1956 Act (s.48(1)) it meant any product of photography or of any process akin to photography.

The 1988 Act seeks to define a photograph in rather more technical terms. Under the new provisions, a photograph is a recording of light or other radiation on any medium on which an image is produced or from which an image may by any means be produced.

The definition therefore covers not only photographs taken by the action of light, but those which are taken by heat-seeking methods and those recorded digitally, as well as holograms.

Individual stills from a film made after the commencement of the 1956   **1.24**
Act are not protected as photographs, but as part of the film. However, films made before the commencement of the 1956 Act are protected as a series of photographs, even where they are also dramatic works as referred to in paragraph 1.14.

The positive as well as the negative comes within the definition of photograph. However, whether or not a positive print will itself be the subject of copyright depends very much in this case on the question of originality. (See paragraph 1.33.)

3. Sculptures (s.4(2))

1.25   There is no exhaustive definition of this, but the expression, as in the 1956 Act, is said to include a cast or model made for purposes of sculpture. The words "for purposes of sculpture" were emphasised by Whitford J. in *J. & S. Davis (Holdings) Ltd.* v. *Wright Health Group Ltd.* ([1988] R.P.C. 403). In that case, it was held that models or casts of plastic dental impression trays were not sculptures, since they were made not for purposes of sculpture, but merely as a step in manufacture of the trays.

4. Collages

1.26   This expression did not appear in the 1911 or 1956 Acts, and accordingly may not have been protected unless it was a sculpture, or a work of artistic craftsmanship. According to the Oxford English Dictionary, a collage is an abstract form of art in which such items as photographs, pieces of paper, matchsticks and so on are placed in juxtaposition or glued to a pictorial surface.

5. "Irrespective of artistic quality"

1.27   All of the four categories of work referred to above are protected irrespective of artistic quality. Although there is no direct decision on the point, the decisions on industrial drawings under the 1956 Act demonstrate that what is meant by this is that it does not matter whether or not the work is artistic in character.

6. Works of architecture (s.4(2))

1.28   As under the 1956 Act (s.3(1)(b)), a work of architecture is defined as a building or a model for a building. Under the 1956 Act, a building was defined as including any structure. Under the 1988 Act the reference is only to any fixed structure. However, the introduction of the qualifying adjective "fixed" does not mean that a structure which is not fixed is incapable of protection as a work of architecture. It simply means that such a structure will not automatically be protected, but it could still be within the ordinary meaning of the word "building".

In *Vincent* v. *Universal Housing Co. Ltd.* ([1928–35] MacG. Cop. Cas. 275), a garden which consisted of a combination of steps, walls, ponds and other structures in stone was held to be a structure.

The 1988 Act also extends the definition of "building" to cover a part of a building or fixed structure. Thus, one room of a building could be protected as a work of architecture.

Under the 1911 Act, it was only architectural works of art which were protected, and emphasis was placed on artistic character and design, as opposed to processes or methods of construction. The reference to "art" was omitted in the 1956 and 1988 Acts, but on the other hand the words "irrespective of artistic quality" which apply to those artistic works already discussed were not included either. The general view however is that artistic quality is still not required because of the way in which the expression is defined simply as a building, rather than a building with artistic quality.

The plans for works of architecture are, of course, protected separately as graphic works.

7. Works of artistic craftsmanship

As in the 1911 and 1956 Acts, no definition of this expression is provided in the 1988 Act. The leading case on the point is *Hensher Ltd.* v. *Restawhile Upholstery (Lancs.) Ltd.* ([1976] A.C. 64), but reading the judgments in this case from that of the trial judge to those in the House of Lords merely demonstrates the difference of opinion which there can be as to the meaning of the phrase. In that case, the House of Lords refused protection for the prototype of a piece of modern furniture.   **1.29**

The problem arises from the use of the word "artistic." Obviously, it is not just any work of craftsmanship which is protected, or there would be no point in the addition of the word "artistic." Some of the judges emphasised that what was important was the intention behind the making of the work, and others not. Some focused on the meaning of the word "artistic," whilst others emphasised the importance of not breaking the phrase up, but simply considering as a matter of fact whether the work was one of artistic craftsmanship.

This is not the place to undertake a full analysis and commentary on the judgments, but one can perhaps best demonstrate the ordinary meaning of the phrase by examples taken from the judgment of Lord Simon. He emphasised not the nature of the craft, but what precisely the craftsman was making. Thus, when a glazier makes a pane of glass, he does not make work of artistic craftsmanship, but he may well do if he is making a stained-glass window. Similarly, a blacksmith might well make a work of artistic craftsmanship when he makes a wrought-iron gate, but not when he shoes a horse.

It is possible that a dress could be a work of artistic craftsmanship but this depends on the particular garment in question. Doubt was expressed in *Burke* v. *Spicers Dress Designs* ([1936] Ch. 400) as to whether an ordinary frock, even one of beauty, would be such a work although the point was left open in *Radley Gowns Ltd.* v. *Spyrou* ([1975] F.S.R. 455). In *Merlet* v. *Mothercare plc* ([1984] F.S.R. 358), Walton J. refused protection to a baby carrier which strapped the baby to its mother. The judge emphasised in that case that whether the work was one of artistic craftsmanship must be decided on the basis of looking at the work itself, not at the way in which it was used. Of course, copyright may in any event subsist in drawings and designs for such garments.

C. ORIGINALITY

1. General

1.30 No literary, dramatic, musical or artistic work can be protected by copyright unless it is an original work. The word "original" has a special meaning in copyright law. The classic summary is that of Peterson J. in *University of London Press Ltd.* v. *University Tutorial Press Ltd.* ([1916] 2 Ch. 601):

> " ... the Act does not require that the expression must be in an original or novel form, but that the work must not be copied from another work—that it should originate from the author."

However, even this statement can be misleading. A work may be substantially based on an earlier work, yet still be an original work in its own right for the purposes of copyright protection.

For a work to originate from an author, that author must have expended his own skill, labour or judgment in his creation of the work to a sufficient degree. Although the degree of skill and labour required is often said to be substantial, in fact the amount may seem to vary from case to case, and it is best to think of "substantial" in this context as meaning "of substance" rather than as importing any quantitative test. Indeed, the borderline between what will be protected as original and what will not is extremely difficult to define, and the cases are not always easy to distinguish on their facts.

2. Works consisting of commonplace material

1.31 Where the work consists of commonplace material, it will be refused copyright protection if there is no more than negligible skill or labour. It is on this basis that the courts have refused protection to titles (such as the titles of novels or songs), and advertising slogans. Most of the cases however on this are old, and with the amount of work which is now put into the development of a catch-phrase for an advertising campaign, the position may be different. In *Exxon Corporation* v. *Exxon Insurance Consultant International Limited* ([1982] Ch. 119) the word Exxon was invented after research and testing to find a suitable word over a long period of time, and Stephenson L.J. accepted that it was therefore "difficult, if not impossible, to say that it is not original."

In *Ladbroke (Football) Ltd.* v. *William Hill (Football) Ltd.* ([1964] 1 W.L.R. 273), a case on football coupons, it was argued that one had to distinguish between on the one hand the skill, labour or judgment in developing the ideas which led to the creation of the copyright work, and on the other hand, the skill, labour and judgment in creating the copyright work, and that only the latter was relevant for the purposes of deciding whether a work was original. Although some of the members of the House of Lords accepted that there could be cases where the distinction could be justified, the majority stressed that preparatory work in developing ideas to the stage when they are ready to be expressed in writing could be taken into account. In the words of Lord Devlin:

> "It is sufficient that the preparation of the document is an object of the work done. If that be so, the work cannot be split up and parts allotted to the several objects. The value of the work as a whole must be assessed when the claim to originality is being considered."

This is particularly important in the case of some lists of information. In *Independent Television Publications Ltd.* v. *Time Out Limited* ([1984] F.S.R. 64), it was argued that there could be no copyright in a list of mere information, such as a railway timetable, since the making of the actual list as opposed to the creation of the schedules which appeared in the list, involved insufficient skill, labour or judgment. The judge rejected this argument. Provided that there was sufficient skill, labour and judgment in the creation of the contents of the list (which he held there to be in the creation of the daily programme schedules which made up the list of programmes in the Radio and TV Times), the work was an original literary work.

3. Works based on existing works

Many literary, dramatic, musical or artistic works are derived from or based on existing works, whether copyright or in the public domain. An abridgement of a book will often attract its own copyright, as will an arrangement of an existing musical work (see *Redwood Music Ltd* v. *Chappell & Co. Ltd.* ([1982] R.P.C. 109)). However, the more the work one is considering is based on or uses one or more existing works (whether or not they are the subject of copyright protection) the more difficulty there is in applying the requirement of originality. **1.32**

A mere slavish copy of an existing work will not usually be an original work. For example, when someone takes a photocopy, they create a photograph, but the photocopy does not enjoy copyright protection since no skill and virtually no labour has been used to create it.

Even where skill, labour or judgment has been used in the process of copying, this will not confer originality where what is created is an exact and literal, or virtually exact and literal, reproduction. As stated by Lord Oliver in *Interlego A.G.* v. *Tyco Industries Inc.* ([1988] 3 All E.R. 949):

> "There must in addition be some element of material alteration or embellishment which suffices to make the totality of the work an original work. Of course, even a relatively small alteration or addition quantitatively may, if material, suffice to convert that which is substantially copied from an earlier work into an original work. Whether it does so or not is a question of degree having regard to the quality rather than the quantity of the addition. But copying per se, however much skill or labour might be devoted to the process could not make an original work."

Some specific problems and examples now need to be addressed:

(a) *Drawings*

1.33 The following passage appears in the judgement of Lord Oliver in the *Interlego* case:

> "Take the simplest case of artistic copyright, a painting or a photograph. It takes great skill, judgement and labour to produce a good copy by painting or to produce an enlarged photograph from a positive print, but no one would reasonably contend that the copy painting or enlargement was an "original" artistic work in which the copier is entitled to claim copyright".

The passage has been criticised as going too far, and certainly could lead to unfair results, particularly when one is considering the skill involved in copying, say, an oil painting.

In the *Interlego* case, design drawings had been regularly updated as minor modifications were made in design or to reflect changes in methods of manufacture. Visually, the deviations from the original drawings were insignificant. The Privy Council held that the deviations were not significant enough to lead to the creation of a new copyright in the revised drawings. Furthermore, although new explanatory material in the form of words and figures had been included in at least one drawing, what one was considering was whether the *artistic* work was original, and the addition of such words or figures could not confer on an artistic work an originality which it did not possess in its own right.

(b) *Photography*

1.34 The question was raised above as to whether a positive print from the negative of a photograph has its own copyright. In our view, the conventional commercial processing of film does not constitute sufficient skill and labour for a new original work to be created. It would be different if the person making positive prints used skill, labour or judgment in deciding the degree of exposure of different parts of the negative in order to create different effects of light and shade in the print.

(c) *Reports*

1.35 In *Walter* v. *Lane* ([1900] A.C. 539), reporters from *The Times* took down public speeches in shorthand, wrote out their notes, and then corrected, revised and punctuated their reports for publication. It was held that copyright subsisted in those reports, with the effect that no one could make a copy of the speech from that report without infringing copyright. Some doubt has been expressed as to whether this case is still good law, particularly since it was decided before the 1911 Act when the word "original" was introduced for the first time. The decision in the case is perhaps also inconsistent with the approach taken in the *Interlego* case.

(d) *Transcription of existing material*

Despite reservations which may arise about *Walter* v. *Lane*, the transcrip-   **1.36**
tion of existing material may still involve the type of skill, labour and
judgment which will mean that the work is protected by copyright. Take
the example of a music manuscript at the British Museum. The manuscript is difficult to decipher in places, and a musician transcribing it has to
decide both on the precise fall of the melody and harmonic progression to
accord with the style of the music of the particular period. He also adds
indications as regards instrumentation, and dynamics. In this type of
case, we believe that there is still copyright in the transcription as an
original work. This does not prevent anyone else from making their own
transcription from the manuscript, but prevents another musician taking
a short-cut by using the first musician's transcription.

(e) *Compilations*

Where the work is a compilation consisting of a collection of existing   **1.37**
material (such as a collection of poems or short stories), the labour and
skill consists of both the selection and arrangement of the existing
material.

4. Computer-generated works

Under a new provision under the 1988 Act (s.178) a computer-generated   **1.38**
work is one which is generated by computer in circumstances such that
there is no human author of the work: see further paragraph 3.54. It is
difficult to see how the normal principles of originality can be applied to a
situation where there is no human author from whom the work orig-
inates, and it seems likely that different principles will need to be evolved.
Since in many ways computer-generated works are treated for copyright
purposes as sound recordings and films, it is possible that the Courts
might say that the requirement of originality is fulfilled where the work is
not simply a copy taken from a previous work (compare for example
paragraph 1.46.)

D. REFUSAL OF PROTECTION

Throughout the eighteenth and nineteenth centuries, the courts fre-   **1.39**
quently refused protection to a work where it was blasphemous, libellous,
immoral or obscene. Even in the twentieth century, this has happened,
such as the cases of *Glyn* v. *Western Feature Film Co.* ([1916] 1 Ch. 261),
where a novel was refused protection on the grounds that it " . . . advo-
cate(d) free love and justifie(d) adultery where the marriage tie ha(d)
become merely irksome," and *A. Bloom and Sons Ltd.* v. *Black*
([1936–45] MacG. Cop Cas. 274), where a leaflet entitled "Last Will and
Testament of Adolf Hitler" was refused protection on the grounds that it
was essentially vulgar and indecent.

In other cases, protection was refused where the work for which protection was sought was fraudulent or intended to deceive the public. For example, in *Slingsby* v. *Bradford Patent Truck Co.* ([1905] W.N. 122), a catalogue of products falsely described the author as "inventor, patentee and sole maker" of these products, and also included misleading pictures of premises which the plaintiff occupied. Protection was refused.

It is uncertain to what extent these cases are still valid, especially where modern views of blasphemy or immorality are considerably different from what they were when many of these cases were decided. (See *Stephens* v. *Avery* 1988 2 All E.R. 477.) For example, there was no suggestion in *Chaplin* v. *Leslie Frewin (Publishers) Ltd.* ([1966] Ch. 71) that the book by Charlie Chaplin's son entitled "I Couldn't Smoke the Grass on My Father's Lawn" was not protected, even though the members of the Court of Appeal thought it "objectionable" and "vulgar trash."

However, that the doctrine is still relevant today is demonstrated by the House of Lords decision in the *Spycatcher* case, *Attorney-General* v. *Guardian Newspapers Ltd. (No. 2)* ([1988] 3 All E.R. 545); all the members of the House of Lords accepted that Peter Wright, as a member of the Security Service, owed a lifelong duty not to disclose confidential information which came into his possession whilst he served with the Security Service, and that publishing the book "Spycatcher" was a breach of that duty. In those circumstances, it was the view of four out of the five Law Lords (Lord Goff not expressing a view) that the Courts would not enforce a claim by Wright to copyright in the book, and three out of the five expressly stated that this extended to his publishers as well. Regrettably, the point was not one considered in detail by any of the four Law Lords, and it is unclear whether their views were based on the special circumstances of the case or whether the same principle would or could be applied to any work published in breach of a duty of confidence. (See paragraph 8.10 for further comment on this case.)

1.40   The remaining question is whether a work made in infringement of copyright can itself be protected by copyright.

It is unclear whether the decision of the House of Lords in the **Spycatcher** case has any bearing on whether copyright protection in a work made in infringement of copyright can be claimed by the infringer. It is certainly possible that the court could take a similar approach, and hold either that the new work is unprotected, or that copyright in equity belongs to the original owner. However, there are fundamental differences between the protection of confidential information and the protection of copyright which would justify a distinction being made.

There are two cases prior to the "Spycatcher" decision which are themselves inconsistent in their approach to the point. In *Redwood Music Ltd.* v. *Chappell & Co. Ltd.* ([1982] R.P.C. 109), Robert Goff J. held that copyright subsisted in arrangements of musical works even where they were made in infringement of copyright, and furthermore that the copyright belonged to the arranger. However in *Ashmore* v. *Douglas-Home*

([1987] F.S.R. 553), Judge Mervyn Davis appears to have denied copyright protection to a part of a play which was derived from an existing copyright play on the grounds that the former was "infringing material". In our view, the better approach is that of Robert Goff J., although the point is not free from doubt particularly in the light of the "Spycatcher" decision.

Of course, even where copyright subsists in the infringing work, and belongs to the infringer, exploitation of that work would usually involve infringement of the original copyright owner's rights, which he would be entitled to restrain or obtain recompense for.

III TYPOGRAPHICAL ARRANGEMENTS OF PUBLISHED EDITIONS

Whether or not a published literary, dramatic or musical work is protected by copyright, copyright subsists separately in the typographical arrangement of a published edition of such a work. This does not apply to published editions of artistic works and if a book includes a literary work with accompanying illustrations, the provision applies only to the words, not the drawings in the book.   **1.41**

Under the 1956 Act, copyright subsisted in the published edition, rather than the typographical arrangement of that edition. However, we do not believe that this change of emphasis has altered the position in practice. Under the 1956 Act, it was only an infringement of copyright to reproduce in certain ways the typographical arrangement of the edition, rather than the edition itself. On that basis, if there was no typographical arrangement, then there could be no infringement. Now, the effect is the same, since where there is no typographical arrangement, there can be no copyright and therefore no infringement.

The 1988 Act contains no definition of typographical arrangement. Neither did the 1956 Act. In debate before the House of Lords Committee considering the Bill, it was described by a Government representative as the layout of letters or symbols on the printed page.

Apart from the copyright in the typographical arrangement, there may be a separate copyright in an artistic work consisting of the design of a typeface. Where printing is carried out by engraving, there could also be protection in that way, and, particularly in the case of musical works, there may be protection by means of an original drawing.   **1.42**

Under the 1988 Act, the published edition may be of the whole or *any part* of one or more literary, dramatic or musical works. The 1956 Act only referred to any one or more such works. The limitation does not appear to have been a problem in practice, but it is clear now that if there is a published edition of one movement from a symphony or concerto, that would now be covered.   **1.43**

There is no use of the word "original" in relation to the typographical arrangement, or the published edition. However, a similar effect is achieved by stating that copyright does not subsist in the typographical arrangement of a published edition if, or to the extent that, it reproduces the typographical arrangement of a previous edition. If therefore some amendments have been made to the printed text of a Shakespeare play for the purposes of a new edition, then it is only the altered parts which would remain protected, assuming that the copyright in the original typographical arrangement has expired. It is arguable in any event that if these alterations were *de minimis*, there would no longer be a typographical arrangement left which could be protected, except to the extent that the original typographical arrangement was still in copyright.

IV SOUND RECORDINGS

1. The basic definition

1.44   A sound recording is defined under the 1988 Act (s.5(1)) as either of the following:

(a) A recording of sounds, from which the sounds may be reproduced

(b) A recording of the whole or any part of a literary, dramatic or musical work, from which sounds reproducing the work may be produced

The medium on which the recording is made (for example, a tape or a microchip) is irrelevant to whether there is protection, as it is the method by which the sounds can be reproduced or produced (for example, hi-fi equipment or a computer).

One distinction between the two alternatives is as follows. Where a musical work is performed in a recording studio, and that performance is recorded, that is a recording of sounds from the performance. However, not every recording from which sounds may be reproduced is a recording of sounds. An old example is a piano roll where the recording is created by perforations on paper made by registering the hammers of a piano. A more modern example might be where electronic digital patterns rather than sounds are embodied in a computer chip from which sounds can be produced. These recordings are therefore still protected provided that the recording is of the whole or any part of a literary, dramatic, musical or artistic work.

The other more obvious distinction between the alternatives is that it is not necessary under (a) that the recording be of a literary, dramatic or musical work. For example, recordings of non-musical sound effects could be protected under that provision.

Most modern recordings of music are made in the form of a master tape. It is arguable that the new definition of sound recording allows one to break down the constituent parts of a master tape further than under the 1956 Act for the purposes of defining what is protected. A modern master tape can be divided horizontally into individual tracks, and separate instrumental or vocal lines may be recorded on each individual track. Each individual track is capable of being reproduced separately, and accordingly may well now be a separate recording. This was arguably not so under the 1956 Act (s.12(9)), because copyright subsisted in the "aggregate" (that is the total) of the sounds embodied in the master tape, and an individual track or part of a track may not have been a substantial part of the whole. (See paragraph 5.09.) If each individual track is protected, this may well have an important practical effect as regards a copyright owner's ability to prevent sampling, where very often a small part of an individual track is taken and inserted into another recording.

Whether or not this means that individual tracks of existing sound recordings are now protected is not clear. As already stated (see paragraph 1.05), under the transitional provisions copyright subsists in an existing work after commencement of the new Act only if it subsisted immediately before the commencement of the Act. The problem is whether the reference to the existing work is to the whole sound recording as opposed to the individual track, and it is difficult to be certain on this.

2. Film sound-tracks

Under the 1956 Act, the sound-track of a film was not protected as a **1.45** sound recording, but as part of a film. The precise relationship between the relevant provisions of the 1956 Act on sound recordings and cinematograph films was the subject of some controversy. In our view, the provision in the 1956 Act did not prevent a sound recording embodied in the sound-track of a cinematograph film from ever having an independent copyright of its own. Taking the example of music, a master recording of music for a film could be used both in the film itself and for a sound-track album. When used as the latter, it was the subject of the sound recording copyright, but, when forming part of the film, it was protected as a cinematograph film.

Under the transitional provisions to the new Act (schedule 1, paragraph 8(1)), sound-tracks of existing films made under the 1956 Act which were formerly protected as part of the film will in future be treated as sound recordings. This is subject to the condition that copyright in the sound-track will subsist only if copyright subsisted in the film immediately before the commencement of the new Act. Thus, if the film failed to qualify for protection under the rules referred to in Chapter 2 below, the sound-track of the film will not be protected.

3. "Originality"

Although the word "original" is not used in connection with sound **1.46** recordings, a similar effect is achieved by a provision that copyright does not subsist in a sound recording which is, or to the extent that it is, a copy taken from a previous sound recording. One question is how this relates to restoration of old recordings. The development of digital recording techniques and other technological advances has made it possible to restore old recordings so that the sound which is reproduced by such recordings is much improved. The technique of restoration is in many cases both time-consuming and costly, and there would seem no reason in principle why there should not be protection for such a recording in its restored form. This would not prevent someone from copying the original form of the recording, but only the restored form. However, whether or not such a recording will receive fresh protection under the 1988 Act depends on the provision referred to in this paragraph. Whilst the point is not free from doubt, it is at least arguable that the use of the words "to the extent that it is" would allow the protection of the work involved in restoring such an old recording.

V FILMS

1.47   Before going into the detail on this, it is worth reiterating the following:

(a) Films made before the commencement of the 1956 Act are not protected as films, but are only capable of protection as dramatic works (see paragraph 1.14 above), photographs, (see paragraph 1.24 above), and, in the case of cartoons, drawings (see paragraph 1.21 above). The making of films very often extends over a long period of time, and the 1956 Act provided that a film was made after the commencement of the 1956 Act unless the making of it was completed before commencement. (See schedule 7, paragraph 45(2).) We believe this still applies, and it is not always easy to decide when completion takes place, particularly in the case of cartoons.

(b) Film sound-tracks are now protected as sound recordings, whether or not they are contained in new films or films made under the 1956 Act. (See paragraph 1.45.)

(c) It is arguable that a film is now also protected as a dramatic work. (See paragraph 1.12.)

1.48   Under the 1988 Act a film is defined as a recording on any medium from which a moving image may by any means be produced. (See s.5(1).) The definition obviously covers theatrical motion pictures and television films, as well as the visual part of material on video cassettes and compact disc video. It will also extend to cartoons (which will still also be protected as drawings), and other techniques such as the use of time-lapse photography.

The definition in the 1956 Act (s.13(10)) was a little more complex. There, a film was defined as any sequence of visual images recorded on material of any description so as to be capable, by the use of that material, either of being shown as a moving picture, or being recorded on other material by the use of which it could be shown as a moving picture. In *Spelling Goldberg Productions Inc.* v. *B.P.C. Publishing Ltd.* ([1981]

R.P.C. 283), it was the view of the Court of Appeal that every part of a complete film which was itself of sufficient duration to be shown a moving picture could also be a cinematograph film. This was because the reference was to "*any* sequence of visual images."

The point is an important one again because of the issue of substantiality which is referred to in paragraph 5.09 below. Whilst again the point is not free from doubt, it is our view that the same effect is achieved in the 1988 Act, because of the reference to "*a* moving image."

As with sound recordings, neither the medium from which the moving **1.49** image may be produced, nor the means of producing the image is relevant. For that reason again, computer programs and in particular many computer games, could be protected as films, as well as in their own right.

Again, as with sound recordings, copyright does not subsist in a film which is, or to the extent that it is, a copy taken from a previous film (see s.5(2)). If a documentary in 1988 includes newsreel footage from 1958, that footage will not be protected as part of the documentary. (Of course, assuming the newsreel footage qualified for copyright protection under the rules referred to in Chapter 2 it will still have an independent copyright). Furthermore, in our view, it does not matter if the film was made before the 1956 Act. Such a film is still within the definition of a film in the 1988 Act for these purposes.

VI BROADCASTS

1. Broadcasts made before commencement of the 1988 Act

No copyright subsists in a broadcast made before the commencement of **1.50** the 1956 Act. (See schedule 1, paragraph 9(a).) This does not affect the copyright in works included in a broadcast, for example, a film or sound recording, and the main effect is therefore on live broadcasts made before the 1956 Act and which were not recorded.

Under the 1956 Act, copyright only subsisted in broadcasts made by the BBC and the Independent Broadcasting Authority, and, as a result of various Orders in Council, in certain foreign broadcasts. If the broadcast was made before commencement of the 1988 Act, it will still only be protected under the new Act if it was one of these broadcasts. The definition of broadcasting under the 1956 Act only contained a reference to the 1949 Wireless Telegraphy Act, and there was no indication as to whether all transmissions by wireless telegraphy were covered or only those which were intended for direct reception by members of the public. Although there was much controversy about the precise meaning of broadcasting, generally it was accepted that fixed service satellite (or point to point) transmissions were not covered because these were not intended for direct reception by the public. Again, such transmissions if they took place before the commencement of the 1988 Act will not be protected under that Act.

2. Broadcasts protected under the 1988 Act (s.6)

1.51   Under the 1988 Act, a broadcast is protected whoever transmits it provided that it is a transmission by wireless telegraphy of visual images,
sounds or other information which is either capable of being lawfully
received by members of the public, or is transmitted for presentation to
members of the public. It therefore covers conventional terrestrial broadcasting, direct broadcasting by satellite, and fixed satellite service (or
point-to-point) transmissions. It also covers not only the transmission of
entertainment programming, but also such services as Oracle or Ceefax.
It obviously applies whether the broadcast is for radio or television
receivers.

There is a special provision on encrypted or coded transmissions.
These are to be regarded as capable of being lawfully received by members of the public only if decoding equipment has been made available to
members of the public. The equipment must have been made available by
or with the authority either of the person who is making the coded
transmission, or the person providing the contents of that coded transmission. It does not matter whether decoding equipment has only been made
available to a limited section of the public. The example used before the
House of Commons Standing Committee was the BBC's proposed night-
time service for the medical profession. Such broadcasts will therefore
still be protected by copyright.

The expression "capable of being lawfully received by members of the
public" is therefore extremely wide. It does not matter whether the
broadcast is primarily aimed at general reception by the public or not. A
transmission via satellite is often primarily intended for reception by a
cable programme service operator, for onward transmission by cable, but
still capable of being received by the public through a satellite dish. If
such reception is lawful, then the broadcast is one which is protected by
copyright.

The use of the alternative phrase "transmitted for presentation to
members of the public" was intended by the Government to cover the
situation where transmission, perhaps at a low level, takes place for the
purpose of presentation to public audiences at particular venues. An
example was given in debate of relays of sporting events or concerts to a
stadium or theatre, where at least part of the chain of transmissions is by
wireless telegraphy.

For a transmission to be protected as a broadcast, it must take place by
wireless telegraphy. This is defined in the 1988 Act as the sending of
electro-magnetic energy over paths not provided by a material substance
constructed or arranged for that purpose. (See s.178.) It therefore
excludes transmission by cable. However, it must be remembered that a
transmission may ultimately be received by cable, but originate as a
broadcast.

3. Infringing broadcasts

1.52   Copyright does not subsist in a broadcast which infringes, or to the extent
that it infringes, the copyright in another broadcast or in a cable pro-

gramme (s.6(6)). Thus, for example, if a broadcast by the BBC is picked up by an earth station in the United Kingdom and then transmitted in infringement of copyright to a satellite, that latter broadcast does not create a new copyright vested in the person making it.

4. Repeat broadcasts

Where a broadcast is repeated, that broadcast has its own copyright. **1.53** However, no copyright subsists in a repeat broadcast which is transmitted after the expiry of the copyright in the original broadcast (s.14(2)). For these purposes, one ignores any broadcast which was made before the commencement of the 1956 Act. (See schedule 1, paragraph 9.) If a pre-1956 Act broadcast is repeated after commencement, that will then be a protected broadcast which will then have to be taken into consideration in applying the repeat broadcast provisions thereafter.

VII CABLE PROGRAMMES

1. Cable programmes made before commencement of the 1988 Act

No copyright subsists in a cable programme included in a cable pro- **1.54** gramme service before January 1, 1985, which was the date on which the relevant provisions of the Cable and Broadcasting Act 1984 came into force. (See schedule 1, paragraph 9(b).) Once again, that would not deny protection to the programme if, for example, it was also a film.

2. Cable programmes protected under the 1988 Act

Under the 1956 Act, as amended by the 1984 Act, one had to look to the **1.55** provisions of the 1984 Act in order to find out which cable programmes were protected. One then also had to look to the Telecommunications Act 1984 for certain exclusions. Fortunately, all the relevant provisions are now contained in the new Act.

A cable programme is any item which is included in a cable programme service. A cable programme service is one which consists wholly or mainly in sending visual images, sounds or other information by means of a telecommunications system (but not by wireless telegraphy), provided that this is for reception:

(a) At two or more places, whether simultaneously or at different times in response to requests by different users, or

(b) For presentation to members of the public.

The expression "telecommunications system" is defined very widely as a system for conveying visual images, sounds or other information by electronic means, although, as stated, transmission by wireless telegraphy (that is, broadcasting) is specifically excluded.

The consequent breadth of the definition of cable programme service is such that a wide variety of cable programmes are protected, not only those which are included in services which provide entertainment, but those which are included in services which transmit any type of information, whether of a public or private nature.

The scope of the definition has however been cut down by excluding specifically certain services. The excluded services are at the moment five in number, but there is power for the Secretary of State to add to or even remove exceptions.

The definition of cable programme service is very similar to that under the 1956 Act. The same applies as regards the services excluded from that definition, although important changes in relation to premises in single occupation are referred to in paragraph 1.59. Two other points by way of comparison with the 1956 Act should be mentioned now:

(i) Although the words "or other information" are an addition to the definition of cable programme service under the 1984 Act, it is generally thought that the position under the 1956 Act was the same because of section 14A(12) of the 1956 Act.

(ii) The definition of cable programme service under the 1988 Act is the same whether the service is run from inside or outside the United Kingdom. Under the 1956 Act, where the service was provided outside the United Kingdom, the exclusions from the definition of cable programme services under the Telecommunications Act 1984 did not apply. This was somewhat anomalous, and the exclusions under the 1988 Act apply wherever the service is provided.

3. Cable programmes excluded from protection under the 1988 Act

The excluded services are at the time of writing as follows:

(a) *Interactive services* (s.7(2)(a))

1.56   The Act excludes services and parts of services of which it is an essential feature that while the visual images, sounds or other information are being conveyed by the person providing the service, there will or may be sent from each place of reception, by means of the same system or the same part of it, information (other than signals sent for the operation or control of the service) for reception by the person providing the service or other persons receiving it.

The best way to explain this somewhat complicated definition is by an example. Some services within the definition not only give information to the person receiving the service, but they also allow the user to communicate with the person providing the service. This could happen for example where cable programme services are used for conducting banking and other business transactions. The exception takes out of the definition of cable programme service any such service.

Cable programme services which communicate information do not neatly either fall into the category of those transmitting information, and those which are used for carrying on transactions as set out above. Many such systems are mixed, and the exception is only intended to apply to the part of such a system which covers the latter. The example given by the Government representative before the Standing Committee was that of teleshopping. In so far as such a service consists of transmitting a catalogue of goods to the user of the service, that is still a cable programme service to which the 1988 Act applies. To the extent however that the service includes a process of ordering goods and confirming orders for such goods and so on, it is outside the definition.

(b) *Services for business purposes* (s.7(2)(b))

This provision excludes a service run for the purposes of a business where **1.57** three conditions are fulfilled:

(i) No one except the person carrying on the business is concerned in the control of the apparatus comprised in the system

(ii) The visual images, sounds or other information are conveyed by the system solely for purposes internal to the running of the business, and not by way of rendering a service or providing amenities for others. If therefore members of the public are admitted to the premises of the business, or can even phone in to the business, and thus have access to the material, the exception does not apply

(iii) The system must not be connected to any other telecommunications system

(c) *Services run by a single individual* (s.7(2)(c))

The exception referred to in paragraph 1.57 above could apply whether **1.58** the business was run by a large company or one person. This exception goes further in removing from the definition of cable programme service services run by a single individual for that person's domestic purposes.
    The conditions which must apply are as follows:

(i) All the apparatus comprised in the system must be under that person's control

(ii) The visual images, sounds or other information which is included in the system is conveyed by the system solely for the domestic purposes of that particular person

(iii) The system must not be connected to any other telecommunications system

(d) *Premises in single occupation*

A service is not a cable programme service if all the apparatus comprised **1.59** in the system is situated in, or connects, premises which are in single occupation, provided that the system is not connected to any other telecommunications system.

The exception would therefore not apply where there is a block of flats, but it would apply where the system links several different buildings but which are occupied by the same person or firm or company.

There is a major exception here which is new to the 1988 Act, and that relates to services operated as part of the amenities provided for residents or inmates of premises run as a business. Thus, the provision of entertainment facilities by closed circuit cable systems in hotels is not in any event within the exclusion, even if the premises could be said to be in single occupation. Such a system is therefore a cable programme service for the purposes of the 1988 Act.

One other difference between the 1988 Act provision on premises in single occupation and that which applied under the 1956 Act should be noted. Under the Telecommunications Act 1984 the reference was to the apparatus being situated "on a single set of premises in single occupation". Now the reference is to the apparatus being situated in *or connecting* premises in single occupation.

(e) *Services run for persons providing broadcasting or cable programme services* (s.7(2)(e))

1.60   This exclusion covers services which are, or to the extent that they are, run for persons providing broadcasting or cable programme services or providing programmes for broadcasting or cable programme services.

4. Retransmission of broadcasts (s.7(6)(a))

1.61   If a broadcast is received by the operator of a cable programme service, and later transmitted, then, subject to paragraph 1.62 below, a separate copyright will subsist in the cable programme, apart from any copyright which subsisted in the broadcast. However, this does not apply where it is a broadcast which is received and then immediately retransmitted in a cable programme service.

5. Infringing cable programmes (s.7(6)(b))

1.62   Copyright does not subsist in a cable programme which infringes, or to the extent that it infringes, the copyright in another cable programme or the copyright in a broadcast. If therefore a cable programme service operator receives a satellite broadcast and later retransmits it, if the owner of the copyright in the broadcast had not consented to this, no separate copyright will arise when the broadcast is included in the cable programme service.

6. Repeat cable programmes (s.14(2))

1.63   Where a cable programme is repeated, that cable programme has its own copyright. However, no copyright subsists in such a repeat if it is transmitted after the expiry of the copyright in the original transmission. For these purposes, one ignores any transmission prior to January 1, 1985. (See schedule 1 paragraph 9(b).)

2 QUALIFYING FOR COPYRIGHT PROTECTION

I INTRODUCTION

1. General

2.01 No work is protected by the law of copyright unless it qualifies for copyright protection under the rules set out in the 1988 Act. This Chapter deals with those rules.

No formality such as registration is required in order for a work to qualify for protection. Although some authors do register their works at the Stationers' Hall Registry, this merely helps to establish the date when a work was created if there is any dispute about that. Such works can be registered there only if they are in written or printed form, not on tape or film.

For the same reason, some authors either lodge a copy with a solicitor, or send a copy to themselves by registered post. In the latter case, it is of course important not to open the envelope on receipt! None of these matters have any bearing however on whether the work qualifies for copyright protection.

The same applies to the use of the copyright symbol ©. It is certainly important to place this symbol on copies of literary, dramatic, musical, and artistic works and films, together with the name of the copyright proprietor and the year of first publication. This is because doing this fulfils any formalities for copyright protection in countries which are parties to the Universal Copyright Convention.

For similar reasons, on sound recordings, it is advisable to include on all copies the symbol ℗, with the year of first publication, and name of the copyright owner or exclusive licensee. If these provisions are followed, this may also help to establish title in infringement proceedings (see paragraph 10.34), but again they are not conditions for protection under the 1988 Act.

2. Summary of rules under the 1988 Act

2.02 In summary, under the 1988 Act, works can qualify for protection in the following manner:

(a) In the case of all works, if the author of the work is a qualifying person at the time the work was made or published. Whether or not an individual or company is a qualifying person depends on nationality, domicile or residence in the case of an individual and the place of incorporation in the case of a company.

(b) In the case of all works except for broadcasts and cable programmes, if the work is first published in the United Kingdom, or in any country to which the provisions of the Act have been extended or applied as regards works of authors of such a country or first published in any such country.

(c) In the case of a broadcast, if it is made from the United Kingdom, or any country to which the provisions of the Act have been extended or applied as regards broadcasts made by individuals or companies of, or made from, that country.

(d) In the case of a cable programme, it is sent from a place in the United Kingdom, or any country to which the provisions of the Act have been extended or applied as regards cable programmes included in cable programme services provided by individuals or companies of, or sent from, that country.

The above rules do not apply where the relevant work is the subject of Crown or a related copyright, or vests in an international organisation under the rules referred to in paragraph 3.84. These works qualify for copyright protection without having to comply with any such requirements.

The above rules also do not apply to existing published works, nor to existing unpublished works which were protected under the 1956 Act. (See section III below for these works.)

3. Extending and applying the provisions of the 1988 Act.

In paragraph 2.02 there are references to provisions of the 1988 Act being   **2.03**
extended or applied in relation to other countries or their works. These expressions will appear frequently in this Chapter, and it is necessary to summarise them briefly at this stage. The same expressions were used under the 1911 and 1956 Acts, and appear when the pre-1988 Act rules are discussed in paragraph 2.55 below.

Under the 1988 Act, there is power to *extend* the operation of the Act to certain other territories. This includes the Isle of Man, the Channel Islands, and the remaining colonies. This has two aspects to it. First, the Act is thereby made part of the internal law of the country to which it is extended, although certain modifications as to procedure and works protected may be introduced for those countries. That aspect is beyond the scope of this book. Secondly, the works of authors of those countries and works first published in those countries will be protected in the United Kingdom, and possibly also broadcasts made and cable programmes sent from those countries.

There is also power to *apply* the 1988 Act to works created by authors of other countries, and works first published in those countries, as well as to broadcasts made and cable programmes sent from such countries. These works will then also qualify for copyright protection in the United Kingdom.

Such extensions or applications of the 1988 Act will take place by the making of Orders in Council. At the time of writing, no such Orders have been made, but see the table in Appendix 1 which explains the position under the 1956 Act at the time of writing. It is likely that the position under the 1988 Act will be similar, but it must be remembered that the copyright status of countries can change.

There are important transitional provisions in relation to countries to which the 1911 Act or 1956 Act extended. These and further details of extensions and applications are dealt with in paragraph 2.26 onwards.

4. Comparison of the 1988 Act with the 1956 Act

2.04   By and large, the method of qualifying for copyright protection is similar in the 1988 Act to that which applied under the 1956 Act. There are however two important changes. The first relates only to broadcasts. Under the 1956 Act, certain foreign broadcasts were protected in the United Kingdom as a result of various Orders in Council, but protection was only possible where the broadcast was **both** made from a place in the relevant country **and** made by an organisation constituted in or under the laws of that country. Now, the latter requirement has been dispensed with. (See paragraph 2.23 onwards.)

The second change relates to literary, dramatic, musical and artistic works. Under the 1956 Act, it was possible for a work to be protected whilst it was unpublished but lose protection on publication, because the rules on qualifying for protection had to be reapplied when publication took place. This will no longer be so. Once a work is protected under the 1988 Act, no subsequent event will deprive it of protection. (See paragraph 2.06.)

5. The practical importance of the rules on qualifying for protection

2.05   The vast majority of works created or published in most countries of the world are protected by copyright in the United Kingdom, either because of a British connection, or connection with a country to which provisions of the 1911 Act or the 1956 Act were extended or applied. The problem is proving it. In an action for infringement of copyright, as will be seen, the copyright owner must prove on the balance of probabilities that the work he owns qualifies for copyright protection. This Chapter summarises how one does this.

However, this is not just a subject which can safely be ignored until an action for infringement appears to be necessary. Where someone is acquiring the copyright in a work, or entering into an exclusive licence agreement, it is advisable if feasible to establish at that stage how the relevant work is protected in the United Kingdom, in order to prevent problems of proof arising later at a time when it may be much more difficult to establish the facts. Where it is not possible to get the assignor or grantor of the exclusive licence to provide the necessary documentation or information, then at least a clause should be inserted in the agreement requiring them to do this later if it becomes necessary because of an action for infringement or some other relevant reason.

Establishing whether or not or how a work qualifies for protection is particularly complex for works existing before commencement of the 1956 Act, but has its difficulties even for works first protected under that Act. The rules in sections III and IV below are only a summary and guide, and some of the more difficult problems which can arise have been omitted.

As stated, works connected with most countries of the world are protected in the United Kingdom, although in many cases there are difficulties with works created or published before a certain date which differs from country to country. The most important countries where there may still be problems are China, Vietnam, Afghanistan, Ethiopia, Sudan, Bolivia and many of the Middle Eastern States.

The rules are also of particular practical importance in relation to sound recordings. Assuming that the same rules continue to apply as under the 1956 Act (see paragraph 2.67), whether or not a sound recording qualifies for copyright protection as having been made by a British person or company or first published in the United Kingdom or by connection with another country will be vital as regards performance, broadcasting and cable transmission rights.

II THE NEW PROVISIONS ON QUALIFYING FOR PROTECTION UNDER THE 1988 ACT

The rules in this section apply only to: 2.06

(a) Works made after the commencement of the 1988 Act. In our view, this also includes works the making of which was completed after commencement.

(b) Works made before commencement if:

(i) they were unpublished as at the commencement of the 1988 Act, and

(ii) they did not qualify for protection when they were made, as referred to in the rules contained in section III below.

The methods of qualifying for protection under the 1988 Act were set out in the summary in paragraph 2.02. The detail of the first two methods, qualifying by reference to the author of the work, and qualifying by reference to first publication, is set out respectively in sections A and B. In relation to both these provisions, it is necessary to know what is meant by publication and Section C explains that. This is followed by Section D dealing with special qualifying rules for broadcasts and cable programmes, and Section E explaining further the extension and application of the Act to works of other countries.

As stated, once a work qualifies for protection under the rules set out below, it remains protected, even where the relevant circumstances have changed. A further example can be given of this: if the works of an author of Chinese nationality qualify for protection because he is resident in Hong Kong, those works do not cease to be protected if he decides to move to China. However, neither residence in China nor Chinese nationality are qualifying criteria for protection of works in the United Kingdom, and whether or not works written after the author moves to China qualify will depend on where and when such works are first published.

A. QUALIFICATION BY REFERENCE TO THE AUTHOR (s.154)

2.07   If the author is a qualifying person at the relevant time referred to below, then the work will be protected under the 1988 Act. In the case of a work of joint authorship, only one of the authors needs to be a qualifying person.

1. Who is a qualifying person?

2.08   The definition of a qualifying person is as follows:

(a) A British citizen, a British Dependent Territories citizen, a British National (Overseas), a British Overseas citizen, a British subject, or a British protected person. All these expressions are defined in or under the British Nationality Act 1981.

(b) An individual domiciled or resident in the United Kingdom.

(c) An individual domiciled or resident in a country to which the 1988 Act has been extended.

(d) A citizen or subject of a country in respect of which the provisions of the 1988 Act have been applied.

(e) An individual domiciled or resident in a country in respect of which the provisions of the 1988 Act have been applied.

(f) A body incorporated under the law of:

(i) any part of the United Kingdom.

(ii) any country to which the 1988 Act has been extended.

(iii) any country in respect of which the provisions of the 1988 Act have been applied.

2. Domicile

2.09   The following is a summary of the rules on domicile. When a child is born, he or she acquires a domicile of origin, that of the father if legitimate, that of the mother if illegitimate. The place of birth is immaterial. Until, generally, the child is 16, his or her domicile will follow that of his parent or relevant parent. After that, he or she can acquire a domicile of choice by taking up residence in another country with the intention of making his or her sole or main home there permanently. A domicile of choice can be abandoned, in which event the domicile of origin revives until another domicile of choice is taken.

The above applies even where the country of domicile under the above rules has different rules for determining where a person is domiciled.

3. Residence

The test for residence is less exacting. Someone may be domiciled in one   **2.10** country, but resident in another, and he may in fact be resident in two or more countries if he spends regular periods of time in each. There must be some element of permanence or continuity—having a house or flat in a territory which is occupied from time to time will probably be good evidence of residence by the occupant.

4. The relevant time

The relevant time for ascertaining whether the author is a qualifying   **2.11** person is determined in accordance with the following rules.

(a) *Literary, dramatic, musical or artistic works*

If the work is unpublished, the relevant time is when the work is made. If the making of the work extends over a period, the author must be a qualifying person for a substantial part of that period.

Most literary, dramatic, musical and artistic works will qualify for copyright protection on the above basis when they are made. If so, it is unnecessary to consider again whether or not the work qualifies at the time of first publication. (See s.153(3).) It is sufficient that it qualified at the time it was made.

If however the work failed to qualify at the time it was made, it has another opportunity to qualify when it is first published. If the author is a qualifying person when that happens, the work then qualifies for protection.

(b) *Typographical arrangements*

The relevant time is when the edition is first published.

(c) *Sound recordings and films*

The relevant time is when the sound recording or film is made.

(d) *Broadcasts*

The relevant time is when the broadcast is made.

(e) *Cable programmes*

The relevant time is when the programme is included in a cable programme service.

B. QUALIFICATION BY REFERENCE TO COUNTRY OF FIRST PUBLICATION (s.155)

2.12   This provision only applies to literary, dramatic, musical and artistic works, typographical arrangements, sound recordings and films.

Any such work qualifies for copyright protection under the 1988 Act if it is first published:

(a) In the United Kingdom or

(b) In any other country to which the 1988 Act has been extended.

(c) In any other country in relation to which the provisions of the 1988 Act have been applied.

C. PUBLICATION (s.175)

2.13   In section B above, it is necessary to know when a work is first published. This may also be necessary in order to ascertain whether a work qualifies under the rules referred to in section A. This section deals with the meaning of publication for these purposes.

1. The basic rule

2.14   The basic rule is that publication of a work takes place upon the issue of copies of that work to the public. Issue to the public means the act of first putting copies of the work into circulation, but it does not matter whether this takes place by way of sale, offer for sale, exposure for sale, hiring, or other distribution.

2. Modifications to the basic rule

2.15   There are some modifications to the basic rule set out in paragraph 2.14. These are as follows, by category of work:

(a) *Literary, dramatic and musical works*

These works are also issued to the public when they are made available to the public by means of an electronic retrieval system. They are not however issued to the public when they are performed or broadcast. They are also not issued to the public when they are included in a cable programme service, otherwise than for the purposes of an electronic retrieval system.

(b) *Artistic works*

An artistic work is also issued to the public when it is made available to the public by means of an electronic retrieval system. If the artistic work is a work of architecture in the form of a building, or an artistic work incorporated in a building, publication also takes place by the construction of the building, but only if this is begun after commencement of the 1988 Act. (See schedule 1, paragraph 45.) There is no explanation as to what is an artistic work incorporated in a building. Although it is possible that this was intended to cover the plans for a building, it is arguable that this is not so because architectural drawings are not incorporated into buildings, although the building may be based on them. Examples might be stained-glass windows or mosaics.   **2.16**

    Artistic works are not published by being exhibited, nor by the issue to the public of copies of a film including such a work. Furthermore, the issue to the public of copies of a graphic work (such as a drawing) or photograph representing a work of architecture or a sculpture or a work of artistic craftsmanship does not constitute publication of the work represented, although it would constitute publication of the graphic work or photograph.

    Finally, the broadcasting of a work or inclusion of a work in a cable programme service does not constitute publication, except in the latter case where done for the purposes of an electronic retrieval system.

(c) *Sound recordings and films*

These works are not published by being played or shown in public. Neither are they published by being broadcast or included in a cable programme service.   **2.17**

3. The difference between publication under the 1956 and 1988 Acts

The major differences between the above rules and the rules under the 1956 Act are the following: **2.18**

(a) Under the 1956 Act, there was no reference to making the work available by means of an electronic retrieval system.

(b) The issue to the public of records of literary, dramatic or musical works now constitutes publication of such works. It did not under the 1956 Act.

(c) In the case of works of architecture, sculptures and works of artistic craftsmanship, the issue to the public of copies of any graphic work (and not just engravings as defined under the 1956 Act) representing such a work does not now constitute publication.

(d) Artistic works are not now published by the issue to the public of copies of a film including the work.

(e) Works of architecture are now published by construction of the building.

4. How much of the work?

2.19   Under the 1956 Act, publication of literary, dramatic, musical or artistic works, or published editions only took place if the whole of the work, or virtually the whole of the work, was included. The position was different in relation to sound recordings or films. (See paragraph 2.50.) What the position is under the 1988 Act is by no means clear. Section 175 contains the new rules on publication, and there is no provision in that section which allows for publication to take place where only part of the work is included in the copy issued to the public. (However, it is possible that, as under the 1956 Act, the Courts would hold that including all but a very small part would still constitute publication.) So, on the basis of section 175, it would seem that the 1956 Act rules remain for literary, dramatic, musical and artistic works, and the typographical arrangement of published editions, and that these rules will also apply for the future to sound recordings and films.

The problem, however, is that the issuing of copies to the public is now also a restricted act, and by section 16(3) references to the doing of a restricted act are to the doing of it in relation to the whole *or any substantial part* (for the meaning of this, see paragraph 5.09). On this basis it might be argued that publication now takes place where a substantial part is included in the copies issued to the public. The position becomes more confusing however when one is considering the specific method of publication of literary, dramatic, musical and artistic works by making such works available to the public by means of an electronic retrieval system. This is not expressly a restricted act, although it will in many cases involve one. Hopefully, however, the above will not cause difficulties in practice.

5. Colourable publication

2.20   By using the word "copies," it is clear that the issue to the public of one copy will not count as publication. However, the 1988 Act also repeats the provision in the 1956 Act which said that publication which was merely colourable, and not intended to satisfy the reasonable requirements of the public, does not constitute publication. It is the intention here which is important, and not whether the number of copies is in practice sufficient to meet demand.

In *Francis Day and Hunter Ltd.* v. *Feldman and Co.* ([1914] 2 Ch. 728), 12 sheet music copies of a song were sent by an American publisher to a publisher in England. Six of those copies were put on sale in their shop, and, as required by law, one copy was sent to the British Museum, and four copies to other libraries. The song was not advertised, and the copies on sale were not in fact sold. It was held that this was not colourable publication, and that the work had been published when the copies were put on sale in the shop.

6. Unauthorised acts

The unauthorised issue of copies of a work to the public does not consti- **2.21**
tute publication. For example, if bootleg copies of a song which had up
until then only been performed in public are sold at a record fair, that
does not constitute publication of the music or lyrics.

7. Simultaneous publication

As referred to in section B above, a work qualifies for copyright protec- **2.22**
tion if it is first published in the United Kingdom or in a country to which
the 1988 Act has been extended or in relation to which it has been
applied. However, for these purposes one can ignore any publication
which has taken place in any other country within the previous 30 days.
To take an example, records of a musical work are first put into circulation in China on September 1. Copies are then distributed in the United
Kingdom on September 30. This still counts as first publication in the
United Kingdom, because the publication in China took place within the
30-day period prior to publication in the United Kingdom.

In another change from the 1956 Act, the simultaneous publication
rule does not apply when one is considering whether an author is a
qualifying person at the time of first publication. This is because section
154 contains no reference to the simultaneous publication rule, and
accordingly in those cases the author must be a qualifying person when
actual first publication takes place, wherever that is.

D. QUALIFICATION BY REFERENCE TO PLACE OF TRANSMISSION (s.156)

These rules are only relevant to broadcasts and cable programmes, not to **2.23**
the works included in them, and can be used as an alternative to qualifying by reference to the author as referred to in section A above.

1. Broadcasts

A broadcast qualifies for copyright protection under the 1988 Act if it is **2.24**
made from:

(a) The United Kingdom.

(b) Any other country to which the 1988 Act has been extended.

(c) Any other country in relation to which the provisions of the 1988 Act
have been applied.

Where the broadcast is a satellite transmission, the place from which a
broadcast is made is the place from which the signals carrying the broadcast are transmitted to the satellite.

2. Cable programmes

A cable programme qualifies for copyright protection if it is transmitted **2.25**
from a place in:

(a) The United Kingdom.

(b) Any other country to which the 1988 Act has been extended.

(c) Any other country in relation to which the provisions of the 1988 Act have been applied.

E. EXTENSIONS AND APPLICATIONS IN RELATION TO OTHER COUNTRIES

2.26 A summary has already been provided in paragraph 2.03 above of what happens when the 1988 Act is extended to other countries or when the provisions on qualifying for protection have been applied to works first published in other countries, or works created by authors who are citizens or subjects, domiciled or resident, or incorporated in other countries. A few more details are now necessary.

1. Extensions (s.157)

2.27 The above provisions may be extended, as opposed to applied, to any of the Channel Islands, the Isle of Man, or any colony. Any of the provisions of the 1988 Act may be modified or excluded in such a case, and the Orders in Council when made will deal with any such modifications or exclusions.

The question then arises as to what happens if a country ceases to be a colony. If this happens, it will still be treated as a country to which the provisions extend for the purposes of qualifying for copyright protection, until one of two events happens. These are as follows (s.158):

(a) An Order in Council is made applying the provisions to authors of that country, or works first published in that country.

(b) An Order in Council is made terminating the extension of the provisions because the government of the former colony has repealed the 1988 Act in that country.

The extension of the 1988 Act to the UK's remaining colonies may take some time to implement, because of local consultation, and the possibility of local modifications to the Act. Accordingly, there is a transitional provision in the Act which states that a dependent territory in which the 1956 Act remains in force will be treated in the United Kingdom as a country to which the copyright provisions of the 1988 Act extend. This applies also to territories in which the 1911 Act remains in force— somewhat surprisingly there are territories in which this is so, including Jersey! In all such cases the effect of a country ceasing to be a United Kingdom colony is the same as set out above, subject to substituting references to the 1988 Act with references to the 1911 or 1956 Acts.

2. Applications (s.159)

2.28 As regards countries in relation to which the provisions are applied, again the Order in Council providing for this can modify the provisions of the 1988 Act, or apply only some of them, whether generally or in specific cases. This was done in particular under the 1956 Act in the case of sound recordings, where in some cases the copyright does not include the right to perform in public, or broadcast the recording or include it in a cable programme. (See paragraph 2.67.)

Except in the case of countries making up the EEC, or Member States of copyright conventions such as the Berne Copyright Convention, or the Universal Copyright Convention, there is an obligation not to make an Order in Council applying the provisions unless the Government is satisfied that provision has been or will be made under the law of the relevant country for giving adequate copyright protection in that country to works protected in the United Kingdom. (See s.159(3).) Apart from this, there is also in similar situations a discretion for the Government to restrict the rights conferred by the provisions of the 1988 Act as regards the works of authors connected with the relevant country if there is inadequate protection in that country for British works. (See s.160.)

There are no transitional provisions relating to countries in respect of which the provisions of the 1956 Act were applied. Accordingly, the provisions of the 1988 Act will not apply unless and until an Order in Council has been made.

III WORKS WHICH QUALIFIED FOR PROTECTION UNDER THE 1956 ACT

If a work qualified for protection under the 1956 Act immediately before the commencement of the 1988 Act, it is deemed to qualify for protection **2.29** under the 1988 Act. (See schedule 1, paragraph 35.) It is necessary therefore to summarise the rules which applied under the 1956 Act. The special rules relating to works made before July 1, 1912 are summarised in section IV.

This section is divided into three sections. Section A deals with the basic rules on qualifying for copyright protection under the 1956 Act by reference either to the author's British status or to the relevant work having first been published in the United Kingdom. Section B deals with works which qualified for protection under the 1956 Act either because of their author's connection with a foreign country, or because the work was first published in such a country. Neither of the first two parts deals with broadcasts and cable programmes, and these are covered separately in Section C.

The rules referred to below have no relevance to works the subject of Crown copyright or works the copyright in which vested under the 1956 Act in certain international organisations. As under the 1988 Act, such works qualified for protection in the United Kingdom without having to comply with any such requirements.

A. THE BASIC RULES

2.30   Differing rules applied to various categories of works, and each such category is dealt with separately below. In many cases, it will be necessary to know when the relevant work was first published, and paragraph 2.44 onwards deals with the meaning of publication under the 1956 Act.

1. Literary, dramatic, musical and artistic works (1956 Act, ss. 2(1) and (2) and 3(2) and (3))

2.31   These rules had to be applied both when the work was made, and, if subsequently published, when it was first published. So, a work which qualified for copyright protection when made might lose protection on publication. However, as already stated, if a work qualified for protection when made, and remains unpublished at the commencement of the 1988 Act, it qualifies for protection under the 1988 Act, and it is not necessary to examine the position again if and when it is published.

As under the 1988 Act, a work of joint authorship qualified for protection if any of the authors fulfilled the relevant criteria.

(a) *Unpublished works*

2.32   An unpublished work qualified for protection if the author came into any of the following categories when the work was made. If the making of the work extended over a period, the author had to come into one of the following categories for a substantial part of that period:

(i) A British subject.

(ii) A British protected person.

(iii) A citizen of the Republic of Ireland.

(iv) A person domiciled in the United Kingdom.

(v) A person resident in the United Kingdom.

(vi) Where the work was a photograph:

—A company or other corporate body with an established place of business in any part of the United Kingdom, if the photograph was taken before June 1, 1957.

—A company or other corporate body incorporated under the laws of any part of the United Kingdom, if the photograph was taken on or after June 1, 1957.

For works made between January 1, 1949 and October 30, 1981, the expression "British subject" is construed in accordance with the British Nationality Act 1948. If the work was made before then, the statute dealing with nationality which was in force at the time of making must be applied.

For works made after October 30, 1981, the expression "British subject" means any person who had the status of a Commonwealth citizen under the British Nationality Act 1981.

Although the expression "British protected person" was in use prior to the 1948 Act, a person can only be a British protected person for copyright purposes if he was the author of a work made on or after January 28, 1949.

(b) *Published works*

(i) Publication Prior to June 1, 1957

A work published before June 1, 1957 qualified for copyright protection if   **2.33**
it was first published in the United Kingdom.

(ii) Publication On or After June 1, 1957

A work published on or after June 1, 1957 qualified for copyright protec-   **2.34**
tion in two circumstances. First, it would qualify if it was first published in the United Kingdom. Secondly, it would qualify if the author was in any of the categories referred to in paragraph 2.32 above at the time of first publication, or, if the author was an individual and had already died by the time of publication, was such a person immediately before his death.

The same comments apply to the expressions "British subject" and "British protected person" as are contained in paragraph 2.32, but in this case of course the relevant time for testing whether the author was of such a status was at the time the work was first published.

2. Sound recordings (1956 Act, s.12(1) and (2))

Unlike the position with literary, dramatic, musical or artistic works, the   **2.35**
rules below did not have to be applied both when the sound recording was made, and, if subsequently published, when published. Provided a sound recording qualified for copyright protection when it was made, it remained protected thereafter, wherever it was first published.

(a) *Qualifying for protection by reference to the maker of the sound recording*

For the identity of the maker of a sound recording, see paragraph 3.37.   **2.36**
A sound recording qualified for copyright protection in the United Kingdom if the maker was one of the following at the time when the recording was made:

(i) A British subject.

(ii) A British protected person.

(iii) A citizen of the Republic of Ireland.

(iv) A person domiciled in the United Kingdom.

(v) A person resident in the United Kingdom.

(vi) If the sound recording was made before June 1, 1957, a company with an established place of business in any part of the United Kingdom.

(vii) If the sound recording was made on or after June 1, 1957, a company or other body corporate incorporated under the laws of any part of the United Kingdom.

(b) *Qualifying for protection by reference to publication*

2.37   A sound recording also qualified for copyright protection in the United Kingdom if first publication of the recording took place in the United Kingdom.

3. Films (1956 Act, s.13(1) and (2))

2.38   The rules set out here do not apply where the film was both made and first published prior to June 1, 1957. These films can only be protected as dramatic works, photographs, or (in the case of cartoons) drawings. (See paragraph 1.14.) In such cases the rules referred to in paragraphs 2.31 to 2.34 must be applied.

The rules contained in this section did apply either in the case of films made after June 1, 1957, or films first published after June 1, 1957.

If a film was made before June 1, 1957, but first published on or after that date, and qualified for protection both when it was made and when it was published, it could be protected both as a dramatic work, series of photographs or (in the case of cartoons) drawings, and as a film.

As in the case of sound recordings, films to which the rules below apply qualified for copyright protection either on the basis of the status of the maker of the film, or on the basis of the country of first publication. If the film qualified by reference to the maker, it did not matter thereafter where it was published.

The rules below also applied to the sound-tracks of the films. Although such sound-tracks after the commencement of the 1988 Act will be protected as sound recordings, copyright subsists in the sound recording only if copyright subsisted in the film immediately before commencement of the 1988 Act. (See Schedule 1, paragraph 8(2).)

(a) *Qualifying for protection by reference to the maker*

2.39   For the identity of the maker, see paragraph 3.40.

A film qualified for copyright protection in the United Kingdom if the maker was any one of the following for the whole or a substantial part of the period during which the film was made:

(i) A British subject.

(ii) A British protected person.

(iii) A citizen of the Republic of Ireland.

(iv) A person domiciled in the United Kingdom.

(v) A person resident in the United Kingdom.

(vi) A company or other body corporate incorporated under the laws of any part of the United Kingdom.

(b) *Qualifying for protection by reference to publication*

A film also qualified for copyright protection in the United Kingdom if **2.40** first publication of the film took place in the United Kingdom.

4. Typographical arrangements of published editions (1956 Act, s.15 (1))

A published edition could qualify for copyright protection in the United **2.41** Kingdom on either of the following two grounds.

(a) *Qualifying for protection by reference to the publisher*

A published edition qualified for copyright protection if the publisher of **2.42** the edition came into one of the following categories at the time when the edition was first published:

(i) A British subject.

(ii) A British protected person.

(iii) A citizen of the Republic of Ireland.

(iv) A person domiciled in the United Kingdom.

(v) A person resident in the United Kingdom.

(vi) A company or other body corporate incorporated under the laws of any part of the United Kingdom.

(b) *Qualifying for protection by reference to publication*

A published edition also qualified for copyright protection if the edition **2.43** was first published in the United Kingdom.

5. Publication

As under the 1988 Act, what constituted publication under the 1956 Act **2.44** depended on the category of work.

(a) *Literary, dramatic and musical works* (1956 Act, s.49(2))

Such a work was published if, but only if, reproductions of the work had **2.45** been issued to the public. This obviously did not happen where there was broadcasting or cable transmission of the work, but a specific provision stated that performance did not constitute publication.

A further provision not repeated in the 1988 Act stated that the issue of records of such works did not constitute publication. This obviously extended to audio-only records, but, because of the breadth of the definition of record in the 1956 Act, it probably also covered audio-visual material such as video cassettes.

(b) *Artistic works* (1956 Act, s.49(2))

2.46   Such a work was published if, but only if, reproductions of the work had been issued to the public.

Exhibition of such a work did not constitute publication. Neither did the construction of a work of architecture, or the issue of photographs or engravings of a work of architecture or sculpture.

(c) *Published editions* (1956 Act, s.49(2))

2.47   Publication of such a work took place if, but only if, reproductions of the edition had been issued to the public.

(d) *Sound recordings* (1956 Act, s.12(9))

2.48   Publication of a sound recording took place only by the issue to the public of records embodying all or any part of such a recording.

(e) *Films* (1956 Act, s.13(10))

2.49   For films protected as dramatic work, photographs, or drawings, see paragraphs 2.45 and 2.46.

Publication of a film *qua* film took place only upon the sale, letting on hire, or offer for sale or hire, of copies of the film to the public.

(f) *How much of the work?* (1956 Act, s.49(2))

2.50   Under the 1956 Act, publication of literary, dramatic, musical or artistic works or published editions did not take place where only part of the work was included in the relevant copy, even where that part was a substantial part. However, where all but a very small part was omitted, there were instances where the courts would hold that the work or edition had been published.

In the case of sound recordings, the issue to the public of records embodying any part of the sound recording constituted publication.

In the case of films (*qua* films), publication took place if the relevant copies contained any part of the film.

(g) *Colourable publication* (1956 Act, s.49(2))

2.51   The same rule applied as is referred to in paragraph 2.20.

(h) *Unauthorised acts* (1956 Act, s.49(3))

2.52   The same rule applied as is referred to in paragraph 2.21.

(i) *Simultaneous publication*

The meaning of this phrase is set out in paragraph 2.22. The same rule   **2.53**
applied under the 1956 Act (1956 Act, s.49(2)), but with two differences:

(1) The simultaneous publication rule also applied when one was looking
at the author's status at the time of first publication.

(2) Where publication took place before commencement of the 1956 Act,
the period of grace was only 14 days, not 30 days (1956 Act, schedule 7,
paragraph 33(1)).

B. PROTECTION OF WORKS OF FOREIGN ORIGIN

As stated, this section does not deal with broadcasts and cable pro-   **2.54**
grammes, which are covered separately in paragraphs 2.73 onwards.

1. General comments

Under the 1956 Act, a work of foreign origin could qualify for copyright   **2.55**
protection in the United Kingdom in a number of different ways:

(a) If it was first published in the United Kingdom, it would qualify under
the rules referred to in section A above. It is important to bear in mind
here the rules on simultaneous publication referred to in paragraph 2.53,
under which a work might in reality be first published in another country,
but, if published in the United Kingdom within a certain number of days
of the real date of first publication, would still count as being first
published in the United Kingdom for copyright purposes.

(b) The author might be a citizen or subject of another country, but he
might also be a British subject or British protected person, in which case
again the rules referred to in section A above would apply. The citizens of
many countries formerly part of the British Empire or of Commonwealth
countries were qualifying persons on this basis.

(c) The 1956 and 1911 Acts were extended or deemed to extend to many
countries outside the United Kingdom. These again were countries which
were at the relevant time part of the British Empire or Commonwealth. If
this was so, the works of authors of those countries would qualify for
copyright protection in the United Kingdom. The same applied to works
first published in such countries.

(d) The provisions of the 1956 and 1911 Acts were applied to works by
authors of many other countries and works first published in such countries. For the most part, these were countries which were members of
international conventions such as the Berne Copyright Convention and
the Universal Copyright Convention.

Determining whether or not a work of foreign origin qualified for copyright protection in the United Kingdom is not an easy matter, particularly in the case of those works which did not qualify under the first two categories above. The table in Appendix 1 lists the relevant countries which come into either category (c) or (d) above, and will hopefully help in determining whether or not a work of an author of such a country or first published in such a country qualifies for copyright protection in the United Kingdom. It also indicates where nationals of foreign countries were treated as British subjects or British protected persons. (See paragraph 2.32.) It is however intended as a summary of the position only.

2. A guide to the table in Appendix 1

2.56 The following provides an explanation of the information contained in the table:

(a) *Country*

2.57 This refers to the country as constituted today. There are obvious difficulties where the boundaries of a country have changed over the years.

(b) *Nationality status*

2.58 This indicates whether nationals of the relevant country will also be British subjects or British protected persons. In some cases, this will only be before or after a certain date or during a certain period, and, where this is so, the date or dates are indicated. If nationals of such countries were British subjects or British protected persons the remainder of the table may be ignored in relation to the works of such authors, and the rules set out in section A (paragraph 2.30 onwards) applied as normal.

(c) *"Extended" countries*

2.59 This indicates whether the country is one to which the provisions of the 1956 Act extended or were deemed to extend. Where there are date limitations, this information is included. If the country is one to which the 1956 Act extended or was deemed to extend, then the rules set out in Section A (paragraph 2.30 onwards) can be applied to the works of authors of such a country and works first published in such a country, but subject to the other matters referred to in the table and the special provisions set out in Section 3. (See paragraph 2.68.) However, it is important to remember that the work may have qualified because it was first published in the United Kingdom, or be the work of a British subject or protected person.

In all cases dealing with extended countries, there is a risk that the information contained here is out-of-date. This is because local legislation may have had an effect on the previous extension or deemed extension of the 1956 Act to such countries and in each case the up-to-date position must be checked.

(d) *"Applied" countries*

This indicates whether the country is one where the 1956 Act was applied   **2.60**
to the works of authors of such countries, or works first published in those
countries. Again, where a date is relevant, this is inserted. If the country
is one to which the provisions of the 1956 Act were applied, then the rules
set out in Section A (paragraph 2.30 onwards) can be applied to the works
of authors of such a country and works first published in such a country,
but subject to the other matters referred to in the table and the special
provisions set out in Section 3 (paragraph 2.68). However, it is again
important to remember that the work may have qualified because it was
first published in the United Kingdom, or be the work of a British subject
or protected person.

(e) *Conventions*

This indicates which of the major conventions, if any, a country is a   **2.61**
member of. These include:

(i) The Berne Copyright Union for the protection of literary and
artistic works founded by the Berne Convention in 1886 ("Berne")

(ii) The Universal Copyright Convention ("UCC")

(iii) The Rome Convention ("Rome") for the protection of performers, producers of phonograms and broadcasting organisations.

(iv) The Geneva (Phonograms) Convention ("Geneva") for the protection of producers of phonograms against unauthorised duplication
of their phonograms.

(f) *Full retroactivity*

This indicates whether the rules referred to in section A (paragraph 2.30   **2.62**
onwards) above can be applied to works of authors of such countries
whenever they were made, and works first published in such countries
whenever they were published. If so it does not matter whether such
works were made or first published, as the case may be, before the date of
the Order in Council extending or applying the provisions of the 1956 Act
came into effect.

(g) *Partial retroactivity*

This indicates whether the rules referred to in section A (paragraph 2.30   **2.63**
onwards) above can be applied to unpublished works of authors of such
countries whenever they were made, even though this was before the date
of the Order in Council extending or applying the provisions of the 1956
Act came into force. Obviously, it is not necessary to apply this where
there is full retroactivity.

(h) *Date for publication purposes*

Where a date is indicated here, publication in the relevant country before   **2.64** that date cannot qualify the relevant work for copyright protection in the United Kingdom. However, with effect from that date, the rules referred to in section A (paragraph 2.30 onwards) can be applied both as regards the country of first publication and the author's status at the time of such publication. Again, it is obviously not necessary to apply this where there is full retroactivity.

(i) *Date of commencement of the 1956 Act*

2.65 The 1956 Act came into effect on June 1, 1957 for works of British authors and works first published in the United Kingdom. This is the date referred to throughout section A (paragraph 2.30 onwards). However, in some cases indicated here, the commencement date was different and, where this is so, the relevant date must be substituted for June 1, 1957 when applying the rules in section A in relation to works which qualify for protection in the United Kingdom because they are of authors of the relevant country, or works first published in the relevant country.

Furthermore, the expression "before the commencement of the 1956 Act" is frequently used throughout this book. Where the work is one which qualifies for copyright protection in the United Kingdom because it is a work of an author of such a country or a work first published in that country, the date in this row is likely to be the relevant date for these purposes as well. The reason why the words "likely to be" are used is that in the transitional provisions to the 1988 Act the date June 1, 1957 is always used. When Orders in Council are made in relation to the relevant countries it will be necessary for the Orders to specify that the dates referred to in these columns should be substituted for June 1, 1957 if the pre-1988 Act position is to be preserved.

(j) *Translation rights*

2.66 This indicates whether the country is one to which the provisions referred to in paragraph 2.70 below apply.

(k) *Limited sound recording rights*

2.67 This indicates whether protection for a sound recording which qualified for protection in the United Kingdom because of its maker's connection with such country, or because it was first published in such a country, did not extend to the right to cause the sound recording to be heard in public, broadcast a sound recording, or include the sound recording in a cable programme service. (See paragraph 2.71.)

(l) *Vested rights*

See paragraph 2.72.

(m) Broadcasts

See paragraph 2.73.

3. Special rules and problems

(a) *The meaning of "works of authors" of the relevant countries*

This term has been used above as a short description of the works of the following: **2.68**

(1) In the case of a country in respect of which the provisions have been *extended*:

  (i) A person domiciled in such a country.

  (ii) A person resident in such a country.

  (iii) Before commencement of the 1956 Act, a company with an established place of business in such a country.

  (iv) On or after commencement of the 1956 Act, a company or other body corporate incorporated under the laws of such a country.

(2) In the case of countries in relation to which the provisions have been *applied*:

  (i) A citizen of such a country.

  (ii) A subject of such a country.

  (iii) A person domiciled in such a country.

  (iv) A person resident in such a country.

  (v) Before commencement of the 1956 Act, a company with an established place of business in such a country (but see below).

  (vi) On or after commencement of the 1956 Act, a company or other body corporate incorporated under the laws of such a country.

The above rules for countries in relation to which the provisions were applied must be qualified as regards works made before commencement of the 1956 Act of which a company or other corporate body was the author. This would only be so in the case of photographs and sound recordings. Although one would expect it to be necessary for the company or corporate body only to have an established place of business (in line with companies in the United Kingdom and "extended" countries) there was a problem in the drafting of the 1956 Act on this. It may therefore be that the company or other corporate body had to be incorporated under the laws of such a country and not just have an established place of business in that country, as with works made on or after commencement of the 1988 Act.

(b) *American works*

From the table, it will be seen that a work first published in the United States prior to September 27, 1957 will not qualify for protection in the United Kingdom by reason of such publication. Prior to that date, it was   **2.69** customary for American publishers to use the rules on simultaneous publication referred to in paragraph 2.53 above in order to ensure that the relevant work was protected in the United Kingdom. So, it was quite common for American publishers to ensure that publication in the United Kingdom or Canada took place within 14 days of publication in the United States. There were difficulties however in doing this in the United Kingdom during the two World Wars, and special rules were applied in order to overcome those problems.

The rules applied where works were first published in the United States either between August 1, 1914 and January 10, 1920, or between September 3, 1939 and December 28, 1950.

In the first case, if republication had not taken place in any one of His Majesty's Dominions, colonies or possessions (excluding Australia, Canada, Newfoundland, New Zealand and South Africa) prior to February 2, 1920, such a work could still qualify for protection if it was published in the United Kingdom before July 11, 1920.

In the second case, if republication had not taken place in any one of His Majesty's dominions, colonies and possessions (again excluding the same countries as before) within 14 days of publication in the United States, the work would still qualify for protection if published in the United Kingdom before December 29, 1950. As regards this Order, it was held by Scott J. in *Warner Brothers Inc.* v. *The Roadrunner Ltd.* ([1988] F.S.R. 292) that the latter publication could also take place in Canada, and not just the United Kingdom, but the correctness of this decision has been doubted.

(c) *Translation rights*

2.70 An Order in Council made under the 1911 Act deprived the copyright owners of literary or dramatic works of their exclusive right originating from certain territories to make translations of the work into another language, and to perform such translations in public, unless within 10 full calendar years after first publication of the original work, an authorised translation into that language was published in the United Kingdom, or in a country of the British Empire, or in certain countries of the Berne Union.

The rules are too complex to set out here in detail, and much depends on the date when the original literary or dramatic work was first published. The table in Appendix 1 lists the relevant countries where works originating from those countries may be subject to this problem.

(d) *Limited rights for sound recordings*

2.71 In some cases, copyright protection for sound recordings did not extend to causing the sound recording to be heard in public, broadcasting the sound recording or including the sound recording in a cable programme. In such cases, although the copyright in the sound recording will be infringed if it is copied, it will not be infringed if it is publicly performed, broadcast or included in a cable programme. The relevant sound recordings are those which qualified for copyright protection in the United Kingdom because of the maker's connection with or because the sound recording was first published in certain countries, and those countries are indicated in the table.

(e) *Vested interests*

As stated in paragraphs 2.62 ad 2.63, in some cases where an Order in Council extended or applied the relevant provisions as regards countries outside the United Kingdom, this had retroactive effect, and works which were in the public domain in the United Kingdom when made or first published would become subject to copyright protection. **2.72**

This did not mean that acts done by a person whilst the work was in the public domain would become actionable for infringement of copyright. However, it did mean that someone could have incurred expense or liability before the date when the work qualified for copyright protection in the United Kingdom, expecting that he would be able to use or exploit the work, but after the provisions were extended or applied was unable to do so without infringing copyright.

In order to mitigate against the harshness of this, provision was made for such persons to be able to fulfil their expectations, unless the copyright owner paid such compensation as might be agreed or determined by arbitration. Countries in relation to which this may be relevant are indicated in the table.

C. BROADCASTS AND CABLE PROGRAMMES

1. Broadcasts

As stated, neither the rules in Section A nor Section B applied under the 1956 Act in relation to broadcasts or cable programmes. This section deals with the rules which determine whether a broadcast made or cable programme included in a cable programme service prior to commencement of the 1988 Act qualified for copyright protection in the United Kingdom. **2.73**

A television or sound broadcast made from a place in the United Kingdom by the BBC or IBA qualified for protection under section 14 of the 1956 Act. **2.74**

In addition various foreign broadcasts could also qualify for protection. The availability and extent of such protection is indicated by the entries in the last two rows of the table set out in Appendix 1.

Television and sound broadcasts made by either the BBC or the IBA or any person lawfully authorised to make broadcasts to the public in countries to which section 14 of the 1956 Act extended by virtue of an Order in Council made pursuant to section 31 of the 1956 Act also qualified for protection. Extension countries to which this applied are indicated by a "yes" in the table.

In countries to which section 14 of the 1956 Act was only deemed to extend, only BBC and IBA broadcasts will qualify for protection. For such countries the entry on the table is "yes, BBC and IBA only".

A television or sound broadcast made from a place in an "applied" convention country could have qualified for protection and whether such protection was available for a particular country is indicated on the table. Such broadcasts only qualified if they were made by an organisation constituted in or under the laws of that country. Where a date is indicated, only broadcasts made after that date attracted copyright protection in the United Kingdom.

2. Cable programmes

2.75 A cable programme qualified for protection in the United Kingdom if it was included in a cable programme service after January 1, 1985 provided by any of the following in the United Kingdom:

(a) A British subject.

(b) A British protected person.

(c) A citizen of the Republic of Ireland.

(d) A person domiciled in the United Kingdom.

(e) A person resident in the United Kingdom.

(f) A company or other body corporate incorporated under the laws of any part of the United Kingdom.

Although there were provisions for the above rules to be extended or applied in relation to other countries, this appears never to have been done.

IV WORKS MADE BEFORE JULY 1, 1912

2.76 The rules set out in section III for works made after July 1, 1912 are complex enough, but investigating whether a work made before that date qualified for copyright protection in the United Kingdom is daunting in the extreme. The following is only a summary of the basic rules, and it is necessary to emphasise even more here that, if the copyright in such a work is in issue, the precise facts relating to the authorship and publication or other exploitation of the work, and the precise rules relevant to those facts, must be considered in detail.

1. Unpublished and unperformed works

2.77 Under the law in force before the commencement of the 1911 Act, so long as works were not published or performed in public, they were protected under common law. In the case of unpublished literary and artistic works, it did not even matter if the work was performed in public, provided that the manner of such public performance did not amount to a dedication of the work to the public.

It is uncertain whether the protection of such works depended on the nationality, domicile or residence of the author. However, in any event the works of the following were protected:

(a) British subjects.

(b) Residents in the British dominions.

(c) Nationals or residents of those countries which were members of the Berne Union on July 1, 1912. The main relevant territories were Belgium, France, Germany, Luxembourg, Italy, Spain, Denmark, Sweden, Norway, Switzerland and Japan.

(d) Nationals or residents of the Austro-Hungarian Monarchy.

2. Paintings and drawings

Where the work was a painting or drawing, copyright protection was also **2.78** given by the Fine Arts Copyright Act 1862. This was so whether or not the work was published. A work qualified for copyright protection provided that its author was one of the persons listed in paragraph 2.77 above.

3. Works published or publicly performed before the 1911 Act

Assuming that any other work was published or publicly performed **2.79** before July 1, 1912, copyright could only subsist under one of the various statutes in force before that date. Generally, such a work would only be protected if first publication took place in:

(a) The United Kingdom

(b) In any part of the Crown's dominions outside the United Kingdom (although there may have been a problem where this took place prior to the commencement of the International Copyright Act 1886).

(c) In one of the countries referred to in paragraph 2.77(c) above.

(d) In any of the territories of the Austro-Hungarian Monarchy.

4. Protection under the 1911 Act.

If the relevant work was protected by copyright under the rules referred **2.80** to in the above paragraphs, then, provided that the relevant period of copyright had not expired before July 1, 1912, the work would generally have been protected under the 1911 Act. (See further paragraph 8.45.)

5. Works published or performed after the 1911 Act

The question then arises as to the position where the work had not been **2.81** published prior to July 1, 1912, but was then, before the commencement of the 1956 Act, published. If the rules under section III are applied, the work would cease to be protected if first publication took place outside the United Kingdom or in a country in relation to which the relevant provisions had not been extended or applied. However, it is arguable that these rules do not apply, because once the work was through the gateway of the 1911 Act, it was protected for the full period of copyright. If however the work was not published until after the commencement of the 1956 Act, no such problem would arise, and the work would be protected, assuming that the copyright had not by then expired under the rules referred to in Chapter 4.

6. Translation rights

2.82   The rules on translation rights also existed under the laws in force prior to the commencement of the 1911 Act. These rules applied to any work originating from one of the countries referred to in paragraph 2.77(c), and also to works originating from the territories of the Austro-Hungarian Monarchies.

3 FIRST OWNERSHIP OF COPYRIGHT

I INTRODUCTION

This Chapter deals with the identity of the person who is or was first owner of the copyright in a work when created.

1. Distinction between first ownership and other forms of ownership arising upon creation of a work

Although under the rules set out in this Chapter, someone may be the **3.01** first owner of the copyright in a work, the copyright will not necessarily belong to him when the work is created. In many cases, an agreement may have been signed by which the potential first owner agrees that the copyright will vest in someone else on creation. Furthermore, the work may have been created in circumstances in which the copyright in equity belongs to someone else, and not the first owner. These aspects of ownership are dealt with in Chapter 8, but whatever the position, the identity of the first owner is always determined on the basis of the rules set out in this Chapter.

One reason why the distinction is one of importance is in proving title. A plaintiff in a copyright infringement action if required to prove ownership must show a chain of title stemming from the first owner. It is also important in relation to moral rights (see paragraphs 11.12 and 11.25), and for the purposes of establishing who is entitled to enter into an agreement as to prospective ownership of copyright by which the copyright vests in someone else on creation. (See paragraph 8.13.)

2. Summary of the 1988 Act

In summary, first ownership under the new Act is determined in accor- **3.02** dance with the following rules:

(a) The first owner of the copyright in a literary, dramatic, musical or artistic work which is not computer-generated or made by an employee in the course of his employment is the creator of that work.

(b) The first owner of the copyright in a literary, dramatic, musical or artistic work which is generated by computer in circumstances such that there is no human author of the work is the person by whom the arrangements necessary for the creation of the work are undertaken.

(c) The first owner of the copyright in a literary, dramatic, musical or artistic work which is made by an employee in the course of his employment is his employer, subject to any agreement to the contrary.

(d) The first owner of the copyright in a sound recording or film is the person by whom the arrangements necessary for the making of the recording or film are undertaken.

(e) The first owner of the copyright in a broadcast is the person making the broadcast.

(f) The first owner of the copyright in a cable programme is the person providing the cable programme service in which the programme is included.

(g) The first owner of the copyright in the typographical arrangement of a published edition is the publisher.

3. Existing works

3.03   The above provisions do not apply to existing works, even though the transitional provisions which apply to such works may lead to the same result. The first ownership of existing works is normally determined by reference to the rules applying when the work was first created.

4. Differences between the 1956 Act and the 1988 Act

3.04   The 1988 Act has made some substantial changes to the rules on first ownership which existed under the 1956 Act. The main alterations are as follows:

(a) The question of who is the owner of the copyright in a photograph is no longer dependent on who owns the material on which the photograph is taken, and the normal rules on ownership of the copyright in artistic works apply.(See paragraph 3.56.)

(b) The concept of joint authorship now extends not just to literary, dramatic, musical and artistic works, but to all works. (See paragraph 3.66.)

(c) The question of who owns the copyright in a literary, dramatic, musical or artistic work which is computer-generated depends not on the normal rules of authorship, but on who makes the arrangements necessary for the creation of the work.(See paragraph 3.54.)

(d) The question of who is the owner of the copyright in a sound recording no longer depends on who owns the first record embodying the recording, but on who makes the arrangements for the making of the recording. (See paragraph 3.57.)

(e) The special rules relating to ownership of certain artistic works and sound recordings if commissioned have been removed. (See paragraph 3.51.)

(f) The rules as to whether a work is the subject of Crown copyright have altered. (See paragraph 3.80.)

(g) The special rules as to ownership of literary, dramatic or artistic works made by someone in the course of employment by the proprietor of a newspaper have been removed.

(h) The first owner of the copyright in a broadcast is the person making the broadcast, and is no longer restricted to the BBC, IBA or certain foreign organisations. (See paragraph 3.58.)

II FIRST OWNERSHIP OF EXISTING WORKS

A. GENERAL

As stated, the question of who was the first owner of copyright in an existing work must be determined in accordance with the law in force at the time the work was made. (See schedule 1, paragraph 11(1).) This seems a fairly simple rule to apply, but in some cases it produces strange results (see for example paragraph 3.49). However, the transitional provisions of the 1988 Act also state that any event occurring before commencement affecting the ownership of the copyright in an existing work, or creating an interest in relation to the copyright in an existing work, has the same effect as regards copyright under the 1988 Act. (See schedule 1, paragraph 25(1).) Although the wording here is somewhat vague, it is arguable that this allows one to preserve the position on ownership which subsisted under the 1956 Act where there is otherwise a problem. For the sake of convenience, the two rules described in this paragraph are respectively referred to as "the basic rule" and "the alternative rule."   **3.05**

Existing works are works made before commencement of the 1988 Act. Where the making of the work extended over a period of time the work is not made until completed. However, where a photograph, portrait, engraving or sound recording has been commissioned prior to commencement in the circumstances referred to in paragraphs 3.24 and 3.38 below, the work is still treated as an existing work even if it was made, or its making was completed, after commencement of the new Act. (See schedule 1, paragraph 11(2).)

In this section each category of work is dealt with separately, except for works the subject of Crown Copyright which are all covered in paragraph 3.41 onwards.

B. EXISTING LITERARY DRAMATIC MUSICAL AND ARTISTIC WORKS

1. General

The author of a literary, dramatic, musical, or artistic work was the first   **3.06** owner of the copyright in such a work under both the 1911 and 1956 Acts, subject to special rules for:

(a) works made by an employee in the course of employment

(b) commissioned engravings, portraits and photographs

(c) copyrights vesting in certain international organisations

(d) works subject to Crown copyright.

Section 2 below deals with the identity of the author, and the following section with works of joint authorship. Commissioned works are dealt with in section 4, and works made by employees in sections 5 and 6. Copyrights vesting in certain international organisations are briefly dealt with in section 7.

Finally, section 8 deals with pre-1911 Act works, where there are some special rules which may still have some application.

2. The author

(a) *No statutory definition*

3.07   No copyright statute prior to the 1988 Act defined who the author of a work was, and a number of cases over the years have dealt in particular with the situation where more than one party was involved in the conception and creation of a work.

(b) *The general approach taken by the courts*

3.08   As stated in Chapter 1, it is only original literary, dramatic, musical or artistic works which are protected by the laws of copyright. For a work to be original, a sufficient amount of skill, labour or judgment must have been used to create that work. If therefore a party claiming to be an author of a work did not exercise sufficient skill, labour or judgment, he was not an author. In each case, it was a question of fact as to whether the relevant party expended sufficient skill or labour, and there has been no hard and fast rule as to what is sufficient.

(c) *Specific examples*

Some examples of the application of the above general rule to specific situations and works are set out below:

(i) *Plays*

3.09   In *Tate* v. *Thomas* ([1921] 1 Ch. 503), a man who conceived the idea of a plot, suggested some of the incidents in the plot, and some of the words and catchlines used was held not to have contributed sufficient for him to be regarded as a joint author. This old case has recently been followed in *Wiseman* v. *George Weidenfeld & Nicolson Ltd.* ([1985] F.S.R. 525).

Here, the title page of the play in printed form bore the name of two people as authors by agreement between them, but the judge still rejected one of them as an author for copyright ownership purposes.

(ii) Amanuensis

If the writer of a work used an amanuensis to write down words or music   **3.10**
which he dictated or played, the writer was the author and therefore the
first owner: *Donoghue* v. *Allied Newspapers Ltd.* ([1938] Ch. 106).

(iii) Copyright in Reports

The above should be contrasted with the situation where copyright sub-   **3.11**
sisted in a report of a speech, because sufficient skill and labour had been
involved in writing down the words of the speaker. In this case, the author
was the person who wrote down the words: *Walter* v. *Lane* ([1900] A.C.
539). However, this assumes that *Walter* v. *Lane* is still good law following *Interlego A.G.* v. *Tyco Industries Inc.* ([1988] 3 All E.R. 949). (See
paragraph 1.35.)

(iv) Ghost Writers

If a writer was granted interviews by a well-known personality, and then   **3.12**
wrote a work using the material from the interviews, he, and not the
personality, was the author of the work: *Evans* v. *E. Hulton & Co. Ltd.*
([1923–28] MacG. Cop. Cas. 51). It would be different where the
personality took an active part in the actual writing of the work.

(v) Works Created by Computer

In *Express Newspapers plc* v. *Liverpool Daily Post* ([1985] F.S.R. 306),   **3.13**
copyright was claimed in grids with different sequences of letters on
them. The grids were printed on cards. Those in possession of the cards
checked them against sequences in a newspaper to see whether they had
won a prize. The grids and letter sequences were produced by computer,
and it was argued that the writer of the program was not the author of
what appeared on the cards (which were tables and therefore protected as
literary works). This was rejected by Whitford J. who said in his
judgment:

> "The computer was no more than the tool by which the varying grids
> of five-letter sequences were produced to the instructions, via the
> computer programs, of Mr. Ertel. It is as unrealistic as it would be to
> suggest that, if you write your work with a pen, it is the pen which is
> the author of the work rather than the person who drives the pen."

However, in that case, the creator of the computer program was also the
person who operated the program to create the work generated by the

computer. No case seems to have arisen where the two were different. If they were, and the person operating the program was held to have used sufficient skill, labour or judgment in the creation of the work he might be the author of the work for copyright purposes.

It is clear that the Judge in the *Express Newspapers* case was striving to establish a sufficient nexus between the creator of the computer program and the work generated by the computer. No case seems to have arisen where the connection was so remote that the former could not be the author, and where the person using the computer program did not use sufficient skill, labour or judgment in the process by which the work was created. This would be the situation now covered by the new provisions under the 1988 Act relating to computer-generated works. (See paragraph 3.54.) However, there is doubt whether such works existing prior to commencement of the 1988 Act would have been protected by copyright, since there was no author in whom the copyright could vest.

(vi) Drawings and Paintings

3.14 In *Kenrick and Co.* v. *Lawrence and Co.* ([1895] 25 Q.B.D. 99), it was said by Wills J. that the author of such a work "must mean a person who has at least some substantial share in putting the touches on to paper." There, the representation embodied in the drawing was conceived by someone who could not draw but who had another make a drawing of the representation under his direction. It was held that the first person could not be the author, although it was suggested by the court that he might be a joint author.

(vii) Works of Architecture.

3.15 The author of an artistic work which is a work of architecture was held in a case under the 1911 Act to be the author of the architect's plans from which the building was built, and not the builder (*Meikle* v. *Maufe* ([1941] 3 All E.R. 144)). It is not thought that the position was any different under the 1956 Act.

(viii) Works of Artistic Craftsmanship

3.16 The author of a work of artistic craftsmanship in *George Hensher Ltd.* v. *Restawhile Upholstery (Lancs) Ltd.* ([1976] A.C. 64) was considered to be the craftsman who made the work, even where some of the ideas for the work were supplied by someone else. However, in *Burke* v. *Spicers Dress Designs* ([1936] Ch. 400), Clauson J. refused to hold that a company whose employees had made a dress to a design not by them could be the copyright owners of the dress as a work of artistic craftsmanship, since the artistic element did not originate with the craftswomen. By analogy with the *Kenrick* case, however, in many cases the input of skill and labour will be provided by several different people so that there may be joint authors.

(ix) Works made in Infringement of Copyright

In *Redwood Music Ltd.* v. *Chappell and Co. Ltd.* ([1982] R.P.C. 109), it   **3.17**
was held by Robert Goff J. that the copyright in a work made in infringement of copyright of another work belonged to the author of the maker of
the infringing work, and not to the owner of the work infringed. (See
paragraph 8.10 for further comments on this in the light of the *Spycatcher*
decision.)

(d) *Special rules for photographs*

Both the 1911 and 1956 Acts contained special provisions on who was the   **3.18**
author of the copyright in a photograph. Under the 1911 Act (s.21), the
author was deemed to be the person who was owner of the original
negative from which the photograph was directly or indirectly derived at
the time when that negative was made. Under the 1956 Act (s.48(1)), the
author was deemed to be the owner of the material on which the photograph was taken at the time when it was taken.

On the above basis, the author of a positive print from the negative of a
photograph might have been different under the 1956 Act than it was
under the 1911 Act. Under the latter, the author would be the owner of
the original negative, whereas under the former, it would have been the
owner of the paper on which the positive was printed.

3. Joint authors

(a) *Definition of work of joint authorship*

Under the 1956 Act, a work of joint authorship was defined as "a work   **3.19**
produced by the collaboration of two or more authors in which the
contribution of each author is not separate from the contribution of the
other author or authors". (See 1956 Act, s.11(3).) The definition in the
1911 Act was much the same, except that the word "distinct" was used
instead of "separate". (See 1911 Act, s.16(3).)

(b) *Who was a joint author?*

Whether or not a person was a joint author still depended on whether he   **3.20**
contributed sufficient skill, labour and judgment to the creation of the
work, and this has been dealt with in paragraphs 3.08 onwards.

(c) *Collaboration*

The expression "collaboration" was not defined, but in our view, requires   **3.21**
some degree of working together in co-operation (if not in harmony) to
create the work. Although there seem to be no cases on the point, it must
be a question of fact and degree as to whether the skill, labour and
judgment expended on a work by one party was rendered so long after
another party's contribution that it is no longer factually true to say that
there was collaboration. In such circumstances, the revised work may be

the subject of a separate copyright, and the second contributor the author of that copyright in so far as it consists of the skill, labour and judgment which he applied to the work.

(d) *Distinct contributions*

3.22   Where the contribution of each author is separate or distinct from the contribution of the other author or authors, each separate or distinct part will be regarded as the subject of a separate copyright, and the authorship of each part must be considered separately. An example would be a book in which some of the chapters were written by one person, and some by another.

4. Commissioned works

(a) *Engravings or portraits made and photographs taken between July 1, 1912 and the commencement of the 1956 Act* (1911 Act, s.5(1)(*a*))

3.23   In the case of these works, the 1911 Act provided that where the original work (or the block or negative used for the making of the work) was ordered by some person other than the author, and was made for valuable consideration in pursuance of that order, then the person ordering it was the first owner of the copyright. This was subject to any agreement to the contrary. This rule could still be of practical importance as regards films made before commencement of the 1956 Act, where these were protected as photographs.

   Under the 1911 and 1956 Acts, engravings included etchings, lithographs, woodcuts, prints or other similar works.

   In *Leah* v. *Two Worlds Publishing Co. Ltd.* ([1951] Ch. 393), discussions took place between the artist and the alleged commissioner prior to the portrait (which incidentally was of a dead person) being made, but the agreement to buy the drawing did not take place until after it was completed. In those circumstances, it was held by Vaisey J. that the work was not "ordered," and therefore copyright vested in the author.

   In *Wood* v. *Sandow* ([1911–16] MacG. Cop. Cas. 142), Scrutton J. held that one good test as to whether the copyright vested in someone other than the taker of a photograph was whether that person could have been sued by the photographer if the other party had refused to take any copies or pay for the sitting.

(b) *Photographs taken, portraits painted or drawn and engravings made between the commencement of the 1956 Act and the 1988 Act* (1956 Act, s.4(3))

3.24   Where a person commissioned any such work, and paid or agreed to pay for it in money or money's worth, and the work was then made in pursuance of that commission, the commissioner was entitled to the copyright, subject to any agreement to the contrary.

Unlike the 1911 Act, the 1956 Act contained no reference to the block used for the making of an engraving. However, in *James Arnold and Co. Ltd.* v. *Miafern Ltd.* ([1980] R.P.C. 397), it was held that the provision also applied where the plate or block from which an engraving could be made was commissioned.

5. Employment: special rules relating to newspapers and periodicals

Under both the 1911 and 1956 Acts, there were special rules for owner- **3.25** ship of the copyright in such material as articles in newspapers, magazines or similar periodicals. The rules, however, were slightly different both as regards the works covered, and the effect of the provisions.

(a) *Works made after July 1, 1912 and before commencement of the 1956 Act* (1911 Act, s.5(1)(*b*))

The following provision applied to any work which was an article or other **3.26** contribution to a newspaper, magazine or similar periodical. Unlike the parallel provision in the 1956 Act, it included musical works.

If such a work was made in the course of employment under a contract of service or apprenticeship, the employer was the first owner of the copyright. However, in the absence of any agreement to the contrary, the author retained a right to restrain publication of the work otherwise than as part of a newspaper, magazine or similar periodical. Unlike the 1956 Act, it was not necessary that the employer be a newspaper proprietor.

It is uncertain what the nature of the right retained by the author was, and there was authority under a similar provision in the Australian Copyright Act that the result of this was merely to give the author a right of veto over such publication, rather than a right to publish or authorise publication himself. Although there is no express provision preserving the author's right in relation to such an existing work under the 1988 Act, it is likely that the right will survive under the general provision relating to existing works under paragraph 25 of schedule 1.

(b) *Works made after commencement of the 1956 Act and before commencement of the 1988 Act* (1956 Act, s.4(2))

The following provision applied only to literary, dramatic or artistic **3.27** works made by an author in the course of the author's employment by the proprietor of a newspaper, magazine or similar periodical under a contract of service or apprenticeship.

If such a work was made for the purpose of publication in a newspaper, magazine or similar periodical, the 1956 Act provided that the copyright was split. In so far as the copyright related to publication of the work in any newspaper, magazine or similar periodical, the copyright belonged to the proprietor. In all other respects, the copyright belonged to the author.

In such a case the proprietor's rights extended to publication in *any* newspaper and so on, not just in that of which he was proprietor.

In the case of both the 1911 and 1956 Acts, the work must have been made in the course of employment under a contract of service or apprenticeship. For comments on these terms, reference should be made to paragraphs 3.67 onwards.

6. Employment: other cases

3.28   The general provisions on employment in the 1911 Act (s.5(1)(*b*)) and 1956 Act (s.4(4)) were to the same effect. Where any literary, dramatic, musical or artistic work was made in the course of the author's employment by another person under a contract of service or apprenticeship, that other person was entitled to the copyright.

In both cases, this was subject to any agreement to the contrary. Furthermore, in each case, the provision was subject to the special rules which applied to journalist employees, and which are set out in paragraphs 3.26 and 3.27 onwards above.

The question is therefore what constitutes a contract of service or apprenticeship. The modern law on this is dealt with in paragraph 3.64 onwards below, but the application of the basic rule defining who is the first owner for existing works is not entirely easy to construe here. There was no definition in the 1911 or 1956 Acts on what constitutes a contract of employment for copyright purposes, nor is there in the 1988 Act. It is therefore to be determined on the basis of case law, and such case law in the context of employment has developed considerably since the 1911 Act came into effect. Accordingly, although one might think it necessary to examine what the state of case law was at the time when the work was made, on the other hand case law in situations such as this is meant not to change the law but to be declaratory of what the law is. In these circumstances, one can only pray for a sensible and practical approach by the courts.

As regards works of joint authorship, under the 1956 Act, where a work was written by joint authors, one of whom, but not all of whom, were employed under a contract of service or apprenticeship, the provisions on employment did not apply, and the first owners of the work were the joint authors. The position was not so clear under the 1911 Act, and it remains doubtful what the position is in relation to such works.

7. International organisations (1956 Act, s.33)

3.29   Under the 1956 Act, power was given to the Crown to order that in certain cases, the copyright in literary, dramatic, musical or artistic works vest in appropriate international organisations. Orders were made to this effect, and applied to organisations such as the United Nations, the Organisation of American States, and the Council of Europe.

The provisions only applied in the following circumstances:

(a) Where the work was made by or under the direction or control of the relevant organisation and in circumstances where, if the author had been a British subject, copyright would have vested, when made, in the organisation.

(b) Where the work was first published by or under the direction or control of the organisation and in circumstances where either:

(i) the work was first published in pursuance of an agreement with the author not reserving the copyright to him, or

(ii) if the work had been first published in the United Kingdom the organisation would have been entitled to the copyright.

Furthermore, in each case, the provision only applied where copyright would not otherwise have subsisted in the work at the time it was made or first published as the case may be.

If under these provisions, the organisation in question was the first owner of the copyright, the same is so under the 1988 Act.

8. Pre-1911 Act works

In general, the first owner of the copyright was the author, and indeed **3.30** many of the cases on who the author is were decided before the 1911 Act came into force. However, some special cases must be briefly summarised.

(a) *Pre-1911 Act engravings and similar works*

In the case of engravings, etchings, or works in mezzotinto or chiaro **3.31** oscuro made before July 1, 1912, the first owner was either the inventor or designer of that work, or the person who caused or procured that work to be designed, engraved, etched or worked. (See 1734 Engraving Copyright Act.)

(b) *Paintings or drawings made between the commencement of the 1862 Fine Arts Act and July 1, 1912*

Under the 1862 Act, where a painting or drawing was made or executed **3.32** for or on behalf of any other person for good or valuable consideration, the copyright belonged to the person on whose behalf the painting or drawing was made or executed, unless the author expressly reserved the copyright to him by agreement in writing signed by the person on whose behalf the painting or drawing was made or executed. (See 1862 Fine Arts Act.)

(c) *Pre-1911 Act sculpture*

In the case of sculptures made before July 1, 1912, the first owner could **3.33** be either the person making the sculpture, or a person causing the sculpture to be made. (See 1814 Sculpture Copyright Act.)

(d) *Employment provisions before July 1, 1912* (Copyright Act 1842)

The following provision only applied where a publisher or other person **3.34** projected or was the proprietor of an encyclopedia, review, magazine, periodical work, work published in a series of books or parts, or any book of whatever type. If in those circumstances, the publisher or proprietor employed someone else to write the whole or any portion of that work on terms that the copyright should belong to the publisher or proprietor and the writer was paid by such person, then assuming that the relevant part was in fact written under such employment, the copyright vested in the publisher or proprietor. This is only a summary of the relevant provision, which is even more cumbersome and complex in its actual terms.

In certain cases, the right to publish separately a work written for inclusion in another work (such as an article in a periodical) reverted to the author 28 years after first publication, and during the first 28-year period the publisher or other person could not publish such a work separately. Furthermore, the author could expressly or by implication reserve to himself the right to publish such a work in separate form during the first 28-year period.

This provision extended not only to contracts of service but contracts for services. Not surprisingly, the section was a somewhat litigious one, and it should be noted in particular that, although the section referred to the necessity for an agreement that the copyright was to belong to the publisher or other person, this could be implied as well as express, and indeed would readily be implied in many circumstances.

(e) *Musical works published before July 1, 1912*

3.35 Before the 1911 Act, there was no right to prevent a musical work being reproduced in the form of a sound recording. The 1911 Act introduced this for the first time. By section 19(7)(*c*) of the 1911 Act, the rights conferred by the 1911 Act in respect of the making, or authorising the making, of what were described as "contrivances by means of which the work may be mechanically performed" belonged to the author or his legal personal representatives. This was so despite any assignment made before the passing of the 1911 Act, that is, December 16, 1911. The somewhat cumbersome "contrivances" expression is probably not as wide as the definition of sound recording under the 1988 Act.

Although the transitional provisions to the 1988 Act contain no express reference to the preservation of this right, in our view it has survived through the operation of the general provisions on existing works under paragraph 25 of schedule 1. Of course, in many cases, the right will by now have been assigned to a publisher.

C. SOUND RECORDINGS

The following provisions do not apply to film sound-tracks. (See paragraph 3.40 below.)

(a) *Application of the previous legislation*

3.36 The 1911 Act contained rules specifying who owned the copyright in a sound recording, the effect of which in practice may have been similar to that of the 1956 Act, but was not necessarily so. The 1956 Act abolished these provisions and applied the 1956 Act rules to sound recordings made under the 1911 Act, not without some odd effects. In our view, pre-1956 Act sound recordings must still be dealt with in the same way, because of the alternative rule. (See paragraph 3.05 above.)

(b) *The first owner under the 1956 Act*

Under the 1956 Act, the first owner of the copyright in a sound recording   **3.37** was the maker of that recording. (See 1956 Act, s.12(4).) The maker was deemed to be the person who owned the first record embodying the recording at the time when the recording was made. (See 1956 Act, s.12(8).) On first reading, this sounds strange, but the 1956 Act distinguished rather more clearly between the sound recording in which copyright subsisted and the artefact in which the recording could be embodied. "Record" was defined under the 1956 Act as any disc, tape, perforated roll or other device in which sounds are embodied so as to be capable (with or without the aid of some other instrument) of being automatically reproduced therefrom. (See 1956 Act, s.48(1).) In most modern cases this would mean the original master tape.
   Of course, the first record embodying the recording such as a master tape could belong to more than one person. In such a case, the copyright would have been jointly owned.

(c) *Commissioned sound recordings*

The 1911 Act contained no special rules on commissioned recordings, but   **3.38** new provisions relating to such recordings were introduced under the 1956 Act (s.12(4)). Taking the approach referred to under paragraph 3.05 above, it follows that these provisions apply to sound recordings made under the 1911 Act, even though whilst the 1911 Act was in force those recordings vested in the owner of the original plate as defined under that Act!
   The commissioning provisions under the 1956 Act applied where someone commissioned the making of a sound recording, and paid or agreed to pay for it in money or money's worth. If the recording was made in pursuance of that commission, the commissioner owned the copyright, subject to any agreement to the contrary, and subject to special provisions as regards Crown copyright.

D. FILMS

(a) *Films made before commencement of the 1956 Act*

As already stated, films made before the commencement of the 1956 Act   **3.39** could only be protected as photographs, dramatic works, or (in the case of cartoons) drawings. In those circumstances, the rules outlined in section B (paragraph 3.06 onwards) above apply.

If such a film was protected as a species of dramatic work, the most likely sole author was the director. Frequently, however, the first owner would still have been the production company, because of the common practice for such companies to employ all creative parties involved in a film. The same probably applies as regards photographs, particularly bearing in mind the commissioning provisions (see paragraph 3.23 above) and the fact that ownership was tied to ownership of the negative.

(b) *Films made between the commencement of the 1956 Act and the 1988 Act*

3.40   Here, the first owner of the copyright was the maker of the film (1956 Act, s.13(4)). The maker was defined in the same way as under the 1988 Act, namely the person by whom the arrangements necessary for the making of the film were undertaken (1956 Act, s.13(10)). This would usually be the production company. If more than one person undertook those arrangements, the copyright might be jointly owned.

Although the sound-tracks of films made under the 1956 Act will be protected as sound recordings under the 1988 Act, the author and first owner of copyright is deemed to be the first owner of copyright in the film. (See 1988 Act, schedule 1, paragraph 8(2).)

E. CROWN COPYRIGHT

3.41   This section applies only to literary, dramatic, musical and artistic works and sound recordings and films, and defines the circumstances in which the first owner of the copyright in such works was the Crown, and not as referred to in Sections B, C and D above.

1. Literary, dramatic, musical and artistic works

3.42   No special rules on ownership of copyright by the Crown applied until the 1911 Copyright Act. The 1911 Act introduced such rules for the first time, and these applied to works prepared or published by or under the direction or control of the Crown, whether or not this had been done before or after the commencement of the 1911 Act (s.18). However, although under the basic rule one needs to look to see who was the first owner of the copyright at the time the work was made, the alternative rule provides that any event having any effect on ownership prior to commencement of the Act retains that effect. Since the effect of the 1956 Act was to repeal the provisions of the 1911 Act, and treat works in this respect as if the provisions under the 1956 Act had always applied (1956 Act, schedule 7, paragraph 45(1)), it is those provisions which it is necessary to consider.

If the work was made by or under the direction or control of the Crown or any government department, then under the 1956 Act the first owner was the Crown. (See 1956 Act, s.39(1).)

Even where the work was not made by or under the direction or control of the Crown, the Crown was the first owner if the work was first published in the United Kingdom (or in another country to which the provisions of the Act on publication extended) under the direction or control of the Crown or a government department. (See 1956 Act, s.39(2).)

These provisions had effect subject to any agreement with the author of the work which was to the contrary.

The precise scope of the term "direction or control" was unclear. In *British Broadcasting Co.* v. *Wireless League Gazette Publishing Co.* ([1926] Ch. 433), it was held that simply because an act was done in pursuance of a licence from the Crown and in accordance with the requirements of that licence did not mean that the act was done under direction or control of the Crown. A work commissioned by a government department will not necessarily have been made under the direction or control of the Crown, and accordingly it is not correct to regard the expression as having been a mere substitute for the usual employment and commissioning provisions.

2. Sound recordings and films

Under the 1956 Act, the copyright in a sound recording or film made by or **3.43** under the direction or control of the Crown or a government department vested in the Crown, subject to any agreement to the contrary with the maker of the sound recording or film (1956 Act, s.39(5) and (6)).

These provisions, however, did not apply to pre-1956 Act films. (See 1956 Act, schedule 7, paragraph 31(2).) Whether or not these were the subject of Crown copyright depended on whether as a dramatic work or series of photographs the copyright would have vested in the Crown under the rules referred to in paragraph 3.42.

F. BROADCASTS

As already stated, no copyright subsists in a broadcast made before the **3.44** commencement of the 1956 Act.

1. Broadcasts made by the BBC or IBA

If the broadcast was made by the BBC or the IBA then the copyright **3.45** belonged to the BBC or IBA. (See 1956 Act, s.14(2).) This applied whether or not the broadcast was made from the United Kingdom or a country to which the provisions of the 1956 Act on broadcasts had been extended.

2. Other broadcasts

Where the broadcast was not one made by the BBC or the IBA, it was **3.46** protected in the United Kingdom only if it came into either of the following categories:

(a) It was made by any person or class of persons lawfully authorised to broadcast to the public in any country to which the provisions of the 1956 Act on broadcasts were extended. (See 1956 Act, ss.31 and 34 and 1961 Copyright (Broadcasting Organisations) Order.)

(b) It was made from a place in any country to which the provisions of the 1956 Act on broadcasts were applied and was so made by any organisation constituted in or under the laws of the country in which the broadcast was made. (See 1956 Act, s.32(1).)

In each of these cases, the copyright in the broadcast was owned by the person who or organisation which made it. For details of the main relevant countries see paragraph 2.73.

3. Direct broadcasting by satellite

3.47   With effect from January 1, 1985, it was provided that, where the broadcast was a DBS broadcast, it was deemed to be made by the body by whom the visual images and/or sounds were transmitted to the satellite transponder. (See 1956 Act, s.14(10)(*b*).)

G. CABLE PROGRAMMES

3.48   As already stated, no copyright subsists in a cable programme included in a cable programme service before January 1, 1985. The first copyright owner of a cable programme included after that date was the person providing the cable programme service in which the programme was included. (See 1956 Act, s.14A(3).)

H. TYPOGRAPHICAL ARRANGEMENTS

3.49   This is another instance where in relation to pre-1956 Act works, the transitional provisions need to be treated with some care.

This copyright did not exist until the 1956 Act, but was retrospective as regards editions published before that date. For pre-1956 Act works therefore, under the basic rule (see paragraph 3.05) there was no first owner, but, having regard to the alternative rule, the first owner of the copyright is the same as in the case of editions published for the first time after commencement of the 1956 Act.

Under the 1956 Act the publisher of an edition was entitled to the copyright in that edition (1956 Act, s.15(2)). No definition was provided of who the publisher was, and by analogy with the decision of the House of Lords in *Infabrics* v. *Jaytex* ([1981] 1 All E.R. 1057) it is unlikely that it simply meant the person issuing copies of the edition to the public. This could have been a mere distributor, and the distributor was not necessarily the party who would ordinarily be described as the publisher. The Shorter Oxford Dictionary defines a publisher as one whose business is the issuing of books, periodicals, music and so on as the agent of the author or owner, or one who produces copies of such works and distributes them to booksellers and other dealers or to the public.

III THE PROVISIONS OF THE 1988 ACT

A. INTRODUCTION

The author is the first owner of the copyright in all cases, except for works **3.50** the subject of Crown or related copyrights, works the copyright in which vests in certain international organisations and works made by an employee in the course of employment. However, for the first time, the term "author" is defined, and this is done not only in general terms, but also specifically in relation to some categories of works. The new provisions on authorship are dealt with first below followed by a section on joint authorship. Subsequent sections deal with the three exceptions to the author being first owner as referred to above. Although strictly speaking not a first ownership point, the special rules on certain anonymous or pseudonymous unpublished literary, dramatic, musical or artistic works are dealt within the final section.

As already stated, one of the major changes under the 1988 Act is the **3.51** abolition of the old commissioning provisions. Accordingly, where a work is commissioned in the future, and the commissioner wishes to own the copyright, he must make special arrangements to ensure that the copyright vests in him through the provisions as to future copyright referred to in paragraph 8.13 onwards. If this is not done, problems may arise over the extent to which the commissioner may exploit the work, although some assistance may be obtained from what is set out in later chapters on equitable ownership (paragraph 8.06 onwards) and implied terms (paragraph 9.07 onwards).

B. THE AUTHOR AS FIRST OWNER

As stated, under the 1988 Act the author of any work is the first owner of **3.52** the copyright in that work (s.11(1)), subject to the provisions on employment (s.11(2)), Crown and related copyrights (ss.163–167) and the copyright of certain international organisations (s.168).

   The author is defined as the person who creates the work (s.9(1)), but there are special rules for certain categories of work, and each category of work is therefore examined in turn.

1. Literary, dramatic, musical and artistic works

Under the 1988 Act, different rules apply depending on whether or not the work is computer-generated.

(a) *Computer-generated works*

(i) The Author of such Computer-Generated Works

3.53   If the work is computer-generated, the author is the person by whom the arrangements necessary for the creation of the work are undertaken (s.9(3)). This is similar to the approach which applies as regards sound recordings and films.

(ii) What is a Computer-Generated Work?

3.54   A work is computer-generated if the work is generated by computer in circumstances such that there is no human author of the work (s.178). It is obvious therefore that not all works which involve the use of a computer in their production fall within the definition of computer-generated work. There will be many cases where it is not clear whether a work is computer generated or whether it is a work with a human author generated with the use of a computer. The distinction is of significance since it affects the duration of copyright in the work, subsistence of moral rights and may also affect title to the work. An example of a work by human author generated with the use of a computer would be an engineering drawing created by the engineer with the assistance of Computer Aided Design (CAD) techniques. An example of a computer-generated work as defined by the 1988 Act would be a list of share prices which is automatically created by the input of raw data from many different sources. In such a case the computer which produces the work may well be unconnected to the author of the program it uses and accordingly one could not meaningfully consider the work as having a human author.
    The situation is therefore not one which is free from difficulty. It may well be that the choice of what instructions to give the computer is such that independent skill and labour has been used, and in those circumstances although the work may have been generated by the computer, the provisions would not apply because there was a human author. Alternatively, it might be that the link between what is embodied in the computer program and what is created by means of that program is so strong that the author of the program is really the author of the work. In these circumstances again, the normal provisions as to first ownership would apply because there is a human author. The point seems already to have been anticipated in *Express Newspapers plc* v. *Liverpool Daily Post*. (See paragraph 3.13 above.)

(iii) Computer-generated works and employees

3.55   It should be noted that the employment provisions contained in the 1988

Act (s.11(2)—see paragraph 3.67) are drafted in such a way that it does not appear that they could apply to computer-generated works. This is because such a work is not made by an employee, but generated by computer in circumstances where no human author has made it. However, where an employee makes the *arrangements* necessary for the creation of the work, his employer will presumably still own the copyright because the employee will usually have made those arrangements on behalf of the employer.

(b) *Non-computer-generated works*

There are no special rules for other literary, dramatic, musical or artistic   **3.56**
works, and accordingly it will be necessary in all other cases to determine who is the person who created the work.

In one case, the new rule represents a fundamental change in the law. The ownership of the copyright in photographs will no longer be tied to the negative, or the material on which the photograph was taken, but to the person who creates the photograph. Under the 1988 Act, a photograph is a recording of light or other radiation on any medium on which an image is produced or from which an image may by any means be produced. It follows therefore that when one is discussing the negative of a photograph, the owner of the copyright will usually be the person who takes the photograph. This is because the film itself is a medium from which an image may be produced. The position might be different when someone sets everything up for the taking of a photograph, but for some reason is not the person who actually takes it. As regards positive prints, assuming that these qualify for protection on the basis of originality (see paragraph 1.34), the copyright owner would be the person who created the print. However, the latter would not be able to exploit his copyright without the consent (express or implied) of the owner of any copyright in the negative.

As regards other works, it is difficult to assess whether the new definition will produce a different result from that under the previous law. Of course, in considering who the "creator" is, one must bear in mind still that it is the copyright work (that is, the literary, dramatic or musical work which has been recorded, or the physical form of the artistic work) which one is considering, and not simply the ideas and concepts embodied in such a work (see paragraph 5.16). On the whole, it seems unlikely that the courts will take a radically different approach from that under the cases referred to in paragraph 3.08 onwards.

2. Sound recordings and films

The first owner of the copyright in a sound recording or film is the person   **3.57**
by whom the arrangements necessary for the making of the recording or film are undertaken (s.9(2)(*a*)). If this is more than one person, then the copyright will be jointly owned, even where the persons are not joint authors, as referred to in paragraph 3.66 below.

3. Broadcasts

(a) *The first owner*

3.58   The first owner of the copyright in a broadcast is defined as the person making that broadcast (s.9(2)(*b*)).

(b) *Who is the person making a broadcast?*

3.59   The person making a broadcast is defined as:

(i) the person transmitting the programme, if he has any responsibility to any extent for its contents, *and*

(ii) any person providing the programme who makes with the person transmitting it the arrangements necessary for its transmission (s.6(3)).

For the position where there is more than one person to whom the above provisions apply, see paragraph 3.66 below.
   A programme is defined as any item included in a broadcast (s.6(3)). This provision is obscure, and gives rise to some difficulties.

(c) *The person transmitting the programme*

3.60   Whether the person transmitting the programme is a first owner or not depends on the meaning of "responsibility," and on what "its contents" refers to. If "its contents" refers to the contents of the broadcast, then whatever the meaning of "responsibility" as referred to below the meaning would seem reasonably clear. For example, the BBC decide on what they intend to broadcast, and therefore are responsible both in the sense of making that decision, and in bearing any liability which may ensue from such transmission. On the other hand, if "its contents" refers (as seems more likely) to the programme, then the BBC may have no responsibility for the contents of that programme, in the sense of deciding what it will contain, where the programme is one which has been bought by the BBC from a third party. However, it may still be "responsible" in the sense of it having responsibilities to ensure that what it broadcasts complies with certain requirements arising under its Charter and its Licence from the Secretary of State for the Home Office.

(d) *The person providing the programme*

3.61   It may also be difficult to determine who is within the second limb of the definition. The BBC transmits its own broadcasting service. Where the programme is one which the BBC has not made, the person supplying the programme to the BBC may be the producer of that programme, or he may be a distributor of television programmes. Which of those two parties actually provides programmes is likely to depend on the contract under which the programme is provided. However, can it be said in those circumstances that such a person makes with the BBC the arrangements necessary for its transmission? In one sense, it may be so, in that arrangements will have to be made for the actual supply of a copy of the programme for the purposes of broadcasting it, but this is simply one step necessary in order for transmission to take place, and may not be sufficient to constitute the whole of "*the* arrangements".

(e) *The IBA*

The definition of who makes a broadcast is easier to apply in the case of 3.62 the IBA, and the independent television companies whose programmes are transmitted by the IBA. The IBA not only transmits the programmes but has responsibility for the contents (see ss.2 and 4 of the 1981 Broadcasting Act). Accordingly, they come within the first limb of the definition. The television companies provide the programmes to the IBA to transmit them and would presumably be held to make the arrangements necessary for transmission. Accordingly, they would come within the second limb of the definition.

(f) *Broadcast relays*

Where the broadcast is one which relays another broadcast by reception 3.63 of the broadcast and immediate retransmission of that broadcast, the first owner is the person making the broadcast which is received and immediately retransmitted. (See s.9(2)(*b*).)

4. Cable programmes

The first owner of the copyright in a cable programme is the person 3.64 providing the cable programme service in which the programme is included (s.9(2)(*c*)). Here, the exclusions from the definition of cable programme service should be borne in mind. (See paragraph 1.56 onwards.)

5. Typographical arrangements

The first owner of the copyright in a typographical arrangement of a 3.65 published edition is the publisher. (See s.9(2)(*d*).)

As under the 1956 Act, there is no definition of publisher, and it is likely that if the point was ever raised the courts would take the view as set out in paragraph 3.49 above. However, there is one material difference in the 1988 Act which must be mentioned. "Publication" is defined as the issue of copies to the public, and unlike the similar provisions in the 1956 Act, the words are added "and related expressions shall be construed accordingly." The question therefore arises whether "publisher" is a related expression. In many ways, it is related in that the origin of the word is the same, but it is to be hoped that the courts would take the view that the reference to related expressions was only to expressions used in the same context such as "published" and "unpublished." If this were not so, the publisher could be a mere distributor of copies to the public, and in order to avoid any doubt in the matter, it would be sensible for publishers to ensure that contracts with their distributors confirm that the copyright is owned by the former.

C. JOINT AUTHORSHIP (s.10)

3.66   The expression "work of joint authorship" is defined in the same way as that appearing in the 1956 Act, except that the draftsman has reverted to the use of the word "distinct" rather than "separate." Although members of the House of Lords in debate appeared to be somewhat concerned about the implications of the use of the word "separate", it seems unlikely that reverting to the use of the word "distinct" as under the 1911 Act will make much difference in practice.

     The expression now extends to all works, although it is not one which lies comfortably with the definition of who is said to be the owner of the copyright in such works as sound recordings or films. This is because first owner in these cases is defined by reference to a time prior to completion of the film or sound recording ("the arrangements necessary for the making of . . ."), whereas the word "contribution" in the definition of a work of joint authorship probably refers to the contribution of the authors in relation to the finished product. However, as with the 1956 Act, where the contributions are not distinct, there will in those circumstances still be two or more people involved in the creation of the work, and accordingly they will be joint first owners, even if they are not joint authors.

     As regards broadcasts, it is specifically provided that in any case where more than one person is to be taken as making the broadcast, then the work is one of joint authorship. Thus, in some circumstances, the person transmitting the programme, as well as one or more persons providing the programme may together be joint authors. (See for example the circumstances referred to in paragraph 3.62.)

D. EMPLOYMENT (s.11(2))

3.67   Where a literary, dramatic, musical or artistic work is made by an employee in the course of his employment, the employer is the first owner of the copyright. This is subject to any agreement to the contrary. Employment means a contract of service or of apprenticeship. (See s.178.) See paragraph 3.55 for comments in relation to computer-generated works.

     There are no similar provisions relating to other works. It is therefore important in such cases for an employer who wishes to ensure that he owns the copyright for example in a sound recording the arrangements for which were made by his employee that the contract of employment makes it clear that any arrangements which the employee makes for the creation of sound recording are made on behalf of his employer.

For the work therefore to be owned by the "employer" there are two necessary criteria. First, the "employee" must be employed under a contract of service or apprenticeship. Secondly, the work must have been made in the course of the author's employment. Where an employer wishes to ensure that he owns the copyright in a work by an employee, he will often include a clause in the contract of employment confirming or providing that copyright in works by the employee will vest in him. This would save arguments as to whether the contract was one of service, or whether the work was one made in the course of employment. However, for the future it may still be important to know whether the work is one to which the employment provisions of the 1988 Act apply, because of the position on moral rights. As referred to in paragraphs 11.12 and 11.25, the ability to enforce moral rights is restricted in the case of works to which the employment provisions apply. An employer however can still protect his position by requiring from his employee a waiver of such rights.

The application of the employment provisions to works of joint authorship is not as clear as it was under the 1956 Act, but we believe that, as there, all the joint authors must be employees for the employer to be first owner. It is arguable however that the employees need not be employed by the same person, in which case two or more employers might own a copyright as joint authors.

1. Contract of service

The distinction which is crucial here is between a contract of service and a contract for services, although recent more general employment cases make it clear that there may be a contract coming into neither of those categories, or indeed no contract at all. (See paragraph 3.76 below.)   **3.68**

Whether an employment contract is a contract of service or a contract for services will often be easy to determine, but there is a difficult grey area which has been the subject of some considerable judicial comment recently. Unfortunately, the "grey" area is of relevance to the law of copyright, because it is precisely in that area, where the degree of control which the employer may have over the creation of the copyright work is limited, that problems may arise.

This is another area where one can do no more than provide a basic summary of what the courts have taken into account in considering whether the contract is one of service or for services. It must be stressed that this is an area in which the courts can only provide guidelines, and where each case is very much one to be decided on the basis of its own facts. None of the tests below is conclusive, and the courts may well apply more than one test in seeking to decide whether a contract is one of service or for services.

(a) *The control test*

The test very often favoured by the courts, particularly in early cases, is   **3.69** one of control. One of the leading cases on this was *Simmons* v. *Heath Laundry Co.* ([1910] 1 K.B. 543), and in the copyright case of *University of London Press Ltd.* v. *University Tutorial Press Ltd.* ([1916] 2 Ch. 601), Peterson J. summarised the judgments in that case as follows:

> " . . . Fletcher Moulton L.J. pointed out that a contract of service was not the same as a contract for service, and that the existence of direct control by the employer, the degree of independence on the part of the person who renders services, the place where the service is rendered, are all matters to be considered in determining whether there is a contract of service. As Buckley L.J. indicated in the same case, a contract of service involves the existence of a servant, and imports that there exists in the person's serving an obligation to obey the orders of the person served. A servant is a person who is subject to the commands of his master as to the manner in which he shall do his work."

(b) *Skilled employees*

3.70   It is apparent that the above test needs to be heavily qualified in the case of skilled employees. Many creators of copyright works have little or no control exercised over them as to the manner in which they create those works. Thus Ungoed-Thomas J. in *Beloff* v. *Pressdram Ltd.* ([1973] 1 All E.R. 241) (a copyright case in which one of the issues was whether the Political and Lobby Correspondent of the *Observer* newspaper was employed):

> "It thus appears, and rightly in my respectful view, that the greater the skill required for an employee's work, the less significant is control in determining whether the employee is under a contract of service. Control is just one of many factors whose influence varies according to circumstances. In such highly skilled work as that of the plaintiff it seems of no substantial significance."

(c) *The Ready Mixed Concrete test*

3.71   A further test which has received some support from higher courts is that originally adopted by McKenna J. in *Ready Mixed Concrete Ltd.* v. *Minister of Pensions and National Insurance* ([1968] 2 Q.B. 497). Here, it was said that a contract of service exists if the following three conditions are fulfilled:

(i) The servant agrees that in consideration of a wage or other remuneration he will provide his own work and skill in the performance of some service to his master.

(ii) He agrees, expressly or impliedly, that in the performance of that service he will be subject to the other's control in a sufficient degree to make that other master. The judge here did not refer to the cases involving skilled workers, but the use of the word "sufficient" implies that the degree of control necessary will still fluctuate from case to case.

(iii) The other provisions of the contract are consistent with its being a contract of service.

(d) *The "economic reality" test*

Remuneration may be an important factor. A regular salary or one which **3.72** is fixed can be good evidence of a contract of service. Conversely, a share in the profits of the business, or carrying the financial risk of the venture, may be evidence that the worker is self-employed. Other relevant financial considerations include provision of sick pay and holiday pay, responsibility for tax and national insurance, and payment and provision of tools, premises and equipment.

(e) *The "organisational" test*

A further test is one which concentrates on the degree of integration of a **3.73** worker into his employer's organisation. Thus, Denning L.J. in another copyright case, *Stevenson, Jordan and Harrison Ltd.* v. *Macdonald and Evans* ([1952] 69 R.P.C. 10) stated:

> "Under a contract of service, a man is employed as part of the business, whereas under a contract for services his work although done for the business is not integrated into it but only accessory to it."

However, this test is not one which has been used much recently, and poses more questions than it answers in such borderline cases as the so-called "umbrella" contracts. (See paragraph 3.72 below.)

(f) *The "label" test*

If when the factors are taken into account they are evenly balanced, then **3.74** the label attached to the position of the "employee" may be the determining factor. Thus Lord Denning in *Massey* v. *Crown Life Insurance Company* ([1978] 1 W.L.R. 676) stated:

> "If their relationship is ambiguous and is capable of being one or the other, then the parties can remove that ambiguity by the very agreement itself which they make with one another. The agreement itself becomes the best material from which to gather the true legal relationship between them."

(g) *The "own boss" test*

A more general test which seems to have found favour is that which **3.75** appears in the judgment of the Employment Appeal Tribunal in *Withers* v. *Flackwell Heath Football Supporters Club* ([1981] I.R.L.R. 307):

> "It is clear from the authorities that when you have to decide whether you have to deal with a contract of employment or a contract for

services by an independent contractor . . . there is no rule of thumb for reaching the right conclusion. The degree of control exercised by the person for whom the work is being done, the terminology the parties use, whether the man doing the work uses his own gear, all are to be taken into account. 'Is he on his own business rather than the business of the party for whom the work is being done?' is the ultimate question."

Later in the judgment, the Employment Appeal Tribunal put the question in an even more basic way. If one asked the "employee" whilst he was in "employment" "are you your own boss?" and if on the facts he could honestly have given no other answer than "no," he will be employed under a contract of service.

(h) *The "mutuality of obligation" test*

3.76   Most recent emphasis has been based on so-called mutuality of obligation. In the words of Dillon L.J. in *Nethemere (St. Neots) Ltd.* v. *Taverna*
([1984] I.R.L.R. 240):

"It is said nonetheless that there is one *sine qua non* which can firmly be identified as an essential of the existence of a contract of service and that is that there must be mutual obligations on the employer to provide work for the employee and on the employee to perform work for the employer. If such mutuality is not present, then either there is no contract at all or whatever contract there is must be a contract for services or something else, but not a contract of service."

However, this mutuality of legally binding obligations on each side may be inferred from the regular provision and acceptance of work, provided that there is the necessary element of continuity. This is the so-called "umbrella" contract case. Thus in the *Nethermere* case, the workers worked from home, using sewing machines to put pockets into trousers. They could decide how much work, if any, they did, but this was subject to the overriding consideration that they must accept sufficient for it to be worthwhile for the company van to visit them. This was obviously a case very near the line, but it was held that the workers were employed on a contract of service. Stephenson L.J. put it in such a way that one can see parallels with such situations as when writers make regular contributions to one newspaper or journal:

"I cannot see why well-founded expectations of continuing home-work should not be hardened or refined into enforceable contracts by regular giving and taking of work over periods of a year or more, and why outworkers should not thereby become employees under contracts of service like those doing similar work at the same rate in the factory."

(i) *Directors*

3.77   A director is not necessarily employed on a contract of service with the company of which he is an officer. Whether or not the company is the first owner of the copyright must be examined on the same basis as above, namely is there a contract of service separate from the holding of office as a director. However, even where there is no such contract of service, the company may be entitled to the copyright under the rules as to equitable ownership. (See paragraph 8.08 below.)

2. Contract of apprenticeship

A contract of apprenticeship is one where the employer agrees to teach someone the skills of a trade and that person agrees to serve his employer in learning that trade. **3.78**

3. In the course of employment

Just because an employee creates a literary, dramatic, musical or artistic work in his employer's time does not mean that he does this in the course of his employment. The leading copyright case here is *Stevenson Jordan and Harrison Ltd.* v. *MacDonald and Evans* ([1952] 69 R.P.C. 10). Here, a man was employed under a contract of service as what might be termed today a management consultant. After he left the employment of the company, he published a book which contained various types of material. One section of the book was taken from a report on one of his cases. This was regarded as covered by the term "in the course of employment." Other sections of the book however consisted of the text of lectures given by the employee whilst he was employed. It was held by the Court of Appeal that, although the giving of the lectures was helpful to the employer, the terms of employment were such that he could not be required to give the lectures under his contract of service, and accordingly the lectures were not done in the course of employment. Denning L.J. put the difference in this way: **3.79**

> "In so far as Mr. Evans-Hemming prepared and wrote manuals for the use of a particular client of the company he was doing it as part of his work as a servant of the company under a contract of service; but, in so far as he prepared and wrote lectures for delivery to universities and to learned and professional societies, he was doing so as an accessory to the contract of service and not as part of it. The giving of lectures was no doubt very helpful to the company in that it might serve directly as an advertisement for the company, and on that account the company paid Mr. Evans-Hemming the expenses he incurred. The lectures were in a sense part of the services rendered by Mr. Evans-Hemming for the benefit of the company. But they were in no sense part of his service. It follows that the copyright in the lectures was in Mr. Evans-Hemming."

Both Denning L.J. and Lord Evershed M.R. considered that if someone was employed as a lecturer, that did not mean that the copyright in lecture notes vested in the employer. Again, in the words of Denning L.J.:

"Other instances occur when a doctor on the staff of a hospital, or a master on the staff of a school, is employed under a contract of service to give lectures or lessons orally to students. If he, for his own convenience, puts the lectures in writing, then his written work is not done under the contract of service. It is most useful as an accessory to his contracted work but it is not really part of it. The copyright is in him and not in his employers."

The case is not entirely an easy one, and the situation might be different with modern teaching practices. Of course, it is always possible for contracts to be drafted in such a way that notes for lectures and the recording of the lectures themselves are part of the employee's duties, and thus created in the course of employment.

E. CROWN AND RELATED COPYRIGHTS

Both the usual provisions on ownership by reference to the author, and the provisions on works made by employees in the course of employment are excluded in relation to the works referred to in this section.

1. Crown copyright (s.163(1) and (4))

3.80 This category applies where any work is either made by the Crown or by an officer or servant of the Crown in the course of his duties. In these circumstances, the Crown is the first owner of the copyright in the work. "In the course of his duties" should probably be looked at in the same way as "in the course of employment". (See paragraph 3.79 above.)

A similar provision applies in relation to works of joint authorship as is referred to in paragraph 3.81 below.

2. Parliamentary copyright (s.165(1))

3.81 This provision applies where any work is made by or under the direction or control of the House of Commons or the House of Lords. Here, the House by whom, or under whose direction or control, the work is first made is the first owner. The two Houses are joint first owners of copyright if the work was made by or under the direction or control of both Houses.

The 1988 Act contains no exclusive definition of the meaning of "by or under the direction or control," but some guidance is provided. If a work is made by an officer or employee in the course of his duties, then that is covered, as is any sound recording, film, live broadcast or live cable programme of proceedings in either House. However, the position set out in paragraph 3.41 above is also confirmed, in that the provision specifically states that a work is not made by or under the direction or control of either House by reason only of its being commissioned.

Where the work is one of joint authorship, and not all of the authors make the work under the direction or control of either House, the section applies only in relation to those authors to whom the provision applies and to the copyright subsisting by virtue of their contribution to the work as a whole. This is a strange provision, because the whole point of a work of joint authorship is that the parts contributed are not distinct. In those circumstances, it is difficult to know how one can say that the provision applies only to the copyright subsisting by virtue of their contribution.

3. Bills (s.166(1))

Copyright in every Bill introduced into Parliament belongs to one or both   **3.82**
Houses of Parliament. The precise provisions depend on whether the Bill is a public or private or personal one.

If the Bill is public, it belongs in the first instance to the House into which the Bill is introduced. When the Bill is carried to the second House, it then belongs to both Houses jointly. Personal Bills are treated in the same way, except that in the first instance the copyright always belongs to the House of Lords.

Copyright in a private Bill belongs to both Houses jointly.

4. Acts and Measures (s.164(1))

Copyright in every act of Parliament or Measure of the General Synod of   **3.83**
the Church of England vests in the Crown.

F. COPYRIGHT OF CERTAIN INTERNATIONAL ORGANISATIONS

This provision only applies to literary, dramatic, musical or artistic   **3.84**
works.

Where such a work is made by an officer or employee of or is published by a relevant international organisation, then the organisation is the first owner of the copyright if the work would not otherwise qualify for copyright protection under the provisions as to qualification by reference to author or by reference to the country of first publication.

The organisations to which this provision applies will be provided for by Order in Council.

By section 178, the international organisations to which this provision can apply are limited to those whose members include one or more states.

This provision is considerably less complex than the equivalent one under the 1956 Act. (See paragraph 3.29.) Furthermore, the relevant works no longer have to be made or published by or under the direction or control of the organisation, and there is no requirement in relation to the publication of such works that they be published in pursuance of any agreement with the author not reserving the copyright to him.

G. FOLKLORE: s.169

3.85 This provision only applies to unpublished literary, dramatic, musical or artistic works of unknown authorship, and is principally intended to apply to folklore. The meaning of the expression "unknown authorship" is referred to in paragraph 4.39.

If there is evidence that the author (or, in the case of a joint work, any of the authors) was someone whose works at the material time (see paragraph 2.11) qualified for copyright protection under section 154 (see paragraph 2.08) then it is presumed until the contrary is proved that he was a qualifying individual and copyright subsists in the work.

If under the laws of the relevant country, there is a body appointed to protect and enforce copyright in such works, then there is power to designate the body by Order in Council as having authority in the United Kingdom to do in place of the copyright owner anything which it is empowered to do under the law of the relevant country. In particular it may sue in its own name. It may not however assign the copyright.

It should be noted that the provision does not make the designated body first owner, but simply capable of exercising the relevant rights in the works. If subsequently it becomes possible to ascertain the identity of the author by reasonable inquiry, then the provision will no longer apply and the copyright will be exerciseable by the first owner according to normal rules, assuming of course that the author was indeed a qualifying individual.

The provision does not apply if there has been an assignment of copyright in the work by the author of which notice has been given to the designated body. Furthermore the provision does not affect the validity of any assignment of copyright made, or licence granted, by the author or a person lawfully claiming under him.

4 DURATION OF COPYRIGHT

I INTRODUCTION

This Chapter deals with the period of time during which copyright in **4.01**
works continues to subsist. After the expiry of the relevant period, the
work in question is said to be in the public domain in the United Kingdom. This means that the work may be used and exploited freely without
the necessity of permission from the former owner. A work may however
be in the public domain in the United Kingdom, but still be protected in
one or more countries outside the United Kingdom.

1. Works based on existing copyright material

Many literary, dramatic, musical and artistic works are altered from time **4.02**
to time in order to update them. In some cases, the updated version will
attract a new copyright. (See Chapter 1.) Where this is so, the duration of
the copyright in the new work may be different from that of the old
version, and expiry of the copyright in the latter will not affect that of the
former. Upon expiry of the copyright in the old version of the work,
exploitation of that work will not infringe the copyright in the new work,
but use of any of the new material in the later work will infringe. Of
course, in many cases, it will be difficult if not impossible to separate out
what is protected as a result of the skill labour or judgement used in
creating the new work.

The effect is similar in the case of sound recordings, films, broadcasts,
cable programmes and typographical arrangements. Where such a work
is in part an existing work and in part new material, the latter will
continue to be protected notwithstanding the expiry of copyright in the
old work.

Furthermore, expiry of the copyright in a work which has embodied in
it other copyright works will not affect the continued requirement for
permission to do the restricted acts in relation to any underlying works
still in copyright. Thus, with the repeal of section 13(7) of the 1956 Act,
once the copyright in a film has expired, consent is still required to
perform publicly the music of the sound-track of the film if it is shown in a
cinema.

2. Summary of the 1988 Act

In summary, the main provisions on duration under the 1988 Act are as **4.03**
follows:

(a) The basic rule for literary, dramatic, musical and artistic works is that copyright expires 50 years from the end of the calendar year in which the author dies. However, there are special rules for works of joint author-ship, works of unknown authorship, and computer-generated works.

(b) Copyright in a sound recording or film expires 50 years from the end of the calendar year in which it is made. However, if it is released before the end of that period, the copyright expires 50 years from the end of the calendar year in which it is released.

(c) Copyright in a broadcast or cable programme expires 50 years from the end of the calendar year in which the broadcast is made or programme is included in a cable programme service.

(d) Copyright in the typographical arrangement of a published edition expires 25 years from the end of the calendar year in which the edition is first published.

(e) Special rules apply for literary, dramatic, musical and artistic works which are the subject of Crown Copyright or the subject of other similar copyrights or which vest in certain international organisations.

3. Existing works

4.04   All this looks reasonably straightforward, but the problem is that the above rules do not necessarily apply in relation to works made before the commencement of the 1988 Act. The transitional provisions are complex and cumbersome, and in order to find out what period copyright subsists for there, it is necessary to go through the following process:

(a) If any of the rules referred to in section II of this Chapter apply, copyright will subsist for the period referred to there, subject to (c) below.

(b) If none of the rules referred to in section II apply, copyright will subsist for the same period as applies to new works and is referred to in section III of this Chapter, subject to (c) below.

(c) In the case of pre-1956 Act works of joint authorship and pre-1911 Act literary, dramatic, musical and artistic works, copyright may already have expired, and section IV must be checked to ensure that this has not happened.

4. Differences between the 1956 Act and the 1988 Act

4.05   The 1988 Act does not radically alter the approach to duration embodied in the 1956 Act. Nevertheless, a number of significant specific changes have been introduced in relation to post-1988 Act works. In summary, the major ones are as follows:

(a) The change in duration of copyright for photographs from 50 years from the end of the calendar year in which the photograph was first published (or taken, in the case of pre-1956 Act photographs) to the normal copyright period for artistic works. (See paragraph 4.37.)

(b) The extended period of copyright protection for Crown Copyright literary, dramatic, musical and artistic works. (See paragraph 4.48.)

(c) Unexploited literary, dramatic and musical works, engravings and photographs will no longer have perpetual copyright protection, and the normal rules as to duration will apply. (See paragraph 4.37.)

(d) Unpublished sound recordings and films will no longer have perpetual copyright protection, and new rules based on the date of making or release will apply. (See paragraph 4.56.)

(e) The new period of protection of 50 years from the making of the relevant work for computer-generated works. (See paragraph 4.43.)

(f) The change in the period of protection for anonymous and pseudonymous works to 50 years from when the relevant work is first made available to the public, not first published. (See paragraph 4.38.)

5. Publication and making a work available to the public abroad

One further point needs to be borne in mind, both in relation to existing **4.06** works and new works. In many cases below, duration is linked to an event which has happened in relation to the relevant work as opposed to the author—publication, or making the work available to the public, for example. If this event happens outside the United Kingdom, before it happens (if at all) in the United Kingdom it still operates so as to start the period of copyright running, assuming of course that the work qualifies for copyright protection under the rules set out in Chapter 2.

II EXISTING WORKS NOT ALREADY IN THE PUBLIC DOMAIN

An existing work is one made before the commencement of the new Act **4.07** Sched. 1, paragraph 1(3). In the case of a work the making of which extended over a period of time, the making must have been completed prior to the commencement of the new Act for it to be treated as an existing work. (See also paragraph 3.05.)

Special rules on duration for existing works are contained in the transitional provisions to the 1988 Act. As stated above, unless a particular existing work is specifically referred to in this section, its duration must be considered in accordance with the provisions in section III below, but in addition the "trap" rules referred to in section IV must be considered.

In summary, the categories of existing works dealt with in this section are as follows:

(a) Works not the subject of Crown Copyright:

  (i) anonymous and pseudonymous works.

  (ii) works not exploited before the death of the relevant author.

(iii) photographs.

(iv) sound recordings.

(v) films.

(b) Works the subject of Crown or similar copyrights.

(c) Works the copyright in which is vested in certain international organisations.

(d) The remaining perpetual university copyrights.

The following points should also be borne in mind in considering what is said below:

(i) Where there is a reference to dramatic works, photographs or artistic works, these include films made before the commencement of the 1956 Act. (See paragraph 1.14.)

(ii) In some instances, duration is tied to publication, and what constitutes publication is determined in accordance with the rules under the 1956 Act not the 1988 Act. (See paragraph 2.44 onwards.)

A. WORKS NOT THE SUBJECT OF CROWN COPYRIGHT

1. Anonymous and pseudonymous works (schedule 1 paragraph 12(3))

(a) *The relevant works*

4.08 The following provisions apply to all literary, dramatic and musical works. They also apply to artistic works except photographs.

(b) *Difference in treatment under 1956 and 1988 Acts*

4.09 An anonymous work is one where the author is not named. A pseudonymous work is one where the author is named, but the name is not his real name. The 1956 Act provisions referred to works published anonymously or pseudonymously (1956 Act, s.11(1)), whereas the transitional provisions of the 1988 Act refer to anonymous and pseudonymous works, both published and unpublished. This difference in treatment makes the application of the transitional provisions under the 1988 Act very difficult, and the following summary of what we believe to be the effect of the provisions is not without its problems.

(c) *Anonymous and pseudonymous works published prior to the 1988 Act*

4.10 If the work has been published prior to the 1988 Act then copyright subsists until the date on which it would have expired under the 1956 Act.

This was 50 years from the end of the calendar year in which the work was first published. (See 1956 Act, schedule 2, paragraph 1(b)). However, two reservations have to be made to this:

(i) If before the 50-year period expired, it became possible for a person without previous knowledge of the facts to ascertain the identity of the author (or one of the authors in the case of a work of joint authorship) by reasonable inquiry, then the normal period of life plus 50 years applied. In our view, had that happened prior to the commencement of the 1988 Act, the work would no longer have been anonymous or pseudonymous, and accordingly the normal provisions of the 1988 Act, and not the transitional provisions, would apply. If this had *not* happened before commencement of the 1988 Act, but it became possible to ascertain the identity after the commencement of the 1988 Act then, in our view, the basic rule referred to above still applies, and one goes back to the normal duration under the 1956 Act (which for those purposes would be the same as in the 1988 Act). However, what is somewhat confusing here is that the 1988 Act transitional provisions state that duration is not tied to the 1956 Act if the identity of the author *becomes known* before the expiry of the 50-year period; a different test from whether it is *possible* to ascertain his identity. However, the practical result is still probably the same because in that situation the transitional provisions state that one must apply the normal provisions on duration under the 1988 Act.

(ii) Where a work of joint authorship was first published prior to the commencement of the 1988 Act under two or more names of which one or more (but not all) were pseudonymous, the work was not treated as published pseudonymously under the 1956 Act and special rules applied for the purposes of calculating duration. (See 1956 Act, schedule 3, paragraph 3). This also applied where first publication was pseudonymous, but it later became possible to ascertain the identity of one or more (but not all) of the authors as referred to in (i) above. We suggest that any such work is not one which can be called a pseudonymous work as at the commencement of the 1988 Act, and therefore one applies the normal provisions of the 1988 Act. Fortunately, in any event, the result again seems to be the same as under the 1956 Act.

(d) *Anonymous and pseudonymous works unpublished prior to the 1988 Act*

The application of the provisions as regards anonymous and pseudony-   **4.11**
mous works unpublished prior to the commencement of the 1988 Act involves a rather less tortuous process. Here, copyright will subsist only until 50 years after the end of the calendar year in which the 1988 Act comes into force, unless either of the following apply:

(i) If the work is made available to the public during that period, then the period of subsistence switches to that applying under the new rules relating to works of unknown authorship. These are referred to in paragraph 4.40 below, and paragraph 4.41 deals with when a work is made available to the public.

(ii) If, before the relevant period of copyright expires, the identity of the author (or, in the case of a work of joint authorship, any of the authors) becomes known then the normal provisions on duration under the 1988 Act apply. (See paragraph 4.45.)

2. Unexploited works (schedule 1, paragraphs. 12(2)(a), (b) and (4) (a), (b))

(a) *The relevant works*

4.12   The following provisions apply only to literary, dramatic and musical works and engravings.

(b) *The rules under the 1956 Act*

4.13   Under the 1956 Act, if certain acts of exploitation in relation to such works had not been carried out prior to the death of the relevant author, (or, in the case of a work of joint authorship, the death of the author who died last) copyright continued to subsist until 50 years from the end of the calendar year when any one of those acts was first carried out. (See 1956 Act, ss.2(3) and 3(4).)

As regards literary, dramatic and musical works, the relevant acts of exploitation were publication of the work, performance in public of the work, the offer for sale to the public of records of the work, broadcasting the work, transmitting the work to subscribers to a diffusion service (up until December 31, 1984) or including the work in a cable programme (from January 1, 1985). As regards engravings, only one act was relevant, and that was publication. The 1988 Act does not contain such provisions for new works.

(c) *Survival of the rules for existing works*

4.14   For existing works, duration of copyright under the 1988 Act depends on whether one of the relevant acts of exploitation referred to above has already taken place prior to commencement of the 1988 Act. If it has, copyright expires in accordance with the rules under the 1956 Act. If it has not, copyright expires 50 years from the end of the year when the new Act comes into force.

(d) *The practical effect*

4.15   If a music publisher has the rights to several unexploited compositions of a composer who died prior to the commencement of the 1988 Act, there can only be one further period of 50 years after the commencement of the Act before all the works fall into the public domain. It may well be therefore that a policy of making such works available one by one over a period of time will need to be reviewed.

3. Photographs (schedule 1, paragraphs 12(2)(c) and (4)(c))

(a) *Photographs taken prior to commencement of the 1956 Act*

4.16   Copyright subsists until 50 years from the end of the year when the photograph was taken.

(b) *Photographs taken after commencement of the 1956 Act and published prior to commencement of the 1988 Act*

Copyright subsists until 50 years after the end of the year in which the photograph was first published. **4.17**

(c) *Photographs taken after commencement of the 1956 Act and not published prior to commencement of the 1988 Act*

Copyright subsists until 50 years after the end of the year in which the 1988 Act comes into force. **4.18**

4. Sound recordings (schedule 1, paragraphs 12(2)(a) and (5)(a))

The rules below do not apply to film sound-tracks. (See paragraph 4.23.)

(a) *Sound recordings made before commencement of the 1956 Act*

Copyright subsists until 50 years from the end of the calendar year in which the sound recording was made. **4.19**

(b) *Sound recordings made after commencement of the 1956 Act and published prior to commencement of the 1988 Act*

Copyright subsists until 50 years from the end of the calendar year in which the sound recording was first published both here and in relation to paragraph 4.21. One should remember that whether or not the sound recording has been published depends on the rules under the 1956 Act (see paragraph 2.44) not the 1988 Act. **4.20**

(c) *Sound recordings made after commencement of the 1956 Act and not published prior to commencement of the 1988 Act*

Prima facie, copyright will expire 50 years from the end of the calendar year in which the 1988 Act comes into force. However, if before the expiry of that period, the sound recording is published, copyright will not then expire until 50 years from the end of the calendar year in which it is published. **4.21**

5. Films (schedule 1, paragraphs 12(2)(e) and (5)(b))

(a) *The relevant films*

The rules here do not apply to films made before commencement of the 1956 Act, and which are protected as dramatic works, photographs or drawings. **4.22**

(b) *Film sound-tracks*

The rules below do apply to the sound-tracks of the relevant films, even **4.23** though they will be treated as sound recordings for other purposes under the 1988 Act. (See schedule 1, paragraph 8(2)(a).)

(c) *Registration of films*

4.24   Under the 1956 Act, the copyright period depended on whether or not the film was registered under the Films Act 1960 or its predecessor the Cinematograph Films Act 1938. The requirement for registration was abolished by the Films Act 1985, but provisions were made in the 1985 Act to preserve the register as it existed on repeal.

(d) *Registered films*

4.25   If the film was so registered, then copyright subsists until 50 years from the end of the calendar year in which the film was registered.

(e) *Unregistered films*

4.26   In the case of unregistered films (including post-1985 Act films), duration again depends upon whether or not the film has been published before the commencement of the 1988 Act, and the rules are exactly the same as for sound recordings. (See paragraphs 4.20 and 4.21 above.)

B. CROWN COPYRIGHT AND RELATED RIGHTS

1. The relevant works

4.27   The following provisions apply basically to all those works which vested in the Crown as first owner of the copyright by virtue of the provisions of the 1956 Act. (See paragraph 3.41 onwards.) There are however a number of situations where the provisions under the 1988 Act and referred to in section III below apply, and not those set out here. These are as follows:

(a) Acts of Parliament, and Measures of the General Synod of the Church of England. (See schedule 1, paragraph 42.)

(b) Unpublished, literary, dramatic or musical works made by or under the direction or control of one or both of the House of Commons and House of Lords. (See schedule 1, paragraph 43(1).)

(c) Public Bills introduced into Parliament and published before commencement of the 1988 Act. (See schedule 1, paragraph 43(2)(a).)

(d) Private Bills of which a copy was deposited in either House of Parliament before commencement of the 1988 Act. (See schedule 1, paragraph 43(2)(b).)

(e) Personal Bills given a first reading in the House of Lords before commencement. (See schedule 1, paragraph 43(2)(c).)

The duration of copyright in relation to existing Crown Copyright works apart from those excepted above depends again on the category of work. As regards literary, dramatic, musical and artistic works, the provisions apply whether or not such a work is anonymous or pseudonymous.

2. Literary, dramatic and musical works

(a) *Published prior to commencement of the 1988 Act* (schedule 1, paragraph 41(2))

Copyright subsists until 50 years from the end of the calendar year in which it was first published.   **4.28**

(b) *Unpublished prior to commencement of the 1988 Act* (schedule 1, paragraph 41(3))

The position is more complicated with works unpublished at that date.   **4.29**
First, one looks to see on what date the copyright would expire under the new provisions in relation to Crown Copyright. This, as will be seen (see paragraph 4.48), is either 125 years from the end of the calendar year in which the work was made, or, if commercial publication takes place before the end of a period of 75 years from the end of the calendar year in which it was made, 50 years from the end of the calendar year in which first commercial publication takes place. Copyright will expire in accordance with these provisions unless this would mean that copyright would expire prior to 50 years from the end of the calendar year in which the new Act comes into force. If that is so, then copyright continues to subsist until the end of that 50-year period.

3. Artistic works, excluding engravings and photographs (schedule 1, paragraph 41(2))

The copyright in all such works expires 50 years from the end of the   **4.30**
calendar year in which the work was made.

4. Engravings (schedule 1, paragraph 41(2))

Duration depends upon publication. If the engraving has been published   **4.31**
prior to the commencement of the 1988 Act, then copyright subsists until 50 years from the end of the calendar year in which first publication took place. If the work is unpublished at this date, it expires 50 years from the end of the calendar year in which the 1988 Act comes into force.

5. Photographs (schedule 1, paragraphs 41(2) and (4))

The provisions here are exactly the same for photographs not the subject   **4.32**
of Crown Copyright.

6. Sound recordings and films (schedule 1, paragraphs 41(2) and (5))

4.33   Again, the provisions are the same as sound recordings and films not the subject of Crown Copyright.

C. COPYRIGHTS VESTED IN INTERNATIONAL ORGANISATIONS (schedule 1, paragraph 44)

4.34   The transitional provisions on existing works here apply only to literary, dramatic, musical or artistic works, if they are unpublished. For when such copyrights vested in certain international organisations, see paragraph 3.29.

On the basis of the transitional provisions, copyright in any such work expires on the date it would have expired under the 1956 Act. Copyright expired under the 1956 Act when the work was published. However, this is subject to the following:

(a) Copyright in such an unpublished work will in any event expire 50 years from the end of the calendar year in which the new Act comes into force.

(b) If the work is first published under the direction or control of a relevant organisation and under the rules referred to in paragraph 3.29, a fresh copyright would then vest in the organisation, and the work continue in copyright until the date it would expire under the 1988 Act. (See paragraph 4.56.)

D. PERPETUAL COPYRIGHTS (Sched. 1, paragraph 13(1))

4.35   Under the 1775 Copyright Act, certain universities were given the sole right in perpetuity to print and reprint books where the copyright in those books had been bequeathed to them. Although the 1911 Copyright Act repealed the 1775 Act, rights obtained prior to that date were preserved. The only examples given to the Whitford Committee of works in print to which these provisions applied were selections from Clarendon's *History of the Rebellion* and *Life*. The 1988 Act provides that any remaining rights will continue only until 50 years from the end of the calendar year in which the new copyright provisions come into force, and then expire.

III NEW WORKS

4.36   Fortunately, the rules here are somewhat simpler than the transitional provisions which were detailed in section II of this Chapter. Duration here is dealt with by reference to the relevant category of work. Crown Copyright is only dealt with separately for literary, dramatic, musical and artistic works: for all other works the period of copyright is the same as works not subject to Crown Copyright.

A. LITERARY, DRAMATIC, MUSICAL AND ARTISTIC WORKS

In relation to all such works, the normal rule is that copyright subsists for   **4.37** the life of the author and thereafter until 50 years from the end of the calendar year during which he or she died. This applies whether or not the author was first owner. (See s.12(1).)

The above rule is however subject to a number of exceptions:

1. Works of unknown authorship (s.12(2))

(a) *Comparison with 1956 Act*

These provisions replace those on anonymous and pseudonymous works.   **4.38** Although the provisions are somewhat differently organised, the expressions used are by and large the same, and the only substantive change is that the 50-year period of copyright runs not from publication, but from first making the work available to the public.

(b) *Definition of works of unknown authorship*

The expression "unknown authorship" is defined in such a way that it   **4.39** covers both anonymous and pseudonymous works. A work is of "unknown authorship" if the identity of the author is unknown or, in the case of a work of joint authorship, if the identity of none of the authors is known. The identity of an author is regarded as unknown if it is not possible for a person to ascertain his identity by reasonable inquiry. Once the identity is known, it cannot subsequently be regarded as unknown.

For the position in the case of joint authorship where one or more but not all of the authors is unknown, see paragraph 4.46 below.

(c) *The period of copyright for works of unknown authorship*

If the work is of unknown authorship under the above rules, copyright   **4.40** expires 50 years from the end of the calendar year in which it is first made available to the public. If during that 50-year period the work ceases to be of unknown authorship, the normal life-plus-50-year provisions referred to will apply. If *after* the expiry of the 50 year period the work ceases to be of unknown authorship, then the copyright is not revived.

(d) *Meaning of "made available to the public"*

The expression "made available to the public" is not defined exclusively,   **4.41** but is said to include, in the case of a literary, dramatic or musical work, performance in public, being broadcast or included in a cable programme service, and, in the case of an artistic work, exhibition in public, showing in public of a film including the work and being included in a broadcast or cable programme service. However, none of these acts are taken into account if they are unauthorised.

(e) *Comparison with copyright in unexploited works under the 1956 Act*

4.42   As already stated above in dealing with existing works, under the 1956 Act a work unexploited at the author's death remained in copyright until 50 years from first exploitation. This possibility of an extended or even perpetual term of copyright has largely been removed for new works, but it remains for works of unknown authorship. So long as such a work is not made available to the public, it remains in copyright.

2. Computer-generated works

4.43   For what constitutes such a work see paragraph 3.54 above.
       In the case of such a work, copyright subsists only for 50 years from the end of the calendar year in which the relevant work was made. (See s.12(3).) This should not be confused with when the *arrangements* for the creation of the work were made, which could be much earlier.

3. Works of joint authorship

(a) *What is a work of joint authorship?*

4.44   A work of joint authorship is a work produced by the collaboration of two or more authors in which the contribution of each author is not distinct from that of the other author or authors. (See s.10 and see paragraph 3.66.)

(b) *Duration: the basic rule (s.12(4)(a))*

4.45   Copyright in a work of joint authorship expires 50 years from the end of the year in which the last surviving joint author died.

(c) *Duration: works partially of unknown authorship (s.12(4)(a) and (b))*

4.46   If the identity of one or more of the authors is known and the identity of one or more others is not, the 50-year period runs from the end of the calendar year in which the last surviving author whose identity is known died. However, the position may change on this even after the death of the person who appears to be the last surviving author. As soon as the identity of a joint author becomes known or it becomes possible for a person to ascertain his identity by reasonable inquiry, he becomes a surviving joint author to be taken into account for the purposes of deciding duration, unless the 50-year period referred to has already expired.

(d) *Works in which the contributions are distinct*

If a work is produced by the collaboration of two or more authors in which   **4.47**
the contribution of each author is distinct from that of the other author or
authors, then each contribution is a separate work, and the copyright in
each such contribution will expire 50 years from the death of the author of
that contribution.

4. Crown Copyright

Duration of copyright in relation to these works depends on whether or   **4.48**
not the work has been published commercially.

(a) *What is commercial publication?*

Commercial publication is defined as: **4.49**

(i) Issuing copies of the work to the public at a time when copies made in
advance of the receipt of orders are generally available to the public, or

(ii) Making the work available to the public by means of an electronic
retrieval system. (See s.175(2).)

However, in deciding whether commercial publication has taken place,
one must also bear in mind that certain acts do not constitute publication,
and cannot therefore constitute commercial publication. For details of
this, see paragraph 2.13 onwards.
     The first part of the definition of commercial publication is not happily
worded. It seems, however, that no such publication can take place unless
copies of the work have both been made in advance of the receipt of
orders, and have been made generally available to the public. This latter
requirement means that first publication can never be commercial publication because at that stage copies would not be generally available to the
public.
     For the purposes of proceedings relating to literary, dramatic or
musical works in which Crown copyright subsists, where there appears on
printed copies of the work a statement of the year in which the work was
first published commercially, this is admissible as evidence of the fact
stated and is presumed to be correct in the absence of evidence to the
contrary (s.106).

(b) *Duration for works not commercially published* (s.163(3)(a))

So long as no commercial publication has taken place, the duration of   **4.50** copyright is 125 years from the end of the calendar year in which the work was made.

(c) *Duration for works commercially published* (s.163(3)(b))

4.51   If the work is then published commercially before the end of the period of 75 years from the end of the calendar year in which it was made, then copyright expires 50 years from the end of the calendar year in which it was first published commercially.

(d) *Joint authors* (s.163(4))

4.52   In the case of a work of joint authorship where one or more (but not all) of the authors are officers or servants of the Crown, it is provided that the special rules on duration for Crown copyright works only apply to the copyright subsisting by virtue of his or their contribution to the relevant work. This means that the parts of the work which the various authors contributed to will need to be separated out in order to consider to what extent the period of copyright is based on the rules in this section or that dealing with works of joint authorship. As with the position on first ownership (see paragraph 3.81) this causes great difficulties since the whole essence of a work of joint authorship is that the contributions are not distinct.

5. Parliamentary Copyright (s.165(3))

4.53   Parliamentary Copyright expires 50 years from the end of the calendar year in which the relevant work was made. Literary, dramatic and musical works are made at the time at which the relevant work is recorded (in writing or otherwise) for the first time. There is no definition as to when an artistic work is made, as this is presumably considered to be readily ascertainable.

6. Copyright in Acts and Measures (s.164(2))

4.54   Copyright in an Act of Parliament or a Measure of the General Synod of the Church of England expires 50 years from the end of the calendar year in which Royal Assent is given.

7. Copyright in Parliamentary Bills (s.166(5))

4.55   Copyright in such Bills ceases either on Royal Assent, or, if the Bill does not receive such assent, either on the withdrawal or rejection of the Bill or the end of the relevant Parliamentary Session. Where such a Bill is rejected by the House of Lords, copyright does not expire if it is still possible for it to be presented for Royal Assent during the relevant Session.

8. Copyright vesting in certain international organisations

4.56   For when this occurs, see paragraph 3.84. Such copyrights generally subsist until 50 years from the end of the calendar year in which the work was made. However, there is power by Order in Council to extend this period for the purpose of complying with any of the United Kingdom's international obligations.

B. SOUND RECORDINGS AND FILMS

1. Duration under the 1956 Act

Under the 1956 Act, copyright continued to subsist so long as the sound   **4.57** recording or film remained unpublished, and thereafter subsisted for a further 50 years from the end of the calendar year in which first publication took place. (See 1956 Act, ss.12(3) and 13(3)(*b*).) In the case of films, this was subject to special rules as regards those films registered under the Films Act. (See paragraph 4.24 above.)

2. Duration under the 1988 Act (s.13(1))

Under the new rules, the 50-year period runs from the end of the calendar   **4.58** year in which the sound recording or film was made. If however the sound recording or film is released before the end of that period, copyright expires 50 years from the end of the calendar year in which release took place.

3. What constitutes release of a sound recording or film? (s.13(2))

Release is defined as first publication, broadcasting or inclusion in a cable   **4.59** programme service. In relation to films and film sound-tracks, release also takes place when the film is first shown in public, but none of these acts are to be taken into account if they are unauthorised.

C. BROADCASTS AND CABLE PROGRAMMES

1. Duration for broadcasts (s.14(1))

Copyright in a broadcast subsists until 50 years from the end of the   **4.60** calendar year in which the broadcast was made.

2. Duration for cable programmes (s.14(1))

Copyright in a cable programme subsists until 50 years from the end of the   **4.61** calendar year in which the programme was included in a cable programme service.

3. Repeat broadcasts and cable programmes (s.14(2))

If the broadcast is a repeat of a broadcast previously made then copyright   **4.62** expires at the same time as the copyright in the original broadcast, and no further period of copyright can arise after the expiry of the copyright in the original broadcast. Similar provisions apply in relation to cable programmes.

What does not appear clear is whether the repeat of the broadcast or cable programme has to be an exact one. In relation to the copyright in sound recording and film, copyright does not subsist in a work if it is, or to the extent that it is, a copy of a previous sound recording or film. Similar provisions do not apply in relation to broadcasts and cable programmes, but the same result is achieved by the rules on duration, certainly as regards an exact repeat. Arguably however, if the same result was to be achieved in relation to broadcast or cable programmes which were partially repeats of previous broadcasts or programmes and partially new, the reference should have been to "copyright in a repeat or to the extent that it is a repeat of a broadcast or cable programme." On the other hand it could be said that the natural meaning of the word "repeat" is that the broadcast or cable programme must be exactly the same.

D. TYPOGRAPHICAL ARRANGEMENTS (s.15)

4.63   Copyright subsists until 25 years from the end of the calendar year in which the edition was first published.

IV EXISTING WORKS ALREADY IN THE PUBLIC DOMAIN

4.64   Although the 1988 Act states that if there are no specific rules on duration of copyright in existing works, the normal rules apply, it is also provided that no copyright can subsist in an existing work unless it subsisted immediately prior to commencement. (See schedule 1, paragraph 5(1).) The purpose of this section is therefore to identify those categories of works which were already in the public domain then, even where they might still seem to be in copyright if one applied the rules contained in sections II and III above. These can be divided for convenience into three categories:

1. Pre-1956 Act works of joint authorship

4.65   Under the 1911 Act, the copyright in a literary, dramatic, musical or artistic work if one of joint authorship subsisted until 50 years after the death of the first author to die or upon the death of the last author to die, whichever was the later. (See 1911 Act, s.16(1).) If, on the basis of this rule, copyright had already expired before commencement of the 1956 Act, it was not revived by that Act, and remains in the public domain. (See 1956 Act, schedule 7, paragraph 10.)

2. Pre-1911 Act works of architecture and artistic craftsmanship

Works of architecture and works of artistic craftsmanship were not pro- **4.66**
tected by copyright prior to the 1911 Act. If any such work was published
prior to July 1, 1912, the work is in the public domain.

3. All other pre-1911 Act works

Pre-1911 Act works were only protected under the 1911 Act if copyright **4.67**
had not already expired (1911 Act, s.24); since in some cases the period of
protection applying under the previous legislation was very short, many
works did not obtain protection under the 1911 Act, notwithstanding the
relative youth of the author. The following table sets out the duration of
the relevant pre-1911 Act works, and if this period expired before July 1,
1912, the work is in the public domain:

Work	Duration
Literary, dramatic and musical works	42 years after publication, or 7 years after death of the author, whichever was longer. (See Copyright Act 1842.) However, in relation to musical works first published after August 10, 1882, the performing right ceased if any copy of the work did not bear a notice reserving the performing right. (See Copyright (Musical Composition) Act 1882.)
Paintings and drawings	Either: (a) Upon first sale or other disposition of the work, unless upon or before such sale or disposition the copyright was expressly assigned to the person acquiring the work, or reserved to the owner, in each case in writing, or (b) if the copyright was so assigned or reserved, 7 years after the death of the author. (See Fine Arts Copyright Act 1862.)
Engravings	Either: (a) Upon first publication, if the copyright owner's name and date of first publication was not on the work then, or (b) If the name and date was on the work then, 28 years from first publication. (See Engraving Copyright Acts 1734 and 1766, Prints Copyright Act 1776.)

Work	Duration
Sculptures	Either:
	(a) Upon first publication, if the copyright owner's name and the date of the work was not on the work then, or
	(b) If the name and date was on the work then, 14 years from publication, plus a further 14 years if the author was still living at the end of that period. (See Sculpture Copyright Act 1814.)

V ABANDONMENT OF COPYRIGHT

4.68   Although old eighteenth- and nineteenth-century cases suggest that it might be possible to abandon a copyright, the only modern authority on the point relates to material included in a patent specification. In *Catnic Components Ltd.* v. *Hill & Smith Ltd.* ([1975] F.S.R. 529) Whitford J. said as follows:

> "In my view, by applying for a patent and accepting the statutory obligation to describe and if necessary illustrate embodiments of his invention, a patentee necessarily makes an election accepting that, in return for a potential monopoly, upon publication, the material disclosed by him in the specification must be deemed to be open to be used by the public, subject only to such monopoly rights as he may acquire on his application for the patent and during the period for which his monopoly remains in force, whatever be the reason for the determination of the monopoly rights."

In that particular case, Whitford J. went on to hold that the plaintiffs had abandoned their copyright not just in the patent drawings but "drawings the equivalent of the patent drawings." On appeal, the Court of Appeal declined to express any concluded view on the point.

It is uncertain whether the judge's finding was correct. Another judge declined to follow it in relation to pending patents. The finding by Whitford J. is also inconsistent with a previous decision of the Court of Appeal *Werner Motors Ltd.* v. *A.W. Gamage Ltd.* ([1904] 2 Ch. 580) which does not appear to have been cited to the judge. In that case, the court refused to hold that an application for a grant of a patent invalidated registration of a design. Several Commonwealth decisions have also failed to follow Whitford J.'s finding. It is doubtful whether the decision has any implications outside the specific area in question, and in any event the ability to use copyright law in these circumstances is severely restricted under the 1988 Act by what is referred to later in Chapter 13.

5 THE RESTRICTED ACTS

I INTRODUCTION

Copyright consists of the exclusive right to do certain acts. These acts are **5.01** known as the restricted acts. Any person who without the licence of the copyright owner does or authorises another to do any of those acts infringes copyright, unless the act is one permitted under the provisions referred to in Chapter 7 or is deemed to be licensed under the provisions relating to the Copyright Tribunal referred to in Chapter 9. The restricted acts are sometimes also referred to as acts of primary infringement, to distinguish them from the acts of secondary infringement referred to in the next Chapter.

1. Summary of the 1988 Act

Under the 1988 Act, the restricted acts are as follows: **5.02**

(a) Copying the work.

(b) Issuing copies of the work to the public.

(c) Performing or playing or showing the work in public.

(d) Broadcasting the work.

(e) Including the work in a cable programme service.

(f) Adapting the work, and doing any of the acts referred to above in relation to an adaptation of the work.

However, not all of these acts apply to every work referred to in Chapter 1, and, where they do apply, they do not always do so in the same way.

2. Differences between the 1956 Act and the 1988 Act

The 1988 Act has made important changes to the law in three ways. These **5.03** are as follows:

(a) The exclusive rights extend now not only to acts done on the territorial waters and the continental shelf of the United Kingdom, but also to acts which take place on British ships, aircraft, or hovercraft. (See paragraph 5.06.)

(b) A new restricted act of issuing copies of a work to the public has been introduced for all works. The restricted act of publishing a work which applied to literary, dramatic, musical and artistic works has accordingly been dispensed with. (See paragraph 5.22.)

(c) The scope of the restricted act of broadcasting and including works in a cable programme service have been extended. (See paragraphs 5.44 and 5.47.)

3. Territory

(a) *Location of the restricted acts*

5.04   The copyright owner only has the exclusive right to do the restricted acts in the United Kingdom (s.16(1)), subject to what is said in paragraph 5.06 below. Whether or not he has rights outside the United Kingdom depends on the laws of those countries. However, a person who grants authority outside the United Kingdom for an act to be done within the United Kingdom may still infringe copyright. For example, a person in Germany who authorises someone to copy a musical work in the United Kingdom without licence is still liable for infringement under United Kingdom copyright law. However, if the authority is given to manufacture in Germany, that is not an infringement of the United Kingdom copyright. (*Def Lepp Music* v. *Stuart Brown* ([1986] R.P.C. 273.)

(b) *Extending the 1988 Act*

5.05   For these purposes, the United Kingdom includes England, Wales, Scotland and Northern Ireland. (See s.157(1).) However, there is power to extend the provisions of the Act to the Channel Islands, the Isle of Man (and also to any colony), subject to exceptions and modifications if desired (s.157(2)). If the Act is so extended, then the local legislature is able to modify the operation of the Act as regards procedure and remedies, and also as regards works qualifying for protection. (See s.157(4).) Although at the time of writing, no measures had been taken in this respect, the Government has said that it does intend to extend the 1988 Act to the Channel Islands and the Isle of Man, subject to consultations with the local legislature. Until then, the 1911 Act (still applicable for example in Jersey) or the 1956 Act will remain in force in the relevant territories.

(c) *Acts beyond the United Kingdom coast*

5.06   Under the 1956 Act, it was doubtful whether the law applied to acts done in the territorial waters of the United Kingdom, and it certainly did not apply to acts done in the United Kingdom sector of the continental shelf or, for example, on a British ship beyond the territorial waters. This has now changed, so that, in relation only to acts done after the commencement of the 1988 Act, it is an infringement of copyright to do those acts:

(i) On the territorial waters of the United Kingdom. (See s.161(1).) Under the Territorial Sea Act 1987 this is 12 nautical miles.

(ii) In the United Kingdom sector of the continental shelf, if the act is done on a structure or vessel present there for purposes directly connected with the exploration of the seabed or subsoil or the exploitation of their natural resources. (See s.161(2).) The obvious example of this is an oil rig. In order to find out whether such a structure or vessel is in the United Kingdom sector, one must look to the various detailed orders made under section 1(7) of the Continental Shelf Act 1964 (s.161(3)), and these are too complex to set out here.

(iii) On a British ship, aircraft or hovercraft wherever situated. (See s.162.) British ships are those which are British ships for the purposes of the Merchant Shipping Acts (see the definition in section 2 of the Merchant Shipping Act 1988). In some cases, a ship can still be a British ship even though it is registered in a country outside the United Kingdom. These ships are however excluded from the definition for copyright purposes. Ships of the Royal Navy are not within the definition.

A British aircraft or hovercraft is one registered in the United Kingdom. It should be noted therefore that the nationality of the airline operating the aircraft is not the criterion here.

Thus, by way of example, British aircraft showing feature films with music on the sound-track will in future require a licence for performing the music in public, even after they have departed from the airspace of the United Kingdom.

4. Acts done before the commencement of the 1988 Act

The 1988 Act only applies to acts done after the commencement date.   **5.07**
The provisions of the 1956 Act continue as regards acts done before commencement. (See schedule 1, paragraph 14(1).) For the most part, the similarity between the new and old provisions should not give rise to any difficulty, but this obviously has importance as regards the changes in the law which are referred to in paragraph 5.03 above. Other differences between the 1956 and 1988 Acts are referred to when the restricted acts are dealt with separately.

5. Direct and indirect acts (s.16(3))

The 1988 Act states that it does not matter whether the restricted act is   **5.08**
done directly or indirectly. This simply codifies what had previously been held to be the law. Thus in *King Features Syndicate, Inc.* v. *O. & M. Kleemann, Ltd.* ([1941] 2 All E.R. 403), the copyright in a cartoon of "Popeye the Sailor" was infringed where the defendants copied not the cartoon but dolls which were three-dimensional copies of the cartoon and which had been made by licensees of the copyright owners.

Furthermore, the 1988 Act states that it is immaterial whether any intervening acts themselves infringe copyright. An intervening act may itself not be an infringement either because it has been done with the licence of the copyright owner, or it is a permitted act (see Chapter 7), or it is authorised under an order made by the Copyright Tribunal (see

Chapter 9). Thus, to take an example, it may be that the making of a copy of a work for the purposes of a school examination is not an infringement of copyright, but if a copy is made from that copy for other purposes then there will be infringement.

6. Substantial part (s.16(3))

5.09   An act is only a restricted act if it is done in relation to the work as a whole or any substantial part of it. Thus, a copyright owner may only take action for infringement of copyright in a musical work where a part of the work is reproduced on a record, if the part reproduced is a substantial part.

This is not one of the more easy topics in copyright law, because, although it might be convenient that there be some hard-and-fast rule as to what constitutes infringement, in reality whether a part of a work is a substantial part is entirely a matter of fact and degree in each case. Although one often still hears of, for example, the "four-bar rule" (meaning that if one only takes four bars from a musical work, this does not infringe copyright), the plain fact is that the rule does not exist and there are no precise rules which can be used to determine whether what someone wishes to use is substantial.

The difficulty can be shown by a comparison between two cases where in each four lines of a literary work were taken, but where in one case it was held to be an infringement and in one case not. In *Kipling* v. *Genatosan Ltd.* ([1917–23] MacG. Cop. Cas. 203), the defendants took four lines from Rudyard Kipling's famous poem "If" for the purposes of an advertisement for the product Sanatogen, and the judge robustly dismissed any argument that the part taken was not substantial. In *Chappell and Co. Ltd.* v. *D.C. Thompson and Co. Ltd.* ([1928–35] MacG. Cop. Cas. 467), four lines of the lyrics of a popular song called "Her Name is Mary" were placed at the head of a magazine story of the same name, and the judge perhaps even more robustly dismissed an action for infringement on the basis that the part taken was (in the judge's view) clearly not substantial.

This then indicates the danger of looking for precedents to find out whether or not a part taken is substantial. All one can do in examining the question is to bear in mind the following factors:

(a) There is high judicial authority for the view that "what is worth copying is prima facie worth protecting". (*Ladbroke (Football) Ltd.* v. *William Hill (Football) Ltd.* ([1964] 1 W.L.R. 273).)

(b) Although the quantity taken is a matter to be taken into account, whether or not a substantial part has been taken depends much more on the importance or quality of that part in relation to the whole. Thus, in one of the leading cases, *Hawkes and Son (London) Ltd.* v. *Paramount Film Service Ltd.*, ([1934] Ch. 593) a part of the well-known march "Colonel Bogey" was used. The whole march took four minutes to play, and only 20 seconds was reproduced, but this was the principal melody. A comparison of the works the subject of the *Kipling* and *Chappell* cases referred to above shows that the four lines of "If" were a smaller percentage of the whole, than the four lines of "Her Name Is Mary".

(c) One test is to examine whether the part taken is in itself novel or striking or just commonplace. (See the judgment of Lord Reid in the *Ladbroke* case.)

(d) Although it is correct to examine whether the part taken itself has originality, this is not the same as saying that one must look to see whether the part taken could itself be the subject of copyright as an original work. A part of a work may be protected even though it could not stand on its own as an original work.

(e) One factor which has been taken into account is whether the amount taken is so slender that it would be impossible to recognise it.

(f) Particularly in relation to works which comprise some original material and some unoriginal material, if a part of a work only attracts copyright by reason of its collocation with a work which is as a whole original, then the part taken is not a substantial part. (See *Warwick Film Productions Ltd.* v. *Eisinger* [1963] 1 W.L.R. 756.)

(g) For the most part, it seems accepted that it does not matter whether the amount taken was enough to cause damage to the copyright owner. However, this was a matter which was taken into account in the *Chappell* case referred to above.

(h) The cases are unclear as to whether the purpose for which the part of the work has been taken or the intention behind taking it are relevant in deciding whether the part taken is substantial. An argument that the purpose is a relevant factor was rejected in *Hawkes and Son Ltd.* v. *Paramount Film Services Ltd.*, where the part taken was reproduced in the sound-track of a newsreel film about the visit of the then Prince of Wales to a school when members of the school marched past the Prince to the strains of the music. Conversely, in *Ravenscroft* v. *Herbert* [1980] R.P.C. 193, Brightman J. seems to have accepted that two factors to be taken into account were first whether the defendant had taken the relevant part for the purpose of saving himself labour, and secondly the extent to which the work in which the allegedly substantial part of another work was used was competing with the work from which the part was alleged to have been taken.

(i) The question is always whether a substantial part of the copyright owner's work has been taken, not whether a substantial use of that work has been made in the defendant's work.

7. Knowledge and intent

It is worth remembering that in relation to the restricted acts dealt with in this Chapter, there is no requirement of either knowledge that use is being made of a copyright work, or of intent to infringe (except in relation to adaptations—see paragraph 5.50 below).   **5.10**

II THE RESTRICTED ACTS THEMSELVES

A. COPYING

5.11   The owner of the copyright in a work has the exclusive right to copy the work in the United Kingdom. (See s.17(1).) Thus, to make a record from a master recording is to copy the sound recording embodied in the master and any music or words included in the sound recording. In relation to some categories of work, the expression "copying" is defined further, and there are also special rules referred to below relating to some works. Whatever the category of work, it does not matter whether the copy made is transient or intended to have permanent existence. (See s.17(6).) The Act also states that it does not matter whether the copies made are incidental to some other use of the work (s.17(6)).

1. Literary, dramatic, musical and artistic works

5.12   As regards these works, what constitutes copying is defined as reproducing the relevant work in any material form. (See s.17(2).) This is the same expression as that used in the 1956 Act.

In *Foley (Brigid) Ltd.* v. *Ellott* ([1982] R.P.C. 433) Megarry V.-C. held that the essence of a reproduction was that it should be some copy or representation of the original work. That case concerned a knitting guide which consisted of written words and numbers stating how garments were to be produced from the guide. The garments knitted using the guide were held not to be reproductions of the literary work consisting of the words and numbers. In general terms, the effect of this is that the reproduction of a work in a different dimension does not infringe the restricted act of copying, although special rules apply to artistic works. (See paragraph 5.17 below.)

More obviously, it is not reproduction of a work such as a picture cut out from a book to paste the picture on to a card for the purposes of selling it.

(a) *Inexact reproduction*

5.13   Reproduction can take place even where it is not exact. One definition of "reproduction" in the Shorter Oxford English Dictionary is "a representation in some form or by some means of the essential features of a thing." Thus, in music plagiarism cases, it is just as important to consider aural similarity as to examine whether the notes are exactly the same. Again, for there to be reproduction of a dramatic work, the words of the characters in the play need not be used exactly. In *Rees* v. *Melville* ([1911–16] MacG. Cop. Cas. 96) Lord Justice Swinfen-Eady said that:

"In order to constitute any infringement it was not necessary that the words or the dialogue should be the same. The situation and incidents, the mode in which the themes were worked out and presented might constitute a material portion of the whole play, and the Court must have regard to the dramatic value and importance of what, if anything, was taken. . . . "

For there to be infringement by copying where the reproduction is not exact, the test is twofold:

(i) There must be a sufficient degree of objective similarity between the two works, and

(ii) There must be a causal connection between the copyright work and the infringing work: in other words the infringing work must have been derived from the other work.

If either of these two elements is missing, there is no infringement by copying.

(b) *Objective similarity*

The "objective similarity" point is demonstrated by the "parody" cases.   **5.14**
Although there is no rule that a parody by its nature cannot be a reproduction, in many cases the parody version will be so far from the original that it is no longer a reproduction. Thus in *Joy Music Ltd.* v. *Sunday Pictorial Newspapers Ltd.* ([1960] 2 Q.B. 60) it was admitted that the parody was derived from the chorus of the lyrics of a popular song, but the judge held that there was no reproduction of a substantial part of the lyrics.

There is no precise formula for determining how much objective similarity is sufficient. It is, however, vital to remember first the nature of the skill, labour and judgement which makes the work an original one (paragraph 1.30 onwards) and the question of substantiality. (See paragraph 5.09.)

(c) *Causal connection*

Even if there is a marked similarity between the works, if the defendant's   **5.15**
work is not copied from the plaintiff's work, then there is no infringement. Thus in *Francis Day and Hunter Ltd.* v. *Bron* ([1963] Ch. 587), there was considerable similarity between the two works in a number of different ways, but the court accepted the evidence of the author of the second work that he had not copied his work from the plaintiff's work, and that he had created his work independently.

The requirement of a causal connection is one which cannot be emphasised too highly, because in some cases a copyright owner may believe on the face of it that copying is proved by the considerable similarity between his work and another work. Although there are cases where the degree of similarity is such that the judge will infer that one man's work has been appropriated by another, there are many instances in which it has been held otherwise. Some details are therefore necessary:

109

(i) What is protected is the skill, labour and judgment used in creating the work alleged to have been copied. If this has not been taken, there is no infringement. In *Dicks* v. *Brooks* ([1879] 15 Ch.D. 22), a woolwork pattern was alleged to have been copied from an engraving of Millais' picture, "The Huguenots." This was held not to be an infringement of the copyright in the engraving. What had been taken was the skill of the artist of the original picture not the engraver.

(ii) Although the works may show some degree of similarity, this may be because they both come independently from a common source or repro-duce commonplace material or material which will necessarily be included because of the nature of the work. In *Geographia Ltd.* v. *Penguin Books Ltd.* ([1985] F.S.R. 208), the issue was whether one map was a copy of another. The two maps differed in their general presenta-tion, but on the face of it there were many similarities in detail. However, it was shown by expert evidence that no modern map could be described as totally original in detail, since it must necessarily be a compilation from source data including many other maps, gazetteers and other geograph-ical and statistical information. The judge accepted that for the most part the allegedly infringing map had been derived from such sources or the cartographer's own independent work, and the amount which had been taken was not substantial.

(iii) However, merely because the allegedly infringing work *could* have been created independently from public information or material from which the allegedly infringed work was taken will not help the person who took a short-cut by copying the former. In *Elanco Products Ltd.* v. *Mandops (Agrochemical Specialists) Ltd.* ([1980] R.P.C. 213), the works in issue were a label and leaflet accompanying a herbicide product. The allegedly infringing work reproduced much of the information, but the form and language of the defendant's leaflet was not the same. Although much of the information could have been obtained from public sources, the view taken by the Court of Appeal was that if it was not but was taken from the plaintiff's work, there would be infringement.

(iv) The causal connection need not however be direct (see paragraph 5.08). A further interesting example of this is the case of *Solar Thomson Engineering Co.* v. *Barton* ([1977] R.P.C. 537). This was a case on infringement of an original engineering drawing of a rubber liner which fitted into the rim of a pulley wheel. When the defendant began to copy the liners to make replacements, a claim was made for infringing the copyright. The defendant then instructed someone independent to pro-duce a "new" design, but supplied the designer with a pulley wheel without the liner in it and also gave him various explicit instructions on what he wanted. The designer not surprisingly came up with a design very similar to the copyright one, and it was held that there was a clear causal connection.

(v) The *Francis Day & Hunter* case referred to earlier is also interesting for its comments on so-called subconscious copying. The question here is whether it is an infringement of copyright if the defendant honestly believes that he did not take the plaintiff's work, but the court finds that there was access by the defendant to the plaintiff's work, and that the defendant did in fact make use of the plaintiff's work, albeit subconsciously. The judges were not in complete agreement on this subject, but the question is really one of evidence. If the resemblance between the two works is so striking, and familiarity with the original work firmly established, however much a judge were to believe a defendant that he was not conscious of having copied, it is likely that reproduction would still be found.

(vi) A final warning. In many cases, the plaintiff is in difficulties because although he may strongly suspect copying, he has no proof because the precise circumstances of the making of the allegedly infringing work are unknown to him. In such cases, there is always a risk that the connection is not such as might seem to him obvious. In *The Regent Publishing Co. Ltd.* v. *Bamforth & Co. Ltd.* ([1923–28] MacG. Cop. Cas. 154), the plaintiff alleged that two postcards the copyright in which he owned had been infringed. One showed a coloured person in bathing trunks with a caption above the picture. The second showed a back view of two coloured children with no clothes on and a caption based on but not exactly the same as the first card. The allegedly infringing card had two coloured children in bathing costume in the same position as the second card and a caption which was similar to both the first and the second card. The detail of the drawing on the cards was not the same. It was admitted that the defendants knew the first card, and they also had another card of a different firm which showed two coloured children clothed. They did not know of the second card. The judge refused to grant an injunction, on the basis that the second card had not been copied, and the similarity with the first card was insufficient.

(d) *The copying of ideas*

As stated, reproduction of a copyright work need not be exact for there to   **5.16**
be infringement. But in emphasising the dictionary meaning of "reproduction" of taking the essential features of a work, one must be careful not to go too far. If the defendant merely takes the general idea behind a work, that does not constitute reproduction of the work or a substantial part of that work.

In all writings on the essence of copyright, one finds reference to the maxim that there is no copyright in ideas and that what is protected is the expression of those ideas. This is a somewhat misleading and simplistic statement, but it is useful to bear in mind when considering the question of whether there has been reproduction. The law of copyright does not protect a general theme or concept which inspired or lies behind the work.

Thus, going back to the case of *Rees* v. *Melville* referred to in paragraph 5.13 above, if there had been not only no use of the language of the play, but also the precise dramatic incidents did not appear, and only the general theme had been taken, that would not constitute infringement. For example in *Wilmer* v. *Hutchinson and Co. (Publishers) Ltd.* ([1936–45] MacG. Cop. Cas. 13) a short story had the same central theme as a film, namely the legal doctrine which prevents a man who has once been convicted of a crime from being tried again for the same offence. There was evidence that the plaintiff who had written the story of the film had told the writer of the published story details of his film version, but the judge found that the characters, scenes and incidents worked out in the defendant's version were so different that there was no reproduction and there could not be infringement simply on the basis of copying the central idea or theme.

The problem of course lies in determining where the line is drawn between taking a general theme or concept behind a copyright work and taking elements of a work which represent the development of that theme or concept into the work. Regrettably, no firm rule can be provided to resolve this issue, and it is evident from many of the reported cases that this is a very grey area. One particular problem which the British Courts seem not to have faced yet is where the line is drawn in the case of computer programs. Here, much of the originality (using that word in its copyright sense) of a program will often lie in its overall structure and organisation. It remains to be seen whether the British Courts would hold that a program which took just that structure, but not the source or object code, infringed copyright.

(e) *Copying of artistic works*

5.17   In relation to artistic works, the 1988 Act repeats the provision contained in the 1956 Act that the making of a copy in three dimensions of a two-dimensional work is covered, as is the making of a copy in two dimensions of a three-dimensional work. (See s.17(3).) An example of the former has already been seen in the *King Features* case referred to in paragraph 5.08 above, and perhaps a more surprising example is *Bradbury, Agnew and Co.* v. *Day* ([1916] W.N. 114), where the elements of a cartoon were reproduced by actors dressing up and posing to look like the original. An example of the latter would be making a drawing of a sculpture.

Copying in relation to photographs is a difficult area, although the principles set out above on causal connection are the same. If a photographer arranges the constituent parts of a scene which he then photographs, a drawing or painting copied from the photograph will infringe copyright in the latter. What happens where the photographer takes a photograph of a live incident? If the view of the majority of the Court of Appeal in *Bauman* v. *Fussell* ([1978] R.P.C. 485) is taken, it will be difficult to show infringement by a drawing taken from the photograph, because the live incident is not his creation. In the *Bauman* case itself, the photograph was a very striking one, two cocks fighting, but it was held that a drawing admittedly taken from the photograph did not infringe copyright. In a dissenting judgment, Romer L.J. emphasised that although the live incident might not be the photographer's creation, "the positions in which the camera caught them are of the essence of the plaintiff's skilful presentation of that activity." The decision is not an easy one, and one is tempted to prefer the approach of Romer L.J. but it has to be admitted that the line is again difficult to draw in such cases.

(f) *Computers and computer programs*

Finally, some special comments are necessary as regards the use of **5.18** computers. What was never tested under the 1956 Act was whether storing a work in an electronic memory such as a floppy disk or a computer's RAM (Random Access Memory) constituted reproduction in a material form. The 1985 Copyright (Computer Software) Amendment Act clarified the position by making special reference to such storage, but even this was not considered wide enough, since it might not have extended to storage elsewhere—the example referred to in the debate before the Standing Committee examining the proposed 1988 Act was a portable non-volatile random access memory, where the store is completely disconnected from the computer. In order to ensure that this type of storage is covered, the 1988 Act goes further and states that reproduction in a material form includes storing the work in any medium by electronic means.

Aside from storing a work in a computer, the use of a computer program will normally involve copying of the program and any work embodied in it. Both the loading of a program and running it involve reproduction in a material form. Although the copies made are not permanent ones and in many cases incidental to the operation of the program, the 1988 Act makes it clear that there is still reproduction in those circumstances. (See s.17(6).)

The question then arises whether the display of a stored work on a computer's VDU screen will constitute reproduction in a material form. Certainly, the act of throwing a work up on to a screen will normally involve such reproduction in the bowels of the computer. However, it has been argued that display itself is a reproduction, although if this is so the same would equally well apply to the display by any means of works on a conventional television screen.

One of the fundamental problems with copyright reform is of course keeping pace with new technology, and the rapid advances made in the computer industry since the Whitford Committee reported in 1977 make one wonder whether in another 10 years' time the terminology of the Act will be wide enough to give adequate protection. One doubt already expressed was whether the words "material form" might cause difficulties in requiring substance to the form in which reproduction takes place. The Government view was that anything which influences the state of matter is material, and that accordingly whether reproduction took place in the form of a floppy disk or a bubble memory, this was still a material form. There are however problems with this approach, and one must certainly hope for flexibility from the courts which may have to apply the 1988 Act to future technology.

2. Sound recordings

5.19 Under the 1956 Act (s.12(5)), the parallel restricted act was not copying the sound recording but "making a record embodying the recording." The definition of record was very wide (s.48(1)) and covered for example not only a conventional phonograph record, but also tape. However, it was clear that one did not infringe the copyright in a sound recording by creating a completely new recording which simply sounded like the copyright recording.

Although expressing the restricted act as "copying" may seem on the face of it to amplify its scope, in our view there is still no infringement where what is created is simply a "sound-alike" recording. This is because although the new recording might be held to be a copy of the sounds contained in the existing recording, infringement requires the copying of the *recording* of those sounds.

3. Films, television broadcasts and cable programmes

5.20 The 1988 Act provides that, in relation to the above works, copying includes making a photograph of the whole or any substantial part of any image forming part of the film, broadcast or cable programme. (See s.17(4).)

This to a large extent reflects the decision of the Court of Appeal in *Spelling Goldberg Productions Inc. v. B.P.C. Publishing Ltd.* ([1981] R.P.C. 283). Under the 1956 Act, one of the restricted acts in relation to the copyright in a film was making a copy of the film, and "copy" was defined as "any print, negative, tape or other article on which the film *or part of it* is recorded." The Court of Appeal held that one still photograph from a film was a part of a film, and accordingly making a copy of that was still an infringement. Otherwise, it may be readily imagined that an argument would have been used that the still was not a substantial part of the film, and therefore could not be protected by itself. The 1988 Act has extended the provision to broadcasts and cable programmes (where what is being broadcast or included in the cable programme service may or may not be a film), but, the expression "any print, negative, tape or other article" has now been limited to a photograph, although, as has been seen, the definition of that term is very wide.

As with sound recordings (see paragraph 5.19), copying of these works does not take place where what is created is simply a "look-alike" or "sound-alike" version of the film, broadcast or cable programme.

4. Typographical arrangements of published editions

5.21 In relation to these works, the meaning of copying is restricted. The 1988 Act provides that it means making a facsimile copy of the arrangement. (See s.17(5).) A facsimile is an exact copy, counterpart or representation, but the 1988 Act says that it includes a copy which is reduced or enlarged in scale. The process of making the facsimile does not matter. The most obvious example of a facsimile is a photocopy, but it will also extend to a fax.

B. ISSUING COPIES TO THE PUBLIC

The owner of the copyright in a work has the exclusive right to issue copies of the work to the public. (See s.18(1).) **5.22**

1. Comparison with the 1956 Act

This is one of the major changes to the restricted acts introduced by the 1988 Act. Under the 1956 Act, there was no such restricted act. Instead, in relation only to literary, dramatic, musical and artistic works, one of the restricted acts was "publishing" the work. There was no definition of publishing in the 1956 Act, although there was a definition of publication. In a leading case, *Infabrics* v. *Jaytex Ltd.* ([1981] 1 All E.R. 1057), the House of Lords held that publishing did not mean the issuing of copies to the public (which constituted publication under the 1956 Act), but, in the words of Lord Reid, "making public what had not previously been made public in the territory." It is clear that the Lords did not find the 1956 Act easy to construe and there was an element of policy in the decision, because, if the word "publishing" had the meaning of issuing copies to the public, it would have deprived innocent distributors and retailers of a defence based on lack of knowledge. (See Chapter 6.)

2. What constitutes issuing copies of a work to the public?

The 1988 Act provision applies to all works, and defines the issuing to the public of copies of a work as the act of first putting those copies into circulation whether in the United Kingdom or elsewhere. (See s.18(2).) It then goes on to say that any subsequent importation of those copies, or any subsequent distribution, sale, hiring or loan of those copies is not included within the term, subject to what is said below about rental. Thus the distinction seems clear. The 1956 Act referred to publishing *the work*, not copies of the work, whereas the 1988 Act refers to the act of first putting *copies of the work*, not the work itself, into circulation. **5.23**

The words "those copies" must be emphasised. The provision does not mean that once the copyright owner has authorised the first batch of articles to be circulated, he has no further distribution right in relation to any other copies of the same article. Each article must be looked at separately, so that each such article requires the consent of the copyright owner for it to be first put into circulation.

It must also be emphasised that for the purposes of this restricted act it does not matter whether or not the copies were made with the consent of the relevant copyright owner. Whether or not they are pirate copies, the United Kingdom copyright owner's right under this provision is limited to preventing first circulation of those copies and whether or not he can prevent further circulation depends on the secondary infringement provisions referred to in Chapter 6.

3. "In the United Kingdom or elsewhere"

The addition of these words was one of the last amendments made to the **5.24**

Bill before it completed its passage through Parliament. It means that once a copy has been put into circulation abroad, the copyright owner has no right to prevent its importation and distribution within the United Kingdom, again unless the provisions of secondary infringement referred to in the next Chapter apply. In many cases, there will be difficulty in knowing whether a particular article imported into this country has already been put into circulation first abroad.

4. The meaning of "circulation"

5.25   In essence therefore, this is a limited distribution right, and it will readily be appreciated that it does to some extent impinge on the provisions on secondary infringement which are referred to in Chapter 6. What is not clear however is when the act of first putting copies into circulation occurs. Say that a record company has no pressing plant or distribution facilities itself, and instructs the pressing plant which manufactures records for it to transfer the records to the warehouse of its distributor, which then distributes the records. Presumably the act of first putting those copies into circulation occurs when that distributor himself distributes the records, and not when the pressing plant transfers the records to the distributor for the purposes of distribution. However, it will be appreciated there can be no hard-and-fast rule because much depends upon the particular facts.

5. Rental

5.26   There is one exception to the provision that it is only the act of putting the copies into circulation for the first time which is a restricted act. This relates to sound recordings, films and computer programs only, and provides that the rental of copies to the public is a restricted act. (See s.18(2).) However, the rental right as regards a computer program expires 50 years from the end of the calendar year in which copies were first issued to the public. (See s.66(5).)

The rental does not therefore apply to literary works (except computer programs) or dramatic, musical or artistic works, whether or not they are embodied in the form of sound recordings, films or computer programs. Of course, this would not prevent the copyright owner of such a work laying down as a condition of granting a licence to copy his work that no rental take place, or that rental be subject to further fees. Furthermore, although rental is not a restricted act in relation to such works, one must not forget that fees may be generated under the provisions of the Public Lending Right Act 1979.

(a) *Definition of rental* (s.178)

5.27   Rental is defined as any arrangement under which a copy of a work is made available either for payment (in money or money's worth) or in the course of a business as part of services or amenities for which payment is made on terms that the copy will or may be returned.

The precise ambit of rental under this provision however is not entirely clear. One can only say this with reasonable confidence:

(i) It will obviously apply both to public libraries and commercial rental operations if a charge is made.

(ii) It does not matter that the monetary consideration was not provided directly for the rental of the copy. Thus, the provision is likely to catch the situation where rental of a record is free but is conditional upon payment for other goods such as blank tapes.

(iii) A scheme by which rental takes place on terms that there is an option to buy and therefore not to return the relevant article will still be caught. Hire-purchase schemes are obvious examples. To give another example, a record rental shop might rent out a compact disc on a nightly charge, but give the person borrowing it the option to buy it at a reduced price. Such rental will infringe copyright unless licensed.

(b) *"In the course of a business"*

The example used by the Government to illustrate this aspect of rental **5.28** was where a hotel has a library of discs or videos which it makes available for no extra charge to hotel guests.

The word "business" is defined as including any trade or profession. Although a charity is not of itself a business, it may run a business as part of its fund-raising operations and would to that extent be subject to the provision. A public library is also not of itself a business, but the 1988 Act amends the Public Libraries and Museums Act 1964 to apply the rental provisions to free lending by such libraries. By section 8(6) of the amended 1964 Act, all the provisions of the 1988 Act relating to rental of copies of sound recordings, films and computer programs apply to any lending by a library authority of copies of such works, whether or not a charge is made.

(c) *Pre-existing copies*

Finally, there is a specific transitional provision to deal with pre-existing **5.29** copies of sound recordings, films or computer programs. (See schedule 1, paragraph 14(2).) Where such a copy has been acquired by any person before commencement of the Act for the purpose of renting it to the public, then the copyright owner has no right to control rental of that copy. This would extend to any other person subsequently renting such copy, for example after the assets of a business have been sold. Subject to this, the rental provisions apply to copies in existence at the date of commencement of the new Act as they do to copies made after commencement.

C. PUBLIC PERFORMANCE

1. Literary, dramatic and musical works

In relation to literary, dramatic and musical works, the copyright owner **5.30** has the exclusive right to perform the work in public. (See s.19(1).) The expression "performance" is not defined exclusively. It includes delivery, in the case of lectures, addresses, speeches and sermons. (See s.19(2).) In general it also includes any mode of visual or acoustic presentation, including presentation by means of a sound recording, film broadcast or cable programme of the work. (See s.19(2).) All of these provisions are repeated from the 1956 Act.

2. Pre-1911 Act musical works (schedule 1, paragraph 17)

5.31   The copyright owner of a musical work first published before July 1, 1912 may however have lost the exclusive right to perform the work in public. If the work was first published on or after August 10, 1882, the right was lost unless it was expressly reserved on each copy of the work. If it has been lost, the copyright owner will also not be able to prevent broadcasting of the work or inclusion of the work in a cable programme service.

3. Sound recordings, films, broadcasts and cable programmes

5.32   In relation to these works, the owner of the copyright has the exclusive right to play or show the work in public in the United Kingdom. (See s.19(3).)

4. Broadcasting can now amount to performance

5.33   The 1956 Act stated that broadcasting and including works or other subject-matter in a cable programme service did not constitute performance. (See 1956 Act, s.48(5).) This provision has been removed. Although broadcasters and those who include works in cable programme services (even in some cases those excluded from the definition of cable programme services under Clause 7(3)) could therefore find themselves involved in the public performance, playing or showing of works (see *Mellor* v. *Australian Broadcasting Commission* [1940] A.C. 491), the circumstances in which they will be liable for infringement are restricted by reason of the provision referred to in paragraph 5.34.

5. Public performance via television and radio

5.34   What is repeated in the 1988 Act however is the special provision which relates to the situation where a work is performed (or played or shown) in public by means of apparatus for receiving visual images or sounds conveyed by electronic means. The obvious example of this is television or radio equipment situated in a public place such as a discotheque and which receives broadcasts or cable programmes. In this case, the person by whom the visual images or sounds were sent is not to be regarded as responsible for infringement by public performance. (See s.19(4).) Of course that person may be liable instead for broadcasting or including the work in a cable programme provided that this was being done in the United Kingdom and was unlicensed.

The exemption now also applies to any performer whose performance is included in the visual images or sounds which are transmitted.

It is only the person by whom the visual images or sounds are sent who is exempted from liability and the drafting leaves it open to argue that anyone who authorises the sending of such visual images or sounds may still infringe. However, the purpose of the exemption is clear, namely that if someone chooses to perform or play or show works in public via a television set or radio set, that person and not the broadcaster or cable programme service provider should be liable for infringement.

6. The meaning of "in public"

It remains therefore to consider what the expression "in public" means. **5.35**
No definition of this was provided in the 1956 Act and is not provided in this Act either, so that one has to look to the cases under the old law. This is another area where the courts have refused to lay down any hard-and-fast rule as to what constitutes a performance or showing or playing of a work in public. In each case, it is again a matter of fact and degree, but again some guidelines and factors which have been taken into account are set out below:

(a) *Domestic or quasi-domestic gatherings*

The most favoured test is to consider whether or not the performance **5.36**
took place in a domestic or quasi-domestic situation. Even this is in itself difficult to construe. In *Harms (Inc.) and Chappell and Co.* v. *Martans Club* ([1927] 1 Ch. 526), Lord Hanworth M.R. said that domestic was used "in the sense that it was private and domestic, a matter of family and household concern only." Obviously, the expression "quasi-domestic" takes this further and in *Duck* v. *Bates* (1884), it was held that a performance at Guy's Hospital before nurses who lived at the hospital, together with doctors, students, members of the administration of the hospital and in each category some of their family members was quasi-domestic and not a performance in public. There was obviously great sympathy for the hospital in that situation, but the judges clearly regarded the case as a borderline one. An attempt to expand it in *Jennings* v. *Stephens* ([1936] 1 All E.R. 409) where the performance of the play took place before members of a Women's Institute all from one village, and excluded all guests, failed. This was held to be a performance in public.

(b) *Number of people*

Mere numbers alone cannot determine whether a performance is in **5.37**
public or not. The expression "public" can encompass a performance before a limited section of the public.

(c) *Presence of guests*

Neither is it material whether or not guests are present at the **5.38**
performance.

(d) *Relevance of payment*

5.39   It does not matter either whether the performers are paid or whether the audience is charged an admission fee. Although in the *Harms* case, it was said that the fact that the performance was profit-motivated was an important factor, in the *Rangers F.C.* case, it was also said that absence of a profit motive does not mean that the performance cannot be one in public.

(e) *Nature of the location*

5.40   Neither is the nature of the place at which the performance takes place material. Several of the cases are concerned with performances which took place at a club, whether proprietary or members', and on the whole arguments which have been used by such clubs that there was no performance in public have failed. Nevertheless, it was said in the case of *Performing Right Society Ltd.* v. *Rangers Football Club Supporters Club*, (Greenock, 1973 S.L.T. 195) that that did not mean that every performance in a club came within the expression "in public". Even where the performance was outside a reserved room there might be occasions where on a true construction of the fact, the performance was not in public.

(f) *Relevance of damage to the performing right*

5.41   On some occasions, emphasis has been laid on the damage caused to the owner of the copyright, and diminution in the value of the copyright. However an attempt to turn this on its head by arguing that it followed that a performance which did not injure the author but was in fact promotional and helped to sell further copies of articles embodying the relevant copyright work (in the relevant case, the playing of records in a record shop) would not be a performance in public was rejected in *Performing Right Society Ltd.* v. *Harlequin Records Shops Ltd.* ([1979] 1 W.L.R. 851). In that case the judge emphasised that such considerations as injury to the author were only likely to come into play when the case was a borderline one—one still first had to look and see whether the case was plainly one which fell within the meaning of the expression "performance in public."

(g) *The Jennings v. Stephens test*

5.42   A more sophisticated test developed in the 1930s was to consider the expression "in public" in relation to the owner of the copyright. Thus Greene L.J. in *Jennings* v. *Stephens*:

> "If the audience considered in relation to the owner of the copyright may properly be described as the owner's 'public' or part of his 'public,' then in performing the work before that audience he would in my opinion be exercising the statutory right conferred upon him; and anyone who without his consent performed the work before that audience would be infringing his copyright."

However, if, as the judge in the *Harlequin* case assumed, this means that one has to look to see whether the owner would expect a fee to be paid, it is not an entirely reliable test.

7. The unresolved problem

During the passage of the Copyright, Designs and Patents Bill through Parliament, various attempts were made (but resisted by the Government) to define the circumstances in which a performance would be in public. One motive was to try and clear up the unresolved issue of whether circumstances such as the relay of films by hotels to individual rooms within a hotel constituted performance in public of, say, any musical work included in the film. Opinion is divided as to whether this is so, although there may under the 1988 Act be infringement by inclusion of the relevant work in a cable programme service. The point is however still one of practical importance in cases where a service is excluded from the definition of cable programme service—for example, a service run for prison inmates.

D. BROADCASTING AND CABLE TRANSMISSION (s.20)

The rights here apply to all categories of works except the typographical **5.43** arrangement in a published edition.
  The owner of the copyright in a work has the exclusive right to broadcast the work in the United Kingdom. He also has the exclusive right to include the work in a cable programme service.

1. Broadcasting

(a) *The meaning of broadcasting* (s.6(1))

Broadcasting consists of the act of transmitting by wireless telegraphy **5.44** visual images, sounds or other information which is either capable of being lawfully received by members of the public, or transmitted for presentation to members of the public. For the meaning of this, see paragraph 1.51. On the basis of this new definition, the restricted act of broadcasting now not only covers direct broadcasting by satellite, but also transmission both from an earth-station to a Fixed Service Satellite and from the latter to an earth-station.
  Several different theories have been propounded as to when and where the broadcast of a work takes place, the arguments being particularly complex in relation to satellite transmissions where one is considering not only the up-leg from the originating station to the satellite but the down-leg from the satellite to the earth station or receiving equipment. Under the 1988 Act, it is only the broadcasting of a work in the United Kingdom which is an infringement of copyright. So far as satellite transmissions are concerned, it is specifically provided that the place from which the

broadcast is made is the place from which the signals carrying the broadcast are transmitted to the satellite. (See s.6(4).) Whilst the provisions on infringement by broadcasting (ss.16 and 20) and the definitions relating to broadcasts (s.6) do not inter-relate particularly well, it appears that infringement by broadcasting takes place where the station transmitting the broadcast to a satellite is in the United Kingdom, even though the footprint does not or is not intended to include the United Kingdom. Conversely, it appears that where the original transmission takes place in France, no infringement occurs in the United Kingdom even though the broadcast was intended purely to be received in this country.

(b) *The person liable for broadcasting* (s.6(3))

5.45 The person who broadcasts a work is defined as:

(i) The person who transmits the programme which embodies the work, if he has responsibility to any extent for its contents.

(ii) A person providing the programme which embodies the work and who makes with the person transmitting it the arrangements necessary for its transmission.

For the meaning of those definitions see paragraph 3.59 onwards.

The two definitions are not alternatives in the sense that only one or other can apply to a particular broadcast. If in the case of any broadcast, more than one person comes within either or both definitions, then more than one person will infringe.

The practical effect of these definitions is in one way to widen the ambit of liability for broadcasting and in another way perhaps to narrow its scope. Transmission for the future is only an infringement if the person transmitting has responsibility for the contents of the programme, and, as stated in paragraph 3.60, the problem here is the meaning of the word "responsibility." However, the alternative allows the copyright owner to go back along the chain to the person who supplied the programme if he made the arrangements with the person transmitting it for its transmission.

2. Cable transmission

(a) *Comparison with the 1956 Act*

5.46 Under the 1956 Act as originally passed, the owner of the copyright had the exclusive right to cause the relevant work to be transmitted to subscribers to a diffusion service. This expression was replaced under the 1984 Cable and Broadcasting Act with the phrase "the inclusion of the work in a cable programme." This has changed slightly so that the restricted act is now its inclusion in a cable programme *service*. This change was effected in order to prevent confusion between, for example, the synchronisation of a musical work with the cable programme, and the transmission of that programme.

(b) *The meaning of cable programme service* (s.7(1))

This is covered in paragraph 1.55 onwards. If the service is one excluded **5.47**
from the provisions of the 1988 Act as referred to in that section, then the
copyright owner has no right to prevent it from being included in such a
service. However, in such circumstances, there could be liability on other
grounds, if for example the work has been copied for the purposes of
inclusion in the service. Generally, however, there will be no liability for
performing or playing or showing the work in public, because of the
exemption referred to in paragraph 5.34.

The changes effected by the 1988 Act in relation to services excluded
from the definition of cable programme services and which are referred to
in paragraph 1.59 are obviously an important extension to the scope of
the restricted act of including works in a cable programme service.

(c) *The meaning of inclusion* (s.7(5))

A work is included in a cable programme service if it is transmitted as part **5.48**
of the service.

(d) *The person liable for including a work in a cable programme service*
(s.7(5))

A person includes a work in a cable programme service if he is the person **5.49**
providing that service.

E. ADAPTATION

1. The making of an adaptation

The copyright owner of a literary, dramatic and musical work has the **5.50**
exclusive right to make an adaptation of such a work. (See s.21(1).)
Under the 1956 Act there was no definition as to when an adaptation was
taken to be made, but under the 1988 Act an adaptation is only made
when it is recorded, in writing or otherwise. Writing includes any form of
notation or code, whether by hand or otherwise, and regardless of the
method by which or medium in, or on which, it is recorded. (See s.178.)

Unlike the other restricted acts considered in this Chapter, the making
of an adaptation is something which involves a conscious and deliberate
process, and thus in this area knowledge is an essential ingredient. As
Willmer L.J. said in the *Francis Day & Hunter* case, "a man cannot
arrange or transcribe without knowing that he is doing so."

2. Other restricted acts and adaptations

The owner of the copyright in a literary, dramatic or musical work also **5.51**
has the exclusive right to copy an adaptation of the work, to issue to the

public copies of an adaptation of the work, perform an adaptation of the work in public, broadcast an adaptation of the work and include an adaptation of the work in a cable programme service. (See s.21(2).) For the meaning of all these expressions, one obviously looks to the section above dealing with the restricted act in question as it applies to the works themselves. For these purposes, it does not matter whether the adaptation has been recorded at the time the act is done, or whether the adaptation was made with or without the licence of the copyright owner.

In a case where the adaptation is unlicensed and is itself the subject of a separate copyright (see paragraph 1.40), it is at first sight difficult to reconcile the provisions with the decision in *Redwood Music Ltd.* v. *Chappell & Co. Ltd.* ([1982] R.P.C. 109) that the copyright in an infringing arrangement belongs to the infringer not the owner of the work infringed. Both would appear then to have conflicting exclusive rights. The answer in our view lies in ensuring that one clearly distinguishes ownership of rights and infringement. Ownership of copyright gives a person the exclusive right to (for example) copy an adaptation of a work, but he still does not own any copyright in the adaptation (assuming that *Redwood* is still good law), and will infringe the owner's rights if he exercises his exclusive right. Likewise, the owner of the copyright of the work made in infringement of copyright has the exclusive right to (for example) copy his work, but he will again infringe the copyright in the work which he has already infringed if he exercises that exclusive right.

3. The meaning of adaptation

5.52   The word "adaptation" has a defined meaning, depending on whether it is used in relation to a literary or dramatic work on the one hand, or a musical work on the other hand.

(a) *Musical works* (s.21(3)(b))

5.53   An adaptation of a musical work is either an arrangement or transcription of the work. In music, the word "transcription" is used in several different senses, but here it probably means a species of arrangement where a work in one medium is changed to another medium—for example, the reduction of an orchestral work to a piano version of that work.

The word "arrangement" is on the other hand not so easy to define, and it may encompass fairly simple changes to a work carried out in order to make it more acceptable on the basis of the musical fashion of the day, and to more extensive changes where a work is completely rewritten to suit other purposes than those for which it was originally composed. There is therefore some possible overlap here with the considerations which were set out above in relation to reproduction. If a work is reproduced not in the exact form it was written, but retaining the essential features of the work, there may be both reproduction of the work itself and reproduction of an adaptation of the work. What never seems to have been decided is whether there reaches a stage when the version reproduced has gone so far away from the original that it ceases to be a reproduction within the ordinary meaning of that word, but remains a reproduction of an adaptation of the work.

(b) *Adaptation of literary and dramatic works* (s.21(3)(a))

An adaptation of a literary or dramatic work can be any of the following: **5.54**

(i) A translation of the work. The obvious example here is translation into a foreign language, but it could also be translation into or out of code, or translation into or out of computer language.

(ii) A dramatic version of a non-dramatic work (for example, a play based on a book), and a non-dramatic version of a dramatic work (for example, a novel based on a play).

(iii) A version of the work in which the story or action is conveyed wholly or mainly by means of pictures in a form suitable for reproduction in a book, newspaper, magazine or similar periodical (for example, a strip cartoon version of a novel).

It is not therefore an infringement of copyright simply to alter some of the words in the lyrics of a song or in a play. However, if any of the other restricted acts are carried out in relation to the altered version, that will usually be an infringement of copyright of the original version, provided that a substantial part of the latter has been used. (See paragraph 5.09.)

(c) *Computer programs*

In relation to a computer program, a translation includes a version of the   **5.55**
program in which it is converted into or out of a computer language or code or into a different computer language or code, otherwise than incidentally in the course of running the program. (See s.21(4).) The meaning of the expression "version of the program" is not entirely clear, but the wording of the section as a whole suggests that it could include flow-charts or human language descriptions.

Computer programs are often translated in order to allow them to be used with computers which are not able to function in the language in which the program was originally written. Where such a translation is created independently, perhaps in the form of a new software package, then it is clear that the translation will not have occurred incidentally in the course of running the program. An example of a case where the "in the course of running the program" exemption might apply is the translation from high level language into source or object code which is required in order for the computer to function. The exemption is clearly intended to ensure that such use does not amount to an actionable adaptation. However, even in such a case, there is a technical argument that the compilation and translation which takes place in order for the computer to work occurs before and independently to the running of the program and accordingly that the exemption does not work.

Although a translation done incidentally in the course of running the program would not constitute adaptation, copying in the course of running a program is a restricted act since under section 17(6) in the 1988 Act copying includes the making of transient copies. (See paragraph 5.18.) If the translation still involves copying the computer program, it must be emphasised that the exemption only applies to infringement by adaptation, and not to infringement by copying of the original program. In many cases, there will either be an express or implied licence to carry out such acts. (See paragraphs 9.08 and 7.91.)

It should be noted that this provision only states that translation "includes" the making of such a version of the program. The precise scope of the work "translation" in relation to computer programs is unclear, but it could be useful perhaps where there are difficulties with the restricted act of copying where the program has been decompiled and a new program created with the same structure but using a different source or object code.

6 SECONDARY INFRINGEMENT

I INTRODUCTION

Chapter 5 dealt with the acts which the copyright owner has the exclusive **6.01** right to do and to prevent others from doing. There, the mere doing of any such act without consent constitutes an infringement of copyright, and in general infringement takes place whether or not the person doing the act, or authorising it to be done, knew that he was infringing copyright or intended to infringe. However, the 1988 Act, like its predecessors, provides that certain other acts will also infringe copyright, provided that an added ingredient of knowledge on the part of the person doing the act is present. Breach of such provisions is commonly called secondary infringement of copyright.

1. Summary of the 1988 Act

In summary, acts which constitute secondary infringement of copyright if **6.02** done with the requisite degree of knowledge are as follows:

(a) Possessing in the course of a business an infringing copy of a work or an article specifically designed or adapted for making infringing copies of a work.

(b) Selling, letting for hire, offering or exposing for sale or hire, in the course of a business exhibiting in public or distributing infringing copies of works or articles specifically designed or adapted for making infringing copies.

(c) Transmitting a work by a telecommunications system where an infringing copy of the work is made on receipt of the transmission.

(d) Permitting a place of public entertainment to be used for infringing copyright in a literary, dramatic or musical work by public performance.

(e) Where an infringing performance or playing or showing of a work takes place by means of apparatus such as juke-boxes, radios and television sets:

   (i) in the case of an occupier of premises, giving permission for the apparatus to be brought on to the premises,

   (ii) supplying the apparatus,

   (iii) supplying a copy of a sound recording or film for use by means of the apparatus.

127

For the sake of convenience, the civil provisions on fraudulent reception of transmissions and devices designed to circumvent copy-protection have also been included in this chapter, although the rights granted by those provisions are not necessarily exerciseable by copyright owners.

2. Differences between the 1956 Act and the 1988 Act

6.03   A number of important changes have been made in this area by the 1988 Act. These are as follows:

(a) The standard of knowledge required has been modified in certain cases, so that actual knowledge will no longer be required, but only "reason to believe." (See paragraph 6.06.)

(b) Possession of an infringing copy in the course of a business has been added to those dealings with infringing copies which constitutes acts of secondary infringement. (See paragraph 6.36.)

(c) The acts of secondary infringement referred to in (c) and (e) of paragraph 6.02 above are new. (See paragraphs 6.58 onwards and 6.16 onwards.)

(d) The provisions relating to secondary infringement by importation and dealing with imported copies have been changed in order to resolve the difficulties faced by exclusive licensees as a result of the decision in *CBS (U.K.) Ltd.* v. *Charmdale Record Distributors Ltd.* [1981] Ch. 91. (See paragraph 6.30.)

(e) In the case of secondary infringement by permitting the use of premises for an infringing performance, it is no longer a defence to show that permission was given gratuitously or for nominal consideration. (See paragraph 6.13.)

3. The requirement of knowledge

6.04   In the case of most of the provisions on secondary infringement referred to below the person doing the relevant act does not infringe copyright unless he knows or has reason to believe a certain fact or set of facts. This section deals with the meaning of that phrase: other requirements as to knowledge are dealt with in the context of the relevant provisions.

(a) *The position under the 1911 and 1956 Acts*

6.05   Under the 1911 and 1956 Acts, for there to be secondary infringement by dealing with a copy of a work made in the United Kingdom, the person doing the relevant act had to know that the article which he was dealing with was made in infringement of copyright (see, for example, 1956 Act ss.5 and 16). The words "or had reason to believe" which are now in the 1988 Act were not present in the 1956 Act.

Although therefore it seemed that in all cases it was actual knowledge which was required, in practice the courts were often prepared to regard the requirement as being fulfilled if there was knowledge of the material facts in such a way as should have put the defendant on notice that copyright had been infringed. However, this was not so in every case. For example, in *Columbia Picture Industry* v. *Robinson* ([1987] Ch. 38) (a case concerned with the sale of pirate video cassettes), it was said by Scott J. on the facts before him:

> "If a check had been made by Mr. Robinson in order to identify those tapes which were pirates he would, in my view, by reason of his professional expertise, have had a good degree of success. I do not doubt that there would have been some pirates that he would not have identified but he would, I think, have identified most of them. The question for decision is whether this general knowledge on Mr. Robinson's part, coupled with his ability to have made a reasonably successful check, coupled with his own concern as to whether or not the shop was selling or hiring pirate tapes, is sufficient to fix him with the requisite knowledge for the purposes of section 16(3). In my judgment, it is not."

The judge did however qualify the requirement as to actual knowledge in the following way:

> "I accept that actual knowledge is necessary but subject to this proviso. In this area of jurisprudence, as in many others, the person who deliberately refrains from enquiry and shuts his eyes to that which is obvious cannot be heard to say that he lacked the requisite knowledge."

A standard of knowledge of this degree certainly puts difficulties in the way of a plaintiff. Under the 1956 Act, this was particularly so in the case of importation of articles manufactured abroad, where, as will be seen, it might be necessary to examine whether the article would have been made in infringement of copyright if the circumstances under which it had been made were hypothetically transferred to the United Kingdom.

(b) *Knowledge under the 1988 Act*

The 1988 Act modifies the requirement as to knowledge, in adding the alternative ground that the relevant person "had reason to believe" the relevant facts or circumstances.   **6.06**

Although at this stage it is hard to know what construction the courts will place on this phrase, it seems likely that the standard of knowledge required will be lower. In our view, whether a defendant has reason to believe that he is dealing with an infringing copy involves a two-stage inquiry. First, one must consider what the defendant "has": that is, what are the facts and circumstances which he was aware of or which were committed? Secondly, did they constitute "reason to believe" that the copy was an infringing copy? Where a proper warning letter has been received and read by the defendant, then that of itself will almost inevitably mean the requirement is fulfilled: the defendant has the letter and it constitutes reason to believe. However, where the warning letter is not received or read, the position is less clear-cut. Then one must inquire what the defendant was aware of, and examine whether that was "reason to believe." So the test is both subjective and objective.

In the case of a pirated product, in many cases now it will be easier to show that the defendant has the required degree of knowledge. However, there will still be many cases where a trader in articles made in infringement of copyright has no idea and no reason to believe that articles which he has purchased in entire good faith were made in infringement of copyright. In those circumstances, putting the trader on notice that the articles were made in infringement of copyright is and will still be necessary.

In a case under the 1911 Act, *Van Dusen* v. *Critz* [1936] 2 K.B. 176, it was held that even where a warning letter had been sent, a defendant must still have a reasonable opportunity of finding out whether the work infringes the copyright or not, assuming that the relevant article was acquired in good faith and without any knowledge that it infringed copyright. Until that reasonable opportunity had passed, it was said that no knowledge could be imputed to the defendant.

In our view, it is unlikely that the same principle will apply under the 1988 Act where a warning letter has been received by the defendant. As stated above, if the letter is received, and has been read by the defendant, that will constitute "reason to believe," and there is little room for any requirement that the defendant be given the opportunity to consider the position. Of course, in practice it may still be sensible for a copyright owner to give a seemingly respectable trader an opportunity to consider his position and desist from the relevant act before proceedings commenced.

4. Acts done before the 1988 Act

6.07 As in the case of the restricted acts referred to in Chapter 5, the provisions of the 1956 Act continue to apply in relation to acts done before commencement of the new Act. (See schedule 1, paragraph 14(1).)

5. Authorising

6.08 It is only the person who does the relevant acts referred to in this Chapter who is liable. The concept of liability by authorising such acts does not apply here, although another party may be liable as a joint infringer, for which see paragraph 10.48 below.

II ACTS OF SECONDARY INFRINGEMENT RELEVANT TO PERFORMANCE OR PLAYING OR SHOWING IN PUBLIC

A. PERMITTING USE OF PREMISES FOR INFRINGING PERFORMANCE (s.25)

1. The relevant works

This provision only applies in the case of literary, dramatic or musical **6.09** works.

2. Summary of the provision

Where such a work is infringed by performance at a place of public **6.10** entertainment, any person giving permission for that place to be used for the performance is also liable for infringement of copyright. However, if at the time he gave permission he believed on reasonable grounds that the performance would not infringe copyright, he has a defence to an action against him.

A place of public entertainment obviously covers theatres and discotheques, but the provision also extends to premises occupied mainly for other purposes but from time to time made available for hire for the purposes of public entertainment. An example would be a village hall used for a variety of different purposes, including dances.

A similar provision was contained in both the 1911 Act (s.2(3)) and 1956 Act (s.5(5)), although modifications have been made with each change in legislation.

3. Necessity of primary infringement

The provision applies only where the performance is an infringement. **6.11** Thus, if the performance occurs at a place of public entertainment, but in circumstances where the performance was not in public (see paragraph 5.35 above), it does not apply.

4. Burden of proof

The burden of proof is on the person giving permission to show that he **6.12** believed on reasonable grounds that the performance would not infringe.

5. Gratuitous/nominal consideration

In the 1956 Act, a person giving permission could also escape liability **6.13** where he showed that he gave the permission gratuitously or for a nominal consideration or for a consideration not exceeding a reasonable estimate of his expenses. This no longer applies.

However, where the premises are occupied mainly for other purposes, they must still be available for hire from time to time for the purposes of public entertainment or the provision will not apply (see paragraph 6.10 above). Hiring requires some monetary or other remuneration and accordingly if, say, a barn is only ever made available for dances free of charge, there will be no infringement.

6. Time for considering defendant's belief

6.14   Under the 1956 Act, it was not clear whether the defendant would be liable where he gave permission without there being reasonable grounds for suspecting that the performance would be an infringement of the copyright, later found out that it would infringe copyright, but still allowed the performance to go ahead. The 1988 Act clarifies the position by providing that the relevant time for considering whether there was belief on reasonable grounds is when permission is given.

7. Possible limitations on the usefulness of the provision

6.15   This provision at first sight looks useful to copyright owners, particularly in cases where it is difficult to identify the actors or musicians who performed, or where they might have insufficient means to satisfy any judgment. However, the precise scope of the equivalent section in the 1911 Act was limited as a result of the decision of the Court of Appeal in *Performing Right Society Ltd.* v. *Ciryl Theatrical Syndicate Ltd.* [1924] 1 K.B. 1. In that case, the defendant was the holder of a licence from the Lord Chamberlain to have plays performed at a theatre, and entered into an agreement with a professional musician that the latter should provide an orchestra to perform at the theatre. Despite the plaintiff society showing that they had drawn the attention of the licensee to the fact that the performances by the orchestra were not licensed and that further performances still took place, it was held by the Court of Appeal that the licensee had no liability under the section. Lord Justice Atkin said that the permission given to use the relevant premises must relate to the specific work the performance of which was complained of, and this was not fulfilled where there was merely a general authority to perform music in the theatre. Since the licensee did not know that the orchestra were performing the particular pieces complained of and had no reason to consider that they were the subject of copyright, accordingly it was held that there was no liability for infringement.

This is not a satisfactory case, and it is difficult to assess whether the provision in the 1988 Act alters the situation. In the 1911 and 1956 Acts, the layout of the section was similar, and it was not thought that the 1956 provision altered that subsisting under the 1911 Act. However, the 1988 Act expresses the provision in rather simpler terms and it may be that the courts would now hold that it is not necessary for the permission to relate to the specific work or works the subject-matter of the proceedings.

B. PERFORMANCE, PLAYING OR SHOWING OF A WORK IN PUBLIC BY MEANS OF CERTAIN APPARATUS

1. Position under the 1956 Act

Under the 1956 Act, where public performance of a literary, dramatic or **6.16** musical work or the showing or playing of sound recordings or films took place by means of such apparatus as a television set or a juke-box, the occupier of the premises where the apparatus was situated was treated as the person responsible for public performance or playing or showing, if the apparatus was provided by him or with his consent. (See 1956 Act s.48(6).) If therefore the occupier of a club allowed a disc jockey to bring hi-fi equipment on to his premises, the occupier was liable for public performance of the relevant musical works, even if he had no knowledge that this would infringe copyright.

2. Effect of the 1988 Act

The 1988 Act changes this position, and makes it possible for the copy- **6.17** right owner in certain circumstances to call to account not only the occupier of premises, but also the supplier of both the software and the hardware used in the infringement. However, in doing this, it also places new limits on the circumstances where the occupier is liable.

3. Necessity of primary infringement

Each of the possible infringers is dealt with separately below, but in every **6.18** case there must be an infringement of copyright by public performance or by playing or showing, and this must have taken place by means of apparatus either for playing sound recordings, or showing films, or receiving visual images or sounds conveyed by electronic means. (See s.26(1).) One must therefore bear in mind the extensive exemptions from infringement in relation to broadcasts, cable programmes, films and sound recordings (see Chapter 7), and that the performance must be in public. (See paragraph 5.35.)

4. Requirement of knowledge

Furthermore, the person must know that the hardware or software is used **6.19** "to infringe copyright." In other words, in many cases it will probably be insufficient simply to show that the likelihood was that the apparatus would be used for public performance or playing or showing purposes, since this is only an infringement of copyright when done without the consent of the copyright owner. The actual requirement of proof of course will depend on each case, and it may well be that it will be easier to show that an occupier of premises normally used for public entertainment is liable than the supplier of hardware and software.

5. The relevant apparatus

6.20 As under the 1956 Act, not only audio juke-boxes are covered by the above, but also video juke-boxes, and not only the use of a television receiving broadcasts and simultaneously showing the visual images in public (see, however, paragraph 7.113), but also where a video cassette recording is used.

6. The occupier (s.26(3))

(a) *Liability*

6.21 The occupier of the premises is liable if he gave permission for the apparatus to be brought on to the premises, and if, when he gave that permission, he knew or had reason to believe that the apparatus was likely to be so used as to infringe copyright.

(b) *Comparison between the 1956 and 1988 Acts*

6.22 In the provision referred to under the 1956 Act, the occupier of the premises was liable whether or not he had knowledge. Conversely, the operator of the apparatus was not liable even though he knew that he was infringing, although it was never settled under United Kingdom copyright law whether or not an operator could be liable by reason of his authorising the performance, or because he was a joint infringer. (See paragraph 10.48.)

Under the 1988 Act, there is no exemption for the operator of the apparatus, so he would be liable if he could be said to be performing or playing or showing the work in public, or authorising any such act. If that is so, it will not be necessary to prove knowledge, because the act will be one of primary infringement. Conversely, the occupier of premises, if he is not the operator, will only be liable under this provision referred to in this section if he has knowledge.

7. Supplier of the hardware (s.26(2))

6.23 This provision applies to the person who supplies the apparatus referred to or any substantial part of that apparatus.

In these circumstances, there are two possible ways in which the supplier may be liable for infringement. First, he will be liable if he knew or had reason to believe that the apparatus was likely to be so used as to infringe copyright. Secondly, in the case of apparatus the normal use of which involves a public performance, playing or showing, he will be liable if he did not believe on reasonable grounds that it would not be so used as to infringe copyright.

As regards the first of these two alternatives, this is unlikely to apply in the case of a normal retail trader. A retailer may know that certain types of equipment are likely to be used in public rather than private, but that does not mean that the use in public will infringe copyright. If however, the owner of a discotheque boasts to his supplier that he has managed to get away with avoiding obtaining a public performance licence from the Performing Right Society Ltd., then there may be liability. For that reason, it may be that some suppliers in future would find it sensible to make purchasers sign a suitable warranty.

As regards the second of the alternatives, this will only apply to apparatus such as an audio juke-box, and not domestic hi-fi equipment. Again, it is unlikely to apply simply to a normal television set. Here the requirement as to knowledge is expressed differently, and is likely to be of a higher standard than where the expression "has reason to believe" is used. Again however, there should be a two-stage inquiry. First, one has to consider what the defendant actually believed, and this goes beyond assessing what facts and circumstances he was aware of, and requires one to consider what the defendant concluded from them. Secondly, one has to look to see whether the defendant's belief was on reasonable grounds. It may be therefore that the defendant's conclusions were incorrect, but provided that he reached them on reasonable grounds, there would be no liability.

8. Supplier of the software (s.26(4))

This provision applies to the person who supplies a copy of a sound **6.24** recording or film which is used for the infringing performance or playing or showing, for example a video cassette for a video juke-box. That person is liable for infringement if when he supplied the copy, he knew or had reason to believe that the copy or a copy made directly or indirectly from it was likely to be used to infringe copyright. Again, it must be emphasised that knowledge that the software was to be used for public performance is insufficient. The supplier must know or have reason to believe that the copy is likely to be used to infringe copyright.

9. Usefulness of the provisions

Of course these new provisions will be much welcomed by copyright **6.25** owners. It is always possible for a copyright owner to write a sufficiently detailed warning letter to put an occupier or supplier of software or hardware on notice. Thus, it gives the owner of the copyright much more power in practice to deprive the person responsible for the primary infringement of public performance or playing or showing in public of his ability to infringe, by for example persuading those who supply hardware or software to such a person to cease supply.

III POSSESSION AND DEALING WITH INFRINGING COPIES

A. THE MEANING OF "INFRINGING COPY"

6.26 An article can be an infringing copy on three possible grounds. First, it will be an infringing copy if its making constituted an infringement of the copyright in the work in question. (See s.27(2).) Secondly, an article is an infringing copy if it has been or is proposed to be imported into the United Kingdom, and its making in the United Kingdom would have constituted either an infringement of the copyright in the work in question, or a breach of an exclusive licence agreement relating to that work. (See s.27(3).) Thirdly, the making of the article may have been permitted for certain purposes as referred to in Chapter 7, but be an infringing copy if dealt with for other purposes. Each of these must be dealt with in turn.

1. Where the making of the copy constituted an infringement of copyright

6.27 The equivalent provisions in the 1956 Act made it clearer that the relevant copyright was the copyright subsisting under the 1956 Act, and not in some other country. The drafting of the 1988 Act is rather looser, and there is no indication on the face of the provision itself as to whether one could apply it to, say, articles manufactured in France under the law of copyright subsisting there. However, in our view the position is still that one must look to see whether the making of the article constituted an infringement of copyright under the 1988 Act, and not under the law of some other country. This appears from section 1(1) of the 1988 Act which provides that copyright is a property right which subsists *"in accordance with this Part"*, that is in accordance with Part I of the 1988 Act. Of course, manufacture abroad could still be relevant if it took place in a country to which the 1988 Act had been extended. Where, however, manufacture took place in a country to which the 1988 Act does not extend, whether or not the manufacture in that country was an infringement of the copyright subsisting there is not relevant to whether its making constituted an infringement for the purposes of this provision. In such cases, one can only look to the second of the three grounds on which an article can be an infringing copy.

2. Where the making of the copy would have constituted an infringement or breach of an exclusive licence agreement if done in the United Kingdom

6.28 Here, it does not matter whether the article was made in infringement of any copyright subsisting outside the United Kingdom, or whether its manufacture was licensed in that country and royalties paid to the copyright owner there, subject to the provisions of the Treaty of Rome referred to in paragraph 6.43 onwards.

(a) *Problem under the 1956 Act*

Here one faces one of the more complex considerations in copyright law.   **6.29**
The provision in the 1956 Act was similar in relation to the importation of articles, but omitted the reference to exclusive licence agreements. (See 1956 Act, ss.5(2) and 16(2).) The absence of this provision resulted in an exclusive licensee being deprived of any ability to control importation in certain circumstances following the case of *CBS (U.K.) Ltd.* v. *Charmdale Record Distributors Ltd.* [1981] Ch. 91.

In the *Charmdale* case, the court said that one had to take the facts relating to the manufacture of the article in the country of manufacture, and hypothetically imagine the same manufacture in the same circumstances taking place in the United Kingdom. If on that basis, if there would have been an infringement of copyright in the United Kingdom, then the relevant provision applied, subject of course to the question of knowledge.

The problems arising from this are perhaps best illustrated by the *Charmdale* decision itself. There, the owner of the copyright in a sound recording both in the United States and the United Kingdom manufactured copies of the sound recording itself in the United States. The owner had granted an exclusive licence to manufacture and market records embodying the sound recordings in the United Kingdom to a British company. The company in the United Kingdom tried to prevent copies of the sound recording manufactured in the United States from being imported into the United Kingdom. It was held by Mr. Justice Browne-Wilkinson that the United Kingdom company could not prevent this, because if those particular copies of the sound recording had been manufactured in the United Kingdom rather than in the United States, it would not have been an infringement of copyright. This was because manufacture was by the owner of the copyright himself, and an owner of the copyright could not infringe the copyright in his own sound recording.

One can contrast this position with that where the owner of the copyright in the United States does not grant an exclusive licence in relation to the United Kingdom, but assigns the copyright. Applying the same facts as in the *Charmdale* decision, there would have been an infringement of copyright because the manufacturer in the United States would have had no licence from the United Kingdom copyright owner to manufacture the records in the United Kingdom. Thus, whether it was possible to prevent importation of articles into the United Kingdom, and subsequent dealing with those articles, depended in many cases on whether the person controlling the rights in the United Kingdom was an owner of the copyright or simply an exclusive licensee, and, as will be seen later (paragraph 8.35), this is not an entirely easy distinction to make.

The *Charmdale* case was not universally regarded as correctly decided. Although the issue was not directly addressed by the Court of Appeal in

Polydor and R.S.O. Records Inc. v. *Harlequin Record Shops and Simons Records* ([1980] F.S.R. 194) the approach taken there by Templeman L.J. was inconsistent with some parts of the judgment in *Charmdale*, and the latter was not followed in at least one Commonwealth case where a similar provision was under consideration.

(b) *The new provision under the 1988 Act*

6.30   The 1988 Act extends the circumstances in which importation can be prevented to cover the *Charmdale* situation. For the future therefore, a copy will be an infringing copy if its making in the United Kingdom would have been a breach of an exclusive licence agreement relating to the work. Exclusive licence has a specific meaning for the purposes of the 1988 Act, it being a licence in writing signed by or on behalf of the copyright owner authorising the licensee to the exclusion of all other persons, including the person granting the licence, to exercise a right which would otherwise be exerciseable exclusively by the copyright owner. (See s.92(1).) An exclusive licence agreement is an agreement by which an exclusive licence is granted.

The 1988 Act uses slightly odd language to overcome the difficulties of the *Charmdale* case, bearing in mind that, in the case of an exclusive licence, only the parties themselves can breach that agreement. If therefore the copyright owner in the United States does not make the article himself, but grants a licence to someone else to make it, without restricting where the manufacture can take place, it is not the making of the article which is a breach of the exclusive licence agreement, but the grant of a licence to manufacture without providing that manufacture must not take place in the territory of the exclusive licensee.

However, applying the new section to the facts of the *Charmdale* decision, one sees that the making of copies of the sound recording in the United Kingdom by the owner of the copyright would have breached the exclusive licence agreement, since this excluded the copyright owner from manufacturing in the United Kingdom.

Where the copyright has been assigned to the person exploiting it in the United Kingdom, instead of exclusively licensed, the effect would seem to be the same as under the 1956 Act and referred to in paragraph 6.29 above.

(c) *The continued effect of Charmdale*

6.31   There must be either an assignment of copyright or an exclusive licence for one to be able to apply the provision successfully where the article was manufactured in another territory by someone who owns the copyright in both that territory and the United Kingdom. In some situations such as the music publishing business, it is quite common for the copyright owner to appoint not an exclusive licensee in the local territory but someone who acts as an agent or administrator of the rights locally. Such a party usually has the exclusive right to collect royalties arising from the exploitation of the rights in the United Kingdom, and will be entitled to a percentage of what he collects. His ability to earn remuneration may well be undermined by the importation of copies of the relevant works from another country, such as records or sheet music, but because of the *Charmdale* decision he will not be able to prevent importation in such cases, even assuming a contractual right to take proceedings in the name of the copyright owner. Because of this, it is obviously sensible for such a party to try to persuade the United Kingdom copyright owner to assign the copyright or grant an exclusive licence.

3. Existing copies (schedule 1, paragraph 14(3))

6.32 The new provisions relating to infringing copies do not apply to articles made before the 1988 Act. Thus, if an article was made during the subsistence of the 1956 Act, the question of whether or not it was made in infringement of copyright, or would have been made in infringement of copyright had it been made in the United Kingdom, must be determined according to the rules under the 1956 Act. For that reason, *Charmdale* may continue to be a problem in relation to old stocks of records. Similarly, although less likely to be a problem in practice, articles made before the 1956 Act are considered by reference to the 1911 Act.

4. Copies the making of which was permitted for certain purposes but which are used for other purposes (s.27(6))

6.33 Under the provisions referred to in Chapter 7, the making of copies of works and the issuing of copies of works to the public is in certain circumstances permitted without infringing copyright. Some of the provisions state however that if there is any dealing with such copies, or, in some instances, dealing with such copies for any purpose other than the permitted purpose, the copy is to be treated as infringing copy. In those circumstances, provided that the requirements as to knowledge are fulfilled, the copyright owner may be able to take action in respect of that dealing, or any further dealing, under the provisions referred to in paragraph 6.35. The relevant provisions referred to in Chapter 7 are as follows:

(a) Copies made for the purpose of instruction by persons giving or receiving instruction. (See paragraphs 7.17 and 7.22.)

(b) Reprographic copies of literary, dramatic and musical works made by or on behalf of educational establishments for the purposes of instruction. (See paragraphs 7.18 and 9.108.)

(c) Copies made for the purpose of examinations. (See paragraph 7.29.)

(d) Recordings of broadcasts or cable programmes made for the educational purposes of an educational establishment. (See paragraph 7.23.)

(e) Copies of certain literary, dramatic, musical and artistic works and published editions made by or on behalf of a librarian or archivist or made on reliance on a false declaration. (See paragraph 7.35.)

(f) Copies of works in electronic form retained after the original purchaser of the copy or a subsequent transferee has transferred the original or another copy to another party. (See paragraph 7.91.)

(g) Copies of an artistic work made for the purpose of advertising of sale of the work. (See paragraph 7.105.)

(h) Copies of works other than broadcasts or cable programmes made for the purposes of broadcasting the work or including it in a cable programme service. (See paragraph 7.99.)

5. Presumption as to making of infringing copy (s.27(4))

6.34   This presumption applies in any proceedings where the question arises as to whether an article is an infringing copy. If it is shown that the article is a copy of the work, and that copyright subsists in the work or has subsisted at any time, it is presumed until the contrary is proved that the article was made at a time when copyright subsisted in the work.

B. POSSESSION OR DEALING WITH INFRINGING COPIES (s.23)

1. The relevant acts

6.35   A person infringes copyright if, without the licence of the copyright owner, he does any of the following acts in relation to an article, and he knows or has reason to believe that the article is an infringing copy:

(a) Imports the article into the United Kingdom otherwise than for private and domestic use.

(b) Possesses the article in the course of a business.

(c) Sells the article.

(d) Lets the article for hire.

(e) Offers the article for sale.

(f) Offers the article for hire.

(g) Exposes the article for sale.

(h) Exposes the article for hire.

(i) Exhibits the article in public in the course of a business.

(j) Distributes the article in the course of a business, or to such an extent as to affect prejudicially the owner of the copyright.

2. The new act of secondary infringement by possession

6.36   Possession in the course of a business is a new act of infringement, and there was no equivalent under the 1956 Act, unless the provisions on conversion applied. (See paragraph 10.96 below.) Possession can occur even when the articles are not owned by the person holding them. Thus, a transport firm carrying goods might be liable, or a storage company. Although the question of whether the article is an infringing copy has to be determined by reference to the law in the United Kingdom when the article was made, possession in the course of a business after the commencement of the 1988 Act of articles made before commencement of the new Act will still be infringement, provided that there is the requisite degree of knowledge.

3. Removal of "by way of trade" under the 1956 Act

Infringement by offering or exposing for sale or hire is no longer qualified by the words "by way of trade," and otherwise references to "by way of trade" are replaced by "in the course of a business." **6.37**

The expression "business" includes any trade or profession. (See s.178.) Were it not therefore for the defence referred to in paragraph 7.71 below, solicitors dealing with copyright actions might find themselves potentially liable for infringement of copyright as regards articles the subject of proceedings in their possession, if they lost the action! **6.38**

4. Retention of title clauses

In many cases now, goods are supplied on terms and conditions which include a retention of title clause, by which property in the goods remains with the supplier until the purchaser has paid for those goods or other goods, and by which the supplier has the right to repossess the goods if payment is not made. The purchaser is allowed to sell the goods even though he is not the owner, but in doing this he often acts as agent for the supplier. **6.39**

Various issues must be addressed here. First, if the purchaser possesses or deals with such goods knowing or having reason to believe that they are infringing copies, he cannot escape liability by saying that he was only doing so as agent. Secondly, where the purchaser is so liable, but the supplier did not know or have reason to believe that the goods were infringing copies at the time the relevant dealing by the purchaser took place, can the supplier be made liable? This is less clear but we incline to the view that he is not liable unless he ratifies the unlicensed dealing. The position may not be the same if the supplier supplies the goods to a purchaser and later gets to know or has reason to believe that the goods were infringing copies before the purchaser deals with them. In that situation, whether or not the purchaser deals subsequently with the goods with the requisite knowledge, it is arguable that the supplier may be liable, but this is not an easy question and the precise terms and conditions of supply may have a significant bearing on the possibility of liability.

5. Groups of companies

In relation to secondary infringement by importation or subsequent **6.40**

141

dealing with imported copies, very often the copyright owner or exclusive licensee which granted a licence to manufacture in the territory of manufacture is a member of the same group of companies as the company which is the copyright owner or exclusive licensee in the United Kingdom and which is trying to prevent importation. This was so for example in the *Charmdale* case. In a similar situation in the *Polydor and R.S.O. Records Inc.* v. *Harlequin Record Shops and Simons Ltd.* [1980] F.S.R. 194 case, an argument that there was no infringement by importation because a sale in one country by one member of the group gave rise to an implied consent to import by all members of the group was rejected by the Court of Appeal.

6. Issuing of copies to the public

6.41   Of course, many of these acts overlap with the act of primary infringement by issuing copies to the public if the relevant copy is being put into circulation for the first time, or, in the case of sound recordings, films and computer programs, is being rented.

C. DEALING WITH ARTICLES DESIGNED OR ADAPTED FOR MAKING INFRINGING COPIES (s.24)

6.42   Under the 1956 Act, the provisions relating to conversion (see paragraph 10.96) applied not only to infringing copies, but also to what was termed as any "plate" used or intended to be used for making infringing copies (1956 Act, s.18). "Plate" was defined to include any stereotype, stone, block, mould, matrix, transfer, negative or other appliance. The result of this was that not only could a copyright owner obtain delivery-up of such a plate, since he was deemed under the conversion provisions to be the owner of that plate, but he was also entitled to damages for any use or dealing with the plate inconsistent with his rights as its deemed owner. The rights of conversion having now been abolished, a new act of secondary infringement has been introduced to cover the situation where a person makes or deals with such a "plate" knowing or having reason to believe that it is to be used for making infringing copies.

The new provision relates only to articles specifically designed or adapted for making copies of a particular work. Thus, in relation to records, it could mean a matrix but it will not apply to the machine which actually carries out the pressing of the records.

Where a person knows or has reason to believe that such an article is to be used to make infringing copies, it is an infringement of copyright to make the article or to do any of the acts referred to in paragraph 6.35 as regards that article, the only difference being that there is no reference to "private and domestic use" in the case of importation.

D. THE EEC AND INFRINGING COPIES

6.43   As stated in paragraph 6.28 above, articles made in territories outside the

United Kingdom may still be infringing copies for the purposes of United Kingdom law, even though they were manufactured lawfully there, and even though the rights owner there has been paid a royalty in that territory. It will readily be appreciated that this territoriality or insularity is in fundamental conflict with the provisions of the Treaty of Rome relating to free movement of goods throughout the European Economic Community. Thus one finds a series of decisions from the European Court of Justice placing severe restrictions on the ability of a copyright owner in one territory of the EEC to prevent the importation into that territory of articles manufactured in another territory of the EEC.

1. The basis of the case law

The case law is based on the following premise. Article 30 of the Treaty of   **6.44**
Rome provides that quantitative restrictions on imports and all measures having equivalent effect are prohibited between Member States. A quantitative restriction is a rule or regulation which limits the quantity (whether by weight, value, number or otherwise) of goods which may be imported into a country. A national law which allows a copyright owner to prevent the importation of goods from another Member State of the EEC is regarded by the European Court as a measure having equivalent effect to a quantitative restriction. One then turns to Article 36 of the Treaty which provides for an exception to Article 30 in the case of prohibitions or restrictions on imports justified on the grounds of protection of industrial and commercial property. Copyright is regarded as a species of such property. However, the prohibitions or restrictions will still infringe Article 30 if they constitute a means of arbitrary discrimination or a disguised restriction on trade between Member States. Although, according to the European Court, Article 36 preserves the existence of such rights of property, the exercise of those rights may still be affected. In this respect, the European Court has said that Article 36 "allows derogations to the free movement of goods only to the extent that such derogations are justified for the protection of the rights which constitute the specific object of such property."

2. The doctrine of exhaustion of rights

Unlike the position with patents and trade marks, the European Court of   **6.45**
Justice has so far not expressly stated what it considers the rights which constitute the specific object of copyright to be, although there is reference in the *Warner Bros. Inc.* v. *Christiansen* (*The Times,* June 1, 1988) case to the two crucial rights of an author being the exclusive right of performance and the exclusive right of reproduction, and there are some other relevant comments in *Coditel S.A.* v. *Cine Vog Films S.A.* ([1982] 2 C.M.L.R. 328). However, what the court has done is to apply to copyright as with other species of industrial property its so-called doctrine of exhaustion of rights. Indeed, its first statement of that doctrine was in a quasi-copyright case, *Deutsche Grammophon Gesellschaft mbH* v.

Metro-SB-Grossmarkte GmbH ([1971] C.M.L.R. 631) which dealt with the rights subsisting in sound recordings in Germany which are protected as rights analogous to copyright. The court said in that case:

> " . . . it would conflict with the provisions regarding the free movement of goods in the Common Market if a manufacturer of recordings exercised the exclusive right granted to him by the legislation of a Member State to market the protected articles in order to prohibit the marketing in that Member State of products that had been sold by him himself or with his consent in another Member State solely because this marketing had not occurred in the territory of the first Member State."

Set out like this, the meaning at first sight does not seem clear, but what effectively the court has said is that once goods have been put on to the market by or with the consent of the copyright owner the copyright owner's rights are exhausted in relation to those goods, and he cannot exercise national laws controlling importation or distribution to prevent or control further distribution of the goods. The practical effect of this is that once the rights owner has obtained a royalty for putting the article on to the market within one country of the EEC, neither he nor the rights owner in another territory will usually be able to claim a further royalty when the articles are distributed elsewhere in the EEC.

3. The applicability of EEC rules in the United Kingdom

6.46   Community law has direct effect in the United Kingdom, and the doctrine of exhaustion of rights has therefore always applied to the exercise of copyright in the United Kingdom, notwithstanding the fact that there was no express provision in copyright legislation in the United Kingdom embodying it. However, the 1988 Act states specifically that the second limb of the definition of infringing copy (see paragraph 6.28) must not be construed as applying to an article which may lawfully be imported into the United Kingdom by virtue of any enforceable Community right under the European Communities Act 1972. (See s.27(5).)

4. Detailed aspects of the doctrine of exhaustion

6.47   This is not the place for an in-depth examination of the decisions promulgated by the European Court in this area. Nevertheless, some further substantive comments are necessary, in order to summarise the development of the case law since *DGG* v. *Metro*.

(a) *Parallel assignments or exclusive licences*

6.48   The owner of a copyright work in one territory of the EEC may have no assignment or licence from the owner of the copyright in another territory of the EEC. This would be so for example where the original owner of the copyright is situated in America, and grants rights under different contracts for different territories in the EEC. Although there is no copyright case which addresses directly the situation where the rights owners in the country of marketing and the country of importation derived their rights entirely independently, it is apparent that arguments based simply on the territorial nature of copyright will not succeed—see *Musik-Vertrieb Membran GmbH* v. *GEMA* ([1981] 2 C.M.L.R. 44). Furthermore, arguments to this effect have been rejected specifically in trade mark cases. In *Terrapin (Overseas) Ltd.* v. *Terranova Industrie C.A. Kapferer & Co.* ([1976] 2 C.M.L.R. 482), the court put the position in this way:

" . . . the proprietor of an industrial or commercial property right protected by the law of a Member State cannot rely on that law to prevent the importation of a product which has been lawfully marketed in another Member State by the proprietor himself or with his consent. It is the same when the right relied on is the result of the subdivision either by voluntary act or as a result of public constraint of a trade mark right which originally belonged to one and the same proprietor."

It is said by some experts on Community law that the last sentence only applies in the case of trade marks which are different from patents and copyrights in that they may continue to subsist in perpetuity. Certainly in a case involving design copyright, *Keurkoop BV Rotterdam* v. *Nancy Kean Gifts BV* ([1983] 2 C.M.L.R. 47) the European Court put the point in a narrower way, and one which might not at first sight for example apply in the situation postulated above as regards an American rights owner:

" . . . The court has consistently held that the proprietor of an industrial or commercial property right protected by the legislation of a Member State may not rely on that legislation in order to oppose the importation of a product which has lawfully been marketed in another Member State by, or with the consent of, the proprietor of the right himself *or a person legally or economically dependent on him.*"

(b) *Arbitrary discrimination and disguised restriction on trade*

Where the copyright owner is justified in exercising the rights given to him under national laws of copyright to control the free movement of goods, he may still be deprived of his right to exercise such rights if he does so in such a way as to constitute an arbitrary discrimination or a disguised restriction on trade. This will happen for example if he discriminates between goods manufactured in his own territory, and goods imported from another Member State of the EEC. It may also happen where he exercises his rights by prohibiting importation or marketing as part of an agreement or practice in restraint of competition contrary to such provisions as Article 85. (See Chapter 9.) Thus, going back to *Keurkoop BV Rotterdam* v. *Nancy Kean Gifts BV*, it was suggested by the court there that it might infringe Article 85 and therefore be outside   **6.49**

Article 36 in a "situation where persons simultaneously or successively file the same design in various Member States in order to divide up the markets within the Community among themselves." See further however paragraph 9.151.

(c) *Articles placed on the market without consent*

6.50   If however the article was placed on the market *without* the consent of the relevant party, the doctrine of exhaustion of rights will prima facie not apply. This is so obviously where the product is a pirate one, but this also applies where a compulsory licence has been granted (*Pharmon BV* v. *Hoechst AG* ([1985] 3 C.M.L.R. 775)) and where the copyright in the relevant territory has expired but continues to subsist in one or more other member-States *(EMI Electrola GmbH* v. *Patricia Im-und Export Verwaltungsgesellschaft mbH* (*The Times*, February 13, 1989)).

At first sight, this would appear to conflict with the position in *Musik-Vertrieb Membran GmbH* v. *GEMA* referred to above, where some of the records had been manufactured in the United Kingdom in accordance with the provisions of section 8 of the 1956 Act. Although the position is not clear on this, it appears however that the court regarded section 8 as simply defining the maximum amount which a rights owner could require payment of for the reproduction of his work in the form of a record, rather than there having been no consent to place the record on the market.

(d) *Articles placed on the market with consent but in a territory where there are no subsisting rights*

6.51   If the appropriate consent has been granted, the doctrine applies even though the article was placed on the market in a territory where there was no subsisting right of protection. Thus in *Merck & Co. Inc.* v. *Stephar BV* ([1981] 3 C.M.L.R. 463), a drug was marketed in Italy by the Merck company. The drug was the subject of patents owned by Merck in other territories of the EEC, but not in Italy, where the Italian Patent Acts at the relevant time prohibited the grant of patents for drugs. It was held by the court that the fact that the drug was not patentable in the country of first marketing did not affect the doctrine of exhaustion of rights, because it had in any event been marketed by Merck.

(e) *Quality of goods*

6.52   Arguments based on the need to control quality of goods will not succeed: *Centrafarm B.V.* v. *Sterling Drug Inc* ([1974] 2 C.M.L.R. 480).

(f) *Lower royalties*

6.53   Neither will any arguments succeed that the royalties are lower in the country of first marketing. In *Musik-Vertrieb Membran GmbH* v. *GEMA* referred to above, the German collecting society GEMA tried to claim the difference between the royalties which had already been paid in the country of manufacture and the higher royalties which would have applied in Germany had the articles been manufactured there. This was denied by the court.

(g) *Instances where the exhaustion of rights doctrine has not prevented the exercise of copyright laws to control exploitation*

Nevertheless, there have been situations where the court has held that the   **6.54**
right is not exhausted and where the rights owner is entitled to exercise national laws restricting exploitation of the right. These have very much been regarded as exceptions to the doctrine, and it is hard to formulate a general rule from them, but in essence the court has applied exceptions where the rights owner is deprived of earning remuneration from the exploitation of the copyright in some other manner than the mere distribution of the article.

Thus, in *Basset* v. *S.A.C.E.M.* ([1984] 3 C.M.L.R. 233), the French copyright society claimed an additional reproduction royalty when records manufactured for retail sale with the consent of the copyright owner were used for public performance purposes. This royalty was separate from a performing royalty. The question was whether this conflicted with the doctrine of exhaustion of rights when it was applied to records manufactured and marketed in another Member State where such a charge was not levied. The court held that it did not conflict with Community law to levy such a charge, especially since it was calculated like a performance royalty on the turnover of the discotheque using the record, rather than on the basis of the number of discs purchased.

Again in *Warner Bros Inc.* v. *E.V. Christiansen*, the court said that a copyright owner in one Member State was justified in exercising a right under copyright law to prohibit rental of video cassettes where the relevant video cassette there had been placed on the market in another Member State where there was no right under copyright law to prohibit rental with the consent of the copyright owner.

The decision of the European Court in *Coditel S.A.* v. *S.A. Cine Vog Films S.A.* ([1981] 2 C.M.L.R. 362) may also be seen as part of this approach, even though it does not strictly speaking deal with the distribution of goods. The question there was whether a company having exclusive distribution rights in a film in one territory of the EEC could exercise national copyright laws to prevent the cable diffusion within that territory of a broadcast of the film made from another territory of the EEC. The broadcast was made under licence from the party which had granted the exclusive distribution rights in the first territory referred to. In this situation Articles 30 to 36 of the Treaty of Rome did not apply because one was not dealing with the free movement of goods. In this case and a subsequent one between the same parties, the court held that the applicable provisions of the Treaty of Rome were those relating to the freedom to supply services, but still applied the same sort of considerations as in the case of goods.

Although the court held that similar principles should apply in this situation, it allowed the rights owner to exercise its rights under national copyright law. It did so because:

> " . . . the right of a copyright owner and his assigns to require fees for any showing of a film is part of the essential function of copyright in this type of literary and artistic work . . . (and) . . . the exploitation of copyright in films and of fees attaching thereto cannot be regulated without regard being had to the possibility of television broadcast to those films."

The court distinguished between this situation and the situation where one was dealing with distribution of goods in saying that " . . . the problems involved in the observance of copyright in relation to the requirements of the Treaty are not the same as those which arise in connection with literary and artistic works the placing of which at the disposal of the public is inseparable from the circulation of the material form of the work, as in the case of books or records." The logic of this statement is not impeccable because the true distinction is not between the category of copyright work, (that is films as opposed to records) but the method of exploitation (that is performance, as opposed to reproduction). In truth, the doctrine of exhaustion of rights is not really consistent with the nature of performing rights.

(h) *Licences of right*

6.55   In a patent case, *Allen and Hanburys Ltd.* v. *Generics (U.K.) Ltd.* ([1988] 1 C.M.L.R. 701) the court has held that where licences as of right are available under a patent in the United Kingdom, the owner of the patent may not use national laws to prevent the importation of products from another Member State if the importer undertakes to take a compulsory licence on the same terms as would apply if the product had been manufactured in the United Kingdom. Although the cases are very much tied to the availability of licences as of right under the 1977 Patents Act, one can see that it might be argued that the same principles could apply to licences available as of right under an order from the Copyright Tribunal (see Chapter 9).

(i) *Treaties between the EEC and other countries*

6.56   The EEC has many treaties with non-EEC territories and organisations of such territories. Some of these treaties contain similar wording to that appearing in Articles 30 to 36 of the Treaty of Rome, but it has been held by the European Court that such provisions do not have the same effect as they do in the case of movement of goods between Member States of the EEC and that therefore "restrictions on trade in goods may be considered to be justified on the ground of the protection of industrial and commercial property in a situation in which their justification would not be possible in the Community". (See *Polydor Ltd.* v. *Harlequin Record Shops Ltd* ([1982] 1 C.M.L.R. 413).)

5. 1992

It is difficult to predict at this stage whether the creation of the Single   **6.57**
European Market will result in a different approach being taken by the
Commission and the Court. One might consider that a single market will
make it even more difficult to use national laws to prevent the distribution
of lawfully manufactured articles. However, in the recent *EMI Electrola*
v. *Patricia Import* case referred to above, the Court made it clear that so
long as there was no harmonization of copyright laws, it was for national
legislatures to lay down the conditions and procedures for protection, and
it may well be that 1992 will simply act as a spur towards achieving
harmonization. There are those who say that intellectual property law has
been through its own "1992" already.

IV TRANSMISSION BY A TELECOMMUNICATIONS SYSTEM (s.24 (2))

1. Background to the provision

Paragraph 5.18 above dealt with the question of infringement by copying   **6.58**
in relation to computer programs. As may be recalled, such infringement
takes place not only when a floppy disk is created, but when the relevant
work is stored in a computer. In many cases, where computers "speak" to
·each other, the information embodied in a computer program is conveyed by means of a telecommunications system, which is defined as a
system for conveying visual images, sounds or other information by
electronic means. This is common where computer programs or works
held in computers are made available to a large number of different
terminals. If the system is one which is within the definition of a cable
programme service, then there may be infringement by including the
information in a cable programme service. However, one problem is that
the system may be outside that definition.
    The second problem is as follows. If the transmission of the informa-
tion results in a copy being made in the United Kingdom, then the
copying itself is an infringement under the 1988 Act. The same would not
be so however where reception of the transmission took place in another
country, because the copying took place outside the territory covered by
the 1988 Act.
    It was primarily for these reasons that the provision dealt with below
was incorporated into the 1988 Act, although as will be seen in many ways
it fails to resolve the problems.

2. Liability by transmission

It was for these and other reasons that a new provision was introduced to   **6.59** the 1988 Act and which applies where a person transmits any copyright work by means of a telecommunications system, otherwise than by broadcasting the work or including the work in a cable programme service (where those primary acts of infringement will apply). If he transmits that work knowing or having reason to believe that infringing copies of the work will be made by means of the reception of the transmission in the United Kingdom or elsewhere, then he infringes copyright.

As stated, one of the main reasons for including this provision in the 1988 Act was to give better protection to computer programs and other works held in electronic form. However, it does not only apply to those areas. There is no requirement that the work be held in electronic form, and the provision could therefore apply to normal fax transmission of any document which embodies a literary, dramatic, musical or artistic work, as well as other transmission of sound recordings and films unless the transmission is within the definition of broadcasting or inclusion in a cable programme service.

3. Transmission

6.60   There is no definition in the 1988 Act as to what constitutes transmission. On one interpretation, it may refer to the act of starting a transmission. On another, it could extend to the whole process from start of the transmission to receipt. If the latter definition is correct, it would be possible to put any operator of a telecommunications system, such as British Telecom or Mercury, on notice as regards transmissions which they carry as part of their system. This would be particularly useful where the transmission commences outside the United Kingdom.

4. Potential problems with the provision

6.61   The provision only applies where the person carrying out the transmission knows or has reason to believe that infringing copies will be made on receipt of the transmission. However, according to section 27(1) "infringing copy" must be construed in accordance with the provisions of that section, and this has already been dealt with in paragraph 6.26 onwards. Leaving aside the situation where the making of a copy is permitted for certain purposes but is an infringing copy because it is used for other purposes (see paragraph 6.33 above), the definition of infringing copy only refers to "articles". (See s.27(2) and (3).) In many cases however, no "article" will be made when the transmission is received, the obvious example being where the work is merely stored in a computer on receipt. In these circumstances, we assume that since there is no relevant meaning of "infringing copy" under section 27, one must look to the ordinary meaning of that phrase. Infringing must mean made in infringment of copyright and copy must be construed in accordance with section 17 (see paragraph 5.18). The result of this is that, if the transmission is, upon receipt, stored in the computer, copying in infringement of copyright will have taken place. One assumes therefore, that an infringing copy has also been made. However, the position is not clear.

Where an "article" is made upon reception of the transmission, then the provisions of section 27(2) and (3) need to be applied, and it is difficult in those circumstances to imagine how the requirements of those provisions will be fulfilled where reception of the transmission is outside the United Kingdom. This is first, because section 27(2) in our view does not generally apply to articles made abroad, since this would not be an infringement of the 1988 Act. (See paragraph 6.27.) However, this might be different where the article was made in a country to which the 1988 Act had been extended. Secondly, section 27(2) would not normally apply because it is unlikely that one would be able to show that the article has been or was proposed to be imported into the United Kingdom. It might be possible to show this where an infringing copy made on receipt of a transmission is then used to make further copies which are intended for export to the United Kingdom.

Even where it is possible to overcome these problems, there may be difficulties arising from the requirement of knowledge on the part of the person transmitting the work. If "infringing copy" is to be construed not in accordance with section 27 of the 1988 Act but in accordance with the laws of the country where the transmission is received, then there may be problems in showing that reception will cause infringing copies to be made. It could be for example that there is no relevant copyright protection in the relevant country (many countries of the Middle East for example), or that storage of the work will not be an infringement and will not therefore result in the making of an infringing copy.

Where reception of the transmission is in the United Kingdom, the above problems will not arise. However, since it is necessary to show knowledge that infringing copies will be made upon reception of the transmission, it is probably advisable to ensure in granting a software licence that the licence does not extend to transmitting the program or works contained in it to others. There is no requirement that infringing copies actually be made, where there is reason to believe that they will be made.

V COPY-PROTECTION (s.296)

1. Background to the provision

As stated, the Government eventually rejected the blank-tape levy solu-   **6.62** tion on home-taping. One other possible solution has been to incorporate into records or tapes something which either prevents copying taking place, or affects the quality of any copy made. Although such systems have been developed, so far they have not been introduced commercially because of the possible effects on the sound quality of the original record or tape. Nevertheless, the Government was convinced by the argument that if such technology did become commercially acceptable, it would be right to legislate to prevent the manufacture of, or commercial dealing with, devices designed to circumvent the copy-protection.

2. Who may sue?

6.63   The right to sue the persons referred to below is not given to any copyright owner or exclusive licensee whose works are reproduced on the relevant copy. It is only exerciseable by a person issuing copies of a copyright work to the public in an electronic form which is copy protected.

The obvious examples of copies of works in an electronic form are discs and tapes, whether audio only or audio visual. Not only discs and tapes for entertainment purposes are covered but computer software. Copy-protection is defined as including any device or means intended to prevent or restrict copying of a work or to impair the quality of copies made.

For the identity of the person who issues copies to the public, and the meaning of that expression, see paragraph 5.23 onwards. That person could be the copyright owner or exclusive licensee, or he could be a distributor.

6.64   ### 3. Who can be sued?

The following are liable

(a) Anyone who makes, imports, sells or lets for hire, offers or exposes for sale or hire, any device or means specifically designed or adapted to circumvent the form of copyright-protection.

(b) Anyone who publishes information intended to enable or assist persons to circumvent that form of copy-protection.

However, no such person is liable unless he knows or has reason to believe that the device or means or information will be used to make infringing copies.

4. Remedies and proceedings

6.65   The person issuing copies to the public has the same rights as a copyright owner has in respect of an infringement of copyright. The remedies in such cases include injunctions and monetary claims such as for damages or an account of profits. (See Chapter 10.)

The seizure or delivery-up provisions referred to in paragraphs 10.96 onwards also apply, but only in relation to any such device or means as is referred to in paragraph 6.42 above which a person has in his possession, custody, or control with the intention that it should be used to make infringing copies of copyright works.

Two other specific provisions should be referred to. First, the presumptions contained in sections 104 to 106 of the 1988 Act (see paragraph 10.29 onwards) can also be used here, although it is difficult to see how they will be of much practical use. Secondly, the withdrawal of privilege against self-incrimination referred to in paragraph 10.58 also applies to such proceedings.

VI BROADCASTING AND CABLE TRANSMISSION RECEPTION (s.298)

1. Background to the provision

Broadcasting and inclusion in a cable programme service are restricted acts which most copyright owners have the right to control. *Reception* of a broadcast or cable programme is not a restricted act and the Cable and Broadcasting Act 1984 (sections 53 and 54) introduced criminal and civil liability provisions relating to fraudulent reception of transmissions. The provisions have been re-enacted with some modifications in the 1988 Act. Civil liability is dealt with here, and criminal liability in paragraph 10.119.   **6.66**

2. Who may sue?

The right to sue the persons referred to below is exerciseable by either of the following: **6.67**

(a) Anyone who makes charges for the reception of programmes included in a broadcasting or cable programme service provided from a place in the United Kingdom.

(b) Anyone who sends encrypted transmissions of any other description from a place in the United Kingdom.

   The word "programme" in relation to broadcasts is widely defined in s.6(3) so as to apply to any item included in a broadcast. There is no definition of "programme" in relation to cable programme services, but presumably the reference is intended to be to a cable programme which is defined (s.7(1)) as any item included in a cable programme service.

   The expressions "broadcasting" and "cable programme service" have the same definitions as for copyright purposes, so services excluded from the definitions of the latter will generally not benefit from the provision.

   However, as in the case of section 297 (see paragraph 10.119), where the provision applies in relation to broadcasting or a cable programme service, it also applies to any service run for the person providing the relevant broadcasting or cable programme service, or for a person providing programmes for the latter, provided that the service run for the latter consists wholly or mainly in the sending by means of a telecommunications system of sounds or visual images or both. (See s.299(4).)

   There is also power for section 298 to be applied by Order in Council in relation to programmes and encrypted transmissions sent from other countries or territories, but no such Order has been made at the time of writing.

3. Who can be sued?

6.68   The remedies referred to below apply as against any of the following:

(a) Anyone who makes, imports or sells or lets for hire any apparatus or device designed or adapted to enable or assist persons to receive the programmes or other transmissions when they are not entitled to do so.

(b) Anyone who publishes any information which is calculated to enable or assist persons to receive the programmes or other transmissions when they are not entitled to do so.

The remedies do not therefore lie against someone who fraudulently receives a transmission: there only the criminal provisions will apply.

4. Remedies and proceedings

6.69   The parties referred to in paragraph 6.67 have the same rights as a copyright owner has in respect of an infringement of copyright. The remedies in such cases include injunctions and monetary claims such as for damages or an account of profits. (See Chapter 10.)

The provision does not require that the defendant know or have reason to believe that what he was selling was designed or adapted as referred to above or that the information he was publishing was calculated to enable or assist fradulent reception of transmissions. However, the defence of innocent infringement referred to in paragraph 10.92 has been adapted for the purposes of this provision. Where therefore in an action for infringement of these rights, it is shown that the defendant did not know and had no reason to believe that his acts infringed the rights, no action lies against him for damages. (See s.298(5).) However, it would still be possible to apply for an injunction or account of profits.

The provisions on seizure and delivery up contained in sections 99, 100 and 114 also apply to any apparatus or device designed or adapted to enable or assist persons to receive programmes or other transmissions when they are not entitled to do so. (See paragraphs 10.96 onwards for these provisions.)

Finally, the withdrawal of privilege against self-incrimination referred to in paragraph 10.58 again applies to such proceedings.

7 PERMITTED ACTS

I INTRODUCTION

The restricted acts which the copyright owner has the exclusive right to do **7.01**
are extremely broad in nature. In certain circumstances, it is deemed
inappropriate for the copyright owner to have the right to prevent others
from doing such acts, and accordingly the 1988 Act contains a large
number of specific provisions which permit one or more restricted acts to
be done without infringing copyright. These are referred to as the permitted acts.

In the 1956 Act, the equivalent provisions were spread widely throughout the Act. The 1988 Act groups all the permitted acts together, but it is
not always easy for a copyright owner to find out with ease what acts by
others he cannot control. This Chapter categorises most of the permitted
acts by reference to the restricted acts referred to in Chapter 5. Thus,
those permitted acts which would provide a defence to an action for
infringement of copyright based on any of the restricted acts are considered first, then those permitted acts relevant to copying, and so on. The
only exceptions dealt with as individual subjects are first those relating to
education, and secondly those relating to libraries, archives, and other
similar bodies. In Appendix 2 however a schedule is provided of the
permitted acts relevant to particular areas of use, such as printers, television broadcasting and so on, with cross-references back to this Chapter.

1. Summary of the 1988 Act

In summary, the permitted acts under the 1988 Act are as follows: **7.02**

(a) Use in an educational context or in educational establishments. The
permitted acts here extend not only to copying for certain purposes, but
also public performance, and in certain circumstances to use both within
and outside the classroom.

(b) Copying by libraries and archives. In certain circumstances, the
copying of articles in periodicals, parts of works, the supply of copies to
other libraries and the replacement of destroyed or damaged copies of
works does not infringe copyright. There are safeguards however
intended to discourage multiple copying.

(c) Fair dealing with some works for certain purposes does not constitute
infringement of copyright. In general, the purposes are research or
private study, criticism or review, and reporting current events.

(d) Certain acts relating to matters of public administration are permitted. These include Parliamentary and judicial proceedings, Royal Commissions, material open to public inspection or on official registers, and material communicated to the Crown in the course of public business.

(e) There are certain acts which although separate acts requiring the consent of the copyright owner under the principles referred to in Chapter 5, are regarded as consequential upon or necessary to the doing of other acts. If the latter act is licensed (and even in some circumstances where it is not licensed), then the copyright owner in some circumstances cannot prevent the consequential restricted act. Into this category come the use of copies of works in electronic form, such as computer programs, the so-called ephemeral clause, the reception and retransmission of broadcasts, and the showing or playing of broadcasts or cable programmes in public.

(f) Permitted acts which the legislature has determined do not damage copyright owners' rights to a material degree. This covers incidental inclusion of one work in another work, reading and recitation in public, recording for the purposes of time-shifting, and taking photographs of television or cable programmes for private and domestic use.

(g) Use where the copyright owner has failed to negotiate or obtain approval of reasonable terms for licensing. This covers subtitled copies of broadcasts and cable programmes for the deaf, and rental of sound recordings, films and computer programs.

(h) There are certain permitted acts which relate purely to artistic works, such as making copies of artistic works exhibited in public, copying artistic works for the purposes of advertising the sale of those works, the making of subsequent works by the same artist, and the reconstruction of buildings.

In addition, an act which would otherwise be an infringement of copyright may not be actionable on the grounds that it was done in the public interest.

2. Differences between the 1956 Act and the 1988 Act

7.03   With something like 48 sections now covering permitted acts, it looks at first sight as if a copyright owner's ability to exercise his rights is considerably more restricted under the 1988 Act than it was under the 1956 Act. In part this is true, but a number of provisions have been introduced which do no more than reflect the reality of the situation, where a copyright owner would be unlikely to exercise his rights—this is particularly so in the field of public administration. Nevertheless, it is also fair to say that the 1988 Act has introduced a number of extremely important changes. Although the list below is not exhaustive, the major ones are as follows:

(a) Fair dealing for the purposes of research or private study is now restricted in certain cases of multiple copying. (See paragraph 7.70.)

However, the provisions on fair dealing for the purposes of criticism and review, and reporting current events, have been extended to works other than those to which the equivalent provisions under the 1956 Act applied. (See paragraphs 7.65 and 7.66.)

(b) A new permitted act of incidental inclusion of one work in another work has been introduced, although the scope is restricted in the case of musical works and associated words. (See paragraph 7.86.)

(c) The so-called compulsory licensing scheme for the making of records of musical works and associated words has been abolished. (See paragraph 7.103.)

(d) Two new permitted acts have been added in relation to education. The first permits the making of recordings of broadcasts or cable programmes (see paragraph 7.23), and the second permits the making of a limited number of reprographic copies of literary, dramatic or musical works. (See paragraph 7.18.) In addition, the educational exemptions will apply in future not only to schools, but also to other designated educational establishments. (See paragraph 7.10.)

(e) Some new provisions have been introduced in relation to libraries and archives. First, it is no longer a statutory requirement that the relevant libraries or archives must not be established or conducted for profit. (See paragraph 7.33.) Secondly, the provisions on supply of replacement copies of works to other libraries have been amended (see paragraph 7.47). Thirdly the provisions as regards supply of copies of articles or parts of works now have restrictions imposed on them in an attempt to control multiple copying. (See paragraph 7.41.)

(f) New permitted acts have been added which relate to public administration. These include use of copyright works in the context of Royal Commissions, Statutory Inquiries, material open to public inspection or on an official register, and communication of material to the Crown in the course of public business. (See respectively paragraphs 7.72, 7.96 and 7.100.)

(g) A permitted act has been introduced which applies particularly to computer programs but also to other works in electronic form whereby copying expressly or impliedly permitted in connection with the use by a purchaser of the relevant copy of the work will also on certain conditions be permitted by a subsequent transferee. (See paragraph 7.91.)

(h) The permitted act relating to reading or recitation in public of a reasonable extract from a published literary or dramatic work has been extended to cover the recording, broadcasting and cable programme transmission of such a reading or recitation. (See paragraph 7.110.)

(i) The provision under the 1956 Act allowing the playing of recordings in public at premises where persons reside or sleep as part of the amenities there has been repealed. (See paragraph 7.112.)

(j) The defence available under the 1956 Act in relation to copies of sound recordings not bearing the year of first publication has been repealed.

(k) The provision under the 1956 Act whereby the playing or showing of sound recordings or films by means of the reception of a BBC or IBA broadcast or a cable programme was not generally an infringement of copyright has been repealed, but the same rules now apply as relate to the playing or showing in public of such broadcasts and cable programmes. (See paragraph 7.113.)

(l) The so-called ephemeral clause dealing with incidental recording for the purposes of broadcast or cable programme transmission has been extended to artistic works, sound recordings and films, and now allows the broadcaster or operator of the cable programme service not only to carry out the recording himself but also to authorise others to record for those purposes. (See paragraph 7.99.)

(m) Two provisions under the 1956 Act in relation to films have been repealed. First, after the copyright in a film expires, consent is now required to do any restricted act in relation to the underlying works comprised in the film. Secondly, the provision by which it was not an infringement of copyright to cause a newsreel film to be seen or heard in public 50 years after the principal events depicted in the film occurred no longer applies.

7.04   (n) New permitted acts have been added as follows:

(i) As regards literary, dramatic, musical and artistic works, any act may be done if the author is not identifiable by reasonable inquiry, and it is reasonable to assume the work is no longer in copyright. (See paragraph 7.75.)

(ii) As regards artistic works, a work may be copied and copies of it issued to the public for the purposes of advertising the sale of the work. (See paragraph 7.105.)

(iii) As regards literary works, a recording of spoken words may be made directly from the speaker and used for the purposes of reporting current events or broadcasting or cable programme transmission. (See paragraph 7.82.)

(iv) Abstracts of articles on scientific or technical subjects may be copied and issued to the public. (See paragraph 7.102.)

(v) There is provision for schemes to be introduced permitting the rental of sound recordings, films and computer programs. (See paragraph 7.109.)

(vi) Recordings of broadcasts and cable programmes may be made0for the purposes of time shifting. (See paragraph 7.97.)

(vii) Photographs may be taken from television broadcasts or cable programmes, for private and domestic use. (See paragraph 7.107.)

(viii) There is power for designated bodies to make copies of television broadcasts or cable programmes for the purposes of providing the deaf or handicapped with subtitled copies. (See paragraph 7.98.)

3. Designs

The 1988 Act also contains important permitted act provisions relating to   **7.05**
artistic or other works which are designs or design documents. These are
dealt with in Chapter 13.

4. Acts done before commencement of the 1988 Act

The permitted acts referred to in this Chapter only apply as regards things   **7.06**
done after commencement of the new Act. Whether an act done before
commencement was an infringement depends on the rules subsisting
then.

5. Relevance of the permitted acts to secondary infringement

The permitted acts are also important in considering liability by way of   **7.07**
secondary infringement. Thus a copy of a work will not be an infringing
copy if its making was permitted under those provisions or would have
been permitted had the copy been made in the United Kingdom. (As will
be seen, there are some reservations to this where a copy is made for one
purpose but then exploited in a different way.) Similar considerations
apply where there is a question whether performance or playing or
showing of a work in public is an infringement.

6. Permitted acts in relation to adaptations

Some of the provisions below state that the relevant act is permitted not   **7.08**
only as regards a literary, dramatic or musical work but also in the case of
an adaptation of such a work. In other cases, it will be seen that copyright
is not infringed by *anything* done, say, for a particular purpose, so there
adapting the work, or exploiting an adaptation of a work, will not infringe
copyright. However, there is also a general provision applying to all
permitted acts which states that any act which may be done without
infringing copyright in a literary, dramatic or musical work does not,
where that work is an adaptation, infringe any copyright in the work from
which the adaptation was made (s.76).

   The meaning of this provision is not entirely clear. The 1956 Act said
that the permitted acts applied to the doing of an act in relation to an
adaptation of a work as they applied to the doing of that act in relation to
the work itself. (See 1956 Act, s.6(8).) Thus, if the act was permitted as
regards a literary, dramatic or musical work, it was equally well permitted
as regards an adaptation of that work. However, unless the permitted act
was one which deprived the copyright owner of all his rights it still left
open the possibility of a copyright owner suing on the basis of the making
of the adaptation itself.

   Whether or not it was intended that the provision in the 1988 Act
achieve the same effect, it is doubtful whether it does. The provision only
seems to apply where the copyright work "is an adaptation". In some
cases, an adaptation of a work will itself attract copyright, in other cases it

will not. (See paragraph 1.31.) So the position seems to be left open where there is no copyright in the adaptation, and here one must remember here that the restricted acts are distinct, so that, for example, it is an infringement of copyright to copy a work, and it is a separate infringement of copyright to copy an adaptation of a work. (See paragraph 5.51.) This seems at first to produce the somewhat strange result that where the adaptation is not the subject of copyright, the permitted act provisions do not allow an act to be done in relation to an adaptation of the work, unless this is either expressly allowed in the provision, or the provision states in general terms that no act will infringe copyright. It is possible alternatively that the words "is an adaptation" were intended to be a short way of saying "used in the form of an adaptation", and, if this were so, this would probably achieve the same result in practice as under the 1956 Act. This would again leave it open for a copyright owner to make a claim on the basis of the making of the adaptation, except of course where the permitted act allows the doing of any act without infringing copyright.

Where the relevant literary, dramatic or musical work is an adaptation the subject of copyright, an example of how the provision operates is as follows. Under section 34 of the 1988 Act (see paragraph 7.26), certain performances of dramatic works at educational establishments are permitted without infringing copyright. If the dramatic work is a play in a foreign language, but the performance is of a translation of the play, the performance of that translation would not infringe copyright in the original foreign language version or the translation.

7. Miscellaneous

7.09   There are three rules which should be borne in mind in considering the permitted acts referred to below:

(a) They are only relevant to the question of infringement of copyright. If there is some other right or obligation which has been infringed (for example, breach of confidentiality) they do not act as a defence in relation to any claim based on that right (s.28(1)).

(b) The fact that an act is outside the scope of one permitted act provision does not mean that is not covered by another provision (s.28(4)).

(c) The permitted act provisions must not be used so as to interpret what is within or outside the scope of the restricted acts referred to in Chapter 5.

II EDUCATION

This section deals with those permitted acts which relate specifically to education. However, the permitted acts relating to libraries, and the more general permitted acts could still be relevant in an educational context.

A. GENERAL

1. Educational establishments

In some cases in this section, the permitted act is restricted to acts done on   **7.10**
the premises of or for the purposes of what are called "educational
establishments." This is defined as any school, but will also apply to any
other educational establishment specified by order of the Secretary of
State (s.174(1)). Although at the time of writing, no such order has been
made, it was made clear by the Government in debates on the Bill that
orders would be made in relation to universities, including the Open
University, and presumably other institutions such as polytechnics will be
covered as well. Under the 1956 Act, some of the equivalent provisions
(in particular those relating to public performance) were confined to
schools.

In addition, there is provision for the Secretary of State to apply those
provisions which are restricted to educational establishments to situations where teachers are employed by a local education authority to give
instruction to pupils unable to attend an educational establishment
(s.174(2)).

2. Acts done by or on behalf of such establishments

In some cases below, it is not only where the act is done by an educational   **7.11**
establishment that it is permitted, but also where it is done "on behalf of"
such an establishment. In those cases copying could for example be
carried out by a printer, or photocopying shop, subject to the specific
restrictions contained in the relevant provision.

3. Secondary infringement

Four of the permitted acts below, those in paragraphs 7.17, 7.18, 7.22 and   **7.12**
7.23, allow copies of works to be made for certain purposes. In each case,
if the copy is then sold or let for hire or offered or exposed for sale or hire,
it becomes an infringing copy as regards that dealing and for any subsequent purposes. This would allow the provisions of Chapter 6 to be
applied provided that the person carrying out the relevant act knows or
has reason to believe that it is an infringing copy.

B. ANTHOLOGIES FOR EDUCATIONAL USE (s.33)

Under this provision, a short passage from a published literary or dra-   **7.13**
matic work can be included in a collection intended for use in educational
establishments. The provision is very similar to that contained in the 1956
Act. (See 1956 Act, s.6(6).)

There are a number of conditions which are attached to the provision, and these can be divided into two parts, those conditions relating to the work or works which can be included in the collection, and those relating to the collection itself.

1. Conditions relating to the work or works in the collection

7.14 These are as follows:

(a) The work must be a literary or dramatic work. Thus, it does not apply to musical works, although it could apply to the lyrics of a song.

(b) The work must be published (see paragraph 2.13 onwards above).

(c) Only a short passage from the work may be included.

(d) The literary or dramatic work must not be one which is intended for use in educational establishments. Use in an educational establishment is defined as any use for the educational purposes of such in establishment.

2. Conditions attaching to the collection in which the work or works is or was included

7.15 These are as follows:

(a) The collection must be intended for use in educational establishments, which again means any use for the educational purposes of such an establishment.

(b) It must be stated in the title of the collection that it is so intended, as well as in any advertisements issued by or on behalf of the publisher of the collection.

(c) The collection must consist mainly of material in the public domain.

(d) No more than two excerpts from copyright works by the same author may be included in collections published by the same publisher over any period of five years. There are special rules here which apply to the situation where authors collaborate in the making of a work. A literary or dramatic work written by an author in collaboration with someone else is treated for these purposes as a work by that author. Furthermore, if the excerpt in question is from a work where two or more authors have collaborated, any literary or dramatic work by any of those authors must be taken into account, whether any such work was written alone or in collaboration with someone completely different.

(e) The inclusion must be accompanied by a sufficient acknowledgement. This must identify the work in question by its title or other description, and must also identify the author, unless it was published anonymously.

3. Inclusion does not extend to issuing copies to the public

7.16 Provided that all these conditions are complied with, then the inclusion of the short passage in the collection is not an infringement of copyright. However, the section only refers to such inclusion, and does not appear to extend to the issue of such copies to the public. It is not clear whether this was intended or not. Under the 1956 Act, issuing copies to the public was not a restricted act, and, although there was a restricted act of publishing, this was not relevant because the provision only related to works which had been published. Thus if the short passage could be included in the work, it could be distributed freely. It does not appear that this is so now, because other permitted acts make the distinction quite clear between copying and issuing copies of the work to the public. Although the situation is slightly different here in that the word used is "inclusion," in our view it is probably stretching the meaning of the word "inclusion" too far in order to say that it covers putting copies of the work into circulation. It may well be of course that if the circulation of the relevant collection was restricted, that would not infringe the restricted act of issuing copies to the public, but this will be a question of degree in each case.

C. NON-REPROGRAPHIC COPYING OF LITERARY, DRAMATIC MUSICAL AND ARTISTIC WORKS FOR THE PURPOSES OF INSTRUCTION (s.32(1))

It is not an infringement of copyright to copy a literary, dramatic, musical **7.17** or artistic work in the course of instruction or of preparation for instruction. There are two conditions. First, the copying must be done by a person giving or receiving instruction. Secondly, the copying must not be by means of a reprographic process.

As in the 1956 Act, this permitted act is not tied in any way to an educational establishment. Thus, the provision is as relevant to commerce and the professions, as it is to schools. The provision does not apply to typographical arrangements of published editions. The much more limited equivalent provision relating to sound recordings and films is dealt with in paragraph 7.22 below.

Under the 1988 Act, a reprographic process is any process for making facsimile copies or involving the use of an appliance for making multiple copies (s.178). A facsimile copy includes one which is reduced or enlarged in size (s.178).

In the case of works held in electronic form (that is, for example, in the form of a semi-conductor chip, floppy disc, compact disc or tape) reprographic copying now includes any copying by electronic means. Examples of copying a work in electronic form would be both storing a work in a computer's memory, and printing out a computer program stored in a computer's memory.

So far as works not in electronic form are concerned, the obvious example is photocopying, but it could for example include the situation where duplication is for the purposes of overhead projection.

Whether or not the work is in electronic form, it is specifically provided that the making of a film or sound recording does not constitute a reprographic process. This means that using a conventional tape duplicating machine to copy a compact disc which embodies a copyright musical work could be permitted under this provision.

D. REPROGRAPHIC COPYING OF LITERARY DRAMATIC MUSICAL OR ARTISTIC WORKS (s.36)

1. Position under the 1956 Act

7.18 The 1956 Act contained no specific provisions permitting reprographic copying of literary, dramatic, musical or artistic works by schools, and the provision relating to fair dealing for the purposes of research or private study (see paragraph 7.70 below) was unlikely to be helpful in many cases because of the use of the word "private." However, a body representing publishers and authors called the Copyright Licensing Agency did enter into agreements with local education authorities by which limited extracts from books and periodicals could be copied in return for payment of a blanket fee.

The 1988 Act now introduces a permitted act for reprographic copying, but it is much more limited than the Copyright Licensing Agency scheme as regards the amount of the relevant works which can be copied.

2. Conditions for the provision to apply

7.19 The conditions which must be complied with for reprographic copying to be permitted are as follows:

(a) It only applies to published literary, dramatic or musical works, and thus does not extend to illustrations in books. If however there is copyright in the typographical arrangement of the published edition from which the work is copied, it applies to the copying of that.

(b) The copies must be made by or on behalf of an educational establishment.

(c) The copies must be made for the purposes of instruction, but there is no provision stating that this must be instruction at the educational establishment in question.

(d) Not more than 1 per cent. of any work may be copied by or on behalf of an establishment in any calendar quarter, that is from January 1 to March 31 and so on. It must be remembered that a book may contain many different works, and each one must be considered separately for these purposes, although where there is a separate copyright in the compilation that must be considered as well. There is no provision which states how one calculates the 1 per cent., whether it is in terms of page numbers, or words, or number of notes, and so on. This lacuna was recognised by the Government in debate, and the hope was expressed that the courts would apply common sense to the facts.

3. Meaning of reprographic copy

The meaning of reprographic copy is referred to in paragraph 7.17 above, **7.20** and includes any copying by electronic means where the work is held in electronic form. There are difficulties here however in applying the provision when a work is stored in a computer. Copying the work will usually take place when the work is displayed on a screen (see s.17(2) and paragraph 5.18), but this, in the case of a purchased or rented program, would be expressly or impliedly allowed anyway. It is likely that the 1 per cent. excludes any copying otherwise expressly or impliedly licensed.

4. Implication of availability of licences

This is the first provision examined where the Government has tried to **7.21** introduce limitations to the permitted act in order to encourage licensing schemes. In this case, it is provided that copying is not authorised under this provision if or to the extent that licences are available authorising the copying in question, and the person making the copies knew or ought to have been aware of that fact. In other words, if the Copyright Licensing Agency promulgates a scheme after the new Act comes into force which extends to such copying, an educational establishment cannot plead this section as a defence, unless it had no reason to be aware of the scheme. However, the benefit of this provision cannot be used where the licence contains provisions restricting the proportion of a work which may be copied to less than the 1 per cent. permitted under this section.

It will be noted that there is no requirement here that the copyright owner or owners obtain certification of the scheme from the Secretary of State, and of course any such scheme may also in any event be referred to the Copyright Tribunal. (See Chapter 9.)

E. COPYING FOR THE PURPOSES OF INSTRUCTION IN THE MAKING OF FILM OR FILM SOUND-TRACKS (s.32(2))

This new provision is somewhat restricted in its scope, and applies only **7.22** where the instruction or preparation for instruction is in the making of films or film sound-tracks. However, this is not as narrow as saying that it is only concerned with institutions which teach the art of film-making. It could apply to a discipline where it is useful to make films or film sound-tracks as an aid to the main subject, but where, in order to use it, the technique of film-making has to be learnt first.

Subject to the above, it is not an infringement of copyright to copy a sound recording, film, broadcast or cable programme in the course of such instruction or of preparation for such instruction. Again, the copying must be done by a person giving or receiving instruction.

F. RECORDING OF BROADCASTS OR CABLE PROGRAMMES (s.35)

7.23 This provision was not contained in the 1956 Act. It permits an educational establishment, or someone acting on its behalf, to record a broadcast or cable programme (or make a copy of a recording of a broadcast or cable programme) for the educational purposes of that establishment. In these circumstances, copying does not infringe the copyright in the broadcast or cable programme, or in any work (such as a musical work or sound recording) included in it. Although on the face of the provision, the recording may not be made for the educational purposes of another establishment, in fact this can be done provided that the educational establishment is making the recording on behalf of another educational establishment.

This is the first permitted act examined where the provision does not apply if or to the extent that there is a licensing scheme certified by the Secretary of State for Trade and Industry as referred to in paragraph 9.47 onwards. Thus, to use an example, if copyright owners of musical works wish to obtain royalties for the copying of their works carried out by recording such broadcast or cable programmes, they must lay down a licensing scheme, and have that certified by the Secretary of State. If this is not done, such copying may be carried out without the copyright owners obtaining any recompense for it.

G. PERFORMANCE (s.34)

1. Position under the 1956 Act

7.24 Under the 1956 Act, certain performances in the course of activities of a school did not constitute public performance or playing or showing in public, and did not therefore infringe copyright. The provision is retained in the 1988 Act, but there are some differences in emphasis, and the provisions now apply to educational establishments, not just schools.

2. The audience at the performance

7.25 In every case referred to below, the performance or playing or showing of a work must be before an audience consisting of no one else but the teachers and pupils of an educational establishment or other persons directly connected with the activities of that establishment. That last phrase does not necessarily apply because the person is the parent of a pupil at the establishment, although it could apply to parents who are also governors or who serve in some other capacity.

3. Permitted acts in relation to literary, dramatic and musical works

7.26 Where the work is a literary, dramatic or musical work, there are two relevant provisions. First, performance before such an audience by a teacher or pupil in the course of the activities of the establishment is permitted. This would cover for example a concert even where this did not take place on the premises of the establishment, provided that the requirements as to the audience are met. Secondly, performance before such an audience at the establishment by any person for the purposes of instruction is also permitted. This for example would extend to a visiting drama company presenting a play which is on a relevant examination syllabus, provided again that the audience restrictions are met. Here however, the performance must take place at the same educational establishment as the one which the teachers and pupils are from.

4. Permitted act in relation to sound recordings, films, broadcasts and cable programmes

Where the work is a sound recording, film, broadcast or cable pro- 7.27 gramme, the permitted act consists of playing or showing the work before such an audience at an educational establishment for the purposes of instruction. Although the playing or showing must therefore take place at an educational establishment, this need not be the educational establishment from which the teachers and pupils come.

H. EXAMINATIONS

1. Position under the 1956 Act

Under the 1956 Act, *copying* of literary, dramatic, musical or artistic 7.28 works or adaptations of such works was allowed where the work was reproduced as part of a question to be asked in an examination, or in an answer to such a question. The 1988 Act extends this provision.

2. The new permitted act

Now, copyright is not infringed by *anything* done for the purposes of an 7.29 examination by way of setting the questions, communicating the questions to the candidates or answering the questions. The provision applies to all works. The expression "communicating the questions to the candidates" is probably wide enough to cover not only the printing of examination papers, but also an oral examination where a work is performed. This is another provision which is not limited to educational establishments, and could apply to any examination of whatsoever nature.

3. Exception for musical works

There is one exception relating to musical works. If the examination 7.30

involves performance of a musical work, what is not permitted is the making of a reprographic copy of the musical work (for example, a photocopy of sheet music) for use by an examination candidate. It would, however, permit the making of a sound recording (see the definition of reprographic process in s.178) and of a manuscript copy.

III LIBRARIES, ARCHIVES AND OTHER SIMILAR BODIES

7.31   The first part of this section deals with those provisions in the 1988 Act which replace what was contained in section 7 of the 1956 Act. Some new provisions relating to the copying of works for archive purposes are then examined, and lastly the provision in the 1988 Act replacing that in the 1956 Act relating to public records.

      This section only deals with those permitted acts which specifically relate to libraries. The provisions referred to on education may also be relevant to school libraries, and some of the general permitted acts referred to later in this Chapter—for example, s.57. (See paragraph 7.75.)

A. COPYING BY LIBRARIANS AND ARCHIVISTS

1. Points of general application

(a) *The person carrying out the copying* (s.37(6))

7.32   As under section 7 of the 1956 Act, the copying which is referred to in the provisions below is only allowed where it is done by a librarian, or, as the case may be, an archivist, of a prescribed library or archive, or someone on behalf of such a person.

(b) *The libraries* (s.37(1))

7.33   Unlike the 1956 Act however, there is no requirement in the 1988 Act that the library be one which is not established or conducted for profit. The libraries to which the permitted acts apply will be prescribed by regulations, which, at the time of writing, have not yet been made. However, the 1988 Act states that the regulations may make different provision for different descriptions of libraries or archives and for different purposes, and the Government have already made it clear that, for example, those to which they will apply the provisions relating to replacement copies may not be the same as those in other cases.

(c) *Reliance on signed declaration* (s.37(2))

7.34   In the case of copying of articles contained in periodicals, and copying of parts of works, the 1956 Act required that the copies in question be supplied only to persons satisfying the librarian (or the person acting on his behalf) that they required them for purposes of research or private study. There was no express obligation on the librarian to make enquiries, and the Regulations made under the 1956 Act required that a declaration and undertaking in writing be signed and delivered to the librarian or some person appointed by the librarian. The provisions were in any event widely ignored.

The 1988 Act states expressly that the new regulations may provide that if the librarian or archivist has to be satisfied as to any matter before making or supplying of copy, he may rely on a signed declaration as to that matter by the person requesting the copy. This will not apply however if the librarian or archivist is aware that the declaration is false in a material particular.

The 1988 Act also states that the regulations may provide that the librarian or archivist must not make or supply any copy without a signed declaration having been made in a form to be prescribed under regulations.

(d) *False declarations* (s.37(3))

Under the 1956 Act, if the librarian or archivist failed to observe the conditions contained in the Act or the Regulations under the Act, an infringement of copyright took place. However, the 1956 Act did not contain any provision dealing with the situation where the declaration was obtained but was false, for example where the person asking the librarian to make a copy did not require it for private study at all. The 1988 Act states that where a person requesting a copy makes a declaration which is false in a material particular and is supplied with a copy which would have been an infringing copy if made by him, first he is liable for infringement as if he had made the copy himself, and secondly, the copy is to be treated as an infringing copy. As a result of the latter, all the provisions on secondary infringement referred to in Chapter 6 would apply. Of course, the practical difficulties in enforcement in these circumstances are unlikely to make the provision as much use to copyright owners as they would like. **7.35**

(e) *Copying*

For what constitutes copying in relation to the relevant works, see Chapter 5. In relation to literary, dramatic, musical and artistic works, it will be appreciated that this is much wider than photocopying. **7.36**

2. Copying of articles and parts of published works (ss.38 and 39)

In certain circumstances, the librarian of a prescribed library may make and supply a copy of an article in a periodical or a copy of a part of a literary, dramatic or musical work contained in a published edition. If the **7.37** conditions are complied with, this does not infringe any copyright in the article or work, or in any illustrations accompanying the work, or in the published edition.

(a) *Conditions applicable in all cases*

7.38   The relevant conditions will be prescribed in Regulations, which have not yet been made. However, the 1988 Act provides that they must contain certain conditions. In each case, copies must be supplied only to persons satisfying the librarian that they require them for purposes of research (and this need not be private research) or private study, and will not use them for any other purpose. As will be seen (see paragraph 7.70), fair dealing with any work for the purpose of research or private study is not an infringement of copyright, but the provisions here avoid problems for librarians in deciding whether what they are asked to do constitutes fair dealing.

Furthermore, the persons to whom the copies are supplied must pay for them a sum not less than the cost (including a contribution to the general expenses of the library) attributable to their production. The equivalent of this latter requirement in the 1956 Act was again widely ignored.

(b) *Conditions applicable to copying of an article in a periodical*

7.39   Here the regulations will have to provide that no person is furnished with more than one copy of the same article, and also that no person is furnished with copies of more than one article contained in the same issue of a periodical. These requirements are not subject to any limit in time, so that, in order not to infringe, librarians will probably in the future have to check their records to see what, if anything, that person has been supplied with in the past.

(c) *Conditions applicable to copying of parts of literary, dramatic or musical works*

7.40   Here the regulations must contain a condition that no person is furnished with more than one copy of the same material or with a copy of more than a reasonable proportion of any work. The expression "reasonable proportion" is not defined, and again it will be necessary for librarians to keep records to see what has been supplied in the past. It should also be remembered that this provision is tied to literary, dramatic or musical works, and a book may contain more than one work—for example, a collection of short stories. On that basis, the librarian may only copy part of the individual work contained in the book, not for example one complete story.

(d) *Multiple copying*

7.41   As well as being impracticable, and therefore widely ignored, the 1956

Act also contained various loopholes. Having regard to the drafting of the provisions of the Act and the Regulations, it was perfectly possible for multiple copying to take place and not infringe copyright. Thus, it was thought that if one person asked a librarian to make 30 copies of an article, and provided 30 declarations, that would comply with the provisions of the 1956 Act and its regulations.

The 1988 Act introduces new provisions intended to prevent multiple copying which apply in the case of both articles in periodicals and parts of literary, dramatic or musical works. These state that the regulations will have to contain a provision to the effect that a copy shall be supplied only to a person satisfying the librarian that his requirement is not related to any similar requirement of another person. The regulations will probably provide more detail on this, but the 1988 Act says that they may provide that a requirement is similar if it is for copies of substantially the same material at substantially the same time and for substantially the same purpose. Furthermore, the regulations will be able to define the requirement of persons being related so as to include a situation where persons receive instruction (presumably in the sense of teaching) to which the material is relevant at the same time and place. Such provisions would therefore apply where the librarian has a succession of students from the same institution asking for the same article from a periodical.

(e) Practical problems

The provisions referred to above on the face of it would appear to be   **7.42** helpful in relation to multiple copying. They certainly place a far greater onus on libraries to ensure that the provisions are not abused. However, use of the provisions may in practice be limited assuming that the regulations do provide that a librarian may rely on a signed declaration by the person requesting a copy unless he is aware that it is false in a material particular. Whether or not the regulations will simply repeat this without qualification remains to be seen, but, if it does, it seems that the librarian will be able to rely on such a declaration even where it is likely that multiple use is involved. Of course, if any case were to come before the court, it might well be that the judge would take the same view as Scott J. in the *Columbia Pictures* v. *Robinson* ([1987] (Ch.38) case, and hold that a librarian must be aware of the situation where he deliberately refrains from inquiring and shuts his eyes to that which is obvious.

(f) Availability of name and address of person entitled to grant licence to copy

In the case of copying of parts of published editions of literary, dramatic   **7.43** or musical works, the equivalent section under the 1956 Act did not apply if, at the time when the copy was made, the librarian knew the name and address of a person entitled to authorise the making of the copy, or could by reasonable enquiry ascertain the name and address of such a person. This provision no longer applies.

3. Unpublished literary, dramatic or musical works (s.43)

7.44   This is a new provision, which allows a librarian or archivist of a prescribed library or archive to make and supply a copy of the whole or any part of a literary, dramatic or musical work from a document in the library or archive. Provided that certain conditions are complied with, such copying and supply does not infringe any copyright in the work or any accompanying illustrations.

     The provision does not apply if at the time of the making of the copy, the librarian or archivist is or ought to be aware either that the work had been published before the document was deposited in the library or archive, or that the copyright owner has prohibited copying of the work. This presumably relates to the copyright owner at the time of copying.

     Again, regulations are to be prescribed in relation to such copying and supply. These will also contain conditions relating to payment, and also that the copies must be supplied only to persons satisfying the librarian or archivist that they require them for purposes of research or private study. For both these requirements see paragraphs 7.34 and 7.38

     In addition, no person must be furnished with more than one copy of the same material.

4. Copying for library purposes (ss.41 and 42)

7.45   There are two provisions here which to some extent are based on those in the 1956 Act.

(a) *Copying for another library where the identity of the copyright owner is not known*

7.46   The first of the two provisions states that the librarian of a prescribed library may in certain circumstances make and supply to another prescribed library a copy of an article in a periodical, or indeed the whole or part of a published edition of a literary, dramatic or musical work. If the conditions are complied with, copying is not an infringement of the copyright in the text of the work, or in any accompanying illustrations, or in the typographical arrangement of the published edition.

     The provision does not apply if at the time the copy is made, the librarian making it knows, or could by reasonable inquiry ascertain, the name and address of a person entitled to authorise the making of the copy. It would also not apply where the person acting on behalf of the librarian in making the copy knew or could by reasonable inquiry ascertain that information.

     The conditions here will be contained in regulations again not made at the time of writing. There are no specific requirements for such regulations in this case, but the regulations under the 1956 Act provided for a wider class of libraries than in other cases, both as regards the library doing the copying, and the library for which the copy was made.

(b) *Copying for the purposes of preservation or supplying a replacement copy to another library*

The second provision extends to any item in the permanent collection of a **7.47** library or archive. If the relevant conditions are complied with, the librarian or archivist of a prescribed library or archive may make a copy from such an item for either of two purposes. The first purpose is in order to preserve or replace that item by placing the copy in its permanent collection in addition to or in place of the item itself. The second purpose is in order to replace in the permanent collection of another prescribed library or archive an item which has been lost, destroyed or damaged.

If the prescribed conditions are complied with, there is no infringement of the copyright in any literary, dramatic or musical work, in any accompanying illustrations, or, in the case of a published edition, in the typographical arrangement of that edition.

Although again the Regulations have not at the time of writing been promulgated, they will restrict the making of copies to cases where it is not reasonably practicable to purchase a copy of the item in question in order to fulfil the relevant purpose.

B. COPYING OF UNPUBLISHED MANUSCRIPTS IN MUSEUMS AND LIBRARIES (Sched. 1, para. 16)

1. Survival of the 1956 Act provision

Under the 1956 Act, it was not an infringement of copyright to copy or **7.48** exploit copies of a manuscript of any unpublished literary, dramatic or musical work kept in a library or museum after a certain length of time. The 1988 Act preserves the provision but only for existing works. Unlike the provisions referred to in section A above, there are no restrictions in relation to the libraries to which it applies, or in relation to who can carry out the copying.

2. Conditions for the provision to apply

The provision applies in the following circumstances: **7.49**

(a) It only applies to literary, dramatic and musical works and any accompanying illustrations.

(b) The work must not have been published.

(c) The author of the work must have been dead for more than 50 years before the calendar year in which someone wishes to take advantage of the provisions, and 100 years must have passed since the work was made.

(d) The manuscript or a copy of the work must be kept at a library, museum or other institution where it is open to public inspection.

3. Permitted acts where the conditions apply

7.50   In these circumstances, the following can be done without infringing copyright:

(a) The work may be reproduced by anyone for the purposes of research or private study or with a view to publication.

(b) The work may in whole or in part be included in another literary, dramatic or musical work and then published, so long as, immediately before publication (and for these purposes each part if published separately must be regarded separately) the identity of the copyright owner was not known to the publisher of the new work.

(c) If the conditions in paragraph (b) above are fulfilled, the work or relevant part thereof may be broadcast, publicly performed or included in a cable programme. Records may also be made of it.

The requirement under the 1956 Act of advertising notice of intended publication will no longer apply.

C. ARTICLES OF CULTURAL OR HISTORICAL IMPORTANCE OR INTEREST (s.44)

7.51   In certain circumstances, articles of cultural or historical importance or interest such as manuscripts cannot lawfully be exported from the United Kingdom without an export licence. Under a new provision in the 1988 Act, where the Department of Trade and Industry requires as a condition for the grant of such a licence that a copy be made for deposit in an appropriate library or archive, it is not an infringement of copyright to make that copy. There is no reference to regulations being made as to appropriate library or archives, so this may be wider than under the regulations to be prescribed for the purposes referred to in paragraph 7.33 above.

D. RECORDINGS OF MUSIC WITH WORDS WHICH ARE UNPUBLISHED AND OF UNKNOWN AUTHORSHIP (s.61)

1. Scope of the provision

7.52   If a song becomes very popular, one sometimes finds it being sung to different words in a non-commercial context. Perhaps the best example is football supporters replacing the lyrics of a song with other words about their team. Provided that certain conditions apply, the recording of such words and music for the purposes of including it in an archive, and the supply of copies of that recording for research or private study, is now allowed without infringing copyright.

174

2. Conditions for the provisions to apply

The conditions are as follows: **7.53**

(a) The recording must be of a performance of a song, that is both the words and the music.

(b) The words must be unpublished and of unknown authorship at the time the recording is made.

(c) The making of the recording must not infringe any other copyright.

(d) The making of the recording must not have been prohibited by the person or any of the persons performing the song.

3. Permitted acts where the conditions apply

Provided that these conditions are complied with, it is not an infringe-   **7.54** ment of copyright to record the words or music for the purposes of including the recording in an archive maintained by a designated body. At the time of writing, no such bodies have been designated, but there is a requirement that the Secretary of State must not designate a body unless satisfied that it is not established or conducted for profit.

In addition, the archivist of such an archive will be able to make and supply copies of the sound recording without infringing copyright in the recording or any works included in it, provided that conditions to be prescribed are complied with. Again, these conditions have not yet been prescribed, but will have to include two stipulations. First, the copies must only be supplied to persons satisfying the archivist that they require them for purposes of research or private study and will not use them for any other purpose. There is no mention of the archivist being able to rely on a signed declaration as referred to in the case of libraries in paragraph 7.34 above, but presumably the order could contain something to this effect. Secondly, no person must be furnished with more than one copy of the same recording. Again, an archivist can appoint someone on his behalf to make and supply the copies of the recording.

E. RECORDING OF BROADCASTS OR CABLE PROGRAMMES FOR ARCHIVAL PURPOSES (s.75)

This again is a new provision, which permits the recording of certain   **7.55** broadcasts or cable programmes, or the making of a recording from a copy of such a broadcast or cable programme, for the purposes of being placed in an archive maintained by a designated body. There is provision for an order to be made by the Secretary of State designating not only the bodies to which this provision will apply, but also the broadcasts or cable programmes to which the provision will apply. The Secretary of State must not designate such a body unless he is satisfied that it is not established or conducted for profit.

In the above circumstances, the recording does not infringe any copyright in the broadcast or cable programme, or in any work included in the broadcast or cable programme.

F. PUBLIC RECORDS (s.49)

7.56 The Public Records Act 1958 provides for the safe-keeping and preservation of certain public records, such as records of Government Departments, court and tribunal records, and so on. Although there are restrictions on public access to certain records held by the Public Record Office, there is a duty on the Keeper of Public Records to arrange that reasonable facilities are available to the public for inspecting and obtaining copies of public records in the Public Record Office. Such material as is open to public inspection may be copied, and a copy supplied to any person, by or with the authority of any officer appointed under the 1958 Act without infringing any copyright in the material.

The provision also applies to the Public Records (Scotland) Act 1937, and the Public Records Act (Northern Ireland) 1923.

IV PROVISIONS RELATING TO ALL RESTRICTED ACTS

7.57 Where the provisions below apply, any of the restricted acts referred to in Chapter 5 can be done without infringing copyright.

A. FAIR DEALING

1. General comments

7.58 Three of the permitted acts referred to below contain reference to the expression "fair dealing"—fair dealing for the purposes of criticism and review (see paragraph 7.65), fair dealing for the purposes of reporting current events (see paragraph 7.66) and fair dealing for the purposes of research or private study. (See paragraph 7.70.) This section deals with certain basic principles which arise out of the cases on the equivalent sections in the 1956 Act.

In general terms, there are no precise rules which can be applied to determine whether a particular dealing with a copyright work is fair. The following considerations have however been held to be relevant:

(a) *Quality and quantity*

7.59 Although again there can be no general rule as to the amount taken and the importance of what has been taken, quantity and quality will be relevant. If, for example, there are long extracts from a copyright work with short comments attached, the dealing may well be unfair where it is for the purposes of criticism or review. Conversely, short extracts and long comments may well be fair. (See *Johnstone* v. *Bernard Jones Publications Ltd.* ([1938] Ch. 599.) Of course, where only a part of a work is taken, it is not an infringement of copyright in any event to do any of the restricted acts unless the part is substantial. (See paragraph 5.09.) Where however the relevant work is extremely short, it could even be fair dealing to reproduce the whole of such work—an example given in one case was the reproduction of an epitaph on a tombstone.

(b) *Unpublished works*

The dealing is less likely to be fair when it relates to an unpublished work. (See *British Oxygen Co. Ltd.* v. *Liquid Air Ltd.* ([1925] Ch. 383.) This is not so however when the work has already been circulated widely. (See *Hubbard* v. *Vosper* ([1972] 2 Q.B. 84.) **7.60**

(c) *Fairness in relation to the relevant purpose*

The question of fairness must be judged in relation to the relevant purpose. Dealing which might be fair for some other purpose or fair in general is not covered. Where the dealing is simply an adjunct to the relevant purpose, it will probably not be fair—for example coupling a newspaper report on injuries sustained to an author in a car crash is unlikely to justify the publication of a substantial part of a work of his. In *Beloff* v. *Pressdram Ltd.* ([1973] 1 All E.R. 241) the magazine *Private Eye* published an internal memorandum from the Political and Lobby Correspondent of the *Observer* newspaper to the editor of the newspaper about a Cabinet Minister and a "campaign" in *Private Eye* against him. It was held by the judge that the publication of this memorandum was not fair dealing when viewed in relation to the purpose either of criticism or review, or reporting current events. **7.61**

(d) *Specific dealing, not surrounding circumstances*

It is necessary to look at the specific dealing in question, and not simply the surrounding circumstances. Thus, in the *Beloff* case, the judge said that he was not concerned with the conduct of *Private Eye* in general, but only with the specific circumstances of the publishing of the relevant memorandum. **7.62**

(e) *Competition with normal exploitation*

A good test is to examine whether the dealing competes with the normal exploitation of the relevant work. It is thus not fair dealing for a rival in the trade to take copyright material and use it for his own benefit. (See *Hubbard* v. *Vosper per* Lord Denning.) **7.63**

(f) *Motive*

7.64 An oblique motive for the dealing may be relevant to whether it is fair, but this is subject to what we say below in relation to fair dealing for the purposes of criticism and review. In *Associated Newspapers Group plc* v. *News Group Newspapers Ltd.* ([1986] R.P.C. 515) (referred to in more detail below under paragraph 7.69) the Judge's decision rejecting the arguments on fair dealing was clearly influenced by his view that the real motive for publication was that of attracting readers.

2. Fair dealing for the purposes of criticism and review (s.30(1))

7.65 Fair dealing with a work for the purpose of criticism or review does not infringe any copyright in the work, provided that it is accompanied by a sufficient acknowledgement. A sufficient acknowledgement is defined as one which identifies the work in question by its title or other description and identifies the author (s.178). It is not necessary to identify the author if, in the case of a published work, it is published anonymously, or, in the case of an unpublished work, it is not possible for a person to ascertain the identity of the author by reasonable enquiry. The first part of the definition of "sufficient acknowledgement" was the same under the 1956 Act, and in *Sillitoe* v. *McGraw-Hill Book Company (UK) Ltd* ([1983] F.S.R. 545) Judge Mervyn Davies Q.C. held that simply identifying the work by title and author was not an acknowledgement. It was held that in addition there must be something which acknowledged the position or claims of the author or copyright owner. So in that case it was insufficient that one could easily ascertain the author and title of the work.

The criticism or review may be of the work itself, or another work, or a performance of a work. Under the 1956 Act there was no reference to a performance of a work, and the 1956 Act only applied to literary, dramatic, musical and artistic works.

In cases under the 1956 Act, it was established that criticism could relate not only to the literary style of the work, but also the thoughts underlying it (*Hubbard* v. *Vosper*). However, the criticism must be criticism of the plaintiff's work, and not the plaintiff's conduct in general.

In the *Sillitoe* case, the Judge refused to apply the equivalent provision under the 1956 Act to study notes containing extracts from two well-known literary and dramatic works on the grounds that they contained an exposition of the works with virtually no critical content. The Judge held that "for the purposes of criticism" meant "for the purpose of estimating the qualities and character of the original work."

3. Fair dealing for the purposes of reporting current events (s.30(2))

7.66 Fair dealing with any work other than a photograph for the purpose of reporting current events does not infringe any copyright in the work. There must be a sufficient acknowledgement (for which see paragraph 7.65 above), except in connection with the reporting of current events by means of a sound recording, film, broadcast or cable programme.

(a) *Comparison with the 1956 Act*

The equivalent section in the 1956 Act did not apply to artistic works, sound recordings, films, broadcasts or cable programmes. Furthermore, the current events had to be reported in a newspaper, magazine or similar periodical, or by means of broadcasting or in a cinematograph film. It did not therefore apply to books, or sound recordings.

7.67

(b) *Photographs*

Although photographs are excluded from the provision, a still from a film, broadcast or cable programme is not a photograph for copyright purposes (s.4(2)), and the permitted act could therefore apply as regards such stills.

7.68

(c) *Scope of the provision*

The scope of this permitted act is uncertain, because there is a fine line between reporting current events and reporting something which may currently be of interest to, for example, readers of a newspaper. Thus, it may be of interest to such readers to read an article on or an interview with a famous author whose works are currently much in demand, but this in our view would not justify the inclusion of substantial parts of such an author's work under this fair dealing exception.

7.69

In *Associated Newspapers Group plc* v. *News Group Newspapers Ltd.* ([1988] R.P.C. 515) Walton J. said that although the provision to succeed did not require the person claiming the fair dealing exemption to show necessity, this was a good start. In the judge's view the test was, "is it reasonably necessary to refer to these matters in order to deal with current events." That case concerned the publication of correspondence between the Duke and Duchess of Windsor, and the judge held that the death of the Duchess did not justify the publication of such correspondence.

The judge in that case also doubted whether the Duchess's motive and intention in wanting the correspondence published (it was then being serialised by another newspaper) was a current event within the meaning of the provision.

Of course, it does not matter that the material being dealt with is much older than the current event. The judge in the *Associated Newspapers* case gave an example:

> "One has only to think, for example, of correspondence dealing with nuclear reactors which have just blown up or have had a core melt-down: that might date from a very considerable period previous to the event happening, but would be of a topical nature in order to enable a report on what had actually happened to be properly prepared."

4. Fair dealing for the purposes of research or private study (s.29)

Fair dealing with a literary, dramatic, musical or artistic work for the **7.70** purposes of research or private study does not infringe any copyright in the work. Where the literary, dramatic, musical or artistic work is in the form of a published edition, neither does it infringe the copyright in the typographical arrangement.

In addition, fair dealing with the typographical arrangement of a published edition for the purposes of research or private study does not infringe any copyright in the arrangement. This would apply for example where the edition was of a work which was out of copyright.

In the *Sillitoe* case referred to in paragraph 7.65 above, the Judge held that the equivalent provision under the 1956 Act did not apply where the person claiming the defence was not himself engaged in research or private study, but was merely facilitating someone else's research or private study. No case however seems to have arisen under the 1956 Act where the person engaged in research or private study specifically asked someone else to carry out the relevant act. The 1988 Act seems to assume that the permitted act could apply in such circumstances, since a new provision has been added with the intention of attempting to limit abuse of the provision.

Where dealing with the work involves copying by a person other than the researcher or student himself, the dealing will not be fair in the following circumstances:

(a) Where a librarian carrying out the copying (or a person acting on behalf of a librarian) does anything which regulations under section 40 would not permit to be done under sections 38 or 39. The latter sections dealing with copying of articles from periodicals, and parts of published works are considered in paragraph 7.37 above. For example, if restrictions under the regulations on the amount of a work which can be copied are not complied with, then there is no defence under this provision or the library provisions.

(b) In any other case, where the person carrying out the copying either knows or has reason to believe that it will result in copies of substantially the same material being provided to more than one person at substantially the same time and for substantially the same purpose. An example here might be conference facilities in a hotel. If for example, a conference of scientists is held at a hotel to discuss research being done into a particular matter, the hotel would infringe copyright if at the request of one of the delegates it photocopied enough copies of an article in a journal for more than one of the delegates to use.

Although the Government stated that it intended to amend the law to exclude commercial research from the scope of the permitted act, a provision to this effect was abandoned during the passage of the Bill through Parliament.

B. OTHER PROVISIONS RELEVANT TO ALL COPYRIGHT WORKS

1. Parliamentary and judicial proceedings (s.45)

Copyright is not infringed by anything done for the purposes of Parlia-   7.71
mentary or judicial proceedings. The 1956 Act had the same reference to
judicial proceedings in respect of all works except, somewhat strangely,
sound recordings and published editions. The reference to Parliamentary
proceedings is new.

    Copyright is also not infringed by anything done for the purposes of
reporting such proceedings. However, there is a special exception here in
the case of published reports of such proceedings, where it will still be an
infringement of copyright to copy the whole or a substantial part of such a
report.

    Judicial proceedings are widely defined as including proceedings be-
fore any court, tribunal or person having authority to decide any matter
affecting a person's legal rights or liabilities (s.178). Parliamentary proceedings include proceedings of the Northern Ireland Assembly and the
European Parliament.

2. Royal Commissions and Statutory Inquiries (s.46)

This is another provision which was not in the 1956 Act, and states that   7.72
copyright is not infringed by anything done for the purposes of the
proceedings of a Royal Commission or Statutory Inquiry.

    Copyright is also not infringed by anything done for the purpose of
reporting any such proceedings which are held in public. However, again
there is the same exception in relation to the copying of a work which is a
published report of such proceedings.

    Finally, copyright in a work is not infringed by the issue to the public of
copies of a report of a Royal Commission or Statutory Inquiry containing
the work or material from it.

3. Acts Done Under Statutory Authority (s.50)

Where a particular act is specifically authorised by Act of Parliament,   7.73
that act does not infringe copyright unless the statute provides otherwise.
It does not matter whether the Act is one already in force, or one passed
in the future.

    Furthermore, any defence of statutory authority otherwise available
under or by virtue of any enactment can also be used as a defence to an
infringement action.

    This provision was not in the 1956 Act, and looks at first sight as if it
might deprive a copyright owner of his rights in many cases. There are
many Acts of Parliament which in general terms authorise acts which a
copyright owner has the exclusive right to do under the 1988 Act.
However, the requirement here is that the authority be specific and relate

to the particular act which is done. Thus, certain statutes authorise broadcasting and cable programme transmission, but they do not authorise the specific use of copyright musical or literary works.

4. Supervision and Control of Broadcasts and Cable Programmes (s.69)

7.74   The making or use of recordings by the British Broadcasting Corporation or the Independent Broadcasting Authority or the Cable Authority for the purposes of maintenance of supervision and control over programmes does not infringe copyright.

Section 21 of the Broadcasting Act 1981 requires contracts between the IBA and programme contractors to contain certain provisions to secure compliance with the Act. Every such contract must in particular contain provision whereby the Authority can obtain scripts or copies of programmes in advance, and copyright is not infringed by anything done under or in pursuance of any provision included in such a contract.

It is also not an infringement of copyright to do anything under or in pursuance of a notice or direction given under section 16 of the Cable and Broadcasting Act 1984 or a condition included in a licence by virtue of section 35 of the 1984 Act. Section 16 gives power to the Cable Authority to require scripts or programmes to be produced in advance of transmission. Section 34 of the 1984 Act allows police officers of a certain rank to order production of a script of a programme or a copy of the programme. Section 35 requires that the Cable Authority do all that it can to secure that any person against whom such an order is made will be able to comply with the requirement, and the fulfilment of any condition in a licence granted to a person providing a licensed service relating to compliance with such an order does not infringe any copyright.

C. OTHER PROVISIONS RELEVANT ONLY TO LITERARY, DRAMATIC, MUSICAL AND ARTISTIC WORKS AND THEIR TYPOGRAPHICAL ARRANGEMENTS

1. Anonymous or pseudonymous works where it is reasonable to assume that copyright has expired (s.57)

7.75   The 1956 Act denied a plaintiff damages for infringement of copyright where at the time of the infringement the defendant did not know and had no reason to believe that copyright existed in the relevant work. As will be seen (paragraph 10.92), the 1988 Act repeats the provision, but goes further in depriving the copyright owner of any rights where the work is of unknown authorship and it is reasonable to assume that it is no longer in copyright.

(a) *Conditions for the provision to apply*

7.76   The provision states that copyright in a literary, dramatic, musical or artistic work is not infringed by an act done at a time when, or in pursuance of arrangements made at a time when, two conditions are satisfied. These conditions are as follows:

(i) It is not possible by reasonable inquiry to ascertain the identity of the author. This is the same wording as is used to define the meaning of "unknown" in relation to works of unknown authorship. (See paragraph 4.39 above.)

(ii) It is reasonable to assume **either** that copyright has expired, **or** that the author died 50 years or more before the beginning of the calendar year in which the act was done or the arrangements were made.

(b) *Works of joint authorship*

There are special rules in relation to works of joint authorship. As regards   **7.77** the first condition, the reference to the author is to any of the authors. As regards the second condition, the reference to the author is to all of the authors.

(c) *Reasonable to assume that copyright has expired*

The second condition gives two alternatives. The first could be relevant to   **7.78** a computer-generated work, or, indeed, a work of unknown authorship under the provisions referred to in paragraph 4.39. The second does not apply where the work is one in which Crown copyright subsists, or where copyright originally vested in an international organisation as referred to in paragraph 3.84 and in respect of which the Order under that section specified a copyright period longer than 50 years.

(d) *Existing works* (Sched. 1, para. 15)

The two alternatives referred to in the second condition are further   **7.79** modified in the case of existing works. The first does not apply as regards photographs or the perpetual copyrights referred to in paragraph 4.35.
    The second alternative only applies to existing works in two cases. Where the work is an unpublished anonymous or pseudonymous work, it takes effect 50 years from the end of the calendar year in which the 1988 Act comes into force. In all other cases, it only applies where the duration of copyright is the same under the new copyright provisions as under the "previous law" (which presumably is meant to refer to the 1956 Act). This would not be so for example in the case of an unexploited work (see paragraph 4.12).

(e) *Comparison with provisions on works of joint authorship*

Under the provisions as to duration referred to in paragraph 4.39   **7.80** onwards, once it becomes possible by reasonable inquiry to ascertain the identity of an author, the work can never again be a work of unknown authorship as defined in those provisions. The same is not so here. The test as to whether it is possible by reasonable inquiry to ascertain the identity of the author is applied at the time the relevant act is done or arrangements made. Thus, it may be that if a work was published anonymously it was possible at that stage to ascertain the identity of the author by reasonable inquiry, but 50 years later this might no longer be so.

(f) *Particular problems with the provision*

7.81   At first sight, the provision looks useful, particularly since it extends to acts done in pursuance of arrangements made when the conditions applied. Thus, if a film company makes a film of a novel when the conditions apply to that novel, and enters into a long-term distribution contract with a film distributor, it is arguable that acts done in accordance with that contract by the distributor will not infringe copyright, even if the identity of the author becomes known at a later date.

     Despite this, it is doubtful whether the provision will be of much comfort to users of copyright works, particularly in areas where it is customary to insure anyway. There are two problems. First, it may be that the party doing the relevant act or making arrangements for the doing of the relevant act himself made reasonable inquiries, but that it is not the question. The first condition is that "it is not possible by reasonable inquiry," and others may have found it possible. The test is therefore objective not subjective. Secondly, it must be remembered that each fresh exploitation may involve a fresh restricted act. Thus, to use the example above, after the distribution agreement has expired, if at that stage the identity of the author is known, licences would be required both for the making of further copies of the film, and for subsequent public performance or broadcasting.

2. Use of notes or recordings of spoken words in certain cases (s.58)

(a) *Scope of the provision*

7.82   This new permitted act relates only to literary works, and will be particularly relevant to newspaper, television or radio journalism. Before going on to the detail, an example will perhaps best explain its relevance. A television company is making a documentary about medical malpractice. An eminent doctor makes a public speech about the subject, and television cameras are allowed by him to film his making of the speech. The speech was written down beforehand. In those circumstances it would not be an infringement of copyright to film the making of the speech, because the writer would be held to have consented to that in allowing television cameras to do so. However, any further copying of the whole or part of the speech would be a fresh restricted act, and the question might arise whether the consent given to film the making of the speech extended to the incorporation of that film into the documentary. Provided that the writer did not place restrictions on its use, the new provision in the 1988 Act would allow the incorporation of the material into the documentary.

(b) *Conditions for the provisions to apply*

The provision states that where a record of spoken words is made, in **7.83** writing or otherwise, either for the purpose of reporting current events or of broadcasting or including in a cable programme service the whole or part of the work, it is not an infringement of the copyright in the words as a literary work to use the record or material taken from it (or to copy the record, or any such material, or use the copy) for that purpose, provided certain conditions are met. The conditions are as follows:

(i) The record is taken directly from the spoken words, not from another record or broadcast or cable programme.

(ii) The speaker did not prohibit the making of the record.

(iii) Where copyright already subsisted in the work, the making of the record did not infringe copyright.

(iv) The use made of the record or material taken from it is not of a kind which has been prohibited by or on behalf of the speaker or copyright owner before the record was made.

(v) Any person lawfully in possession of the record has given authority for the use of it or is using it himself.

(c) *Comparison with fair dealing*

The permitted act therefore goes further than that relating to fair dealing **7.84** for the purposes of reporting current events, because it could extend to the recording of any speech for the purposes of broadcasting or including in a cable programme service the whole or part of that speech, of course, there is also no need to fulfil any requirement of fair dealing provided that all the conditions referred to above are fulfilled. However, the use of the recording of the speech has to tie up with the purpose for which it was made. Thus, if a speech is made by someone about a specific case of medical malpractice decided in the courts, and recorded for the purposes of inclusion on television news, the defence would not extend to the copying of that recording for the purposes of a subsequent documentary about the person who made the speech.

3. Reconstruction of buildings (s.65)

The 1988 Act provides that anything done for the purposes of recon- **7.85** structing a building does not infringe any copyright either in the building, or in any drawings or plans in accordance with which the building was, by or with the licence of the copyright owner, constructed. The relevant copyright owner is the one at the time of construction.

The 1956 Act contained a similar provision, although it was slightly narrower in effect. It provided that copyright was not infringed by the reconstruction itself, whereas the 1988 Act states that anything done for the purposes of reconstruction does not infringe copyright. Thus for example, it is arguable that if funds are needed for reconstruction, an appeal can be launched raising funds by selling copies of the original architect's drawings of the building.

It is somewhat strange that neither in the 1956 Act nor in the 1988 Act is there any reference to a model of the building, which has a separate copyright from the building or the plans.

V PROVISIONS RELATING TO INFRINGEMENT BY COPYING

A. THOSE RELEVANT TO ALL WORKS

1. Incidental inclusion (s.31)

(a) *Comparison with the 1956 Act*

7.86   Under the 1956 Act, it was not an infringement of copyright in an artistic work to include that work in a film or television broadcast if its inclusion was only by way of background or was otherwise incidental to the principal matters represented in the film or broadcast. (See 1956 Act, s.9(5).)

This provision does not appear in this form in the 1988 Act, but instead a much broader defence has been introduced relating to all works. The precise scope of the new provision is, however, somewhat uncertain.

(b) *The defence*

7.87   The provision states that copyright in any work is not infringed by its incidental inclusion in an artistic work, sound recording, film, broadcast or cable programme. The problem for both copyright owners and users therefore in practice is what the word "incidental" means. The Shorter Oxford English Dictionary defines this as "occurring or liable to occur in fortuitous or subordinate conjunction with something else."

(c) *Uncertain scope*

7.88   If the provision prevents a copyright owner exercising his exclusive rights where the inclusion is simply fortuitous, then that may be defensible on policy grounds. However, to deprive the copyright owner of his rights where the use is simply subordinate to something else could deprive the copyright owner of his rights on occasions when it would not (in our view) be right to do so. This is particularly relevant in the case of films, and an example may help. A feature film has as its subject a love story. A scene is included at a theatre where the couple are so engrossed with each other that they talk to each other and ignore the play, which is simply heard going on in the background, but which happens to be a major West End success. Assuming that a substantial part of the play is used (see paragraph 5.09) is the inclusion of the play merely incidental because it is subordinate to the main plot of the film? It could be argued either way, and it is to be hoped that the courts will not construe the provision too widely.

(d) *Exception for music*

There is one major exception to this provision, which can again best be demonstrated by an example. The film referred to has another scene where the couple are in a cafe, and in the background a radio is playing a number one hit. In these circumstances, the inclusion will not be incidental, because of the special exception in the 1988 Act which states that a musical work is not to be regarded as incidentally included in another work if it is deliberately included. The same applies to any words spoken or sung with music, and so much of a sound recording, broadcast or cable programme as includes a musical work or such words.   **7.89**

Even here however, it is difficult to be certain of the scope of this exception. Using the example of the feature film again, a further scene is shot on the streets of London, and the footage includes film of a union demonstration. Amongst those marching past in the demonstration is a brass band playing a well-known copyright melody. In those circumstances, it might well be argued that if the cameras continue to film whilst the brass band is playing, that in itself would be deliberate. In any event, when the editing stage comes and the decision is taken to include in the film the part of the demonstration when the brass band is playing, that in itself will be deliberate, and consent would be required.

(e) *Issuing copies to the public*

If the making of a copy of a work was not an infringement of copyright because of this provision, it is also not an infringement of copyright to issue such a copy to the public, or to use such a copy for broadcasting or inclusion in a cable programme service or playing or showing in public. These provisions also apply to copies made before the commencement of the 1988 Act. So even though an action for infringement would still lie as regards any infringement of copyright which took place before commencement, any copy made prior to commencement which would not have been made in infringement of copyright had it been such after commencement may be exploited freely as if it had been made after commencement. (See schedule 1, paragraph 14(4).)   **7.90**

2. Transfer of copies of works in electronic form (s.56)

(a) *Background to the provision*

This is a new provision, which applies to copies of works in electronic   **7.91** form. The obvious example of this is a computer program, and it was in fact computer programs which prompted the inclusion of the provision in the 1988 Act. However, computers and other forms of electronic memory are increasingly used to store other works such as dictionaries and lists of information, and these in themselves will be literary works held in electronic form. In addition, a musical work or sound recording embodied on a tape or compact disc is a work held in electronic form.

As referred to in paragraph 5.18, the normal use of a computer program will usually involve copying of the program and of any underlying works such as musical or artistic works embodied in the program. Where a purchaser buys a computer program, the terms and conditions on which he purchases it may expressly state that certain acts are allowed in relation to the computer program. Even when they do not, it will usually be implied that such copying as may occur in the normal use of a program is licensed and it might be implied that the making of back-up copies is licensed, unless of course express restrictions are included in the terms and conditions of supply. However, if the purchaser has no further use for the computer program, and wishes to sell or otherwise transfer to someone else, the question then arises as to whether the new owner is also licensed to carry out the same acts. He was not a party to the original contract of supply, and, although the vendor to him could probably expressly pass on the benefit of his licence, it is unlikely in practice that the transferor would remember to do this. It is this situation which the provision below is intended to deal with.

(b) *Effect of the provision and conditions for it to apply*

7.92 In order to deal with such subsequent transfer, the 1988 Act provides that anything which the original purchaser was allowed to do, whether expressly or impliedly, may also be done by the new owner without infringing copyright.

The provision does not apply where any of the following terms are expressly included in the original purchase contract:

(i) A term prohibiting the transfer of the copy.

(ii) A term imposing obligations which continue after a transfer.

(iii) A term prohibiting the assignment of any licence.

(iv) A term terminating any licence on a transfer.

(v) Any provision relating to the terms on which the transferee may do the things which the original purchaser was allowed to do.

Obviously, the provision will also not apply where the copy is not purchased, but only rented out. The same would probably be so where title to the copy is retained, and the person to whom it is supplied is merely given certain rights to use it.

(c) *Retention of copies after transfer*

7.93 It was clear that leaving the provision as set out above would have introduced a loophole by which a copy of a computer program might be retained for use by the original purchaser, with the result that one computer program could be copied for use by a whole chain of transferees, without infringing copyright. However, this has been dealt with by providing that any copy, adaptation or copy of an adaptation made by the original purchaser which is not also transferred shall be treated as an infringing copy for all purposes after the transfer. The meaning of the word adaptation is referred to in paragraph 5.52 onwards. This would then allow the provisions on secondary infringement to apply, so that the owner of the copyright in the computer program would have a right of recourse for example against the original purchaser for possession in the course of a trade. There must of course always be the requisite degree of knowledge for the secondary infringement provisions to apply. (See paragraph 6.04.)

(d) *Extension of the provisions to related circumstances*

The provision also applies in the following circumstances: **7.94**

(i) Where the original article is no longer usable, and what is transferred is a copy used in its place. This provision takes account of the fact that such articles as floppy discs fade after a period of time, and become increasingly difficult to load. If in such a case the work held in that form is transferred on to another article, then the provisions referred to above apply to that article.

(ii) To further transfers after the original one. In this way, computer programs can continually be transferred, and use made in accordance with the original terms on which the computer program was supplied without infringing copyright. In each case of course, any copies retained by the transferor will become infringing copies.

(e) *Purchases prior to commencement of the 1988 Act*

The provision does not apply to any copy where its purchase took place before commencement of the 1988 Act. (See schedule 1, paragraph   **7.95**
14(6).)

3. Material open to inspection on a public register

There are three separate new provisions here. The first two of these relate   **7.96**
to material either open to public inspection pursuant to a statutory requirement, or to a register maintained in pursuance of a statutory requirement.

The first provision states that the copyright in any such material as a literary work is not infringed by the copying of so much of the material as contains factual information of any description, provided that the copying is not for a purpose which involves the issuing of copies to the public (s.47(1)). This provision would apply for example to making a copy of a company's annual accounts from that lodged with the Registrar of Companies.

The second permitted act applies where such material contains information about matters of general scientific, technical, commercial or economic interest. Here, copyright is not infringed by the copying or the issuing to the public of copies of the material for the purpose of disseminating that information (s.47(3)). The example given by the Government in debate was a patent specification, although arguably this is a matter of specific rather than general scientific or technical interest.

The last provision relates only to material open to public inspection pursuant to a statutory requirement. Here, copyright is not infringed by the copying of the material or the issuing of it to the public for the purpose of enabling the material to be inspected at a more convenient time or place or otherwise facilitating the exercise of any right for the purpose of which the requirement was imposed (s.47(2)). This for example would apply to planning documents, where someone wants to consider plans with a view to making a submission about a planning application.

There is also power to extend the above provisions to material made open to public inspection by an international organisation, and to any register maintained by an international organisation. No such order has been made at the time of writing.

In each of the above cases, the copying or issuing to the public must be done by or with the authority of the person required to make the material open to public inspection, or, where appropriate, the person maintaining the register.

The Secretary of State also has the power to provide in any of the above cases that the provisions shall only apply to copies which are appropriately marked. No such order has been made at the time of writing.

4. Recording for purposes of time-shifting (s.70)

7.97   Under the 1956 Act, it was not an infringement of copyright in a broadcast or cable programme to make a recording of the broadcast or programme for private purposes. However, this did not apply to works included in the broadcast or programme, whether films or sound recordings, or literary, dramatic, musical or artistic works.

Although the Government did not carry out its proposal to legalise all private recording, it has introduced a new provision which applies to all works and which in practice achieves the same result where the recording is made from a broadcast or cable programme. The provision states that the making for private and domestic use of a recording of a broadcast or cable programme solely for the purpose of enabling it to be viewed or listened to at a more convenient time does not infringe any copyright in the broadcast or cable programme or in any work included in it.

The provision does not require that the recording must be made for the use of the person carrying out the recording. Recording is therefore permitted for a friend or neighbour, provided that it is for such a person's private and domestic use.

It is not certain whether the provision allows anything more than the recording of a broadcast or cable programme for viewing or listening to it once, and once only. The reference is to "*a* more convenient time." However, in practice the point is largely academic because if the person carrying out the recording or the person for whom the recording was made decides later that he wants to retain the recording, the mere retention and continued private use will not render unlawful what was lawfully done in the first place.

A provision in the Bill stating that the recording must be destroyed within 28 days of being carried out was later deleted. In any event, it is unlikely that copyright owners will ever have the evidence to sue on the basis of infringement of copyright where the private recording is carried out for the purposes of retaining the copy permanently, even if they were willing to risk the media opprobrium which would probably follow.

The section does not contain the provision which is found in many other permitted act provisions and which states that any dealing with the copy for other purposes will make that copy an infringing copy. This may in practice bring difficulties of proof where copies of television or radio programmes are found on sale to the public. If the recording was made under the exemption, it would not be possible to apply the acts of secondary infringement, because the original making would not have been an infringement of copyright. It would be possible to prevent such a copy from being issued to the public, but this would only apply to putting it into circulation for the first time, and not to any subsequent dealing with it. All in all, it is hard to resist the feeling that this provision was enacted with little regard for the rights of copyright owners.

5. Subtitled copies of broadcast or cable programmes (s.74)

This provision allows copies of television broadcasts or cable pro-   **7.98**
grammes to be made and issued to the public where this is done for the purpose of providing people who are deaf or hard of hearing or physically or mentally handicapped in other ways with copies which are sub-titled or otherwise modified for their special needs. If the copies are made or issued for that purpose, this does not infringe any copyright in the broadcast or cable programme or any work included in it.

The copying and issuing to the public must be carried out by a designated body, and designation will take place by order of the Secretary of State. This is another instance in which he may not designate a body unless he is satisfied that it is not established or conducted for profit. No order has been made at the time of writing.

Furthermore, this is another instance where the provision does not apply if or to the extent that there is a licensing scheme certified under the provisions referred to in paragraph 9.47 below. Thus again, there is encouragement for copyright owners to put in place and obtain approval for a scheme regulating such recording and providing for the payment of royalties at an acceptable level. If this is not done, the defence will apply, and copyright owners will receive nothing in the way of remuneration.

B. THOSE RELEVANT TO ALL WORKS EXCLUDING BROADCASTS AND CABLE PROGRAMMES

1. The ephemeral exemption (s.68(1))

7.99   The 1956 Act allowed someone who was licensed to broadcast or include in a cable programme a literary, dramatic or musical work, to record the work for the purposes of such broadcasting or inclusion without a separate licence being required for the recording of the work, provided that certain conditions were fulfilled. (See 1956 Act, s.6(7).) This provision has become known as the ephemeral exemption. In its 1988 Act form, the scope has been extended to other works, and to recording by those authorised by the person holding the broadcasting or cable licence.

The new provision applies where by virtue of a licence or assignment of copyright someone is authorised to broadcast or include in a cable programme service a literary, dramatic, musical or artistic work (or an adaptation of such a work), or a sound recording or film.

In the above circumstances, the person who is authorised to broadcast the work or include the work in a cable programme service is treated as being licensed by the copyright owner to do or authorise the doing of any of the following for the purposes of the broadcast or cable programme:

(a) In the case of a literary, dramatic or musical work, to make a sound recording or film of the work.

(b) In the case of an artistic work, to take a photograph or make a film of the work.

(c) In the case of a sound recording or film, to make a copy of it.

There are two conditions, both of which must apply for the relevant copying to be permitted. First, the copy must not be used for any purpose other than for the relevant broadcast or cable programme. Secondly, the copy must be destroyed within 28 days of being first used for broadcasting the work or including it in a cable programme service. If either of these conditions is not fulfilled, the copy is treated as an infringing copy, and provisions relating to secondary infringement could be applied, as referred to in paragraph 6.35, provided that the requisite degree of knowledge is there.

C. THOSE RELEVANT TO LITERARY, DRAMATIC, MUSICAL AND ARTISTIC WORKS

1. Material communicated to the Crown in the course of public business (s.48)

7.100   This is a new provision which applies where a literary, dramatic, musical or artistic work has been communicated to the Crown in the course of public business for any purpose by or with the licence of the copyright owner, and where a document or other material thing recording or embodying the work is owned by or in the custody or control of the Crown. The expression "public business" includes any activity carried on by the Crown. A simple example might be a written submission to a Government Department on a matter of current public interest.

In these circumstances, the Crown may copy the work and issue copies of the work to the public, provided that this is for the purpose for which the work was communicated to the Crown, or any related purpose which could reasonably have been anticipated by the copyright owner. Thus, taking the above example, this would probably allow copying of the submission and distribution to other Government Departments for comment, and perhaps including the submission or an extract from it in a Green Paper inviting comments on a proposed change in legislation.

The provision does not apply where the work has previously been published, but for these purposes one ignores any publication which takes place by virtue of the provision itself.

The provision is also subject to any agreement to the contrary between the Crown and the copyright owner. There must be an agreement for this to have effect, not merely a statement by the copyright owner that no consent was granted for copying or issuing to the public.

2. Sound recordings of public readings or recitations (s.59(2))

The making of a sound recording of a reading or recitation which is permitted under the provision referred to in paragraph 7.110 below is not an infringement of copyright. See that paragraph for further details of this.

7.101

3. Abstracts of scientific or technical articles (s.60)

This provision applies where an article on a scientific or technical subject is published in a periodical accompanied by an abstract indicating the contents of the article. An abstract is a summary, and this might be given at the start of the article, or in a general index of the contents of the periodical. The scope of the phrase "scientific or technical" is not entirely clear. In particular, the word "technical" is commonly used to describe not only industrial, practical or mechanical disciplines, but also particular aspects of many of the arts.

7.102

In these circumstances, it is not an infringement of copyright in the abstract or in the article to copy the abstract or issue copies of it to the public. Thus, it would be possible in the future for a scientific periodical not only to include its own material on a particular subject, but also to include summaries of other articles on the same subject if those summaries were taken from other periodicals. It would not however allow the periodical to make its own summary of an article, although this might not in any event amount to copying a substantial part of the abstract or article. The provision also does not apply to the typographical arrangement of published editions.

This is another instance where the provision does not apply if or to the extent that there is a licensing scheme certified as referred to in paragraph 9.47 below. Again therefore, if the copyright owners obtain certification for such a scheme, they will receive recompense for such use, but if they do not, there is an absolute defence to an infringement of copyright claim.

4. The statutory recording licence (Sched. 1, para. 21)

7.103   Under the 1956 Act, it was not an infringement of copyright to make records of a musical work and any associated words such as the lyrics in the case of a song, provided that certain conditions were complied with (1956 Act, s.8). The conditions were as follows:

(a) Records of the work had previously been made in or imported into the United Kingdom for the purposes of retail sale by or with the licence of the owner of the copyright in the work.

(b) Before making the record, the manufacturer gave to the owner of the copyright notice in prescribed form of his intention to make it. This for example had to include details of the number of records which he intended to sell.

(c) The manufacturer intended to sell the record by retail, or to supply it for the purpose of its being sold by retail by another person, or intended to use it for making other records which were to be sold or supplied.

(d) In the case of a record sold by retail, the manufacturer paid the copyright owner a royalty of 6¼ per cent. of the ordinary retail selling price of the record, subject to a statutory minimum rate for each work.

The Copyright Royalty System (Records) Regulations 1957 laid down what had to appear in the notice referred to above, and details as to the timing and calculation of the royalties. Both the provisions in the Act itself and in the Regulations were complex and cumbersome, and in practice agreements were entered into between representatives of the record industry and representatives of the music copyright owners providing for a more workable system, although still within the context of the Act and Regulations.

The 1988 Act repeals the provision, and for the future licences will be required for the making of records embodying copyright musical works and their associated words just as with the copying of any other work. Transitional provisions however provide that a notice to make records given before the commencement of the 1988 Act will continue to have effect but only as regards the making of records within one year of the repeal coming into force and up to the number of records specified in the notice.

Although service of such notices before the commencement of the 1956 Act will allow a record company to make records without infringing copyright (provided the other conditions such as payment of royalties are observed), the *issuing* of the records to the public is a separate restricted act, and no provision has been made permitting the issue of such records. It is arguable therefore that consent for this will still be necessary, since the provisions of the 1988 Act apply to all acts done after commencement.

5. Copying of artistic works on public display (s.62)

The 1988 Act re-enacts the provision in the 1956 Act allowing copying for   **7.104**
whatever purpose of certain artistic works on public display (1956 Act, s.9(3)).

The provision in the 1988 Act applies to any building, and the definition of this now includes any part of a building. So it would apply to a room in a building, even though it was not normally open to the public, although of course the proprietor would still be able to impose a contractual condition of entry that, for example, no photography should take place. It also applies to sculptures, models for buildings, and works of artistic craftsmanship, but only if they are permanently situated in a public place, or in premises open to the public.

The copyright in such a work is not infringed by either making a graphic work representing it, or making a photograph or film of it. In addition, the issue to the public of copies made in accordance with this provision is permitted without infringing copyright. The same applies where such a copy is broadcast or included in a cable programme service. Such exploitation is also allowed where the copy was made before commencement of the 1988 Act. (See schedule 1, paragraph 14(4).)

6. Copying of artistic works for the purposes of advertising the sale of a work (s.63)

This provision applies to all artistic works, and states that it is not an   **7.105**
infringement of copyright in such a work to copy it for the purpose of advertising the sale of the work. Neither is it an infringement of copyright to issue copies to the public for the same purpose. There was no similar provision in the 1956 Act.

The provision only applies to the sale of a work, not a copy of a work. Thus, it would apply in the case of the sale of a painting, but not the sale of a book which includes a copy of that painting.

If a copy the making of which was permitted as a result of this section is then sold or let for hire, offered or exposed for sale or hire, or distributed or exhibited in public for any other purpose, then the copy is treated as an infringing copy as regards any such act and for all subsequent purposes. This would enable the provisions on secondary infringement to be applied, provided that the requisite degree of knowledge was present. (See paragraph 6.04 above.)

7. Making of subsequent works by the same artist (s.64)

This provision is another re-enactment from the 1956 Act (1956 Act,   **7.106** s.9(9)) and again applies to all artistic works. Where the author of an artistic work is not the copyright owner, he does not infringe the copyright by copying the work in the course of making another artistic work. However, he will infringe copyright if he repeats or imitates the main design of the earlier work.

The subsequent artistic work need not be of the same type as the earlier one. Thus, the first work may be a sculpture, and the second a painting.

Although the expression "making another artistic work" could apply to a photograph, it would appear to be impossible to take a photograph certainly of the whole work without this being a repeat or imitation of the main design of the earlier work.

Only copying is not an infringement of copyright, and the issue of copies to the public could still be an infringement.

D. PROVISION RELEVANT TO OTHER WORKS

Making photographs of television or cable programmes

7.107   As stated above in paragraph 7.97, the making for private and domestic use of a recording of a broadcast or cable programme for the purposes of time-shifting does not infringe copyright in the broadcast or cable programme or any work included in it. The provision here goes further, and allows the making for any private and domestic use of a photograph of the whole or any part of an image forming part of a television broadcast or cable programme. It also allows the making of a copy of such a photograph, again if it is for private and domestic use. In these circumstances, the copying does not infringe any copyright either in the broadcast or cable programme or in any film included in it. It might, however, infringe the copyright in another work such as an artistic work, although it must be remembered here that the definition of artistic work does not include a photograph which is part of a film.

As with the time-shifting exemption, there are again no provisions relating to subsequent dealing with any such photograph, although the issuing to the public of such a copy would be an infringement.

VI PROVISIONS RELATING TO INFRINGEMENT BY ISSUING COPIES TO THE PUBLIC

A. THE ISSUING TO THE PUBLIC OF COPIES OF WORKS THE MAKING OF WHICH WAS A PERMITTED ACT

7.108   In some cases, copies of works the making of which was permitted under the provisions referred to in section v above can be issued to the public without infringing copyright. These are as follows, and reference should be made to the relevant paragraph for fuller details:

(a) The issuing to the public of copies of a work in the form of an artistic work, sound recording, film, broadcast or cable programme or copy thereof where the making thereof was not an infringement of copyright because the work was only included there incidentally. (See paragraph 7.86.)

(b) The issuing to the public of copies of the report of a Royal Commission or Statutory Inquiry containing a work or material from it. (See paragraph 7.72.)

(c) The issuing to the public of copies of certain material open to public inspection. (See paragraph 7.96.)

(d) The issuing to the public of copies of television broadcasts or cable programmes for the purpose of providing people who are deaf or hard of hearing or otherwise physically or mentally handicapped with copies which are subtitled or otherwise modified for their special needs. (See paragraph 7.98.)

(e) The issuing to the public of copies of an abstract of an article on a scientific or technical subject. (See paragraph 7.102.)

(f) The issuing to the public of certain copies of certain artistic works on public display. (See paragraph 7.104.)

(g) The issuing to the public of copies of an artistic work for the purpose of advertising the sale of the work. (See paragraph 7.105.)

B. RENTAL OF SOUND RECORDINGS, FILMS AND COMPUTER PROGRAMS (s.66)

The 1988 Act contains a provision whereby the Secretary of State is able **7.109** to order that the rental of a copy of a sound recording, film or computer program be treated as licensed by the copyright owner, subject only to the payment of such reasonable royalty or other payment as may be agreed, or (in default of agreement) determined by the Copyright Tribunal. It is possible for such an order to lay down different provisions for different cases, by reference to the nature of the copies, the identity of the rental operation or the circumstances in which rental takes place.

This is another provision where there is encouragement for the relevant copyright owners to obtain certification of a licensing scheme as referred to in paragraph 9.47 onwards. If or to the extent that there is such a licensing scheme certified, no order under this provision will apply.

At the time of writing, no such order has been made. Before the Standing Committee dealing with the Bill in its passage through the

House of Commons, the Government representative made it clear that this would for example be applied in the case of rental or loan of records by public libraries, if the copyright owners were unable to obtain agreement or approval for a scheme for such rental with representatives of such public libraries.

If the Secretary of State were to make such an order as is referred to above, and no agreement could be reached as to the level of royalties, then either the copyright owner or the person claiming to be treated as licensed by him may apply to the Copyright Tribunal (s.142). The Tribunal will make such order as it may determine to be reasonable in the circumstances. (See paragraph 9.93.) Applications to vary an order may be made by either party, but not for 12 months after the relevant order, unless the Tribunal gives special leave. Orders varying an original order only take effect from the date on which they are made, or such later date as the Tribunal may specify.

VII PROVISIONS RELATING TO INFRINGEMENT BY PUBLIC PERFORMANCE OR PLAYING OR SHOWING IN PUBLIC

A. PUBLIC READING OR RECITATION (s.59)

7.110 As under the 1956 Act (see s.6(5)) the reading or recitation in public by one person of a reasonable extract from a published literary or dramatic work does not infringe copyright, provided that it is accompanied by a sufficient acknowledgement. See paragraph 7.65 for comments on the definition of the sufficient acknowledgement.

The defence was lost under the 1956 Act if the reading or recitation was carried out for the purposes of broadcasting. This no longer applies, and indeed the provision has been extended. It is now possible to make a sound recording (which would include the sound-track of a film), or broadcast or include in a cable programme service such a reading or recitation, provided that this consists mainly of material in relation to which it is not necessary to rely on the defence. This would be so if for example the material is in the public domain, or the relevant use has been licensed.

It should be noted that the new provisions do not extend as far as playing or showing in public a sound recording, the making of which was not an infringement of copyright because of this section. Thus, it may not be an infringement of copyright to make a sound-track of such a reading or recitation for the purposes of inclusion in a film, but it might be an infringement of copyright to play the sound-track in public, unless one of the other permitted acts applied.

B. PLAYING OR SHOWING IN PUBLIC OF COPIES OF WORKS INCIDENTALLY INCLUDED IN OTHER WORKS (s.31 (2))

The playing or showing in public of a sound recording, film, broadcast or cable programme which incidentally includes another work is not an infringement of copyright. (See paragraph 7.86 above.)   **7.111**

C. PLAYING OF SOUND RECORDINGS FOR CLUB OR SOCIETY PURPOSES (s.67)

The 1956 Act contained various exceptions as regards the exclusive right of causing a sound recording to be heard in public. One of these is referred to in paragraph 7.113. A further exception (1956 Act, s.12(7) (a)), where the sound recording was caused to be heard in public at any premises where persons reside or sleep as part of the amenities provided exclusively or mainly for residents or inmates, has been repealed. The other main exception has been re-enacted in the 1988 Act.   **7.112**

The provision states that it is not an infringement of copyright in a sound recording to play it as part of the activities of, or for the benefit of, a club, society or other organisation, provided that certain conditions are fulfilled. It should be noted that the permitted act only applies to sound recordings, not to works (such as musical works) included in them.

These conditions are as follows:

(a) The club, society or other organisation must not be established or conducted for profit. This does not mean that the relevant organisation must not *make* a profit, but this must not be what it was founded for or run for.

(b) The main objects of the club, society or other organisation must be charitable or otherwise concerned with the advancement of religion, education or social welfare. The scope of this provision is not certain, but, having regard to the second half of the phrase, it is clear that the relevant organisation need not be charitable in the technical sense of that word. There is no requirement therefore that the club or society must be both beneficial and available to a sufficient section of the community, or that the purposes must be exclusively charitable.

(c) The proceeds of any charge or admission to the place where the recording is to be heard must be applied solely for the purposes of the relevant organisation. So, the provision would not apply where the proceeds are to be applied for another such organisation.

D. FREE SHOWING OR PLAYING OF BROADCASTS OR CABLE PROGRAMMES (s.72)

1. Comparison with the 1956 Act

Under the 1956 Act, copyright owners of films and sound recordings were   **7.113**

199

not able to enforce the exclusive right of causing their works to be seen or heard in public, where this was by means of the reception of a broadcast made by the BBC or the IBA (1956 Act, s.40(1) and (2)). These provisions no longer apply, but the circumstances in which such a copyright owner may enforce the exclusive right under the 1988 Act of playing or showing the work in public will still be limited. This is because the 1956 Act provision relating to broadcasts and cable programmes by which it was only an infringement of copyright to cause them to be heard or seen in public if the audience was a paying audience has been extended to sound recordings and films included in such broadcasts or cable programmes.

2. The new provision

7.114 The provision states that the showing or playing in public of a broadcast or cable programme to an audience who have not paid for admission to the place where the broadcast or programme is to be seen or heard does not infringe any copyright in the broadcast or cable programme, or in any sound recording or film included in either of them.

If the audience has paid for admission to a place of which the place where the showing or playing in public is taking place forms part, then the exemption does not apply. This would apply for example to a leisure park where payment is made at the entrance for all the facilities, and one of those facilities is a discotheque.

3. Paying for admission

7.115 An audience is also treated as having paid for admission to a place if certain conditions in relation to the price of goods or services supplied at that place (or a place of which it forms part) are fulfilled. The goods or services may be of any type, and need not be related to the broadcast or cable programme or the playing or showing thereof. The conditions are either that the prices are substantially attributable to the facilities afforded for seeing or hearing the broadcast or programme, or exceed those usually charged there and are partly attributable to those facilities.

Here, the 1988 Act has introduced a change, although it is hard to assess in practice what difference the change will make. The 1956 Act stated that the prices must **both** exceed those usually charged at the relevant place **and** be partly attributable to those facilities. Now, the prices may be the same, but the exception will still not apply if they are substantially attributable to the facilities for seeing or hearing the broadcast or programme.

The problem obviously lies in construing what "substantially" means in this context. It may not have the same effect as stating that a substantial portion of the price has to be attributable to the cost of the provision of facilities for seeing or hearing the broadcast or programme. What it seems to envisage is that one looks at the total price, and examines whether that is substantially attributable to such facilities. In practice, this may well be difficult to show in many cases such as cafes and restaurants where the presence of large numbers of television screens provides an attraction to the public, but where the cafe or restaurant cannot charge that much more than prices at other cafes or restaurants not having those facilities without driving its customers away.

4. Further cases where the provision applies

Even if the audience is one which has paid for admission to a place or is **7.116** treated as having paid for admission under the above rules, there are some instances in which the exception still applies so that no licence will be required. These are as follows:

(a) Where the relevant person is admitted as a resident or inmate of the place. One must be careful here to identify the place referred to. If a discotheque in a hotel admits a resident free of charge, he is not to be regarded as having paid for admission simply because he has paid for his hotel room. On the other hand, if there is an additional charge for going into the discotheque, the exception does not apply. This is because the person is not admitted as a resident or inmate of the place for which admission was charged, that is the discotheque itself.

(b) Persons admitted as members of a club or society, where the payment is only for membership of the club or society and the provision of the facilities is only incidental to the main purposes of the club or society. There is some overlap here with the provision referred to in paragraph 7.112 above. The club could be a members' club or a proprietary club. However, any club whose main purpose is the entertainment of people involving the use of music is unlikely to fall within this provision.

5. Infringing broadcasts or cable programme transmissions

The defence applies even where the making of the broadcast or inclusion **7.117** of the programme in a cable programme service was an infringement of copyright. If it was, the fact that it was heard or seen in public is a matter to be taken into account in assessing damages for infringement by broadcasting or including the programme in a cable programme service. Somewhat oddly, the relevant part of the provision does not state that it is material only where there was an audience which had paid for admission to the relevant place, although this might be a matter taken into account by the courts under the normal rules as to damages.

6. No application to literary, dramatic, musical or artistic works

The exception only applies to sound recordings or films included in the **7.118** relevant broadcast or cable programme. A licence is still required for public performance of any literary, dramatic or musical works included in the broadcast or cable programme.

VIII PROVISIONS RELATING TO INFRINGEMENT BY BROADCASTING

A. BROADCASTING AND INCIDENTAL INCLUSION (s.31(2))

7.119   A broadcast which incidentally includes another work of any nature does not infringe the copyright in that work. Furthermore, the broadcasting of an artistic work, sound recording, film, broadcast or cable programme which incidentally includes a work is not an infringement of copyright in that latter work. (See paragraph 7.86 above.)

B. PUBLIC READING AND RECITATION (s.59(2))

7.120   The broadcasting of a reading or recitation in public by one person of a reasonable extract from a published literary or dramatic work does not in certain circumstances infringe any copyright in the latter work. (See paragraph 7.110 above.)

C. ARTISTIC WORKS ON PUBLIC DISPLAY (s.62(3))

7.121   The broadcasting of certain artistic works on public display does not infringe copyright in the latter, and neither does the broadcasting of a graphic work representing any such artistic work, or a photograph or film of any such work. (See paragraph 7.104 above.)

IX PROVISIONS RELATING TO INFRINGEMENT BY CABLE PROGRAMME SERVICE TRANSMISSION

A. CABLE PROGRAMMES AND INCIDENTAL INCLUSION (s.31(2))

7.122   The incidental inclusion of a work in a cable programme does not infringe the copyright in that work. Furthermore, the inclusion in a cable programme service of an artistic work, sound recording, film, broadcast or cable programme which incidentally includes a work is not an infringement of copyright in that latter work. (See paragraph 7.86 above.)

B. PUBLIC READING AND RECITATION (s.59(2))

The inclusion in a cable programme service of a reading or recitation in   **7.123**
public by one person of a reasonable extract from an published literary or
dramatic work does not infringe any copyright in the latter work. (See
paragraph 7.110 above.)

C. ARTISTIC WORKS ON PUBLIC DISPLAY (s.62(3))

The inclusion in a cable programme service of certain artistic works on   **7.124**
public display does not infringe copyright in the latter, and neither does
the inclusion in a cable programme service of a graphic work representing
any such artistic work, or a photograph or film of any such work. (See
paragraph 7.104 above.)

D. RECEPTION AND RETRANSMISSION OF BROADCASTS IN CABLE PROGRAMME SERVICES (s.73)

This provision re-enacts (with some modifications to reflect new defini-   **7.125**
tions for broadcasting and cable transmission) the provisions in the 1956
Act by which in certain circumstances a cable operator was able to receive
and immediately retransmit a broadcast without infringing copyright by
the inclusion of the broadcast (or the underlying works) in a cable
programme (1956 Act, s.40(3)). This is a matter of some controversy,
particularly in relation to works the subject of the Berne Convention
(literary, dramatic, musical and artistic works, and films) by which the
author is meant to have the exclusive right of authorising any communication to the public of the performance of their work. Where a broadcast
takes place, is received and then transmitted by a cable service operator,
two restricted acts occur, firstly the original broadcast, and secondly the
cable service transmission. However, in circumstances where the broadcast is immediately re-transmitted by cable, many jurisdictions, including
the United Kingdom, take the view that the cable transmission is merely
an extension to the original broadcast, and accordingly should not require
a separate licence. The provision dealt with in this paragraph defines the
circumstances in which this applies.

The provision applies only where a broadcast is made from a place in
the United Kingdom and where the broadcast is by reception and immediate retransmission included in a cable programme service. It does not
therefore apply in the case of a satellite broadcast unless the place from
which the signals carrying the broadcast are transmitted to the satellite is
in the United Kingdom. It also therefore does not apply to delayed relays.

Under section 13 of the Cable and Broadcasting Act 1984, there is a
duty on the Cable Authority to require that licensed cable services

provided by any person in any area transmit as part of their service the
local BBC or IBA programming. Where the BBC (or as the case may be
IBA) broadcasts are contained in two or more programme schedules, the
duty relates first to those programmes broadcast for reception in the
greatest part of the relevant area, but, if this cannot be applied, the
relevant broadcasting authorit may designate whichever schedule it
chooses. Whichever broadcasts the Cable Authority requires the cable
service operator to include under these provisions, the inclusion of such
broadcast in the service does not infringe the copyright in the broadcast or
in any work included in the broadcast.

Inclusion of a broadcast in a cable programme service by reception and
immediate retransmission is also not an infringement of copyright even
where there is no such requirement under the 1984 Act, but where the
cable programme service operator in any event receives and immediately
transmits a broadcast which is made for reception in the area in which the
cable programme service is provided. This might apply for example to
local programming which was one of the alternatives which the Cable
Authority could have designated under the 1984 Act but where it chose
another schedule instead. In the case of the copyright in the broadcast
itself (as opposed to the copyright in the underlying works), there is an
additional requirement for the permitted act to apply, and that is that the
broadcast must not be a satellite transmission nor an encrypted transmission. (See paragraph 1.51.)

As regards the copyright in the works included in the broadcast, the
provision applies whether or not the original broadcasting of the work
was authorised. However, if it was unauthorised, the fact that retransmission took place as part of a cable programme service is a factor to be taken
into account in assessing damages for infringement of copyright by the
original broadcast.

X COPYRIGHT AND THE PUBLIC INTEREST

7.126   The1988 Act states that nothing in the copyright provisions contained in
the Act affects any rule of law preventing or restricting the enforcement
of copyright, on grounds of public interest or otherwise (s.171(3).)

It has long been settled that the courts will protect the secrecy of
confidential information by restraining breaches of confidence, unless
such breaches can be justified. Until recently, there was doubt as to
whether any such breach could ever be justified except where some
iniquity such as a serious misdeed or misconduct was being disclosed.
There was also doubt whether such a defence would in any event operate
in the same way in an action for infringement of copyright. These two
points were however dealt with by the Court of Appeal in *Lion Laboratories Ltd.* v. *Evans* ([1985] Q.B. 526).

Very often, a breach of confidence will involve infringement of copyright. If an employee of a company leaks a document to the press, he may well have taken a copy of the document and supplied that copy. Such a copy would have been made in infringement of copyright, and under the 1956 Act the copyright owner was deemed to be the owner of the copy, and therefore entitled to its return. If the document is then included in a newspaper, further infringement will take place by the newspaper, first by reproducing the document in the form of the newspaper, and secondly by issuing copies of the newspaper including the document to the public.

In the *Beloff* v. *Pressdram* case ([1973] 1 All E.R. 241), Ungoed-Thomas J. held that a breach of confidence could be justified not only where there was some serious misdeed or criminal misconduct, but also where it was otherwise in the public interest:

> "The defence of public interest clearly covers and, in the authorities does not extend beyond, disclosure, which as Lord Denning M.R. emphasised must be disclosure justified in the public interest, of matters carried out or contemplated, in breach of the country's security, or in breach of laws, including statutory duty, fraud, or otherwise destructive of the country or its people, including matters medically dangerous to the public; and doubtless other misdeeds of similar gravity. Public interest, as a defence in law, operates to override the rights of the individual (including copyright) which would otherwise prevail and which the law is also concerned to protect. Such public interest, as now recognised by the law, does not extend beyond misdeeds of a serious nature and importance to the country and thus, in my view, clearly recognisable as such."

This broader approach was confirmed by the Court of Appeal in the *Lion Laboratories* case, and in the *Spycatcher* case *A.-G.* v. *Guardian Newpapers Ltd. (No. 2)* ([1988] 3 All E.R. 545). In the *Lion Laboratories* case, employees of a company manufacturing the Intoximeter machine used by the police for measuring intoxication by alcohol leaked to the press confidential internal memoranda casting doubt on the accuracy of the machine's readings. The Court of Appeal refused to grant an interlocutory injunction restraining the publication of some of the memoranda, on the basis that the relevant documents raised a serious question as to whether wrongful convictions of a serious criminal offence were taking place.

None of the judges in the *Lion Laboratories* or *Spycatcher* case were prepared to define the circumstances in which a public interest defence would apply. However, all the members of the Court of Appeal in *Lion Laboratories* made it clear that it was an exceptional case. In emphasising that the judgment was not intended to be a "mole's charter," it was said by one or more of the members of the Court of Appeal as follows:

(a) In considering whether it is in the public interest to make known certain information, one must not confuse this with making known what is interesting to the public.

(b) One must also beware of confusing the public interest with the media's interest in publishing what appeals to the public thereby increasing the public's interest in the relevant newspaper or other media.

(c) It is not in every case that the public interest will be best served by publication in the media. One must also consider whether it would not be better for an informer to give the confidential information not to the press but to the police or some other responsible body.

It was also held by the Court of Appeal that the defence operated both in relation to breach of confidence and infringement of copyright. Although there is no requirement that the relevant restricted act involved be carried out or threatened in the context of disclosure of confidential information, it seems more likely that the defence will operate in a copyright infringement action where there is also an action for breach of confidence.

Both the *Beloff* v. *Pressdram* and *Lion Laboratories* cases were cited with approval in the *Spycatcher* case. Some of the judges in that case in the Court of Appeal also emphasised that a mere allegation of iniquity will be insufficient. In the words of Lord Goff:

> "A mere allegation of iniquity is not of itself sufficient to justify disclosure in the public interest. Such an allegation will only do so if, following such investigations as are reasonably open to the recipient, and having regard to all the circumstances of the case, the allegation in question can reasonably be regarded as being a credible allegation from an apparently reliable source."

8 SUBSEQUENT OWNERSHIP

I INTRODUCTION

Chapter 3 dealt with the provisions in the 1988 Act on first ownership. This Chapter deals with ownership apart from ownership under those provisions. **8.01**

   In the circumstances referred to in sections II and III below, the copyright in a work may belong to someone other than the first owner with effect from when it is created. However, it is still important to keep in mind the identity of the first owner. This is so partly because there are circumstances in which the interest in a copyright acquired by such means may be defeated (see paragraph 8.13), and also because of the provisions on moral rights (see Chapter 11).

1. Gifts and sales of articles

The gift or sale of an article which embodies a copyright work or a copy of such a work does not prima facie include the copyright. For example, the purchase of a painting does not operate so as to vest its copyright in the purchaser. At all times, one must bear in mind the distinction between the physical property in the article, and the copyright embodied in that article. The sole exception to this rule is referred to in paragraph 8.21 below. **8.02**

2. Summary of the law

In summary, copyright in a work, or a right which forms part of the copyright, may be acquired as follows: **8.03**

(a) Although the legal title to the copyright may belong to the first owner or a subsequent owner, the beneficial ownership may under equitable rules lie elsewhere.

(b) The work may be the subject of an agreement as to future copyright, and the copyright thereby automatically vest in the assignee as soon as it is created.

(c) After the death of an owner, it may have either been transmitted under the will of the deceased, or under an intestacy.

(d) Upon liquidation of a company, or bankruptcy of an individual, it may form part of assets to be dealt with upon liquidation of a company, or bankruptcy of an individual.

(e) The copyright may have been assigned, wholly or in part.

(f) The rights may have reverted to the author or his personal representatives, either under the so-called substituted right provisions or reversionary right provisions previously in the 1911 Act. The former apply only to pre-1911 Act works and the latter only to grants of rights between the 1911 and 1956 Acts.

(g) An agreement under which the copyright was assigned may have been set aside, and an order made by the court for the return of the copyright to the assignor.

3. Changes under the 1988 Act

8.04   The 1988 Act has made few changes to the previous law in this area. The only one of substance relates to devolution by will. Under the 1956 Act, the bequest in a will of an unpublished manuscript or artistic work included the copyright in the work, unless there was a contrary intention in the will. The 1988 Act extends this to *any* document or article embodying such a work, and also to the copyright in sound recordings and films. (See paragraph 8.24.)

II EQUITABLE OWNERSHIP

8.05   In certain limited circumstances, the copyright in a work will belong in law to one person as a result of the rules on first ownership or otherwise, but, because of the relationship between that person and another party, ownership of the copyright in equity lies with the latter.

1. Circumstances giving rise to ownership in equity

It is not possible to define precisely the circumstances in which this can happen, but examples appear below:

(a) *Where someone who is not an employee is commissioned to create a copyright work in circumstances where it is an implied term of the contract that copyright will vest in the commissioner*

8.06   Unlike the 1988 Act, the 1911 and 1956 Acts both contained provisions by which the copyright in certain commissioned works vested automatically in the commissioner as first owner. Even where these provisions did not apply, the courts were on occasions prepared to imply a term into the agreement under which the copyright work was created to the effect that the party commissioning the creation of the work owned its copyright in equity. These cases are probably still of relevance today, but not every commissioned copyright work will belong to the commissioner in equity, and the circumstances in which this will happen must to some extent be regarded as exceptional. It is as well here to remember that a court will only imply terms into a contract in very limited circumstances. It will generally only do so where it is necessary to give business efficacy to the contract or, as it is sometimes put, where if the parties had been asked by an officious bystander whether or not a particular term applied they would have replied testily "of course."

One example is as follows. The creation of such works as films, operas, ballets and musical plays very often necessarily involves the prior creation of individual constituents of the work which are copyright works in their own right. If such an individual constituent is created by another party for the specific purpose of it being incorporated into the larger work under a contract by which that party is paid for creating the work, it may be possible to argue successfully that the copyright in the individual constitutent part is owned in equity by the party paying for the work to be done. This happened for example in *Massine* v. *de Basil* ([1936–45] MacG. Cop. Cas. 223). There, one of the principal dancers at the Ballets Russes was contracted not only as a dancer but a choreographer, and was bound under his contract to create and supply the choreography for ballets to be produced by the company. He was paid a monthly salary for doing this, and indeed one of the grounds for the decision that the person responsible for creating the ballet as a whole owned the copyright in the choreography was because the choreographer was an employee. However it was said by the Court of Appeal that even if he were not, the copyright would in equity belong to the creator of the ballet. This was because:

> "The choreography was but one part of a composite whole. The defendant had paid the money under the agreement for the supplying to his ballet of a part which was necessary for its completeness, and unless he was entitled to the copyright in that part of the ballet he would not be getting that benefit from the contract which must have been the intention of the parties."

It is however very difficult to draw a line between a case such as the one above and the situation where the party ordering the work to be done only obtains an implied licence to use the copyright work for the purposes for which it was created. The court in the *Massine* case was undoubtedly influenced by the fact that their view was that the choreographer was an employee anyway.

The same result can occur in circumstances other than where the work is being created for inclusion in a larger whole. This is particularly so in the area of designs, where an independent contractor is commissioned to design an article on the basis of instructions from the party contracting for the creation of the design. The greater the degree of control over the design, whether by way of the original specification or requirement for subsequent amendment, the more likely it is that it will be held that in equity the copyright is owned by the person ordering the work to be done. Thus, in *Ironside* v. *H.M. Attorney-General* ([1988] R.P.C. 197) the plaintiff won a competition for the design of the new 1971 decimal coinage. After his designs were selected, many alterations and additions were made as required by the Royal Mint. It was held by Whitford J. that the payment made to the plaintiff included the copyright in the designs.

(b) *Where a work is created by one or more partners in a firm, and is partnership property*

8.07   Under the rules referred to in Chapter 3, it is possible for the partners of a firm to be first owners of the copyright in a work jointly either as joint authors or joint owners. There no problem arises as regards legal title to the copyright. Where one or more but not all of the partners create a copyright work or acquire it, they will hold the copyright in trust for the partners as a whole if the copyright is partnership property. The rules on when property is treated as partnership property are too complex to be set out here. In general, there is a presumption that the property is owned by the partnership either where it is purchased out of partnership money or where it is both used and treated as being owned by the partners. In *Roban Jig & Tool Co. Ltd.* v. *Taylor* ([1979] F.S.R. 130), it was accepted by the court that engineering drawings were prepared by one of the partners for the partnership and that therefore the partnership owned the copyrights in such drawings in equity.

(c) *Where a director of a company who is not an employee creates a work either for the company of which he is a director or in the course of his duties as a director of that company*

8.08   In *Antocks Lairn Ltd.* v. *I. Bloohn Ltd.* ([1971] F.S.R. 490), it was held that the managing director of a furniture manufacturing company who created certain drawings of chairs held the copyright in the drawings in trust for the company, and would have to assign the copyright in them to his company if and when called upon to do so.

(d) *Where an enforceable contract is entered into by which one party agrees to assign the copyright to another, but fails to effect a written assignment*

8.09   Provided that the contract is supported by consideration, the contract will create an equitable interest in favour of the party to whom the copyright was intended to be assigned. This is clearly so where the agreement to assign is in writing, and in *Western Front Limited* v. *Vestron Inc.* ([1987]) F.S.R. 66), it was held by Peter Gibson J. that an oral contract to assign could also create such an equitable interest.

(e) *Where a work is written in breach of a duty of confidence*

8.10   In the *Spycatcher* case, *Attorney-General* v. *Guardian Newspapers Ltd.* ([1987] 1 W.L.R. 1248) four out of five judges in the House of Lords suggested that the copyright in the literary work might belong in equity to the Crown, since it had been written in breach of the duty of confidence which the writer of the work owed to the Crown as a former member of the British Secret Service. It is not clear whether this view was based on the specific relationship between a member of the Secret Service with the Crown, or whether it is of more general application. Certainly, in the judgment of Lord Goff the suggestion is put in very wide terms.

If the views expressed by the House of Lords in that case are of general application, the question arises whether similar considerations might apply to a copyright work based on existing copyright material and made without the consent of the copyright owner of the latter. In *Redwood Music Ltd*. v. *Chappell & Co. Ltd*. ([1982] R.P.C. 109) Robert Goff J. held that the copyright in such a work would still vest in the writer of that work whether or not this is still good law remains to be seen, but there are fundamental differences between the law on breach of confidence and the law of copyright which would justify a distinction being made.

2. The effect of ownership in equity

Where under the above rules a party is in equity entitled to a copyright, **8.11** that party is prima facie able to compel the transfer of the legal interest to him. However, there are circumstances in which the courts will refuse to grant an order requiring such transfer. (See paragraph 8.13(e) below.)

Unless the owner in equity acquires the legal title to the copyright, he may be faced with two problems. First, as referred to in paragraph 10.18, he may be faced with procedural problems in actions for infringement of copyright. Secondly, if the legal owner assigns the copyright to a bona fide purchaser for value without notice of the equitable interest, the equitable owner's interest will be defeated, and he will be left only with a claim for damages against the party who assigned the legal title.

III ASSIGNMENT OF FUTURE COPYRIGHT (s.91)

1. Pre-1956 Act future assignments

Before the 1956 Act, it was not possible to assign the copyright in a work **8.12** prior to the work coming into existence. A purported assignment was valid in equity, and would prima facie entitle the intended assignee to call for an assignment to be made, as referred to in paragraph 8.11. Although the 1956 Act made provision for the assignment of future copyrights, the provision had no effect (and continues to have no effect under the 1988 Act) as regards agreements made before commencement of the 1956 Act. In those cases, it is still necessary to examine whether there has been a subsequent assignment of the copyright after the work is created, and, if not, whether the owner in equity is entitled to call for an assignment of the legal title to be made.

2. 1988 Act provision

The provision in the 1988 Act is virtually identical to that in the 1956 Act **8.13**

(1956 Act, s.37), except in one respect which will be dealt with later in this section. What is set out below may therefore be applied to assignments under the 1956 Act as well as the 1988 Act. The provision applies where there is an agreement made in relation to future copyright which is signed by or on behalf of the prospective owner of the copyright, and where the prospective owner purports to assign the future copyright in whole or in part to another person. If, on the copyright coming into existence, the assignee or another person claiming under him would be entitled as against all other persons to require the copyright to be vested in him, the copyright vests in the assignee or his successor in title.

A number of specific points need to be made about this provision:

(a) *Prospective owner*

The prospective owner of the copyright may be the author of the work, or, in the case of a work made by an employee in the course of employment, his employer. Care must be taken in order to ensure that the correct person assigns.

(b) *Purports to assign*

In order to ensure that an agreement falls within the provision, it is necessary that the prospective owner purports to assign the copyright, not simply to agree to assign it at a later date.

(c) *Subsequent purported assignment*

If after such an agreement is entered into, the prospective owner purports to assign the future copyright again, even if to a bona fide purchaser for value without notice, that person's claim will rank behind the claim of the first assignee.

(d) *Assignment by assignee*

The provision not only applies to an assignment by the prospective first owner of the copyright, but also to subsequent assignments on from the prospective assignee before the copyright comes into existence.

(e) *Entitlement to require vesting*

The major problem with the provision is that it only applies where the assignee or person claiming under him would be entitled as against all other persons to require the copyright to be vested in him. If therefore under equitable rules, the assignee of future copyright would not be entitled to an order from the court requiring the previous owner to assign the copyright, it might be argued that the provision will not apply so as to vest legal title in the prospective assignee. Aside from this provision, the same rules will govern whether or not an equitable owner under the rules

212

referred to in paragraph 8.05 onwards will be entitled to an order that the legal interest be conveyed to the equitable owner. It is not possible in this work to deal with all the circumstances where such an order would not be made, but some relevant instances would be as follows:

(i) Where there was no consideration given for the assignment.

(ii) Where the contract is not "equal and fair," or the circumstances under which the agreement was entered into are such that it is inequitable that an order should be made. It is likely that the burden of showing this is less than that required in relation to undue influence as referred to in paragraph 8.64 onwards below, but mere inadequacy of consideration would not usually be a sufficient ground in itself.

(iii) The prospective owner may already have assigned his future copyright to someone else.

(iv) The contract under which the copyright was assigned may contain some other term which would lead a court to refuse specific performance, such as making the assignee's entitlement to the copyright dependent upon some other event which has not happened, or some obligation on the part of the assignee with which the assignee has failed to comply.

(f) *Partial vesting of rights*

The provision can be used to vest different rights in different parties in the same way as it is possible for a copyright owner to partially assign his copyright. (See paragraph 8.31.)

(g) *Licence by prospective owner*

If before the copyright comes into existence, the prospective owner grants a licence to someone to do any of the restricted acts, then such a licence will be binding on the assignee of the future copyright, and any successor in title, unless he is a purchaser in good faith for valuable consideration and without actual or constructive notice of the licence, or he is a person deriving title from such a purchaser. (See further paragraph 9.15.) For this reason, it is advisable to insert in agreements as to future copyright a warranty and representation that no such licences have been or will be granted before the copyright comes into existence.

(h) *Only applies to copyright in the United Kingdom*

The provision of course only applies to copyright subsisting in the countries to which the 1956 or 1988 Act extends or extended. If therefore the assignment as to future copyright is expressed to be for the whole world, whether or not this will vest the copyright in the assignee for a country outside the countries to which the Act extends or extended will depend upon the local laws of those countries.

3. Death of the prospective owner

In one respect, the 1988 Act appears to have made a change to the 8.14

provisions on assignment of future copyright. Under the 1956 Act if when the copyright came into existence, the assignee of the future copyright was dead, title to the copyright devolved as it if had subsisted immediately before his death and he was then the owner of the copyright. This meant that copyright devolved under the deceased's will or intestacy as referred to in the next section. The provision however has been repealed under the 1988 Act, although it continues to have effect in relation to agreements entered into prior to the commencement of the 1988 Act, even where the copyright does not come into existence until after commencement of the 1988 Act. It is not clear why this provision was repealed, and it is uncertain what happens now in such circumstances. It seems possible to argue that even without the 1956 Act provision, the copyright in many circumstance would have belonged to the deceased's estate in equity.

4. Practical importance of the provisions

8.15   The provisions on assignment of future copyright are extremely important. With the repeal of all provisions relating to the commissioning of works, it is under the provisions referred to in this section that a commissioner of copyright works can best ensure that the copyright wholly or partially vests in him.

IV DEVOLUTION UPON DEATH

A. WILLS AND INTESTACIES

8.16   How copyright devolves upon the death of the owner depends upon whether or not the owner left a valid will or whether there is an intestacy.

1. Title to the copyright where there is a will

If the copyright owner left a will, then, assuming one or more of the executors named in the will are still alive, the copyright will vest in them. Their title derives from the will, and they can, for example, commence proceedings for infringement of copyright even before they obtain a grant of probate. However, since a court is not able to look at a will except where probate has been granted, the executors must obtain a grant in order to *prove* their entitlement to the copyright.

2. Title to the copyright in the case of an intestacy

8.17   Where there is no will, or the executors named in the will are dead or cannot be found, the copyright vests in the President of the Family Division of the Supreme Court. Copyright does not vest in the administrators until letters of administration have been granted. Accordingly, no proceedings for infringement of copyright can be commenced until after letters of administration have been granted, although, since the administrator's authority takes effect retrospectively to the date of death, it is possible then to take proceedings for an infringement of copyright which has occurred between the date of death and the grant of letters of administration.

3. Bequests of copyrights under a will

Where there is a will, the copyright may have been bequeathed to someone as a specific legacy, or it may form part of the general residue of the deceased's estate. Prior to the 1988 Act, it was uncertain whether the copyright could be bequeathed in parts in the same way as partial assignment. The better view was that this was possible, but for deaths occurring after the commencement of the 1988 Act, it is now clear that part of the copyright may be bequeathed—for the various possibilities see paragraph 8.32. **8.18**

Whether or not the copyright is bequeathed as a specific legacy or as part of the residue, the executors must upon the administration of the deceased's estate being completed assent to the vesting of the copyright in the relevant beneficiary under the will. Such assents are necessary in the case of any property in order to show that the property is no longer required for the payment of funeral expenses or debts and so on. Although it is normal and advisable that such an assent be in writing, this is not strictly necessary, and such an assent may be implied.

4. Copyrights under an intestacy

The position is different where the copyright falls to be dealt with under an intestacy, whether whole (where there is no valid will) or partial (where a bequest fails). In these circumstances, the administrators hold the copyright on trust to sell it and to apply the proceeds in accordance with the rules as to the entitlements of the various beneficiaries under such an intestacy. However, the administrators also have power to appropriate the copyright to a beneficiary under the intestacy. If they do this, they must again vest the copyright in the beneficiary, and this is normally done by an assignment of the copyright. **8.19**

5. Deaths of persons domiciled outside the United Kingdom

The rules set out above will also apply where the deceased died domiciled in a foreign country, unless the law of domicile is different. Thus, in *Redwood Music Ltd.* v. *B. Feldman & Co. Ltd.* ([1979] R.P.C. 1), it was held that the executors named in the will of someone who died domiciled in the State of Michigan acquired on his death a good title to the reversionary interest in his copyrights which devolved upon the legal personal representatives under the provisions referred to in paragraph 8.51 onwards below, since there was no evidence that the law of the State of **8.20**

Michigan was different in any material respect from that in England as regards the vesting of property in the executors. For the same reason, it was held that an assent to the copyright vesting in the beneficiaries under the will could be implied from the executors' conduct, and need not be express.

B. BEQUESTS OF ARTICLES EMBODYING COPYRIGHT WORKS

8.21   As stated above, where the owner of the copyright gives or sells an article which embodies the copyright (such as the manuscript of a literary work) to someone else, the gift or sale of the article will not normally be effective to transfer the copyright in the work. There is however an exception to this, and this relates to dispositions by will. The precise provisions depend on the date of death.

1. Deaths before commencement of the 1956 Act (1911 Act, s.17(2))

8.22   Where the testator died before the commencement of the 1956 Act, the following presumption applies, but only where the bequest is made by the author of the relevant work.
       If the author bequeathed the manuscript of a work under his will, then if that work had not previously been published or performed in public, the bequest was prima facie proof of the copyright passing to the person to whom the manuscript was bequeathed.
       The presumption was relatively easy to rebut. In *Re Dickens* ([1935] Ch. 267), an action concerning a work by Charles Dickens known as *The Life of Christ*, the will bequeathed Dickens's private papers (which expression was held by the court to include the manuscript) to one party absolutely, and the residue of his estate (including the copyrights of the author, which were expressly referred to as part of the residue), to that party and another on trust for sale. The Court of Appeal held that this reference of the copyrights in the context of describing the residue meant that the copyright in *The Life of Christ* passed with the residue. The presumption that the copyright in the unpublished work had passed with the manuscript was therefore defeated.
       The presumption clearly applies to literary, dramatic and musical works. Whether it applies to artistic works is more difficult. It would seem that the expression does not cover paintings or drawings, although it might extend to illustrations included in a manuscript.

2. Deaths after commencement of the 1956 Act and before commencement of the 1988 Act (1956 Act s.38)

8.23   Where the testator died and bequeathed an original document embodying a literary, dramatic, or musical work, or an artistic work, to someone, then the bequest, whether by way of a specific legacy or part of the general residue, included the copyright in the work in so far as the testator owned the copyright immediately before his death. This provision applied whether or not the testator was the author.

If a contrary intention was indicated in the testator's will or a codicil to it, then the provision did not apply. It is possible that *Re Dickens* would have been decided in the same way under the 1956 Act because of this.

3. Deaths after commencement of the 1988 Act (s.93)

Here, the provision under the 1956 Act has been re-enacted, but has been   **8.24** extended as follows:

(a) It applies not only where the bequest is of an original document embodying the literary, dramatic, or musical work or the artistic work, but where it is of any other material thing (such as perhaps a master tape) embodying the work.

(b) The provision also applies to the copyright in sound recordings and films, where there is a bequest of any material thing which embodies such a work.

V INSOLVENCY

1. The effect of bankruptcy of an individual

Where an individual owning a copyright is declared bankrupt, the copy-   **8.25** right vests in the Trustee in Bankruptcy. The Trustee may then sell the copyright, and apply the proceeds of sale for the benefit of the creditors. Alternatively, he may retain the copyright and exploit it, applying the royalties flowing from exploitation again for the benefit of the creditors.

2. The effect of liquidation of a company

Where a limited company owning a copyright goes into liquidation, the   **8.26** copyright remains vested in the company, but the liquidator has the power to sell the copyright in the name of the company. Again, he may decide not to sell the copyright, but to apply royalties to which the company is entitled by reason of the exploitation of the copyright for the benefit of the creditors.

3. Royalty entitlement

Where the bankrupt or company in liquidation acquired the copyright   **8.27** from another party under a contract providing for the payment of royal- ties to that other party, the above rules can produce harsh results. As regards royalties due to be paid by the company, whether those royalties arise before or after the date of liquidation, the relevant party is only entitled to prove in the liquidation for the amount owed to him. Furthermore, if as referred to above, the copyright is sold, the purchaser, whether or not he knows of the existence of the contract, takes the copyright free of any obligation to pay royalties, or indeed any other obligation under the contract by which the bankrupt or company in liquidation acquired the copyright.

It is for this reason that a party assigning the copyright in a work to a limited company needs to be cautious. The assignor could ask for a provision in the assignment that upon a petition for the winding-up of the company being validly presented to the court, the copyright in the work will automatically revert to or revest in the assignor. Alternatively, it could be provided that reversion takes place where a petition is presented and not dismissed within so many days, or upon a winding-up order being made.

The problem with provisions of this kind is that they may well be regarded as devices to contract out of the statutory provisions governing the liquidation of the assignee and thus be ineffective. The provisions could be seen as an attempt to usurp the rules governing the distribution of the company's assets on winding-up (See *British Eagle International Air Lines Limited* v. *Compagnie Nationale Air France* [1975] 1 W.L.R. 758). A possible way round this may be to include only a partial assignment of copyright, where the duration of the assignment is limited to the period from the date of the assignment until the moment just beore the presentation of a petition to wind up the assignee. Such an assignment may also be vulnerable to attack, but we consider that it is more likely to succeed than a provision for reversion of copyright on liquidation. The partial assignment could conceivably be attacked as a charge, which would be unenforceable unless registered. However, we consider it unlikely that such an attack would succeed.

It is likely that any of these provisions are preferable to a provision whereby the assignor is entitled to terminate the contract and require the reassignment of the copyright, because the liquidator of the company may before termination is validly effected disclaim the contract under which the right of termination was granted. Similar problems may arise where the copyright is vested in the assignee conditionally upon payment of royalties.

4. Special rule for bankruptcy

8.28 The ability to exploit a copyright or assign a copyright free of any obligation to pay royalties to the party from whom the copyright was acquired is subject to one exception. The exception applies only where the assets of a bankrupt include the copyright in any work or any interest in such a copyright. It does not therefore apply to companies in liquidation, so the practical effect of the exception is therefore extremely limited.

Where the bankrupt is liable to pay to the author of the relevant work royalties or a share of profits from exploitation of the copyright, the Trustee in Bankruptcy is limited in his powers to exploit or assign the copyright. These limitations are twofold:

(a) He may not sell or authorise the sale of any copies of the work, or perform or authorise the performance of the work, except on terms of paying to the author such sums by way of royalty or share of profits as would have been payable by the bankrupt.

(b) He may not without the consent of the author or of the court assign the copyright or transfer an interest in the copyright or grant any interest in the right by licence, except on terms which will secure to the author payments by way of royalty or share of the profits at a rate not less than that which the bankrupt was liable to pay.

This provision was enacted by the Bankruptcy Act 1914 and repealed by the Insolvency Act 1985. Notwithstanding its repeal, it continues to have effect in any case where a petition in bankruptcy was presented, or a receiving order or an adjudication in bankruptcy was made before namely December 29, 1986.

The provision also continues to apply where a person is adjudged bankrupt on a petition presented on or after December 29, 1986, if the liability to pay royalties or a share of profits arose by virtue of a transaction entered into before that date (Insolvency Act 1986 Sched. 11, paragraph 15). Except to that extent, the provision has no effect as regards bankruptcies after December 29, 1986.

VI ASSIGNMENTS OF COPYRIGHT

An assignment of the copyright by the owner of the copyright to another **8.29** party transfers the copyright to that other party, subject to any terms and conditions which may be agreed will apply to such assignment. It is thus distinct from a licence, even an exclusive licence, where no property passes, and where the licensee has only certain rights (sometimes exclusive and sometimes non-exclusive) to exploit the copyright without infringement taking place.

A. THE REQUIREMENT OF WRITING (s.90(3))

No assignment of copyright is effective unless it is in writing signed by or **8.30** on behalf of the assignor. This seems to apply not only to the legal title to a copyright, but also to any equitable interest in a copyright, as referred to in Section II above: *Roban Jig & Tool Co. Ltd.* v. *Taylor* ([1974] F.S.R. 130). However, as referred to in paragraph 8.09, an agreement to assign the copyright, even if not in writing, may take effect in equity.

Where a person signs a document assigning a copyright on behalf of the copyright owner, the assignment will have no effect unless that person had authority to sign from the owner: *Beloff* v. *Pressdram* ([1973] 1 All E.R. 241). If no express authority has been granted, the assignment will still be valid if either the party signing it usually had authority to sign, or was held out by someone having actual authority as having authority. However, neither of the latter cases applies where the party to whom the copyright is being assigned knows that the party signing the document of assignment had no authority to do so.

Some further comments are necessary as regards assignments on behalf of companies:

(a) Whether or not a person signing an assignment on behalf of a company had authority to do so will prima facie be governed by the Articles of Association of the company.

(b) Where the assignee is a party dealing with the company in good faith, and the assignment was decided on by all the directors of the company, it is deemed to be one within the capacity of the company to enter into, and therefore the power of the directors to bind the company is free of any limitation on this under the Memorandum or Articles of the company. (See section 35 Companies Act 1985.)

(c) Under a new provision in the 1988 Act, the requirement that the assignment be signed by or on behalf of a person is also satisfied by the affixing of the company's seal (s.176(1)). The provision does not state whether or not this is subject to any requirement arising by reason of the company's Articles of Association that the seal be affixed in the presence of one or more directors. It would certainly be sensible for an assignee to ensure that any such provisions be complied with.

B. PARTIAL ASSIGNMENTS

8.31 The copyright in a work may be assigned as a whole, or in part.

1. Definition of partial assignment (s.90(2))

A partial assignment is one which is limited so that it applies:

(a) To one or more, but not all, of the things the copyright owner has the exclusive right to do. The meaning of this phrase is referred to in paragraph 8.32 below.

(b) To part, but not the whole, of the period during which the copyright is to subsist. For example, where the assignment of copyright is for the life of the author, this will be a partial assignment of the copyright.

Unlike the equivalent provision in the 1956 Act (s.36(2)(*b*)), the 1988 Act does not state that an assignment can be limited so as to apply to any one or more, but not all, of the countries in relation to which the owner of the copyright has the relevant right. The 1956 Act provision meant for example that the copyright owner could divide the rights by reference to territory, so that he could assign the copyright subsisting in, say, Gibraltar, to one party, and, say, the copyright subsisting in Hong Kong to another party. The provision of course only applied to territories to which the Act extended, so, for example this provision did not authorise separate assignments for France, Germany and so on—the ability to assign separately for each such territory would arise anyway by virtue of the copyright in each case being territorial. It is unlikely that the removal of this provision therefore will have much effect, and in any event it is arguable that the drafting of section 90(2)(*a*) is wide enough to cover this.

2. Partial assignments of rights

As stated, one type of partial assignment occurs where the copyright **8.32** owner assigns one or more, but not all, of the things the copyright owner has the exclusive right to do. This could apply to:

(a) The whole of one of the restricted acts which the copyright owner has the exclusive right to do—for example, the right to perform a work in public, or the right to copy a work.

(b) Classes of rights which are not separate restricted acts. For example, in relation to musical works, rights commonly referred to are "the print rights" and "the mechanical rights," the former referring to the right to print the musical work in sheet music form, and the latter to reproduce the musical work in the form of records and film sound-tracks and so on. Both of those fall within the restricted act of copying a musical work, but may be assigned separately.

(c) The right to do certain restricted acts for defined purposes only. An example of this would be assigning the right to print an article as part of a magazine, but not separately.

(d) Very limited rights. For example, where a film company wishes to use music in a film, it will usually require an assignment of the exclusive right to use the music in that film, (as opposed to films in general). Whilst the point is not free from doubt, this could operate as a partial assignment of copyright, thus entitling the film company to sue for infringement of copyright if a copy of the part of the film which included the music is made without the consent of the copyright owner of the film sound-track.

   The examples above are given on the basis of the 1988 Act provision. The equivalent provisions in the 1956 and 1911 Acts were differently worded, and some doubt has been expressed as to the scope of those provisions. In particular, it is uncertain whether under the 1911 Act a purported assignment of the type referred to in (c) or (d) above could have operated as a partial assignment, and the same uncertainty exists in relation to (d) under the 1956 Act. It is specifically provided in the transitional provisions to the 1988 Act that any document made before commencement which had any operation transferring an interest or right

221

in respect of the copyright in an existing work continues to have the same effect under the 1988 Act (Schedule 1, paragraph 25).

The position is even more uncertain as regards assignments made before the commencement of the 1911 Act. The general view appears to be that an assignment of copyright could then be limited in terms of duration and in terms of the territories to which it applied. However, it is thought that partial assignment of the rights comprising copyright could not be effective in law, except of course for the reproduction rights and performing rights in dramatic and musical works which arose under different statutes. (See paragraph 8.46.)

C. WHAT CONSTITUTES AN ASSIGNMENT?

1. No particular form necessary

8.33 No particular form of document or even form of words is required in order to effect an assignment of the copyright, whether in whole or in part. It is possible for words included on a receipt to be wide enough to constitute an assignment of copyright. In *E. W. Savory Ltd.* v. *The World of Golf Ltd.* ([1914] 2 Ch. 566), a receipt from an artist which stated "Received of Messrs. E. W. Savory Ltd., Bristol, the sum of two pounds six shillings and six pence for five original card designs inclusive of all copyrights" was held to be sufficient to assign the copyrights in those designs. It did not matter that some of the designs were not precisely referred to, and evidence was admitted as to which particular designs were intended to be included.

2. Importance of clear words

8.34 Although no particular form of words is required for there to be an assignment, it is obviously highly desirable that the parties entering into an agreement by which rights are granted in relation to a copyright work define as clearly as possible what rights are being granted, and the nature of those rights, that is whether a grant of rights amounts to an assignment of copyright, whether wholly or partially, or a licence, whether exclusive or non-exclusive.

Where someone wishes to acquire rights exclusively, it might be said that it does not matter whether or not this is by way of assignment or grant of an exclusive licence, but in fact the distinction is still an important one, for the following reasons:

(a) If the party granting the rights retains the copyright, and then in breach of the grant does one of the acts which he gave the other party the exclusive right to do, the latter will only have a cause of action for breach of contract, not for infringement of copyright. This could limit the remedies available to the exclusive licensee, and also deprive him of his ability to use the provisions on secondary infringement, except where articles are imported from abroad. (See paragraph 6.30.)

(b) Although exclusive licensees have certain rights to take proceedings for infringement of copyright, provided that the exclusive licence is one to which the 1988 Act applies, the procedure involved in such an action may present difficulties, and there may be problems as regards the remedies for infringement. (See paragraph 10.93.)

(c) If the grant of rights only constitutes an exclusive licence, a subsequent purchaser of the copyright in good faith for valuable consideration and without actual or constructive notice of the licence will take the copyright free of the licensee's rights. (See paragraph 9.15.)

(d) In the absence of any material express or implied terms, an assignee of the copyright has the right to assign it on to another party. An exclusive licensee will not be able to assign if the contract is a personal one. (See paragraph 9.32.) See also the problem with insolvency (paragraph 8.26).

(e) Again in the absence of any express or implied terms, an assignee of the copyright may do anything in relation to the copyright work which the assignor could. The rights of an exclusive licensee may be more limited. (See for example paragraph 9.30.)

The best way in which the parties to an agreement by which rights are granted can define the nature of those rights is to state expressly whether the grant operates by way of assignment of the whole copyright, or by way of partial assignment, or by way of exclusive or non-exclusive licence only. Whilst the words used by the parties may not be absolutely conclusive, express provisions to this effect are much more likely to determine the position.

3. Construing whether a document is an assignment or exclusive licence

Where there are no clear words, it is extremely difficult to determine **8.35** whether or not the grant of a right is by way of assignment or licence, and, in truth, the cases dealing with this are not entirely consistent. Factors which need to be borne in mind are as follows:

(a) In modern cases, the use of expressions such as "grant the sole and exclusive right" or "shall have the exclusive right" accompanied by a reasonably wide description of the acts which the grantee can do will normally constitute an assignment. (*Messager* v. *British Broadcasting Corporation Ltd.* ([1929] A.C. 151), *Loew's Inc.* v. *Littler* ([1958] Ch. 650.)

(b) Conversely, the mere use of expressions such as "assign the rights" or "license the rights" or "assignee" or "licensee" will not be conclusive of there being an assignment or licence. (*Jonathan Cape Ltd.* v. *Consolidated Press Ltd.* ([1954] 1 W.L.R. 1313).)

(c) Even less formal language may in an appropriate case constitute an assignment. In *Lacy* v. *Toole* ((1867), 15 L.T. 512, N.P.), an author in debt to someone else wrote a letter to that person agreeing "to let you have my drama of 'Doing the Best' in discharge of £10 of the sum due." This was held to be an assignment.

(d) A limited grant of rights can still constitute an assignment because of the provisions on partial assignments of copyright. However, the more restricted the rights are, the less likely it is that a court would, in the absence of clear wording, hold that the grant constituted an assignment. In *Frisby* v. *British Broadcasting Corporation* ([1967] Ch. 932), the words were "the exclusive right to televise during a period of two years from the date of delivery of the full script," but it was held that since this was limited to one performance, and wider rights were comprised only in an option clause, the grant only constituted a licence. In *Landeker & Brown* v. *L. Wolff & Co. Ltd.* ((1907) 52 Sol.Jo. 45), the agreement was expressly stated to be an assignment of copyright, but was so qualified by conditions, such as an undertaking on the part of the assignee not to use the copyright in any way without consent, that the court held that the assignment was ineffective.

(e) If the agreement is personal as between the parties, and provides for continuing personal obligations to be rendered by the party to whom the rights are granted, it is less likely that the document will be construed as an assignment. In *Sampson Low & Co.* v. *Duckworth & Co.* ([1923–28] MacG. Cop. Cas. 205) publishing rights were granted to a publisher and its "assigns, successors for the time being *in their business and firm.*" The fact that the contract was not with the publisher and its assigns generally and the fact that there were continuing obligations to pay a share of the profits from exploitation of the work influenced the court in holding that the grant was not an assignment.

(f) Where there is a clause dealing with cessation or termination of rights, one indication of an assignment will be if this is expressed in terms of reversion of rights rather than cessation of a licence. (*Messager* v. *British Broadcasting Corporation Ltd.* ([1929] A.C. 151).)

(g) Where the agreement under which the grant of rights is made is subject to foreign law, United Kingdom law determines whether the relevant right is assignable, but the foreign law will determine whether the grant of rights constitutes an assignment.

D. THE EFFECT OF ASSIGNMENTS

1. Assignments of the whole copyright

8.36 Once the full copyright has been assigned, the assignor is left with no rights, unless there is an express or implied reservation under the agreement by which assignment took place.

2. The effect of partial assignment

8.37 Where partial assignment takes place, the copyright is divided so that the assignee is the owner of the copyright in the rights assigned and the assignor is the owner of the copyright in the rights reserved. Unless there is an express or implied agreement to the contrary, the assignee can exploit the rights assigned and the assignor can exploit the rights reserved without permission from or indeed consultation with the other. This is so even where exploitation of one party's rights would damage the exploitation of the rights of the other party, and it is for this reason that one very often sees clauses in which the timing or manner of exploitation of rights either retained or granted is restricted. For example, if a film production company grants rights to a distribution company to enable the distributor to authorise the showing of the film in public in cinemas, but no other rights, the film distribution company will usually require that the right to copy the film in the form of videograms and distribute those to the public, or to authorise the broadcasting of film, is restricted for a period of time.

3. Subsequent acts by the assignor

Once assignment has taken place, assuming that there has been no express or implied reservation of rights, the assignor will infringe copyright if he does or authorises the doing of any of the relevant restricted acts. If a copyright owner retains copies of a work in his possession made whilst he was owner, he will then infringe copyright if he issues them to the public after he has assigned the copyright. **8.38**

If the author of a literary, dramatic or musical work assigns the copyright in that work, and then creates another work which reproduces a substantial part of the first work, then he will infringe copyright if he does or authorises the doing of any of the restricted acts in relation to the new work. The same is so as regards artistic works, subject to the permitted act referred to in paragraph 7.106. In *Metzler & Co. (1920) Ltd. v. J. Curwen & Sons Ltd.* ([1928–35] MacG. Cop. Cas. 127), a composer wrote incidental music for the performance of a play. He then arranged extracts from the incidental music as a suite, and assigned the copyright in the suite to the plaintiffs. After his death, his widow, as personal representative, assigned the copyright in one of the songs which was included both in the incidental music and (with some minimal variations) in the suite, to another party. It was held that the printing and publishing of copies of the song by the subsequent assignee was an infringement of copyright. This was obviously a case where the two pieces of music were in substance the same, but where the writer of a literary, dramatic, musical or artistic work creates a fresh work after assigning the copyright in the original work, there may be more difficulty in showing an infringement of copyright in relation to a substantial part since the style and themes used by the author of such a work will very often be consistent.

4. Effect of assignment on prior acts

Assignment of the copyright in whole or in part does not nullify the effect of acts carried out or authorised by the copyright owner whilst he owned **8.39** the rights. Thus, he will still be entitled after assignment to collect royalties in respect of acts done prior to assignment.

Furthermore, a licence granted by a copyright owner is binding on every subsequent assignee, except that it is not binding on a purchaser in good faith for valuable consideration without actual or constructive notice of the licence, or a person deriving title from such a purchaser (s.90(4)). (See further paragraph 9.15.)

5. Further assignment

8.40   Unless an assignment of copyright restricts the ability of the assignee to himself assign the rights whether wholly or partially, the assignee will be free to do this. The point is an important one because the original assignor can only sue the party to whom he assigned the right for breach of any terms and conditions contained in the assignment, and not the subsequent assignee. For this reason, the original assignor will usually try to protect himself either by an absolute prohibition on assignments, or a prohibition on assignments without consent, or requiring a clause to the effect that no assignment is valid unless the proposed assignee has entered into a contract direct with the original assignor undertaking to comply with the terms and conditions of the original agreement.

6. Revocability

8.41   An assignment of copyright cannot be revoked by the assignor unless there is a provision to this effect in the contract by which the copyright was assigned.

7. Effect of assignment on moral rights

8.42   Where an author assigns the copyright in a work created by him to another party, he still retains his moral rights, if any, and such rights are not assignable. (See Chapter 11.)

VII REVERSION OF RIGHTS

8.43   Two surviving provisions from the 1911 Act are dealt with here. The first is the reversion of the substituted right arising under section 24 of the 1911 Act to the author or his personal representatives for any extended term of copyright which arose by virtue of that provision. The second is the reversion of rights granted under an assignment made by an author between the passing of the 1911 Act and the commencement of the 1956 Act to the legal personal representatives of that author 25 years after his death.

A. REVERSION OF THE SUBSTITUTED RIGHT

8.44   This provision only applies to literary, dramatic, musical and artistic works which were protected by copyright immediately prior to July 1, 1912, that is the commencement date of the 1911 Act.

1. The scheme of the 1911 Act

The scheme of the 1911 Act as regards such works was intended to ensure 8.45
that once such works could be shown to have been passed through the
"gateway" of the 1911 Act, they would be protected in accordance with
that Act, and not in accordance with the confusing array of statutes in
force prior to commencement of the 1911 Act. Accordingly, the Act
provided that where any person was immediately before the commencement of the 1911 Act entitled to a particular right as regards any copyright
work or to any interest in such a right, he was from the commencement of
the Act entitled to a substituted right under the 1911 Act or to the same
interest in such a substituted right. In that way the owner of the relevant
right prior to the commencement of the 1911 Act became the copyright
owner under the 1911 Act.

2. Musical and dramatic works

Since in the case of these works, the copyright (that is, the reproduction 8.46
right) in any such work and the performing right in any such work arose
under different statutes and could be owned by different people, the
position here was as follows:

(a) If someone owned the copyright *and* the performing right before the
commencement of the 1911 Act, he owned the full copyright after the
commencement of the Act.

(b) If he only owned the performing right prior to commencement of the
1911 Act, after commencement he only owned the right to perform the
work in public.

(c) If he owned the copyright but not the performing right prior to the
commencement of the 1911 Act, then after the commencement of the
1911 Act he would own the full copyright except for the right to perform
the work in public.

The owner of the performing right under the above rules also today owns
the right to broadcast the work and to include it in a cable programme
service.

3. Extended term of copyright under the 1911 Act

The rules on duration of copyright prior to commencemement of the 1911 8.47
Act were summarised in paragraph 4.66. Where the work was published,
copyright protection was often considerably shorter than the life plus 50
years term introduced by the 1911 Act, and in such cases an extension of
the original term of copyright was given by the 1911 Act. This can best be
illustrated by the facts of *Coleridge-Taylor* v. *Novello & Co. Ltd.* ([1938]

3 All E.R. 506). The musical work there was first published in September 1911, that is prior to the commencement of the 1911 Act. Under the law which subsisted prior to commencement, the copyright would have subsisted for 42 years from the date of publication, and would therefore have expired in 1953. The composer died on September 1, 1912, and accordingly under the 1911 Act the copyright in the work expired in 1962. An additional nine years was therefore added to the term of copyright by the 1911 Act.

4. Ownership of the extended term

8.48   Under section 24 of the 1911 Act, this additional period ordinarily belonged to the author. If he was dead, the rights would devolve in accordance with his will. The provision stated that if the author of any work before commencement of the 1911 Act had assigned the right or granted any interest in the right for the whole term of the right, then at the date when, but for the passing of the Act, the right would have expired, the substituted right under the 1911 Act would, in the absence of express agreement, pass to the author of the work.
    Two points need to be made about this provision:

(a) It did not apply where someone other than the author was the first owner of the copyright, and assigned the relevant right or interest.

(b) The phrase "in the absence of express agreement" was held to refer to an agreement which refers to the substituted right in terms " ... clearly identifying the right by naming it ... ": *Redwood Music Ltd*. v. *B. Feldman & Co. Ltd*. ([1979] R.P.C. 385). It does not therefore apply to wide general words, and, in particular, could not apply to general words in an agreement entered into before the passing of the 1911 Act.

5. Options for the former owner

8.49   However, the person who owned the relevant right or interest immediately before the right reverted to the author or his personal representatives had an option to do either of the following:

(a) Upon giving notice not more than one year nor less than six months before the date of reversion to the author or the author's personal representatives, he could require an assignment of the right or the grant of a similar interest therein for the remainder of the term of the right for a consideration to be determined by arbitration, failing agreement. The notice had to be sent by registered post to the author or if he could not with reasonable diligence be found, advertised in the *London Gazette* and two London newspapers.

(b) He could continue to reproduce or perform the work in the same way as he was previously entitled to. This however was subject to the payment, if demanded by the author within three years after the date the right reverted, of royalties to the author to be determined by arbitration, if not agreed. If however the work was incorporated in a collective work (see paragraph 8.52), and the owner of the right or interest prior to reversion was the proprietor of that collective work, no payment was required.

6. Preservation of the provisions under the 1988 Act (Sched. 1, para. 28)

The 1988 Act preserves the above provisions with some modifications: 8.50

(a) If, before commencement of the 1988 Act, the substituted right has reverted, then the author or his personal representatives retain the right. If either of the options referred in paragraph 8.49 to has also been exercised, the effect of exercising that option is retained under the 1988 Act. Any assignments or other dispositions prior to the commencement of the 1988 Act which have been made by the author or his personal representatives, or, where the appropriate notice had been served, the previous owner, would also continue to have the same effect. If the second of the two options was exercised prior to the commencement date of the 1988 Act, but the three-year period referred to has not expired, then the author or his personal representatives can still give the notice which is referred to there.

(b) If reversion is not due to take place until after the commencement of the 1988 Act, and a period of notice under the first option has begun but not expired prior to the commencement of the 1988 Act, then that option can still be exercised after the commencement of the 1988 Act.

(c) Subject thereto, any reversion to the author or his personal representatives after the commencement of the 1988 Act is not subject to either of the options referred to above.

B. THE REVERSION OF RIGHTS UNDER ASSIGNMENTS AND OTHER DISPOSITIONS MADE BETWEEN THE COMMENCEMENT OF THE 1911 AND 1956 ACTS

1. Reversion 25 years after death

Under the proviso to section 5(2) of the 1911 Act, where the author of a 8.51 work was the first owner of the copyright in that work, no assignment of the copyright, and no grant of any interest in the copyright, which was made by him (otherwise than by will) after the passing of the Act could vest in the assignee or grantee any rights relating to copyright beyond the expiration of 25 years from the death of the author. The reversionary right for the last 25 years devolved on the death of the author on his legal personal representatives as part of his estate. Any agreement entered into by the author as to the disposition of that reversionary interest was null and void, so the author could not contract out of the provision.

2. Exclusion for collective works

8.52   The above provision did not apply to the assignment of the copyright in a collective work, or a licence to publish a work or part of a work as part of a collective work. "Collective work" was defined as:

(a) An encyclopedia, dictionary, year book, or similar work;

(b) A newspaper, review, magazine, or similar periodical;

(c) Any work written in distinct parts by different authors, or in which works or parts of works of different authors are incorporated.

3. Preservation under the 1988 Act

8.53   Although the provision did not appear in the 1956 Act, its effect was preserved for assignments and grants of interest made before the commencement of that Act. This position is preserved under the 1988 Act. (See schedule 1, paragraph 27.)

4. Author had to be first owner

8.54   The provision only applied where the author of a work was the first owner of the copyright. Accordingly, it had and has no effect as regards works which vested in an employer or commissioner under the relevant provisions in the 1911 Act.

5. Assignments between passing and commencement of the 1911 Act

8.55   Although the proviso stated that it applied to assignments of copyright or grants of interest made after the passing of the 1911 Act (that is, December 16, 1911), it was held in *Coleridge-Taylor* v. *Novello & Co. Ltd.* ([1938] 3 All E.R. 506), that assignments and grants of interest made between the passing of the Act and the commencement of the Act were not covered because the provisions referred to in paragraph 8.45 were a complete code on the rules relating to works in existence at the date of commencement of the 1911 Act.

6. Photographs and sound recordings

8.56   It is uncertain, but unlikely, that the provisions applied to photographs and sound recordings, where the duration of the copyright was not tied to the life of the author.

7. Meaning of the collective work exclusion

8.57   The exclusion to the proviso for collective works only applies where there is a separate copyright in the collective work, apart from the copyright in the individual constituents of the work. This was the meaning placed on the exception to the proviso by the House of Lords in *Chappell & Co.*

Ltd. v. *Redwood Music Ltd.* ([1980] 2 All E.R. 817), where it was decided that a song in which the lyrics were written by one person and the music by another person was not excluded from the proviso, because there was no separate copyright in such a song. Apart from the specific instances of the collective work referred to in the definition, an example might be an anthology of poems. One of the members of the House of Lords, Lord Keith, also said that the position might be different in the case of complicated works comprising musical and literary components such as an opera.

8. Works of joint authorship

The application of the reversionary rights provisions to works of joint authorship is complex. The generally held view seems to be that reversion takes place either 25 years from the death of the first author to die, or upon the death of the last author to die, whichever first happens. The alternative contention (in cases where the first author to die did so less than 25 years before the commencement of the 1956 Act) is that reversion occurs 25 years from the death of the last author to die, but this is not consistent with the judgment in *Redwood Music Ltd.* v. *B. Feldman & Co. Ltd.* ([1979] R.P.C. 1).   **8.58**

9. Post-1956 assignment of reversionary rights

Under the 1911 Act, it was not possible for an author to assign or sell his reversionary rights during his lifetime. It is uncertain whether the 1956 Act changed this so as to enable an author to enter into a new agreement after the commencement of the 1956 Act covering the last 25-year period. The better view is that it was possible. Under the transitional provisions of the 1988 Act, it is now clear that an author can assign his reversionary rights after commencement of the 1988 Act.   **8.59**

10. Assignment by legal personal representatives

Although it was not possible for an author to assign the reversionary rights during his lifetime, it was possible for his legal personal representatives to assign those rights after the author's death but before the reversionary period commenced. Such an assignment could for example have taken place when American renewal rights under the old United States copyright law were dealt with, if the language in the relevant document was wide enough, but it was held by the House of Lords in the *Chappell* case that such an assignment would not be implied simply by clauses stipulating the rate at which royalties were to be paid for the future in the United Kingdom.   **8.60**

VIII THE AVOIDANCE OF CONTRACTS

This subject is dealt with here because of the possible recovery of copyrights assigned under such contracts. However, the principles involved are equally important in relation to the validity of licensing agreements.   **8.61**

A. MINORS

8.62   The 1969 Family Law Reform Act reduced the age of majority in the United Kingdom to 18. If someone below that age enters into a contract such as a publishing contract or an exclusive song-writing agreement, then such a contract is treated in the same way as contracts of apprenticeship, service, education and instruction, namely that it is binding on the minor only if beneficial to him.

Whether or not the contract is beneficial to the minor depends on whether at the time the contract was made it was, taken as a whole, one of benefit to him. This does not mean that all the terms and conditions contained in the contract have to be in the minor's favour, provided that the relevant clause is common to such contracts and reasonably justified for the protection of the party contracting with the minor. This however is subject to the agreement not being one which can be avoided on the grounds of undue influence or restraint of trade: see below.

Contracts such as publishing contracts and exclusive song-writing agreements very often vest the copyright in the works created under such contracts either wholly or in part in the party with whom the minor enters into the contract. However, even if such a contract is held not to be beneficial to the minor, and can therefore be avoided, any copyrights which have already vested in the other party remain with that party, and do not revert to the minor. (See *Chaplin* v. *Leslie Frewin (Publishers) Ltd.* ([1966] Ch. 71).)

B. UNDUE INFLUENCE AND RESTRAINT OF TRADE

8.63   In a series of decisions from 1974 onwards, the courts have considered whether or not certain music industry contracts like exclusive recording agreements and exclusive song-writing agreements should be set aside upon the grounds either that they were in restraint of trade or procured by undue influence or both. Under such contracts, copyrights created by the author are very often assigned to the other contracting party, and one of the issues at stake in these cases has been whether or not the copyrights should be returned to the author.

Although there appear to be no reported cases where the same principles have been applied to agreements by which copyrights pass in other areas, the principles are of general application, and not confined to music industry contracts.

1. Undue influence

8.64   A party induced to enter into a contract by undue influence may be able to avoid that contract. Undue influence is the unconscionable use by one person of power possessed by him over another in order to induce the other to enter into the contract. It may be express, or it may be presumed from a confidential relationship between the parties and it is this latter case which is dealt with here.

(a) *The relationship of confidentiality*

The courts have refused to put strictly defined limits on the relationships **8.65** to which the presumption of confidentiality can apply. In general terms the relationship exists where "the degree of trust and confidence is such that the party in whom it is reposed, either because he is or has become an adviser of the other or because he has been entrusted with the management of his affairs or everyday needs or for some other reason, is in a position to influence him into effecting the transaction of which complaint is later made." (See *Goldsworthy* v. *Rickell* [1987] 1 All E.R. 853 *per* Nourse L.J.). It is not necessary for the party in whom the trust and confidence is reposed to dominate the other party in any sense in which that word is commonly understood. In the music industry cases, the relationship of confidentiality has been held to apply as between a manager and artist, writer and publisher and record company and performing artist.

(b) *Manifestly disadvantageous transaction*

Once the relationship of confidentiality is established, it is also necessary **8.66** for the person alleging undue influence to show that the transaction was to his manifest disadvantage. This can be for various reasons—it may be a gift, or a "hard and inequitable" agreement, or "immoderate and irrational" transaction or an unconscionable transaction if it is a sale at an undervalue. The terms which the courts have taken into account in music industry cases are referred to in paragraphs 8.78 below.

(c) *Avoiding the contract*

Once both a confidential relationship and a manifestly disadvantageous **8.67** transaction have been established, the onus of proof shifts to the party alleged to have influenced the person trying to set the agreement aside to rebut the presumption that it was procured by the exercise of undue influence. If he cannot, the contract can be avoided.

(d) *Application to copyright cases*

The application of these principles to transactions where copyrights are **8.68** assigned is shown by the case of *O'Sullivan* v. *M.A.M. Ltd.* ([1985] Q.B. 428). The performing artist and song-writer Gilbert O'Sullivan had no success in his musical career until he met Gordon Mills who was a director and shareholder in the defendant companies of which he had *de facto* control. O'Sullivan looked upon Mills as a father figure and trusted him implicitly in all matters. Mills asked him to sign several contracts over the years which O'Sullivan did without question. A management contract was entered into with a company controlled by Mills in February 1970, and, during the currency of that agreement, further contracts were entered into with other companies in the group, for exclusive recording and song-writing services. All the contracts were held to be manifestly disadvantageous, and the judge had no hesitation in setting aside the contract, and ordering that all the copyrights vested in the defendants be returned to the plaintiff. He did this even in relation to the recordings on which O'Sullivan performed and of which O'Sullivan was not the original copyright owner.

(e) *Voidable not void*

8.69   On appeal from the decision of the judge in the *O'Sullivan* case, the Court of Appeal held that whilst the judge was right to set the agreements aside in this case, there could be circumstances in which it would no longer be right to do so. The question in each case was "what does the justice of the case require?" However, the court also confirmed that if the agreements under which the copyrights were assigned were set aside, then it would ordinarily follow that the copyrights should be reassigned.

(f) *Effect of delay*

8.70   In *John* v. *James* (unreported), the court refused to order that copyrights be returned, because of the length of time since the agreement had been entered into, and the fact that the plaintiff had not acted promptly in pursuing his claim.

(g) *Subsequent assignment*

8.71   If the party to the contract who used undue influence has transferred the copyrights to a bona fide purchaser for value without notice of the undue influence, then no order for the return of the copyrights will be made.

(h) *Independent expert advice*

8.72   The presumption of undue influence may be rebutted by showing that the party alleging undue influence took independent expert advice on the contract. For this reason, one commonly sees in music industry contracts a clause to the effect that the writer or performer acknowledges that the publisher or record company has encouraged him to take independent advice on the contract, and either that he has taken that advice or consciously opted not to take advice. However, simply putting such a clause in a contract is not sufficient in itself. If it is not true then it will not help to rebut the presumption. In any event, if the writer or performer fails to or decides not to take advice the contract may still be held to be one procured by undue influence. The important thing is that independent expert advice is actually taken.

2. Restraint of trade

(a) *Definition of contracts in restraint of trade*

8.73   A contract in restraint of trade is one in which one party agrees with another party to restrict his liberty in the future to carry on trade with other persons not parties to the contract in such manner as he chooses. Such a contract is only enforceable if it is reasonable.

(b) *Application in copyright cases*

In *Schroeder (A.) Music Publishing Co. Ltd.* v. *Macaulay* ([1974] 3 E.R. 616), the doctrine was applied to an exclusive song-writing agreement under which a composer had agreed that he would write songs exclusively for a music publisher for a period of five years (with a possible automatic extension for a further five years) and under which all the copyrights in the songs written during that period would vest in the publisher for the full period of copyright throughout the world. The House of Lords decided that the contract was one in restraint of trade, and that its terms were unreasonable. Accordingly, the contract was set aside. **8.74**

The test laid down by Lord Reid in the *Schroeder* case for such contracts was as follows:

> "Are the terms of the agreement so restrictive that they cannot be justified at all, or that they must be justified by the party seeking to enforce the agreement? Then if there is room for justification, has that party proved justification—normally by showing that the restrictions were no more than what was reasonably required to protect his legitimate interest."

(c) *Standard form contracts*

It is no answer to a claim that a contract is in restraint of trade that it is in a standard form in common use between those who create copyright works and those who exploit them. It may be a defence to an action based on restraint of trade where the form of a contract has been settled over the years by negotiation by representatives of the commercial interests involved and widely adopted on that basis, but that is completely different from the position where one party lays down the terms of a contract on a "take it or leave it" basis. **8.75**

(d) *Independent expert advice*

Unlike undue influence, it is not possible to avoid restraint of trade problems by the creator of the copyright work taking independent expert advice. If the contract is one which is in unreasonable restraint of trade, that is an end of the matter. (See *ZTT Records Ltd.* v. *Johnson* (unreported).) **8.76**

(e) *Voidable not void*

In the *Schroeder* case, Lord Reid held that the effect of the contract being in unreasonable restraint of trade was that so far as unperformed it was unenforceable. This appears to be the same result as the undue influence cases, namely that the agreement is voidable but not void *ab initio*. In the **8.77**

Court of Appeal ([1974] All E.R. 171) it was held that insofar as assignments of copyright had been executed prior to the contract being avoided, those assignments remained valid, and the assignee remained entitled to the copyright on the agreed terms as to division of royalties.

3. Terms on the basis of which contracts have been set aside on the grounds of restraint of trade or undue influence

8.78 This section contains a list of the relevant terms which have expressly or impliedly been disapproved by the courts in music industry restraint of trade and undue influence cases. The list does not distinguish between the two, because in practice the same type of clauses have been held relevant.

(a) *Too long a term*

8.79 So far, criticism appears to have been confined to the term during which the publisher or the record company is entitled to the services of the writer or performer, not the term during which the copyrights are held. In the *Schroeder* case, the term was for five years, with an option to renew for a further five years. Although the option was only exercisable if the royalties generated achieved a certain level, the level was not very difficult to achieve. In *Z.T.T. Records Ltd.* v. *Johnson* (unreported), an exclusive recording agreement contained a detailed product commitment, specifying the recordings which had to be made and delivered in one initial period and seven successive option periods. The duration of the various periods was not defined. Since the record company could decide when the particular recording was to be made, and whether it was up to standard when made, the effect was that if the record company decided to do nothing about arranging recording, the artists were in a position whereby they had no work and no opportunity to earn royalties. This was held to be in unreasonable restraint of trade.

(b) *Indemnities*

8.80 An indemnity by the writer or performer against claims being made against or proceedings commenced against the publisher or record company, if the indemnity is too wide, or could be used oppressively.

(c) *Assignment*

8.81 Power for the publisher or record company to assign the benefit of the contract or the rights vested in them to any party without the approval of the writer or performer.

(d) *No obligations or no substantial obligations on the part of the publisher or record company under the contract*

8.82 In this respect, a clause providing that the publisher or record company will use its best endeavours to exploit the copyright works is unlikely to be sufficient. In the *O'Sullivan* case, the judge took into account the fact that in his view there was too low a commitment on the part of the record company in relation to the number of tracks to be recorded. In the *Z.T.T.* case, the judge took into account as regards the exclusive song-writing agreement the fact that there was an absolute discretion on the part of the publisher to refrain from taking proceedings where the copyright had been infringed. As regards the exclusive recording agreements he took account of the provision that the record company had an unqualified discretion to decide time, place, budget, record producer and even the works to be recorded.

(e) *No clause in the agreement, or too restrictive a clause, to terminate the contract or to obtain the return of copyrights if the publisher or record company does little or nothing to exploit them*

In the *Z.T.T.* case, the exclusive song-writing contract contained a provi-   **8.83**
sion whereby the writers could recover the rights to the various compositions if they had not been exploited within three years from the date of
expiration of the term. The term was an initial period of one year with
options to extend it for two additional periods of two years each.
However, the right to require return of the rights could only be exercised
within six months from the end of the three-year period, and was in any
event subject to any then subsisting sub-publishing rights. The judge
seems to have objected to both of these provisions, as well as the length of
time before there was any possibility of recovering the relevant work.

(f) *Inadequate consideration*

In the *O'Sullivan* case, the judge took into account the fact that the   **8.84**
royalty rate was well below that for another artist who was contracted to
the same company but who was less well-known, and also the fact that
there was no advance against royalties. In the *Z.T.T.* case, the judge as
regards the exclusive recording contract took into account the "modest"
rates of royalty and advance, the fact that there was no provision for
control as regards recording costs, and the fact that there was provision in
the contract for exploitation of the rights by methods securing no return
to the artist.

(g) *Alterations to the copyright work*

In the *Z.T.T.* case, the judge took into account the unfettered right to   **8.85**
edit master recordings in the exclusive recording agreement, and the
publisher's absolute right to alter and change compositions in the exclusive song-writing agreement.

237

9 LICENSING

I INTRODUCTION

1. General

9.01 This chapter deals with various aspects of copyright licensing and exploitation. First, it covers the different types of situation in which the Court would hold that a licence has been granted, or has been deemed to have been granted. Secondly, it deals with the construction of copyright agreements, their termination and remedies for breach. Finally, it covers the various ways in which the copyright owner's ability to exploit his copyright freely is restricted, the main topics being the Copyright Tribunal and competition law, both United Kingdom domestic law and that of the EEC.

The contents of this chapter cannot be read in isolation from what is in Chapter 8, and vice versa. Many of the aspects dealt with in this chapter are equally important in considering contracts by which the ownership of copyright is transferred. Some of the rules covered in Chapter 8 will have a bearing on the validity of copyright licences. Some of the important points to bear in mind are as follows:

(a) The validity of a licence depends upon it having been granted by the correct owner. The rules referred to in Chapter 8 are therefore important to bear in mind on this.

(b) Reversionary rights covered in paragraph 8.51 onwards affect licences granted by the owner of the copyright prior to reversion as well as the assignment itself.

(c) Restraint of trade and undue influence principles dealt with in paragraph 8.63 onwards could affect licensing agreements as well as assignments.

(d) The principles on construction of licensing agreements in paragraph 9.23 onwards apply also to construction of assignments of copyright.

(e) Competition law could affect assignments of copyright as well as licences.

2. Differences between the 1956 and 1988 Act

9.02 The 1988 Act has made several important changes in this area which are dealt with in this chapter:

(a) Exclusive licensees have been given a direct right of recourse against a successor in title of the copyright owner who granted them their exclusive licence. (See paragraph 9.46.)

(b) Provision has been made for an indemnity to be implied into licensing schemes and licences granted by licensing bodies for reprographic copying as regards the works covered by such schemes and licences. (See paragraph 9.103.)

(c) The jurisdiction of the Copyright Tribunal has been greatly extended. See paragraph 9.58 for a fuller summary of the changes from the 1956 Act.

(d) The Secretary of State for Trade and Industry has been given powers to provide for compulsory licensing in certain situations following a report by the Monopolies and Mergers Commission that particular practices are against the public interest. (See paragraph 9.135.)

(e) Provision has been made for the Secretary of State to certify licensing schemes where such certification is a condition of copyright owners being able to exercise their exclusive rights in some areas. (See paragraph 9.47.)

(f) Other powers to extend the scope of licensing schemes and even to provide compulsory licences in the area of reprographic copying by or for educational establishments have been given to the Secretary of State. (See paragraph 9.108.)

II GENERAL ASPECTS OF LICENSING

A. GRANT OF LICENCES

1. Validity

Obviously, no licence is valid unless it is granted by or with the authority of the person entitled to grant it. Where therefore the person granting the licence owns some of the rights comprised in the copyright in the work, but not the particular right which is being licensed, the licence is of no effect against the true owner. (See *Performing Right Society Limited* v. *Coates* [1923–28] MacG. Cop. Cas. 103.) **9.03**

Where the licence is granted by an agent, it will be invalid unless the agent either had authority to grant it or was held out by the person entitled to grant it as having authority to grant it. (See *Heinemann* v. *Smart Set Publishing Co.* [1905–10] MacG. Cop. Cas. 221.) This is particularly important in relation to companies. Whether or not a director or employee is entitled to grant a licence on behalf of a company depends on whether he has express or implied authority to grant such a licence, or has been held out as having such authority.

In practice, it is not common for proposed licensees to call for proof that a proposed licensor is entitled to grant a licence. Although a warranty as to title will usually be implied in to the licence, an indemnity is often called for by the licensee to cover any damage or loss which the licensee may suffer in the event that the licensor was not entitled to grant the licence.

If a licence is invalid, copyright is infringed by doing or authorising any restricted act as referred to in Chapter 5, even though the licensee was innocent. However, innocence will act as a defence to a claim for secondary infringement of copyright as referred to in Chapter 6, unless and until the licensee can be shown to have reason to believe that the licence was not validly granted. (See paragraph 6.06.)

Where the copyright in a work is owned jointly by more than one person, the licence in order to be fully effective must have been granted by or with the authority of all the owners. One co-owner does not prima facie have authority to grant a licence on behalf of his other co-owners, although such authority may have been granted expressly or impliedly.

2. Express licences

9.04 A licence may be granted in writing or orally. However, an exclusive licence must be in writing if it is to come within the definition under the 1988 Act for the purposes of such provisions as those relating to infringement proceedings. (See paragraph 10.20.)

An express licence can be granted to named parties, or generally. In *Mellor* v. *Australian Broadcasting Commission* ([1940] A.C. 491), the copyright owners issued pamphlets stating that "all our music is free for public performance." This was held to be an effective licence to anyone to perform the relevant music in public.

3. Derogation from grant

9.05 Many of the reported copyright cases in the late 1970s and 1980s had as their subject-matter the copyright in drawings of articles of purely functional or utilitarian value. The basis of such actions is explained in Chapter 13. Not surprisingly, some judges displayed a marked reluctance to allow copyright law to be used to its full extent in order to prevent the manufacture of articles derived from such drawings.

One major issue which arose during the 1980s was whether spare parts for motor cars copied from the original parts could be manufactured without infringing the copyright in the engineering or production drawings of the original parts. It was argued by many legal experts that such manufacture was permitted on the basis of an implied licence to repair similar to that applied in relation to patents. However, in *British Leyland Motor Corporation* v. *Armstrong Patents Company Ltd.* [1986] A.C. 577, the House of Lords rejected the implied licence argument, but preferred instead the argument that British Leyland could not derogate from their supply of motor cars to the public by exercising copyright law in such a way as to prevent the car from being repaired. On those grounds, not only could the owner of the car repair it, but others manufacture replacement parts for supply to owners.

The above is a very basic summary of the effects of the judgments of the majority in the House of Lords, and the two leading judgments of Lord Bridge and Lord Templeman are not entirely easy to interpret. Whilst the practical effect of the decision in relation to the copyright in such drawings will not be as great under the 1988 Act because of the new provisions on designs (see Chapter 13), it is still unclear what if any effect the decision has in other areas.

It is possible to argue that the effect of the decision is for the most part limited to the exercise of copyright law in relation to functional or utilitarian articles which are direct or indirect copies of engineering or production drawings. However, it is also possible to argue that the same principles could be applied to other articles. An example might be computer programs. As stated in paragraph 5.18, the ordinary use of a computer program will often involve copying that program. Assuming that there are no express conditions attaching to the supply of the program, it seems clear that the user will impliedly be licensed to carry out such copying as is involved in the ordinary use of that program. The question then arises as to what happens if faults develop in the program. If the rectification of such faults involves further copying or adaptation of the computer program, it may be argued either that this is impliedly licensed as well, or alternatively permitted on the same basis of non-derogation as referred to in the *British Leyland* case.

It is possible to envisage other circumstances where similar considerations might be invoked. Take the example of an artist who is commissioned to paint a mural. If the materials used by the artist turn out to be defective, and the mural deteriorates, it could perhaps be argued on the same basis that the owner of the mural could have it repainted without seeking further consent from the artist even where this amounts to a reproduction of a substantial part of the artistic work. Whether or not such a claim would be upheld by the Courts is still unclear, and, as stated, the precise scope of the *British Leyland* decision is a matter of some difficulty.

4. "Implied licences"

This is a generic term which is used to describe a number of different situations. It is not really possible to formulate any one principle which adequately covers all the cases where a licence to use a copyright work will be implied, and the examples given below may not be the only ones where a Court might in future be prepared to imply that the copyright owner has consented to a particular act.   **9.06**

(a) *Where A commissions B to create a copyright work in circumstances that it is clearly within the contemplation of the parties that A would use the work in the manner in which he did use it.*

As stated in paragraph 8.06, the commissioning of a work will sometimes lead to the copyright being owned in equity by the commissioner. Even where it does not, the circumstances will very often be such that it is   **9.07** clearly contemplated by both parties that A will be able to use the work for the purposes for which it was created. An example of this is *Harrold Drabble Ltd*. v. *The Hycolite Manufacturing Company* ([1923–28] MacG. Cop.Cas. 322) where the plaintiffs who were advertising agents made some alterations to a newspaper advertisement for the defendants who owned the copyright in the advertisement. The plaintiffs sued for infringement when the defendants approached newspapers direct to insert the advertisements. Astbury J. dismissed the action, one of the grounds being as follows:

> "In my opinion there must be inferred from the circumstances of this case a plain consent on the part of Mr. Drabble that if he altered these advertisements they should remain the property of the defendants to this extent that they should be entitled as and when they thought fit to insert them in the newspapers provided the papers would consent to do so."

Problems arise however in determining the extent of use permitted under the licence and these problems are well illustrated by the cases on architects' plans. In *Blair* v. *Osborne & Tomkins* ([1971] 2 Q.B. 78), an architect was engaged to prepare plans in connection with an application for planning permission. He was paid his fees for doing so in accordance with the RIBA scale. He imposed no limitations on the use of the plans, and indeed when sending in his account noted on it "wishing you all the very best in this venture." In these circumstances, it was held by the Court of Appeal that the plans could be used for all purposes connected with the erection of the houses on the site to which the plans related. The *Blair* case should be contrasted with the case of *Stovin-Bradford* v. *Volpoint Ltd*. ([1971] Ch. 1007), where the architect charged only a nominal fee for preparation of the drawings in sufficient detail to apply for planning permission, and the Court of Appeal held that the licence only extended to the use of the drawings and plans for the purpose of obtaining that planning permission.

No test appears to have been formulated by the United Kingdom courts as to how one determines the extent of the licence in such circumstances. Some support (particularly in the *Stovin-Bradford* case) has been given for the following dictum of Jacobs J. in the Australian case of *Beck* v. *Montana Construction Pty. Ltd*. [1964–65] N.S.W.R. 229:

> " ... it seems to me that the principle involved is this: that the engagement for reward of a person to produce material of a nature which is capable of being the subject of copyright implies a permission, or consent, or licence in the person giving the engagement to use the material in the manner and for the purpose in which and for which it was contemplated between the parties that it would be used at the time of the engagement."

However, this test is not universally regarded as satisfactory, and may be too wide in its terms. Salmon L.J. in the *Stovin-Bradford* case seems to have had reservations about the dicta of Jacobs J. in the *Beck* case.

Commenting on the *Blair* case, he said that he was by no means convinced that even if an architect charged the full scale fee for preparation of drawings, a licence to use the drawings for erecting the building would necessarily be implied in every case.

The example given by Salmon L.J. shows that the *Beck* test although useful may be misleading in some circumstances:

"Take the case of an architect who is world-famous for the brilliance and originality of his designs. He normally, with good reason, commands a fee considerably in excess of the minimum prescribed in clause 1 of the RIBA scale. A building owner is anxious to have, say, a large hotel designed by this architect. He engages him to prepare drawings for the purpose of planning permission at what for this architect is the comparatively modest maximum fee prescribed in clause 3(ii) of the scale. Planning permission is granted. Can the owner then refuse to employ the architect any further and yet have the benefit of his design for the purpose of erecting his hotel without having any express licence to use the copyright design for this purpose? I do not propose to express any concluded view on this point until it arises for decision. It may be that the answer is that a licence to use the drawings for building purposes would be implied if the building owner offers to appoint the architect as architect under the contract at what would be a reasonable fee for this architect, and the architect capriciously refuses or demands an exorbitant fee. Such an answer would at any rate protect both the building owner and the architect. In the circumstances postulated, the licence, if it exists, can exist only by implication. Accordingly, it seems reasonable that when it is implied it should be implied only on terms which are fair to both parties."

In these circumstances, it is in our opinion probably better to regard the test as similar to one of those referred to in paragraph 9.28 below, namely, as a matter of ordinary business efficacy, was it necessarily implied that the commission could carry out the particular restricted act? The "business efficacy" approach was certainly taken by Salmon L.J. in the *Stovin-Bradford* case, although not by the other judges in either that or the *Blair* case.

(b) *Where an article which is a copy of a copyright work is sold or supplied by or with the consent of the copyright owner, and the ordinary use of that article necessarily involves doing a restricted act*

A good example of this is a computer program, where using the software 9.08 will often necessarily involve copying of the program and the works embodied in it. (See paragraph 5.18 for further comments.)

The word "necessarily" is important here. The consumer who purchases a record buys it in order to play it and listen to it. However, even if there were no express words on the record forbidding public performance, a licence to play the sound recording in public would not be implied

243

in our view because the ordinary use of the record would not necessarily involve playing it *in public*. (Compare however the *Monckton* case referred to in paragraph 10.46.)

Again, however, there are problems with the extent of any such implied licence, and these are demonstrated by the case of *Roberts* v. *Handiware Ltd*. ([1980] F.S.R. 352). There the plaintiff owned the copyright in designs for handmade knitted garments. She exploited the designs both by manufacturing the garments, and publishing pattern books by which people could make up the garments from the patterns included in the books. The defendants made garments from the pattern books and sold them through their retail outlets. In granting an interim injunction to prevent the further manufacture and sale, Vinelott J., whilst not deciding the point, doubted whether the licence to make the garments which was clearly conferred on the purchaser of the pattern book extended to doing this for commercial purposes.

Again, a useful test as to the extent of any such licence might be the business efficacy one referred to in paragraph 9.28.

(c) *Where an express licence has been granted to do a particular act for purposes which involve the doing of another restricted act*

9.09   This is best explained by an example. If a writer who owns the copyright in a novel grants the right to a television company to reproduce this in the form of a film for the purposes of broadcasting it, then it is almost certain (in the unlikely event of the point not being covered in an express agreement) that a Court would hold that a licence to broadcast had been granted.

However, again the extent of the licence may be a problem: would it in the example given extend to broadcasting by others or to cable transmission? This might depend on other terms in the agreement, or, like the architects' plans cases, the amount paid.

In these circumstances, it is clearly in the interests of both licensor and licensee to have a properly drafted agreement which states expressly what is and what is not covered by the agreement. Once the 1988 Act is in force it will be even more important to ensure that licence agreements properly deal with the rights covered. This arises in particular from the creation of the new restricted act of issuing copies to the public. Under the 1956 Act, this was not a restricted act, and no separate consent was therefore required to distribute articles once they had been manufactured with consent, unless such distribution amounted to publishing the relevant work. In the context of the 1988 Act, a licence to manufacture articles for the purpose of selling or hiring those articles may (depending on the terms of the agreement) carry with it an implied licence to issue those articles to the public, and, if the person granting the licence wishes to impose conditions on such issue, it will be important to state those conditions expressly.

(d) *Where the behaviour of the copyright owner is such that consent must be inferred*

In *Redwood Music Limited* v. *Chappell & Co. Ltd.* ([1982] R.P.C. 109),   **9.10**
Robert Goff J. held that the test as to whether such a licence had been granted is "whether, viewing the facts objectively, the words and conduct of the alleged licensor, as known to the alleged licensee, in fact indicated that the licensor consented to what the licensee was doing."

In that case the copyrights in the words and music of a song had been assigned to a music publisher through whom the defendants claimed, but the plaintiffs claimed ownership under the reversionary rights provisions of the 1911 Act. (See paragraph 8.51 onwards.) Contemporaneously with making a claim to those rights, representatives of the plaintiff's predecessors in title invited the defendants to negotiate for continued administration of the rights. Various requests for information about the claim made by the defendants were either not answered at all or were not answered satisfactorily, and there were long periods where it might have been reasonable to assume that the claim had been abandoned. During all this time, the defendants continued with the knowledge of the plaintiffs and those through whom they claimed to exploit the song and account for royalties. It does not appear that at any stage an express demand was made to the defendants that they cease to exploit the copyrights or collect the royalties. In those circumstances, the Judge held that there was an implied consent to continue exploiting the copyright.

(e) *Where it is a custom of the trade*

This is probably of limited application today, and the point seems only to   **9.11**
have been addressed in the area of newspapers and magazines. It is said to be a custom of the trade that where a manuscript article is submitted by an author to a periodical without any suggestion as to its publication or the payment of a fee, the article may be published in the periodical without further consent being required, provided that the author is paid the standard rate applicable. (See *Hall-Brown* v. *Iliffe & Sons Ltd.* [1928–1935] MacG.Cop.Cas. 88.) Compare this with the *London Printing* case in the next paragraph.

(f) *Encouragement is not necessarily a licence*

A person entitled to grant licences in relation to a copyright work will   **9.12**
obviously wish to encourage exploitation and use of the work in order to generate income from it. However, encouragement to do so will not necessarily constitute a licence. In *Performing Right Society Ltd.* v. *Coates* ([1923–1928] MacG.Cop.Cas. 103), Tomlin J. said that the sending of complimentary sheet music copies of songs to well-known performers did not amount to a licence to perform the songs in public. Similarly in *London Printing and Publishing Alliance Ltd.* v. *Cox* ([1891] 3 Ch. 291), it was held by the Court of Appeal that a letter from an artist copyright owner to a magazine enclosing a sketch drawn by her and encouraging

them in a desire to print it only amounted to an offer of negotiation to reproduce the sketch, and not a licence.

(g) *Where no other terms or facts inconsistent with implied licence*

9.13   The circumstances dealt with in paragraphs (a) to (e) above depend on there being no other factors inconsistent with such implied licences. If for example in the contracts described in paragraphs (a), (b) and (c) there had been express terms inconsistent with an implied licence, then such a licence would not have been implied. Similarly in the *Redwood* case referred to in paragraph 9.10, if the reversionary rights owners had called upon the publishers to cease exploitation and reserved all rights whilst negotiating, the result of the case might have been different.

5. Acquiescence and estoppel

9.14   Apart from where implied consent has been granted, and where a copyright owner is not entitled to exercise his copyright in the circumstances referred to in paragraph 9.05 above, there may be other situations where the copyright owner is deprived of his ability to enforce his exclusive right. Such circumstances may in particular occur where the copyright owner acts in such a way (either by giving some clear and unequivocal representation, promise or assurance, or even in some cases by standing by and doing nothing) that a third party is led to believe that the copyright owner will not enforce his rights. This is not a rule which is peculiar to copyright, but arises on the basis of the general equitable principles of estoppel and acquiescence. These principles are too complex to set out here, and there are various stringent conditions which must be fulfilled if a defence to an action for infringement is to succeed on that basis.

However, an example of where such a defence did succeed is *Cecil Lennox Ltd.* v. *Metro-Goldwyn-Meyer Pictures Ltd.* ([1928–1935] MacG. Cop.Cas. 453). The plaintiffs here owned the copyrights in the words and music of a song. The song was incorporated into a film without their knowledge, but, after this was drawn to their attention, they approached the film company which had included the song in the film and reached an agreement with them by which the film company allowed the plaintiffs to print the title of the film, the film company's name and photographs of the stars acting in the film on sheet music copies of the song. On that basis, it was held by Clauson J. that the plaintiffs could not afterwards turn round and complain that the defendants were infringing copyright by performing or authorising the performance of the song in public.

Although it is not necessary for such principles to apply that infringement take place before the behaviour of the copyright owner which deprives him of his right to take action, it is more likely that estoppel and acquiescence will be of use as a defence in those circumstances. Otherwise it is likely that the Court would simply take the view that consent was implied. (See paragraph 9.10.)

6. Successors in title

9.15   Where the owner of a copyright in a work grants a licence to someone to exploit or use the work in some way, and then subsequently assigns his copyright to someone else, the question arises whether the licence is effective against the new owner as regards acts done after assignment. Here, the 1988 Act re-enacts the provision in the 1956 Act whereby such a licence is binding on every successor in title to the copyright owner who granted the licence, except a purchaser in good faith for valuable consideration and without notice (actual or constructive) of the licence or a person deriving title from such a purchaser (s.90(4)).

(a) *All types of licence*

The provision applies to all licences, and accordingly even an exclusive **9.16** licensee can lose his licence if the copyright owner assigns the copyright to such a good faith purchaser as is mentioned above.

(b) *Successor in title*

The expression successor in title could refer not only to a subsequent **9.17** assignee but also, for example, to someone to whom the copyright devolves by will, or someone to whom the copyright reverts after a period of time.

(c) *Subsequent assignees*

Once the copyright has been assigned to such a good faith purchaser, any **9.18** subsequent assignee will also take free of the licence, even though he had notice of it.

(d) *Licence must be valid*

In our view, the licence in order to be binding on the successor in title **9.19** must be one which it is within the scope of the copyright owner to grant. For example, if the copyright has been assigned to someone for 10 years with a right of reverter to the original owner at the end of that period, a licence granted by the former to exploit the copyright work for a period longer than the 10 years will not be effective against the original owner once the copyright has reverted.

(e) *Copyright owner*

The provision is expressed only to apply to licences granted by a copyright **9.20** owner, but presumably extends to licences granted on behalf of the copyright owner by someone having authority to do so. Although in theory the provision does not apply to licences granted by, for example, an exclusive licensee, in practice such a licence will be binding because the exclusive licence under which it was granted (assuming that it was one within the scope of the exclusive licensee's rights to grant) would itself be binding on the successor in title.

(f) *Notice*

9.21   Actual notice will include notice to an agent where the agent was given notice of the licence or got to know of the licence, if this happened within the ambit of the agent's employment. This will generally be so even where the agent fails to pass on notice to his principal.

The meaning of the expression constructive notice is unclear, and there appears to have been no copyright case dealing with the point. In land law, constructive notice will generally be imputed to someone either if he knows something which ought to have put him on notice to make further enquiry, or from his wilfully abstaining from making enquiries in order to avoid notice. If therefore a person wishing to acquire a copyright fails to investigate or make enquiries as to what licences have been granted, he may still be held to have constructive notice of them, assuming that the same considerations apply as in land law.

(g) *Prospective copyright owners*

9.22   A similar rule to section 90(4) applies to any licence granted by the prospective owner of a copyright which has not yet come into existence. A licence granted by such a prospective owner is binding on every successor entitled to his interest or prospective interest in the right, except a purchaser in good faith for valuable consideration and without actual or constructive notice of the licence or a person deriving title from such a purchaser (s.91(3)).

This provision applies whether or not the future copyright has been assigned under the provisions referred to in paragraph 8.12 onwards above, even though it appears in the section in the 1988 Act which deals with that provision. However, special problems arise where the copyright is one which is subject to such an assignment. Where that is so, the prospective owner of the copyright could either be the person to whom the future copyright has been assigned, or the person in whom the copyright would vest in the absence of such an agreement. This is because on the basis of what is referred to in paragraph 8.13(e) it is not possible to know with certainty who the copyright will vest in. It seems therefore that a licence granted by either party could be binding on the person owning the copyright with effect from creation.

B. TERMS AND CONDITIONS

9.23   This section in particular is relevant both as regards construction of assignments and licensing agreements.

1. Special copyright rules

9.24   The 1988 Act transitional provisions repeat those in the 1956 Act whereby any document made or event occurring before commencement of the 1988 Act which had any operation affecting the ownership of the copyright in an existing work, or creating, transferring or terminating an interest, right or licence in respect of the copyright in an existing work, has the corresponding operation in relation to copyright in a work under the 1988 Act. (See schedule 1, paragraph 25(1).) The effect of this provision on ownership of copyright has been referred to elsewhere in this book (see paragraph 3.05).

In the context of construction of assignments and licensing agreements, it means in its simplest application that an assignment or licensing agreement made before the commencement of the 1988 Act has the same effect under the 1988 Act. So, if a licence to broadcast is granted just prior to commencement of the 1988 Act, this is construed in accordance with section 48(2) of the 1956 Act, not section 6(1) of the 1988 Act.

A further transitional provision to the 1988 Act states that expressions used in any document made before commencement which had any operation affecting ownership of the copyright in an existing work, or creating, transferring or terminating an interest, right or licence in respect of the copyright in an existing work must be construed in accordance with their effect immediately before commencement of the 1988 Act. (See schedule 1, paragraph 25(2).)

This means for example that if there is a reference in such a pre-1988 Act document to publication this must be construed on the basis of what publication meant under the 1956 Act (see paragraph 2.44 onwards), and not under the 1988 Act.

The transitional provisions to the 1956 Act contained a similar rule in relation to documents made before commencement of the 1956 Act. In our view, the effect of the 1988 Act transitional provision is that the 1956 Act transitional provision is also preserved. So, taking the example of publication again, if a document made before commencement of the 1956 Act has a reference to publication, that will be construed in accordance with the 1911 Act provision, and not the 1956 Act provision.

The table below identifies the main words and expressions which are identical in wording but different in meaning in the three Acts, and which might in practice be important:

Expression	1911 Act	1956 Act	1988 Act
"artistic work"	s.35(1)	s.3(1) & s.48(1)	s.4(1)
"building "	—	s.48(1)	s.4(2)
"collective work"	s.35(1)	—	s.178
"dramatic work"	s.35(1)	s.48(1)	s.3(1)
"literary work"	s.35(1)	s.48(1)	s.3(1)
"photograph"	s.35(1)	s.48(1)	s.4(2)
"publication"	s.1(3)	s.49(2) & (3)	s.175
"sound recording"	—	s.12(9)	s.5(1)
"sufficient acknowledgement"	—	s.6(10)	s.178
"writing"	—	s.48(1)	s.178

2. Normal rules as to construction

(a) *On the basis of normal contractual rules*

Apart from the specific rules referred to in paragraph 9.24 above, assign- **9.25** ments and licensing agreements must be construed in accordance with the normal rules relating to construction of contracts. These rules are too detailed to set out here, but the most important rule which one must bear in mind is that although the purpose of construing agreements is to discover the intention of the parties, this must be done on the basis primarily of the words which they use in the document itself. If these words are clear and unambiguous, and there are no provisions which conflict with each other, the agreement must be construed as it stands, however harsh the effect. This of course is subject to the rules on undue influence and restraint of trade referred to in Chapter 8, and to other contractual rules such as rectification where the written agreement does not reflect the intentions of the parties.

(b) *Problems with new technology and new media*

9.26 The construction of copyright agreements does however pose particular problems because of advances in technology and new media in which copyright works can be exploited. A number of cases in particular have dealt with the development of the film industry, and are useful in demonstrating the problems which arise. In *Ganthony* v. *GJR Syndicate Ltd.* ([1911–1916] MacG.Cop.Cas. 247), it was held that an assignment made in 1899 of "all acting rights whatsoever" in a play only covered the right to perform the play as a play with live actors on stage in the ordinary way, and so did not grant any cinematograph rights. In *Pathe Pictures Ltd.* v. *Bancroft* ([1928–1935] MacG.Cop.Cas. 403) it was held that a grant in 1927 in relation to the copyright in a play of the "sole and exclusive licence to produce the said work in moving picture films" did not extend to a sound film, because the expression "moving pictures" was inappropriate to cover the sound track.

In *Hospital for Sick Children* v. *Walt Disney Productions Inc.* ([1968] Ch.52), the Court of Appeal held that an agreement of 1919 to produce the literary and dramatic works of Sir James Barrie "in cinematograph or moving picture films" would extend prima facie to both silent and sound films, even though the making of silent films at that stage was not a commercially practicable proposition. However, for differing reasons, the members of the Court held that the agreement did not entitle the defendants to prevent the copyright owner/plaintiff granting to another party a licence to make a sound film of the play *Peter Pan*, Lord Denning on the basis that the rest of the agreement demonstrated that sound films were not covered by the original 1919 agreement, Harman L.J. and Salmon L.J. on the basis that the agreement only covered the making of one film of *Peter Pan* which had already been made. The differing approach by the members of the Court demonstrates the problems faced in construing such agreements.

Although there appear to be no recent cases of a similar type, practical problems continue to arise particularly in relation to the exploitation of licensed versions of copyright works in different media. A particular problem has been whether old licences granting the right to use literary, dramatic or musical works in films have extended to the exploitation of the films in the form of video cassettes made for retail sale to the public.

Although of course it is difficult to predict the methods of exploitation and media which will exist far into the future, it is vital both for copyright owners and users to ensure that agreements properly reflect not only present day conditions but those which are known to be on the horizon. It is still sometimes the case unfortunately that standard agreements dealing with the exploitation of copyright works do not adequately reflect new media and methods of exploitation. From the copyright owner's point of view, this can have disastrous effects as regards generating income from exploitation of the work. Merely because the licence or grant of rights extends to areas in respect of which the copyright owner is not entitled to royalties or other fees under the contract will not usually be a ground for terminating the agreement.

(c) *Foreign law*

Particular problems of interpretation may also arise where an assignment or licence is made subject to a foreign law. Here, the rules of construction under the foreign law must be applied, which may not be exactly the same as those which apply under English law. (See *Redwood Music Ltd*. v. *B. Feldman and Co. Ltd*. [1979] R.P.C. 385.) **9.27**

C. IMPLIED TERMS

1. Where terms will be implied

Whether or not a term will be implied into an assignment or licensing agreement depends on the normal principles which apply under the law of contract. A term will not be implied simply because it is reasonable to do so. In the words of Kay L.J. in *Hamlyn and Co.* v. *Wood and Co.* ([1891] 2 Q.B. 488), no term will be implied "unless there arises from the language of the contract itself, and the circumstances under which it is entered into, such an inference that the parties must have intended the stipulation in question that the Court is necessarily driven to the conclusion that it must be implied." **9.28**

This general rule is often expressed in two different ways. First, it is said that a term will be implied in order to give business efficacy to a transaction. (See *The Moorcock* [1889] 14 P.D. 64.) Secondly, a term will be implied if it "is something so obvious that it goes without saying; so that, if while the parties were making their bargain, an officious bystander were to suggest some express provision for it in the agreement, they would testily suppress him with a common, 'Oh, of course' ". See *Shirlaw* v. *Southern Foundaries (1926) Ltd*. ([1939] 2 K.B. 206).

The above general principles are not easy to apply, and in examining the cases on implied terms it is sometimes difficult to understand why in some instances a term has been implied, and why in others it has not. Each case of course very much depends on its own facts, but some examples of issues in copyright cases are addressed below.

2. Implied term to exploit

9.29   In general, where the copyright in a work is assigned to another party, the Court will not imply into the agreement an obligation to exploit it, even where the consideration for the assignment is the payment of royalties. In *Schroeder* v. *Macaulay* ([1974] 3 All E.R. 616), it was even doubted by Lord Reid that one could read into an exclusive songwriting agreement an obligation on the part of the publisher to act in good faith, that is, for example, not to refrain from publishing a work which he would otherwise have published for some oblique or malicious motive. Absence of any undertaking to exploit may however be relevant in deciding whether a contract may be avoided on the principles set out in paragraph 8.63 onwards.

    An obligation to exploit might however be inferred from other clauses in the agreement. In *John* v. *James* (unreported), the exclusive song-writing agreement obliged the writers to supply a minimum number of musical compositions considered suitable and acceptable for publication by the publisher. It was accepted by the publishers here that there was an implied term to use reasonable diligence to publish, promote and exploit compositions which were accepted by the publisher under the agreement.

    Where there is an express obligation to exploit a copyright work, but the time within which exploitation must take place is not specified, the Court may imply a term that exploitation take place within a reasonable time: *Crane* v. *C. Arthur Pearson Ltd.* ([1936–1945] MacG.Cop.Cas. 125). However, even here there may be other provisions which will negate the inference. In *Zang Tumb Tuum Records Ltd.* v. *Johnson* (unreported), a record company had options to require recordings to be made embodying performances of the defendant. It was argued by the record company that there was an implied term that on the exercise of an option the record company would proceed to procure the making of the record within a reasonable time and that if they failed to do so the performers could make time of the essence upon service of some suitable notice. Whitford J. rejected this argument, on the basis that the agreement provided in express terms that the record company could choose the time and place and other aspects of the recording to be made.

3. Implied terms to alter a copyright work

9.30   Where the copyright in a work is assigned, the assignee will normally be entitled to make such alterations to the work as he considers fit, subject to the alterations not being actionable on the basis of defamation, and subject now to the question of moral rights. (See Chapter 11.)

    In the case of a licence, it was held by Goff J. in *Frisby* v. *BBC* ([1967] Ch. 932) that if the user of a copyright work has a licence to copy a work, "he can set that up as a defence equally whether he has copied verbatim or made alterations, unless and save insofar as the terms of the licence expressly or impliedly require him not to make alterations." This rather turns the situation on its head so that prima facie it seems that the question is not whether there is an implied term that the licensee may alter the work but whether there is an implied term that no alterations may be made.

However, Goff J. went on to say that the Court would readily imply a term limiting the right to make alterations. In *Joseph* v. *National Magazine Co. Ltd.* ([1959] Ch. 14), there was not just a licence for a magazine to publish an article, but a contract obliging the magazine to publish. There, Harman J. held that the plaintiff author was amply justified in refusing to allow the article to be published in an altered form both as to content and style.

Although Goff J. in the *Frisby* case held that in the absence of an express or implied prohibition on alterations a licensee had the right to make even substantial alterations, this may not be so where the alterations are such that an adaptation of the work has been made. As referred to in paragraph 5.50, adaptation is a separate restricted act in the case of literary, dramatic and musical works. Whether or not a licence to adapt or exploit a work in the form of an adaptation can be implied in such a case will depend on the considerations set out in paragraph 9.28 above.

4. Implied terms as regards royalties and type of exploitation

In *Nichols* v. *The Amalgamated Press* ([1905–1910] MacG.Cop.Cas.   **9.31**
166), the author of certain songs assigned the copyrights in the words and music of those songs to a music publisher for the world, with a royalty to be paid on every copy of the songs sold by the publisher. The publisher allowed a third party to publish the songs, and it was held by the Court of Appeal that since the sale was not a sale by the publisher, no royalties arose. Although the Court said that a term would be implied that the publisher would not put it out of its power to sell copies, the Court rejected an argument that there was an implied term that the publisher would do nothing whereby the sale of the songs by it might be prejudiced or the author's chance of earning royalties diminished.

This seems a harsh decision and the report of the case is not very detailed. It should be contrasted with the unreported judgment of Plowman J. in *Instone* v. *A. Schroeder Music Publishing Co. Ltd.*, where the contract was not a simple assignment but an exclusive songwriting agreement by which the publishers acquired the future copyright in all compositions written by the composer over a period of years. There the judge expressed the view that there was to be implied into the agreement a term to the effect that the defendant publishers would not enter into any arrangement such as would unfairly, unjustifiably or artificially diminish their receipts. This he held to have been breached where the publisher's associated company in a local territory deducted 50 per cent. of its receipts from the independent subpublisher in that territory before remitting sums to the publisher. The point is not one which was dealt with when the case went to the House of Lords (reported as *Schroeder* v. *Macaulay*—see paragraph 9.29).

D. ASSIGNMENTS AND SUB-LICENSING OF LICENCES

9.32   As referred to in paragraph 8.40, the assignee of the copyright in a work is entitled to assign the copyright on to a third party, unless the assignment to him provides otherwise. Different considerations apply to licences. A properly drafted licensing agreement will expressly deal with the question of assignment, but, in the absence of any such provisions, whether or not the licence is assignable depends on whether the licence is a personal one.

1. Where a licence is personal

9.33   A licence will be personal to the licensee, and therefore not assignable, in broadly two circumstances. First, it will be personal where it was granted because of the licensee's personal reputation. (See *Dorling* v. *Honnor Marine Ltd*. [1964] Ch. 560.) This can be so whether or not the licensee is an individual or a limited company. (See *Griffith* v. *Tower Publishing Co. Ltd*. [1897] 1 Ch. 21.) Secondly, a licence will be personal where it imposes duties of a personal nature, such as to exploit a work, and to account for and pay royalties. (See *Hale* v. *T. Fisher Unwin Ltd*. [1923–1928] MacG.Cop. Cas. 31.)

2. Problems for licensors where assignment allowed

9.34   If the licence is not a personal one, it can be assigned. The same problem may arise here as under assignments of copyright (see paragraph 8.40) in that if the assignee of the licence fails to observe a term contained in the licensing agreement, the licensor will have no agreement with the assignee of the licence, and will only be left with a remedy against the original licensee. Of course, the licence may be expressed in such a way that it is conditional upon observance of the relevant term, in which case the original licensor may be able to take action for infringement of copyright.

3. Sub-licensing

9.35   Under the 1956 Act (s.49(7)), where the express or implied terms of a licence permitted the licensee to authorise a particular act, and the licensee then authorised a third party to do that act, it was specifically provided that the doing of that act by the third party was to be regarded as having been done with the licence of the original licensor and every other person upon whom the licence was binding (for example, a successor in title bound by the terms of the licence under the provisions referred to in paragraph 9.15 above).

Somewhat strangely, this provision is not re-enacted in the 1988 Act. However, it probably follows anyway, since if the original licensee was permitted to authorise someone else to do the relevant act, it could not in any event be said to have been done without the licence of the copyright owner. Obviously, whether or not the licence permits the licensee to authorise others to do the relevant act is another point which should be expressly covered in licensing agreements.

E. TERMINATION AND EXPIRY OF LICENSING AGREEMENTS

Whether or not a licence can be revoked or terminated is a difficult **9.36**
question, and again it must be emphasised that the issue is one which it is
important to cover in a licensing agreement. Many licensing agreements
now contain provisions for termination of the licence in the event that
there is a material breach of the licensing agreement which is not rectified
within so many days of notice specifying the breach. In many cases also, a
licensing agreement will specify that the licence may be terminated in the
event of bankruptcy, liquidation, receivership and so on.

1. Non-contractual licences

If there is no term dealing with the position, whether or not the licence **9.37**
can be revoked or terminated depends on the nature of the licence. If the
licence is nothing more than a bare consent to do an act, it will usually be
possible to revoke it, although not without giving reasonable notice. This
follows from the case of *Hart* v. *Hayman Christy and Lilly Ltd.* ([1911–16]
MacG.Cop.Cas. 302.) However, the fact that the Judge in that case held
that the copyright owner had changed his mind about the licence "with
good reason" may mean that in some circumstances a copyright owner
may not be entitled to revoke a consent once given, particularly where the
licensee has already expended money in reliance on the licence.

2. Contractual licences

Where the licence has been granted under a contract (for example where **9.38**
the copyright owner has agreed to grant a licence in consideration of the
payment of money whether in the form of a lump sum or royalties), the
licence can only be terminated or revoked if there is an implied (assuming
that there is not an express) term to this effect. This is not an easy matter
to determine. Where there is a joint venture between the copyright owner
and the licensee, it seems more likely that the licence is revocable subject
to reasonable notice. See *Dorling* v. *Honnor Marine Ltd.* ([1964] Ch.
560). Conversely, where a licence to publish a work obliges the publisher
to publish it and to pay royalties on the basis of the number of copies sold
as opposed to a share of the profits, it is unlikely that the Court will imply
a term that the licence can be revoked. See *Holland* v. *Methuen and Co.
Ltd.* ([1928–35] MacG.Cop.Cas. 247).

   If a licence is revocable on reasonable notice, what is reasonable will
depend upon the facts of the case. If notice to terminate is given, but the
period of notice is not reasonable, it appears that the notice is not invalid,
and the licensee can only continue to operate under the licence until
expiry of the period which would have been reasonable. (See *Dorling* v.
Honnor Marine Ltd. [1964] Ch. 560.)

3. Termination for breach

Whether or not a licence can be revoked or terminated expressly or **9.39** impliedly, it may also be possible to terminate it on the grounds of breach, even where there is no express provision providing for this. See paragraph 9.42 below.

4. Acts after expiry of termination

9.40   Once a licence has expired or been terminated, the licensee cannot continue to do the relevant restricted act which he was licensed to carry out. However, in the absence of an express or implied term to the contrary, he can do acts which are not restricted acts, even though his ability to do those acts has arisen by reason of the licence which was granted to him. The example often used to illustrate this is the sale or distribution after the licence has expired of articles manufactured in accordance with the licence. Since under the 1911 and 1956 Acts, the sale of articles lawfully manufactured in the United Kingdom was not one of the restricted acts, the licensee could continue to sell off existing stock after the licence expired. (See *Howitt* v. *Hall* [1862] 6 L.T. 348.) However, this is now subject to the operation of the new restricted act of issuing copies to the public, which may in future allow the copyright owner to prevent sale or distribution after the licence has come to an end.

F. REMEDIES FOR BREACH OF A LICENCE

1. Conditional licences

9.41   From the copyright owner's point of view, it is often sensible to ensure that a licence to exploit or use a copyright work is made conditional upon the licensee's compliance with the terms and conditions of the licensing agreement. Assuming that the licence is carefully drafted on this basis, a breach of a term or condition contained in the licensing agreement will then often enable the copyright owner to exercise or claim the rights and remedies of a copyright owner where his copyright has been infringed.

2. Non-conditional licences

9.42   Where a licensing agreement does not on its proper construction make the licence conditional, the remedies for breach of the licensing agreement will be determined in accordance with the normal principles on remedies for breach of contract. This is particularly important where the licensor wishes to terminate the agreement by reason of the breach, because under the law of contract it is not every breach of contract by a licensee which will entitle the licensor to treat the contract as discharged. This will generally only be so where the breach deprives the licensor of substantially the whole benefit which it was the intention of the parties as expressed in the contract that he should obtain as the consideration for the grant of the licence. See *Hongkong Fir Shipping Co. Ltd.* v. *Kawasaki*

Kisen Kaisha Ltd. [1962] 2 Q.B. 26. Not even the late payment of royalties will in all circumstances allow a licensor to treat the licensing agreement as at an end. See in particular *Decro-Wall International S.A.* v. *Practitioners In Marketing Ltd*. [1971] 1 W.L.R. 361.

3. Damages for breach of a licensing agreement

Breach of the licensing agreement will of course also give rise to a claim **9.43** for damages for breach of contract. Where for example there is an obligation to exploit in the licensing agreement which the licensee breaches, the licensor is entitled to claim damages for the failure to exploit, and this may extend to damages for the loss of opportunity to enhance the copyright owner's reputation. See *Joseph* v. *National Magazine Co. Ltd*. ([1959] Ch. 14).

4. Specific performance

Where there is an obligation to exploit, the Court has power to make an **9.44** order for specific performance of the agreement. This was done for example in *Barrow* v. *Chappell & Co. Ltd*. ([1976] R.P.C. 355). However, where the performance of the contract would require constant supervision by the Court, the Court is unlikely to grant such an order— see in particular *Joseph* v. *National Magazine Co. Ltd*. [1959] Ch. 14, where Harman J. refused to make an order for specific performance on the basis that " . . . the exact terms of the article were never agreed on between the parties and the Court would be called on to supervise the editing of the article. . . . "

5. Breach by licensor

Of course, it may not only be the licensee which is in breach of contract. **9.45** Where an author enters into an agreement to supply a publisher with a work of his, but the author fails to do so, the publisher will normally be able to claim damages for breach of the agreement. The Court will in an appropriate case make an order for specific performance of an agreement to allow a publisher to publish the work of an author (see *Macdonald (E.) Ltd*. v. *Eyles* [1921] 1 Ch. 631), but it will not grant an order for specific performance of a contract to write a book.

6. Breach by assignee of licensor

As already stated, where a licence is assignable, the licensor will normally **9.46** only be able to sue the licensee, and not his assignee, for breach of the licensing agreement, unless the failure to observe the relevant terms and conditions of the licensing agreement constitutes an infringement of copyright. Ordinarily, the same applies as regards a licensee's rights under a licensing agreement, in that he will only be able to seek a remedy from his licensor. However, the 1988 Act has here introduced a new provision in relation only to exclusive licences. (See paragraph 10.22.) Where an exclusive licence within the 1988 Act definition has been granted by a copyright owner, and the copyright is then subsequently assigned by the copyright owner to someone else, the exclusive licensee has the same rights against the assignee of the copyright as he has against the person who granted him the exclusive licence (s.92(2)). The provision however only applies in the case of an assignee who is bound by the exclusive licence, so it would not apply as against a purchaser in good faith for valuable consideration and without notice (actual or constructive) of a licence or a person deriving title from such a purchaser. (See paragraph 9.15.) The provision also does not apply in relation to exclusive licences granted before commencement of the 1988 Act.

III CERTIFICATION OF LICENSING SCHEMES (s.143)

1. The relevant licensing schemes

9.47 In some cases set out in Chapter 7, an act is specifically permitted without infringing copyright except to the extent that there is a licensing scheme in force providing for the grant of licences which has been certified by the Secretary of State for Trade and Industry. The meaning of the expression "licensing scheme" is dealt with in paragraph 9.61 below.

The relevant permitted acts are as follows:

(i) s.35: educational recording of broadcasts or cable programmes. (See paragraph 7.23.)

(ii) s.60: abstracts of scientific or technical articles. (See paragraph 7.102.)

(iii) s.66: rental of sound recordings, films and computer programs. (See paragraph 7.109.)

(iv) s.74: sub-titled copies of broadcasts or cable programmes for people who are deaf or hard of hearing or otherwise physically or mentally handicapped. (See paragraph 7.98.)

2. Method of obtaining certification

9.48 Applications to certify such licensing schemes may be made to the Secretary of State by a person operating or proposing to operate the scheme. The Secretary of State *must* certify the scheme if he is satisfied that the following two conditions have been complied with:

(i) The scheme enables the works to which it relates to be identified with sufficient certainty by persons likely to require licences. This in our view does not mean that the scheme has to contain detailed reference to the precise works covered, and this of course would be impractical in many cases. We believe it means that the scheme has to contain a procedure whereby persons likely to require licences will be able to find out which particular works are covered.

(ii) The scheme must set out clearly the charges (if any) payable and the other terms on which licences will be granted.

3. Jurisdiction of the Copyright Tribunal

The fact that the Secretary of State has certified a scheme does not mean   **9.49**
that it cannot be referred to the Copyright Tribunal under the provisions
referred to in paragraph 9.54. In accordance with those provisions, a
proposed licensing scheme could be referred to the Tribunal before
certification has taken place. The scheme could also be referred after
certification. There is no duty placed on the Secretary of State under the
1988 Act to examine whether or not the charges or terms or conditions are
reasonable.

4. Effective date of the scheme

If the Secretary of State certifies the scheme, such certification will take   **9.50**
effect from the date on which the Secretary of State specifies that it will do
so, but this cannot be until the expiry of eight weeks from the date of the
order certifying the scheme. Furthermore, if the scheme is the subject of a
reference to the Copyright Tribunal, certification will take effect from
any later date on which the order of the Copyright Tribunal comes into
force or the reference to the Tribunal is withdrawn. The provision does
not specify the material time at which the scheme must be the subject of a
reference to the Copyright Tribunal for a later date to apply. In our view,
it is likely that the later date will take precedence if at any time before the
date specified by the Secretary of State a reference is made to the
Tribunal.

5. Variation of scheme

No variation of the scheme has any effect unless a corresponding amend-   **9.51**
ment of the order has been made. The Secretary of State must make such
an amendment in the case of a variation ordered by the Copyright
Tribunal on a reference under sections 118, 119 and 120. (See paragraphs
4.68 and 9.72.)

6. Revocation of scheme

The order certifying the scheme must be revoked if the scheme ceases to   **9.52**
be operated. The Secretary of State also has power to revoke the scheme
if it appears to him that it is no longer being operated according to its
terms.

IV THE COPYRIGHT TRIBUNAL

A. INTRODUCTION

9.53   Under the 1956 Act, a tribunal called the Performing Right Tribunal ("the PRT") had jurisdiction in the areas of public performance, broadcasting and cable use over licensing schemes made by licensing bodies, and, in certain restricted cases, the refusal of licences by licensing bodies. Under the 1988 Act, the jurisdiction of the PRT has been greatly extended, and the tribunal has been re-named the Copyright Tribunal.

1. Summary of the Tribunal's jurisdiction

9.54   (a) It can confirm or vary proposed licensing schemes by licensing bodies, and also existing licensing schemes where a dispute arises with the operator of the scheme.

(b) It has jurisdiction over the refusal of licences both in cases covered by licensing schemes, and, in limited circumstances, cases excluded from licensing schemes.

(c) It has power to confirm or vary the terms of a licence proposed by a licensing body, and to order that an existing licence continue even after it has been terminated.

(d) It has jurisdiction over applications to settle the royalty or other sum payable for the rental of sound recordings, films or computer programs. (See paragraph 7.109.)

(e) Where, following a report made by the Monopolies and Mergers Commission, an order is made by the Secretary of State providing for compulsory licences to be available, the Copyright Tribunal has the power to settle the terms of such licences. (See paragraph 9.136.)

(f) As regards performers' rights, it has the power to grant consent to make a recording from a previous recording of a performance, where the identity or whereabouts of a performer cannot be ascertained by reasonable enquiry, or where a performer unreasonably withholds his consent. (See Chapter 12.)

(g) It can determine the royalty or other remuneration to be paid to the trustees for the Hospital for Sick Children for certain uses of "Peter Pan" by Sir James Barrie. (See Chapter 14.)

The powers referred to in paragraphs (a) to (c) above are covered in this section. The other powers are dealt with where indicated above.

The Tribunal has no jurisdiction to make investigations of its own volition. The issue in each case must be referred to the Tribunal by the appropriate party. The identity of that party varies from case to case, and is dealt with below in the context of each separate provision.

2. Constitution of the Tribunal

The Tribunal will consist of a Chairman and two deputy chairmen, **9.55** together with not less than two, or more than eight, ordinary members (s.145(2)). For the purposes of any proceedings, the Tribunal will consist of either the Chairman or one of the deputy chairmen, and two or more ordinary members (s.148(1)). It is therefore possible that three separate divisions of the Tribunal could sit at the same time, and indeed, with the extension of jurisdiction referred to below, this may be necessary. The Tribunal makes decisions by majority vote, and if the votes are equal the Chairman or deputy chairman has a further casting vote (s.148(2)).

The 1988 Act provides that no-one is eligible for appointment as Chairman or a deputy chairman unless he is a barrister, advocate or solicitor of not less than seven years' standing, or has held judicial office s.145(3). The Monopolies and Mergers Commission in its report on the collective licensing of public performance and broadcasting rights in sound recordings (Cm.530) recommended that the Chairman should be either a retired High Court Judge or other person of similar standing available to serve at short notice.

The 1988 Act does not specify any qualifications necessary for the ordinary members. The Monopolies and Mergers Commission in the report referred to recommended that they should include some nominated by collective licensing bodies and the leading users' associations.

3. Procedure of the Tribunal

The procedure of the Copyright Tribunal will be laid down in rules which **9.56** have not at the time of writing been made (s.150). Some guidance as to what will be in the rules is, however, contained in the 1988 Act, as follows:

(a) Some of the provisions below allow applications to be made by an organisation representative of copyright users. In order to entertain such a reference, the Tribunal will have to be satisfied that the organisation is reasonably representative of the class of persons which it claims to represent.

(b) There will be power to make party to any proceedings any person or organisation satisfying the Tribunal that they have a substantial interest in the relevant matter.

(c) The Tribunal will obviously have to give the parties to proceedings an opportunity to state their case, in writing or orally.

The Tribunal has power to make awards of costs in relation to any proceedings before it (s.151(1)).

The Monopolies and Mergers Commission in its report mentioned above also made some recommendations as regards the procedure of the Copyright Tribunal, but it remains to be seen whether, or to what extent, the recommendations will be followed. In particular, the Commission recommended that the procedural rules should empower the Tribunal to stipulate the length of hearings, to limit the length of oral proceedings as much as possible and instead to rely on written submissions to the fullest possible extent. It recommended that the Tribunal should provide a framework within which cases could be considered rapidly, so that the most complex case could be dealt with expeditiously.

4. Appeals

9.57   It will only be possible to appeal from decisions of the Copyright Tribunal on points of law (s.152). Appeal takes place to the High Court, or, in the case of proceedings of the Tribunal in Scotland, to the Court of Session. The procedural rules will lay down any time limits within which an appeal may be brought, and also give powers to suspend the operation of orders of the Tribunal pending the appeal, and to modify the provisions referred to below as to the effect of any order made by the Tribunal.

5. Differences in jurisdiction between the 1956 and 1988 Acts

9.58   The main differences are as follows:

(a) Under the 1956 Act, the PRT only had jurisdiction over literary, dramatic or musical works, sound recordings and television broadcasts. Under the 1988 Act, the jurisdiction has been extended to artistic works, films, all broadcasts, cable programmes and the typographical arrangement of published editions.

(b) The PRT only had jurisdiction over public performance, broadcasting and cable transmission. Under the 1988 Act, there is jurisdiction over most restricted acts, except in some cases issuing copies of the work to the public, and making adaptations of the work.

(c) Under the 1956 Act, proposed licensing schemes could not be referred to the Tribunal. Under the 1988 Act, they can.

(d) The jurisdiction over proposed licences and expiring licences referred to in paragraphs 9.83 and 9.87 is new.

(e) The areas of jurisdiction referred to in paragraphs 9.54 (e)(f) and (g) above are also new.

(f) The 1988 Act extends the guidelines for the Tribunal to follow in certain cases. (See paragraph 9.93 onwards.)

(g) The 1956 Act contained no express right of appeal, although there was power for the PRT to refer any question of law to the Court, and a power for the Court to order that the Tribunal refer such a question to the Court. This was capable of being used in order to try to overturn a decision of the PRT on the grounds that it had misdirected itself, but the 1988 Act goes further and contains an express provision for appeals, as referred to in paragraph 9.57 above.

B. LICENSING BODIES, LICENSING SCHEMES AND LICENCES

9.59   Much of the jurisdiction of the Copyright Tribunal relates to licensing schemes of licensing bodies, and licences offered, granted or refused by licensing bodies. It is therefore necessary to deal first with the meaning of these expressions, before going on to examine the precise aspects of licensing schemes and licences which the Tribunal has jurisdiction over.

Although in practice the Copyright Tribunal is likely to be most concerned with the royalties and other fees payable for the use of copyright works, it should be noted that its jurisdiction in the cases referred to in this section extends to all the terms and conditions of licensing schemes and licences.

1. Licensing body

A licensing body is a society or other organisation which has as its main **9.60** object, or one of its main objects, the negotiation or granting, either as owner or prospective owner of copyright or as agent for him, of copyright licences, and whose objects include the granting of licences covering works of more than one author (s.116(2)).

It is clear that licensing bodies are subject to the Tribunal's jurisdiction whether or not they own the relevant rights (for example, the Performing Right Society Ltd.), or act as agents for the owners (for example, the Mechanical-Copyright Protection Society Ltd.). What is not clear is whether *any* company or firm owning or controlling a catalogue of copyrights can be subjected to the Tribunal's jurisdiction.

The expression "society or other organisation" is exactly the same as that used under the 1956 Act, and indeed the definition of "licensing body" under the 1988 Act is virtually the same as under the 1956 Act. The meaning of the expression was never considered by the PRT, because all the references made to it involved the Performing Right Society or Phonographic Performance Limited, which were clearly within the definition. The issue is however now one which may very well be tested before the Tribunal because of the extension of jurisdiction to works and areas of use where in many instances licensing is not carried out by collecting societies.

In general, it has been assumed by some commentators that many companies owning or controlling a catalogue of copyrights will be subject to the Tribunal's jurisdiction for the future as being licensing bodies, because the objects clauses in the Memorandum of Association of such companies often includes the negotiation and granting of copyright licences, as referred to above. The issue is not entirely an easy one, but we incline to the same view. However, the use of the expression "society or other organisation" is odd, and there may be some scope for an argument, under what is termed the *ejusdem generis* rule of construction, that not all companies are covered even where the objects clause requirements are fulfilled, because the ordinary meaning of the word "society" in this context qualifies the type of other organisation which would be subject to the Tribunal's jurisdiction.

However, even if the expression "licensing body" does not extend to individual companies owning or controlling a catalogue of copyrights, it should be noted that in some cases below (in particular those referred to in paragraphs 9.71, 9.74 and 9.78) jurisdiction of the Copyright Tribunal does not depend on the relevant scheme being operated by a licensing body. In such cases, an application may be made to the Copyright Tribunal, whether the copyright owner is any individual, firm or company.

In practice of course, many such copyright owners will not be subject to the jurisdiction of the Tribunal anyway, either because they do not lay down licensing schemes, or because their licences are exempt under the provisions referred to in paragraph 9.62 onwards below.

The expression "copyright licences" means licences to do or authorise the doing of any of the acts restricted by copyright referred to in Chapter 5, although, as will be seen, some of the restricted acts are specifically excluded in certain cases.

2. Licensing scheme

9.61   A licensing scheme is a scheme setting out the classes of case in which the operator of the scheme, or the person on whose behalf he acts, is willing to grant copyright licences, and the terms on which licences would be granted in those classes of case (s.116(1)).

A scheme need not be called a scheme for it to fall within the definition. It could be called a tariff, and it covers anything in the nature of a scheme. In Case 35/78 (Association of Independent Radio Contractors Ltd. and Phonographic Performance Ltd.), the PRT held that the relevant scheme was contained in a draft standard licence, and correspondence and records of conversations relating to it.

The definition again clearly extends both to the situation where the operator of the scheme (for example, the collecting society) grants the licence, and, in the case of a society acting as an agent for the copyright owner, where the member of the society grants the licence in accordance with the scheme.

As stated in paragraph 9.47, some licensing schemes relating to acts which would otherwise be permitted under the provisions referred to in Chapter 7 need to be certified by the Secretary of State for Trade and Industry. Where certification has taken place, they are still subject to the jurisdiction of the Copyright Tribunal.

3. Limitations on jurisdiction over licensing schemes and licences

9.62   Despite the wide definitions of licensing bodies and licensing schemes referred to above, not all licensing or licensing schemes are potentially subject to the Tribunal's jurisdiction. The parameters of the jurisdiction are restricted in the case of literary, dramatic, musical and artistic works, as well as films. None of the exclusions below apply to sound recordings (except film sound-tracks when accompanying a film), broadcasts, cable programmes or the typographical arrangement of published editions.

(a) *Literary, dramatic, musical and artistic works*

(i) *Works of only one author*

Licensing schemes and licences are only subject to the jurisdiction of the   **9.63**
Copyright Tribunal if they cover the works of more than one author (s.
116(4)). Even where there is more than one author involved, there are
several instances where works are still treated as being only by one
author. These are as follows:

(a) Where the licensing scheme or licence covers only a single work of
joint authorship. So a licensing scheme or licence covering a work written
jointly by A and B is not subject to the jurisdiction of the Tribunal. It
must be remembered here that a song in which the music is written by A
and the lyrics by B is not a work of joint authorship because the music and
lyrics are separate works.

(b) Where the licensing scheme or licence covers more than one work of
joint authorship, provided that *all* the authors of *each* work are the same.
So, this would apply in the case of two works each jointly written by A and
B, but not two works one of which is written by A and B, and one by A, B,
and C.

(c) Where the licensing scheme or licence covers only a single work in
which there are distinct contributions by different authors or in which
works or parts of works or different authors are incorporated (see the
definition of "collective work" in s.178). This definition seems to be
based heavily on that part of the definition of "collective work" under the
1911 Act which caused so many problems in the reversionary rights cases.
(See paragraph 8.52.) It may again cause problems here, because it is not
clear whether the work or works referred to have to be ones in which a
separate copyright must subsist. We think it likely it does not, and, if that
is so, a song with words by A and music by B would be treated as being by
one author.

(d) Where the licensing scheme or licence covers more than one such
work referred to in (c) above provided that the authors of *each* work are
the same. It is not so clear here whether for example this covers the
situation where there are say two songs, one the music of which is written
by A and the lyrics by B, and one where the music is written by A and the
lyrics by B and C. We consider it likely that this is not within the definition
and therefore will not be treated as being by one author.

(e) Licensing schemes and licences covering only works made by, or by
employees of or commissioned by, a single individual, firm, company or
group of companies. Group of companies means a holding company and
its subsidiaries, within the meaning of section 736 of the Companies Act
1985.

(ii) *Restricted acts*

Even where the licensing scheme or licence relates to works of more than   **9.64** one author under the rules referred to above, the Copyright Tribunal has no jurisdiction in so far as it relates to issuing copies of literary, dramatic, musical or artistic works to the public, or adapting such works. Restricted acts which the Tribunal have jurisdiction over as regards these works are therefore only copying, performance in public, broadcasting and inclusion in a cable programme service (ss.117 and 124).

Although licensing schemes and licences relating to adapting literary, dramatic and musical works are not subject to the Tribunal's jurisdiction, it must be remembered that the restricted act of adaptation is distinct from doing restricted acts such as copying in relation to adaptations of works. (See paragraphs 5.50 and 5.51.) The question therefore arises whether licensing schemes and licences covering the doing of restricted acts in relation to adaptations of literary, dramatic or musical works are within the Tribunal's jurisdiction. The 1956 Act expressly provided that adaptations were covered in this way, but the 1988 Act is less clear, there being no specific reference to adaptations under the relevant provisions. We believe it likely that the Tribunal would still regard itself as having jurisdiction in the same way as in the 1956 Act, since in most cases doing the act in relation to an adaptation of a work will involve doing it in relation to the work itself.

(iii) *Special rules for computer programs*

9.65   The limitations on jurisdiction referred to above as regards works of more than one author and the issuing of copies of work to the public need to be modified in the case of computer programs. All licensing schemes and licences in relation to the copyright in computer programs are within the Tribunal's jurisdiction so far as they relate to the rental of copies to the public.

(b) *Films*

9.66   These are basically subject to the same limitations as literary, dramatic, musical and artistic works. This applies both as regards the exclusions for works of only one author, and the exclusions as regards restricted acts. It is important to bear in mind that author means the person by whom the arrangements for the making of the film are undertaken. (See paragraph 3.57.)

However, as in the case of computer programs, all licensing schemes and licences so far as they relate to the rental of copies to the public are subject to the Tribunal's jurisdiction. This provision may not however apply to pre-1956 Act films, because they are not protected as films (see paragraph 1.14), although the drafting is not entirely clear on this.

For all these purposes film soundtracks when accompanying a film are treated in the same way as the films themselves.

4. Authorising restricted acts

Under the 1956 Act, the word "licence" was defined in such a way that it only covered a licence to do the particular act, rather than a licence to authorise the particular act to be done. This obviously limited the Tribunal's jurisdiction so that for example in *The Performing Right Society Ltd. v. Reditune Ltd.* (unreported), Whitford J. held that suppliers of both the equipment and tapes for playing background music in variety of different locations such as pubs, hotels and shops could not apply to the Tribunal on the grounds that the society had refused to grant them a public performance licence. This was because what they were seeking was a licence not to perform the relevant works in public but only to authorise such public performance.

The same limitation is not present in the 1988 Act, and it appears that the Tribunal will have jurisdiction in such a case for the future.

C. CONTROL OVER LICENSING SCHEMES

This section deals with the jurisdiction which the Copyright Tribunal has   **9.67** over licensing schemes.

1. Proposed licensing schemes (s.118)

(a) *First reference*

The terms of a licensing scheme proposed to be operated by a licensing   **9.68** body can be referred to the Copyright Tribunal. However, this can only be done by an organisation claiming to be representative of persons claiming that they require licences in cases of a description to which the scheme would apply.

There is no definition of "proposed licensing scheme." It seems therefore that even early or initial proposals could be referred, but the Tribunal has power to decline to allow the reference on the ground that it is premature.

If the Tribunal does decide to entertain the reference, it can make such order confirming or varying the proposed scheme as it may determine to be reasonable in the circumstances.

The order can be made to last indefinitely or for a particular period in time.

(b) *Further reference*

Unless special leave is given, the scheme cannot be referred to the   **9.69** Tribunal again in respect of the same description of cases as was covered by the order until 12 months from the date of the order, or, if the order was made so as to be in force for 15 months or less, until three months before the expiry of the order (s.120).

A reference to the Tribunal in these circumstances can be made either by the operator of the scheme, or a person claiming he requires a licence in a case of the description to which the order applies, or an organisation claiming to be representative of such persons.

Until such a reference is concluded, the scheme referred again to the Tribunal remains in force.

(c) *Backdating of orders*

9.70   Where an order either under the original reference or a further reference varies the amount of charges payable, the Tribunal has a discretion to make that retrospective, but not earlier than the date on which the reference was made, or, if later, on which the scheme came into operation. If this happens, any payments already made over the amount provided by the Order must be repaid (s.123(1)).

However, in the case only of a further reference of a scheme certified by the Secretary of State under the provisions referred to in Section III above (paragraph 9.47 onwards), any order varying the scheme by reducing the charges *must* take effect from the date on which the reference was made to the Tribunal.

2. Disputes under existing licensing schemes (s.119)

(a) *Licensing schemes to which the provision applies*

These are as follows:

9.71   (i) in the case of literary, dramatic, musical and artistic works, films and film soundtracks when accompanying a film, only licensing schemes operated by a licensing body. Furthermore, this is also subject to the limitations referred to in paragraph 9.62 onwards.

(ii) in the case of sound recordings (except film soundtracks when accompanying a film), broadcasts, cable programmes and the typographical arrangement of published editions, all licensing schemes, whether or not operated by a licensing body.

(iii) in the case of sound recordings, films or computer programs, all licensing schemes so far as they relate to licences for the rental of copies to the public, whether or not operated by a licensing body. There is obviously some overlap here with those licensing schemes referred to above.

(b) *First reference*

9.72   The provision applies where a licensing scheme is already in operation. If then a dispute arises between the operator of the scheme and a person claiming he requires a licence in a case of a description to which the scheme applies, or an organisation claiming to be representative of such persons, the scheme can be referred to the Copyright Tribunal in so far as it relates to cases of that description.

Only the person claiming he requires a licence or the organisation can refer the scheme to the Tribunal. In case 39/84 (The Limes Country Club Ltd. v. PPL) the PRT held that the reference under the 1956 Act to "persons requiring a licence" referred to "persons who genuinely regard it as in their interest to obtain a licence so as to avoid infringement of copyright, and have requested one in order to serve that interest." In that case, the PRT refused jurisdiction where the applicant had already infringed copyright.

There is no limitation on what sort of disputes can be referred. The scheme however remains in operation until proceedings are concluded.

Again, the Tribunal can make such order confirming or varying the scheme as it may determine to be reasonable in the circumstances, but only in so far as it relates to cases of the description to which the reference relates. The Tribunal also again has power to make the order indefinite, or for a particular period.

(c) *Further references and backdating*

The same rules on further references of the scheme, and the same powers   **9.73** of backdating, apply as are referred to in paragraphs 9.69 and 9.70. However, in this case, the obligatory backdating for certified schemes applies both in the case of the first reference and the further reference.

3. Refusal of a licence in a case covered by a licensing scheme (s.121 (1))

(a) *Licensing schemes to which the provision applies*

These are the same as referred to in paragraph 9.71.   **9.74**

(b) *First reference*

In a case covered by a licensing scheme, an application to the Copyright   **9.75** Tribunal can be made by anyone who claims that the operator of the scheme has refused to grant him or procure the grant to him of a licence in accordance with the scheme, or has failed to do so within a reasonable time after being asked.

If the Tribunal is satisfied that any such claim is well-founded, it must make an order declaring that the applicant is entitled to the appropriate licence. It should be noted here that the Tribunal has no discretion even if it thinks the licensing body was perfectly reasonable in refusing a licence. The terms of the licence will be such as the Tribunal determine to be applicable in accordance with the licensing scheme, and the order can be made to be in force indefinitely or for a particular period.

(c) *Further reference*

A further reference to the Tribunal to review such an order can be made   **9.76** either by the operator of the scheme or the original applicant. However, unless special leave is given by the Tribunal, this cannot be done within 12 months from the date of the Order (or of the decision on a previous application under the provision), or, if the Order was made so as to be enforced for 15 months or less (or as a result of the decision on a previous application under the provision is due to expire within 15 months of that decision), until the last three months before the expiry date.

(d) *Backdating*

9.77   There is no power to backdate under an application under this provision.

4. Refusal of a licence in a case excluded from a licensing scheme

(a) *Licensing schemes to which the provision applies*

9.78   These are again the same as referred to in paragraph 9.71.

(b) *Limits on jurisdiction*

9.79   The Tribunal only has jurisdiction here in two cases:

(i) Where the scheme provides for the grant of licences subject to terms excepting particular matters from the licence, and the case falls within such an exception, and

(ii) Where the case is so similar to those in which licences are granted under the scheme that it is unreasonable that it should not be dealt with in the same way.

(c) *First reference*

9.80   Assuming that either of the above apply, an application to the Copyright Tribunal can be made by a person who claims that the operator of the scheme has either:

(i) Refused to grant or procure the grant to him of a licence, or has failed to do so within a reasonable time of being asked, and that in the circumstances it is unreasonable that a licence should not be granted, or

(ii) Proposed terms for a licence which are unreasonable.

Again, if the Tribunal is satisfied that the claim is well-founded, it must make an order declaring that the applicant is entitled to a licence in respect of the matter specified in the order, either indefinitely or for a specified period. However, here the Tribunal does have some discretion in that it has to be satisfied that the refusal of a licence or the terms offered were unreasonable. The terms of the licence will be such as the Tribunal determine to be reasonable in the circumstances.

(d) *Further reference*

9.81   The same provisions as regard reviews of such orders apply as are referred to in paragraph 9.76 above. Again, there are no backdating powers.

D. CONTROL OVER LICENCES

The following provisions apply only to licences which are granted by a **9.82** licensing body otherwise than in pursuance of a licensing scheme. If the licence is one which is granted in pursuance of a licensing scheme, the Copyright Tribunal only has jurisdiction as referred to in paragraph 9.67 onwards.

It is these provisions which make the meaning of "society or other organisation" referred to in paragraph 9.60 so important. There is no limitation on the licensees or proposed licensees who may apply, and the provisions could therefore extend not only to users of copyright works, but those who for example take exclusive licences from the copyright owner and exploit the relevant works by granting licences to users. Of course, the Tribunal might well refuse to interfere on the basis that the copyright owner ought in such circumstances to be left to decide who he wants to exploit his works for him and to grant licences to users, and the terms on which he should do so.

As in the case of licensing schemes all orders can be made so as to be in force indefinitely or for a specific period.

1. Proposed licences (s.125)

(a) *Reference of proposed terms*

The terms on which a licensing body proposes to grant a licence may be **9.83** referred to the Copyright Tribunal. However, this can only be done by the prospective licensee.

As in the case of proposed licensing schemes, the Tribunal has power to decline to entertain the reference on the ground that it is premature. If it does decide to entertain the reference, it can make such order concerning or varying the terms as it may determine to be reasonable in the circumstances.

(b) *Reviews of orders*

See paragraph 9.91 below. **9.84**

(c) *Backdating*

The Tribunal has the power to direct that its order be backdated, in so far **9.85** as it varies the amount of charges payable. It cannot backdate to a date earlier than that on which the reference or application was made, or, if later, on which the licence was granted.

If a backdating order is made, there is provision for any necessary repayments or further payments to be made.

(d) *Assignment*

9.86　The benefit of an order under this provision can be assigned, provided that assignment is not something which is prohibited under the terms of the Tribunal's order.

2. Expiring licences: s.126

(a) *Reference of expiring licence*

9.87　This provision applies where a licence granted by a licensing body is due to expire, whether by effluxion of time or as a result of notice given by the licensing body. Here, a licensee under such a licence may apply to the Copyright Tribunal on the grounds that it is unreasonable in the circumstances that the licence should cease to be in force. No application can be made until the last three months before the licence is due to expire.

Whilst the proceedings on the reference are in progress, the licence remains in operation.

If the Tribunal finds that the application is well-founded, it must make an order declaring that the licensee will continue to be entitled to the benefit of the licence, but on such terms as it may determine to be reasonable in the circumstances.

(b) *Review of orders*

9.88　See paragraph 9.91 below.

(c) *Backdating*

9.89　The Tribunal again has backdating powers. It cannot backdate to a date earlier than that on which the reference or application was made, or, if later, on which the licence was due to expire.

(d) *Assignment*

9.90　The benefit of an order made under this provision may again be assigned, provided that assignment was not prohibited under the terms of the original licence.

3. Review of orders: s.127

9.91　The following provisions apply to both orders as regards proposed licences, and orders as regards expiring licences.

An application to review an order can be made either by the licensing body or the person entitled to the benefit of the order, who could be the original licensee, or an assignee, where assignment of the benefit of the licence is permitted under the rules previously referred to.

Unless special leave is given by the Tribunal, an application cannot be made within 12 months from the date of the order (or of the decision on a previous application) or, if the order was made so as to be in force for 15 months or less (or, as a result of a decision on a previous application, is due to expire within 15 months of that decision), until the last 3 months before the expiry date.

Backdating provisions again apply, although the provisions relating to the earliest date to which the order can be backdated are somewhat confusing. We believe the position is that the earliest date is when the reference or application for review of the order was made.

E. THE EFFECT OF TRIBUNAL ORDERS (s.128(1))

Provided that he complies with certain conditions, the person in whose **9.92** favour an order is made under the provisions referred to in paragraph 9.83 onwards will be treated as if he had at all material times been the holder of a licence granted by the owner of the copyright in question on the terms specified in the order. There is a similar provision in relation to licensing schemes the subject of an order made under the provisions referred to in paragraph 9.68 onwards, but obviously only in relation to cases of a class to which the order applies. There, a person within the ambit of the scheme is treated as the holder of a licence granted by the owner of the copyright in question in accordance with the scheme.

The conditions are as follows:

(a) Any charges payable under the scheme covered by the order or the order itself are paid. Some special rules must be referred to here:

(i) If the amount of the charges cannot be ascertained, he will still be treated as a holder of a licence if he gives an undertaking to pay the charges when ascertained.

(ii) In the case of the provisions referred to in paragraphs 9.68 and 9.72, payment must be made to the operator of the scheme.

(iii) In the case of the provisions referred to in paragraphs 9.83 and 9.87, payment must be made to the licensing body.

(iv) Where an order is made under the provisions referred to in paragraphs 9.68 and 9.72 (including any further reference under those provisions) which is backdated, the reference to the charges payable is to the charges payable under the backdated order.

(v) Where an order has been made under the provisions referred to in paragraphs 9.83 and 9.87, and a review later varies the charges payable under the licence, and backdates the variation, the reference to the charges payable is again to the charges payable under the backdated order.

(b) All the other terms applicable to a licence under the relevant licensing scheme, or specified in the order, must be complied with.

F. EXERCISE OF THE TRIBUNAL'S POWERS

1. General

(a) *Reasonable in the circumstances*

9.93   In most of the provisions referred to above, it is provided quite simply that the Copyright Tribunal has power to make such order as it determines to be reasonable in the circumstances. In those cases where the Tribunal has no alternative but to make an order declaring that someone is entitled to a licence (see paragraphs 9.75 and 9.80), it again can do so on such terms and conditions as it determines to be reasonable in the circumstances, unless the case is one within a licensing scheme, where the terms of the licence must be in accordance with the scheme.

This approach is exactly the same as that which applied in the case of the PRT under the 1956 Act, and of course allows the Tribunal a considerable amount of latitude. Although the 1988 Act contains provisions directing the Copyright Tribunal to take into account certain factors in specific cases, the Tribunal in all cases has a general obligation to have regard to all relevant considerations (s.135).

(b) *The PRT's decisions*

9.94   It is not possible here to analyse in detail the approach which the PRT took in exercising its powers in those applications which came before it under the 1956 Act. In any event, the Copyright Tribunal is not bound by previous decisions, and it is possible that the new Tribunal might take a different approach, given the extensions to its jurisdiction, and some of the provisions referred to below relating to specific matters which it must take into account.

In summary, the PRT in early cases tried to assess the charges for use of the relevant rights on the basis of a willing buyer and a willing seller. In doing this, it laid great emphasis on any previous agreements which have been reached between the parties without recourse to the Tribunal as providing good prima facie evidence of the terms which a willing seller and buyer would agree. This however was subject to considering whether or not there were any factors which meant that either side was not negotiating freely, and also to any material changes in the circumstances since the agreement was reached. Furthermore, the PRT emphasised in case 38/81 (Independent Television Companies Association Ltd. and The Performing Right Society Ltd.) that in considering previous negotiations and agreements, it had the benefit of extended hindsight. If therefore the agreement did not turn out to give proper weight to all of the factors which the PRT with the benefit of hindsight considered to have been relevant, then the PRT might regard those factors as important in deciding the relevance of the previous agreement. Finally, where one of the parties admitted that it was mistaken in having reached agreement providing for a particular level of payment, and had not taken into account certain factors which it should have done, the PRT again took the view that it could have regard to this. (Case 24/71 (British Broadcasting Corporation and The Performing Right Society Ltd).)

In later cases, the PRT emphasised however that the "willing buyer and seller" approach, although helpful in determining what level royalties should be set at, was not a substitute for the statutory formula, which required them to consider all the facts and matters before them and decide what was reasonable in all the circumstances. In case 38/81 (Independent Television Companies Association Ltd. and PRS), the PRT held that in considering the issue of reasonableness, the interests of both parties had to be taken into account, not just the copyright owners.

2. Non-discrimination (s.129)

In determining what is reasonable, the Tribunal must have regard to the   **9.95** availability of other schemes, or the granting of other licences, to other persons in similar circumstances, and the terms of those schemes or licences.

It is also provided that the Tribunal must exercise its powers so as to secure that there is no unreasonable discrimination, not only within a licensing scheme, or as between licensees or prospective licensees of the same licensing body, but also by comparison with any others operating licensing schemes or granting licences.

3. Licensing of reprographic copying (s.130)

Where the Tribunal is examining the licensing of reprographic copying of   **9.96** published literary, dramatic, musical or artistic works, or the typographical arrangements of published editions, it must have regard to the following factors:

(a) The extent to which published editions of the works in question are otherwise available.

(b) The proportion of the work to be copied.

(c) The nature of the use to which the copies are likely to be put.

For the meaning of reprographic copying see paragraph 7.17.

4. Works included in other works

In some cases, the Copyright Tribunal will be examining licensing   **9.97** schemes or licensing of works which include other copyright works—for example, films which contain sound recordings and musical and literary works. There are some specific provisions which in these circumstances direct the Tribunal to have regard to charges or payments for the use of the included works. These are as follows:

(a) Any licensing in relation to the copyright in sound recordings, films, broadcasts or cable programmes (s.133(2)). Here, the Tribunal must take into account any reasonable payments which the copyright owner of such a work is liable to make in respect of any performance included in the recording, film, broadcast or cable programme.

(b) Licences for the rental to the public of copies of sound recordings, films or computer programs (s.133(1)). Here again the Tribunal must take into account any reasonable payments which the owner of the copyright in such a work is liable to make to owners of the copyright in works included in the sound recording, film or computer program.

(c) Licences for the recording by or on behalf of educational establishments of broadcasts or cable programmes which include copyright works, or the making of copies of such recordings, for educational purposes (s.131). Here, the Tribunal must have regard to the extent to which the owners of copyright in the included works have already received or are entitled to receive payment in respect of their inclusion.

(d) Licences relating to sound recordings, films, broadcasts or cable programmes which include or are to include any entertainment or other event (s.132). Here, the Tribunal must have regard to any conditions imposed by the promoters of the event. If such a licence could not have been granted consistently with those conditions, the Tribunal must not hold the refusal or failure to grant a licence to be unreasonable.

The Tribunal need not however have regard to any conditions in so far as they purport to regulate the charges for the grant of licences, or relate to payments to be made to the promoters for the grant of facilities for making the recording, film, broadcast or cable programme.

9.98   (e) Licences to include in a broadcast or cable programme service literary, dramatic, musical or artistic works, or sound recordings or films, where one broadcast or cable programme is by reception and immediate retransmission to be further broadcast or included in a cable programme service (s.134). It should be remembered that in some circumstances the inclusion in a cable programme service of a broadcast by means of reception of the broadcast and immediate retransmission in the service is not an infringing act (see paragraph 7.125).

The provisions here are somewhat complex. References below to the first transmission are to the broadcast or cable programme received and immediately retransmitted. References to the further transmission are to the immediate retransmission.

The factors which the Tribunal must have regard to depend on the area covered by the further transmission:

(1) *To the same area as the first transmission*

Here the Tribunal in considering what charges (if any) should be paid for licences for either transmission, must have regard to the extent to which the copyright owner has already received, or is entitled to receive, payment for the other transmission which adequately remunerates him in respect of transmissions to that area.

(2) *To an area outside that of the first transmission*

(i) Subject to (ii) below, the Tribunal has to ignore the further transmission in considering what charges if any should be paid for the first transmission.

(ii) As explained in paragraph 7.125, the 1984 Cable & Broadcasting Act contains provisions requiring licensed cable programme services to carry local BBC or IBA programming. Where the Tribunal is satisfied that these requirements will result in the further transmission being to areas part of which fall outside the area to which the first transmission is made, the Tribunal must exercise its powers so as to secure that the charges payable for licences for the first transmission adequately reflect that fact.

V THE LICENSING OF REPROGRAPHIC COPYING

A. INTRODUCTION

1. Definition of reprographic copying

Reprographic copying means copying by means of a reprographic process **9.99** (s.178). A reprographic process is a process for making facsimile copies, or involving the use of an appliance for making multiple copies.

The obvious example of a reprographic process is photocopying. However, the meaning is much wider than that because it is specifically provided that any copying by electronic means in relation to a work held in electronic form is included in the term. This extends the concept of reprographic copying to the use of computers and in particular the storage of works in a computer's memory. In relation to such use, *any* copying by electronic means is included (see paragraph 7.17), and, for example, there is no requirement that it be multiple copying. The breadth of this definition is however modified in one important way, in that it is provided that the making of a film or sound recording does not involve a reprographic process.

2. Importance of the definition

The scope of the definition of reprographic copying is important because **9.100** the 1988 Act contains some specific provisions which apply to certain licensing schemes and licences for reprographic copying, but no other form of copying and in relation to no other restricted act. This section deals with those specific provisions, but it should be remembered that the general provisions on references to the Copyright Tribunal set out in the previous section apply in relation to licensing schemes and licences covering reprographic copying as they do in relation to any other form of copying, and any other restricted act.

3. Permitted acts involving reprographic copying

9.101 As referred to in Chapter 7, the 1988 Act permits reprographic copying in the context of fair dealing for the purposes of research or private study, some reprographic copying by or on behalf of libraries, and reprographic copying by or on behalf of an educational establishment. (See respectively paragraphs 7.70, 7.37 and 7.18.) In each case, controls are imposed on multiple reprographic copying, and in one case (reprographic copying by or on behalf of educational establishments) the provision does not apply if or to the extent that licences are available authorising the copying in question and the person making the copies knew or ought to have been aware of that fact.

4. Licensing of reprographic copying

9.102 Under the 1956 Act, the position on multiple copying was much less clear, and in any event the strict rights of copyright owners were to a great extent ignored. However, after a series of successful actions by copyright owners to prevent infringement by photocopying of books and other literary works, a body called the Copyright Licensing Agency was set up by authors and publishers to encourage some of those who were engaged in wide-spread photocopying to obtain licences. As a result of this, the Agency entered into blanket licences with local education authorities allowing a certain amount of multiple copying. The extent to which the arrangements which operated whilst the 1956 Act was in force will be continued under the 1988 Act with its new provisions in relation to reprographic copying remains to be seen.

B. THE IMPLIED INDEMNITY (s.136)

1. The relevant schemes

9.103 The provisions referred to in this section apply to schemes for licensing reprographic copying of published literary, dramatic, musical or artistic works, or the typographical arrangement of published editions. It is important to note that it is not necessary that such a scheme be operated by a licensing body, so that for these purposes the difficulties with that definition referred to in paragraph 9.60 above are not relevant for these purposes. It is clear therefore that any scheme for licensing reprographic copying operated by an individual publisher would be within the provisions. The same is not so as regards licences, as opposed to licensing schemes. There, the provisions below apply only to licences granted by licensing bodies for the reprographic copying of such works.

Neither does it matter for the purposes of these provisions whether or not the licence or licensing scheme is one which covers the works of more than one author.

2. Conditions for the indemnity to apply

Where the scheme or licence does not specify the works to which it **9.104** applies with such particularity as to enable licensees to determine whether a work falls within the scheme or licence by inspection of the scheme or licence and the work, then an indemnity on the part of the operator of the scheme or the licensing body is implied. It would seem therefore that it would not be sufficient to provide a mechanism within the scheme or licence by which the licensee can find out which works are covered. The licensee must be able to determine this simply by inspection of the scheme or licence and the work itself.

3. Scope of the indemnity

The indemnity implied in the relevant scheme or licence is an undertaking **9.105** to indemnify the licensee against any liability incurred by him by reason of his having infringed copyright by making or authorising the making of reprographic copies of a work in circumstances within the apparent scope of his licence. In the case of a licensing scheme, the undertaking is deemed to have been given by the operator of the scheme. In the case of a licence, it is deemed to have been given by the licensing body. "Liability" is defined widely so as to include not only damages for infringement, but also costs, including costs reasonably incurred by a licensee in connection with actual or contemplated proceedings against him for infringement of copyright.

4. Meaning of "apparent scope"

The circumstances are within the apparent scope of a licence if two **9.106** conditions are fulfilled. The first condition is that it must not be apparent from inspection of the licence and the work that it does not fall within the description of works to which the licence applies. So, where a licensing scheme does not specify the works to which it applies with sufficient particularity, but a licence granted under the scheme does, this will prevent the implied indemnity applying.

The second condition is that the licence must fail to provide expressly that it does not extend to copyright of the description infringed. So, where again the licensing scheme does not specify the works to which it applies, if the licence granted under the scheme expressly provides that it does not extend to copyrights of a certain description, then the implied indemnity will not apply as regards such copyrights. The use of the word "description" is somewhat vague, but we assume that it refers not only to whole categories of works, such as musical works, but descriptions of works within those categories, such as, perhaps, choral music or piano music and so on.

5. Terms and conditions relating to the implied indemnity

9.107 The implied indemnity referred to in this section does not prevent a scheme or licence containing reasonable provision with respect to the manner in which, and time within which, claims under the implied undertakings must be made. The same applies as regards reasonable provision enabling the operator of the scheme or licensing body to take over the conduct of any proceedings which might affect the amount of his liability.

C. EXTENSION OF LICENSING SCHEMES AND LICENCES: ss.138–141

1. The relevant licensing schemes and licences

9.108 Unlike the provision on implied indemnity, the following provisions only apply to licensing schemes and licences which are operated or granted by a licensing body. Furthermore, they do not apply unless the scheme or licence is one covering the works of more than one author. (See paragraph 9.63.)

2. Power to extend the operation of the scheme or licence

9.109 If the scheme or licence is one which provides for the grant of licences, or is a licence, authorising the making, by or on behalf of educational establishments for the purposes of instruction, of reprographic copies of published literary, dramatic, musical or artistic works, or of the typographical arrangement of published editions, then the Secretary of State for Trade and Industry has certain powers to extend the operation of the scheme or licence. This power arises where it appears to the Secretary of State, first that works of a description similar to those covered by the scheme or licence are unreasonably excluded from it, and secondly that making them subject to the scheme or licence would not conflict with the normal exploitation of the work or unreasonably prejudice the legitimate interests of the copyright owners. The second of these two requirements is virtually identical to Article 9(2) of the Berne Convention.

Prior to making such an order, the Secretary of State has to go through various notification procedures to relevant parties. If the Secretary of State makes an order, it cannot come into effect until six weeks have expired from the making of the order.

3. Appeals to the Copyright Tribunal

The owner of the copyright in a work which is the subject of an order by **9.110**
the Secretary of State may appeal to the Copyright Tribunal. The Tribunal has a discretion to confirm or discharge the order, or vary it so as to exclude works from it, having regard to the same considerations as are referred to in paragraph 9.109.

An appeal must be brought within six weeks of the making of the order, unless the Tribunal allows a further period. If the appeal is brought within the period of six weeks, then the order will not come into effect until the appeal proceedings are disposed of or withdrawn. If an appeal is brought after the end of that period, the order remains in effect, and any decision of the Tribunal on the appeal does not affect the validity of anything done in reliance on the order before the Tribunal's decision is made.

4. Applications to vary or discharge orders

The owner of the copyright in a work covered by an order may also apply **9.111**
to the Secretary of State for variation or discharge of the order. The Secretary of State cannot entertain such an application within two years of the making of the relevant order, unless it appears to him that the circumstances are exceptional. Again, there are notification procedures which must be complied with before a decision is made whether or not to confirm or discharge the order, or vary it. Similar provisions as regards the effective date of orders and appeals apply in relation to any order made by the Secretary of State following such an application as are set out in paragraphs 9.109 and 9.110.

5. Power to set up inquiry

In addition to the above, the Secretary of State also has power to set up an **9.112**
inquiry to consider whether new provision is required, either in the form of a licensing scheme or general licence, to authorise the making by or on behalf of educational establishments for the purposes of instruction of reprographic copies of published literary, dramatic, musical or artistic works, or the typographical arrangement of published editions, of a description apparently not within an existing licensing scheme or general licence and not subject to the Secretary of State's powers referred to above.

No recommendation for the making of such a new provision can be made unless the person appointed to hold the inquiry is satisfied as to two matters. First, he must be satisfied that it would be of advantage to educational establishments to be authorised to make reprographic copies of the works in question. Secondly, he must be satisfied that making those works subject to a licensing scheme or general licence would not conflict with the normal exploitation of the works or unreasonably prejudice the legitimate interests of the copyright owners.

Where a recommendation for a new provision is made, and the recommendation is not put into effect by the relevant copyright owners or their representatives, the Secretary of State has power to order that the making by or on behalf of an educational establishment for the purposes of instruction of reprographic copies of the works to which the recommendation relates be treated as licensed by the copyright owners.

Under section 27(6) (paragraph 6.33), if reprographic copies the making of which was permitted under section 36(1) (paragraph 7.18) are subsequently sold or let for hire or offered or exposed for sale or hire, they are treated as infringing copies for the purposes of the provisions on secondary infringement referred to in paragraph 6.35. The same will apply as regards any reprographic copies the subject of such an order by the Secretary of State and which the relevant order requires should be treated in the same way.

VI COPYRIGHT AND COMPETITION LAW

9.113 Copyright is often described as a monopoly right. In one sense, this is misleading. Unlike registered designs and patents, copyright does not prevent the exploitation of a work identical or similar to the protected work unless the former is derived from the latter. If the new work has been created independently, the copyright owner of the identical or similar work has no right to prevent the exploitation of the independently created work. Nevertheless, he has exclusive rights in his own work, and, to the extent that use of that work involves an infringement of his rights, he has a monopoly in that work.

The copyright statutes themselves during this century have increasingly introduced curbs on the copyright owner's exclusive rights: compare for example the permitted acts under the 1911 Act with those referred to in Chapter 7. In addition, the 1956 Act introduced controls over collective licensing in the form of the Performing Right Tribunal. However, over the last 20 years, the ability of copyright owners to exercise their exclusive rights has been profoundly affected by the development of laws intended to prevent or control anti-competitive practices. The developments in this area have taken place not only in the context of the Treaty of Rome but also increasingly under domestic legislation. However, as will be seen, there are important distinctions between those provisions in the Treaty of Rome, and those which apply only under United Kingdom law.

The precise extent to which competition law affects the exclusive rights of copyright owners is not easy to determine. The brief summary provided below sets out the potential problems which copyright owners must be aware of, and the rights of recourse which a copyright user may have where he believes that copyright owners are abusing the exclusive rights given to them in such a way as to be anti-competitive. It must be stressed that competition law is an area of law which is particularly volatile, and current political and economic circumstances will often affect the outcome of any investigation or case. This is particularly so as regards decisions of the European Commission and the European Court where in many cases it is difficult to reconcile statements made in one decision with those in another.

A. UNITED KINGDOM DOMESTIC LAW

For the most part, United Kingdom competition law relies on the inter-   **9.114**
vention either of regulatory bodies set up in order to consider competition issues or the Secretary of State for Trade and Industry. Developments over the last few years have shown both such regulatory bodies and Government more willing to intervene in copyright issues.

It should be noted that there are at present proposals for reform of competition law in the United Kingdom: see in particular the Green Paper on Review of Restrictive Trade Practices Policy (Cm.331) and the Department of Trade and Industry's 1988 paper on the policy and procedures of merger control.

1. Monopoly Situations: the Fair Trading Act 1973 (ss.47–56)

(a) *References of monopoly situations*

The Fair Trading Act 1973 allows the Secretary of State for Trade and   **9.115**
Industry or (in most cases) the Director General of Fair Trading to refer what are called under the Act "monopoly situations" to the Monopolies and Mergers Commission ("the MMC") to investigate and report on. Monopoly situations in relation to goods and services exist where at least one-quarter of the goods of any description or services of any description supplied in the United Kingdom are supplied by or to one and the same person carrying on business in the United Kingdom, or by or to closely related persons so carrying on business. Other monopoly situations (called "complex monopoly situations") exist where at least one quarter of the goods of any description or services of any description supplied in the United Kingdom are supplied by or to two or more persons (not being inter-connected companies) who, whether voluntarily or not, and whether by agreement or not, so conduct their respective affairs as in any way to prevent, restrict or distort competition in connection with the production or supply of goods of that description, or the supply of services of that description. There are other provisions which relate to monopoly situations in relation to exports of goods of any description.

(b) *Requirement of goods or services*

Under these definitions, no monopoly situation can exist for the purposes   **9.116**
of the 1973 Act outside the supply of goods or services. This of itself excludes a substantial number of copyright businesses, because it seems to be accepted (at least by the Director General of Fair Trading) that the

grant of a licence to do something which would otherwise be an infringement of copyright is not a supply of services, or, more obviously, a supply of goods. However, the provisions might impinge on copyright exploitation where the copyright owner or his licensee produces and supplies goods embodying copyrights (such as books or records), or supplies services with a copyright element (such as the supply of cable programme services).

(c) *Investigation by the Commission*

9.117 In some cases the MMC may merely be asked to investigate the facts. In most cases, it is required to go beyond that, and consider whether the facts found by the Commission in pursuance of their investigation operate or may be expected to operate against the public interest. "Public interest" is defined extremely widely, and the Commission is entitled to take into account all matters which appear to be relevant in the particular circumstances, although some general guidelines are provided in section 84 of the 1973 Act. "Public" for these purposes does not only apply to the ultimate consumer member of the public, but to users and suppliers of the relevant goods or services.

(d) *Reports by the Commission*

9.118 It is unusual for the MMC to find that the monopoly situation itself is against the public interest. It is much more likely to hold that a certain type of behaviour is against the public interest. However, assuming that it makes a finding that the monopoly situation or a certain type of behaviour is against the public interest, the report of the MMC must specify the particular effects adverse to the public interest which in their opinion those facts have or may be expected to have. The MMC must also consider what action if any should be taken for the purpose of remedying or preventing those adverse effects, and can if they think fit include in their report recommendations as to such action.

(e) *Powers subsequent to report*

9.119 The Secretary of State for Trade and Industry has no duty to make orders carrying out the recommendations of the MMC. If however he decides to take action, he has wide order-making powers referred to in particular in Part I of Schedule 8 to the 1973 Act. One power which did not exist until the 1988 Act however was the power to compel a copyright owner to grant a licence to do an act which would otherwise be an infringing act. This important new provision is referred to later in paragraph 9.135, as it relates to other provisions dealt with in this section.

So far, the order-making powers have rarely had to be used in practice because the 1973 Act contains a consultation procedure involving the Director General of Fair Trading, and as a result of these procedures appropriate undertakings are usually given.

2. Control of Mergers: The Fair Trading Act 1973 (ss.63–77)

The 1973 Act allows the Secretary of State for Trade and Industry to refer   **9.120**
certain mergers to the MMC. He has no duty to do so, and the number of
mergers actually referred to the MMC is small in comparison to those
which could be.

(a) *Definition of merger*

The definition of "merger" is wide. It covers the situation where two or   **9.121**
more previously distinct enterprises come under common ownership, or
under common control, the word "control" being again very widely
defined. A merger also takes place for the purposes of the Act where an
enterprise ceases to be carried on at all in consequence of any arrangement of transaction entered into which prevents competition between
that enterprise and one or more others.

(b) *Qualifying conditions for a merger reference*

A merger as defined qualifies for possible reference by the Secretary of   **9.122**
State to the MMC *either* if it will result in a monopoly situation (see
paragraph 9.115) with respect to the supply of goods or services of any
description (or, where a monopoly situation already exists, increases the
relevant one-quarter share), *or* if the gross value of the assets taken over
exceeds £30 million. Most merger references take place on the basis of
asset value, but if a reference were to be considered on the basis of a share
of the relevant market in goods or services, the same comments made in
paragraph 9.116 above would apply. A reference may only be made
where at least one of the enterprises is carried on in the United Kingdom,
or by a company incorporated in the United Kingdom.

(c) *Investigation by the MMC and subsequent powers*

If a reference is made, the MMC investigates whether the merger does   **9.123**
indeed come within the provisions of the Act, and then whether it may be
expected to operate against the public interest. If by a two-thirds majority
of the members investigating the reference, the MMC does hold that the
merger may be expected to operate against the public interest, then the
Secretary of State has wide powers. These allow him not only to prevent
the merger, but also again to exercise one or more of the powers in
particular referred to in Part I of Schedule 8 to the 1973 Act. Once again,
the 1988 Act has added to this the power to impose compulsory licences,
and this is dealt with in paragraph 9.135.

There are interim powers exerciseable while the MMC investigation is
being conducted.

There is no formal consultation procedure following an MMC report as
there is in relation to monopoly situations. In practice, however, appropriate undertakings are again usually secured from the relevant companies through the offices of the Director General of Fair Trading.

(d) *References in relation to copyright businesses*

9.124   Recently, two mergers of enterprises whose businesses were substantially involved in copyright exploitation were referred to the Monopolies and Mergers Commission, the first being the proposed merger of Book Club Associates and Leisure Circle Book Clubs (Report Cmnd. 277) and secondly the acquisition by Warner Bros Music of the music publishers Chappell. Following reports by the MMC, the Secretary of State refused to allow the first merger to go ahead, but cleared the second (Report Cmnd. 301). It remains to be seen whether in any future reference the Secretary of State might use instead the new powers given to him under the 1988 Act referred to below.

3. Anti-competitive and uncompetitive practices: the Competition Act 1980 and the Fair Trading Act 1973

(a) *Investigation of anti-competitive practices: the 1980 Act*

9.125   The Competition Act 1980 enables the Director General of Fair Trading to investigate whether a person, firm or company is engaged in an anti-competitive practice. This is defined as occurring when someone in the course of business pursues a course of conduct which, of itself or when taken together with a course of conduct pursued by persons associated with him, has or is intended to have or is likely to have the effect of restricting, distorting or preventing competition in connection with the production, supply or acquisition of goods in the United Kingdom, or any part of it, or the supply or securing of services in the United Kingdom, or any part of it.

There are exemptions for the conduct of small businesses, which for these purposes are those with *both* an annual turnover of less than £5 million *and* a relevant market share of less than 25 per cent.

It should be noted again that the legislation only applies in connection with goods and services businesses, and the same point applies on this as is referred to in paragraph 9.116.

(b) *Consequence of finding of anti-competitive practice by Director-General*

9.126   If the Director-General finds that an anti-competitive practice is being carried on, he has power to accept appropriate undertakings offered by a person specified in his report as someone who has or is engaged in the relevant practice. Alternatively, he can make a reference to the MMC. The MMC then also considers whether or not an anti-competitive practice is being pursued. If it finds that this is so, its report must state whether that practice operated or might be expected to operate against the public interest, and, if so, what are, or are likely to be, the effects adverse to the public interest. The MMC must also consider what action, if any, should be taken for the purpose of remedying or preventing the adverse effects, and can include recommendations as to such action.

(c) *Consequence of MMC Report*

Assuming that the MMC confirms the existence of an anti-competitive **9.127** practice, and that this operates or might be expected to operate against the public interest, a consultation procedure may be invoked by which the Director-General of Fair Trading is asked to seek appropriate undertakings. If that procedure is not invoked, or suitable undertakings have not been forthcoming, or have been breached, the Secretary of State has the same order-making powers as in the case of monopoly situations and merger references, in particular those in Part I of Schedule 8 to the 1973 Act. It was in fact the *Ford Motor Company* reference under the Competition Act which revealed that the wide powers of the Secretary of State contained a major defect in not allowing for the grant of compulsory copyright licences. The new provisions to this effect are dealt with in paragraph 9.135 below.

(d) *Restricting, distorting and preventing competition*

The reports of the Director-General of Fair Trading and the MMC fail to **9.128** disclose any firm criteria as to when a course of conduct is likely to be held to have the effect of restricting, distorting or preventing competition. Proponents of competition law may argue that this is an area where flexibility of approach is necessary in order to adapt to new circumstances and practices, but the result of this is that it is almost impossible to advise precisely on whether a given practice is likely to be held to be anti-competitive, particularly in relation to the exploitation of copyrights, where the nature of the rights almost inevitably results in some restriction on competition.

Some useful guidance on the general considerations taken into account by the Director-General in carrying on an investigation is contained in the Office of Fair Trading's own booklet: "Anti-Competitive Practices: A Guide to the Provisions of the Competition Act 1980." From this, it appears that the steps taken by the Director-General are similar to the criteria referred to in paragraph 9.156 as those which determine whether there is an abuse of a dominant position under Article 86:

(i) The Director General first identifies the relevant market in which the firm is operating and in which any adverse effects on competition are to be expected.

(ii) He then identifies the extent and nature of the market power that a firm may hold, and the effect of a firm's practice on its market power.

(iii) He then considers in the light of the above the effects of the relevant practice on competition. The booklet referred to identifies three categories of possible anti-competitive practices:

    – practices which do or could eliminate the competition a firm faces in a market in which it is engaged;

    – practices which do or could prevent the emergence of new competitors or restrict competition in a market in which a firm is engaged by making it difficult for existing competitors to expand in the market;

– practices which have such an effect upon the terms and conditions of supply in some market (not necessarily a market in which the firm itself is engaged) that they distort competition between firms engaged in that market.

(e) *Ford Spare Parts reference*

9.129 Copyright issues have been the subject of investigations by the Director-General and references to the MMC under the 1980 Act in two cases. Both involved to some extent a refusal to grant licences. The *Ford Spare Parts* reference (Report Cmnd. 9437) has already been mentioned. What was being investigated there was Ford's refusal to grant licences to spare part manufacturers to produce spare parts which were reproductions of industrial or engineering drawings the copyright in which was owned by Ford.

Both the Director-General and the MMC held that Ford's policy constituted an anti-competitive practice, and the latter also found that it operated against the public interest. As stated however, no power at that stage existed for the Secretary of State to compel Ford to grant licences. Of course, the result of the *British Leyland* case (see paragraph 9.05) and the new provisions in the 1988 Act on designs (see Chapter 13) have since altered the copyright position fundamentally in relation to such drawings.

(f) *BBC/ITP reference*

9.130 In another investigation, *British Broadcasting Corporation and Independent Television Publications Ltd.* (Report Cm. 9614), the Director-General and the MMC considered whether or not the two parties mentioned were each carrying on an anti-competitive practice in their policies as regards the publication of television and radio programme schedules by other persons. The BBC published its own schedules in the "Radio Times," and ITP published the IBA programme schedules in the "TV Times." Both placed restrictions on the extent to which newpapers or magazines could reproduce the programme schedules, which were held to be the subject of copyright in *Independent Television Publications Ltd.* v. *Time Out Ltd.* ([1984] F.S.R. 64). The Director-General held that both were involved in anti-competitive practices in pursuing a policy and practice of limiting the publication by others of advance programme information, and of not granting licences which would allow other commercial organisations to publish advance programme information for periods in excess of those specified by the parties. The MMC also held that an anti-competitive practice was being pursued by each of the parties, but by the casting vote of the Chairman held that this did not operate against the public interest.

(g) *Uncompetitive practices: the 1973 Act (s.78)*

9.131 The provisions of the 1980 Act on anti-competitive practices depend on a preliminary investigation by the Director-General of Fair Trading. Apart from this procedure, the Secretary of State for Trade and Industry has the power under section 78 of the 1973 Fair Trading Act to require the MMC to submit a report on the general effect on the public interest, first of practices which in his opinion are commonly adopted as a result of or for the purpose of preserving monopoly situations, and secondly any practices which appear to him to be uncompetitive practices.

The Secretary of State can also require the MMC to submit to him a report on the desirability of action to remedy or prevent effects adverse to the public interest which result or might result from monopoly situations or from uncompetitive practices.

Such references can also be made jointly with any other Minister. In practice, these powers are only used to conduct investigations on an industry-wide basis.

(h) *Definition of uncompetitive practices*

For these purposes, uncompetitive practices are defined as practices having the effect of preventing, restricting or distorting competition in connection with any commercial activities in the United Kingdom. Although there are some similarities here with the Competition Act provisions, the most important distinction in relation to copyright exploitation is that there is no requirement that the practice is being carried on in connection with the production, supply or acquisition of goods or the supply or securing of services. It is presumably for this reason that the PPL reference referred to in paragraph 9.134 was made under this provision, and not under the Competition Act or the other provisions of the Fair Trading Act.   **9.132**

(i) *Action following MMC Report*

The breadth of the powers of reference which the Secretary of State has under these provisions to refer matters to the MMC is not matched by powers to effect any recommendations by the Commission. In short, there are no such powers, although of course it is always possible for the Government of the day to introduce new legislation specifically to remedy the position if the relevant parties continue the practices. The provision referred to in paragraph 9.135 below does not therefore apply to reports of the MMC following such a reference.   **9.133**

(j) *Reference of collective licensing of sound recordings*

As stated, it was under this provision that the Secretary of State referred to the MMC certain practices in relation to the copyright in sound recordings. The reference arose following a final decision by the Performing Right Tribunal in October 1986 on a dispute between Phonographic Performance Ltd., (which by assignment of copyright owns the copyright subsisting in the United Kingdom in the vast majority of sound recordings   **9.134** exploited here) and the Association of Independent Radio Contractors. Dissatisfied with the decision of the Tribunal, the Association pressed the Government to investigate PPL's practices, and the Secretary of State and the Home Secretary jointly requested the MMC to report on practices relating to the collective licensing of sound recordings for broadcasting and public performance. The reference was wide-ranging, and required the MMC to investigate not only the terms and conditions of granting copyright licences, but also the practice of owners of copyright in sound recordings assigning their public performance and broadcasting rights to a collective licensing body.

The report by the MMC stated that in its opinion collective licensing bodies were the best available mechanism for licensing sound recordings, provided that they can be restrained from using their monopoly unfairly, and made various recommendations to that effect as well as in relation to some of PPL's specific practices (Report Cmnd. 530).

4. Compulsory licences following MMC Report (s.144)

(a) *Where the powers apply*

9.135   The powers given to the Secretary of State for Trade and Industry referred to below apply where a reference has been made to the Monopolies and Mergers Commission under the provisions referred to in paragraphs 9.119 and 9.127 above, and the MMC has held that a particular situation or behaviour operates against the public interest. It does not apply where the reference to the MMC was made under section 78 of the 1973 Act as referred to in paragraph 9.131 above.

(b) *Scope of the power*

9.136   Under each relevant provision, the MMC is bound to specify the particular matters which operate or may be expected to operate or have operated against the public interest. If these include either conditions in licences granted by the owner of copyright in a work restricting the use of the work by the licensee or the right of the copyright owner to grant other licences, or the refusal by a copyright owner to grant licences on reasonable terms, then the Secretary of State has power to cancel or modify any conditions referred to, and, instead or in addition, to provide that compulsory licences be available.

If the relevant parties cannot agree the terms of such a compulsory licence, these will be settled by the Copyright Tribunal on application by the person requiring the licence. Where this happens, the licence has effect from the date on which the application to the Tribunal was made.

(c) *Conflict with copyright conventions*

9.137   This is a broad power which could be used to deny a copyright owner even his most fundamental rights given under the 1988 Act. Accordingly, it is provided that the powers available can only be exercised by a Minister if he is satisfied that to do so does not contravene any Convention relating to copyright to which the United Kingdom is a party. There is no definition of the word "Convention," and no specific reference to the conventions to which the provision applies. It presumably applies to the Berne Convention, the Universal Copyright Convention, the Rome Convention and the Geneva Convention. Whether it applies to agreements such as the European Agreement on the Protection of Television Broadcasts or the Vienna Agreement for the Protection of Type Faces is not clear.

The provision itself is likely to be difficult to apply. Assuming that a Minister exercises the power referred to and declares himself satisfied that the order made by him does not contravene any relevant Convention, it will be open to an interested party to challenge his decision in the Courts. However, the interpretation of the international conventions is a matter of great difficulty. Although all the Conventions provide for certain fundamental rights in respect of the relevant works, the Conventions also contain not only specific exemptions and limitations, but much broader reservations. For example, Article IV bis of the Paris Revision of the Universal Copyright Convention provides that the rights given to authors and copyright proprietors "shall include the basic rights ensuring the author's economic interests, including the exclusive right to authorise reproduction by any means, public performance and broadcasting." The same article however then goes on to provide that "any contracting state may, by its domestic legislation, make exceptions that do not conflict with the spirit and provisions of this Convention, to the rights mentioned. . . . " This seems to give quite a degree of latitude to the signatories to the Convention, but this latitude is then qualified by the subsequent provision that "Any State whose legislation so provides shall nevertheless accord a reasonable degree of effective protection to each of the rights to which exception has been made." Faced with balancing such provisions as these, it will be very difficult for the Court to determine whether or not a particular order made by a Minister in exercising the powers referred to contravenes such a Convention.

(d) *Effect on infringement proceedings (s.98)*

Where a copyright owner or exclusive licensee takes proceedings for infringement of copyright in circumstances where a compulsory licence is available, the defendant can at any time before final order in the proceedings is made undertake to take a licence on such terms as may be agreed, or in default of agreement, settled by the Copyright Tribunal. He can do this without any admission of liability.   **9.138**

If the defendant gives such an undertaking, the remedies of the copyright owner and/or exclusive licensee referred to in Chapter 10 are limited. No injunction may be granted against him. Neither may an order for delivery up be made under section 99 (see paragraph 10.103). Damages or an account of profits may still be recoverable but these are limited to not more than double the amount which would have been payable by the defendant as licensee if the licence compulsorily available had been granted before the earliest infringement.

The provision does not affect any remedies available in respect of an infringement committed before compulsory licences were available.

5. Restrictive Trade Practices: the Restrictive Trade Practices Act 1976

(a) *Differences between the 1976 Act and other United Kingdom competition provisions*

9.139 The legislation dealt with below differs fundamentally from the provisions of the 1973 Fair Trading Act and the 1980 Competition Act in two ways. First, it is much more specific as to what is covered by the legislation, and indeed has been criticised for its technicality. The Restrictive Trade Practices Act 1976 is one of the most complex pieces of legislation on the statute book. Secondly, if an agreement is one covered by the legislation, but is not registered as referred to below, not only are the relevant provisions in breach of the Act void (which may mean on normal principles as to severability that the whole agreement is void), but also anyone who suffers damage as a result of the relevant provisions has an action against the parties to the contract for breach of statutory duty.

(b) *Agreements which must be registered*

9.140 The 1976 Act provides that certain agreements must be registered with the Director-General of Fair Trading. The most important agreements are those which are described as restrictive agreements as to goods and restrictive agreements as to services, but the provisions also apply to what are called information agreements as to goods and information agreements as to services.

A restrictive agreement as to goods is an agreement between two or more persons carrying on business within the United Kingdom in the production or supply of goods, or in the application to goods of any process or manufacture, whether with or without other parties, being agreements under which certain restrictions are accepted by two or more parties. The relevant restrictions are too extensive to set out here, but include such matters as prices, quantities, terms and conditions of supply, restrictions on who can be supplied and so on. Similar provisions apply to agreements between two or more persons carrying on business within the United Kingdom in the supply of services. There are also complicated provisions on trade associations, which deem an agreement made by a trade association to be an agreement made by all persons who are members of the association. Furthermore, where the association makes certain recommendations to its members as to the action to be taken or not to be taken by them, there is deemed to be an agreement between the members that they will agree to comply with the recommendation. Again, a similar provision relates to associations of those engaged in the supply of services.

Information agreements are agreements between two or more persons carrying on goods or services businesses to which the Act applies under which provision is made for or in relation to the furnishing by two or more parties to each other or to other parties of information in respect of certain matters. These matters are similar to the restrictions referred to above under the definition of restrictive agreements.

The above is a very basic summary of some of the agreements to which the Act applies, and the specific provisions are much more complex. From the above definitions, it will be noted that the Act only applies to agreements where two or more, and not just one of the parties to the agreement accepts restrictions. Some restrictions, such as those which relate exclusively to the goods or services supplied, are disregarded for the purposes of the Act, but other provisions extend the ordinary meaning of the term "restrictions," so that, for example, terms conferring privileges or benefits on those who comply with specified conditions are included within the term.

It is important to emphasise that the Act applies to "arrangements" as well as agreements proper, and any course of conduct can be caught. Legal enforceability is irrelevant.

(c) *Application to copyright agreements*

As with the legislation on monopoly situations and anti-competitive   **9.141** practices, the 1976 Act only applies to agreements as to goods or services. Once again therefore, its effect on copyright licensing would seem to be restricted (see paragraph 9.116), but in this instance unlike the other legislation there is in any event a specific exemption for certain copyright agreements. This was introduced by the 1980 Competition Act (s.30) which provides that the 1976 Act does not apply in relation to first, a licence granted by the owner or a licensee of any copyright, secondly, an assignment of any copyright, and lastly an agreement for such a licence or assignment. This is however subject to the condition that the restrictions being accepted or information provisions being made under such an agreement are only in respect of the work in which the copyright subsists or will subsist.

The exemption for such assignments and agreements seems at first sight somewhat restricted in its scope because of the condition referred to. However it appears from the decision of Vinelott J. in *Academy Sound and Vision Ltd.* v. *WEA Records Ltd.* ([1983] I.C.R. 586) that the words "in respect of the work" are to be construed widely. The Judge there was considering an assignment of the copyright in certain sound recordings, and held that the words referred to any provisions "fairly incidental to an assignment of any copyright." In that case the exemption was held to apply to a restriction relating to the disposal of a stock of records in existence when the copyright was assigned, and also one relating to the disposal of records made by the assignee prior to the assignor's sell-off period having ended. These restrictions were therefore disregarded for the purposes of examining whether the 1976 Act applied.

(d) *Effect of agreements being subject to the 1976 Act*

9.142 Agreements to which the 1976 Act apply must be notified to the Director-General of Fair Trading. Prima facie, the Director-General has a duty to take proceedings as regards each relevant agreement before the Restrictive Practices Court, although in some cases he has a discretion to refrain from taking such proceedings. The Court considers whether or not the relevant provisions in the agreement are contrary to the public interest. The provisions on this are too detailed and complex to set out here, but the criteria are not the same as those under the Fair Trading Act. Where the provisions are found by the Court to be contrary to the public interest, the agreement is void in respect of those provisions. The Court has power then to restrain the relevant parties not only from giving effect to the provisions, but also from entering into any other agreement to the like effect.

It is very rare for an agreement to be exempted on public interest grounds. It is more usual for the parties to cancel an existing agreement which has not been registered and replace it with one excluding the offending provisions. Nevertheless, non-registration is taken very seriously by OFT, who will not accept ignorance of the law as an excuse.

Legislation is expected later in 1989 which will give a power to fine retrospectively for failure to register. Meanwhile, there are powers to obtain Court Orders prohibiting further breaches of the Act, either specifically or generally. Contravention of such an order is a contempt which can result in fine or imprisonment.

B. EEC LAW

9.143 This section deals with those rules on competition contained in the Treaty of Rome which have an important effect on the exploitation of copyright works. The relevant provisions are contained in Article 85, which prohibits anti-competitive agreements and concerted practices, and Article 86, which proscribes abuses of a dominant position. In considering what appears below however, it is also important to keep in mind the provisions on free movement of goods in Articles 30 to 36 of the Treaty which were covered in paragraphs 6.43 onwards.

1. General

9.144 Unlike most of the provisions under United Kingdom domestic competition law, Articles 85 and 86 are directly enforceable against persons, firms and companies who breach the rules. This means first, that the European Commission can impose fines, which can be substantial. Secondly, the provisions can also be used in the United Kingdom courts certainly as a defence, and, it seems, as the basis for an action for breach of statutory duty where loss or damage is caused by the breach of Article 85 or 86. (See *Garden Cottage Foods Ltd.* v. *Milk Marketing Board* ([1984] A.C. 130).)

So-called "Euro-defences" are now not uncommon in infringement of copyright actions: see for example *British Leyland* v. *Armstrong* in the Court of Appeal ([1984] F.S.R. 591).

Applying the broad provisions of Articles 85 and 86 to copyright is not an easy matter. There are not many cases in which the European Court of Justice has considered the issues in detail, and there is therefore a tendency to apply by analogy judgments of the Court and decisions of the Commission on other intellectual property rights or similar rights. It is true that in most cases the same approach has been taken, but in our view some caution must always be exercised before assuming that the principles must be applied in exactly the same way.

Where the Commission decides that Article 85 or 86 is being breached, the relevant party can appeal to the European Court of Justice. The Commission and the European Court have in recent cases not been entirely in accord as regards the application of Articles 85 and 86 to the exercise of intellectual property rights. On the whole, the Court has tended to be more sympathetic to the submissions of rights owners, particularly where, as in the case of copyright, there is as yet no harmonisation between the various domestic laws. Of course, there is no guarantee that the same approach will continue in the future.

2. Trade between Member States

Articles 85 and 86 only apply if the relevant agreement or monopoly abuse affects trade between Member states. However, this phrase has been given a wide meaning by both the Commission and the Court, and it is unusual for a decision of the Commission to be reversed on the grounds that trade between Member States could not be affected. Some specific comments may help to demonstrate the potential breadth of this aspect.   **9.145**

(a) "Trade" itself is construed widely. It covers effectively all commercial activities. The Commission has even held that opera singers are engaged in trade. (See *re Unitel* [1978] 3 C.M.L.R. 306.)

(b) The expression is "*may* affect trade" and therefore not only actual effects but potential effects must be considered.

(c) Somewhat strangely, the Court has held that the requirement is satisfied even where there is an increase rather than a decrease in trade. (See *Consten and Grundig* v. *E.C. Commission* [1966] C.M.L.R. 418.)

(d) The Court has held that the requirement is satisfied not only where it is foreseeable that there may be "an influence, direct or indirect, actual or potential, on the pattern of trade between Member States" (*Sociètè Technique Miniére* v. *Maschinenbau Ulm* [1966] C.M.L.R. 357), but also where there may be an alteration in the structure of competition within the Common Market. (See *Greenwich Film Production* v. *SACEM* [1980] 1 C.M.L.R. 629.)

(e) The fact that the agreement on the face of it only concerns activities within one Member State does not mean that trade between Member

States will not be affected. The requirement may still be satisfied because the agreement tends to reinforce the compartmentalisation of markets on a national basis, or it may simply be that it will discourage exports to or imports from other member-states. (See for example *Re Carlsberg Beers* [1985] 1 C.M.L.R. 735.)

(f) It does not matter that one or other of the parties to an agreement or carrying on a concerted practice or monopoly abuse is outside the EEC: *Re Wood Pulp Cartel* [1988] 4 C.M.L.R. 901.

(g) The requirement may still be satisfied where the trade is between an EEC member-state and a country outside the EEC, if there is a likelihood of re-importation into the EEC. (See *Re Campari* [1978] 2 C.M.L.R. 397.) It should be noted here that a number of the Treaties between the EEC and non-member states contain provisions which are similar to Articles 85 and 86, although the procedure for enforcing them is different. It is not certain whether such provisions have direct effect within the EEC.

3. Article 85

(a) *The rule stated*

9.146   Article 85 of the Treaty of Rome prohibits as incompatible with the Common Market all agreements between undertakings, decisions by associations of undertakings, and concerted practices, which may affect trade between Member States and which have as their object or effect the prevention, restriction or distortion of competition within the Common Market. Certain specific examples of these are given in Article 85. They are as follows:

(i) Those which directly or indirectly fix purchase or selling prices or any other trading conditions.

(ii) Those which limit or control production, markets, technical development or investment.

(iii) Those which share markets or sources of supply.

(iv) Those which apply dissimilar conditions to equivalent transactions with other trading parties, thereby placing them at a competitive disadvantage.

(v) Those which make the conclusion of contracts subject to acceptance by the other parties of supplementary obligations which, by their nature or according to commercial usage, have no connection with the subject of such contract.

(b) *General Comments on Article 85*

9.147   The scope of Article 85 is therefore very broad, and some general comments need to be made in order to demonstrate this:

(i) The word "undertakings" is itself construed widely. It applies to individuals as much as it applies to firms or companies. In *Re Unitel*, the Commission held that performing artists could constitute undertakings within Article 85.

(ii) Article 85 applies to both horizontal agreements (for example, between manufacturer and manufacturer) and vertical agreements (for example, between manufacturer and distributor). This has particular importance in relation to intellectual property rights. (See paragraph 9.150 below.)

(iii) Although the expression is "*decisions* by associations of undertakings," the Court has upheld the Commission's view that this can even apply to a recommendation where such a recommendation is normally complied with, even if it is of no binding effect. (See *IAZ International Belgium S.A.* v. *E.C.C. Commission* [1984] 3 C.M.L.R. 276.)

(iv) The expression "concerted practice" is also extremely widely construed by the Commission. (See for example *Re Peroxygen Cartel* [1985] 1 C.M.L.R. 481.) It does not cover situations in oligopolistic markets where companies unilaterally adapt themselves to the existing and anticipated conduct of their competitors, but in truth the line is sometimes hard to draw.

(v) In some cases, the object of the agreement or concerted practice is so plain that it is not necessary to consider whether or not it has any anti-competitive effect. (See *Verband der Schversicherer* v. *E.E.C. Commission* [1988] 4 C.M.L.R. 264.) If the object is not clear, then it is necessary to consider whether it might have such an effect.

(vi) It is not only existing competition which the Commission and the Court will look at. They also consider potential competition, such as whether or not the parties to an agreement might potentially be competitors, even though they are not at the present time.

(vii) There are some agreements which fall outside Article 85:

— Those which have no appreciable impact on inter-state trade or competition: the so-called "de minimis" rule. The Commission in its notice of September 3, 1986, on Agreements of Minor Importance has stated that agreements between undertakings engaged in the production or distribution of goods or in the provision of services generally do not fall under the Article 85 prohibition if the goods or services which are the subject of the agreement (or are considered by users to be equivalent) do not represent more than five per cent. of the total market for such goods or services in the area of the Common Market affected by the agreement, *and* the aggregate annual turnover of the participating undertakings does not exceed 200 million ECU.

— Agreements between parents and subsidiaries where the subsidiary although having separate legal personality enjoys no economic independence provided the agreement concerns merely the allocation of tasks between the group companies. (See *Beguelin Import* v. *G.L. Import Export* [1972] C.M.L.R. 81.)

— Those agreements which the Commission has indicated (by notice in the Official Journal) are in its view outside the scope of Article 85, one example being agreements between a principal and agent. Such notices are usually very restricted in scope.

(c) *Application of Article 85 to the exploitation of copyright*

(i) *Difference between existence and exercise*

9.148   As in the case of Article 86 and Articles 30 to 36, the Court makes a distinction between the existence of rights and their exercise. This approach was taken as early as 1966 in *Consten & Grundig* v. *EEC Commission* [1966] C.M.L.R. 418 in which the Court upheld the Commission's decision that an agreement providing for registration of a trade mark in one Member State infringed Article 85 in that it ensured absolute territorial protection in favour of the party registering the mark.

This is not however of much help in determining precisely which agreements and practices are consistent with Articles 85 and 86, and which are not, although it does signify that it is more likely to be consistent with such provisions where the copyright owner is protecting rights which are of the essence of copyright, such as the reproduction right and the performing right.

(ii) *Types of agreement*

9.149   Having said this, whether or not a copyright agreement is consistent with Articles 85 and 86 does not depend upon its form or type. The provisions may apply to assignments of copyright and exclusive and non-exclusive licences, as well as other agreements between rights owners. For an example of the latter, see *Re The European Broadcasting Union* [1987] 1 C.M.L.R. 391, where a number of broadcasting organisations belonging to the Union proposed to fix common rates and conditions for supplying television news items to third parties. The proposal was abandoned after the Commission objected.

(iii) *Exclusive licences*

9.150   Most attention under Article 85 has focused on the status of exclusive licences. Exclusive licences for the exploitation of intellectual property raise difficult questions, and the leading judgment of the European Court of Justice in the *Maize Seeds* case on plant breeder's rights (*L.C. Nungesser K.G.* v. *E.C. Commission* [1983] 1 C.M.L.R. 278) raises more questions than it has solved. Nevertheless, it seems clear that the grant of an exclusive copyright licence does not of itself create problems with Article 85. In *Coditel S.A.* v. *Cine Vog Films S.A. (No. 2)* [1983] 1 C.M.L.R. 49, the European Court held as follows:

"The mere fact that the proprietor of a film copyright has granted to a single licensee the exclusive right to exhibit the film in the territory of a member-state, and therefore to prohibit its diffusion by others for a specified period, is not sufficient however for a finding that such a contract must be considered as the object, means or consequence of an agreement, decision or concerted practice prohibited by the Treaty."

In that case, the Court listed those matters which would require investigation in order to consider whether the exercise of the exclusive right would constitute a breach of Article 85. Such an investigation would in particular have to determine "whether exercise of the exclusive right to exhibit a cinematograph film does not create artificial, unjustified barriers, having regard to the requirements of the film industry, or the possibility of royalties exceeding a fair remuneration for the investments made, or an exclusive right for a period which is excessive by reference to these requirements, and whether generally the exercise of such right within a specified geographical area is not likely to prevent, restrict or distort competition within the Common Market."

The decision of the Court in the *Coditel* case is consistent with its decision in the *Maize Seeds* case, in which it made a distinction between so-called "open" exclusive licences or assignments where "the exclusivity of the licence relates solely to the contractual relationship between the owner of the right and the licensee, whereby the owner merely undertakes not to grant other licences in respect of the same territory and not to compete himself with licensing in that territory," and an exclusive licence or assignment with absolute territorial protection "under which the parties to the contract propose, as regards the products and the territory in question, to eliminate all competition from third parties, such as parallel importers or licensees for other territories."

Nevertheless, it is necessary to warn that the Commission has taken a restrictive view of this approach, emphasising in particular that the Court's decision seems to have been based in part on the nature of plant-breeders' rights which require a high degree of protection in order to protect the investment put into the development of new products. The extent to which it would accept that the some should apply with exclusive copyright licences, particularly of existing catalogues of works, is not certain. In a case referred to in the Thirteenth Commission Competition Report, *Re Knoll-Hiller Form*, a copyright licence prohibited the licensor from granting any further licences in the licensee's territory, and from itself carrying out exploitation there. The licensee also agreed not to sell products made under the licence outside its territory. The Commission gave its view that such an exclusive licence was not an "open" one.

(iv) *Territorial Licensing throughout the EEC*

The *Coditel* and *Maize Seeds* cases both deal with the grant of one   **9.151** exclusive licence for a specific Member State. In some copyright businesses, it is common to grant separate exclusive licences for each or most of the individual Member States—for example the music publishing industry. The question then arises whether this would itself be a breach of Article 85.

The issue is not one which has been directly addressed by the Court, although in *Keurkoop B.V.* v. *Nancy Kean Gifts B.V.* [1983] 2 C.M.L.R. 47 it was held in relation to registered designs that a breach of Article 85 could occur where "persons simultaneously or successively file the same design in Member States in order to divide up the markets within the Community among themselves." This however is not the same as one rights owner deciding to grant rights separately for individual territories for the purposes of better protection and administration, and it appears from the Commission's Green Paper on Copyright and the Challenge of Technology that the Commission at present accepts that such a system in itself does not infringe Article 85. Paragraph 4.3.8 of the Green Paper states as follows:

> "It should be noted that the doctrine of exhaustion founded upon Articles 30 to 36 EEC concerns the free circulation of copies of copyright works after they have been lawfully placed on the market. Its effects should not be confused with the effects of competition law on agreements by which publishing rights are allocated on a territorial basis. Such agreements, which are of considerable interest to authors and publishing companies, are to be respected provided they do not run counter to the principles of competition policy in the Treaty, particularly the provisions of Article 85."

(v) *The concept of the Community-wide validity of a licence*

9.152   Before going on to consider some specific terms and conditions which are likely to cause problems with Article 85, one further basic issue must be referred to and that is the Commission's concept of community-wide validity of copyright licences.

This concept is best explained by reference to the situation in which it was most strikingly applied. (See *Re GEMA* [1985] 2 C.M.L.R. 1.) The investigation there concerned the situation where record companies wished to obtain a licence for reproduction of musical words in the form of records from a copyright protection society in one Member State, but have manufacture carried out in another Member State. The Commission held that this was allowed, even where another copyright protection society owned the rights in the territory of manufacture. The press release by the Commission stated that "in the Commission's opinion, a licence granted by a Community copyright protection society is valid throughout the Community, and authorises manufacture, even by way of custom pressing, in any Member State."

It is difficult to accept this extremely broad concept, and it remains to be seen whether the Court would uphold the principle as stated by the Commission if a case on the point were referred to it. It of course comes perilously close to rendering nugatory the supposed distinction between existence and exercise of intellectual property rights, since whether or not the grantor of the licence has any rights in the territory in which the licence is exercised appears to be irrelevant. There is no indication whether the Commission regards the principle as being confined to licences granted by copyright collection societies or whether it could be applied to individual copyright owners.

(vi) *Specific problem clauses*

Aside from these basic issues, it is clear that some specific clauses in   **9.153** copyright agreements will result in problems under Article 85. Unlike the position on patent licences, where a block exemption applies (Regulation 2349/84 of July 23, 1984), there is no absolute guide to what provisions will cause such problems. Nevertheless, the following provisions are likely to be disapproved by the Commission:

(1) So-called "no-challenge" clauses, in which the licensee is prohibited from challenging the validity of the licensor's rights. The Commission took this view in relation to a copyright licence in *Neilson-Hordell/ Richmark* (12th Commission Competition Report). The Commission held that the fact that the clauses formed part of a settlement agreement terminating earlier copyright infringement litigation could not justify such a clause. The patent block exemption prohibits such clauses in patent licensing but allows the insertion of a clause giving the licensor the right to terminate the licensing agreement in the event of such a challenge. It is possible that the Commission might accept such a clause in a copyright licensing agreement but one must beware of assuming that such agreements will be treated in the same way.

(2) Where the licensee is charged royalties on the use of works which are not the subject of copyright. This appears from the approach taken with the Commission under Article 86 and referred to in paragraph 9.159.

(3) Restrictions on prices which may be charged for goods manufactured by the licensee in accordance with the licence.

(4) Obligations to transfer to the licensor the title to a copyright work created in the course of exercising the rights under the licence. This again was disapproved by the Commission in relation to copyright in *Neilson-Hordell/Richmark*.

(5) Restrictions on exports between Member States, whether those restrictions are express or implied. (See *Re "The Old Man and The Sea"* [1977] 1 C.M.L.R. D121.) In *Re STEMRA* [1981] 2 C.M.L.R. 494, the Commission disapproved a clause in a copyright licensing agreement which only authorised exports of products made under the licence to other Member States with the agreement of the collecting society in the country of destination. The same approach was taken in *Re Performing Rights Societies* [1984] 1 C.M.L.R. 308, where the Commission held that sound recordings lawfully manufactured in one Member State, that is made with the copyright owner's permission, and which are marketable in that State may be sold without restriction anywhere in the Community. According to the Commission, it was not necessary for the records to

have been placed on the market in the first Member State for the rules on free circulation to apply.

(d) *Breaches, clearances and exemptions*

9.154 Agreements, decisions and concerted practices prohibited by Article 85 are automatically void. This is particularly important in relation to agreements proscribed by Article 85, because it means that the relevant provisions cannot be enforced in the Courts. Indeed, under normal rules as to severability, it may be that the whole agreement will be void and therefore unenforceable.

The Commission has the power to grant exemptions from the rigours of Article 85. The power to declare Article 85 inapplicable applies in the case of agreements, decisions or concerted practices which contribute to improving the production or distribution of goods or to promoting technical or economic progress, while allowing consumers a fair share of the resulting benefit. This is however on condition that the agreement, decision or concerted practice does not impose on the undertakings concerned restrictions which are not indispensible to the attainment of these objectives, or afford such undertakings the possibility of eliminating competition in respect of a substantial part of the products in question. The words used are those of Article 85(3).

It is not possible here to examine the detail of how the Commission has addressed the question of exemption under Article 85(3), but once again, the breadth of the wording allows it a great deal of latitude in determining whether or not exemption should be granted.

Exemption under Article 85(3) cannot be granted unless the relevant agreement, decision or practice has been notified to the Commission. In many cases, the parties notifying the agreement will seek negative clearance for the agreement, that is a certification that there are no grounds for Article 85 to apply, or, in the alternative, exemption under Article 85(3). If exemption under Article 85(3) is requested, no fine can be imposed on the relevant parties as regards conduct from the date of notification to the date of the Commission's decision, unless the acts of the parties do not fall within the limits of the activity described on the notification, or the Commission informs the parties that after preliminary examination it is of the view that Article 85(1) applies and that an exemption under Article 85(3) is not justified. However, this does not mean that the agreement, decision or practice is lawful during that period, so that for example a party who has suffered damage during the intervening period prior to the decision of the Commission could still in some circumstances maintain an action for damages even though the agreement, decision or practice is abandoned after the Commission's decision.

4. Article 86

(a) *The rule stated*

9.155 Under Article 86, any abuse by one or more undertakings of a dominant position within the Common Market or in a substantial part of it is prohibited as incompatible with the Common Market in so far as it may affect trade between Member States. Specific examples of such abuse are stated to be as follows:

(i) Directly or indirectly imposing unfair purchase or selling prices or other unfair trading conditions.

(ii) Limiting production, markets or technical development to the prejudice of consumers.

(iii) Applying dissimilar conditions to equivalent transactions with other trading parties, thereby placing them at a competitive disadvantage.

(iv) Making the conclusion of contracts subject to acceptance by the other parties of supplementary obligations which, by their nature or according to commercial usage, have no connection with the subject of such contracts.

(b) *Meaning of dominant position and abuse*

Aside therefore from the requirement of affecting trade between Member States (see paragraph 9.145 above) there are two important questions to address. First, there is the question of dominant position. Secondly, there is the question of what constitutes an abuse. Some general comments are necessary on these two requirements: **9.156**

(i) Before considering whether one or more undertakings is in a dominant position in a particular market, it is necessary first to define what the market is. Not surprisingly, the Commission takes a broad or narrow view of the relevant market, depending on which market will enable it to justify best its findings on dominance, and in general the Court has tended to uphold the Commission's findings as regards the market.

(ii) However, the primary test for identifying the relevant product market is based on the concept of interchangeability. If two products can be regarded as interchangeable, then they are both within one product market for the purposes of applying Article 86. In *United Brands* v. *E.C.C. Commission* ([1978] 1 C.M.L.R. 429), the question was whether the supply of bananas was one product market, or whether the market was fruit as a whole. The Court agreed with the Commission that other fruits could not be regarded as a substitute for the banana, and accordingly the relevant product market consisted of bananas alone.

(iii) Again, there are no precise formulae which enable one to determine whether the market power of the relevant undertaking or undertakings constitutes a dominant position in that market. The general test in the *United Brands* case was stated by the court to be as follows.

"The dominant position thus referred to (by Article 86) relates to a position of economic strength enjoyed by an undertaking which enables it to prevent effective competition being maintained on the relevant market by affording it the power to behave to an appreciable extent independently of its competitors, customers and ultimately of its consumers."

Obviously, market share is an important factor here. The larger the market share, the more likely it is that there will be a dominant position within the meaning of Article 86, but this also depends on the market share which other competitors have. Furthermore, other matters may be relevant, such as whether there are factors which make it difficult for competitors to enter the market or expand their share of the market. It is not therefore possible to specify any particular percentage market share below which there can be no dominant position.

(iv) Geographical considerations are vital both in relation to product market, and market power. One member-state can be a "substantial part" of the Common Market, and perhaps even part of a member-state.

(v) As regards abuse, the specific matters referred to in paragraph 9.155 are only examples of practices which will reach Article 86. The Court has held that such abuse can consist of interference in the structure of competition within a particular product market, such as through mergers or company acquisitions. (See *Europemballage Corp. and Continental Can Co.* v. *E.C. Commission* [1973] C.M.L.R. 199.) Refusal to continue to supply goods to an existing customer has also been held to be an abuse: *Commercial Solvents* v. *E.C. Commission* ([1974] 1 C.M.L.R. 309). Even the taking of proceedings for infringement of intellectual property rights may under certain circumstances be an abuse: *Re the Complaint by Yoshida Kogyo KK* ([1978] 3 C.M.L.R. 44.)

(c) *Application of Article 86 to the exploitation of copyright*

(i) *Product market*

9.157   The most difficult question is that of identifying the product market. Most of the cases on copyright and Article 86 concern collecting societies in the music business, and here it is clear that such societies enjoy a dominant position both as regards services to copyright owners and the grant of licences to users. The real problem therefore lies with individual rights owners, where there are difficulties in applying the concept of interchangeability. There are no cases or decisions of the Court or Commission which state precisely how that concept applies in relation to copyright works, and it is not possible to state with any degree of certainty what position the Commission or the Court would take if it became necessary for it to be decided.

Nevertheless, it seems to have been accepted by the Court that prima facie the mere fact of ownership of an exclusive right does not mean that the owner of that right is in a dominant position. That appears to follow from the following statement by the Court in *Deutsche Grammophon GmbH* v. *Metro* ([1971] C.M.L.R. 631):

"A manufacturer of recordings who has a protection right analogous to copyright does not however have a dominant position within the meaning of Article 86 of the Treaty merely because he exercises his exclusive right to market the protected articles."

However, it also appears from the *Deutsche Grammophon* case that there could be circumstances in which an individual rights owner would be held to be in a dominant position. Following the above passage, the Court said as follows:

"If the artistes in the recordings are bound to the manufacturer by exclusive contracts, inter alia their popularity with the public, the duration and the extent of the obligations undertaken by them and the opportunities for other manufacturers of recordings to obtain artistes for comparable performances, must be taken into consideration."

This seems to indicate that the ownership of copyright in the works of one creator could, if those works are so popular that no other work could be regarded as a true substitute for them, give rise to a dominant position. Of course, the problem lies in deciding when that stage is reached.

In some areas, an even more restrictive definition of the relevant market may be identified. This is particularly so as regards the ownership of copyright or similar rights in designs which are applied industrially. In *Hugin Cassaregister A.B.* v. *E.C. Commission* ([1979] 3 C.M.L.R. 345), Hugin manufactured cash registers, and clearly did not have a dominant position in relation to the market for the manufacture or supply of cash registers. However, independent undertakings specialising in the maintenance and repair of cash registers were restricted in their ability to obtain spare parts for Hugin registers, partly because of rights which Hugin may have had in related industrial drawings. The Court held that the relevant market constituted spare parts for Hugin cash registers. So, although the manufacture and supply of original equipment did not give rise to a dominant position, the manufacture and supply of spare parts did. Although the copyright issue was not directly mentioned by the Court, the case seems to be an indication of the position which might be taken. Regrettably, although in *A.B. Volvo* v. *Erik Veng (U.K.) Ltd.* (*The Times*, November 15, 1988) the High Court in London referred a question directly on the point to the European Court in relation to registered designs, the Court declined to answer the point, holding that there was no abuse anyway.

(ii) *Abuse: refusal of licence*

As regards abuse, the main question is whether refusal to grant a licence   **9.158**
is itself an abuse of a dominant position. The Court appears to take the view that a rights owner is prima facie entitled to decide whether or not he wishes to grant or refuse a licence to exercise the rights which constitute the essence of copyright, and that he can refuse a licence without infringing Article 86. In the *Volvo* case referred to above, the Court stated as follows:

" . . . the right of the proprietor of a protected design to prevent third parties from manufacturing and selling or importing, without his consent, products incorporating the design constitutes the very subject-matter of his exclusive right. It follows that an obligation imposed upon the proprietor of the protected design to grant third parties, even in return for a reasonable royalty, a licence for the supply of products incorporating the design would lead to the proprietor thereof being deprived of the substance of his exclusive right, and that a refusal to grant such a licence cannot in itself constitute an abuse of a dominant position."

It appears that the Commission is not entirely happy with the breadth of that decision, although it seems to accept that refusal of a licence will not normally be an abuse. Commissioner Peter Sutherland in a written answer dated February 24, 1988, (reported in [1988] 4 C.M.L.R. 641) accepted that "apart from exceptional circumstances . . . a copyright owner is free to decide whether or not to grant licences for the use of protected works." However, this raises the problem of when there will be such exceptional circumstances, and it is interesting that in oral answers to questions in February and March 1988 the Commission stated that it was investigating both the refusal to supply advance information on programme schedules in the United Kingdom (see paragraph 9.130) and an alleged refusal to negotiate or sell satellite or cable rights to sporting events to a company in the private sector. Since then the Commission has held (Official Journal 1989 L 78/43) that the BBC and ITP have been abusing their dominant position in the market for advance weekly listings of their programme services by limiting the scope of the licences granted by them to only one or two days listings at a time.

It should be noted that the Court in the *Volvo* case referred only to refusal to grant a licence to do an act "which constitutes the very subject-matter of his right." This certainly applies to reproduction rights, and performing/broadcasting rights. The extent to which it would apply to distribution rights is less clear, but the cases on Articles 30 to 36 will presumably be of some guidance here. (See paragraphs 6.43 onwards.)

(iii) *Abuse: general*

9.159 In the *Volvo* case, the Court emphasised that certain conduct by rights owners in exercising their exclusive rights would be an abuse. In particular, the Court gave as examples in relation to the exercise of an exclusive right by the proprietor of a registered design for car body panels "the arbitrary refusal to supply spare parts to independent repairers, the fixing of prices for spare parts at an unfair level, or a decision no longer to produce spare parts for a particular model even though many cars of that model are still in circulation."

This approach of course is very much in line with the general principles on abuse referred to in paragraph 9.156, and also accords with the approach which the Court and the Commission has taken as regards collecting societies in the music business. Specific practices held to be abuses include the following:

(1) In *Re GEMA* ([1971] C.M.L.R. D35), the Commission held that it was an abuse for the German collecting society to require full payment of royalties on the reproduction of musical works in the form of records where the record contained some musical works in the public domain.

(2) In the same case, the Commission also held that it was an abuse for GEMA to impose a licence fee on recordings imported or re-imported into Germany by traders, when the recordings had already had to bear a licence fee in a Member State of the Community. The precise decision by the Commission should however be read subject to the later decision of the Court under Articles 30 to 36 *Musik-Vertrieb Membran GmbH* v. (*GEMA* ([1981] 1 C.M.L.R. 44) (see paragraph 6.53).

(3) Again in that case the Commission held that imposing a higher hardware levy on tape recorders imported into Germany than on those manufactured in Germany was an abuse.

(4) As already stated in the context of Article 85, the Commission has intervened in various cases to prevent restrictions or conditions attached to the exportation of records from one Member State to another (see paragraph 9.153(v)).

(5) In *Basset* v. *SACEM* ([1987] 3 C.M.L.R. 173), the Court held that the level of royalties fixed by a collecting society could be such that Article 86 would be applied if that level were unreasonable.

(6) Both the Court and the Commission have attacked as abuses under Article 86 certain conduct by collecting societies in their relations with members. In *Belgische Radio and Televisie* v. *SABAM* ([1974] 2 C.M.L.R. 238), for example, the Court held that it was an abuse under Article 86 for a collecting society to require an assignment of rights exceeding the limit absolutely necessary for the attainment of the object of the collecting society in protecting the rights and interest of its individual members against users. A similar approach was taken by the Commission in *Re GEMA*. Both the Court and the Commission have disapproved any measures taken by collecting societies which discriminate against members or potential members on the grounds of nationality.

(d) *No power to seek exemption*

Unlike Article 85, there is no power to grant exemption from the provisions of Article 86. It is possible to seek negative clearance from the Commission however. 9.160

10 REMEDIES AND PROCEEDINGS FOR INFRINGEMENT OF COPYRIGHT

I INTRODUCTION

10.01   This chapter deals with the remedies available to copyright owners and exclusive licensees in civil proceedings where an infringement of copyright has taken place. It also covers acts which are criminal offences and the penalties for such offences, and remedies exercisable without the necessity for proceedings.

A. SUMMARY OF 1988 ACT PROVISIONS

10.02   The remedies in the case of infringement can be categorised as follows. Subject to certain restrictions referred to later, they are available both to copyright owners and exclusive licensees.

1. Remedies without the necessity for court proceedings

10.03   (a) Subject to certain stringent conditions, infringing copies may be seized and detained.

(b) In the case of printed infringing copies of published literary, dramatic and musical works, and all infringing copies of sound recordings and films, notice can be given to the Commissioners of Customs & Excise requiring that importation of such copies be prohibited.

2. Remedies available in civil proceedings

10.04   (a) Not only the person doing the relevant infringing act may be liable, but also those who authorise the doing of the act, and those who act pursuant to a common design in the infringement or who procure the infringement.

(b) Injunctions may be granted to prevent an infringement taking place or continuing. Such injunctions can be granted before determination of whether infringement has taken place, in order to protect the position of the plaintiff until trial, and other pre-trial injunctions granted to ensure that the plaintiff is not denied effective relief when the action comes to trial.

(c) A successful plaintiff is normally entitled to damages for infringement of copyright, but may instead ask the court to exercise its discretion to award an account of profits. In appropriate cases, the court has power to award additional damages, for example where the infringement was flagrant. A plaintiff will be denied any damages where the defendant did not know or have reason to believe that copyright subsisted in the relevant work.

(d) The court has power to order delivery up, forfeiture, destruction or other disposal of infringing copies of works in the possession, power or control of someone in the course of a business, whether or not that person is infringing copyright. A similar power exists in relation to an article specifically designed or adapted for making infringing copies of particular copyright works, but only where the person knows or has reason to believe that it has been or is to be used for making infringing copies.

3. Criminal proceedings

(a) In some cases, an infringing act will give rise to criminal as well as civil liability.   **10.05**

(b) Generally, this applies to making infringing copies for sale or hire, and possessing and dealing with such copies in the course of a business, if the relevant party knows or has reason to believe the article is an infringing copy. In addition, causing an infringing performance in public, or public playing or showing is an offence if the defendant knew or had reason to believe that copyright would be infringed.

(c) A private prosecution may be mounted in relation to such infringements. The penalties for offences include both imprisonment or fines, and the court has similar powers to order delivery up, forfeiture, destruction or disposal as referred to in paragraph 10.04 above.

(d) Apart from such infringing acts, it is an offence to dishonestly receive a programme included in a broadcasting or cable programme service from a place in the United Kingdom with intent to avoid payment of any charge applicable to the reception of the programme.

B. COMPARISON WITH THE 1956 ACT

The following are the principal changes introduced by the 1988 Act: **10.06**

(a) The general presumptions on subsistence in and ownership of copyright works for the purposes of civil proceedings have been repealed.

However, new presumptions have been introduced for computer programs and films. (See paragraphs 10.33 and 10.35.)

(b) Restrictions on the granting of injunctions in actions for infringement
of copyright relating to the construction of a building have been removed.
(See paragraph 10.55.)

(c) The remedy of conversion has been abolished. Instead new provisions
have been introduced which allow seizure of infringing copies in certain
limited circumstances, and also give the court power to make orders for
delivery up, forfeiture, destruction or other disposal of infringing copies
and certain apparatus used for making infringing copies. (See paragraph
10.96 onwards.)

(d) The court's discretion to award additional damages has been broa-
dened, it no longer being a requirement that the court be satisfied that
effective relief would not otherwise be available to the plaintiff. (See
paragraph 10.86.)

(e) The power to give notice to the Commissioners of Customs & Excise
requiring them to treat certain articles as prohibited goods has been
extended to infringing copies of sound recordings and films. (See paragraph 10.107.)

(f) In relation to criminal proceedings for infringement:

(i) The knowledge requirement has been modified so that an offence
will now be committed where there is reason to believe the relevant
fact. (See paragraph 10.115.)

(ii) The offence of possession of an infringing copy in the course of
business and the power to grant search warrants have been extended to
all works. (See paragraphs 10.115 and 10.121.)

(iii) The offence of causing an infringing public performance of a
literary, dramatic or musical work has been extended to playing and
showing in public of sound recordings and films, but the offences are
not committed where public performance takes place by reception of a
broadcast or cable programme. (See paragraph 10.117.)

(iv) Some of the penalties have been increased. (See paragraph
10.123.)

II WARNING AND THREATENING LETTERS

1. Necessity for warning letters

10.07   It is not in general necessary to send a warning letter to someone who is
infringing copyright before an action for infringement is started. It may of

course be desirable in order to give the infringer a chance to remedy the situation before costly and time consuming proceedings are commenced.

A warning letter may however be necessary in order to fix someone with knowledge or reason to believe for the purpose of the acts of secondary infringement referred to in Chapter 6. In such cases until that party has the appropriate knowledge or reason to believe, he does not infringe copyright.

2. Actionable warning letters

In order to minimise damage caused by a primary infringer, a copyright owner will very often send letters to those dealing with the infringer, warning them not to do themselves any act which would be an infringement of copyright. For example, if a record is manufactured in infringement of copyright of the sound recording embodied on it, the copyright owner of the latter will often write both to distributors and retailers warning them not to distribute, offer for sale or sell such records. However, such letters should only be sent in a proper case, because they could provide grounds for an action by the alleged infringer, either on the grounds of malicious falsehood or unlawful interference with contractual relations.   **10.08**

3. Malicious falsehood

An action for malicious falsehood will lie where someone has made a false statement to a third party about another person's business or goods, if the statement is made with malice. A false statement that goods made or sold by a trader are infringing copies will be such a statement. Malice in this context means the wilful and intentional doing of damage without just occasion or excuse. (See *Joyce* v. *Motor Surveys Ltd.* ([1948] Ch. 252).) Honest belief in an unfounded claim however is not malice (*Greers Ltd.* v. *Pearman & Corder Ltd.* ((1922) 39 R.P.C. 406)).   **10.09**

4. Unlawful interference with contractual relations

If a person intentionally induces someone else by wrongful means to breach a contract with a third party who thereby suffers damage, the third party can take proceedings for unlawful interference with contractual relations. This will be so for example, where as a result of threats made against him, someone who has contracted for the purchase of goods refuses to take them. However, no such action will lie where "all the defendant has done is to assert in good faith a legal right claimed by him and to threaten proceedings if that right is infringed. (See *Granby Marketing Services Ltd.* v. *Interlego A.G.* ((1984) 81 L.S.Gaz. 1212).)   **10.10**

5. Interlocutory injunction

In an appropriate case, a court will grant an interlocutory injunction to   **10.11** prevent such threats being made. (See *Jaybeam Ltd.* v. *Abru Aluminium Ltd.* ([1957] F.S.R. 734).) For the principles on which such injunctions will be granted see paragraph 10.71 below.

6. Declarations of non-infringement

10.12 Where there are no grounds for taking proceedings on the above basis, the question arises as to what a person receiving threats which he believes are unwarranted can do to resolve the issue if the person making threats then fails to take proceedings. In the law of copyright, there is no action for threats such as exists in relation to patents and the new design right. (See paragraph 13.41 below.) His only remedy is to apply to the Court for a declaration that he is not infringing copyright. (See *Leco Instruments (U.K.) Limited* v. *Land Pyrometers Limited* ([1982] R.P.C. 140).)

7. Malicious communications

10.13 The sending of such letters may also be a criminal offence under the Malicious Communications Act 1988. This provides that any person who sends to another person a letter which contains a threat or information which is false (and known or believed to be false by the sender) is guilty of an offence, if his purpose, or one of his purposes, is to cause distress or anxiety to the recipient, or to any other person to whom he intends that it or its contents or nature should be communicated. However, the offence is not committed if the sender of the letter shows both that the threat was used to reinforce a demand which he believed he had reasonable grounds for making, and he believed that the use of the threat was a proper means of reinforcing the demand. The penalty for such an offence is a fine.

III WHO CAN SUE

A. THE OWNER OF THE COPYRIGHT

10.14 An infringement of copyright is actionable by the copyright owner (s.96(1)).

1. Different owners of different rights

Where different persons are entitled to different aspects of copyright in a work, the copyright owner who can take action is the person entitled to the right which has been infringed (s.173(1)). It is therefore important to identify what act of infringement the defendant has committed, and ensure that the proposed plaintiff is the owner of the right which has thereby been infringed.

2. Owner at the time of infringement

10.15 Furthermore, the copyright owner must have owned the relevant right at the time when the infringement took place. An assignee of the copyright in a work cannot sue for infringements which took place before the copyright was assigned to him. For that reason, one sometimes finds in assignments of copyright an assignment of the right to take proceedings for any prior infringement, and in other cases a right to take proceedings in the name of the former copyright owner for infringements which took place before assignment.

3. Joint ownership

One joint author or joint owner can take proceedings for infringement of copyright without joining his co-owners. This would even enable him to sue a co-owner for infringement of copyright where the co-owner has done one of the restricted acts without the consent of the other owner or owners. (See *Cescinsky* v. *George Routledge & Sons Ltd.* ([1916] 2 K.B. 325).)   **10.16**

4. Joining an exclusive licensee

Where an infringement of copyright is committed in respect of which the copyright owner's exclusive licensee has a concurrent right of action, the copyright owner may commence the action in his own name, and may also seek interlocutory relief (such as an injunction) on his own. Otherwise, he cannot proceed with the action without the leave of the Court unless he joins the exclusive licensee as a plaintiff or defendant (s.102(1)).   **10.17**

5. Equitable ownership

An owner of the copyright in equity (see paragraph 8.05 onwards) may also commence proceedings in his own name and apply for interlocutory orders such as an injunction, but again he cannot continue proceedings without joining the owner of the legal title to the copyright. He could of course also obtain an assignment of the legal title.   **10.18**

6. Importance of the correct plaintiff

It is vital to ensure that copyright proceedings are taken in the name of the correct person. The consequences of not doing this are demonstrated by the case of *Roban Jig & Tool Co Ltd.* v. *Taylor* ([1979] F.S.R. 130). This was a case for infringement of the copyright in certain engineering drawings. Some of the drawings had been prepared for the plaintiff company by independent designers. Others had been prepared by one of the partners of the firm whose assets and goodwill had eventually been transferred to the plaintiffs. As regards the former drawings, there appeared to be no assignment in writing from the independent contractors to the plaintiffs, and there was also no evidence that the plaintiffs owned the copyright in these drawings in equity. As regards the latter, it was accepted that the partnership owned in equity the drawings made by one of the partners, but again there was no evidence of a transfer of the   **10.19** title from the partnership to the plaintiffs. After the commencement of the proceedings, all these defects were cured by assigning the rights to the plaintiffs. However, the court refused to allow the proceedings to be amended, and struck out the claim for infringement. Of course, new proceedings could be taken once the defects had been cured, but in such cases not only does the plaintiff suffer delay, but also, in normal circumstances, an award of costs against him, as well as giving a defendant a tactical victory.

B. EXCLUSIVE LICENSEES

10.20   The provisions below only apply to proceedings for infringement committed after commencement of the 1988 Act and to seizure and applications for delivery up, forfeiture and disposal taking place after commencement. The provisions contained in section 19 of the 1956 Act continue to have effect for infringements committed before commencement, although they are broadly similar to those under the 1988 Act. None of the provisions either under the 1956 or 1988 Acts can be applied in the case of a licence granted before commencement of the 1956 Act.

1. Right to take proceedings

10.21   An exclusive licensee has the same rights and remedies for infringement of copyright as the copyright owner (s.101(1)). He can therefore sue for infringement of copyright, provided that the right infringed is one in respect of which he has an exclusive licence. However, he can only sue in respect of acts done after the grant of the licence, and during its subsistence. His rights do not extend as far as suing the owner of the copyright for infringement.

2. Meaning of exclusive licence

10.22   An exclusive licence is a licence in writing signed by or on behalf of the copyright owner authorising the licensee to the exclusion of all other persons, including the person granting the licence, to exercise a right which would otherwise be exercisable exclusively by the copyright owner (s.92(1)). For comments on the phrase "on behalf of" see paragraph 8.30 above. The right need not be an entire restricted act, and exclusive licences can be granted in the same way as rights partially assigned (see paragraph 8.31). If the copyright owner reserves any power to exercise the right being licensed, then it will not be an exclusive licence for the purposes of the 1988 Act, and will not entitle the exclusive licensee to take proceedings. In order to overcome such a problem, an exclusive licence should be granted without reservation and then a non-exclusive licence granted back by the exclusive licensee.

3. Rights concurrent with copyright owner

10.23   The rights and remedies which an exclusive licensee has are concurrent

314

with those of the copyright owner (s.101(2)). Because of this, some of the remedies referred to in this chapter are subject to special rules where there is both a copyright owner and an exclusive licensee. These are dealt with in the context of each relevant remedy.

4. Joining the copyright owner

An exclusive licensee may commence proceedings in his own name, and **10.24** may seek interlocutory relief on his own, but otherwise he cannot without the leave of the court proceed with the action unless the copyright owner is either joined as a plaintiff or added as a defendant (s.102(1)). The sort of case in which the court will grant such leave is demonstrated by *Bodley Head Ltd.* v. *Flegon* ([1972] 1 W.L.R. 680) where the court granted leave to continue an action for infringement of Alexander Solzhenitsyn's novel "August 1914" where at that time the author was still living in the USSR, and where publication of the novel there would not have been allowed.

5. Defence to action by exclusive licensee

A defendant to an action brought by an exclusive licensee can use any **10.25** defence against the exclusive licensee which would have been good against the owner of the copyright. So, if the defendant had a licence from the copyright owner, the exclusive licensee's claim will be defeated, although he will be left with a claim for breach of contract against the owner of the copyright.

C. OTHER PARTIES

1. Licensee

A licensee who is not an exclusive licensee has no right to take proceed- **10.26** ings for infringement of copyright (*Nicol* v. *Barranger* ([1917–23] MacG. Cop. Cas. 219)).

2. Agent

An agent acting for a copyright owner cannot take proceedings in his own **10.27** name. Although in *Carlin Music Corporation* v. *Collins* ([1979] F.S.R. 548), it was held that an agent might be able to seek relief on the grounds of unlawful interference with business, it is uncertain whether this has survived the decision of the House of Lords in *Lonrho Ltd.* v. *Shell Petroleum Co. Ltd.* ([1981] 2 All E.R. 456).

D. REPRESENTATIVE PROCEEDINGS

Under the Rules of the Supreme Court, where numerous persons have **10.28** the same interest in any proceedings, those proceedings may be begun and (unless the court otherwise orders) continued by any one or more of them as representing all of them. This rule is frequently used in copyright infringement proceedings, for example where a defendant is engaged in large-scale infringement of many different copyrights belonging to members of one collecting society or trade organisation. The procedure has for example been used with great success by the British Phonographic Industry against manufacturers and sellers of pirate records.

E. PRESUMPTIONS ON TITLE

1. Proof of subsistence and ownership

10.29   In order to succeed in an action for infringement of copyright, the owner must prove on the balance of probabilities that the work is one in which copyright subsists, and that he is the owner of that copyright. This means that he must prove that the work is an original one in the case of literary, dramatic, musical and artistic works. He must also in the case of all works prove that the work qualified for protection in the United Kingdom prior to the infringing act being carried out, and that he has a good title to the work deriving ultimately from the first owner of the copyright.

In some cases, particularly where the copyright is an old one, this can present difficulties for the copyright owner. Under the 1956 Act, there were presumptions both that copyright subsisted in the work, and that the plaintiff was the owner of the copyright (s.20). In truth, these presumptions were not of much use, because they did not apply where the defendant put them in issue, and, not surprisingly, most defendants did. These presumptions are not repeated in the 1988 Act, but some special presumptions are re-enacted, and will help to some extent. New presumptions have been introduced for computer programs and films. The presumptions under the 1988 Act apply to infringements committed after the commencement of the 1988 Act, and applications for delivery up, forfeiture or destruction made after such commencement. The 1956 Act presumptions continue to have effect for infringements committed before commencement.

2. Presumptions relating to literary, dramatic, musical and artistic works

(a) *Presumptions as to the author* (s.104(2))

10.30   In order to take advantage of this presumption, a name purporting to be that of the author must appear on copies of the work as published or on the work when it was made. In such a case, the person whose name so appeared is presumed until the contrary is proved to be the author of the work, and not to have made it as an employee in the course of employ-

316

ment. It will also be presumed that it was not a work subject to Crown copyright, Parliamentary copyright, or copyright of certain international organisations.

This presumption therefore only helps to establish ownership. It does not help in establishing either that the work was an original one, or that it qualified for copyright protection in the United Kingdom. Its use may also be limited where a person's name appears as an arranger or adapter of the copyright work, since it will not help establish which part of the work as published constitutes his skill, labour and judgment (*Roberton* v. *Lewis* ([1976] R.P.C. 169)).

The expression "as published" is unclear in meaning, and the question arises as to whether it requires that the plaintiff show that the name appeared on all copies, or merely some. In our view, the drafting of the provision is more consistent with the latter, and it does not matter if some copies were published without the name, even where, for example, first publication was anonymous. However, the point is not free from doubt. What is not entirely clear is whether the word "published" has to be construed in accordance with the 1988 Act (paragraph 2.13) or earlier statutes (paragraph 2.44). On balance, our view is that, in relation to events which happened prior to commencement of the 1988 Act, one looks to see whether this amounted to publication on the basis of the rules then in force. This arises from paragraph 4(4) of Schedule 1 to the 1988 Act which states that references in the 1988 Act to any of the new copyright provisions shall, so far as the context permits, be construed as including, in relation to times, circumstances and purposes before commencement, a reference to corresponding earlier provisions.

In the 1956 Act, the alternative requirement, that the name of the author appeared on the work when made, applied only to artistic works. Under the 1988 Act, a literary, dramatic and musical work is made when it is first recorded (in writing or otherwise) and it is possible that a court might hold in future that the presumption will operate where, for example, the original manuscript bears a name. It could be argued however that this part of the presumption still only applies to artistic works, since in the case of the other works it is only a *copy* of the work which is made when it is recorded, not the work itself.

Where the work is one alleged to be one of joint authorship, the presumption applies separately in relation to each person alleged to be one of the joint authors (s.104(3)).

(b) *Presumptions as to ownership* (s.104(4))

This presumption only applies where no name purporting to be that of the **10.31** author appeared on copies of the work as published or on the work when it was made. It will chiefly be relevant where the work is published anonymously.

In this case, if the work qualified for copyright protection in the United Kingdom by reference to the country of first publication (see paragraph 2.12), and a name purporting to be that of the publisher appeared on copies of the work as first published, then that person's name is presumed until the contrary is proved to have been the owner of the copyright at the time of publication. The word "first" should be noted here in contrast to the presumption referred to in paragraph 10.30. The latter also deals with the meaning of the word "published".

Again, this presumption is only of limited effect. It does not provide any presumption as to originality, or of course as to qualifying for copyright protection, since this is one of the matters which the copyright owner has to prove in order to rely on the presumption. It is also only a presumption as to ownership at the time of publication, and, assuming that the same person is not still the copyright owner, the copyright owner at the time of infringement will have to prove a chain of title from that publisher.

In most cases, a publisher's name will appear on copies of the work as first published. However, this will not always be so, given that publication can now take place by making the work available by means of an electronic retrieval system, which may happen where there is no publisher.

In our view, the accidental omission of the publisher's name from some of the copies when first publication took place will not prevent the presumption from being used.

The presumption is clearly intended to help plaintiffs in infringement proceedings, but it can cause problems where the work is subsequently published with the name of the author. In that event, both presumptions will apply and if the person claiming to be owner of the copyright can only trace title back to the author and not to the publisher, the presumption will defeat his claim unless he can prove that the publisher was not the owner of the copyright at the time of first publication. (See *Warwick Film Productions Limited* v. *Eisinger* ([1963] 2 All E.R. 892).)

(c) *Presumption where the author is dead or unknown* (s.104(5))

10.32   If the author of the work is dead, or his identity cannot be ascertained by reasonable enquiry, it is presumed in the absence of evidence to the contrary that the work is an original work. It is also presumed that the plaintiff's allegations as to where and when first publication of the work took place are correct.

Where copyright does not subsist by reference to the country of first publication, it will not help establish subsistence by reference to the status of the author when the work was made.

This presumption is of more use in practice, particularly if it can be coupled with that referred to in paragraph 10.30.

(d) *Presumptions as regards computer programs* (s.105(3))

10.33   This presumption applies where the action is for infringement of the copyright in a computer program, and where copies of the program have been issued to the public in electronic form.

If such copies bore a statement *either* that a named person was owner of the copyright in the program at the date of issue of copies, *or* that the program was first published in a specified country *or* that copies of it were issued to the public in electronic form in a specified year, those statements will be admitted as evidence of the facts stated, and will be presumed to be correct until the contrary is proved.

The expression "electronic form" means in a form usable only by electronic means. The most common examples would be in the form of cassettes or floppy discs.

It is unclear again whether or not the provision requires that all copies issued to the public bear the relevant statement. Our view in this case also is that the presumption is not defeated if some copies do not bear it.

3. Presumptions relevant to sound recordings (s.105(1))

Where copies of the recording as issued to the public bear a label or other   **10.34**
mark stating *either* that a named person was the owner of copyright in the recording at the date of issue of the copies, *or* that the recording was first published in a specified year, *or* in a specified country, the label or mark is admissible as evidence and is presumed to be correct until the contrary is proved.

Again in our view it is not necessary for the person wishing to use the presumption to show that all copies of the sound recording bore the relevant information.

The presumption only applies to the owner of copyright at the date of issue of the relevant copies. If there has been a change in ownership since then, a chain of title from that owner must be proved, although of course in many such circumstances fresh copies issued to the public will bear the name of the new owner.

4. Presumptions in relation to films

There are two separate presumptions here.   **10.35**
The first applies where copies of the film have been issued to the public. If such copies bear a statement *either* that a named person was the author or director of the film, *or* that a named person was the owner of copyright at the date of issue of the copies, *or* that the film was first published in a specified year in a specified country, any such statement is admissible as evidence of that and is presumed to be correct until the contrary is proved (s.105(2)).

The other presumption applies where the film has been shown in public, broadcast or included in a cable programme service. If the film in those circumstances bore a statement that a named person was *either* the author or director of the film *or* the owner of the copyright in the film immediately after it was made, then any such statement is admissible as evidence of that and is presumed to be correct until the contrary is proved (s.105(5)).

In relation to the first of these presumptions, we are again of the view that it is not necessary to show that all copies of the film bore the relevant information. As in the case of all the other presumptions, the point is not free from doubt, and the same applies to the second presumption. Here however, our view is that all copies of the film as shown in public and so on must bear the relevant statement for the presumption to operate. This is because of the reference to "the film" as opposed to "copies of the film." However, it is possible that a court would still allow use of the presumption where a minimal number of copies accidentally omitted the relevant information.

5. Retrospective effect

10.36   The presumptions relating to copies of works refered to above apply even to proceedings for infringements alleged to have occurred before the date on which the relevant copies were issued to the public. Similarly, the presumption in paragraph 10.35 applies in proceedings for infringements alleged to have occurred before the date on which the film was shown in public, broadcast or included in a cable programme service. The presumptions can obviously be used however infringement took place, not just in cases of infringement by issuing copies to the public and so on.

6. Territoriality

10.37   The presumptions referred to above use the expressions "as published", "as issued to the public" and "as shown in public", without specifying a territory where these acts took place. The question therefore arises whether such acts can or should be taken into account if they took place outside the United Kingdom. Regrettably, no clear answer can be provided here, but it is in our view likely that such acts would enable the presumptions to be used, even though the relevant facts may be entirely different as regards the copyright subsisting in such a territory.

7. Conflicting information

10.38   As stated, our view in the case of publishing and issuing to the public is that the presumptions will not be defeated if some copies do not bear the relevant information. However, the position is more difficult where some copies bear different and conflicting information. It is likely in those circumstances that the law would give little weight to the presumptions and require clearer evidence to establish the facts on a balance of probabilities.

8. Complying with labelling requirements

10.39   In some cases above the presumption applies where copies of the work bear a particular statement, or a label containing a particular statement. It is uncertain whether these provisions would be satisfied by the use of such abbreviations as "© XYZ Ltd 1988" or "℗ ABC Ltd 1987." These might not be considered to be a "statement," and it is advisable to follow strictly what is required in each case. Furthermore, it is on copies of the work or (in two cases) the work itself that the relevant label mark or information must appear, not just the packaging of such a work or copy.

9. Limitations on the presumptions

The provisions above only contain presumptions, and should be treated   **10.40** with some caution. In some cases the presumption operates until the contrary is proved, that is, the burden of proof shifts to the defendant. In other cases, the presumption only applies in the absence of evidence to the contrary, and presumably where there is any evidence to the contrary the presumption fails to have any effect at all. Furthermore, it is not only where the defendant has evidence to the contrary that problems may arise. Under the Rules of the Supreme Court, a plaintiff in any action must disclose all documents relating to the matters in issue and this would extend to all documents relating to subsistence and ownership of copyright. If these documents demonstrate some flaw in the title, then this also can constitute evidence to the contrary, or allow the defendant to rebut the presumption. The moral is always to check subsistence and ownership as rigorously as possible prior to commencement of proceedings, even though this may present difficulties.

10. Infringement prior to commencement of the 1988 Act

The presumptions do not apply to infringements committed prior to   **10.41** commencement of the 1988 Act: here section 20 of the 1956 Act continues in effect. That provision contained:

(a) General presumptions on subsistence and ownership (see paragraph 10.29).

(b) The presumptions referred to in paragraphs 10.30, 10.31 and 10.32.

(c) A similar presumption in relation to sound recordings as is referred to in paragraph 10.34 save that the first alternative required a statement that the person was maker of the sound recording rather than the owner.

11. Practical points

In practice, the presumptions relevant to computer programs, sound   **10.42** recordings and films will be rather more useful than those relating to other literary works, and dramatic, musical and artistic works. In any event, usefulness obviously depends on whether the relevant information is properly included on copies, and the presumptions must be borne in mind and followed when making copies of the relevant works and labelling them. Soundtracks of films are now protected as sound recordings not films, so such articles as video cassettes should in future contain information as to both. As regards the presumptions referred to in paragraphs 10.33, 10.34 and 10.35, it is advisable if possible to include all the relevant information.

12. Notice to admit facts

10.43 Under the Rules of the Supreme Court (Ord. 27 r. 2), a party to an action may serve notice on any other party requiring him to admit a particular fact or facts. This could be used in copyright infringement actions to try to get a defendant to admit facts which would establish both subsistence and ownership. However, the only penalty for not admitting any such facts is in costs, and in practice many defendants take the risk to see whether the plaintiff can in fact prove the facts he alleges.

IV WHO MAY BE SUED

A. THE PERSON DOING THE RELEVANT ACT

10.44 This covers not only the situation where someone is infringing copyright himself, but in certain circumstances where the infringing act is done by a servant, independent contractor or agent. The usual form of injunction granted in copyright cases forbids someone to do an infringing act "whether by himself, his servants, agents or otherwise howsoever. . . . "

An employer will be liable for an infringement of copyright committed by his employee not only where the employer instructs the employee to do the act, but where the employee was acting in the course of his employment (*Performing Right Society Ltd.* v. *Mitchell and Booker (Palais de Danse) Ltd.* ([1924] 1 K.B. 762)).

A principal will be liable for the acts of his agent not only when the principal instructs the agent to do the act, but where he authorises or ratifies it. In an old case, *Monaghan* v. *Taylor* ([1885] 2 T.L.R. 685), a singer was hired to perform at a music hall. He was allowed to choose whatever music he wanted to sing, and the proprietor of the premises exercised no control over performers in ensuring that there was no infringement of copyright. The singer performed a song without permission from the copyright owner, and an action against the proprietor was upheld on the basis that there was sufficient evidence of authority to perform that song. It is uncertain whether the result would be the same today. It is in marked contrast to the approach taken by the court in *Performing Right Society Ltd.* v. *Ciryl Theatrical Syndicate Ltd.* ([1924] 1 K.B. 1) although that was a case of secondary infringement (see paragraph 6.15).

In *Machinery Market Ltd.* v. *Sheen Publishing Ltd.* ([1983] F.S.R. 431), Whitford J. held that the publisher of a magazine was liable for infringing copyright by reproducing the typographical arrangement of another company's published edition, even though the reproduction had been carried out by independent printers for the publishers. Of course, if the plaintiffs had alleged that the publishers authorised the reproduction the defendants would probably have been liable on that basis (see paragraph 10.46 below).

B. AUTHORISING INFRINGEMENTS OF COPYRIGHT

1. Authorising in relation to primary and secondary infringement

If one party authorises another to do one of the acts restricted by the **10.45**
copyright referred to in Chapter 5, the party authorising the act to be
done without the licence of the copyright owner is liable for infringement
of copyright, as well as the person actually doing the act. This does not
however apply in the case of the acts of secondary infringement referred
to in Chapter 6.

2. Meaning of authorising

The question is therefore what constitutes authorising. There is no **10.46**
straightforward answer to this. Until the case of *CBS Songs Ltd.* v.
Amstrad Consumer Electronics plc ([1987] 3 W.L.R. 144), the most
common definition used was that of "sanction, approve and counte-
nance." But it is now clear from the *Amstrad* case that this is misleading.
In the *Amstrad* case, Lord Templeman held as follows:

> " ... In the context of the Copyright Act 1956 an authorisation
> means a grant or purported grant, which may be express or implied,
> of the right to do the act complained of."

It is not however easy to apply this general statement of principle in
practice, especially since in many cases there will be no express grant of
the right to do the act, but only the possibility of an implied one. In
general terms however, the major distinction to bear in mind is between
giving express or implied authority for an act to be done, and merely
facilitating the doing of that act.
  Some additional guidance however may be obtained from the facts of
the *Amstrad* case, and cases cited with approval in the *Amstrad* case.

(a) In *Monckton* v. *Pathe Freres Pathephone Ltd.* ([1914] 1 K.B. 395),
Buckley L.J. said: "The seller of the record authorises, I conceive, the use
of the record, and such user will be a performance of the musical work."
Of course, nowadays most records bear a statement to the effect that no
unauthorised performance in public is allowed of the recording or the
works reproduced thereon, and no authority is therefore granted.

(b) In *Evans* v. *E. Hulton and Co. Ltd.* ((1924) 131 L.T. 534), Tomlin J.
said that: " ... where a man sold the rights in relation to a manuscript to
another with a view to its production, and it was in fact produced, both
the English language and common sense required him to hold that this
man had 'authorised' the printing and publication."

(c) In *Falcon* v. *Famous Players Film Co.* ([1926] 2 K.B. 474), the defendants hired to a cinema a film based on the plaintiff's play. It was clear that this was done for the purpose of allowing the showing in public of the film, as the defendant was entitled to receive a proportion of the receipts from the showing of the film. This was held to amount to authorising.

(d) In the *Amstrad* case itself, the defendants manufactured and sold hi-fi systems which incorporated facilities for high speed copying from pre-recorded cassettes on to blank tapes. This was held not to be authorising the copying of musical works or sound recordings. This was because "Amstrad conferred on the purchaser the power to copy but did not grant or purport to grant the right to copy." In their advertisements for the machines, the defendants drew attention to the advantages of the particular model, and to the fact that they could be used in the copying of records. However, a footnote to the advertisement gave a warning that some copying required permission. It was again held that the advertisements did not authorise the recording, because ". . . the operators of an Amstrad tape recording facility . . . can alone decide whether to record or play and what material is to be recorded . . . (and) . . . no purchaser of an Amstrad model could reasonably deduce from the facilities incorporated in the model or from Amstrad's advertisement that Amstrad possessed or purported to possess the authority to grant any required permission for a record to be copied."

(e) In *CBS Inc.* v. *Ames Records and Tapes Ltd.* ([1981] 2 W.L.R. 973), Whitford J. held that a record library which lent out records and simultaneously offered blank tapes for sale at a discount did not authorise an infringement of copyright in the recordings.

C. WHERE THE ACT AUTHORISED DOES NOT TAKE PLACE

10.47   What is not clear is whether a person is liable for infringement of copyright by authorising an act where the act does not in fact take place. In *Performing Right Society Ltd.* v. *Mitchell and Booker (Palais de Danse) Ltd.* ([1924] 1 K.B. 762), McCardie J. expressed his opinion that there would be no infringement in these circumstances, but of course it would still be possible to apply for a *quia timet* injunction in an appropriate case (see paragraph 10.52).

D. JOINT INFRINGERS

10.48   The term used by Lord Templeman in the *Amstrad* case has been adopted here, although one more commonly finds the expression "joint tortfeasors."

Joint infringers are two or more persons who act in concert with one another pursuant to a common design in the infringement. This extends to the situation where someone procures a breach of copyright, whether by inducement, incitement, or persuasion.

In the *Amstrad* case however, it was held by the House of Lords that Amstrad were not joint infringers. Firstly, there was no common design:

> "Amstrad sold a machine and the purchaser or the operator of the machine decided the purpose for which the machine should from time to time be used. The machine was capable of being used for lawful or unlawful purposes. All recording machines and many other machines are capable of being used for unlawful purposes but manufacturers and retailers are not joint infringers if purchasers choose to break the law."

Secondly, there was no procurement of the infringements:

> "Amstrad do not procure infringement by offering for sale a machine which may be used for lawful or unlawful copying ... (or) ... by advertising the attractions of their machine to a purchaser who may decide to copy unlawfully ... The purchaser will not make unlawful copies because he had been induced or incited or persuaded to do so by Amstrad. The purchaser will make unlawful copies for his own use because he chooses to do so."

E. PERSONAL LIABILITY OF DIRECTORS AND EMPLOYEES

In the case of a small company, very often the day to day activities of **10.49** the company are closely controlled or supervised by the directors. In such cases, it may be possible to join the director to the proceedings personally either for having authorised the particular act or as a joint infringer. This is useful for a copyright owner where a director has or has had a number of companies involved in copyright infringement, and also where the company has no assets with which to satisfy a claim for damages.

However potent a weapon, it must clearly be used with caution, as it is not in every case that a director will be liable as a joint infringer. It was made clear by Slade L.J. in the case of *C. Evans Ltd* v. *Spritebrand Ltd* ([1985] 2 All E.R. 425) that where joining a director to proceedings against a company was demonstrably a tactical move, an application to strike out the proceedings against the director might well be justified. Where the director procures or directs the infringement knowingly or recklessly, he will clearly be liable. Where the director has no knowledge and has not behaved recklessly, the court may be more reluctant to hold him liable, but he could still be liable for infringement in the case of one of the restricted acts referred to in Chapter 5, because knowledge is generally not a necessary ingredient for infringement to take place in the case of such acts (*C. Evans Ltd.* v. *Spritebrand Ltd.*)

An example where a director might be liable was given in the *Spritebrand* case. If a company employee himself manufactures articles in breach of copyright, and carries out this operation under the personal supervision and direction of the director, not only will the employee be liable as having made the copies, but also the director.

F. REPRESENTATIVE DEFENDANTS

10.50   Under the same rules referred to in paragraph 10.28, proceedings may be begun and continued *against* any one or more persons on a representative basis. This for example was done in *EMI Records Ltd.* v. *Kudhail* ([1985] F.S.R. 36). In that case, pirate cassettes were being manufactured and distributed under the trade name *Oak Records*. The plaintiffs had been unable to find out the source of the goods. It was held by the Court of Appeal that there was a common interest in all those engaged in the trade of selling cassettes bearing the name *Oak Records* in that they were all concerned to prevent anybody from finding out where the cassettes came from. Accordingly, orders were made against the two persons sued on their own behalf and on behalf of and as representing all other persons engaged in the trade of selling tapes bearing the trade name *Oak Records*.

V INJUNCTIONS

A. GENERAL POINTS

10.51   An injunction is a discretionary remedy. It can either be in negative (that is, compelling someone not to do something) or mandatory (that is, requiring someone to do something) terms. In proceedings for infringement of copyright, injunctions are often sought both before trial, sometimes even before proceedings are commenced, and at trial. Pre-trial injunctions are dealt with below separately from those at trial, and a final section considers remedies available where injunctions are breached. First however, several points of general importance must be made.

1. Anticipated infringement

10.52   It is not necessary for a copyright owner or exclusive licensee to wait for an infringement to take place before commencing proceedings. Action can also be taken where an infringement is threatened: such proceedings are generally known as *quia timet* proceedings. However, there must be good evidence of a threatened infringement, and not just fear on the plaintiff's part that an infringement might take place.

2. Broad injunctions

10.53   It is on the above basis that a plaintiff often not only applies for an injunction to prevent infringement in relation to a work the copyright in which has already been infringed, but also in relation to other works the copyright in which is owned by or exclusively licensed to him. If the court considers that there is a real threat that such copyrights will be infringed, an injunction extending to such works will be granted. If the court considers there is no real threat it will not. In recent cases, there has been a reluctance to grant injunctions in too broad a form. Even where there is a threat that many other copyrights will be infringed, the court will not grant an injunction in such wide terms that the defendant will not know or readily be able to discover the scope of what he can or cannot do. (See *Columbia Picture Industries* v. *Robinson* ([1987] Ch. 38).)

3. Delay

In applications for pre-trial injunctions, it is vital that the plaintiff acts quickly once the infringement or threatened infringement is discovered. If he fails to do this, his application may be denied on those grounds alone. It is impossible to define exactly what delay will result in a plaintiff being refused relief. This entirely depends on the particular circumstances, but in general a three to four week period between an infringement or threatened infringement being discovered and the commencement of proceedings will not be considered undue.

   Substantial delay in rare cases may lead to the court refusing a final injunction, where it is such that it would be dishonest or unconscionable for the plaintiff to claim an injunction. In some cases, the court will on the grounds of delay award damages in lieu of an injunction under an 1858 statute known as Lord Cairns's Act.

10.54

4. Injunctions in relation to buildings

Under the 1956 Act, in an action for infringement of copyright in respect of the construction of a building, no injunction or other order could be made so as to prevent a building from being completed, or to require it to be demolished after construction had begun. This provision has not been re-enacted under the 1988 Act, but continues to have effect as regards infringements committed before commencement of the 1988 Act. (See schedule 1 paragraph 31(1).)

10.55

B. PRE-TRIAL INJUNCTIONS

1. Injunctions to prevent destruction or disappearance of evidence

(a) *Rationale behind the granting of such injunctions*

In some cases, there is a danger that warning the potential defendant that proceedings for infringement of copyright are being taken will result in

10.56

the destruction or disappearance of evidence vital for the purposes of a trial. In such circumstances, the court has the power to grant an injunction requiring that the potential defendant allow the potential plaintiff to enter his premises, inspect and remove documents or other articles. Applications for such orders are generally, but not always, made before the issue of proceedings against the potential defendant, and they are of course made without the potential defendant being warned of the application.

(b) *Principles on which granted*

10.57   The principles on which such orders are granted were dealt with in *Anton Piller K.G.* v. *Manufacturing Processes Ltd.* ([1976] Ch. 55), and it is from that case that such orders have derived their common description, Anton Piller orders.

As held by the Court of Appeal in the *Anton Piller* case the prerequisites for such an order to be granted are as follows:

(i) In general, an order should be made only where it is essential that the plaintiff should have inspection so that justice can be done between the parties.

(ii) There must be an extremely strong prima facie case for infringement of copyright.

(iii) The damage, potential or actual, must be very serious for the applicant.

(iv) There must be clear evidence that the defendant has in his possession incriminating documents or other articles, and that there is a real possibility that they might destroy such material if notice were given to them.

(v) The inspection must do no real harm to the defendant or his case.

The Court of Appeal in the *Anton Piller* case emphasised that it was only in exceptional cases that such an order would be granted. This has been frequently repeated by the courts over the years, and in several recent judgments comments have been made that such orders have often been granted too readily. See especially *Columbia Picture Industries* v. *Robinson* ([1987] Ch. 38).

(c) *Effect of the order*

10.58   The order if made does not operate as a search warrant. It requires the defendant to give access, allow inspection and (in some cases) the removal of property. If the defendant refuses, the plaintiff cannot use force. His remedy is to return to the court for an order for committal based on the defendant's contempt.

Where the order is made, service is generally required to be effected by the plaintiff's solicitor, who acts as an officer of the court for these purposes. An opportunity must be given to the defendant to consider the order and to consult his solicitors. The defendant can apply to discharge the order.

A person against whom an order is made cannot refuse to comply with it on the grounds that to do so might expose him or his spouse to criminal proceedings (Supreme Court Act 1981, s.72). Likewise, he cannot use the possibility of self-incrimination as grounds for refusing to answer any questions put to him in the course of proceedings.

(d) *Other material points in applying for and executing orders*

Since the *Anton Piller* case was decided, there have been many other cases reported dealing with such orders. It is not possible here to cover all the relevant points, but the following is a summary of the most important practical points: **10.59**

(i) The evidence put before the Court in applying for an order must be full and frank. Failure to tell the whole story may result in the discharge of the order. (See *Thermax* v. *Shott Industrial Glass* ([1981] F.S.R. 209).)

(ii) In many cases it will be impossible to obtain direct evidence of a threat to destroy material or documents, but such a threat will often be inferred from illegal or underhand behaviour by the defendant (*Yousif* v. *Salama* ([1980] 1 W.L.R. 1540)).

(iii) An Anton Piller order must not be used as a fishing expedition in order to find out precisely what claims a plaintiff has. The exact ambit of the claim must be known. (See *Hytrac Conveyors Ltd.* v. *Conveyors International Ltd.* ([1983] 1 W.L.R. 44).)

(iv) Generally, an Anton Piller order should not be used where the alleged infringer is operating his business in a perfectly open manner in a shop to which the public is admitted, and where the only evidence as to infringement is a sale and a suspicion that other sales may be taking place, with nothing to show that the business is being conducted in so underhand and surreptitious a way that there is good ground for believing that without the order being made there would be nothing left to fight on. (See *Systematica Ltd.* v. *London Computer Centre Ltd.* ([1983] F.S.R. 313).)

(v) In *Columbia Picture Industries* v. *Robinson* ([1987] Ch. 38) Scott J. laid down certain additional requirements:

— Documentary material and correspondence should be retained only long enough to copy it and should then be returned.

— Once the defendant has solicitors on the record other seized material should be handed over to them on their undertaking for its safe custody and production in court.

— A detailed record of material taken should be made by solicitor executing the order before it is removed from the premises.

— No material should be taken which is not covered by the order, even with consent, unless the defendant's solicitor confirms that the consent is not subject to pressure and was given with full knowledge.

(e) *Dangers of abuse*

10.60 The dangers of abusing the Anton Piller order rules, either as regards the obtaining of the order, or executing that order, are demonstrated by the *Columbia Picture Industries* case where the court ordered that the plaintiffs pay £10,000 to the defendants in damages, and also made orders for costs against them.

(f) *Orders after judgment*

10.61 An Anton Piller order can also be made after judgment in order to prevent the defendant rendering any judgment nugatory. (See *Distributori Automatic Italia S.P.A.* v. *Holford General Trading Co. Ltd.* ([1985] 1 W.L.R. 1066).)

(g) *Use of documents*

10.62 Where documents are seized or copied during the course of execution of an Anton Piller order, they must not be disclosed to a third party without leave of the court. (See *Commissions of Customs and Excise* v. *A.E. Hamlin & Co.* ([1984] 1 W.L.R. 509).) Whether they can be used without leave for the purposes of proceedings against third parties involved in the manufacture of or dealing with the relevant infringing goods is unclear. Browne-Wilkinson J. said that they could in *Sony Corporate* v. *Anand* (R.S.) ([1981] F.S.R. 398). However, the normal rule that such documents and information must only be used for the purposes of the proceedings in which the order was obtained was re-affirmed by Warner J. in *General Nutrition Ltd.* v. *Pradip Pattni* ([1984] F.S.R. 403).

2. Injunctions to prevent dissipation of assets

(a) *Rationale behind the granting of such injunctions*

10.63 Where there is a danger that a judgment for a sum of money will be worthless because assets which could be used to satisfy the judgment have been dissipated, then the court has a discretion to grant an injunction to prevent the assets being disposed of. Such an injunction is called a Mareva injunction from the case under which the principles applicable to the granting of such an injunction were first laid down. (See *Mareva Compania Naviera S.A.* v. *International Bulk Carriers S.A.* ([1980] 1 All E.R. 213).)

(b) *Principles on which granted*

10.64 The pre-requisites for the making of such an order in an infringement of copyright case will be as follows:

(i) A good arguable case for at least an approximate sum of money. In copyright cases, it is unlikely that the plaintiff will be able to prove an exact sum, but he must be able to provide a properly reasoned estimate of the damages which he would recover.

(ii) There must be a risk of dissipation of the assets, that is that if an injunction is not granted there is a real risk that a judgment would remain unsatisfied.

These are the bare outlines of the grounds on which such an order may be made, and, again, it is not possible here to deal with the large number of cases in which the granting of such orders have been considered. The law relating to *Mareva* injunctions is particularly complex, and is still developing to meet new circumstances.

(c) *"Piling a Piller on a Mareva"*

Applications for Anton Piller orders are very often coupled with applications for Mareva injunctions. This was for example done in *CBS United Kingdom Ltd.* v. *Lambert* ([1983] Ch. 37). In that case, the Court of Appeal ordered delivery-up of motor cars belonging to the defendant.   **10.65**

(d) *Banks*

Where the person against whom the Mareva injunction is granted has a bank account, the plaintiff will serve the bank with a copy of the order, in order to ensure that the relevant account is frozen up to the amount in respect of which the order was granted, subject to any provision for the defendant to draw certain sums of money for living expenses. The plaintiff will in such a case have to undertake to pay the reasonable costs involved in searching to see whether any of the defendant's assets are held by the bank.   **10.66**

3. Injunctions and orders for disclosure of information

(a) *Type of orders*

In granting an Anton Piller order, a court will often also grant an order that the defendant discloses to the plaintiff the names and addresses of all persons, companies or firms responsible for supplying, or offering to supply, or to whom they have supplied or offered to supply, the infringing articles. Indeed, in *Sony Corporation* v. *Anand* ([1981] F.S.R. 398), Browne-Wilkinson J. stated that one of the purposes of granting an Anton Piller order was to enable the plaintiff "to obtain information as to the persons from whom the defendant obtained the supplies of the infringing material and the persons to whom the defendant in turn has supplied the infringing material." Similarly, a Mareva order is often accompanied by an order requiring the defendant to disclose the whereabouts of his assets.   **10.67**

Another disclosure order which may be made when an Anton Piller order is granted is one requiring the defendant to disclose the names and addresses of all persons, firms and companies who are partners of or associated with the defendants in relation to the relevant infringing activity.

As a corollary of such orders in the context of an Anton Piller order, the court will usually order further that the defendant must not directly or indirectly inform or notify any such persons, firm or company of the existence of the proceedings or that proceedings may be brought against them.

Applications for disclosure of names and addresses and other information can also be made where no Anton Piller order has either been sought or obtained.

(b) *Limits on disclosing names of customers*

10.68   Despite the comments of the judge in the *Sony Corporation* case, it is clear that the power to order disclosure particularly of names of customers will be exercised with great caution. As stated by Templeman L.J. in *Sega Enterprises Ltd.* v. *Alca Electronics* ([1982] F.S.R. 516).

> "The power should not be exercised in interlocutory proceedings, and certainly not *ex parte*, unless the court is reasonably satisfied that the plaintiff will, or probably will, suffer irreparable damage if there is any delay in ordering discovery. Where the court is satisfied—and on *ex parte* applications the court cannot be certain; it must act on the evidence which is before it—that the plaintiff will or may probably suffer irreparable damage, then the court may act with all speed with which the court is capable and may impose *ex parte* orders for discovery. But such orders should never be made as a matter of course—never merely as part and parcel of an Anton Piller order—without investigation of the circumstances of each case and without the court coming to the conclusion that it is necessary for the long-term protection of the plaintiff that such a draconian course should be taken."

In that case, the court refused to grant such an order because there was a genuine dispute over infringement, and disclosing the names of the defendants' customers could have damaged the defendants' business. The evidence was also that the relevant customers were all reputable traders.

Furthermore, the court will not make an order for disclosure of the names and addresses of persons to whom defendants supplied infringing articles, where there is no evidence that those persons were themselves infringing copyright. (See (*Roberts* v. *Jump Knitwear Ltd.* ([1981] F.S.R. 527).) The order cannot therefore be used in order to obtain the names and addresses of persons for the purposes of fixing them with knowledge prior to taking proceedings for secondary infringement.

(c) *Disclosure of source of information*

A further possible limitation on the obtaining of such orders occurs where   **10.69**
infringement takes place either by the defendant reproducing material in
a publication for which he is responsible, or by his committing one of the
acts of secondary infringement by dealing with such a publication, and
where the publication is an infringing copy. Here, the defendant may be
able to plead successfully section 10 of the Contempt of Court Act 1981
which states that:

> "No court may require a person to disclose nor is any person guilty of
> contempt of court for refusing to disclose the source of information
> contained in a publication of which he is responsible unless it is
> established to the satisfaction of the court that disclosure is necessary
> in the interests of justice or national security or for the prevention of
> disorder or crime."

This defence was pleaded successfully in *Handmade Films (Productions) Ltd.* v. *Express Newspapers plc.* ([1986] F.S.R. 463).
A plaintiff cannot show that disclosure is necessary in the interests of
justice where it is simply expedient or desirable. He will usually be able to
show necessity where he needs the name of the relevant person for the
purposes of starting an action against a wrongdoer.

(d) *Orders against parties not infringing*

Aside from where a plaintiff seeks such an order as part of infringement   **10.70**
proceedings, he may be entitled to obtain such information from
someone who is not infringing. This follows from the case of *Norwich
Pharmacal Co.* v. *Commissioners of Customs and Excise Commissioners*
([1974] A.C. 133) in which Lord Reid said:

> " ... if through no fault of his own a person gets mixed up in the
> tortious acts of others so as to facilitate their wrong doing he may
> incur no personal liability but he comes under a duty to assist the
> person who has been wronged by giving him full information and
> disclosing the identity of the wrongdoers. I do not think that it
> matters whether he became so mixed up by voluntary action on his
> part or because it was his duty to do what he did. It may be that if this
> causes him expense the person seeking the information ought to
> reimburse him. But justice requires that he should co-operate in
> righting the wrong if he unwittingly facilitated its perpetration."

Again, however this is subject to section 10 of the 1981 Contempt of
Court Act.

4. Injunctions to prevent infringement occurring or continuing

In some cases, the infringing act or acts have been committed, and there is   **10.71**

no immediate danger that further acts will take place. In other cases
however, the defendant is threatening to infringe or continue to infringe,
and the plaintiff will want to prevent this. In those circumstances, he will
want to consider whether or not the court might grant what is called an
interim injunction, that is an injunction to prevent the doing of the
relevant acts until the trial of the action, or some other date.

Such an injunction usually forms part of an Anton Piller order, when it
will be granted over a short period of time to enable the order to be
executed and then to give the defendant an opportunity to come to the
court and for the court to hear argument as to whether the injunction
should be continued further. Similar injunctions may be granted in cases
of extreme urgency where there is no application for an Anton Piller
order. Such a case might arise for example where the copyright owner of a
musical work is notified that a record made in infringement of copyright
of the work is about to be shipped out to wholesalers. Applications may
be made even before commencement of proceedings. In less urgent
cases, the plaintiff commences proceedings, and then gives notice to the
defendant that he intends to apply for an interim injunction.

The principles on which the court will consider whether or not to grant
or extend injunctions preventing infringement until trial were set out by
the House of Lords in *American Cyanamid* v. *Ethicon Ltd.* ([1975] A.C.
396). They are as follows:

(a) The Court will first examine whether there is a serious issue to be
tried. If there is no arguable defence, then an injunction will normally be
granted, subject to the comments made below in relation to final injunctions. Otherwise, a good guide to whether there is a serious issue to be
tried is contained in the judgment of the Vice-Chancellor in *Mothercare
Ltd.* v. *Robson Books Ltd.* ([1979] F.S.R. 466):

> "All that has to be seen is whether the plaintiff has prospects of
> success which, in substance and reality, exist. Odds against success
> no longer defeat the plaintiff, unless they are so long that the plaintiff
> can have no expectation of success, but only a hope. If his prospects
> of success are so small that they lack substance and reality, then the
> plaintiff fails, for he can point to no question to be tried which can be
> called 'serious' and no prospect of success which can be called
> 'real.' "

(b) Assuming that there is a serious issue to be tried, the court examines
whether damages would be an adequate remedy either for the plaintiff or
(under the cross-undertaking as to damages referred to in paragraph
10.72 below) the defendant. If damages would be adequate to compensate the plaintiff, then normally no injunction will be granted. Conversely, if the defendant could be adequately compensated under the
plaintiff's cross-undertaking as to damages, then an injunction will probably be granted. It is obviously also necessary to consider whether it is
likely that the relevant party will have means to satisfy a judgment for
damages.

(c) If it is doubtful whether damages will be an adequate remedy for either party, then the court examines whether on the balance of convenience an injunction should be granted or denied. "Convenience" is a somewhat misleading word here, and it is better to treat it as a question of "balance of justice." It is impossible to define what the court will take into account in applying this, since each case needs to be viewed on the basis of its own facts.

(d) Assuming that the balance is fairly even, the court will often preserve the status quo. Of course, the immediate question is which status quo one should consider, because the facts and circumstances may have changed a number of times. This has given rise to problems, but in *Garden Cottage Foods Ltd.* v. *Milk Marketing Board* ([1984] A1, 130) it was held that the relevant status quo is the state of affairs existing during the period immediately preceding the issue of the writ, or, if there is unreasonable delay between the issue of the writ and the application for an injunction, the period immediately preceding the application. However, the House of Lords also held that the duration of the period during which that status quo existed must be more than minimal, taking into account the total length of any relationship between the parties. Where it is not more than minimal, the relevant status quo is the state of affairs before the last change.

(e) If even then the extent of the disadvantage to each party would not differ widely, it is not improper for the court to take into account in tipping the balance the relative strength of each party's case. This however should only be done where it is apparent upon the facts disclosed by the evidence before the court as to which there is no credible dispute that the strength of one party's case is disproportionate to that of the other party.

(f) In addition to all these rules, there may be other special factors to be taken into consideration in the particular circumstances of individual cases. In *Kennard* v. *Lewis* ([1983] F.S.R. 346), Warner J. refused to grant an interim injunction on the basis that such injunctions should not in general be used to restrain free speech and in particular to restrain political controversy. There, the defendants had published a pamphlet entitled *30 Questions and Honest Answers about CND* which was modelled closely on the plaintiff's leaflet similarly named.

5. Cross-undertaking as to damages

In the case of Anton Piller and Mareva applications, the strength of the copyright owner's case is important. In other cases, under *American Cyanamid* principles, it is a possible subsidiary factor. In practice, the grant or denial of a pre-trial injunction will very often lead to the disposal of the whole action, and is therefore sometimes seen by parties to litigation as to a quick way of resolving a dispute. However, such applications should not be made lightly. 10.72

First, where the court considers that the purpose of such an application is to force the defendant to settle or put him out of business, it is likely to exercise its discretion to prevent such abuse, assuming that the defendant has an arguable case that he is not infringing. This is particularly so in the case of the exercise of such draconian powers as Anton Piller orders. (See *Columbia Picture Industries* v. *Robinson* ([1987] Ch. 38).) Secondly, the party in whose favour an injunction is granted will always have to give to the court an undertaking to pay any damages sustained by the defendant because of the grant of the injunction which the court considers the plaintiff ought to pay. The obvious example is where the plaintiff fails in his action at the trial, but there could be other circumstances as well.

Where for example the court grants an injunction preventing the sale of a particular article, the damages based on loss of sales could be substantial, although difficult to quantify in many cases. The remedy is one which is in the discretion of the court, and it is not something which the defendant is entitled to as of right.

6. Injunctions at trial

(a) *Prima facie will be granted*

10.73   Ordinarily, a copyright owner who is successful at the trial of the action will be granted an injunction to prevent further infringement.

In rare cases, an injunction will not be granted because it is highly improbable that the infringement will be repeated. However, this is not a presumption which the court makes lightly.

(b) *Undertakings*

10.74   Both in relation to final and pre-trial injunctions, the court may accept an undertaking from the defendant not to repeat the infringement in lieu of an injunction. However, sometimes an injunction will be imposed even where such an offer has been made. (See *E.W. Savory Ltd.* v. *The World of Golf Ltd.* ([1914] 2 Ch. 566).)

(c) *Acquiescence*

10.75   As stated in paragraph 10.54, substantial delay may result in the court refusing to exercise its discretion in favour of granting an injunction. Refusal may also occur where the plaintiff has acquiesced in the defendant's infringement, that is where the plaintiff knows of the infringement and acts in such a way that the defendant is encouraged to continue what he is doing. In some cases, such conduct will amount to an implied licence. (See further paragraph 9.10.)

(d) *Damages in lieu of injunction*

10.76   As stated in paragraph 10.54, the court always has power to award damages in lieu of an injunction under the Chancery Amendment Act

1858 known as Lord Cairns's Act. In *Shelfer* v. *City of London Electric Lighting Company* ([1895] 1 Ch. 287) A. L. Smith L.J. held that a good working rule as to when the discretion should be exercised was where the injury to the plaintiff's legal right was small, capable of being estimated in money, adequately compensated by a small sum, and the case was one where it would be oppressive to the defendant to grant an injunction. It appears that the discretion is not often exercised in copyright cases.

7. Remedies where injunction or undertaking breached

(a) Punishment for contempt

If a defendant is in breach of an undertaking which he has given to the **10.77** court, or disobeys an injunction granted by the court, the court has power to punish him for contempt. The most usual way of doing this is either to impose a fine, or a prison sentence. Stringent orders for costs are also made even where the court decides not to make any such order.

Particularly in the case of Anton Piller orders, the courts have emphasised that orders of the court must be obeyed, even where the person against whom the order is made has some justification for objecting to the order. The remedy in such a case is for the relevant party to apply to the court to discharge the order or vary it. He should not simply use any such justification as a defence in proceedings for contempt.

Contempt proceedings are usually commenced by the party in whose favour an injunction is granted, but the object of contempt proceedings is not to compensate that person but to draw the court's attention to disobedience of the order.

(b) *Procedural requirements for contempt*

Under the Rules of the Supreme Court, the person against whom the **10.78** injunction or order was made must have been served with a copy of the order with a penal notice attached. The penal notice is a warning that if the person against whom the order was made disobeys the order (or in the case of a mandatory order, neglects to obey it) he will be liable to process of execution for the purpose of compelling him to obey it.

Where the order is made against a company, it should be served on one or more directors of the company, again with a penal notice attached but this time addressed to the directors. In cases involving companies, contempt applications can either be for sequestration of the company's assets, or committal of the directors to prison.

Where an undertaking has been given to the court, instead of an injunction imposed, the requirement of service of the order is less strict, provided that the court is satisfied that the person giving it knew and understood its effect. In many cases, the practice is still followed of serving the order with a penal notice attached.

(c) *Contempt by third parties*

A third party not subject to an order of the court but knowing of it will be **10.79** in contempt of court if he assists the party subject to the order in disobeying it.

VI FINANCIAL CLAIMS

A. DAMAGES FOR INFRINGEMENT OF COPYRIGHT

1. General principles

10.80   Generally it is said that the measure of damages for infringement of copyright is the depreciation caused by the infringement to the value of the copyright. (See *Sutherland Publishing Co. Ltd.* v. *Caxton Publishing Co. Ltd.* ([1936] Ch. 323).)

This however is not of much help in practice, because it is difficult to assess what depreciation means in relation to copyright. It is therefore perhaps of more use in practice to follow the more general principle in damages cases that the measure of damages is to be, so far as possible, that sum of money which will put the injured party in the same position as he would have been if he had not sustained the wrong. This old principle (the words are those of Lord Blackburn in *Livingstone* v. *Rawyards Coal Co.* ((1880) 5 App.Cas. 25)) was recently confirmed as the correct approach in breach of confidence cases in *Dowson and Mason Ltd.* v. *Potter* ([1986] 1 W.L.R. 1419).

The plaintiff has the burden of proving his loss, and it must always be remembered that the object of damages is to compensate the plaintiff and not, in normal cases, to punish the defendant (but see paragraph 10.86). It is also important to remember that what is being considered is the damage to the copyright owner's property, that is his copyright. It does not extend to damage resulting from the use made by a third party of infringing material which the defendant has not authorised even though its use was reasonably foreseeable. The result might, however, be different where there is actual knowledge of the dishonest purpose.

This is illustrated by the case of *Paterson Zochonis & Co. Ltd.* v. *Merfarken Packaging Ltd* ([1986] 3 All E.R. 522). There the defendants printed cartons and leaflets which were exact copies of those used by the plaintiffs in the manufacture and sale of a particular product, and the copyright in which was owned by the plaintiffs. The defendants supplied the cartons and leaflets to competitors of the plaintiffs who then passed off their products as those of the plaintiffs. It was accepted that the defendants were not involved in the scheme to pass off the products as the plaintiff's. The Court of Appeal held that the plaintiffs could not recover from the defendants damages to compensate passing-off by the third party. The fact that the passing-off was facilitated by the infringement of copyright was not sufficient, and since the plaintiff could not prove any loss flowing from the infringement of the copyright, the claim for damages for infringement had to be struck out.

2. Damages based on loss of profit

If the copyright owner uses the copyright work himself in his business,   **10.81**
damages will usually be assessed on the basis of his loss of profit. This is
usually applied where for example the copyright owner manufactures
and/or sells articles which are reproductions of his copyright work.
However, where the copyright owner would not have been able to sell as
many copies as the defendant, the court will apply the principles referred
to in paragraph 10.83 as regards those copies which the copyright owner
would not have been able to sell.

If the copyright owner has to reduce the price of his product in order to
compete with the defendant, then loss of profit may be assessed on that
basis. (See *Meters Ltd.* v. *Metropolitan Gas Meters Ltd.* ([1911] R.P.C.
157).) Where the plaintiff is forced to withdraw the product from sale
because of competition from the infringing articles, he may recover as
damages for infringement of copyright both the value of his stock of
copies and profit on a future edition. (See *Vivian Mansell & Co. Ltd.* v.
Harold Wesley Ltd ([1936–45] MacG. Cop. Cas. 288).)

3. Damages for injury to trade

In a case where the plaintiff copyright owner uses the copyright work in   **10.82**
his business, and the defendant is competing with him, damages may also
be awarded on the basis of the plaintiff suffering harm to his business
beyond lost sales. This for example was done in *Birn Bros. Ltd.* v. *Keene
& Co. Ltd.* ([1918] 2 Ch. 281) where there was extensive and deliberate
piracy, and the judge accepted that, by offering products at a much lower
price than the plaintiff, the defendants might have caused substantial
injury of a more general nature to the plaintiff's business.

4. Damages by reference to a licence fee

Where the plaintiff copyright owner is not using the copyright himself in   **10.83**
his business, but exploits it by granting licences, the court will normally
assess damages on the basis of what is a fair licence fee. What is fair in
these circumstances is very often construed liberally, but the sum must be
realistic and the court will take into account market forces which might
have an effect on the amount of the licence fees. (See *General Tire and
Rubber Co.* v. *Firestone Tyre and Co. Ltd.* ([1975] 1 W.L.R. 819).)
Subject to this, if there is a range of licence fees the court will very often
award damages based on the top end of the scale. In some circumstances,
the court will also take the view that a normal royalty is too small in all the
circumstances, and increase the amount. An example of this is *Chabot* v.
Davies ([1976] 3 All E.R. 221).

Damages by reference to a reasonable licence fee are often awarded
even in cases where the plaintiff copyright owner does not himself
normally grant licences, or himself use the copyright. (See *Meikle* v.
Maufe ([1941] 3 All E.R. 144).)

5. Where part of the copyright work only is used

10.84 In many cases, an infringing article manufactured and/or sold by the defendant reproduces only part of the plaintiff's work. In such cases, the court may still assess damages on the basis of the whole loss of profit which the plaintiff would have suffered if the whole work had been used, or a licence fee based on the use of the complete work. Examples are *Meters Ltd.* v. *Metropolitan Gas Meters Ltd.* and *Stovin-Bradford* v. *Volpoint Properties* ([1971] 3 All E.R. 570). However, there may still be scope for an argument that the relevant damages should be proportionately reduced, and this could be used particularly where the defendant has himself contributed a substantial amount of his own work to the infringing article.

B. DAMAGES FOR CONVERSION

10.85 Under the 1956 Act, infringing copies of copyright works were deemed to be the property of the copyright owner. This entitled the copyright owner to those articles, so that he could claim their delivery-up (see paragraph 10.96), and it also meant that, in general, he was entitled to damages equivalent to the value of the articles at the relevant time they were dealt with in a manner inconsistent with the copyright owners deemed ownership.

This remedy was considered by most people as penal in its effect, and a claim for conversion damages would very often induce alleged infringers to settle an action before trial.

The right to conversion damages has been abolished by the 1988 Act. The remedy is preserved only for the purposes of proceedings commenced prior to commencement of the 1988 Act (schedule 1, paragraph 31(2)), and it must be remembered for these purposes that the court has no power to award damages in relation to articles manufactured after the date of the writ, since in relation to those articles no cause of action has arisen at the time of the writ.

C. ADDITIONAL DAMAGES

10.86 In an action for infringement of copyright, the court may award such additional damages as the justice of the case may require, having regard to all the circumstances, and in particular to the flagrancy of the infringement and any benefit accruing to the defendant by reason of the infringement (s.97(2)).

1. Comparison between the 1956 and 1988 Acts

10.87 The equivalent section in the 1956 Act was expressed in much more restrictive terms. Under that provision (s.17(3)) the court had to be satisfied that effective relief would not otherwise be available to the plaintiff. This requirement meant that such damages were rarely awarded. The 1956 Act provision continues to have effect for infringements prior to commencement of the 1988 Act.

The discretion under the 1988 Act is much greater, but it remains to be seen whether the court will require flagrancy and benefit in normal circumstances before applying the provision. It is certainly to be hoped that the court will not, particularly as regards the benefit requirement, because in some cases it may be difficult for the plaintiff to show that benefit has accrued to the defendant, for example where his venture has failed.

2. Flagrancy and benefit

In *Ravenscroft* v. *Herbert and New English Library* ([1980] R.P.C. 193),   **10.88** Brightman J. considered the meaning of flagrancy and benefit in the equivalent provision under the 1956 Act, and held as follows:

(a) Flagrancy implied the existence of scandalous conduct, deceit and such like, and included deliberate and calculated copyright infringement.

(b) Benefit implied that the defendant had reaped a pecuniary advantage in excess of the damages he would otherwise have to pay.

3. Other material considerations

Under the equivalent section in the 1956 Act, the Court had to consider   **10.89** not only flagrancy and benefit but also all other material considerations. In *Beloff* v. *Pressdram* ([1973] R.P.C. 765) Ungoed-Thomas J. held that such considerations included "the defendants' conduct with regard to the infringement and motive for it, injury to the plaintiff's feeling for suffering insults and indignities and the like, and also the plaintiff's own corresponding behaviour." Under the 1988 Act, the Court must have regard to all the circumstances, and would be likely to take the same sort of matters into account.

4. Exemplary and aggravated damages

In the law of tort generally, exemplary or aggravated damages can be   **10.90** awarded by the court. However, it seems that the existence of the statutory remedy in copyright precludes any award of such damages. (See *Beloff* v. *Pressdram*.)

D. ACCOUNT OF PROFITS

This is an alternative to a claim for damages, and cannot be claimed in   **10.91** addition to such damages. It is a discretionary remedy.

Under an order for an account of profits, the court assesses the profit which the defendant made as a result of the infringement, and awards that profit to the plaintiff. Of course, in some cases the defendant's use of the copyright work will not have been a success, and an account of profits will plainly not be an attractive remedy. However, even where exploitation appears to have been successful, the amount to which the plaintiff would be entitled under this remedy may not be as much as under the rules on damages for infringement referred to in paragraph 10.80 onwards. Where part only of the defendant's exploitation is attributable to the plaintiff's work, an apportionment may be made, and, as well as the costs incurred by the defendant, it appears from the case of *Redwood Music Ltd.* v. *Chappell & Co. Ltd.* ([1982] R.P.C. 109) that the court will make a liberal allowance for the skill and labour exercised by the infringer in producing the profits for which the defendant is being asked to account. This was however in a case where the defendants honestly believed that they were entitled to exploit the copyright work.

Generally, plaintiff copyright owners do not opt for an account of profits instead of damages. This is not surprising because it is perhaps easier to estimate what damage the copyright owner himself has suffered through infringement, than to guess what the court will determine to be the amount of the profit made by the defendant which the copyright owner is entitled to after the account has been taken.

E. INNOCENT INFRINGEMENT

10.92   Where it is shown at the time of the infringement that the defendant did not know, and had no reason to believe, that copyright subsisted in the work to which the action relates, the plaintiff is not entitled to damages against him (s.97(1)). However, the plaintiff is still entitled to apply for an injunction, account of profits and delivery-up, although all these are discretionary remedies.

This provision is similar to one contained in the 1956 Act (s.17(2)) which continues to have effect for infringements committed prior to commencement of the 1988 Act. That provision used the phrase "had no reasonable grounds for suspecting" rather than "had no reason to believe," but it is unlikely that the court will construe this as being materially different. Also in the 1956 Act, the equivalent provision stated that the plaintiff in such a case was "entitled" to an account of profits, which is normally a discretionary remedy, whereas the 1988 Act provision simply says "without prejudice to any other remedy." It is therefore possible that in such a case in the future the plaintiff will be refused any compensation, even an account of profits.

The defence is very limited in its scope. It cannot be used for example where there was reason to believe that copyright subsisted in the work, but the defendant believed that it belonged to someone else.

In *Infabrics Ltd.* v. *Jaytex Shirt Co. Ltd.* ([1980] 2 All E.R. 669) Buckley L.J. said as follows:

"It is, in my opinion, incumbent upon anyone who proposes to make use of any artistic work in a way which might infringe copyright, if it subsisted in the work, to make such enquiries and investigations as he reasonably can, to satisfy himself that the work is free of copyright ... if no adequate inquiries or investigations are made it must, it seems to me, be difficult to suppose that the person proposing to use the work has no grounds for suspecting that it may be subject to copyright."

F. CONCURRENT RIGHTS OF ACTION OF COPYRIGHT OWNERS AND EXCLUSIVE LICENSEES (s.102(4))

The following provisions apply to any action for infringement of copy- **10.93** right where the copyright owner and an exclusive licensee have concurrent rights of action. (See paragraphs 10.20 onwards.) It does not matter whether they are both parties to the action. The provisions would not of course apply where there is an exclusive licensee, but not in relation to the right which has been infringed.

In assessing damages, the court must take into account the terms of the exclusive licence, and any pecuniary remedy already awarded or available to either of them in respect of the infringement. So, the court must take into account in a claim by an exclusive licensee the amounts which the licensee will have to pay the copyright owner.

As regards an account of profits, no order for an account must be made in favour of a copyright owner or exclusive licensee if an award of damages has been made, or an order for account already made, in favour of the other. If an account of profits is ordered, the court will apportion the profits between them in such manner as the court considers just, subject to any agreement between them.

G. INTEREST

Where there is a contract between the parties specifying a rate of interest **10.94** which will take effect, then the court will award interest on that basis.

The court also has a discretion to award interest on sums recovered by way of damages, or following the taking of an account of profits. It has power to award such interest with effect from the date on which the cause of action arose, that is when the infringement took place.

H. COSTS

The award of costs is in the discretion of the court. However, generally a **10.95** successful plaintiff or defendant will be granted an order for payment of his costs, although the scale of costs will vary from case to case, and in most cases the successful party will not recover the full amount of costs which he has incurred.

However, the plaintiff will usually be at risk as to costs incurred after the defendant has offered an undertaking not to infringe and to pay damages and costs, if he continues the action after that offer has been made. (See *Jenkins* v. *Hope* ([1896] 1 Ch. 278).)

It is possible that the court might also make an award of costs against the plaintiff for costs incurred after an offer has been made by the defendant in a letter marked "without prejudice" but stating that the letter will be drawn to the attention of the court when the issue of costs is dealt with. This is on the general principles relating to such letters known as "Calderbank" letters. However, it is uncertain to what extent such principles apply in copyright proceedings, and it is arguable that the principles would not apply unless the defendant agrees to admit liability.

Where a copyright owner or exclusive licensee is joined as a defendant in proceedings by the other, as referred to in paragraphs 10.17 and 10.24, he is not liable for any costs unless he takes part in the proceedings even where the defendant admits liability and offers compensation before the action is started.

Where the defendant is successful, he may still not receive an award of costs if he is guilty of misconduct. In *Baschep* v. *London Illustrated Standard Co.* ([1900] 1 Ch. 73), the defendant was successful because the plaintiff's work was held to be indecent (see paragraph 1.39), but the court refused to make an order for costs since the defendant had copied the work. Furthermore, where a defendant unnecessarily puts copyright title in issue, but succeeds in resisting the action on other grounds, he may again not obtain an award of costs. (See *West* v. *Moss Empires Ltd* ([1928–35] MacG.Cop.Cas. 388).)

VII SEIZURE, DELIVERY-UP AND DISPOSAL OF INFRINGING ARTICLES

10.96   Under section 18 of the 1956 Act, an infringing copy was deemed to be the property of the copyright owner. The expression "infringing copy" was not quite as wide as that under the 1988 Act, and, in particular, excluded reproductions in the form of a cinematograph film in the case of literary, dramatic, musical and artistic works, and published editions.

The 1956 Act provision was used frequently, and not only for a claim for delivery-up in infringement proceedings. In cases for example of pirate and bootleg records and tapes, the provision enabled copyright owners and their representatives simply to seize such articles when found, without the necessity for proceedings. Of course, if the copyright owners made a mistake, that would have been actionable as a trespass to goods.

The 1988 Act has replaced this reasonably simple provision with a series of complicated inter-related provisions. The provisions are not clearly drafted, and it remains to be seen whether the courts will give them a restrictive or liberal interpretation. At this stage, it is difficult to give anything more than initial impressions as to how the new provisions will operate in practice.

Before considering the individual provisions in detail, some matters of general application must be dealt with.

A. GENERAL

1. Infringing copy (s.27(2) & (3))

All of the statutory provisions below relate to the seizure, delivery-up,   **10.97** forfeiture or disposal of infringing copies of works.

An article is an infringing copy of the work if its making constituted an infringement of copyright in the work in question. An article is also an infringing copy if it has been or is proposed to be imported into the United Kingdom, and its making in the United Kingdom would have constituted an infringement of copyright in the work in question, or a breach of an exclusive licence agreement relating to that work. For the meaning of these provisions see paragraph 6.26 onwards.

There is no requirement that the infringing copy be situated in the United Kingdom. A court might be prepared to make an order for delivery-up or disposal under the provisions referred to below even where the articles are outside the United Kingdom. However, the question of seizure of such goods by the copyright owner is much more difficult, and if the copyright owner attempted to take advantage of those provisions outside the United Kingdom, the fact that seizure appeared to be authorised under United Kingdom law would not prevent such seizure being a breach of the local law.

2. Possession, custody or control

Each of the statutory provisions referred to below can only be used as   **10.98** against someone who has the relevant articles in his possession, custody or control. The scope of this expression is wide.

Possession covers the situation where, for example, a bailee has been entrusted certain goods belonging to someone else. Custody covers the situation where a director or employee holds property of a company. Control covers the situation where someone does not have physical possession of the goods himself, but is able to order the person actually holding them to deal with them as he instructs.

3. In the course of a business

The statutory provisions below which relate to infringing copies only   **10.99** apply in the case of an article in the possession, custody and control of someone in the course of a business. The word "business" includes a trade or profession.

4. Distinction between infringement by possession and delivery-up remedy

10.100   Under the provision referred to in paragraph 6.36, it is an infringement of copyright for someone to possess in the course of a business an article which is and which he knows or has reason to believe is an infringing copy of a copyright work (s.23). If someone infringes copyright on this basis, all the remedies referred to in this Chapter, whether by way of an injunction or damages, are available to the copyright owner.

In contrast, the statutory remedies referred to below apply even where the person having possession, custody or control of the infringing copy does not know or have reason to believe that the article is an infringing copy.

5. Articles made before commencement of the 1988 Act

10.101   As already stated, the remedies for conversion under the 1956 Act, including the remedy of delivery-up, only apply for the purposes of proceedings begun before commencement of the 1988 Act.

The 1988 Act applies to articles made before commencement of the Act. However, the question whether the making of an article constitutes an infringement of copyright, or would have done if the articles had been made in the United Kingdom, is determined by reference to the 1956 Act, for articles made when that Act was in force, and by reference to the 1911 Act, in relation to articles made before commencement of the 1956 Act. (See paragraph 6.32.)

B. SEIZURE (s.100)

10.102   This provision enables the copyright owner in certain circumstances to seize an infringing copy of a work without first taking proceedings. Unlike section 99 (see paragraph 10.103) it does not apply to articles specifically designed or adapted for making infringing copies of a particular copyright work.

The provision states that an infringing copy of a work which is found exposed or otherwise immediately available for sale or hire may be seized and detained by the copyright owner or a person authorised by the copyright owner. The words "for sale or hire" in our view apply both to "otherwise immediately available" and "exposed."

This right however is subject to some stringent conditions which will in practice limit its usefulness. The conditions are as follows:

(a) The right may only be exercised by the copyright owner where he would be entitled to apply for an order under section 99 of the 1988 Act. (See paragraph 10.103 below.) This means that he will only be able to exercise it where someone has an infringing copy of a work in his possession, custody or control in the course of a business.

(b) Before anything is seized, notice of the time and place of the proposed seizure must be given to a local police station.

(c) Only premises to which the public has access may be entered. The word "premises" is widely defined to include land, buildings, moveable structures, vehicles, vessels, aircraft and hovercraft. However, the provision leaves open certain questions. It is not for example clear whether it could be used at a time when premises to which the public normally have access are closed, although this would be subject to what is set out in (d) and (e) below. Furthermore, it is not clear what happens where part of the premises is open to the public, and part not. To give an example, if there is a record fair, and someone is selling pirate or bootleg records, it is not clear whether the provision allows one to seize not only the records on display, but back-up stock kept in a separate room. Such records however might not be within the expression "exposed or otherwise immediately available for sale or hire."

(d) In any event, no-one may seize anything in the possession, custody or control of a person at a permanent or regular place of business of his. This could place severe restrictions on the copyright owner. Obviously, if the infringing copies are displayed at retail premises, the circumstances then in which the copyright owner will be able to seize even blatantly infringing articles will be extremely limited. It is however the use of the word "regular" which causes the most problems. If an itinerant trader turns up every week to the same place selling infringing copies, that might be said to be a regular place of business, in which case no seizure can be effected.

(e) No force may be used in exercising the right. If the copyright owner or person authorised by him merely takes articles, that in our view is not force. If the person having possession of the goods tries to physically restrain the copyright owner or person authorised by him from seizing the goods, then force cannot be used in retaliation in order to effect seizure.

(f) A notice in the prescribed form must be left at the place where the article was seized and at the time when it was seized. The notice must contain prescribed particulars as to the person by whom or on whose authority the seizure is made and the ground on which it is made. "Prescribed" means prescribed by the Secretary of State. At the time of writing, regulations have not been made under this provision.

It is noticeable that the section does not contain any sanction against the person who has possession, custody or control of the article, if he refuses to allow the copyright owner or authorised person to take it.

The provision only allows the copyright owner and an authorised person to seize and detain the infringing copy. He cannot dispose of it or destroy it without some risk, because of the provision referred to in paragraph 10.104 whereby it might have to be returned to the person from whom it was seized.

All in all, it is difficult to know whether this provision will be of much use in practice. It has been called a statutory Anton Piller order, but, in our view, this is misleading. Anton Piller orders for the most part require access to be given to premises not normally open to the public: the seizure provisions do not apply either there or where the infringing copies are in the possession, custody or control of someone at a permanent or regular place of business of his.

C. DELIVERY-UP (s.99)

10.103   This provision allows the copyright owner to apply to the court for an order for delivery-up of an infringing copy, and certain articles used for making infringing copies.

The provision applies in two circumstances. First, it applies where someone has an infringing copy of a work in his possession, custody or control in the course of a business. Here, as stated in paragraph 10.100 above, that person need not know or have reason to believe that it is an infringing copy. Secondly, it applies where a person has in his possession custody or control an article specifically designed or adapted for making copies of a particular copyright work. Here there is an additional requirement that he must know or have reason to believe that it has been or is to be used in making infringing copies. For further comments on this requirement see paragraph 6.06.

Where either of those circumstances apply, the copyright owner in the work may apply to the court for an order that the infringing copy or article be delivered up to him or to such other person as the court may direct. As stated, the application need not be made in the context of infringement proceedings, although in practice it very often will be.

The court cannot make such an order unless it also makes, or it appears to the court that there are grounds for making, an order under section 114 of the 1988 Act. (See paragraph 10.104.) It is difficult however to construe what this means in practice. The two provisions are in fact circular, because section 114 states that an application may be made where an infringing copy or other article *has been* delivered-up! What it probably means however is that the court must first consider whether other remedies available would be adequate to compensate the copyright owner and to protect his interests (s.114(2)). If the court believes on that basis that there are no grounds for making an order under section 114, then no order can be made under section 99.

What is also unclear is whether the existence of other parties having an interest in the relevant article will also have an effect on the possibility of the court making an order under section 99. As will be seen, provision is made under section 114 for the making of rules of court as to the service of notice on persons having an interest in the infringing copy or other article.

The court rules have not at the time of writing been made, but if they require service of notice before an order can be made, then this in turn will affect the stage at which an order can be made for delivery-up of the article under section 99.

Where the claim for delivery-up is included in an action for infringement of copyright, the copyright owner could use section 99 in order to obtain an order for delivery-up pending trial of the action. However, whether or not such an order is made before or at trial, the person to whom the infringing copy or other article is delivered-up must retain it pending the making of an order (or the decision not to make an order) under section 114. Of course, an order under section 114 may be made at the same time as an order under section 99, and in our view in proceedings for infringement of copyright it will be necessary for the copyright owner requiring forfeiture or destruction to claim in the writ both an order under section 99 and an order under section 114.

D. DESTRUCTION, DISPOSAL AND FORFEITURE OF ARTICLES (s.114)

This provision enables the copyright owner to seek forfeiture or destruc-   **10.104**
tion of an infringing copy or article as referred to in paragraphs 10.102 and 10.103. It also enables a defendant to apply for the copy to be returned to him, or perhaps destroyed or otherwise dealt with, and there are provisions relating to other persons who might have an interest in any such article.

Apart from where an order for delivery-up has been made under the criminal provisions referred to in paragraph 10.126, the provision only applies where an infringing copy or other article has been delivered up in pursuance of an order under section 99 (see paragraph 10.103), or an infringing copy has been seized and detained in pursuance of the right conferred by section 100. (See paragraph 10.102.)

In these circumstances, an application may be made to the court for an order that the infringing copy or other article be forfeited to the copyright owner, or destroyed or otherwise dealt with as the court may think fit.

An application may also be made for a decision that no such order should be made. Such an application will presumably be made by defendants, since it is provided that if a court decides that no order should be made, the person in whose possession, custody or control the copy or other article was before being delivered up or seized is entitled to its return.

Provision is to be made by rules of court for the service of notice on persons having an interest in the copy or other article. Any such person is entitled to appear in proceedings for an order under this provision (whether or not he was served with notice) and also to appeal against any order which, whether or not he appeared at the application for the making of the order. An order is not to take effect until the end of the period within which notice of an appeal may be given. If before the end of that period notice of appeal is duly given, the order will not take effect until the final determination or abandonment of the proceedings on the appeal. At the time of writing, no such rules of court have yet been made.

On the basis of this provision, many different people will be entitled to appear in proceedings for an order under this provision, or to appeal against any such order. A person who owns the physical property in the article will be entitled to do so, and also the owner of any other copyright which is embodied in the article. Specific provisions are made for owners of rights in performances, owners of design rights and owners of trade marks to make such an application. With this number of people who could have an interest in a particular article, such proceedings could be extremely complex and expensive, and may well have the effect of discouraging people to make applications for such orders.

E. EXCLUSIVE LICENSEES

10.105   Both copyright owners and exclusive licensees can apply for orders under section 99 and section 114, and an exclusive licensee is also entitled to seize infringing copies under section 100. Of course, these provisions only apply if the right exclusively licensed is that infringed by the making of the relevant article. So, for example, if someone is an exclusive licensee in relation to the right to make audio only copies of a sound recording, he can make no claim in relation to audio-visual copies of the sound recording.

Before applying for an order under section 99, or exercising the right conferred by section 100, the copyright owner must notify any such exclusive licensee (s.102(5)). Although there is no similar reference to an application under section 114, this would follow in any event because an exclusive licensee would be someone having an interest in such an infringing copy or other article.

There is no identical provision in relation to exclusive licensees requiring them to notify the copyright owner prior to applying for a section 99 order or exercising the section 100 right. However, it is provided that on an application for an order under section 99 the court may make such order as it thinks fit having regard to the terms of the exclusive licence. It can also on an application by the licensee prohibit or permit the exercise by the copyright owner of the right of seizure in section 100.

F. JURISDICTION OUTSIDE THE 1988 ACT

10.106   Under Order 29 of the Rules of the Supreme Court, the court has power on the application of any party to proceedings to make an order for the detention, custody or preservation of any property which is the subject-matter of the action. In addition to this, there is the power to make Anton Piller orders referred to in paragraph 10.57 above.

Aside from the above, the court has an inherent jurisdiction in equity to order delivery-up of an article the making of which was an infringement of copyright. All the cases dealing with this inherent right are old, and this is not surprising since under the 1911 and 1956 Acts a plaintiff copyright owner was usually deemed to be the owner of the relevant article, and therefore had no real need to fall back on the equitable jurisdiction. It appears that under the old cases an order would only be made for the purposes of destruction of the relevant article, or that part of the relevant article which infringed the copyright.

It is uncertain to what extent the inherent jurisdiction of the court will be exercised in modern times. Where, perhaps for technical reasons, the court is not entitled to make an order under section 99 or section 114 above, it might use its inherent jurisdiction to make an order in an appropriate case. However, it might also be argued that the court will not save in exceptional cases extend the scope of the jurisdiction beyond what Parliament has made limited provision for on a statutory basis.

VIII CUSTOMS SEIZURE

The 1956 Act contained a provision which allowed the copyright owner of a published literary, dramatic or musical work to give notice to the Commissioners of Customs and Excise that infringing copies of the work in printed form should be treated as prohibited goods (s.22). The provisions were not extensively used. They have been re-enacted in the 1988 Act, and a new provision added relating to copies of sound recordings and films. It remains doubtful whether the provisions will be of much use in practice.   **10.107**

1. Literary, dramatic and musical works (s.111(1) and (2))

The owner of the copyright in a published literary, dramatic or musical work may give notice in writing to the Commissioners of Customs and Excise that he is the owner of the copyright in the work, and requests the Commissioners, for a period specified in the notice, to treat as prohibited goods printed copies of the work which are infringing copies. The period specified in the notice must not exceed five years, or extend beyond the period of copyright for the work.   **10.108**

Unlike its equivalent in the 1956 Act, the 1988 Act provision applies where the infringing copies were made in the United Kingdom, exported and are due to be imported back into the United Kingdom.

The provision obviously applies to books and sheet music. It does not extend to copies of such works in the form of records or films, nor to computer software. Neither does it apply to copies of artistic works.

2. Sound recordings and films (s.111(3))

10.109 The owner of the copyright in a sound recording or film may give notice in
writing to the Commissioners of Customs and Excise that:

(a) He is the owner of the copyright.

(b) Infringing copies of the work are expected to arrive in the United
Kingdom at a time and place specified in the notice.

(c) He requests the Commissioners to treat the copies as prohibited
goods.

Here, there is no restriction as to the type of copies which notices must
relate to. A copy of a sound recording could be in audio only or audio-
visual form. However, the usefulness of the provision may be restricted
by the requirement that the copyright owner gives notice of the time when
and the place where the infringing copies are expected to arrive. This will
often be very difficult.

3. Exclusive licensees

10.110 An exclusive licensee has the same rights and remedies in respect of
matters occurring after the grant of the licence as if the licence had been
an assignment. (See paragraph 10.21.) This in our view entitles an exclusive licensee to use this provision. The notice to the Commissioners must
of course specify that the relevant person is exclusive licensee, not copyright owner.

4. Infringing copies

10.111 The meaning of this expression is referred to in paragraph 10.97 above.
An article will not be an infringing copy if it may lawfully be imported into
the United Kingdom by virtue of EEC law. (See paragraph 6.43.)

5. Procedural matters (s.112)

10.112 Regulations are to be made by the Commissioners of Customs and Excise
as to procedural matters where a copyright owner or exclusive licensee
wishes to use the provisions. Those regulations have not yet been prescribed, but the 1988 Act gives some idea as to their content:

(a) A person giving notice will have to furnish the Commissioners with
any evidence required by them, either when notice is given, or when the
goods are imported, or both. Regulations under the 1956 Act simply
stated that the owner of the copyright must furnish such evidence and
information and produce such books or other documents as the Commissioners might require, without specifying any precise requirements.

(b) Fees will probably be payable on the giving of a notice.

(c) The Commissioners will probably require a person giving notice to give such security as may be required in respect of any liability or expense which the Commissioners might incur because of the detention of any article or anything done to such an article following on from the giving of notice.

(d) The regulations may, and probably will, require the person giving a notice to indemnify the Commissioners against any such liability or expense, whether security has been given or not.

6. Effect of giving notice (s.111(4))

If notice is validly given under this provision, the importation of the relevant goods will be prohibited, unless done by someone for his private and domestic use. However, the only penalty for importing the goods is their forfeiture. **10.113**

IX CRIMINAL PROCEEDINGS

A. ACTS GIVING RISE TO CRIMINAL LIABILITY

The 1956 Act contained provisions relating to criminal liability for infringement of copyright (1956 Act, s.21), and these provisions were extended and strengthened as a result of the Copyright Act 1956 (Amendment) Act 1982 and the Copyright (Amendment) Act 1983. The provisions were in general only used in cases of blatant piracy. The 1988 Act extends and strengthens the provisions further, and in their present form they may be a more effective deterrent, particularly below the level of organised piracy. It is possible for a copyright owner or exclusive licensee to mount a private prosecution where one of the offences below is committed: Prosecution of Offences Act 1985, s.6. **10.114**

The 1988 Act provisions apply only in relation to acts done after commencement of the 1988 Act. The only exception is the provision on search warrants. The 1956 Act provisions continue in effect for the purposes of acts done before commencement.

1. Making, possessing and dealing with infringing copies (s.107(1))

A person commits an offence if he does any of the following acts without the licence of the copyright owner, in relation to an article which is, and which he knows or has reason to believe is, an infringing copy of a copyright work: **10.115**

(a) Makes the article for sale or hire.

(b) Imports the article into the United Kingdom otherwise than for his private and domestic use.

(c) Possesses the article in the course of business with a view to committing any act infringing the copyright.

(d) In the course of a business:

   (i) Sells or lets for hire the article.

   (ii) Offers or exposes for sale or hire the article.

   (iii) Exhibits the article in public.

   (iv) Distributes the article.

(e) Distributes the article otherwise than in the course of a business to such an extent as to affect prejudicially the owner of the copyright.

For comments on these acts see paragraph 6.35, and for what is meant by infringing copy see paragraph 6.26 onwards.

2. Making and possessing articles designed for making infringing copies (s. 107(2))

10.116   A person commits an offence who makes an article specifically designed or adapted for making copies of a particular copyright work, or has such an article in his possession, knowing or having reason to believe that it is to be used to make infringing copies for sale or hire or for use in the course of a business.
   For comments on the articles to which these provisions apply, see paragraph 6.42.

3. Public performance and playing or showing in public (s.107(3))

10.117   Where copyright is infringed by the public performance of a literary, dramatic or musical work, or by the playing or showing in public of a sound recording or film, any person who caused the work to be so performed, played or shown is guilty of an offence if he knew or had reason to believe that copyright would be infringed.
   This provision does not apply however where this takes place by reception of a broadcast or cable programme. So for example, where a music video is broadcast, and the broadcast is then received by television apparatus in a discotheque, the playing and showing in public of the music video by that method will not be a criminal offence. If on the other hand a copy of the music video was purchased or rented, and then displayed on a television screen by means of video apparatus, that could be a criminal offence if the necessary degree of knowledge was present.
   The scope of liability under this provision depends upon the meaning of the expression "caused the work to be so performed, played or showed." Under pre-1911 Act legislation on civil liability, it was not an infringement of copyright to "authorise" a restricted act. Instead, the word "causing" was used. This however was given a very restrictive meaning in

Karno v. *Pathe Freres* ((1909) 100 L.T. 260). In that case, the defendants made a film embodying a copyright work, and supplied it to third parties in the knowledge that such parties would show the film in public. It was held that this did not constitute causing a public performance of the work. It is not clear whether the courts would give such a restrictive meaning to the word "caused" in a case under this provision in the 1988 Act. If it did, this would limit the circumstances in which a supplier of hardware or software could be liable.

It seems clear that someone will be liable if they give instructions for a particular copyright work to be performed, played or showed. The position is more difficult where more general instructions are given for the playing of music or sound recording or showing of films. In that case it could be argued that the defendant did not cause a particular copyright work to be performed in public, played or shown. Much will depend on the precise facts, and if someone, for example, hires performers who are known only to play contemporary music, the causal link will probably be sufficient.

The provision will only apply where copyright is infringed, and in a number of circumstances public performance, playing or showing is not an infringement. (See Chapter 7.)

4. "Knowing or having reason to believe"

Each of the above offences is committed not only where the defendant has actual knowledge, but also where he has reason to believe. This in our view will make it much easier to mount a successful prosecution for criminal infringement. This could help deter some infringers if they realise not only that action in the civil courts will be taken, but also criminal proceedings which could result in not only a fine (or possibly imprisonment) but also a criminal record. For the meaning of the expression "reason to believe," see paragraph 6.06.   **10.118**

5. Fraudulent reception of transmissions (s.297)

A person who dishonestly receives a programme included in a broadcasting or cable programme service provided from a place in the United Kingdom, with intent to avoid the payment of any charge applicable to the reception of the programme, commits an offence.   **10.119**

There is power by Order in Council to extend this provision to programmes included in services provided from a country or territory outside the United Kingdom, but no order has been made at the time of writing.

"Programme," "broadcasting" and "cable programme service" under this provision have the same meanings as are referred to respectively in paragraphs 3.59, 5.44 and 1.55. Where the provision does apply in relation to a broadcasting or cable programme service, it also applies to dishonest reception of a programme included in a service run for the person providing the broadcasting or cable programme service, or a person providing programmes for that service, if in either case the broadcasting or cable programme service consists wholly or mainly in the sending of sounds or visual images (or both) by means of a telecommunications system.

The meaning of "dishonestly" and "with intent to avoid payment" will probably be analogous to the meaning of such expressions under the Theft Act 1968. Dishonesty is a state of mind and a question of fact not law. It requires first that what was done was dishonest according to the ordinary standards of reasonable and honest people, and secondly that the defendant himself realised that what he was doing was by those standards dishonest. (See *R. v. Ghosh* ([1982] 2 All E.R. 689).) True consent is obviously a defence, but not consent brought about by dishonesty. (See *R. v. Lawrence* ([1971] 2 All E.R. 1253).) A person only intends to avoid payment if he intends to avoid it permanently, not where he intends to delay or defer payment. (See *R. v. Allen* ([1985] 1 All E.R. 148).)

A person who makes or supplies any apparatus intended to enable persons to dishonestly receive transmissions will be liable for civil infringement of copyright. (See paragraph 6.66 onwards.)

6. Offences by companies

10.120

Where any of the offences referred to above has been committed by a body corporate, a director, manager, secretary or other similar officer of the body, or a person purporting to act in any such capacity, will also be guilty of the offence if it is proved to have been committed with his consent or connivance.

Where the body corporate is one whose affairs are managed by its members (this will usually mean the shareholders) the word "director" means such a member.

B. SEARCH WARRANTS (s.109)

10.121

It is possible to obtain search warrants in relation to some but not all of the offences referred to above. The relevant offences are those referred to in paragraphs 10.115(a) (b) (d) (iv) and (e).

In England, Wales and Northern Ireland, the power to issue search warrants is exercisable by a justice of the peace following information on oath given by a constable. In Scotland, the power is exercisable by a sheriff or justice of the peace following any evidence on oath.

The justice of the peace (or, in Scotland, the sheriff) has to be satisfied by the information (or evidence) on oath that there are reasonable grounds for believing that one of the offences referred to has been or is about to be committed in any premises, and that evidence that such an offence has been or is about to be committed is in those premises.

The warrant authorises a constable to enter and search the premises, using such reasonable force as is necessary. The warrant however may also authorise persons to accompany any constable executing the warrant. Warrants remain in force for 28 days from the date of issue.

There are limitations on the power to authorise searches relating to certain material. This is material of the kind referred to in section 9(2) of the Police and Criminal Evidence Act 1984, which in summary covers items subject to legal privilege, material held in confidence, and certain limited personal records.

"Premises" includes land, buildings, moveable structures, vehicles, vessels, aircraft and hovercraft.

In executing the warrant, a constable may seize an article if he reasonably believes that it is evidence that any offence as referred to above has been or is about to be committed. This is therefore not limited to the offences in relation to which the search warrant could be issued in the first place, or to infringing copies or articles specifically designed or adapted for making infringing copies of a particular copyright work. It would for example enable duplicating machines to be seized.

C. EVIDENCE

In a criminal case, the standard of proof is different from that which applies in civil cases. In a prosecution under the above provisions, it will be necessary to prove liability beyond reasonable doubt, and not just on the balance of probabilities. However, as stated, in practice the burden will not be too great where it is only necessary to show (for example) that the defendant had reason to believe that the article was an infringing copy, and so on. **10.122**

This assumes however that the prosecutor can prove beyond reasonable doubt all the elements of the relevant offence. As regards the offences referred to in paragraphs 10.115, 10.116 and 10.117, there are no presumptions as to subsistence as there are in civil proceedings (s.107 (6)). This means that in each case, the prosecutor will have to prove that copyright subsisted in the relevant work. This was confirmed in *Musa* v. *Le Maitre* ([1987] F.S.R. 272), a case about possession of infringing copies of cinematograph films. Some of the films in question were Indian in origin, and subsistence was proved by calling various English licensees who derived permission from the holders of the copyright to make copies of the relevant films. They gave evidence as to first publication of the films in India, and Stephen Brown L.J. commented that proving subsistence was unlikely to require the evidence of the actual maker or holder of the copyright.

As regards the offences referred to in paragraphs 10.115 and 10.116, the prosecutor must prove that the relevant article is an infringing copy. This requirement was also dealt with in *Musa* v. *Le Maitre*. It was argued in that case by the defendant that it was necessary for the prosecutor to prove who the copyright owner was at the time the act was done, and then that he had not given his permission. This would inevitably mean that in many cases the owner of the copyright would have to be called. The Divisional Court rejected the argument that this was necessary in every case, and said that in many cases it would be possible to produce expert evidence which would be sufficient. For example, in the *Musa* case itself, the prosecutor gave evidence that he was experienced in the identification of so-called pirate video tapes, and gave reasons why in his view the tapes in that case infringed copyright. This evidence was accepted as sufficient in order to justify a conviction. Of course in many cases, the articles will not so obviously be infringing copies, and it will be necessary to produce more precise evidence.

Although the presumption referred to in paragraph 6.34 does survive in relation to criminal proceedings, this of itself will not prove that the article was an infringing copy, although it may make a court readier to infer that it is.

D. PENALTIES

10.123   All prosecutions for the offences referred to above will commence in a magistrates' court. In many cases, the magistrates will deal with the case themselves. As regards the offences referred to in paragraphs 10.115(a) (b) (d) (iv) and (e), the magistrates in a serious case may commit the defendant for trial at a Crown Court.

1. Imprisonment

10.124   Magistrates' courts have power to impose a prison sentence of not more than six months in the case of all offences referred to in paragraph 10.115.

The Crown Court can go further and impose a sentence of not more than two years, but only in the case of the offences referred to in paragraph 10.115(a) (b) (d) (iv) and (e).

A prison sentence can be imposed in addition to or as an alternative to a fine.

2. Fines

10.125   In the case of any offence under paragraph 10.115(a) (b) (d) (iv) and (e), a magistrates' court can impose a fine not exceeding the statutory maximum, presently £2,000. A Crown Court however can fine without limit.

In any other case, a magistrates' court can impose a fine not exceeding level 5 on the standard scale, presently £2,000.

It must be remembered that the making or possession of, or dealing with, each infringing copy, and each public performance, playing or showing in public, could be a separate offence and therefore subject to a separate fine.

3. Delivery-up in criminal proceedings (s.108)

10.126   The following provisions apply where the court before which proceedings are brought against a person for any of the offences under paragraphs 10.115, 10.116 and 10.117 above is satisfied that at the time of his arrest or charge he had in his possession, custody or control:

(a) An infringing copy of a copyright work, where this was in his possession, custody or control in the course of a business.

(b) An article specifically designed or adapted for making copies of a particular copyright work, knowing or having reason to believe that it had been or was to be used to make infringing copies.

In these circumstances, the court may order that the infringing copy or article be delivered-up to the copyright owner or to such other person as the court may direct.

The provision is very similar to that which applies in civil proceedings and which is dealt with in paragraph 10.103 above.

The court can make such an order of its own volition, or on the application of the prosecutor. It may also be made whether or not the person is convicted of the offence. It must not be made if it appears to the court unlikely that any order will be made under section 114. (See paragraph 10.104.) This should be compared with section 99 (see paragraph 10.103), where the court cannot make an order unless it also makes, or it appears to the court that there are grounds for making, an order under section 114.

A person to whom an infringing copy or other article is delivered up in pursuance of an order under this provision must retain it pending the making of an order, or the decision not to make an order, under section 114.

Aside from these specific provisions on delivery-up, forfeiture and disposal, there are more general powers as to forfeiture in criminal proceedings. For England and Wales these are contained in section 43 of the Power of Criminal Courts Act 1973. For Scotland, the provisions are contained in section 233 and 436 of the Criminal Procedure (Scotland) Act 1975, and for Northern Ireland in Article 7 of the Criminal Justice (Northern Ireland) Order 1980.

X LIMITATION OF ACTIONS

This section deals with the period after which the copyright owner or exclusive licensee is no longer entitled to claim the remedies referred to in this Chapter.   **10.127**

1. Civil proceedings for infringement of copyright

The following rules apply except in relation to applications for delivery-up under sections 99, 108 and 114.   **10.128**

(a) *Normal six-year period*

Under (Section 2) of the Limitation Act 1980, no proceedings for infringement of copyright can be commenced after the expiration of six years from the date on which the infringement took place.

Each infringement must be considered separately for these purposes. Thus, if a defendant continues to manufacture copies of records which infringe the copyright in a musical work, the six year period starts to run separately for each copy made, and not from when the first copy was made.

(b) *Disability*

10.129   Where at the time of the infringement the copyright owner or exclusive licensee was an infant, or of unsound mind, the action may be brought at any time before the expiration of six years from the date when he ceased to be under such a disability, or died, whichever first occurs.

(c) *Concealment of facts*

10.130   In general, the six year limitation period runs from when infringement took place, not from when the plaintiff discovered it.

However, where any fact relevant to the plaintiff's right of action has been deliberately concealed from him by the defendant, the six year period does not begin to run until the plaintiff has discovered the concealment, or could with reasonable diligence have discovered it. The same applies to concealment by the defendant's agent or by any person through whom the defendant claims or his agent. (See 1980 Act, s.32(1).)

The above will principally apply in piracy cases where the defendant is conducting a clandestine operation. It would not for example apply where the defendant openly did something which was an infringement, and simply failed to tell the copyright owner or apply to him for a licence.

The standard of diligence which the copyright owner or exclusive licensee must exercise is quite high. The six year period will start to run if there was something which should have put him on notice, and, if inquiry had then been made, this would have resulted in discovery of the infringement.

2. Civil proceedings for delivery-up

10.131   A claim for delivery-up may be made in proceedings for infringement of copyright, or it can stand as an action in its own right. Whichever the position is, the rules referred to in this section apply.

(a) *Normal six year period*

10.132   No application may be made for delivery-up of an infringing copy or article under section 99 of the 1988 Act (paragraph 10.103) after the end of the period of six years from the date on which the infringing copy or article in question was made.

There is no corresponding provision in relation to an application for forfeiture or destruction under section 114. (See paragraph 10.104.) Such an order can therefore be made more than six years after the making of the infringing copy or article, although the court might take into account the expiry of that period, and any delay in making an application, in considering what order to make.

(b) *Disability*

If during the whole or any part of the six-year period referred to, the copyright owner or exclusive licensee is an infant, or of unsound mind, then an application may be made under section 99 at any time before the end of the period of six years from the date on which he ceased to be under such a disability.   **10.133**

(c) *Fraud or concealment*

If during the whole or any part of the six-year period the copyright owner or exclusive licensee is prevented by fraud or concealment from dis-* covering the facts entitling him to apply for an order, an application under section 99 may be made at any time before the end of the period of six years from the date on which he could with reasonable diligence have discovered those facts.   **10.134**

A comparison with the provision referred to in paragraph 10.130 above shows that this provision is not quite the same. Use of the expression "fraud or concealment" is particularly relevant here. It is probable that no degree of moral turpitude is necessary to establish fraud. What is covered by the term is difficult to define, but it probably extends to conduct which, "having regard to some special relationship between the two parties concerned, is an unconscionable thing for the one to do towards the other". (See *Kitchen* v. *R.A.F. Association* ([1958] 2 All E.R. 241) *per* Lord Evershed M.R.) As regards concealment, the omission of the word "deliberate" probably does not amount to much, because it is arguable that concealment in itself implies some element of intent.

3. Criminal proceedings

(a) *Summary proceedings*

Prosecutions for the offences referred to in paragraphs 10.115(c) (d) (i) (ii) (iii), 10.116 and 10.117 must be commenced within six months of the allegedly offending act taking place.   **10.135**

(b) *Indictments*

Prosecutions for the offences referred to in paragraphs 10.115(a) (b) (d) (iv) and (e) may either be tried in the magistrates' courts, or, on indictment, at the Crown Court. There is no limitation period for these offences.   **10.136**

(c) *Delivery-up in criminal proceedings*

10.137   No order for delivery-up under section 108 (see paragraph 10.126) may be made after the end of the period of six years from the date on which the infringing copy or article in question was made. Neither disability nor concealment of facts delays the period here. As in civil proceedings, there is no time limit as regards orders under section 114. (See paragraph 10.132.)

XI RELATED REMEDIES

10.138   It is beyond the scope of this book to deal with other causes of action which are sometimes linked with proceedings for infringement of copyright. However, the following is a list of possible other causes of action:

1. Breach of confidence

10.139   As already stated, actions for infringement of copyright are often linked with actions for breach of confidence. (See paragraph 7.126.)

2. Passing-off

10.140   Such an action may lie where a trader makes a representation to prospective customers of his or ultimate consumers that his business or goods are the business or goods of the plaintiff. This remedy is also used where there are difficulties with copyright infringement proceedings, common examples being where a work is exploited using the same title as a work of the plaintiff, and in character merchandising.

3. Infringement of trade marks

10.141   Such actions are sometimes linked with copyright infringement action where the defendant is not only dealing with copies made in infringement of copyright, but the copies are being marketed using the plaintiff's trade mark.

4. Defamation and malicious falsehood

10.142   If the defendant exploits the copyright work in a manner or form which would tend to lower the reputation of the owner of the copyright in the eyes of right-thinking members of the public, then an action or defamation could be taken.
For malicious falsehood, see paragraph 10.09.

5. Unlawful interference with contractual relations

10.143   See paragraph 10.10 above.

6. Breach of contract

An act done in breach of an assignment of copyright or a licensing   **10.144**
agreement may amount to an infringement of the copyright. In addition
however, the contract may specify other remedies because of the breach,
in which case an action for breach of contract will lie as well.

Apart from the above, there may also be grounds for taking proceedings for infringement of a moral right (see Chapter 11), a right in a
performance (see Chapter 12) and design right (see Chapter 13).

11 MORAL RIGHTS

I INTRODUCTION

11.01   The 1988 Act, in Chapter IV of Part I, introduces a number of new rights under the general heading of Moral Rights. Some of the rights contained in Chapter IV are entirely new to English law and some represent an amendment and re-enactment of the false attribution of authorship provisions contained in section 43 of the 1956 Act.

    The so-called moral rights of creators of works have long been recognised in some other jurisdictions. The 1948 Brussels Revision of the Berne Convention, which has been ratified by the United Kingdom, contains provisions protecting moral rights. Article 6 bis of the Brussels Revision gives an author two rights in addition to and completely independent of his copyright. These rights in Article 6 bis, which is not part of United Kingdom law, are exercisable during the author's lifetime and consist of the right (i) to claim authorship of his work; and (ii) to object to any distortion, mutilation, or other alteration of his work, or any other action in relation to his work which would be prejudicial to his honour or reputation. These two rights are to remain exercisable by the author, notwithstanding that he has assigned the copyright in the work in question. The purpose of the rights is to give the author some control over his work even though he may have ceased to own the copyright in it. Copyright will provide his economic rewards and moral rights, protect his artistic integrity and reputation.

    The 1971 Paris Revision of the Berne Convention, which has not been ratified by the United Kingdom, requires that more extensive moral rights be conferred on authors. In particular, it requires moral rights to be protected for the same period as copyright rights. The 1988 Act confers additional rights which should make it possible for the United Kingdom to ratify the 1971 Paris Revision.

II EXISTING LAW BEFORE THE 1988 ACT

11.02   The United Kingdom has not until the 1988 Act introduced any new legislation to give effect to the provisions of Article 6 bis. Prior to the 1988 Act, moral rights were protected, if at all, by a number of different remedies. Copyright played an important part, so far as alterations to a copyright work are concerned and copyright could also be used to force a third party to give the author a proper acknowledgment in certain circumstances. However, the author might not own the copyright. It is considered by some that the right to prevent distortion or mutilation of a work is protected, at least in part, by the law of defamation. However, until the 1988 Act there existed no right of an author to require to be named as such, except indirectly in very limited circumstances under the fair dealing provisions in sections 6 and 9 of the 1956 Act. Also, any rights which an author had under the law of defamation would not be infringed by any acts done after his death.

Passing-off proceedings could be used by an author in respect of the publication of a work naming him as author, where he is not in fact the author. Section 43 of the 1956 Act would also apply in this situation. Also, a passing-off action will normally lie in respect of the publication of a work with a title which is too similar to the title of an existing work.

Where a work by one author is published under the name of another, the real author of the work may have a right of action in malicious falsehood against the publisher if he can prove malice on the part of the publisher. In practice, this may not be as difficult as at first appears, as malice has been given a fairly wide interpretation. He may also have to prove special damage, unless the case falls within section 3(1) of the Defamation Act 1952.

The Trade Descriptions Act 1968 may also be relevant to a situation of this kind, as the publisher may be applying a false trade description to goods by representing that the work is written by someone other than the actual author. However, it is unlikely that this Act confers any rights on the author. It merely provides criminal sanctions, where applicable.

Perhaps the most usual way of protecting moral rights prior to the 1988 Act was by contract. It is usual for copyright licences to contain detailed provisions restricting the way in which the copyright work may be used or altered and requiring appropriate credit to be given to the creator of the work. In general, however, contractual provisions will only bind the contracting parties, although they may have implications for third parties who seek to interfere with the contractual provisions. An example of a case where an author successfully relied on a contract term to prevent an alteration to his script being made is *Frisby* v. *British Broadcasting Corporation* [1967] Ch. 932. In that case, which was an interlocutory application for an injunction, the court found that the deletion of two words from one very important line in a play could amount to a "structural alteration" and, as the contract forbade such alterations without the author's consent, which was not forthcoming, the author was entitled to an injunction to prevent broadcast of the play as altered. It is worth also looking at *Joseph* v. *National Magazine Co. Ltd.* [1959] 1 Ch. 14. There, an author of an article was found to be fully justified in refusing to allow a magazine to publish an article written by him which had been substantially altered without his consent.

In addition, a copyright licence may be drafted in such a way that non-compliance leads to termination. In such a situation the copyright owner will be able to enforce copyright rights against the former licensee and third parties.

None of the existing remedies of libel, passing off, malicious falsehood, Trade Descriptions Act 1968 or rights in contract are in any way expressly affected by the 1988 Act and all will therefore continue to be relevant in the field of moral rights. Section 171(4) of the 1988 Act provides expressly that nothing in Part I of the 1988 Act shall affect any right of action or other remedy, whether civil or criminal which is available otherwise than under Part I of the 1988 Act in respect of acts infringing any of the moral rights.

However, section 43 of the 1956 Act is repealed by the 1988 Act, but continues to apply in relation to acts done before the commencement of the 1988 Act. Section 43 applies to literary, dramatic, musical and artistic works and, amongst other things, contains provisions prohibiting a person from falsely attributing authorship of a work to a person who is not the author. Chapter IV of Part I of the 1988 Act contains somewhat similar provisions and a comparison of the provisions will be dealt with below. (See paragraphs 11.26 to 11.32.)

III THE 1988 ACT

A. SUMMARY

11.03   The moral rights contained in Chapter IV fall into four distinct categories:

(a) The right to be identified as author or director of a work ("the paternity right");

(b) The right to object to derogatory treatment of a work ("the integrity right");

(c) The right of a person not to have a work falsely attributed to him as its author or director ("the false attribution right");

(d) The right to privacy in respect of certain photographs and films ("the privacy right").

These new moral rights are not property rights and are not assignable. They are transmissible on death. (See paragraph 11.38.) They vest in the author or director in the case of the paternity right and integrity right. In the case of the false attribution right, it vests in the person to whom authorship is falsely attributed or the person to whom a film is falsely attributed as director. In the case of the privacy right, it vests in the person who commissions the taking of the photograph or making of the film. There is no requirement that the person must be of any particular nationality or the person reside in any particular place. The right will be enjoyed by every person, provided that the requisite circumstances exist. In the case of paternity, integrity and privacy rights, the work concerned must enjoy copyright protection for the moral right to subsist. The requirements of copyright must therefore be satisfied, but those could be satisfied by publication rather than by nationality or residence.

B. APPLICATION TO EXISTING WORKS

(a) References in this Chapter to "commencement" and to "commencement of the 1988 Act" are to the commencement of the new copyright provisions contained in the 1988 Act, which are by and large contained in Part I of and Schedule 1 to the 1988 Act. No action will lie under the 1988 Act in respect of any of the four new rights in respect of any act done before the commencement of the 1988 Act. The new rights will, subject to certain exceptions, subsist in relation to works existing prior to the commencement of the 1988 Act, but those rights will only be enforceable in respect of acts done after commencement. The transitional provisions are set out in paragraphs 10 and 22 to 24 of Schedule 1 to the 1988 Act. References in the transitional provisions to existing works are to works made before commencement. Where the making of a work extends over a period, the work is deemed to have been made when its making was completed. (See schedule 1 paragraph 1(3).)   **11.04**

(b) Neither the paternity right nor the integrity right will apply:

(i) in relation to any literary, dramatic, musical or artistic work whose author died before the commencement of the 1988 Act; or

(ii) in relation to any film made before commencement of the 1988 Act; or

(iii) in relation to anything done in relation to a record made in pursuance of section 8 of the 1956 Act, which dealt with compulsory recording licences.

(c) In addition, the paternity right and integrity right do not apply in relation to any literary, dramatic, musical or artistic work in existence at the date of commencement of the 1988 Act in the following circumstances:

(i) Where the author was the first owner of copyright, the rights do not apply to anything which, by virtue of an assignment of copyright made or licence granted before the commencement of the 1988 Act may be done without infringing the copyright in the work.

(ii) Where the author was not the first owner of the copyright, then the rights will not be infringed by anything done by or with the licence of the copyright owner.

These provisions are not easy to apply. First of all one needs to establish who is the author of the work. To do this one must look at the provisions of the 1988 Act and not to the law in force when the work was made. (See schedule 1 paragraph 10.) It is worth noting that, for the purpose of determining who is the author of an existing work for copyright and other purposes not relating to moral rights, one must look at the law in force at the time the work was made. This may be a different person to the author of a new work for the purposes of the 1988 Act. Then, one needs to ask whether or not the author was alive at the date of commencement of the 1988 Act. If not, then the integrity right and paternity right will not exist in relation to the author's works. If the author was alive, then one must discover whether the author was the first owner of the copyright. In order to do this one must look at the law in force at the time the work was made. (See schedule 1 paragraph 11.) However, where a work has been commissioned prior to the commencement in circumstances falling within section 4(3) of the 1956 Act or section 5(1)(*a*) of the 1911 Act, those provisions will determine first ownership of any work made after commencement in pursuance of the commission. The questions of authorship and first ownership are dealt with more fully elsewhere in this book (see Chapter 3). The rules governing ownership of copyright in commissioned works have been substantially changed by the 1988 Act.

If the author was not the first owner of the copyright in an existing work, the integrity right and paternity right do not apply to anything done by or with the licence of the copyright owner. This presumably means the copyright owner from time to time. So long as the relevant act is done by or with the licence of the person owning the copyright at the time that the act is done, then the rights of paternity and integrity of the author will not be infringed.

If the author is the first owner of copyright in an existing work and before the commencement of the 1988 Act, he has assigned the copyright or granted a licence of the copyright to any third party, the following applies. Any act which is done and which by virtue of such assignment or licence may be done without infringing copyright, may also be done without infringing the author's right of paternity or right of integrity. What is not entirely clear is what happens when the assignee or licensee subsequently assigns or sub-licenses its rights. An assignment or licence granted before commencement would certainly be covered and could be relied on by the assignee or licensee. However, where such subsequent assignment or sub-licence takes place after commencement of the 1988 Act it is not so clear cut. Looking at the wording of paragraph 23(3)(*a*) of Schedule 1 to the 1988 Act, it would seem that the later assignment and licence cannot be relied on because the assignment will not have been made or licence will not have been granted before the commencement of the 1988 Act. However, it could be argued that the later assignment or licence is entirely dependent on the earlier assignment or licence, which does predate the commencement. Therefore, the act could be done without infringing copyright by virtue of both assignments, one made before and one made after the commencement of the 1988 Act.

If the author acquires or reacquires the copyright after the commencement of the 1988 Act, he will also effectively regain control of his paternity and integrity rights. If the author is the first owner of the copyright and he has not assigned the copyright or licensed it prior to the commencement of the 1988 Act, the paternity and integrity rights will vest unfettered in the author, but will, of course, only be enforceable in respect of acts done after the commencement of the 1988 Act.

(d) Finally, the privacy right does not apply to photographs taken or films made before the commencement of the 1988 Act.

C. THE NEW RIGHTS

The new moral rights will come into existence on the commencement of **11.05** the 1988 Act and will apply in relation to certain categories of works, as set out more fully below. It is intended to deal with each of the four rights separately, as different considerations apply to each right. In the course of examining the various rights, a number of expressions are used which are defined in Part I of the 1988 Act and apply to Chapter IV of Part I. Except where those expressions relate solely to the rights contained in Chapter IV, they are not discussed in this part of this book, but are dealt with elsewhere.

1. Right to be identified as author or director of a work

This right, referred to in this book as the paternity right, arises in relation **11.06** to literary, dramatic, musical and artistic works and films, but only where copyright subsists in such works or films. The right does not therefore arise in relation to any work which is in the public domain in the United Kingdom, for whatever reason. The paternity right gives to the author of a copyright literary, dramatic, musical or artistic work and the director of a copyright film, the right to be identified as the author or director of the work in certain specified circumstances. The right vests in the author or director, notwithstanding that he may not be the owner of the copyright in the work or film. Dealings with the copyright will not affect ownership of the paternity right, which is unassignable. (See paragraph 11.38.) The two rights are independent.

The right is not infringed unless it has been asserted in the manner required by the 1988 Act. (See paragraphs 11.14 to 11.17.) The precise nature of the right varies according to the type of work involved. These works are discussed below.

To determine who is the author of a work, one must look at the law as set out in the 1988 Act, notwithstanding that the work was made prior to the commencement of the 1988 Act. The question of authorship under the 1988 Act is dealt with more fully in Chapter 3. The presumptions set out in sections 104 and 105 of the 1988 Act will apply. These are discussed more fully in Chapter 10, and will clearly be of great assistance in identifying who is the author of a work or the director of a film and as to who is the copyright owner in a work or film and as to whether the copyright first rested in the author's employer or in an international organisation and as to whether Crown copyright or parliamentary copyright subsists in a work or film.

The term "director" is not defined in the 1988 Act and no guidance, other than the rebuttable presumption contained in section 105 of the 1988 Act, is given as to how to determine who is a director of a film. Section 88 of the 1988 Act deals with jointly directed films. A film is jointly directed if it is "made by the collaboration of two or more directors and the contribution of each director is not distinct from that of the other director or directors." This seems to suggest that there is some connection between the director of a film and its maker. This doesn't help very much.

Under the 1956 Act the maker of a film was defined, but this is not the case under the 1988 Act. Furthermore, under the 1956 Act the maker was the first owner of the copyright in a film. Under the 1988 Act it is the author. It is true that the definitions of "author" and "maker" under the respective Acts are the same. However, if it had been intended to make a link here between the author of a film and its director it would have been easy to do so, and no express link has been made. On balance, it would seem that the term "director" will have to be given its ordinary and natural meaning for the purposes of the 1988 Act.

First ownership of copyright is in some circumstances relevant to the paternity right. In such cases, the question of first ownership is determined in accordance with the law in force at the time that the work was made, subject to one or two exceptions in the case of works commissioned prior to the commencement of the 1988 Act and made after commencement. (See paragraph 11.04.)

(a) *Works in relation to which the paternity right can subsist:*

(i) *Literary works (other than words intended to be sung or spoken with music) and dramatic works* (section 77(2))

11.07   The author of such a work has the right to be identified whenever the work is published commercially, performed in public, broadcast or included in a cable programme service and whenever copies of a film or sound recording including the work are issued to the public. In addition, whenever any of those events occur in relation to an adaptation of the author's work, the author has the right to be identified as the author of the work from which the adaptation was made. It would seem that the person making the adaptation would have similar rights if the adaptation is capable itself of being a separate copyright work. This will depend on how much new original material is introduced into the adaptation. (See paragraph 5.50.)

In the case of words "not intended to be sung or spoken with music," it is thought that it is the intention of the author which is relevant and it is his intention at the time of creation which matters. For example, a poem written as such and subsequently set to music as a song, would not thereby change in nature. It would not become "words intended to be sung or spoken with music." This may well be relevant because the rights attaching to words intended to be sung or spoken with music differ from those not so intended. (See next paragraph.)

(ii) *Musical works and literary works consisting of words intended to be sung or spoken with music* (section 77(3))

The author of any such work has the right to be identified whenever the **11.08** work is published commercially; or copies of a sound recording of the work are issued to the public; or a film of which the sound-track includes the work is shown in public or copies of such a film are issued to the public. In addition, if any of these events occur in relation to an adaptation of the work, the author has the right to be identified as the author of the work from which the adaptation was made. It is considered that the adaptor will also have similar rights if the adaptation is capable itself of being a separate copyright work. As to what is meant by "intended to be sung or spoken with music," see paragraph 11.07 above).

It is worth noting that the rights in respect of those works are more limited than those attaching to literary or dramatic works discussed in paragraph 11.07. The exclusion of public performance, broadcast and inclusion in a cable programme service are significant and are intended to prevent the need for very lengthy credits in musical programmes and performances.

(iii) *Artistic works* (sections 77(4) and (5))

The author of any artistic work has the right to be identified whenever: **11.09**

(a) the work is published commercially or exhibited in public, or a visual image of it is broadcast or included in a cable programme service, or

(b) a film including a visual image of the work is shown in public or copies of such a film are issued to the public.

The term "visual image" is not defined, although it appears in many places in Part I of the 1988 Act. It will therefore bear its ordinary and natural meaning. It presumably means any representation of the work which is recognisable and can be seen with the eye.

In the case of a work of architecture in the form of a building or a model for a building, a sculpture or a work of artistic craftsmanship, the author has the right to be identified whenever copies of a graphic work representing it or of a photograph of it are issued to the public. In a case of a work of architecture in the form of a building, the author also has the right to be identified on the building as constructed or, where more than one building is constructed to the design, only on the first such building to be constructed.

(iv) *Films* (section 77(6))

The director of a film has the right to be identified whenever the film is **11.10** shown in public, broadcast or included in a cable programme service or copies of the film are issued to the public.

(b) *Method of identification*

Section 77(7) of the 1988 Act sets out the way in which the author or **11.11** director must be identified. In each case, the identification must be clear and reasonably prominent. There is no definition either of the word "clear" or of the words "reasonably prominent" and no doubt it will not be long before a case arises for decision on this point.

In the case of commercial publication or the issue to the public of copies of films or sound recordings, the author or director has the right to be identified in or on each copy or, if that is not appropriate, in some other manner likely to bring his identity to the notice of a person acquiring a copy. For these purposes, provided that the identification is clear and reasonably prominent, it ought to be sufficient to identify the author or director on the packaging, provided that it can be shown that it is not appropriate for the information to be included in or on the physical copy of the film or sound recording itself. To a great extent, this will depend on the amount of space available in or on the film or sound recording and the amount of information which has to be included.

The wording is wide enough to permit the information to be recorded in the film or sound recording itself, but this could conceivably fall foul of the requirement that such identification shall be clear and reasonably prominent, as the identification will only be capable of being seen by playing or showing the film or sound recording. On balance, however, provided that the identification recorded in the film or sound recording is clear and reasonably prominent in relation to the other material recorded, then the wording would seem to be satisfied. However, in such circumstances it will only come to the attention of a person after he has acquired a copy, and not whilst acquiring a copy. This may preclude such a notice from satisfying the alternative requirement of identifying the author "in some other manner likely to bring his identity to the notice of a person acquiring a copy."

In the case of identification on a building, the author, such as the architect, has the right to be identified by appropriate means visible to persons entering or approaching the building. No guidance is given as to what "appropriate" means, but one assumes that a plaque or something similar would suffice, provided that it was clear and reasonably prominent.

In any other case so far not dealt with, the author or director must be identified in a manner likely to bring his identity to the attention of a person seeing or hearing the performance, exhibition, showing, broadcast, or cable programme in question.

The precise form of the identification depends on the way in which the author has asserted his paternity right. If, in asserting his right, the author has specified a pseudonym, initials or some other particular form of identification, that specified form must be used. There is no requirement that the form specified should be reasonable and it could be quite an elaborate logo, for example. In any other case, any reasonable form of identification may be used. No clue is given as to what "reasonable" means. However, it is submitted that any form which names the author and effectively identifies him will be "reasonable."

(c) *Exceptions to paternity right*

As has already been noted, the right does not apply in relation to works in   **11.12**
the public domain in the United Kingdom. Nor does it apply in relation to
any works which do not fall within the categories of literary, dramatic,
musical or artistic works or films. This means that sound recordings,
broadcasts, cable programmes and typographical arrangements are
excluded. In addition, the right does not arise in respect of any computer
program, any computer-generated work or any design of a typeface.

Special rules apply where the copyright in a work vests in the author's
employer by virtue of section 11(2) of the 1988 Act, which covers works
produced in the course of employment. These rules also apply in the case
of a film, where the author and first owner of copyright in the film is, by
virtue of sections 9(2)(*a*) and 11(1) of the 1988 Act, the director's
employer. Section 9(2)(*a*) provides that the person who made the
arrangements necessary for the making of the film, is regarded as the
author of the film and section 11(1) provides that the author is the first
owner of the copyright. Such person may well not be the director's
employer. Normally a director would be self-employed or employed by a
loan-out company owned or controlled by him. This point should be
borne in mind when preparing an agreement securing the services of a
director.

In either case, where the special rules do apply, the paternity right does
not apply to anything done by or with the authority of the copyright
owner. That authority could be given in writing or orally, or by conduct.
It is considered that the reference to "copyright owner" must mean
copyright owner from time to time, rather than the original copyright
owner. It is worth noting that the copyright owner does not acquire the
moral right in these circumstances. It is merely the case that the moral
right will not be exercisable by the author or director in these circumstances, if the thing is done by or with the authority of the copyright
owner. In any other case, where the copyright owner has not authorised
the thing to be done, the paternity right will be enforceable.

Section 79(4) provides a list of situations in which the paternity right is
not infringed. The intention here is to ensure that specified acts, which do
not infringe copyright, will not infringe any paternity right either. The
provisions concerned are:

(i) Section 30 (Fair dealings for certain purposes), so far as it relates to the
reporting of current events by means of a sound recording, film, broadcast or cable programme;

(ii) Section 31 (Incidental inclusion of work in an artistic work, sound
recording, film, broadcast, or cable programme);

(iii) Section 32(3) (Examination questions);

(iv) Section 45 (Parliamentary and judicial proceedings);

(v) Section 46(1) or (2) (Royal commissions and statutory inquiries);

(vi) Section 51 (Use of design documents and models);

(vii) Section 52 (Effect of exploitation of design derived from artistic work);

(viii) Section 57 (Anonymous or pseudonymous works: acts permitted on assumptions as to expiry of copyright or death of author).

All of the above categories are dealt with elsewhere in this book. (See Chapter 7.) The test seems relatively straightforward. If the relevant act does not infringe copyright in the work in relation to which the paternity right subsists, then the paternity right is not infringed.

In addition, the paternity right does not apply in relation to any work made for the purpose of reporting current events. There is obviously no requirement in this case that there should be any sufficient acknowledgment, as is required by section 30(1) of the 1988 Act. What is relevant here is the purpose for which the work is made in the first place. If a work is made for a purpose other than reporting current events, and then subsequently it is desired to use the work for that purpose, the exception will not apply and the paternity right will not be affected.

Section 79(6) provides that the paternity right does not apply in relation to the publication in:

a newspaper, magazine or similar periodical; or

an encyclopedia, dictionary, year book or other collective work of reference;

of a literary, dramatic, musical or artistic work made for the purposes of such publication or made available with the consent of the author for the purposes of such publication.

The wording of section 79(6) is unclear. It could bear more than one meaning. For example, if a literary work were made for the purposes of publication in a particular newspaper, the paternity right will not apply in relation to publication in that newspaper. The question then arises whether the paternity right will arise in relation to a subsequent publication of the same article in a different newspaper or, for example, a year book. The most restrictive reading of section 79(6) would disapply the paternity right in respect only of the publication of the work in the particular newspaper. A more liberal reading would disapply the right in respect of the publication of the work in any newspaper. The freest reading would disapply the right in respect of the publication of the work in any of the categories of publications listed in section 79(6). It is submitted that the more liberal reading is to be preferred to the most restrictive and the freest.

It is worthwhile looking at the equivalent provisions in section 81(4) of the 1988 Act, which deals with the integrity right. There the wording used is the same as in section 79(6) except that a further paragraph has been added to make it clear that the integrity right does not apply to any subsequent exploitation elsewhere of the work published in this way, provided the work is exploited without any modification. The draftsman clearly felt that the additional words were necessary to avoid a restricted meaning being applied. In view of the absence of these additional words from section 79(6) it could be argued that a more restrictive meaning should be adopted, than the freest meaning given in the example above.

Finally, the right does not apply in relation to a work in which Crown copyright or parliamentary copyright subsists, or to a work in which copyright originally vested in an international organisation, unless the author or director has previously been identified as such in or on published copies of the works. It does not specify the circumstances or time when such previous identification should take place. Presumably, the right would arise (subject to being asserted) at the moment after such identification is made for the first time, which might happen at any time. There is no requirement that the identification should be with the consent of the copyright owner and presumably the director or author could identify himself on published copies and thereby cause the right to arise (subject to being asserted).

(d) *Requirement to assert right*

Unlike the other three moral rights, the right of paternity must be asserted before it can be enforced.   **11.13**

Section 78 of the 1988 Act provides that a person does not infringe the paternity right by doing any act which would otherwise infringe the paternity right, unless the paternity right has been asserted by the author or director in such a way as will bind the potential infringer in relation to that act. It is submitted that the assertion of a right will not render infringing an act done prior to assertion and that an act done by a person prior to being bound by an assertion will not be rendered infringing by the person becoming so bound. Nevertheless, it is easy to envisage situations where the assertion of the right could catch a third party in a difficult position. For example, a film company might have a large stock of video recordings in course of distribution. If it becomes bound at that stage by an assertion, the film company will have to comply with the paternity right before the stock can be distributed, although some assistance may be gained from section 78(5) which requires the court, in considering remedies for infringement, to take into account any delay in asserting the right. Presumably no injunction would be given where there had been delay in asserting the right.

The right may be asserted generally, or in relation to any specified act or description of acts. It seems likely that the right will normally be asserted generally, but it may be that in the context of negotiations regarding a work or film, the author or director may agree not to assert his rights in relation to a specified act or a description of acts. It seems more probable that negotiations of this kind will take place in relation to a waiver by the author or director, which will be dealt with in more detail below. However, the existence of the paternity right will probably strengthen the hand of the author or director when it comes to negotiating credit provisions in contracts.

The paternity right may be asserted in a number of different ways.

(i) *On assignment of copyright*

11.14   The 1988 Act requires assignments of copyright to be in writing and signed by or on behalf of the assignor. Where the assignor is a company, the company can affix its seal to satisfy this requirement, but a signature on behalf of the company by a duly authorised signatory would suffice. The paternity right may be asserted on an assignment of copyright in the work. This is done by including in the document effecting the assignment, a statement that the author or director asserts in relation to the work being assigned, his right to be identified. Such an assertion will bind the assignee and anyone claiming through the assignee, whether or not he has notice of the assertion. The assignment does not have to be signed by the author or director and to this extent, the right can be asserted by someone other than the author or director, for example, a subsequent copyright owner. In this case, however, the right will still vest in the author or director.

(ii) *By instrument in writing*

11.15   The right may also be asserted by an instrument in writing signed by the author or director. It seems that this could take place either before or after the copyright in the work has been assigned and whether or not any paternity right has already been asserted in the assignment. For example, in an assignment, an author may assert his right in relation only to a specified description of acts. The author could subsequently assert his right in respect of all other acts and he could do this by an instrument in writing, signed by him.

Assertion by instrument in writing binds anyone to whose notice the assertion is brought. Presumably this will be done by sending copies of the written assertion to anyone whom the author or director wished to bind. It might be possible to place an advertisement giving notice that the right has been asserted in this way, but it would always be difficult to prove that any particular person saw it or noticed it. Also, a notice of assertion could, for example, be put on every copy of a book which is published. The mere appearance of the author's name on the book would not be sufficient to assert the right, even if the author is unmistakably and prominently identified as the author. What is required is that the right should be asserted and notice of the assertion given.

There is no provision permitting an assertion to be signed on behalf of an author or director. This means that an agent cannot sign on behalf of the author or director and rules out the possibility of a collective assertion of rights by an organisation representing a number of authors or directors.

One interesting point emerges in relation to the requirement that the assertion be signed by the author or director. Section 176(2) provides expressly that, in such a case, where the person asserting is a company, the written instrument can be signed on behalf of the company or alternatively the seal can be affixed. However, it is difficult to see how the author or director could be a company. To decide who the author is one must look at the 1988 Act only, even in the case of existing works, by virtue of paragraph 10 of schedule I to the 1988 Act. The 1988 Act provides that the author is the person who creates the work. This could hardly be a company in the case of a literary, dramatic, musical or artistic work, except perhaps a computer-generated work, in respect of which there is no paternity right anyway. It is difficult to see how the director of a film could be a company. It seems that, in fact, section 176(2) has no application in this context.

(iii) *Artistic works—assertion in relation to public exhibition*

The paternity right in relation to the public exhibition of an artistic work   **11.16**
may be asserted in two additional ways.

The first way is by securing that when the author or other first owner of copyright parts with possession of the original work, or of a copy made by him or under his direction or control, the author is identified on the original or copy, or on a frame, mount or other thing to which it is attached. Under these circumstances, the assertion will bind anyone into whose hands that original or copy comes, whether or not the identification is still present or visible. The wording here is very wide and provided that the author is identified on the original copy, the public exhibition paternity right will be effectively asserted, whoever happens to acquire the original or copy. To assert the right in this way, there is no requirement as to the manner in which the author is to be identified or that the identification must be clear or reasonably prominent. Once asserted, however, third parties bound by the assertion will have to satisfy all the requirements of the paternity right in relation to public exhibition of the work. The identification will have to be clear and reasonably prominent. It will not necessarily be sufficient to copy the way in which the author was identified when the right was asserted.

The second way of asserting this paternity right in relation to public exhibition is by including in a licence by which the author or other first owner of copyright authorises the making of copies of the work, a statement signed by or on behalf of the person granting the licence, that the author asserts his right to be identified in the event of the public exhibition of a copy made in pursuance of the licence. In the case of a licensor which is a company, the document can be signed on behalf of the company or, alternatively, the company seal can be affixed.

Under these circumstances the persons bound by the assertion are the licensee, and anyone into whose hands a copy made in pursuance of the licence comes, whether or not that person has notice of the assertion. Again, the wording is very wide. If the right is asserted in the licence in the manner required, then the right will be effectively asserted in respect of all copies made in pursuance of the licence. This assertion will bind anyone into whose hands a copy comes, even if he does not have notice of the assertion. This particular right of paternity can only be asserted by this method by the author or other first owner of copyright and only in licences granted by such a person. If the copyright is assigned to a third party and the right has not been asserted in this way before assignment, another means of asserting the right will have to be found, for example, by an instrument in writing signed by the author or on an assignment of copyright.

(e) *General*

11.17   In an action for infringement of the paternity right, the court, in considering remedies, must take into account any delay in asserting the right. Presumably, this means that the defence of laches will be available in suitable circumstances. It may also have some relevance to the amount of damages recoverable in a given case. It will provide some ammunition for an infringer who is caught in the middle of an infringing act by a late assertion of the right. It will be interesting to see how the courts apply this provision in relation to works in existence at the commencement of the 1988 Act. The court will have to balance the position of the author, who may not have been aware that he had acquired a new right under the 1988 Act against that of the infringer whose innocent course of conduct is rendered infringing by a late assertion of rights.

Although the paternity right may in appropriate circumstances be asserted by persons other than the author or director, it is clear that the right vests in the author or director and can only be enforced by proceedings by either the author or director. It is not assignable, but is transmissible on death. (See paragraph 11.38.)

2. Right to object to derogatory treatment of a work

11.18   Section 80 gives the author of a copyright literary, dramatic, musical or artistic work and the director of a copyright film, the right in certain specified circumstances not to have his work subjected to derogatory treatment. This right is referred to in this book as the integrity right.

As in the case of the paternity right, the integrity right only arises in relation to the works and films just mentioned if they are protected by copyright in the United Kingdom. It does not arise in respect of works in the public domain. The right vests in the author or director, notwithstanding that he may not be the owner of the copyright in the work or film. Dealings with the copyright will not affect ownership of the integrity right, which is unassignable, but transmissible on death. (See paragraph 11.38.) The two rights are independent. As to who is the author or director, please see paragraphs 11.04 and 11.06 and Chapter 3.

(a) *Derogatory treatment*

11.19   "Treatment" of a work is defined to mean any addition to, deletion from or alteration to or adaptation of the work other than:

(i) a translation of a literary or dramatic work; or

(ii) an arrangement or transcription of a musical work involving no more than a change of key or register.

It is clear, therefore, that even a very minor amendment to an existing work is likely to fall within the definition of "treatment." However, there does have to be some addition, deletion, alteration or adaptation. If none of these are present, such as simply putting the work in a different context, even though this is derogatory, there will be no treatment. For example, a song could be included in a nude stage production. The song would not be subject to derogatory treatment but the inclusion of the song might reflect badly on the composer. Also, it would not include a situation where, for example, a painting deteriorated naturally, with no human intervention. There is no obligation to restore, and indeed, restoration itself could amount to a treatment. Total destruction of a copyright work, however, probably would not.

A treatment of a work will be "derogatory" if it amounts to distortion or mutilation of the work or is otherwise prejudicial to the honour or reputation of the author or director. This wording is clearly derived from the Berne Convention and is intended to give effect to its provisions.

The words "distortion" and "mutilation" are rather emotive and seem to envisage damaging, but not necessarily substantial, alterations to a work. It is possible to envisage a number of treatments which would not amount to distortion or mutilation and therefore would not be derogatory. However, quite a small alteration could have a dramatic affect, which would amount to a distortion or mutilation.

The question of what is "otherwise prejudicial to the honour or reputation of the author or director" is less easy to answer. Presumably it is something which will have to be judged by some objective standard. It may be that some assistance will be gained from libel cases, as references to "honour or reputation" seem to have more in common with the law of defamation than the law of copyright. It would clearly apply in a case where a work was altered in such a way as to reflect badly on the author. For example, the insertion of an explicitly pornographic passage in a book might reflect badly on the author in some cases. Clearly, anyone parodying copyright works will have to proceed with extreme caution.

As in the case of infringement of the paternity right, the question of what amounts to infringement differs depending upon the type of work involved.

(b) *Works in relation to which the Integrity Right can subsist:*

(i) *Literary, dramatic and musical works* (section 80(3))

In the case of any such work, the right is infringed by any person who does **11.20** any of the following acts in relation to a derogatory treatment of the work:

(a) Publishes it commercially; or

(b) Performs it in public; or

(c) Broadcasts it or includes it in a cable programme service; or

(d) Issues to the public copies of a film or sound recording of or including it.

It is worth noting that the protection given to musical works by the integrity right is more extensive than that given to musical works by the paternity right.

(ii) *Artistic works* (sections 80(4) and (5))

11.21   In the case of any such work, the right is infringed by a person who:

(a) Publishes commercially or exhibits in public a derogatory treatment of the work; or

(b) Broadcasts or includes in a cable programme service a visual image of a derogatory treatment of the work; or

(c) Shows in public a film including a visual image of a derogatory treatment of the work or issues to the public copies of such a film.

The integrity right is also infringed in the case of a work of architecture in the form of a model for a building, or a sculpture or a work of artistic craftsmanship, by any person who issues to the public copies of a graphic work representing, or of a photograph of, a derogatory treatment of the work.

Where the work of architecture is in the form of a building, the integrity right is not infringed by a derogatory treatment of the work. However, where the author of the work of architecture is identified on the building, he has the right to require the identification to be removed if the work has been the subject of derogatory treatment.

(iii) *Films* (section 80(6))

11.22   The integrity right in the case of a film is infringed by a person who:

(a) Shows in public, broadcasts or includes in a cable programme service a derogatory treatment of the film; or

(b) Issues to the public copies of a derogatory treatment of the film; or

(c) Along with the film, plays in public, broadcasts or includes in a cable programme service or issues to the public copies of a derogatory treatment of the film sound-track.

It is interesting that there is no integrity right in a sound recording as such. However, for these purposes at least, the sound-track is closely associated with the film and the integrity right of the director may be infringed by acts done in relation to a derogatory treatment of the film sound-track, provided those acts are not done independently of the film itself.

(c) *Further acts of infringement*

11.23   Section 83 of the 1988 Act provides additional circumstances when the integrity right will be infringed. It introduces the concept of infringing the right by possessing or dealing with an infringing article. For the purposes of section 83 an infringing article means a work or a copy of a work which has been subjected to derogatory treatment, as defined, and which has been or is likely to be the subject of any of the acts described in section 80 of the 1988 Act in circumstances which infringe the integrity right. These acts are those prohibited by section 80(3), (4) and (6) and are discussed above in paragraphs 11.20, 11.21 and 11.22.

Section 83 provides that the integrity right is infringed by any person who either:

(i) Possesses in the course of a business; or

(ii) Sells or lets for hire or offers or exposes for sale or hire; or

(iii) In the course of a business exhibits in public or distributes; or

(iv) Distributes otherwise than in the course of a business so as to affect prejudicially the honour or reputation of the author or director;

an article which is, and which he knows or has reason to believe, is an infringing article.

In order to prove infringement of the integrity right under section 83, the plaintiff will have to leap over a number of hurdles. First, he will have to prove that the article is an infringing article. In order to do this, he will have to prove that the work has been subjected to a derogatory treatment and also that his integrity right has been or is likely to be infringed in one of the ways set out in section 80.

When the plaintiff has done all that, he must then go on to prove that the person possessing or dealing with the infringing article has done one of the four acts prohibited by section 83 and that the infringer knows or has reason to believe that the article is an infringing article. What is meant by "has reason to believe" is discussed more fully in paragraph 6.06. In most cases, it is going to be extremely difficult for a plaintiff to prove all the requisite elements to establish the infringement of his rights by any of these further acts of infringement.

(d) *Treatments of treatments*

Section 80(7) of the 1988 Act covers "treatments of treatments." This will **11.24** occur where parts of a work have been subject to treatment by a person other than the author or director of the work, under circumstances where those parts as treated are attributed to or are likely to be regarded as the work of the author or director. In such a case a subsequent treatment of those treated parts, will be subject to the integrity right of the author or director, notwithstanding that in fact those particular parts were not the work of the author or director. This seems rather a convoluted provision. It is perhaps best illustrated by an example. Supposing an author writes a novel. That novel is then substantially revised and amended by a ghost-writer who is someone other than the author. The amended work is then published under circumstances where the amended work is attributed to or is likely to be regarded as the work of the author, rather than the ghostwriter. If that amended work is then subjected to a derogatory treatment, the author will have an integrity right to exercise, notwithstanding that the parts of the amended work which have been subject to such treatment were not in fact written by the author, but were written by the ghostwriter. The ghostwriter may also have a right to take action for infringement of his integrity right in these circumstances.

(e) *Exceptions*

11.25   The integrity right only applies to copyright literary, dramatic, musical or artistic works and copyright films. It therefore does not apply to works in the public domain and nor does it apply to sound recordings (except film soundtracks in limited circumstances—see paragraph 11.22), broadcasts, cable programmes or typographical arrangements.

It does not apply to a computer program or to any computer-generated work, although it seems it could apply, unlike the paternity right, to the design of a typeface.

The integrity right does not apply in relation to any work made for the purpose of reporting current events. There is no requirement for a "sufficient acknowledgment" as is required in section 30 of the 1988 Act, dealing with infringement of copyright. As in the case of the paternity right (see paragraph 11.12) one must look at the purpose for which the work is made, and not the use which may at any time in fact be made of the work.

Section 81(4) of the 1988 Act contains a provision in exactly the same terms as section 79(6) of the 1988 Act relating to the paternity right and publication in newspapers and other works. The comments made in relation to the paternity right apply equally in the case of the integrity right (see paragraph 11.12), save that additional wording appears in section 81(4) dealing with subsequent exploitation elsewhere of a work. In the case of the integrity right, it seems that once the derogatory treatment has appeared in the relevant publication, any subsequent exploitation of the work in the form in which it appeared without any modification, will not infringe the integrity right.

It is specifically provided that the integrity right is not infringed by an act which by virtue of section 57 of the 1988 Act would not infringe copyright. This section deals with both anonymous and pseudonymous works. (See Chapter 7.)

Section 81(6) gives various further circumstances where the right will not be infringed. The integrity right is not infringed by anything done for the purpose of:

(i) Avoiding the commission of an offence; or

(ii) Complying with the duty imposed by or under an enactment; or

(iii) In the case of the BBC, avoiding the inclusion in a programme broadcast by them of anything which offends against good taste or decency or which is likely to encourage or incite to crime or to lead to disorder or to be offensive to public feeling;

Provided that in each of those cases, there must be a "sufficient disclaimer" where the author or director is identified at the time of the relevant act or if the author or director has previously been identified in or on published copies of the work in question. "Sufficient disclaimer" is defined to mean a clear and reasonably prominent indication given at the time of the act and,

if the author or director is then identified, appearing along with the identification,

that the work in question has been subject to treatment to which the author or director has not consented.

Section 81(6) is intended to cover, for example, a situation where indecency or obscenity laws would be infringed if a work was not amended. It would also be apt to cover a situation where there was censorship, or where any statute imposed obligations to alter works in any circumstances.

However, in each case, there must be a "sufficient disclaimer."

Under section 82, special provisions apply in the case of the following works:

(i) Works created by an author in the course of employment in which the copyright first vests in the author's employer by virtue of section 11(2) of the 1988 Act; and

(ii) Films in respect of which the arrangements necessary for making the film are undertaken by the director's employer, so that the employer is the author by reason of section 9(2)(*a*) of the 1988 Act; and

(iii) Works in which Crown copyright or parliamentary copyright subsists; and

(iv) Works in which copyright originally vested in an international organisation by virtue of section 163 of the 1988 Act.

In respect of these four categories of works, the integrity right does not apply to anything done in relation to such a work by or with the authority of the copyright owner unless the author or director is identified at the time of the relevant act or has previously been identified in or on published copies of the work. As in the case of the paternity right, it does not specify the circumstances or time when such previous identification should take place or that such identification should have been with the copyright owner's consent.

Even where the right does apply in relation to such categories of work, it is not infringed if there is "a sufficient disclaimer." "Sufficient disclaimer" has the same meaning as in section 81(6) (see above).

In this context, it is submitted that "copyright owner" means the copyright owner at the time of the relevant act and not any previous copyright owner. The authority of the copyright owner does not have to be in writing. It could be oral or given by conduct.

3. The right of a person not to have a work falsely attributed to him as its author or director

11.26　Section 84 of the 1988 Act contains the right not to have a work falsely attributed to a person as author or director. This right is referred to in this book as the false attribution right. This provision substantially reproduces the rights contained in section 43 of the 1956 Act, although there are some differences. Section 43 of the 1956 Act will continue to be relevant as it continues to apply in relation to acts done before the commencement of the 1988 Act. Section 84 of the 1988 Act will only apply to acts done after the commencement of the 1988 Act. For some time, therefore, it will be necessary to look at both provisions. It is not intended to deal with section 43 of the 1956 Act in any detail, but in the course of discussing section 84 of the 1988 Act, significant differences between the old and new law will be pointed out.

Under section 84, a person now has the right, in the circumstances specified in section 84, not to have a literary, dramatic, musical or artistic work falsely attributed to him as author and not to have a film falsely attributed to him as director.

The inclusion of films is new, as section 43 of the 1956 Act conferred rights only in relation to literary, dramatic, musical or artistic works.

In section 84 "attribution" is defined to mean, in relation to any such works, a statement (express or implied) as to who is the author or director. The word "falsely" is not defined and must be presumed to have its ordinary meaning. There is no requirement that the statement be in writing. In appropriate circumstances, it could therefore be oral. It could be either an express statement or a statement implied from the circumstances, presumably by innuendo or by the context. However, the statement must be clear enough to identify a person as author or director. In *Moore* v. *News of the World* [1972] 1 Q.B. 441, Dorothy Squires successfully sued the News of the World in respect of an article which it published. The article was stated to be "By Dorothy Squires talking to Weston Taylor" and was written in the first person. In fact, she had not written the article and she succeeded in her claim under section 43 of the 1956 Act in respect of the false attribution. This situation would also amount to a false attribution under the 1988 Act.

Section 43 of the 1956 Act required (except in the case of public performance, broadcast or inclusion in a cable programme) that the infringer "inserted or affixed" the name of the person in or on a work or a copy of the work in such a way as to imply that the person was the author of the work. The 1988 Act requires a statement (express or implied) as to who is the author of a work or director of a film, together with certain specified acts. The scope of the 1988 Act is wider and does not require that the person be actually named, although clearly the identity of the person must be readily ascertainable from the statement. Section 43 of the 1956 Act expressly provided that "name" included initials or a monogram, and both those would almost certainly be covered by the 1988 Act, as would a recognisable pseudonym or nickname.

The false attribution right is not infringed by the mere act of false attribution. There has to be some further act before there is an infringement. To this extent the law differs from that set out in section 43(2)(*a*) of the 1956 Act, which made the act of false attribution itself an actionable tort.

Section 43 of the 1956 Act was only infringed by acts which took place in the United Kingdom. There is no such requirement in the 1988 Act and acts done outside the United Kingdom may fall within the scope of section 84, if they fall within any of the categories of infringing acts set out in section 84 (but see paragraph 11.40).

Under the 1988 Act there is no requirement that the work or film falsely attributed has to be protected by copyright. Copyright considerations are irrelevant. The right vests in the person to whom false attribution is made, or his personal representatives.

(a) *Acts which infringe the false attribution right*

(i) *Issue of copies to the public and public exhibition*

Section 84(2) sets out the first circumstance where the right will be **11.27** infringed. It will be infringed by a person who issues to the public copies of a work to which the section applies in or on which there is a false attribution, or who exhibits in public either the original or a copy of an artistic work, in or on which there is a false attribution. The equivalent prohibition in section 43 of the 1956 Act prohibited "publishing" a work, rather than issuing copies to the public. "Publishing" under the 1956 Act was held to mean publishing for the first time and the use of the words "issuing copies to the public" will have a wider meaning than this. (See paragraph 5.22.)

There is no requirement under section 84(2) of knowledge on the part of the infringer and this is a departure from section 43 of the 1956 Act, which in these circumstances required the offender to have knowledge that the person concerned was not the author of the work. It should therefore be much easier to prove the necessary elements of section 84(2), than it was to prove those of section 43.

(ii) *Public performance, broadcast and inclusion in a cable programme*

The second circumstance in which the false attribution right is infringed is **11.28** set out in section 84(3). The right is infringed by a person who:

(a) in relation to a literary, dramatic or musical work, performs the work in public, broadcasts it, or includes it in a cable programme service, as being the work of a person; or

(b) in the case of a film, shows it in public, broadcasts it or includes it in a cable programme service as being directed by a person;

knowing or having reason to believe that the attribution is false.

Again, there are similarities to the provisions of section 43 of the 1956

Act. Under the 1956 Act it was necessary to show that the offender knew that the person was not the author of the relevant work. Under the 1988 Act the test is, as elsewhere in the 1988 Act, less stringent and as an alternative to proving actual knowledge, it is sufficient to show that the infringer had "reason to believe" that the attribution is false. What this means is discussed more fully elsewhere in this work. (See Chapter 6.)

Artistic works fall outside the scope of section 84(3), whereas they were included in the equivalent provision under the 1956 Act.

(iii) *Material containing false attribution*

11.29 Section 84(4) gives the third circumstance in which the false attribution right is infringed. In this case, the right is infringed by the issue to the public or the public display of materials containing a false attribution in connection with any of the acts set out in section 84(2) or (3). This extends the rights beyond those granted under the 1956 Act and creates an entirely new right of action. However, the right will only come into existence in connection with acts contravening sections 84(2) or (3). Whether this means that those acts must have taken place before this new right arises or whether it would be sufficient for material to be issued in anticipation of one or more of those acts is not entirely clear. "Materials" is not defined, and will bear its ordinary and natural meaning. It will cover a wide range of articles.

(iv) *Possession and dealing with infringing work*

11.30 The fourth circumstance in which the false attribution right is infringed, is contained in section 84(5), where it is provided that the right is infringed by any person who, in the course of a business:

(a) Possesses or deals with a copy of any work covered by section 84 in or on which there is a false attribution; or

(b) In the case only of an artistic work, possesses or deals with the work itself when there is a false attribution in or on it;

in either case, knowing or having reason to believe that there is such an attribution and that it is false.

The rights conferred in respect of possession are entirely new and create new rights of action which were not available under the 1956 Act. What amounts to possession is not defined in the 1988 Act. It should therefore be given its ordinary meaning. (See Chapter 6.)

"Dealing" is defined in section 84(7) to mean selling or letting for hire, offering or exposing for sale or hire, exhibiting in public, or distributing.

The requirement of knowledge is relaxed in section 84(5), in the same way as in section 84(3). (See paragraph 11.28.)

The right conferred here covers only copies of works and not the originals themselves, except in the case of an artistic work, when both the original and copies fall within the scope of section 84(5). Under section 43 of the 1956 Act equivalent rights were given in respect of both originals and copies of literary, dramatic, musical and artistic works, except in the case of the act of distribution, infringement of which was, for obvious reasons, limited only to copies of works.

Section 84(5) requires that all the infringing acts should be done in the course of a business. Under the 1956 Act the equivalent provisions did not have any such requirement in relation to sale or hire of infringing works or copies. In the case of exhibiting in public, offering and/or exposing for sale or hire the 1956 Act required this to be "by way of trade." This alteration is in keeping with the way copyright infringement is dealt with in the 1988 Act.

(v) *Dealing with artistic works*

Section 84(6) sets out the fifth circumstance where the false attribution **11.31** right will be infringed. It will be infringed by a person who, in the course of a business:

(a) Deals with an artistic work which has been altered after the author parted with possession of it as being the unaltered work of the author; or

(b) Deals with a copy of such a work as being a copy of the unaltered work of the author;

in either case, knowing or having reason to believe that this is not the case. Similar provisions existed under the 1956 Act. In an early case (*Carlton Illustrators* v. *Coleman* [1911] 1 K.B. 771), dealing with the equivalent provisions in the Fine Arts Copyright Act 1862, it was held that the alteration had to be "material" and it seems likely that this would also be a requirement under the 1988 Act. This remedy may overlap in certain circumstances with the new integrity right.

The requirement of knowledge is relaxed in the case of section 84(6) as in section 84(3) so that it is not necessary to prove actual knowledge.

"Dealing" is defined in section 84(7). (See paragraph 11.30.) It does not include "publishing" which is one of the acts prohibited by the provisions of section 43 of the 1956 Act, which are equivalent to section 84(6). It does however include "distributing" and exhibiting in public which were not caught by section 43 in these circumstances.

Section 84(6) requires each infringing act to be done "in the course of a business." Under the equivalent provisions of section 43 there was no such requirement in relation to publishing or selling or letting for hire, but in the case of offering or exposing for sale or hire, there was a requirement that it be done "by way of trade."

(vi) *Adaptations and copies*

Section 84(8) extends the scope of the false attribution right in certain **11.32** situations. The circumstances covered by section 84(8), will give rise to a potentially actionable false attribution. This will become actionable if any of the acts set out in section 84 subsequently takes place. (See paragraphs

11.27 to 11.31.) In each case the provisions relevant to the particular infringing act will have to be looked at to see if infringement has taken place. The rights in this case will arise in favour of the author or, if dead, his personal representatives.

The first circumstance covered by section 84(8) is where, contrary to the fact, a literary, dramatic or musical work is falsely represented as being an adaptation of the work of a person. This provision existed also under the 1956 Act, although in that Act it extended also to artistic works. The wording of section 84(8)(*a*) of the 1988 Act is rather wider than that contained in section 43(3) of the 1956 Act. In particular, section 43(3) refers to an "adaptation of the work of *another* person" whereas section 84(8) refers to "an adaptation of the work of *a* person." Taken literally, section 84(8) could be infringed by falsely representing that the work of an author is an adaptation by the author of a work of his rather than his original unadapted work. Rights could arise in favour of the author in such circumstances.

The second situation covered by section 84(8) applies only to artistic works and arises where, contrary to the fact, a copy of the artistic work is falsely represented as being a copy made by the author of the artistic work.

Similar provisions were contained in section 43(6) of the 1956 Act. In the case of artistic works represented falsely as being a copy made by the author of the artistic works, section 43(6) only provided a remedy where copyright subsisted in the artistic work. This limited the scope of works covered. However, the rights arising under section 43(6) were not fixed by any time limit and would therefore be exercisable for the period of copyright protection of the work. All other rights under section 43 of the 1956 Act were limited in duration to the period expiring 20 years after the death of the person entitled to the right. Also, section 43(6) did not contain the words "without the licence of the author," which do appear in section 43(4) and, *mutatis mutandis*, in section 43(2). It would seem from this that, whether the author licensed the acts or not, the rights would technically be infringed if the acts set out in section 43(6) took place. The position would not be the same under section 84(8) of the 1988 Act.

Also the scope of the acts covered by section 43(6) differs from the scope of equivalent acts covered by section 84(8) of the 1988 Act, in the same way as is discussed in relation to section 84(5) of the 1988 Act. (See paragraph 11.30.)

Section 43(10) of the 1956 Act expressly provided that nothing in section 43 would derogate from any right of action or other remedy (whether civil or criminal) in proceedings instituted otherwise than by virtue of section 43. It also provided that nothing in section 43(10) should be construed as requiring any damages recovered by virtue of section 43 to be disregarded in assessing damages in any proceedings instituted otherwise than by virtue of section 43 and arising out of the same transaction. Section 171(4) of the 1988 Act makes it clear that nothing in Part 1 of the 1988 Act affects any right of action or other remedy, whether civil or criminal, which is available otherwise than under Part 1 in respect of any acts which infringe any of the moral rights conferred by the 1988 Act. Thus, other remedies are expressly preserved. However, there is no provision equivalent to section 43(10) of the 1956 Act. It could be argued that this omission was deliberate and that damages for infringement of this new moral right should be disregarded when assessing damages for infringement of any other right, even if the proceedings arise out of the same transaction. However, it seems unlikely that any court would grant damages twice in respect of the same tortious act without taking into account in each case the amount of damages awarded in respect of each cause of action.

4. The right to privacy in respect of certain photographs and films

Section 85 of the 1988 Act contains the fourth of the moral rights, a right   **11.33**
to privacy in respect of certain photographs and films. This right is referred to in this book as the privacy right. This is an entirely new right which arises where a person commissions the taking of a photograph or the making of a film for private domestic purposes. "Commissions" is not defined for the purposes of Part I of the 1988 Act, but in Part III (dealing with the new design right) a commission is defined as a commission for money or money's worth. Somewhat similar wording to this was used in section 4(3) of the 1956 Act, dealing with, amongst other things, ownership of copyright in commissioned photographs. This may give some guidance for the purposes of Part I. What amounts to a commission will clearly be very important. There are a number of cases going back before the 1911 Act which dealt with the case where a professional photographer took photographs speculatively in the hope of selling some to the subjects being photographed. These cases dealt with ownership of copyright and were covering different circumstances, as there was no requirement under the relevant legislation that the commission should be for private domestic purposes. It is submitted that the correct test will now be whether the commissioner in the circumstances is in fact obliged to pay for the photographs taken or whether he can rightfully decline to pay anything or buy any photographs. If he is not obliged, then it is probably not a commission.

Where copyright subsists in the photograph or film, the person commissioning it for private domestic purposes has the right not to have:

(a) Copies of the work issued to the public; or

(b) The work exhibited or shown in public; or

(c) The work broadcast or included in a cable programme service.

Any person who does or authorises the doing of any of those acts in relation to such photographs or film infringes the privacy right, unless one of the exceptions applies.

The right will only apply where the taking of the photograph or the making of the film has been commissioned. Under the 1988 Act, in such a case, where the commission is made after the commencement of the 1988

Act, the copyright will normally vest in the person taking the photograph or the person making the arrangements necessary for the making of the film, and not in the person giving the commission. The new right would therefore not apply to photographs taken or films made by a person for himself. However, under those circumstances he would almost certainly own the copyright and would have the protection afforded to a copyright owner. This would not assist the people photographed who in such a case would not have any privacy right. Photographs taken socially may therefore still be exploited commercially, for example, in a newspaper, if the social photographer permits it, as copyright owner. If the requirements of section 85 are satisfied, it does not matter who owns the copyright, the privacy right will vest in the person who commissioned the taking of the photograph or the making of the film. No dealing with the copyright will affect the privacy right. The two rights are independent.

The exceptions are listed in section 85(2). These provide that the right is not infringed by an act which, by virtue of any of the provisions set out below, would not infringe the copyright in the work:

Section 31 (Incidental inclusion of work in an artistic work, film, broadcast or cable programme);

Section 45 (Parliamentary and judicial proceedings);

Section 46 (Royal commissions and statutory inquiries);

Section 50 (acts done under statutory authority);

Section 57 (anonymous or pseudonymous works, acts permitted on assumptions as to expiry of copyright or death of author).

The privacy right does not apply to photographs taken or films made before commencement. However, it would seem to apply to photographs taken and films made after commencement, even though the commission was agreed before commencement. In such a case, conceivably the commissioner might own both the copyright and the privacy right. (See paragraph 11.04.)

The greatest limitation is that the privacy right applies only to commissions for private and domestic purposes. It would not arise in the case of a commission for any other purpose, such as for photographs on a modelling assignment, where the photographs will be used in the course of a business. The usual sort of situation which would be covered is commissioned wedding photographs or a commissioned video taken of a wedding.

D. DURATION OF THE NEW RIGHTS

11.34   The paternity right, integrity right and privacy right will continue to subsist for so long as copyright subsists in the work in relation to which the right exists. This will generally be the life of the author plus 50 years, (see

Chapter 4). If for any reason the work concerned falls into the public domain, then the moral rights in relation to that work will come to an end as well.

The false attribution right is not dependent on copyright and exists whether or not copyright subsists in the work falsely attributed. The period of protection in this case will last during the lifetime of the person owning the right and for a period of 20 years after that person's death. This is the same as the period provided for the comparable right under the 1956 Act, save in the case of artistic works in the circumstances governed by section 43(6), where the right endured for so long as copyright subsisted in the artistic work to which the right related.

E. CONSENT AND WAIVER

Section 87 provides that it is not an infringement of any of the four new **11.35** rights to do any act to which the person entitled to the right has consented. There is no requirement that the consent should be in writing and it could therefore be oral or by conduct. Consent in writing would obviously provide more satisfactory evidence of the consent.

Consent also prevented an infringement of rights under section 43 of the 1956 Act.

Section 87(2) provides that any rights comprised in the four new rights may be waived by the person giving up the right, by an instrument in writing signed by the person giving up the right. Section 176(2) provides that where a company signs a waiver, it is permissible either for a person to sign on behalf of the company or for the company seal to be affixed. The use of the word "may" in section 87(2) is permissive and it is not clear from section 87(2) whether the new rights can be waived in any other way.

In section 87(4) there is a general statement making it clear that nothing in Chapter IV of the 1988 Act shall be construed as excluding the operation of the general law of contract or estoppel in relation to an informal waiver or other transaction in relation to any of the new rights. This suggests that the new rights can be waived "informally," by an oral agreement or by estoppel. The use of a written waiver will be preferable, if only from the point of view of evidence. In addition, the precise scope of a waiver will be judged more easily in most cases from a written waiver. The scope of an informal waiver or estoppel may be very difficult to determine.

The scope of the waiver can be limited in a number of different ways. It may relate to a specific work only, or to works of a specified description, or to works generally. It may relate to existing or future works. In addition, it may be conditional or unconditional and may be expressed to be subject to revocation. All of these combinations give immense scope for variation and will no doubt result in interesting negotiations. It seems that a waiver could be framed so broadly that the right could be given up entirely, not only in favour of the person to whom it is given, but in favour of the whole world.

Where a waiver is made in favour of the owner or prospective owner of the copyright in the work or works to which the waiver relates, there is a presumption that the waiver will extend to the owner or prospective owner's licensees and successors in title, unless a contrary intention is expressed.

As stated above, a waiver may be expressed to be subject to revocation. This suggests that if it is not so expressed, then it should be presumed to be irrevocable. The statute does not actually say this, but it seems a reasonable implication. Section 87(4) expressly refers to estoppel, which is preserved in relation to informal waivers. If a waiver is given and relied upon, it should not be difficult to argue that the person giving the waiver is estopped from revoking it, unless of course the waiver was expressly stated to be revocable, when it was granted. It may be a wise precaution to provide for waivers and consents to be expressed to be revocable, subject to appropriate conditions, as moral rights may provide a useful additional remedy where there are difficulties in proving ownership of copyright. If the rights have been irrevocably and generally waived, they may be lost entirely which may not be to the benefit of anyone except an infringer. If the rights are revocably waived, then the author could agree to revoke that waiver in the event of an infringement and to co-operate with the copyright or other rights owner in attacking the infringer. Similar considerations apply to any agreement by an author or director not to assert his paternity right. (See paragraph 11.13.) It would be wise for a rights owner to be able to require the author or director to assert the paternity right, so that the right can be used to assist in infringement proceedings.

Consents and waivers will commonly appear in contracts. Normal contractual considerations will apply to such contracts. The Unfair Contract Terms Act 1977 may possibly apply in appropriate circumstances, although that Act does contain some exemptions to contracts so far as they relate to the creation or transfer of a right in copyright or other intellectual property. Moral rights are not property rights, and could not be classed as intellectual property. This is borne out by Paragraph 24 of Schedule 7 of the 1988 Act which amends the Unfair Contract Terms Act to include a reference to the new design right created by the 1988 Act. No similar amendment is made to incorporate moral rights. In addition, rules relating to the avoidance of contracts entered into under duress or undue influence will apply to consents and waivers. These are discussed more fully elsewhere in this book. (See Chapter 8.)

Care should be taken in drafting consents and waivers, particularly where the person giving the consent or waiver is also the owner of the copyright in the relevant work. A consent or waiver which is too widely worded may give permissions in respect of the copyright work as well and this may not be the intended result. Any consent or waiver should refer clearly to the right to which the consent or waiver relates and should clearly define the precise limits of the scope of the consent or waiver.

F. JOINT WORKS

The paternity right, in the case of a work of joint authorship, is a right of   **11.36**
each joint author to be identified as a joint author and must be asserted by
each joint author in relation to himself. This means that no joint author
can rely on any assertion by any other joint author.

The integrity right, in the case of a work of joint authorship, is a right of
each joint author. If one joint author consents to the treatment in
question, then his right is satisfied and not infringed. However, it seems
that this will not bind any of the other joint authors.

A waiver by one joint author of any moral right does not in any way
affect the rights of the other joint authors.

The false attribution right is infringed by any false statement as to the
authorship of a work of joint authorship and by the false attribution of
joint authorship in relation to a work of sole authorship. Such a false
attribution infringes the right in every person to whom authorship of any
description is, whether rightly or wrongly, attributed.

The effect of this will be that where authorship of a joint work is falsely
attributed for any reason, even if that attribution may be partially correct,
the false attribution right of each person to whom authorship is attributed
is therefore infringed and is actionable if any of the circumstances set out
in section 84 occur in relation to the work whilst it bears such a false
attribution. Approximately equivalent provisions were contained in section 43(7) of the 1956 Act.

The same provisions apply in relation to a film which has been jointly
directed. For these purposes, a film is treated as "jointly directed" if it is
made by the collaboration of two or more directors and the contribution
of each director is not distinct from that of the other director or directors.

In relation to the privacy right, provision is made for the situation
where there is a joint commission. In such circumstances each person who
commissioned the making of the work has a separate right of privacy. The
right of each joint commissioner is satisfied if he consents to the act in
question, but his consent will not bind any of the other joint commissioners. Similar provisions apply in respect of waiver. Waiver by one joint
commissioner will not affect the rights of the others.

G. PARTS OF WORKS

The paternity right and right of privacy apply in relation to the whole or   **11.37**
any *substantial* part of a work. They will not therefore apply to a part of a
work which is not substantial. The word "substantial" is not defined and it
is assumed that in construing "substantial" the courts will look at the
position under the pre-existing law. The expression "substantial part"
was used in both the 1911 Act and 1956 Act and was not defined in either.
There is, however, a body of case law on the subject which makes it clear
that it is the quality of what is produced, rather than the quantity which is
important. (See Chapter 5.)

The integrity right and false attribution right apply in relation to the whole or any part of a work. There is therefore no requirement in the case of these two rights that they should have been infringed in relation to a *substantial* part.

H. ASSIGNMENT AND DEVOLUTION OF MORAL RIGHTS

11.38   Moral rights are not assignable. As has been seen, they may be waived or given up by consent, but they may not be assigned to any third party. Given the wide possibilities for waiver and consent (see paragraph 11.35), one could envisage a situation where almost the same effect as an assignment could be achieved by contractual provisions. For example, the owner of the right could agree to enforce or refrain from enforcing the right strictly in accordance with the instructions of another. Section 94 contains a clear statement that moral rights are not assignable and it may be that this provision would prevent disguised assignments. However, this seems doubtful.

When the person entitled to the right dies then the rights will be transmitted in accordance with section 95 of the 1988 Act.

In relation to the paternity right, integrity right and privacy right, these pass on the death of the owner of the right to such person as he may by testamentary dispositions specifically direct. The use of the word "specifically" means that the right will have to be identified by a sufficient description in the will if the direction in the will is to be effective. It will probably be necessary to refer to the right expressly.

If the owner of the right does not make any provision in his will for these three rights, but the copyright in the work to which the rights relate forms part of his estate, then the rights will pass to the person to whom the copyright passes.

In any other case, these three rights will become exercisable by the deceased's personal representatives.

In the event that the deceased leaves part of a copyright to one person and part of it to another, then the moral right will be correspondingly divided. Section 95 gives two examples of where this might happen. They are only examples, and there may be many other situations where the moral right may be divided. The first example is where some of the copyright rights in a work are left to one person and others to another. For example, the owner of the copyright in a musical work might leave the right to issue copies of the work to the public to one person and all other rights to another person. The other example cited in section 95 is where the copyright is left to a person for part only of the remaining copyright period.

Section 95(3) applies where more than one person becomes entitled to exercise a moral right as a result either of a testamentary disposition of such moral right or alternatively by reason that the moral rights have devolved to beneficiaries along with the copyright. In such a case any one of the joint owners may assert the paternity right. Each owner shall be entitled separately to exercise the integrity right and right of privacy and any one of such owners who consents to any treatment or act, will be bound by that consent. That consent will, however, not bind the other owners of the right in question. Similarly, a waiver given by one owner under these circumstances will not affect the rights of the other owners.

Any consent or waiver given by a testator during his lifetime will bind any person to whom any paternity, integrity or privacy right passes on his death. This will include rights which vest in the testator's personal representatives.

With regard to the false attribution right, this right will only be actionable after the death of the owner of the right, by his personal representatives. Any damages recovered by personal representatives by virtue of section 95 of the 1988 Act in respect of such an infringement after a person's death devolve as part of his estate as if the right of action had subsisted and been vested in him immediately before his death. All this is the same as the position under section 43 of the 1956 Act.

Infringements occurring before the death of the deceased would be actionable by him and will form part of his estate.

In view of the potential effect that moral rights may have on the exploitation of copyright works or films, it is vitally important that it is possible to identify the owner of the rights. This will not usually be a problem during the author's or director's lifetime, but it is essen-tial that anyone owning moral rights should make adequate provision for them in his will. It is also clearly desirable that contracts should comprehensively deal with any moral rights involved in a particular situation. This can also provide for what is to happen after the death of the owner of the rights. It may be advisable in appropriate circumstances to take indemnities from authors and directors.

I. REMEDIES FOR INFRINGEMENT OF MORAL RIGHTS

The remedies available for infringement of moral rights are set out in **11.39**
section 103 of the 1988 Act. Here it is provided that an infringement of any of the moral rights is actionable as a breach of statutory duty owed to the person entitled to the right. Infringement of moral rights is not a criminal offence. Again, the position was the same under section 43 of the 1956 Act. None of the moral rights are property rights and infringement is therefore not treated as an infringement of a property right.

In the case of the integrity right, the court may, if it thinks it an adequate remedy in the circumstances, grant an injunction on terms prohibiting the doing of any act unless a disclaimer is made, in such terms and in such a manner as may be approved by the court, disassociating the author or director from the treatment of the work. It is assumed that this remedy in respect of the integrity right is in addition to all the remedies available in respect of breach of statutory duty, which would, of course, include an injunction, in appropriate circumstances.

In the case of a work of architecture which is a building, the integrity rights of the author are limited, so that the author can only require the removal of any identification of him as the architect which appears on the building (s.80(5)). (See paragraph 11.21.)

In the case of the paternity right, section 78(5) of the 1988 Act provides that the court shall, in considering remedies, take into account any delay in asserting the right. (See paragraphs 11.13 and 11.17.)

The most usual remedies will be for an injunction in appropriate cases, and for damages. It is difficult to guess what approach the courts will take in assessing damages. No doubt the courts will take into account all the circumstances, including annoyance and irritation suffered by the plaintiff. Loss of reputation and other non-pecuniary loss may be relevant in many cases and it may be possible to show that a person's career, and therefore business, has been damaged by an infringement of his moral rights. It may be difficult to quantify damages.

Other remedies such as Anton Piller orders and Mareva injunctions should also be available.

J. PLACE OF INFRINGEMENT

11.40   The 1988 Act in Chapter IV does not expressly limit the application of the four new moral rights to acts taking place in the United Kingdom. On a literal reading of the provisions, acts taking place anywhere in the world would fall within the provisions. No wording equivalent to that appearing in section 16(1) of the 1988 Act appears in Chapter IV. Section 16(1) lists the acts restricted by copyright and specifically states that these consist of "the exclusive right to do the following acts in the United Kingdom." A similar limitation appeared in the 1956 Act in relation to copyright in section 1 and, in relation to the false attribution right, in section 43. It is, therefore, significant that no such wording appears in the moral rights provisions of the 1988 Act.

In *Def Lepp Music and Others* v. *Stuart Brown and Others* [1986] R.P.C. 273 it was held that action could not be brought in England in respect of infringements of copyright occurring by acts done exclusively outside the United Kingdom. The decision was based partly on the wording of section 1 of the 1956 Act, which expressly referred to the United Kingdom. It is thought that the decision will continue to apply to copyright infringement under the 1988 Act (see paragraph 5.04).

It would be an odd result if the new moral rights were enforceable in the United Kingdom in respect of acts done throughout the world, when that is not the case in respect of copyright works. The answer seems to be that the new moral rights are not property rights and are only enforceable as breaches of statutory duty. On this basis, one must look at the countries to which the 1988 Act extends. This is dealt with in Chapter 2. (See paragraph 2.27.) It clearly extends to the United Kingdom and there is no difficulty here. The question is whether there would be a breach of statutory duty by doing an act in all other countries to which the Act extends. There seems no reason why there would not be, save that on normal principles of construction of statutes, there is no extra-territorial effect unless expressly provided. The next question is whether an act done outside those countries would be sufficient to give rise to a right of action. It is thought that the courts will decide this point by ruling that it is not. This will effectively limit the application of the new moral rights provisions to acts done in those countries to which the 1988 Act extends.

12 RIGHTS IN PERFORMANCES

I INTRODUCTION

12.01 Part II of the 1988 Act contains a detailed set of provisions conferring civil rights on performers and persons having recording rights. In addition, it creates a number of criminal offences.

Part II is intended to replace and extend the provisions contained in the Performers' Protection Acts 1958 to 1972 ("the Performers' Protection Acts"), which are repealed by the 1988 Act. There are no transitional provisions as such. However, section 180(3) of the 1988 Act expressly provides that the rights conferred by the 1988 Act will apply in relation to performances taking place before the commencement of Part II of the 1988 Act. This means that some subsequent acts in respect of such performances, such as dealing in recordings of the performances, will give rise to rights and remedies under the 1988 Act. Section 180(3) goes on to provide that no act done before the commencement shall be regarded as infringing the rights contained in the 1988 Act. Furthermore, no act done after the commencement of Part II of the 1988 Act, which is done in pursuance of arrangements made before its commencement will infringe the new rights. The word "arrangements" is not defined, but seems wide enough to encompass not only contractual obligations, but less formal arrangements as well. This provision is going to be particularly important because Part II of the 1988 Act confers some completely new rights, which will apply to performances given before the commencement of the 1988 Act, when the new rights did not in fact exist.

The whole of the Performers' Protection Acts are repealed by the 1988 Act. These statutes will therefore have no bearing on performances rendered after their repeal, but they will continue to have relevance to performances given and acts done before that date. It is assumed that the date of repeal of the Performers' Protection Acts will be the same date as the commencement date of Part II of the 1988 Act. There will be difficulties if the two dates do not coincide.

Section 16 of the Interpretation Act 1978 will be relevant here as it covers the situation where a new Act repeals an existing Act. Unless the contrary intention appears, the repeal will not affect the previous operation of the enactment repealed or anything duly done or suffered under that enactment. Similarly, unless the contrary intention appears, the repeal will not affect any right, privilege, obligation or liability acquired, accrued or incurred under the repealed enactment. Nor will it affect, unless the contrary intention appears, any penalty, forfeiture, or punishment incurred in respect of any offence committed under that enactment and nor will it affect any investigation, legal proceeding or remedy in respect of any such right, privilege, obligation, liability, penalty, forfeiture or punishment.

There is nothing in the 1988 Act which would appear to show a contrary intention and therefore, if an offence is committed and rights have accrued under the Performers' Protection Acts, it will continue to be actionable in respect of performances given and acts done before their repeal by the 1988 Act. Clearly these rights will become less important as time goes by, particularly as civil rights of action become statute-barred. Nevertheless, it is worthwhile summarising the existing law before turning to the new rights conferred and offences created by the 1988 Act.

II EXISTING LAW BEFORE THE 1988 ACT

Rights of performers were first protected in the United Kingdom by the   **12.02** Dramatic and Musical Performers Protection Act 1925 ("the 1925 Act"). This created a new criminal offence where a person knowingly did certain acts, including making a sound recording of the performance of any dramatical or musical work without the consent in writing of the performers. The Act did not expressly create any civil rights or remedies and, indeed, in a case in 1930 (*Musical Performers' Protection Association Limited* v. *British International Pictures Limited* [1930] 46 T.L.R. 485) the court held that no civil rights or remedies were conferred by the 1925 Act.

The 1925 Act was amended by the 1956 Act, which extended the scope of the criminal offence to give protection to performers in films, which was similar in scope to the protection already given to performers in respect of unauthorised sound recordings of their performances.

The provisions contained in the 1925 Act, as amended by the 1956 Act were consolidated in the Dramatic and Musical Performers' Protection Act of 1958 ("the 1958 Act").

The United Kingdom became a Contracting State to the International Convention for the Protection of Performers, Producers of Phonograms and Broadcasting Organisations dated October 26, 1961, which was entered into at Rome ("The Rome Convention"). In order to give effect to The Rome Convention, the 1963 Performers' Protection Act ("the 1963 Act") was passed. It extended the scope of the criminal offence and also covered records made outside the United Kingdom.

Finally, the Performers' Protection Act 1972 ("the 1972 Act") was passed and this increased the fines in respect of the offences contained in the Performers' Protection Acts 1958 to 1963 and also introduced a further offence in the case of offences committed by companies.

None of the Performers' Protection Acts provides expressly for any civil remedy. They simply provide for the creation of criminal offences. Nevertheless, it has now been held that the Acts do in fact confer civil rights on performers. There has been a great deal of litigation on this subject and the courts have had considerable difficulty in deciding whether any civil rights have in fact been conferred and, if so, on whom and to what extent.

The current state of the law was considered in a recent case in the Court of Appeal—*Rickless and Others* v. *United Artists Corporation* [1987] 1 All E.R. 679. The judgment of Sir Nicolas Browne-Wilkinson, the Vice-Chancellor, contains a very useful summary of the existing law and the cases decided so far. The Vice-Chancellor commented at page 688: "The present state of the authorities is not a happy one and as soon as the matter is clarified, either by legislation or by a definitive decision by the House of Lords, the better."

It is perhaps worth summarising the more important cases which preceded *Rickless*. In the case of *ex p. Island Records Limited* [1978] Ch. 122 the Court of Appeal considered the problem of whether the legislation gave rise to civil remedies. In that case proceedings were brought by both performers and record companies claiming civil remedies in respect of breaches of section 1 of the 1958 Act. The Court of Appeal held that both record companies and performers had a valid civil cause of action and all plaintiffs were successful. The judges in the Court of Appeal reached their conclusions for different reasons, which are discussed in the *Rickless* case. The majority decision was that the Performers' Protection Acts did not confer any civil rights either on performers or record companies for breach of statutory duty. However, the majority considered that both record companies and performers would succeed on a more general basis. It decided that where a criminal offence is committed, which is not only an offence against the public generally, but also causes or threatens to cause special damage to a private individual over and above the damage caused to the public generally, then the private individual can obtain relief from the court to protect the private right which is being infringed by the criminal act. In this case, the majority held that the record companies had a legitimate interest to protect, which was the right to exploit records made by them of the performances of the performers. The performers had a legitimate right to receive royalties from the records. Therefore, both the record companies and performers succeeded in obtaining injunctions against the bootleggers in this case.

The *Island Records* case was considered in the House of Lords in the later case of *Lonrho Limited* v. *Shell Petroleum* [1982] A.C. 173. Lord Diplock, with whom all the other Law Lords agreed, cast doubt on the reasoning of the Court of Appeal judges in the *Island Records* case. He thought that the basis of the decision in the *Island Records* case was wrong and, ironically, took the view that the court could, in that case, have found for the performers, at least, on the basis of breach of statutory duty.

Shortly after the *Lonrho* decision, there was a further decision of the Court of Appeal in *RCA Corporation* v. *Pollard* [1983] Ch. 135. In that case, the plaintiffs were all record companies, who brought proceedings to prevent the making and selling of unauthorised recordings of performances given by artists who were bound by exclusive recording contracts to RCA. The Court of Appeal regarded itself as bound by what had been said in the *Lonrho* case and held that record companies did not have any civil rights of action under the Performers' Protection Acts.

In the *Rickless* case, the Court of Appeal held firmly that performers did have civil remedies under the Performers' Protection Acts. However, the *RCA* v. *Pollard* decision will still govern the situation so far as record companies are concerned and they will continue to have no such civil rights under the Performers' Protection Acts, unless the *RCA* v. *Pollard* decision is reversed by a later decision of the House of Lords.

The civil remedy available to performers is for breach of statutory duty. All the usual remedies for breach of statutory duty will be available, including injunctions, Anton Piller orders and damages. The right of action vests in the performer alone. It is not assignable, but the performer can authorise someone to give consent on his behalf. The consent must be in writing whether given by the performer or on his behalf.

According to the *Rickless* case, the rights do not die with the performer, but will continue indefinitely after the performer's death. However, after the performer's death consent can be given by his personal representatives and again, this consent must be in writing. If the performer has granted a third party authority to give consent on his behalf, then this authority will come to an end on the death of the performer and the right to give consent will then vest in the performer's personal representatives. It is not clear whether the personal representatives could then authorise some third party to give consent on their behalf. It seems a slightly unlikely situation. The rights are not restricted by any statutory provision, such as the fair dealing provisions applicable to copyright and there are no statutory provisions governing the way in which the rights may be enforced.

The long duration and unrestricted nature of the rights of performers under the Performers' Protection Acts should not now in practice give rise to any real difficulty. The Performers' Protection Acts are repealed by the 1988 Act and will therefore only apply in relation to performances given and other acts done prior to the commencement of the 1988 Act. The 1988 Act expressly applies to performances given prior to the commencement of that Act, but only in respect of infringing acts done after commencement. The Performers' Protection Acts having been repealed, it will no longer be necessary to obtain consents under those Acts in respect of acts done after their repeal. Consent will be required under the 1988 Act in respect of such acts, if required at all. Effectively therefore, the duration of the rights which arise under the Performers' Protection Acts has been curtailed by the 1988 Act, which sets out in full the duration of the rights which arise under the 1988 Act.

It should be remembered that there is no copyright in a performance. This was the position under the old law and it remains unchanged under the 1988 Act.

A. THE 1958 ACT

12.03   The primary purpose of the Performers' Protection Acts was to protect the live performances of performers, so that they were not "fixed" or recorded without the consent of the performer. Section 1 of the 1958 Act prescribes three circumstances when a person will commit a criminal act. The person will only be guilty of the criminal act if he does the act "knowingly." "Knowingly" has been held to mean both that the person knows that he is doing the act and also that he knows that he does not have the consent in writing of the performers to do it. In section 1 the prohibited acts are committed if a person knowingly:

(a) makes a record, directly or indirectly from or by means of the performance of a dramatic or musical work without the consent in writing of the performers; or

(b) sells or lets for hire or distributes for the purposes of trade or by way of trade exposes or offers for sale or hire, a record made in contravention of paragraph (a); or

(c) uses such a record for the purposes of a public performance.

It is a defence to a charge of making such a record, for the person charged to prove that the record was made for his private and domestic use only. This defence would not cover any act subsequently done in relation to that record, so that even if the defence was available to the charge of making the record, it would not be available if copies of the record were, for example, subsequently sold.

Section 2 of the 1958 Act is in similar terms to section 1, except that it relates to films, rather than to records. Section 3 of the 1958 Act provides that it is an offence knowingly to broadcast (otherwise than by the use of a record or film) a performance of a dramatic or musical work, or any part of such a performance, without the consent in writing of the performers.

Section 3 is intended to cover only live performances. However, sections 1 and 2 are worded much more widely. The inclusion in sections 1(*a*) and 2(*a*) of the words "directly or indirectly" would seem to cover recording both a live performance and a recording of that live performance. Thus the recording of an existing recording without the consent of the performers will be a contravention of the 1958 Act. In addition, section 8(1) of the 1958 Act makes it clear that a performance includes a mechanical or other performance rendered audible by mechanical or electrical means. This would include the playing back of a recording.

Section 4 of the 1958 Act creates a further offence where the person makes, or has in his possession, a plate or similar contrivance for the purpose of making records in contravention of the 1958 Act. Section 5 of the 1958 Act gives the court power to order the destruction of records, films, plates or similar contrivances in the possession of an offender, which appear to the court to have been made in contravention of the 1958 Act or to be adapted for the making of records in contravention of the 1958 Act. However, the order can only be made on the conviction of the offender and then only in respect of those items in respect of which the offender has been convicted. This severely limits the scope of any destruction order.

Section 6 provides two additional defences to any proceedings brought under the 1958 Act:

(a) The first is to prove that the record, film, broadcast or cable programme concerned was made or included only for the purpose of reporting current events.

(b) The second defence is to prove that the inclusion of the performance in question in the record, film, broadcast or cable programme concerned was only by way of background or was otherwise only incidental to the principal matters comprised or represented in the record, film, broadcast or cable programme.

These two defences are in addition to the specific defence to charges brought under section 1(*a*) or 2(*a*), which is to prove that the record is made for private and domestic use only.

Section 7 covers the situation where someone has consented on behalf of a performer. The section is framed in the form of a defence. A person charged with an offence under the Act will have a defence if he can prove that the record, film, broadcast or cable programme concerned was made or included with the consent in writing of a person who, at the time of giving the consent, represented that he was authorised by the performers to give it on their behalf and that the person making the record, film, broadcast or cable programme had no reasonable grounds for believing the person giving the consent was not so authorised. If this can be proved, then the performers themselves are deemed to have consented in writing to the making or including of the record, film, broadcast or cable programme concerned. If the consent given is wide enough, it will cover not only the making of the record, film or broadcast, but all the other acts prohibited by the 1958 Act.

B. THE 1963 ACT

This Act was passed in order to give effect to the Rome Convention and it came into operation on September 1, 1963. It is expressly stated that it applies only in relation to performances taking place on or after September 1, 1963.   **12.04**

Section 1 of the 1963 Act inserts a new wider definition into the 1958 Act of what is meant by a performance of a dramatic or musical work. Section 1 defines this as: "The performance of any actors, singers, musicians, dancers or other persons who act, sing, deliver, declaim, play in or otherwise perform literary, dramatic, musical or artistic works." This is a very wide definition, but nevertheless would not be wide enough to cover certain types of performance. In its Report, the Whitford Committee felt that it would not cover performances by variety artists such as acrobats or jugglers, because those performers did not perform "works."

Section 1(2) of the 1963 Act provides that the 1958 Act applies to performances given outside the United Kingdom, but it is made clear that nothing done outside the United Kingdom is to be treated as an offence. In addition, section 1(2) will only apply to performances given on or after September 1, 1963. Although acts done outside the United Kingdom in relation to performances will not be covered by the 1963 Act, section 2 of the 1963 Act may apply to acts done subsequently in the United Kingdom. In addition, an unauthorised recording made outside the United Kingdom before September 1, 1963 of a performance given outside the United Kingdom will not be covered by the 1958 Act and no offences under the Performers' Protection Acts will be committed by carrying out any of the prohibited acts in relation to that recording, whenever or wherever those prohibited acts are done. As will be seen, the position may be different under the 1988 Act.

Section 2 of the 1963 Act covers records made outside the United Kingdom in certain circumstances. Again, it will only apply to performances given on or after September 1, 1963. This provision does not cover films, and applies only to offences under section 1(*b*) and 1(*c*) of the 1958 Act, covering dealings in and public performances of an unauthorised record. It applies to records made outside the United Kingdom directly or indirectly from or by means of a performance given after September 1, 1963 to which the 1958 Act applies. Where the civil or criminal law of the country where the record is made, contains a provision for the protection of performers under which the consent of any person to the making of the record is required, then the record will be deemed to have been made in contravention of the 1958 Act if, whether knowingly or not, the record was made without the consent required by the local law and without the consent in writing of the performers. The meaning of this provision is not at all clear. The Whitford Committee considered that at least three meanings were possible.

The first meaning is that for the section to apply, the law of the place where the record is made must contain an appropriate provision for the protection of performers. If it does not, then section 2 does not apply at all and no consents are required in such a case. If this is the right construction, then there is a requirement of reciprocity.

The second meaning does not require reciprocity. On this construction, the section merely stipulates that where consent is required under the law of the place where the record is made, then that consent must be obtained and, in addition, the consent in writing of the performers must be obtained. If no consent is required by the local law, then the only consent required is the consent in writing of the performers.

The third construction argues that the section is dealing with the situation where the law of the country where the record is made requires consent, but not in writing. If such unwritten consent was obtained, then no further consent is required in the United Kingdom.

Section 3 of the 1963 Act as amended by the Cable and Broadcasting Act 1984, creates a new offence. An offence is committed by a person who knowingly includes a performance to which the 1958 Act applies, or any part of such a performance, in a cable programme without the consent in writing of the performers. The performance must be included otherwise than by the use of a record of film or the reception and immediate retransmission of a broadcast. Effectively, this therefore means that live performances only are covered.

The offence is committed by the person who includes the offending performance in a cable programme. A cable programme is defined to mean a programme included in a cable programme service. Section 48(3) of the 1956 Act applies for these purposes and provides that references to the inclusion of a programme in a cable programme service are references to its inclusion in such a service by the person providing that service. This means that the person who commits the offence under section 3 of the 1963 Act is the person who provides the cable programme service, who will normally be the person licensed to do so under the Cable and Broadcasting Act 1984.

The defences set out in section 6 and section 7 of the 1958 Act also apply to offences under section 3 of the 1963 Act and sections 6 and 7 of the 1958 Act are amended to include appropriate references to cable programmes and the inclusion of performances in cable programmes.

Section 4 of the 1963 Act, as amended, contains a further offence. It arises in a situation where a record, film or broadcast is made or a cable programme is included with the consent in writing of a person who, at the time that he gives the consent, represents that he is authorised by the performers to give it on their behalf, when to his knowledge he was not so authorised. That person will only be guilty of an offence if the consent which he gave would, by virtue of section 7 of the 1958 Act, afford a defence to proceedings brought against the person to whom the consent is given. In other words, the person to whom the consent is given must have had no reasonable grounds for believing that the person giving the consent was not authorised to give it. If he does have any reasonable grounds, then the person receiving the consent has no defence under section 7 and is guilty of an offence. If he did have reasonable ground for believing that the person giving the consent was duly authorised, then the person giving the consent will be guilty of the offence, if he knew he was not authorised to give the consent.

C. THE 1972 ACT

This Act increased the penalties for offences committed under the two   **12.05**
earlier Acts. It also introduced, in section 3, a new offence. Where an offence under the 1958 Act or 1963 Act is committed by a body corporate and the offence is proved to have been committed with the consent or connivance of, or to be attributable to any neglect on the part of, any director, manager, secretary or other similar officer of the company or by any person who was purporting to act in any such capacity, that person is guilty of an offence as well as the body corporate.

The wording of this provision is very wide. The words "attributable to any neglect on the part of" would seem be wide enough to cover a large number of situations, including a situation where somebody failed to take due care.

The offences created under the Performers' Protection Acts are completely independent of the law of copyright and it is immaterial whether the work performed is protected by copyright or not. The position is the same under the 1988 Act.

III THE 1988 ACT

12.06 Part II of the 1988 Act contains the provisions conferring rights in respect of performances. The new rights are not property rights, unlike copyright rights. As has been mentioned already, the 1988 Act repeals in their entirety the Performers' Protection Acts. Part II of the 1988 Act will apply in relation to performances taking place before the commencement of Part II of the 1988 Act, but only in respect of infringing acts done after commencement in relation to those performances. However, no act done before the commencement of the 1988 Act or done in pursuance of arrangements made before commencement shall be regarded as infringing the rights conferred by Part II (s.180(3)). What exactly amounts to "arrangements" is not defined, but it is clearly wider than contractual obligations and would include less formal arrangements. The Performers' Protection Acts will continue to apply to acts done prior to their repeal, in relation to performances given before repeal. It is hoped that repeal of these Acts will be timed to coincide with the commencement of Part II of the 1988 Act as this will minimise confusion. Even assuming this is so, the position of acts done after commencement in pursuance of arrangements made before commencement is unclear. These may not be caught by the Performers' Protection Acts unless the "arrangements" themselves are caught and they will not be caught by the 1988 Act. There is a potential loophole in this case. However, it is thought that this will only affect the position of civil remedies under the 1988 Act and not the new criminal offences. The wording of section 180(3) refers to "the rights conferred by this part" and that wording would not be apt to cover the criminal offences. For this reason, criminal acts done after commencement should be covered notwithstanding that they are done in pursuance of arrangements made prior to commencement.

The provisions of Part II are intended to put right a number of shortcomings in the previous law. It was considered desirable to create civil remedies expressly, rather than relying on the rather precarious position existing before the 1988 Act as discussed above, and to define clearly the limits and scope of such remedies. It was also considered wrong that record companies should not have civil remedies, as decided in *RCA Corp.* v. *Pollard* [1983] Ch. 135 and the 1988 Act therefore confers civil rights on persons having recording rights.

It was also felt that the previous law operated somewhat capriciously, in that certain types of performer were not protected at all, such as variety artists. The 1988 Act expressly confers rights in respect of variety acts and the scope of performances covered is expanded.

Section 180(4) makes it clear that the new rights created in Part II of the 1988 Act are entirely independent of any copyright in or moral rights relating to any work performed or any film or sound recording or broadcast or cable programme including the performance. Indeed, the new rights are stated to be independent of any other right or obligation arising otherwise than under Part II of the 1988 Act. It will therefore continue to be immaterial as to whether or not there is copyright or any other right in the work performed. One will simply have to look at the performer or person having recording rights and at the performance. It is quite possible that out of the same course of events there could arise infringements of rights in a performance and of copyright and of moral rights. All would be actionable separately by the owners of the relevant rights.

Part II of the 1988 Act aims to achieve three objects. The first is to confer civil rights on a performer, by requiring his consent to the exploitation of his performances. The second is to confer civil rights on a person having recording rights in relation to a performance as regards recordings made without his consent or that of the performer, depending on the circumstances. The third is to create a number of criminal offences, which relate to dealing with and using illicit recordings and certain other related acts.

The definitions contained in Part I of the 1988 Act do not apply to Part II, except where Part II provides that they shall apply. Nevertheless the definitions in Part I are useful in construing Part II, where Part II contains no relevant definition in a particular provision. Two definitions appear in section 180, which are central to the whole of Part II and which are crucial to determining the scope of the rights. The expressions defined are "performance" and "recording."

A. PERFORMANCE

Performance means a *live* performance only. This follows on the philosophy of the Rome Convention, which seeks to give performers the right to prevent their performances being "fixed" or recorded without their prior consent. The definition is to this extent, narrower than that contained in the Performers' Protection Acts, which included non-live performances, such as the playback of recordings.   **12.07**

To fall within the definition, the live performance must be given by one or more individuals. The word "individual" is not defined, but must mean any person whether professional or amateur and whether skilled or not. This would exclude a corporation and a machine. It is difficult to envisage a machine giving a "live" performance, as, in order to perform, a machine would need to have instructions given to it, either by a recording, in which case the performance would not be live, or by a person transmitting instructions live, in which case that person would be the individual giving the performance. The word "performer" is not defined, but must be taken to mean any individual who gives a live performance. Under the 1988 Act, in order to fall within the definition, a performance must fall into one of four categories.

(a) *Dramatic performance*

12.08   The first is a dramatic performance, which is stated to include dance and mime. "Dramatic" is not defined. In Part I of the 1988 Act a "dramatic work" is stated to include a work of dance or mime, but is otherwise not defined. In any event, it is unlikely that the expression "a dramatic performance" was intended to be limited to the "performance of a dramatic work," which was one of the definitions of "performance" under the Performers' Protection Acts. Clearly there has been an attempt to move away from the earlier definition and create something wider.

(b) *Musical performance*

12.09   The second category is "a musical performance." Again, it is considered that this must be intended to cover more than just the performance of a musical work. A musical work is defined in Part I of the 1988 Act as a work consisting of music, exclusive of any words or action intended to be sung, spoken or performed with the music. If, indeed, only the performance of a musical work is intended to be covered then part of the performance of a song would not be covered in so far as the performance of the singer is concerned, although the performance of the accompaniment would no doubt fall within the definition. The singing of the melody by the singer would also be covered, but not the singing of the words. However, if the performance by singing of the words is not covered under this definition, then the singing of the words (as opposed to the melody) will not be covered at all, as it would not fall within either of the other two categories of performance which are discussed below. This may not matter in practice, but it would be a strange result and it would be more satisfactory to conclude that, in this context, a "musical performance" includes also the singing of the words.

(c) *Reading or recitation of a literary work*

12.10   The third category of performance is "a reading or recitation of a literary work." Section 203 of the 1988 Act expressly provides that the expression "literary work" shall have the same meaning in Part II as in Part I of the 1988 Act. This provides that "literary work" means any work, other than a dramatic or musical work, which is written, spoken or sung. Going back to the point raised in relation to a musical performance, it is clear that the words of a song are a literary work. However, performance only means "a reading or recitation" and would not therefore include the singing of the song.

(d) *Performance of a variety act or any similar presentation*

The fourth category is a performance of a variety act or any similar **12.11** presentation. "Variety act" is not defined. However, it seems likely that it is intended to have a wide interpretation and this is borne out by the inclusion of the words "or any similar presentation." However, it would probably not be wide enough to include the performance of a sportsman taking part in a sporting event, for example. An innings of a batsman would probably not be included, but some iceskating or synchronised swimming events probably would be included.

Under the Performers' Protection Acts it was necessary for there to be **12.12** a performance of any actors, singers, musicians, dancers or other persons who act, sing, deliver, declaim, play in or otherwise perform literary, dramatic, musical or artistic works. The idea of the performance of an artistic work seems rather bizarre and difficult to imagine, and there is no reference in the 1988 Act to performances of artistic works, or indeed any other work, except a literary work.

The definition of "performance" in the 1988 Act does not require the performer to be anything other than "an individual." A performance is covered if it is, or so far as it is, a live performance given by one or more individuals. It is not clear whether the words "so far as it is" qualify just "live performances" or also the words "given by one or more individuals." It would seem to qualify both. The question then arises as to whether, for example, a circus act would be covered. It is certainly a variety act. However, for example, an act involving performing dogs might not involve a human being appearing at all. In such a case, there will certainly be a human trainer, even if invisible to the audience. It is considered that the trainer would be the individual performing, but the words "so far as it is" might exclude the performance by the dogs. This would be an unfortunate result and would go against the clear intention of the 1988 Act, which is to broaden the scope of performances covered. A circus act would certainly fall within the general meaning of a "variety act." For this reason, it is thought that the courts would try to protect the whole variety act. In this example, provided that the performance was live and the trainer of the dogs took part in it, then the whole performance should be covered, including the performances of the dogs.

Finally, in the 1988 Act, the only express requirement that a work be performed is in relation to a literary work. In this particular case the 1988 Act is more limited than the Performers' Protection Acts where any performance of a literary work would be covered, whereas under the 1988 Act it is only a reading or recitation of a literary work which is covered. In other respects the definition of performance under the 1988 Act is rather wider than that under the Performers' Protection Acts.

B. RECORDING

The second crucial definition is that of a recording. A recording in **12.13** relation to a performance means a film or sound recording, both of which expressions are defined to have the same meaning as that given to them in Part I of the 1988 Act, made in certain circumstances. These definitions are extremely wide (see paragraphs 1.44 and 1.48) and are rather more up-to-date than those contained in the Performers' Protection Acts. However, the definitions in both pieces of legislation would seem wide enough to cover all forms of sound recordings and films.

In order for a film or sound recording to fall within the definition of recording in Part II of the 1988 Act, it must satisfy one of three requirements in relation to a live performance.

(a) *Live performance*

12.14   The first requirement is that it must be made *directly* from the live performance. Under the Performers' Protection Acts, the words "directly or indirectly" were used and these words also appear in the third circumstance set out below. It seems therefore that "directly" is intended to have a limited meaning and must be intended to cover the situation where the live performance itself is recorded without anything being interposed between the performance and the recording being made. If this is right, it would only cover the situation where the recording device directly records the live performance concerned. For example, recording a live broadcast from the radio or television would not satisfy this first requirement, although it would satisfy the second (see below).

It is interesting that in defining this circumstance the words "live performance" are used, whereas in the other two circumstances below only the word "performance" is used. Performance is, of course, defined to mean "live performance," as explained above. It is not clear what (if any) significance is to be attached to the use of the word "live" in this particular case, when it is not used elsewhere. It probably has none.

(b) *Broadcast and cable*

12.15   The second alternative requirement is that it must be made from a broadcast of or a cable programme including the live performance. This will cover the case where a live performance is broadcast or included in a cable programme and the recording is made from the broadcast or cable programme and is therefore, to this extent, recorded indirectly.

(c) *Recorded performances*

12.16   The third alternative requirement is that it is made either directly or indirectly from another recording of the live performance. This wording is extremely wide. It would cover any situation where a recording is made of a live performance and that recording is then re-recorded directly or indirectly. For example, a live performance might be recorded for later broadcast. If that later broadcast were recorded by anyone, that recording would fall within this third circumstance, rather than the second circumstance above. It would also be wide enough to cover the situation where a studio recording of a live performance is made in the normal way and that studio recording is subsequently re-recorded.

C. RIGHTS OF PERFORMERS

This section will deal with the civil remedies given to a performer to prevent the exploitation of his performances without his consent. The criminal sanctions are dealt with below. (See paragraph 12.44.) **12.17**

1. Definitions

Wherever the expressions "performances" and "recordings" are used in this chapter, they have the particular meanings given to them in Part II of the 1988 Act, as already outlined. To analyse the new rights some further definitions need to be examined. **12.18**

(a) *Qualifying performance*

As has been seen (see paragraph 12.04), the application of the Performers' Protection Acts in relation to performances outside the United Kingdom had given rise to some confusion, particularly in the meaning to be given to section 2 of the 1963 Act and in the question of whether there existed any requirement of "reciprocity." The situation is grasped rather more comprehensively under the 1988 Act by the introduction of a requirement that a performance must be a "qualifying performance" if it is to give rights to the performer. A performance will be a qualifying performance either if it is given by a qualifying individual or if it takes place in a qualifying country. **12.19**

(b) *Qualifying individual*

The expression "qualifying individual" is defined in section 206 of the 1988 Act and means a citizen or subject of or, an individual resident in a qualifying country. No definition is given of "resident". (See paragraph 2.10.) Perhaps some guidance can be gained from tax legislation and cases. If that is so, then it may not be very difficult to establish residence in a qualifying country. It may only be necessary for an individual to have accommodation available to him in a country to become resident in that country and an individual may be resident in more than one country at the same time. **12.20**

Section 206 does expand on what is meant by a person being a citizen or subject of a qualifying country. This shall be construed in relation to the United Kingdom, as a reference to being a British citizen. In relation to a colony of the United Kingdom, it shall be construed as a reference to being a British Dependent Territories' citizen by connection with that

411

colony. What the requirements are, in each case, are set out in the British Nationality Act 1981.

(c) *Qualifying country*

12.21   A qualifying country is also defined in section 206 of the 1988 Act and means the United Kingdom or another Member State of the EEC and certain further countries enjoying reciprocal protection. The United Kingdom, for all purposes of Part II, includes its territorial waters. Part II also applies to things done on a British ship, aircraft or hovercraft or in the United Kingdom sector of the continental shelf on a structure or vessel which is present there for purposes directly connected with the exploration of the seabed or subsoil or the exploitation of their natural resources, as it applies to things done in the United Kingdom.

    Qualifying country also includes a country designated under section 208 of the 1988 Act as enjoying reciprocal protection. Under section 208 an Order in Council may be made in respect of a convention country (see below) or a country as to which the Government is satisfied that provision has been or will be made under its law giving adequate protection for British performances.

(d) *British performances*

12.22   A British performance means a performance taking place in the United Kingdom or a performance given by an individual who is a British citizen or resident in the United Kingdom, wherever that performance took place.

(e) *Convention country*

12.23   A convention country means a country which is a party to a convention relating to performers' rights to which the United Kingdom is also a party. At the moment, the Rome Convention is the only relevant convention.

    Section 208(4) of the 1988 Act gives scope for the Government to give limited reciprocal protection where the relevant overseas country provides adequate protection only for certain descriptions of performance. Under those circumstances the Government is empowered only to give limited reciprocal protection so that the protection granted in the United Kingdom is no greater than that granted in the overseas country. It is made clear that an Order under section 208 can be made in respect of the Channel Islands, the Isle of Man or any colony of the United Kingdom, as well as in relation to any foreign country.

2. The rights granted

12.24   A number of rights are granted to performers and these are split up into three separate categories. The first is the right to require consent for recording or live transmission of a performance. The second is the performer's rights in respect of recordings made without his consent. The third category of rights deals with the importation, possessing or dealing with illicit recordings.

(a) *Recording or live transmission of performance*

Under section 182 of the 1988 Act, a performer's rights are infringed by a   **12.25** person who, without his consent:

(a) Makes, otherwise than for his private and domestic use, a recording of; or

(b) broadcasts live or includes live in a cable programme service;

the whole or any substantial part of a qualifying performance.

It is first worth noting that there is no requirement of knowledge on the part of the infringer. All that is required is that the performer has not consented to the infringing act being done. One of the difficulties in taking action under the Performers' Protection Acts was that it was necessary to prove knowledge on the part of the offender and this could raise evidential and practical problems. For example, it is generally difficult for a performer to attend to give evidence, particularly if that performer spends a lot of time working overseas.

The performer's rights are not infringed if a recording is made for the private and domestic use of the person making the recording. These words are not defined, but did appear in the 1958 Act as a defence to a charge of making an unauthorised recording in contravention of the 1958 Act. There has been no reported decision as to what "private and domestic use" meant under the 1958 Act. It will bear its ordinary and natural meaning.

If the person making the recording for his private and domestic use subsequently makes an unauthorised use of that recording, he may at that stage infringe the rights of the performer.

In relation to broadcasting and including in a cable programme service, this must be done "live" to infringe this right of a performer.

Both in the case of making the recording of the qualifying performance and broadcasting it and including it in a cable programme service, it is sufficient if a "substantial part" of a qualifying performance is used. No definition of "substantial part" is to be found in Part II of the 1988 Act. It presumably relates to quality, rather than quantity and no doubt guidance can be obtained from the cases dealing with this point in relation to copyright infringement. (See paragraph 5.09.)

Whilst knowledge is not required for the rights of a performer to be infringed, there is a partial defence of innocence contained in section 182(2). This provides that in an action for infringement of these rights of a performer, damages shall not be awarded against a defendant who shows that, at the time of the infringement, he believed on reasonable grounds that consent had been given. No guidance is given as to what "reasonable grounds" might mean. The burden of proof is on the infringer. The infringer will have to satisfy the court that he held the belief and will have to go on to provide some evidence that grounds existed on which the belief was based. The court will then decide whether the grounds proved are "reasonable" and presumably the court will apply an objective test when deciding this.

This defence will not prevent the owner of the rights from enforcing remedies other than damages, such as an injunction and delivery up.

(b) *Use of recordings made without consent of the performer*

12.26   Under section 183 of the 1988 Act, a performer's rights are infringed by a person who, without his consent:

(a) shows or plays in public the whole or any substantial part of a qualifying performance; or

(b) broadcasts or includes in a cable programme service the whole or any substantial part of a qualifying performance;

by means of a recording which was, and which that person knows or has reason to believe was, made without the performer's consent.

The requirement of knowledge reappears here, but not as stringently as in the Performers' Protection Acts. Under the 1988 Act it will be necessary for the person seeking to enforce these rights to prove that the recording was, in fact, made without the performer's consent and that the infringer knew or "had reason to believe" that the recording was made without the performer's consent. The meaning of "reason to believe" has already been discussed in relation to infringement of copyright (see section 6.06) and much the same considerations apply here. It will also be necessary to prove that one of the infringing acts mentioned above has taken place without the consent of the performer.

The burden of proof will be on the plaintiff, whereas under section 182 of the 1988 Act, covering performer's rights in relation to recordings and live transmission, the onus was on the defendant to show that he believed that on reasonable grounds consent had been given. It is therefore likely that it will be more difficult to enforce the rights relating to use of recordings made without consent, than it will be to enforce the right against the making of the recording or the live transmission.

The consent of the performer is required not only for the making of the recording in the first place, but also for the act of showing or playing in public or broadcasting or including in a cable programme service. Both consents must be missing before these rights are infringed. For example, if the recording is made with consent, its subsequent playing in public will not infringe the rights of the performer, even if no consent for the playing in public has been given.

In some respects, the rights granted in section 183 are more limited than those under the Performers' Protection Acts, but overall they are much wider. Under the Performers' Protection Acts it was an offence to use a recording made without consent for the purposes of a "public performance." In section 183 the acts restricted are "showing or playing in public," which are the restricted acts contained in section 19(3) of the 1988 Act, and which are more limited than "public performance."

On the other hand, the Performers' Protection Acts only restricted broadcast and inclusion of a performance in a cable programme "otherwise than by the use of a record or cinematograph film." This meant that only live performances would be covered. Section 183 extends the rights of a performer to cover broadcast and inclusion in a cable programme by means of a recording.

(c) *Infringement by importing, possessing or dealing with illicit recordings*

Section 184 of the 1988 Act includes the third set of rights of a performer.   **12.27**
This provides that performer's rights are infringed by a person who, without his consent:

(a) imports into the United Kingdom otherwise than for his private and domestic use; or

(b) in the course of a business possesses, sell or lets for hire, offers or exposes for sale or distributes;

a recording of a qualifying performance which is, and which that person knows or has reason to believe is, an illicit recording.

For these purposes, an illicit recording is a recording of the whole or any substantial part of a performance of a performer, if it is made, otherwise than for private purposes, without the performer's consent. This definition is contained in section 197(2) of the 1988 Act. Some other recordings described in Schedule 2 to the 1988 Act are also included (see paragraph 12.43), but otherwise no recording made in accordance with the provisions set out in Schedule 2 will be an illicit recording. The expression "private purposes" is not defined. It differs from the wording in section 184 itself, which refers to "private and domestic use." It is difficult to be certain whether the decision not to use the word "domestic" is significant or is intended to have any particular effect. If it is, then presumably "private purposes" are intended to cover a wider range of purposes than those which would be encompassed by the expression "private and domestic use." "Domestic" use carries a suggestion of use in the home, whereas "private" use could cover use anywhere, provided the use is private. If the recording is originally made for private purposes, that recording cannot subsequently become an illicit recording, even if it was made without the performer's consent. However, if that recording were duplicated for commercial purposes, those duplicated copies might well be illicit recordings as they would fall within the wide definition of recordings set out in secton 180(3) and would be made without the performer's consent.

Section 184 sets out a series of acts involving illicit recordings which will infringe the rights of the performer if done without his consent. Section 184 introduces two entirely new rights, which did not previously exist. The first is the right to prevent importation of an illicit recording of a performance of a qualifying performer, except where such importation is for the importer's private and domestic use. The second is the right to prevent a third party possessing such an illicit recording in the course of a business.

Selling or letting for hire such recordings must now be done "in the course of a business" before the performer's rights will be infringed. This was not a requirement of the Performers' Protection Acts. Otherwise, apart from the two entirely new rights mentioned above, the scope of the rights conferred by section 184 of the 1988 Act are comparable to the equivalent provisions of the Performers' Protection Acts, with the exception of the replacement of the words "by way of trade" and "for the purposes of trade" by the words "in the course of a business."

In addition, the requirement of knowledge is less onerous under the 1988 Act than it was under the Performers' Protection Acts. However, it will still be necessary for the performers to prove that the infringer "knew or had reason to believe" that the relevant recording was illicit, and the burden of proof will fall on him. He will also have to prove that the recording was, in fact, an illicit recording.

As in the case of section 183, the consent of the performer is required at two stages. The first is to the making of the recording. The second is to the doing of the act restricted by section 184. The consents are required at different times. The absence of both consents must be established before the section 184 rights are infringed.

In section 184(2) there is a separate partial defence to an infringement action brought under section 184 by a performer. Where, in such an action, a defendant shows that the illicit recording was innocently acquired by him, or a predecessor in title of his, the only remedy available against him in respect of the infringement is damages not exceeding a reasonable payment in respect of the act complained of. There is no indication as to what is "reasonable" and this will be up to the court to decide. It will probably be related to the rate of royalty which would have been required for a legitimate use. However there seems ample scope for producing evidence of damage to a court in a case like this. It is not entirely clear whether this provision will prevent the other ancillary remedies, such as delivery up, seizure, forfeiture and destruction (see paragraph 12.42) being available to a plaintiff in circumstances where this partial defence is proved. It could be argued either way, but it is thought that these ancillary remedies were not intended to be affected by section 184(2).

The expression "innocently acquired" is defined in section 184(3) and means that the person acquiring the recording did not know and had no reason to believe that it was an illicit recording. The burden is on the defendant to show that the recording was innocently acquired. This may be fairly difficult because, for this defence to become relevant, the plaintiff will have had to prove that, at the time of importation, for example, the defendant knew or had reason to believe that it was an illicit recording. The defendant will have to show that he only discovered that the recording was illicit after he, or a predecessor in title of his, acquired it.

D. RIGHTS OF PERSON HAVING RECORDING RIGHTS

Entirely new rights have been introduced by the 1988 Act. These are conferred on "persons having recording rights."   **12.28**

1. Definitions

To understand the new provisions, it is worth first examining some detailed definitions before going on to look at the new rights themselves.   **12.29**

(a) *Exclusive recording contract*

Before any rights can vest in a person, there must be an "exclusive recording contract." By virtue of section 185(1) of the 1988 Act, this means a contract between a performer and another person under which that other person is entitled, to the exclusion of all other persons (including the performer) to make recordings of one or more of his performances with a view to their commercial exploitation. "With a view to their commercial exploitation" is defined in section 185(4) to mean, "with a view to the recordings being sold or let for hire or shown or played in public." It seems that there is no requirement in the case of showing or playing in public that any fee or charge should be made to those to whom it is shown or played.   **12.30**

The contract does not have to be long-term. It can relate to one performance only, provided that the contract is exclusive. Also there seems no requirement that the contract must be in writing. However, in practice, it would be most unusual for such a contract to be oral. Recordings has the wide meaning discussed in paragraph 12.13 and includes both films and sound recordings.

(b) *Qualifying person*

The right will vest in the "person having recording rights." In order to discover who this is, it is necessary to look at one further definition, that of "qualifying person," which is found in section 206. It means a qualifying individual or a body corporate or other body having legal personality which   **12.31**

(a) is formed under the law of a part of the United Kingdom or another qualifying country; and

(b) has in any qualifying country a place of business at which substantial business activity is carried on.

Qualifying country has the same meaning in this context as in relation to the rights of performers. (See paragraph 12.21.)

Section 206(3) gives some guidance as to what is meant by substantial business activity. In determining whether substantial business activity is carried on at a place of business in any country, no account shall be taken of dealings in goods which are at all material times outside that country. There is no requirement to disregard services in such circumstances, although this may be implied. Presumably the intention here is to prevent people setting up shell companies in order to obtain rights under Part II of the 1988 Act. What is meant by "substantial" is not clear, but it implies at least some quantitative requirement. There is no requirement that the business activity should relate to the recording business, and it could presumably be in any business, whether dealing in goods or services.

(c) *Person having recording rights*

12.32   Section 185(2) provides that the "person having recording rights" in relation to a performance is the person

(a) who is party to and has the benefit of an exclusive recording contract to which the performance is subject; or

(b) to whom the benefit of such a contract has been assigned;

and who is a qualifying person.

First of all, therefore, one has to look and see whether there exists an exclusive recording contract. If that exists, then one must look at the performance in question and see whether that performance is covered by the exclusive recording contract. Then one must identify the person who is both a party to and has the benefit of the exclusive recording contract. If he is a qualifying person, he will be the person having recording rights. If he has assigned the benefit of the exclusive recording contract to a third party, he will cease to have the benefit of it and will cease to be a "person having recording rights" by virtue of that contract. The third party will replace him as the "person having recording rights" provided that that third party is a qualifying person.

There are provisions covering the situation where neither the original contracting person nor an assignee is a qualifying person and these will be dealt with below. However, it is interesting to see the way in which section 185(2) can work. For example, where the original contracting party is not a qualifying person, then he will not be a "person having recording rights" and it may well be that there is no such person in existence. However, if that person subsequently assigns the benefit of the contract to a third party who is a qualifying person, then that third party will then become the "person having recording rights," notwithstanding that no such person existed before the assignment. Of course, this could work the other way around where the original contracting party is a qualifying person and the assignee is not. Whilst the original contracting party retains the benefit of the contract, he will be the "person having recording rights". As soon as he assigns to the party who is not a qualifying person, then neither he nor the assignee will be the "person having the recording rights" and it may be that no such person will exist.

Section 185(3) does provide some relief in the situation just discussed. This subsection covers the situation where a performance is subject to an exclusive recording contract, but the relevant person who would normally have the rights under section 185(2) is not a qualifying person. Under those circumstances, "the person having recording rights" in relation to the performances is any person

(a) who is licensed by the non-qualifying person to make recordings of the performance with a view to their commercial exploitation; or

(b) to whom the benefit of such a licence has been assigned;

who, in either case, is a qualifying person.

"With a view to commercial exploitation" has the same meaning as above (see paragraph 12.30).

Section 185(3) envisages a person who is licensed by the non-qualifying person to make recordings of the performance with a view to their commercial exploitation. There is no requirement under section 185(3) that such a person licensed should be exclusively licensed. All that is required is that he should be a qualifying person and have an appropriate licence from a non-qualifying person in appropriate circumstances. That licence could be either to make recordings from live performances, or alternatively, because of the extended definition of "recording" in section 180, to reproduce recordings which are made directly or indirectly from a recording of the live performance. So, the existence of a non-exclusive master-tape licence in favour of a licensee might be sufficient to establish that person as a "person having recording rights." If that person were to assign the non-exclusive licence to another person, then that other person, providing that he is a qualifying person, will become the "person having recording rights." If more than one non-exclusive licence is granted, then there may be several "persons having recording rights."

However, it must be remembered that for there to be any "person having recording rights," there must be an exclusive recording contract and the performance must be subject to that contract. It is only where for some reason the person who would otherwise have the recording rights is not a qualifying person, that the rather curious position just discussed can arise. Given these rather complicated rules, it is not always going to be easy to establish who is the "person who has recording rights" or how many of them there are in relation to a particular performance.

Finally it is worth noting that, for the purposes of the rights conferred on persons having recording rights, it does not matter who the performer is or where the performance takes place. What is important is that the "person having recording rights" is a qualifying person and that the contractual requirements are satisfied.

2. Rights conferred

As in the case of the rights of a performer, the rights of a person having **12.33** recording rights are infringed in three different sets of circumstances. The first is where a recording is made without his consent of a performance subject to an exclusive contract. The second is where use is made of recordings made without appropriate consent. The third is where illicit recordings are imported, possessed or dealt with. Each set of rights will be dealt with separately.

(a) *Making of recordings*

12.34 This is covered by section 186. It provides that a person infringes the rights of a person having recording rights in relation to a performance who, without the consent either of such rights owner or the consent of the performer, makes a recording of the whole or any substantial part of the performance, otherwise than for the private and domestic use of the person making the recording.

It is worth noting that the rights under section 186 of the person having recording rights can be defeated entirely by the performer who can give consent in relation to a performance, notwithstanding the existence of the exclusive recording contract. Clearly, it will now become usual in recording contracts to cover this situation by an appropriate undertaking by the performer not to give such consent. The performer cannot assign his right, but he can bind himself contractually not to give consent. Breach of such a contract will give to the person having recording rights a right of action against the performer, but it will not normally affect the position of the infringer. This might not be the case where the infringer knew of the contractual terms and induced a breach of them.

The expressions "substantial part" and "private and domestic use" are not defined in relation to these rights. However, see paragraphs 12.25 and 5.09.

In an action for infringement of section 186 rights, damages will not be awarded against a defendant who shows that at the time of the infringement he believed on reasonable grounds that consent had been given. This defence is similar to that applying under section 182. (See paragraph 12.25.)

Section 186 does not cover live broadcasts or live inclusions in a cable programme service of a performance. These acts may infringe the rights of the performer, but not of the person having recording rights.

(b) *Use of recordings made without consent*

12.35 Section 187 grants additional rights to a person having recording rights, which are roughly equivalent to those contained in section 183 in relation to a performer. (See paragraph 12.26.) There are some differences. Most importantly, the performance concerned under section 187 does not have to be a qualifying performance.

Under section 187, a person infringes the rights of a person having recording rights in relation to a performance who, without the consent of the rights' owner, or, in the case of a qualifying performance, the consent of the performer

(a) shows or plays in public the whole or any substantial part of the performance; or

(b) broadcasts or includes in a cable programme service the whole or any substantial part of the performance;

by means of a recording which was, and which that person knows or has reason to believe was, made without the appropriate consent.

Appropriate consent, means either the consent of a performer or the consent of the person who, at the time that the consent was given, had recording rights in relation to the performance (or if there was more than one such person, the consent of all of them).

The principal elements of this right have been discussed in relation to section 183. (See paragraph 12.26.) First of all, there has to be in existence a recording of a performance which was made without appropriate consent. In all cases, whether the performance is qualifying or non-qualifying, the consent of the performer will be sufficient and will defeat the rights of the person having recording rights. In the absence of such consent, the consent of all the persons having recording rights in the particular performance will be required. As has been discussed above, there could be quite a large number of persons having recording rights in relation to a performance and it may not be easy to identify all or any of them. This is clearly an area of possible difficulty.

As in the case of section 183, it is necessary to show that recording was made without appropriate consent and that the person infringing the section 187 right knew or had reason to believe that the recording was made without the appropriate consent. The burden of proof is therefore on the person seeking to enforce the right.

In addition, consent is required to the doing of the acts listed in section 187. The consent of the rights owner will suffice in all cases. The consent of the performer will suffice in the case only of a qualifying performance, as an alternative to obtaining the consent of the rights owner. As in the case of performers' rights, the rights in section 187 are only infringed if neither consent for the making of the recording nor for its subsequent exploitation was obtained. Either consent would prevent infringement of section 187 rights taking place.

(c) *Importing, possessing or dealing with illicit recordings*

Section 188 is the equivalent of section 184 which confers similar rights on a performer. (See paragraph 12.27.) However, again there are differences. **12.36**

It is necessary to look at the definition of "illicit recording" contained in section 197. In relation to a person having recording rights, it means a recording of the whole or any substantial part of a performance subject to the exclusive recording contract, if it is made otherwise than for private purposes, without the consent of the rights owner or that of the performer. It also includes some recordings described in Schedule 2 to the 1988 Act (see paragraph 12.43), but otherwise no recording made in accordance with the provisions set out in Schedule 2 will be an illicit recording. Once again, one has the rather curious use of "for private purposes". See paragraph 12.27 for an examination of the meaning of this expression and of the effect of subsequent commercial use of a recording originally made for private purposes. Also, the consent of the performer can always defeat the rights of the person having recording rights, and this is so whether or not the performance recorded is a qualifying performance.

Section 188 provides that a person infringes the rights of a person having recording rights in relation to a performance who, without the rights owner's consent or, in the case of a qualifying performance, that of the performer

(a) imports into the United Kingdom otherwise than for his private and domestic use; or

(b) in the course of a business, possesses, sells or lets for hire, offers or exposes for sale or hire or distributes;

a recording of the performance which is, and which that person knows or has reason to believe is, an illicit recording.

As in section 187, there is no requirement here that there should be a recording of a "qualifying" performance. However, the consent of the performer to the doing of the acts set out in section 188 will only be adequate in the case of a qualifying performance.

As in section 184, the burden of proof falls on the rights owner to prove that the recording is an illicit recording and that the infringer knew or had reason to believe that the recording was an illicit recording.

There is a defence in section 188(2) of innocent acquisition, which is the same as that in section 184, save of course, that the definition of "illicit recording" is different. (See paragraph 12.27.)

E. EXCEPTIONS TO RIGHTS CONFERRED

12.37 There are a number of exceptions to the new rights of performers and persons having recording rights. These take the form of permitted acts and there are also provisions enabling consent to be given on behalf of a performer by the Copyright Tribunal in certain circumstances.

1. Permitted Acts

12.38 Section 189 provides that the acts set out in schedule 2 to the 1988 Act may be done without infringing any of the rights conferred by Part II of the 1988 Act. Schedule 2 lists a large number of permitted acts, which by and large follow the relevant permitted acts in relation to infringement of copyright. The list is not co-extensive with the copyright permitted acts, which are more numerous. It is not intended to go through these in detail here as the permitted acts in relation to infringement of copyright have been dealt with at length in Chapter 7 of this book. However, a list of the permitted acts follows.

Paragraph 1 of schedule 2 approximately mirrors the provisions of section 28 of the 1988 Act.

Paragraph 2 of schedule 2 is the equivalent of section 30 (Criticism, reviews and news reporting).

Paragraph 3 of schedule 2 is the equivalent of section 31 (Incidental inclusion of performance or recording).

Paragraph 4 of schedule 2 is the equivalent of section 32 (Things done for purposes of instruction or examination).

Paragraph 5 of schedule 2 is the equivalent of section 34 (Playing or showing sound recording, film, broadcast or cable programme at educational establishment).

Paragraph 6 of schedule 2 is the equivalent of section 35 (Recording of broadcasts and cable programmes by educational establishments).

Paragraph 7 of schedule 2 is the equivalent of section 44 (Copy of work required to be made as condition of export).

Paragraph 8 of schedule 2 is the equivalent of section 45 (Parliamentary and judicial proceedings).

Paragraph 9 of schedule 2 is the equivalent of section 46 (Royal commissions and statutory inquiries).

Paragraph 10 of schedule 2 is the equivalent of section 49 (Public records).

Paragraph 11 of schedule 2 is the equivalent of section 50 (Acts done under statutory authority).

Paragraph 12 of schedule 2 is the equivalent of section 56 (Transfer of copies of works in an electronic form).

Paragraph 13 of schedule 2 is the equivalent of section 58 (Use of recordings of spoken works in certain cases).

Paragraph 14 of schedule 2 is the equivalent of section 61 (Recordings of folk songs).

Paragraph 15 of schedule 2 is the equivalent of section 67 (Playing of sound recordings for purposes of club, society, etc.).

Paragraph 16 of schedule 2 is the equivalent of section 68 (Incidental recordings for purposes of broadcast or cable programme).

Paragraph 17 of schedule 2 is the equivalent of section 69 (Recordings for purposes of supervision and control of broadcasts and cable programmes).

Paragraph 18 of schedule 2 is the equivalent of section 72 (Free public showing or playing of broadcast or cable programme).

Paragraph 19 of schedule 2 is the equivalent of section 73 (Reception and retransmission of broadcast in cable programme service).

Paragraph 20 of schedule 2 is the equivalent of section 74 (Provision of sub-titled copies of broadcast or cable programme).

Paragraph 21 of schedule 2 is the equivalent of section 75 (Recording of broadcast or cable programme for archival purposes).

2. The Copyright Tribunal

Section 190 provides that the Copyright Tribunal may give consent on   **12.39** behalf of a performer in certain cases. These only arise in the case where someone wishes to make a recording of an existing recording, and would not cover the making of a recording of a live performance. Performers will in future need to be careful when agreeing to contractual limitations on their right to give consent. In such cases, the performer should always exclude any liability in a case where the Copyright Tribunal gives consent on the performer's behalf.

Section 190 provides that the Copyright Tribunal may, on the application of a person wishing to make a recording from a previous recording of a performance, give consent in a case where

(a) the identity or whereabouts of a performer cannot be ascertained with reasonable inquiry; or

(b) a performer unreasonably withholds his consent.

The consent given by the Tribunal has effect as consent of the performer for the purposes of the provisions of Part II dealing with the rights of the performer and also in relation to section 198(3)(a), which deals with criminal liability.

The consent may be given subject to any conditions specified in the Tribunal's order. It is provided that the Tribunal should not give consent where the identity or whereabouts of a performer cannot be ascertained by reasonable inquiry, except after the service or publication of notices, as set out in section 190(3).

Where a performer unreasonably withholds his consent, the Tribunal should not give consent unless satisfied that the performer's reasons for withholding consent do not include the protection of any legitimate interest of his. However, it is for the performer to show what his reasons are for withholding consent and in default of evidence as to his reasons, the Tribunal may draw such inferences as it thinks fit. There is no indication of what is meant by "legitimate interests." However, it is thought that it would include the question of how much the performer should be paid for giving his consent.

The Tribunal is obliged under section 190(5) to take into account the following factors:

(a) Whether the original recording was made with the performer's consent and is lawfully in the possession or control of the person proposing to make the further recording;

(b) Whether the making of the further recording is consistent with the obligations of the parties to the arrangements under which or is otherwise consistent with the purposes for which, the original recording was made.

This seems to imply that the Tribunal should look favourably on any application for consent where these factors can be answered in the affirmative. It is also implicit that the Tribunal could, in an appropriate case, grant consent even though the performer had not consented to the making of the recording in the first place.

One would suspect that in the normal course of events, if the recording was made with the performer's consent in the first place, the person making the recording will ensure that he has obtained at the same time all other consents he may require to exploit the recordings. However, it must be remembered that the 1988 Act applies to performances rendered prior to the commencement of the 1988 Act and it may be that the consents obtained when the performance was given did not envisage the introduction of civil rights of the kind contained in Part II of the 1988 Act. It is presumably for this reason that the second factor listed above is included.

Also, it is possible that permissions might not have been obtained for the making of recordings for purposes not known when the recording was made, such as satellite broadcasts. This provision will enable consent to be obtained for such uses subject to safeguards. It will also prevent one performer, perhaps not a very important one, from standing in the way of a use of a recording which most other performers on the recording have consented to. It will also cover the situation where a performer cannot be traced.

Finally, it is provided in section 190(6) that, where the Tribunal gives consent, it shall in default of an agreement between the applicant and the performer, make such order as it thinks fit as to the payment to be made to the performer in consideration of consent being given. Once again, one can see that there is going to be a great deal of scope for argument in front of the Copyright Tribunal and no doubt a body of precedent will be built up in time. However, to begin with, the Tribunal is going to have to feel its way through a mass of evidence, which no doubt will conflict wildly.

F. DURATION AND TRANSMISSION OF RIGHTS

One of the difficulties in the *Rickless* case (see paragraph 12.02) was the **12.40** question of how long a performer should have rights under the Performers' Protection Acts and also the question of what was to happen to those rights on his death. In *Rickless*, the Court of Appeal decided that the rights would indeed last forever, even though this is clearly a longer period of protection than that conferred in the case of copyright. It was also decided that the rights would be exercisable by the performer's personal representative after his death. As discussed above (see paragraph 12.02) the Performers' Protection Acts are going to have limited importance in future, inasmuch as they will only apply to acts done before the commencement of the 1988 Act.

Under the 1988 Act it is expressly provided that the rights conferred by Part II of the 1988 Act continue to subsist in relation to a performance until the end of the period of 50 years from the end of the calendar year from which the performance takes place. This period is generally likely to be the same as the period of copyright protection in a sound recording or film, except where that sound recording or film is released after the end of the calendar year in which it is made, but within 50 years from that year. (See paragraph 4.58.) The two rights are, of course, quite unrelated. As

Part II of the 1988 Act applies to performances given prior to the commencement of Part II, performances given in the last 50 years are going to be eligible for the new rights, subject to the relevant requirements being satisfied.

Section 192 of the 1988 Act deals with the transmission of rights. It is expressly provided that the rights conferred by Part II of the 1988 Act are not assignable. Performers' rights are transmissible, but only in accordance with the provisions set out in section 192. Section 192 also provides that the provisions of section 185(2)(*b*) and (3)(*b*), which relate to the rights of a person having recording rights, are an exception to this prohibition on assignment. These provisions cover the case where an exclusive recording contract is assigned to a third party or where a licence to make recordings is assigned, in either case in circumstances where the assignee has rights conferred by section 185 of the 1988 Act. It is clear that the rights of the person having recording rights are not freely assignable and are tied to the existence of an exclusive recording contract and must generally follow that exclusive recording contract. If that contract expires or is terminated the rights will expire. Very often an exclusive recording contract will entitle the recording company to exploit recordings for the life of copyright. However, this is not always the case. What is really important is the term during which the recording company is exclusively entitled to record the performances of the performer. The recording company's rights will only arise in respect of performances rendered during that term. It will usually be apparent fairly soon after a performance if recordings have been illegally made and to this extent the duration and assignability of recording company's rights may not be crucially important.

So far as the rights of a performer are concerned, his performer's rights will pass to such person as he may by testamentary disposition specifically direct. There is no definition of what is meant by "specifically direct." However, it is submitted that this means that the rights must be expressly referred to in the will, otherwise the word "specifically" would be unnecessary. Similar wording is used in relation to moral rights in section 95 of the 1988 Act. (See paragraph 11.38.)

If there is no such direction in a performer's will, or if there is no will, the performer's rights are exercisable by his personal representatives, for so long as the rights subsist. In view of the fact that performances given over the last 50 years may be covered, a large number of performers whose performances will be covered by the 1988 Act will already have died. Problems may arise in identifying the personal representatives in some cases. The Copyright Tribunal may not be of assistance here, as it is not a case where the identity or whereabouts of a performer cannot be ascertained, but rather the identity or whereabouts of the performers personal representatives. (See paragraph 12.39.)

Section 192 provides that references in Part II of the 1988 Act to the performer, in the context of the person having performer's rights, shall be construed as references to the person for the time being entitled to exercise those rights. Therefore, after the death of a performer, where the consent of a performer is required in any particular circumstance, it will be necessary to investigate whether the performer left a will and, if so, whether it contained any disposition specifically directing that the performer's rights should pass to any particular person or persons.

Section 192(3) covers the situation where a performer specifically directs by testamentary disposition that his performer's rights will pass to more than one person. Section 193(3) provides that in these circumstances a right is exercisable by each of such persons "independently of the other or others." This means that any one of such persons can enforce the right against a third party. The question arises as to whether one of such persons could give a consent which would be binding on the others. Section 193 does not expressly deal with consents, which are dealt with in section 194. Unfortunately, section 194 does not deal expressly with the question of what is to happen in these circumstances.

There are two express references in Part II of the 1988 Act to the consent of *all* rights owners being required. These are where "appropriate consent" is required under section 187 and where "sufficient consent" is required under section 198. Under these circumstances, one would have expected the 1988 Act to provide expressly that the consents of all persons were required where more than one person inherits by testamentary disposition. However, in view of the fact that the rights are exercisable by each such person independently of the other or others, it does suggest that the consent of all of them would be required. It is analogous to the situation where there are joint owners of copyright. Either owner may sue for infringement of copyright independently of the other. But, the consent of all copyright owners is required to the use of the copyright work.

Section 192(5) provides that any damages recovered by personal representatives by virtue of section 192 in respect of an infringement after a person's death, shall devolve as part of his estate as if the action had subsisted and been vested in him immediately before his death. This section is in exactly the same terms as section 95(6) dealing with moral rights (see paragraph 11.38). Essentially the same considerations will apply. Any damages recovered by personal representatives will form part of the estate of the deceased performer and be distributed in accordance with whatever rules govern the distribution of the particular estate. If the right of action accrues before the performer's death, then that right of action will form part of the estate and be dealt with accordingly.

The wording of section 192(3) clearly permits a performer to direct that his performer's rights will go to more than one person. However, it makes no provision permitting the rights of the performer to be divided up so that some rights go to one person and some to another, as is permitted in the case of moral rights. (See paragraph 11.38.) One could envisage a situation where one person would have control of the showing and playing in public and broadcast and inclusion in a cable programme service of performances of a deceased individual and another person would have the right to prevent importation and sales of recordings of such performances. However, the 1988 Act does not specifically permit this and it is probably therefore not possible to do it. The wording of section 192(1) is restrictive, in that it provides that the rights are not transmissible "except to the extent that performer's rights are transmissible in accordance with the following provisions." As the provisions do not expressly cover this situation, it seems unlikely that such a splitting of rights will be permitted.

G. CONSENT

12.41   Perhaps the biggest departure from the Performers' Protection Acts is that it is not now necessary for the consent of the performer to be in writing. An oral consent will be sufficient, as would consent by conduct. An oral consent will also suffice in relation to the new rights conferred on persons having recording rights. The effect of this is likely to be that it will be much easier for those requiring consent to prove that consent was in fact obtained. For example, it would be quite difficult for a performer to argue that he has not consented to a recording being made, where he voluntarily went to the recording or film studio and allowed the recording to be made, knowing exactly what was going on. Of course, arguments will arise as to the extent of the consent and what acts beyond the simple making of the recording were consented to. Here again, one can see plenty of scope for litigation and a great deal of conflicting evidence. Any problems should be forestalled by careful documentation.

Section 193 deals with consent for the purposes of Part II of the 1988 Act. It is provided that consent may be given in relation to a specific performance, a specified description of performances or performances generally, and may relate to past or future performances. Clearly in future it is going to be even more important to ensure that adequate consents are provided for in recording contracts. The wording of such consent clauses will have to be carefully drafted from the performer's point of view as well, particularly where the performer is also a creator of copyright works and an owner of moral rights. It is easy to envisage a situation where a performer may give consent to recordings of his performances being made. If that consent refers generally to all rights under the 1988 Act, then it may be wide enough to cover the recording of copyright works under Part I of the 1988 Act and may cover moral rights as well. Any consent given by a performer should clearly define the scope of the consent being made and, in all circumstances, be limited strictly to rights conferred by Part II of the 1988 Act.

Section 193(2) of the 1988 Act provides that a person having recording rights in a performance is bound by any consent given by a person through whom he derives his rights under the exclusive recording contract or licence in question, in the same way as if the consent had been given by him. The wording of this provision is quite wide and would seem to cover the consent of the performer, which, in any event, will usually override the consent of the person having recording rights. It will also cover consents given by predecessors in title to persons having recording rights by way of an assignment of contract or licence. It seems the predecessor in title could give consent at any time, even after the assignment has taken place. The wording of the subsection is certainly wide enough to include this meaning.

One could also envisage the situation where consent might be given under section 185(3) by a person who is not a qualifying person, but who would otherwise be a person having recording rights. In such a case a person having recording rights under section 185(3) will "derive his rights" through a person who is not a qualifying person. If the non-qualifying person gave a consent, it would be binding on the qualifying person who in fact holds the rights.

Section 193(3) provides that where a right conferred by Part II of the 1988 Act passes to another person, any consent binding on the person previously entitled, will bind the person to whom the right passes, in the same way as if the consent had been given by the person to whom the right passes. This seems quite logical and will protect recipients of consents.

Section 193 does not deal expressly with the question of whether a duly authorised person can give consent on behalf of a person whose consent is required under Part II of the 1988 Act. It was expressly provided for in section 7 of the 1958 Act, but this was in the context of a defence to a criminal offence. Even though not expressly mentioned, there seems no reason on general agency principles why a person cannot authorise another person to give consent on his behalf for the purposes of the 1988 Act. This would be consistent with the relaxing of the requirement that consent be given in writing. Also, it would be consistent with section 201 of the 1988 Act, which makes it a criminal offence for a person to represent falsely that he is authorised to give consent for the purposes of Part II of the 1988 Act in relation to a performance, unless he believes on reasonable grounds that he is so authorised. This clearly presupposes that consent can be given for these purposes.

H. REMEDIES FOR INFRINGEMENT

The civil remedy provided is, as in the case of moral rights, breach of   **12.42**
statutory duty. Like moral rights, rights in performances are not property rights. Any infringement of the rights conferred by Part II of the 1988 Act is actionable by the person entitled to the right as a breach of statutory duty. The remedies available will include injunctions and damages. It will also be possible to use remedies such as Anton Piller orders and Mareva injunctions. However, in the case of the rights in Part II, additional remedies are provided. There are also criminal sanctions for breaches of rights in performances, which are not available in the case of breaches of moral rights.

The quantification of damages for infringement may not always be straightforward. The normal rules for assessing damages will apply. The court will consider the consequences of the breach. Also, it may be relevant to consider the sort of remuneration a person might have received in respect of the wrongful use of the right infringed, had such use been legitimate.

In section 195 of the 1988 Act, provisions similar to those in section 99 of the 1988 Act are incorporated giving a person having performer's rights or recording rights in relation to a performance, a right to delivery up of illicit recordings of that performance. The rights contained in section 195 are, to all intents and purposes, identical to those in section 99 of the 1988 Act, which relate to infringing copies. (See paragraph 10.103.)

Section 196 gives a right to seize illicit recordings to any person who would be entitled to apply for an order under section 195 of the 1988 Act. Again, these provisions mirror those contained in section 100 of the 1988 Act which relate to infringing copies. (See paragraph 10.102.)

Sections 203, 204 and 205 contain ancillary provisions relating to orders for delivery up similar to those contained in sections 113, 114 and 115 of the 1988 Act relating to infringing copies. (See paragraph 10.104.)

I. ILLICIT RECORDINGS

12.43 The concept of illicit recordings has been discussed already, but it is perhaps worth setting out the definitions contained in section 197 of the 1988 Act.

For the purposes of a performer's rights, a recording of the whole or any substantial part of a performance of his is an illicit recording if it is made, otherwise than for private purposes, without his consent. The meaning of this has already been discussed at paragraph 12.27. For the purposes of the rights of a person having recording rights, a recording of the whole or any substantial part of a performance subject to the exclusive recording contract is an illicit recording if it is made, other than for private purposes, without his consent or that of the performer. The meaning of this definition has been discussed more fully above. (See paragraph 12.36.)

For the purposes of the criminal offences, a recording is an illicit recording if it is an illicit recording for the purposes set out in the two definitions above.

In addition "illicit recording" will include any recording falling to be treated as an illicit recording by virtue of the following provisions of schedule 2 to the 1988 Act (which deals with permitted acts):

(a) Paragraph 4(3) (recordings made for the purposes of instruction or examination).

(b) Paragraph 6(2) (recordings made by educational establishments for educational purposes).

(c) Paragraph 12(2) (recordings of performance in electronic form retained on transfer of principal recording).

(d) Paragraph 16(3) (recordings made for purposes of broadcast or cable programme).

In all these instances, there are mirror provisions which relate to permitted acts in relation to infringement of copyright. Paragraph 4(3) is equivalent to section 32(5). Paragraph 6(2) is equivalent to section 35(3). Paragraph 12(2) is equivalent to section 56(2). Paragraph 16(3) is equivalent to section 68(4). These are discussed more fully in relation to infringement of copyright. (See Chapter 7.)

Section 197 provides that, except for those exceptions just listed, a recording made in accordance with any of the provisions of Schedule 2 is not an "an illicit recording."

Section 197(6) expressly states that for the purposes of deciding whether a recording is an "illicit recording," it is immaterial where the recording was made. It would therefore cover recordings made in non-qualifying countries. However, to enforce rights in relation to illicit recordings a person having recording rights must be a qualifying person and this will involve the person seeking to enforce the right satisfying the qualifications set out earlier in this chapter. A performer can only enforce rights in relation to an illicit recording, if that illicit recording is of a qualifying performance, and the qualification requirements set out earlier in this chapter will have to be satisfied in relation to that performance. A person having recording rights can enforce those rights in relation to an illicit recording of a performance, whether it is qualifying or not, subject to all the other necessary requirements being satisfied.

J. OFFENCES UNDER THE 1988 ACT

A number of criminal offences are created in Part II of the 1988 Act.   **12.44**
These are set out in section 198 of the 1988 Act.

A further definition must be considered in relation to criminal offences. This is the concept of "sufficient consent."

In the case of a qualifying performance, this means the consent of the performer.

In the case of a non-qualifying performance subject to an exclusive recording contract, it means

(a) in the case of recordings made for sale or hire, the consent of the performer or the person having recording rights; and

(b) for all other purposes of section 198, the consent of the person having recording rights.

Sufficient consent can also be given in relation to a qualifying performance, in appropriate circumstances, on behalf of a performer by the Copyright Tribunal. (See paragraph 12.39.)

References in this definition to the person having recording rights are to the person having those rights at the time the consent is given or, if there is more than one such person, to all of them. This means that in order to avoid criminal liability, consent may have to be obtained from a large number of persons. The effect of this has been discussed above (see paragraph 12.32) in relation to civil remedies.

It is important to note that consent in relation to criminal proceedings is now not required to be in writing, as was required under the Performers' Protection Acts.

The new criminal offences are listed in section 198(1) and (2).

A person commits an offence, who, without sufficient consent:

(a) makes for sale or hire; or

(b) imports into the United Kingdom otherwise than for his private and domestic use; or

(c) possesses in the course of a business with a view to committing any act infringing the rights conferred by Part II of the 1988 Act; or

(d) in the course of a business sells or lets for hire; or offers or exposes for sale or hire; or distributes;

a recording which is, and which he knows or has reason to believe is, an illicit recording.

These are the offences contained in section 198(1) and it is perhaps worth commenting on these offences before going on to those contained in section 198(2). The requirement of knowledge has been watered down from that set out in the Performers' Protection Acts so that it is now only necessary to prove that the offender "has reason to to believe" that a recording is an illicit recording. The meaning of this has been discussed above. (See paragraph 6.06.)

In order to secure a conviction under section 198(1), a large number of matters will have to be proved. First, it will be necessary to prove that the person did not have "sufficient consent." As consent can now be given orally, lack of consent may be more difficult to prove than was previously the case.

It will also be necessary to prove that the recording is an illicit recording. In order to prove this, it is necessary to prove that it was made otherwise than for private purposes (note the change from private and domestic use only) and that it was made without the requisite consent, which again could be oral.

Thirdly, it is necessary to prove that the offender knows or has reason to believe that the recording is an illicit recording.

Finally, in addition, it will be necessary to prove that one of the acts set out in section 198(1) has taken place. The first of these acts is that the recording is made for sale or hire. In this case it will be necessary to prove that the recording was made for these purposes. This was not a requirement under the Performers' Protection Acts. Under those Acts it was an offence just to make the record of the performance, provided that it was done knowingly. There was a defence available that the record was made for private and domestic use only. However, it was up to the defendant to prove his defence. Under the 1988 Act, the onus of proof has shifted, so that the prosecution will now have to prove that the illicit recording was made for sale or hire. Whilst it may be easier to prove the requisite knowledge, the other elements of the offence which now have to be proved may make it more difficult to secure a conviction under the new law than under the old law.

The second act deals with importation of the illicit recording into the United Kingdom otherwise than for the private and domestic use of the importer. This is a new offence, as importation was not an offence under the Performers' Protection Acts although dealings after importation could be.

The third act is possession of an illicit recording in the course of a business with a view to committing any act infringing the rights conferred by Part II of the 1988 Act. This is a rather wider offence, in most respects, than that contained in section 4 of the 1958 Act, which made it an offence for a person to have in his possession a plate or similar contrivance for the purpose of making records in contravention of the 1958 Act. However, under section 4 of the 1958 Act it was not necessary for the person to be in possession of the plate "in the course of a business," as required by the 1988 Act. Furthermore, the 1958 Act referred to possessing a "plate or similar contrivance for the purpose of making records in contravention of the 1958 Act." The 1988 Act requires possession to be "with a view to committing any act infringing the rights conferred by Part II of the 1988 Act." These infringing acts cover many more circumstances than simply the making of records in contravention of the 1988 Act.

The fourth act occurs where a person, in the course of a business, sells or lets for hire, or offers or exposes for sale or hire, or distributes an illicit recording in the requisite circumstances.

Under the 1958 Act the offence of selling or letting for hire was committed whether or not done in the course of a business. Under the 1988 Act it will only be an offence if the selling or letting for hire is done in the course of a business. Under the 1958 Act distribution was required to be "for the purposes of trade" and the offer or exposure for sale or hire or distribution was required to be "by way of trade." Under the 1988 Act, those acts are only offences, if done in the course of a business.

Section 198(2) contains two further offences. A person commits an offence who causes a recording of a performance made without sufficient consent to be:

(a) shown or played in public; or

(b) broadcast or included in a cable programme service;

thereby infringing any of the rights conferred by Part II of the 1988 Act, if he knows or has reason to believe that those rights are thereby infringed. Many of the remarks made in relation to offences under section 198(1) of the 1988 Act apply in this case as well.

To secure a conviction under this subsection, it will be necessary to prove that a recording has been made without sufficient consent. The difficulties which this may pose have been discussed already (see previous paragraph).

It will also be necessary to prove that rights conferred by Part II of the 1988 Act have been infringed by the showing or playing in public or broadcast or inclusion in a cable programme service. It will also be necessary to prove knowledge, albeit in a watered-down form, on the part of the offender.

The new offence differs considerably from the equivalent offence under the Performers' Protection Acts. Under the 1958 Act the offence was committed by a person who knowingly used for the purposes of a public performance a record made in contravention of the 1958 Act. The expression "public performance" was wider than merely "showing or playing in public." However, under the 1988 Act the requirement of knowledge is less onerous than under the 1958 Act. Under the 1988 Act it will be necessary to prove that Part II rights have been infringed by the showing or playing in public and there was no equivalent requirement under the 1958 Act.

So far as broadcast or inclusion in a cable programme service is concerned, it was not an offence under the Performers' Protection Acts to do either of these acts in relation to a recording. The offences in section 3 of the 1958 Act and section 3 of the 1963 Act, which were the equivalent provisions, related only to live performances. There are no equivalent criminal offences under the 1988 Act in relation to live performances, although there are civil remedies.

Section 198(4) of the 1988 Act provides that no offence is committed under section 198 by the commission of an act which by virtue of any provision of schedule 2 to the 1988 Act may be done without infringing the rights conferred by Part II of the 1988 Act. This means that all the permitted acts defences contained in schedule 2 will apply. These go considerably further than the special defences contained in section 6 of the 1958 Act (see paragraph 12.03).

The penalties for conviction under section 198 are set out in section 198(5) and (6).

Section 201 contains a further offence, which roughly equates to the offence contained in section 4 of the 1963 Act, dealing with the case where someone gives consent without authority. Section 201 provides that it is an offence for a person to represent falsely that he is authorised by any person to give consent for the purposes of Part II of the 1988 Act in relation to a performance, unless he believes on reasonable grounds that he is so authorised. The offence under section 4 of the 1963 Act has been discussed above (see paragraph 12.04), from which it will be seen that that offence was rather complicated and convoluted. The new offence under section 201 is very much simpler. Under the 1963 Act it had to be shown that the offender made a false representation of authority "when to his knowledge he was not so authorised." Now all the prosecution will have to prove is that a false representation of authority has been made and the defendant will then have to prove that he believed on reasonable grounds that he had the authority. The burden of proof has therefore shifted. Section 201 sets out the penalties relating to offences under that section.

Section 202 contains a further offence. Where an offence under Part II of the 1988 Act committed by a body corporate is proved to have been committed with the consent or connivance of a director, manager, secretary or other similar officer of the body, or a person purporting to act in any such capacity, he, as well as the body corporate, is guilty of the offence and liable to be proceeded against and punished accordingly. A similar provision was introduced by the 1972 Act, which inserted a new section 4(A) in the 1963 Act. The wording of section 202 is very similar to that contained in section 4(A) of the 1963 Act, except that the 1963 Act contains further wording to cover the situation where an offence was proved to be attributable to "any neglect on any part of" any director or other person as is mentioned in the section. The scope of the offence has therefore been reduced by the absence of this wording.

Section 202 goes on to provide that in relation to a body corporate whose affairs are managed by its members, a "director" means a member of the body corporate. This did not appear in the 1963 Act.

The penalties for offences under section 202 will depend on the nature of and be the same as for the offences committed by the body corporate under section 198 or section 201.

K. OTHER REMEDIES IN CRIMINAL PROCEEDINGS

Section 5 of the 1958 Act gave power to the court in criminal proceedings   **12.45**
to order destruction of various items. However, the power of destruction was limited and could, in any event, only arise where a conviction had been obtained against the offender and even then, the destruction order could only relate to items which were not only made in contravention of the 1958 Act but which were also covered by the conviction. The power was therefore subject to many limitations.

Under the 1988 Act, various further remedies are included in the case of criminal proceedings. Section 199 of the 1988 Act contains provisions relating to the forfeiture of illicit recordings which are parallel to those provisions relating to infringing copies contained in section 108 of the Act (see paragraph 10.126), dealing with criminal proceedings relating to copyright. Section 199 gives wide powers to the court to order delivery up of illicit recordings. The order can be made whether or not any person is convicted of an offence and is subject to various limitations, all of which have been discussed in relation to section 108 (see paragraph 10.126).

Section 200 gives power for search warrants to be issued in relation to illicit recordings. The provisions of section 200 are equivalent to those contained in section 109, which relates to infringing copies and section 109 is discussed above (see paragraph 10.121). It is not intended to comment further on section 200, except to say that the power of seizure appearing in section 109(4) of the 1988 Act is not repeated in section 200.

There are consequential provisions in section 204 which are similar to the consequential provisions relating to copyright contained in section 114, which relates to section 108 of the 1988 Act. Again, these are discussed above. (See paragraph 10.104.)

As is apparent, the remedies available where there has been an infringement of rights contained in Part II of the 1988 Act, are very much wider and more far-reaching than those available under the Performers' Protection Acts. It seems likely that this will encourage more people to enforce rights than was the case previously. The express creation of civil remedies will make the taking of proceedings a much safer exercise for performers. This will be even more true of persons having recording rights, who would, before the 1988 Act, have had to overcome the difficulties of *RCA Corp.* v. *Pollard* [1983] Ch. 135.

13 DESIGN RIGHT

I INTRODUCTION

In the 1988 Act the concept of an unregistered "design right" has been **13.01** introduced. This right is a property right subsisting in original designs. There is no requirement of registration and the protection afforded by the new design right is more limited than that provided in respect of artistic works under either the 1956 Act or the 1988 Act and of a shorter duration than registered design right under the Registered Designs Act 1949 ("the 1949 Act") as amended by the 1988 Act.

The 1988 Act attempts to separate the new design right from copyright and to regulate the relationship between copyright, the new design right and registered design rights. The aim of the 1988 Act is to restrict copyright in the design field to artistic, rather than industrial works and to leave the design right and registered design rights to provide protection in respect of industrial designs. Inevitably there is an overlap between the three rights.

Substantial amendments to the 1949 Act are made by the 1988 Act, extending the duration of registered design rights and altering the types of designs which will be registrable. It is not within the ambit of this book to deal with registered designs, but some reference to registered designs is necessary to appreciate the relationship between copyright, the new design right and registered design rights.

Under the 1956 Act, the full benefit of copyright protection was indirectly given in certain circumstances to ordinary functional objects of no particular artistic merit. One of the aims of the 1988 Act was to bring this situation to an end and to introduce a system which worked more logically and more fairly.

The position under the 1988 Act is, subject to a number of exceptions, as follows. Protection will be given to purely functional original designs and to certain other designs which have not been registered, for a period of between 10 and 15 years, subject to licences of right during the last five years of the term of the new design right. Designs which have "eye-appeal" and are registered as designs under the amended 1949 Act will enjoy protection for up to 25 years from the date of registration, subject to more limited compulsory licence and licence of right provisions. Copyright protection will be available for artistic works for the full copyright period of the life of the author, plus 50 years from the end of the calendar year in which the author dies. However, if an artistic work is exploited industrially and marketed, then full copyright protection will continue only for the period of 25 years from the end of the calendar year in which copies of the artistic work are first marketed. In addition, copyright protection will be cut down in certain circumstances where new designs and registered designs come into existence in relation to an artistic work.

The interrelation of copyright, the new design right and registered design rights is extremely complicated and some of the provisions of the 1988 Act are difficult to understand. As a first step, it is worthwhile briefly summarising the position of artistic works under the 1956 Act. Artistic works are the works protected by copyright which are most relevant to the area of the new design right and registered design rights. Some literary works now also have relevance, as design documents.

II EXISTING LAW BEFORE THE 1988 ACT

13.02 Under the 1956 Act artistic works protected by copyright enjoyed protection for the life of the author, plus a period of 50 years from the end of the calendar year in which the author died, subject to certain exceptions. Copyright subsisted in every original artistic work, which included, *inter alia*, any drawing irrespective of whether it had any artistic quality or not. It also included a work of artistic craftsmanship, which would require some artistic quality to qualify for protection. There were other classes of artistic works, but these two were the most important in the context of protecting designs. Of these, drawings were by far and away the most important category. See Chapter 1 for a fuller discussion of the various types of artistic works.

Under the 1956 Act, any person who did a restricted act in relation to an artistic work would infringe the copyright in that work, unless the person doing the act was the copyright owner or had the licence of the copyright owner to do the act. The only really relevant restricted act in the case of artistic works in the field of design copyright, was "reproducing the work in any material form."

In relation to an artistic work, "reproduction" is defined by the 1956 Act to include a version produced by converting the work, if in two dimensions, into a three-dimensional form, or, if it was in three dimensions, by converting it into a two-dimensional form and references to reproducing the work were construed accordingly.

Industrial drawings were held to be protected as artistic works. In view of the wide definition of "reproduction," the production of a three-dimensional object from the industrial drawing would be treated as a reproduction of the drawing. Very often, the three-dimensional object produced was not itself an object in which copyright was capable of subsisting. An obvious example is the exhaust pipe in the case of *British Leyland Motor Corporation Ltd.* v. *Armstrong Patents Co. Ltd.* [1986] 2 W.L.R. 400.

That case also confirmed that a copy of the exhaust pipe itself (rather than of the drawing) made by the process of indirect copying known as "reverse engineering," was itself a copy of the drawing, even though those who carried out the reverse engineering process never saw the original industrial drawing. Such indirect reproduction was held to amount to a reproduction of the original industrial drawing. Lord Griffiths, in a dissenting judgment in the *British Leyland* case, agreed that this is what previous cases had decided, but took the view that the previous cases were wrongly decided in so far as they held that "reproducing" drawings included "indirect copying" in cases in which the drawing was of a purely functional object. He considered that the House of Lords should overrule the previous cases on this point, even though this would have meant overruling the House of Lords' own decision in *L.B. (Plastics) Limited* v. *Swish Products Limited* [1979] R.P.C. 551. The *British Leyland* decision has been dealt with in more detail elsewhere in this book (see paragraph 9.05), but it is worthwhile mentioning here the importance of the spare part exception which was established in that case.

For copyright protection to arise under the 1956 Act, it was not necessary that the artistic work should be a drawing. Other artistic works, such as photographs and engravings, would give a similar basis for protection, not always for the same period and subject to certain exceptions. It is not intended to go into detail here, except to mention works of artistic craftsmanship, which are perhaps the more likely candidates for industrial use. The courts have tended to give a fairly narrow interpretation of what, in this area, amounts to a work of artistic craftsmanship (see paragraph 1.29). For example a prototype of a piece of modern furniture was held not be be a work of artistic craftsmanship in *George Hensher Limited* v. *Restawile Upholstery (Lancs.) Limited* [1976] A.C.64.

A further provision of the 1956 Act which needs to be considered is the defence contained in section 9(8) of the 1956 Act. This provided that the making of an object of any description which is in three dimensions, shall not be taken to infringe the copyright in an artistic work in two dimensions, if the object would not appear to persons who are not experts in relation to objects of that description, to be a reproduction of the artistic work. This provision was considered by Graham J. in *Merchant-Adventurers Limited* v. *M. Grew & Co. Limited* [1972] Ch. 242. In that case, Graham J. commented as follows: "There is infringement of drawings by three-dimensional reproduction of those drawings if they are sufficiently clear for a man of reasonable and average intelligence to be able to understand them and from an inspection of them, to be able to visualise in his mind what a three-dimensional object if made from them would look like." This is as clear an explanation of the provision as one is likely to find anywhere.

The provision caused considerable difficulty and could operate capriciously, as in the case of *Merlet* v. *Mothercare PLC* [1986] R.P.C. 115. Mme. Merlet designed a rain cape and prepared drawings of all the separate parts of the cape, but not of the whole. Mothercare caused the cape to be copied and Mme. Merlet sued for infringement of copyright in the drawings. Mothercare successfully raised a defence under section 9(8). Walton J. held that it was not permissible notionally to dissect the garment into its component parts and compare these to the drawings. The complete garment had to be compared with the plans to see whether the garment was a reproduction of the two-dimensional plans. He decided that it was not, but his decision might have been different if Mme. Merlet had also done a drawing of the complete garment, in addition to the drawings of the parts. The case went to appeal and Walton J.'s judgment was confirmed by the Court of Appeal. There is no provision in the 1988 Act which is equivalent to Section 9(8).

Under the 1956 Act the relationship between registered designs and copyright was regulated by section 10 and schedule 1. Section 10 has given rise to considerable difficulty in construction, but it now seems clear in the light of the *British Leyland* case and of the Privy Council decision in *Interlego AG* v. *Tyco Industries Ltd.* [1988] 3 W.L.R. 678 that section 10 only applies to artistic works in respect of which a corresponding design can be registered under the 1949 Act. A corresponding design in relation to an artistic work, means a design, which when applied to an article, results in a reproduction of the artistic work. The effect of this was that an artistic work incorporating a design which is not registrable, fell completely outside the ambit of section 10 and enjoyed unfettered copyright protection under the 1956 Act, subject to the limitations set out in the *British Leyland* case in respect of spare parts.

However, if the design was registrable then the position under section 10 was as follows. If a corresponding design was applied industrially (see paragraph 13.09) by or with the licence of the owner of the copyright in the work and, articles to which the design had so been applied were sold, let for hire or offered for sale or for hire anywhere in the world, then the copyright protection in the artistic work was cut down. There was full copyright protection for a period of 15 years from first sale, etc., but thereafter it was not an infringement in the copyright in the work to do anything which would have infringed the registered design right, had such a design been registered. If the design were registered, the position was the same, except that there would, in addition, be full registered design right protection during a period of up to 15 years from the date of registration. As to what was registrable under the unamended 1949 Act, see *Amp Inc.* v. *Utilux Proprietary Limited* [1972] R.P.C. 103.

The absurd result is that functional designs which could not be registered under the 1949 Act enjoyed copyright protection for the full period of copyright, whereas designs which could be so registered and which satisfied all the requirements of the 1949 Act, including the "eye-appeal" requirement, would only enjoy very limited copyright protection after the expiry of the 15-year period.

A case which illustrates the absurdity of the situation is the *Interlego* v. *Tyco* case. Interlego had various registered design registrations which had expired. In an attempt to obtain copyright protection in respect of the designs, Interlego argued that the designs were, in fact, unregistrable and should never have been registered in the first place. This argument was rejected.

The *British Leyland* case also highlighted the absurdity of the state of the law under the 1956 Act. The exhaust pipe in that case would not itself have qualified for copyright protection, but did so indirectly, because it was a reproduction of a drawing in which copyright subsisted. As a result, the exhaust pipe effectively enjoyed copyright protection for the full copyright period applicable to an artistic work. It was not registrable as a design, because it was a purely functional object and had no appeal to the eye. It contained no invention which was protectable by patent. Nevertheless, the period of copyright protection given was longer than that given either in the case of patent or registered design. However, the protection was limited by the spare part exception.

In addition, it is clear that if the exhaust pipe had been made as a prototype, without any drawings, it would not have qualified for any copyright protection, because the prototype would not have been an artistic work. In other words, it was only because it originated in the form of drawings that copyright subsisted. To take the example further, suppose the exhaust pipe had been made as a prototype without any preliminary drawings and subsequently production drawings were made of the prototype. The question arises whether copyright would subsist in those production drawings, even though there was no copyright in the original prototype. In *L.B. (Plastics) Ltd.* v. *Swish Products Limited* [1979] R.P.C. 551, Whitford J. thought that such drawings would enjoy copyright protection. This view was commented on in the *Interlego* v. *Tyco* case without disapproval [1988] 3 W.L.R. 678 at p. 705.

However, whether in such circumstances it would be possible to use that copyright protection to prevent third parties from "reverse engineering" copies of exhaust pipes legitimately made to the design of the copyright drawings is not completely clear. It could be argued that what has been copied is, in fact, the original prototype, in which no copyright subsists. The better view is probably that the copyright in the drawing would be infringed, provided that the "reverse engineering" was done in relation to an exhaust pipe which had been made from the design set out in the drawing.

In the light of this, one can understand why the House of Lords reached the conclusion that the rights of the copyright owner should be overridden by the rights of the car owner to repair his car, even if that resulted in an infringement of copyright.

The state of the law may also help to explain the decision of the Privy Council in *Interlego* v. *Tyco* (see above), which shows the attitude of the court towards industrial drawings which are based heavily on pre-existing industrial drawings. In that case the court could see an attempt being made to create a perpetual copyright by producing new drawings periodically which differed only to a very small degree from pre-existing drawings. If the new drawings had enjoyed copyright protection, then effectively the period of protection could have been extended indefinitely. In the *Interlego* v. *Tyco* case, it was made clear that there had to be a substantial degree of originality before a fresh copyright would be created.

III THE 1988 ACT

13.03   It is intended to deal first of all with copyright, then with design right and finally, and very briefly, with registered design rights and topography rights in semi-conductorships. Inevitably there is an overlap between these rights and a certain amount of cross-referencing will be necessary.

A. COPYRIGHT

1. Copyright Protection

13.04   The status of works existing at the commencement of the 1988 Act is set out in the earlier chapters of this book. However, it is worthwhile summarising very briefly the most relevant provisions of the 1988 Act relating to artistic works, which are the only really relevant works for copyright purposes, and then to consider the impact on copyright protection of the new permitted acts which have been introduced in the 1988 Act in the design field and also to consider the effect of the new design right. Finally, it is intended to deal with the transitional provisions to determine the effect of the new regime on existing works.

Among many other categories, artistic works under the 1988 Act include graphic works, irrespective of artistic quality and, works of artistic craftsmanship, which are required to possess some artistic quality. Amongst other things, a graphic work includes a drawing, diagram, map, chart or plan. The duration of copyright protection in artistic works has already been discussed. (See Chapter 4.) One of the restricted acts in relation to an artistic work under the 1988 Act is copying the work, which means reproducing the work in any material form. This is expressed to include the making of a copy in three dimensions of a two-dimensional work and the making of a copy in two dimensions of a three-dimensional work. It is provided that an act restricted by the copyright in a work is done, if it is done:
in relation to the work as a whole or any substantial part of it; and
either directly or indirectly; and
it is immaterial whether any intervening acts themselves infringe copyright.

The protection afforded to artistic works under the 1988 Act is therefore broadly similar to that afforded under the 1956 Act, subject to the amendments made by the 1988 Act referred to in previous chapters. Under the 1988 Act express reference is made to indirect copying, which should get over any potential obstacles raised by the dissenting judgment of Lord Griffiths in the *British Leyland* case. (See paragraph 13.07.) However, the limitations on copyright promulgated by the majority of the Law Lords in that case, in the form of "the right to repair" will continue to be a factor to be considered in relation to copyright under the 1988 Act.

An important difference between the 1956 Act and the 1988 Act is that there is no provision in the 1988 Act which is equivalent to section 9(8) of the 1956 Act. (See paragraph 13.02.) This will mean that a plaintiff will have one less hurdle to overcome in an infringement action based on three-dimensional reproduction of a two-dimensional artistic work.

In considering the copyright position of works in which copyright subsists it is necessary to consider the interrelation between copyright and the new design right. In this connection, the definitions of "design" and "design document" are critical.

(a) *Design*

"Design" means the design of any aspect of the shape or configuration   **13.05**
(whether internal or external) of the whole or part of an article, other than surface decoration. (See section 51(3).) "Article" is not defined but it is thought that it may exclude a drawing or design document itself (see paragraph 13.08). Otherwise it must bear its ordinary and natural meaning and will cover most objects. In fact, it is difficult to think of examples of man-made things which would not be covered. The use of the words "shape or configuration" are perhaps more apt to apply to three-dimensional, rather than two-dimensional objects. However, this alone should not be sufficient to limit the meaning of "article" to three-dimensional objects. If it was intended for the meaning of "article" to be so limited, one would expect this to be done expressly, and it is not.

Design is defined in terms of itself, which is not very helpful. It will cover both internal and external aspects of shape and configuration. There is no requirement of "eye-appeal" or that the design should have aesthetic or artistic quality. Also it does not matter if the shape or configuration are dictated by the function the article has to perform and so purely functional objects are included. Also the design can be either of the whole or part of an article. The only exclusion for the purposes of Part I of the 1988 Act is surface decoration.

(b) *"Design Document"*

"Design Document" means any record of a design, whether in the form of   **13.06**
a drawing, a written description, a photograph, data stored in a computer or otherwise. (See section 51(3).) This is a very interesting definition when one considers that normally a design will be of the shape or configuration of a three-dimensional article. Drawings are usual enough, as are photographs. However, the inclusion of a written description and data stored in a computer is novel. The words "or otherwise" seem to refer to "any record of a design", which gives a wide meaning to the expression. It would include any kind of a record, whether of the kind given as examples, or of any other type. The record could be tangible or intangible. This wide definition seems to support the view that a design document will not itself be an article. (See paragraph 13.08.) Clearly data stored in a card-index system, on tape, on punch cards or tape or in any

other manner or medium would be included. From the copyright point of view the design document is going to be either an artistic work or a literary work.

It is worth noting here that under the 1956 Act it would not be an infringement of copyright in a written description of an article to make a three-dimensional article to that description. In *Brigid Foley Limited* v. *Ellott* [1982] R.P.C. 433, which was a decision on an interlocutory application, it was held that the words and numerals in a knitting guide were not reproduced by following the instructions contained in the words and numerals and thereby making the garment. The position under the 1988 Act remains the same in relation to copyright, but, as will be seen, the position in relation to design right will be different (see paragraph 13.30).

In the Shorter English Dictionary "Design" has many meanings, including "a preliminary sketch for a work of art," "a delineation" and a "pattern." There does seem to be a requirement that the design is a precursor of something else. For this reason a finished artistic work, such as a sketch or painting, which is not intended to be used as a design to which articles will be made, will probably not be a design document, notwithstanding that articles could be made to a design embodied in the sketch or painting.

From these definitions it can be seen that, whilst design documents may well be works protected by copyright, articles made to the design will very often not be. The purpose of the 1988 Act is to prevent such articles from gaining copyright protection indirectly by virtue of the copyright in the design document. The extent to which this purpose is achieved can be judged from the later parts of this Chapter. In some, but not all cases, the new design right protection is conferred instead of copyright protection.

2. New Permitted Acts

13.07   Existing literary and artistic works and new literary and artistic works coming into existence after the commencement of the 1988 Act will enjoy copyright protection as described in the earlier chapters of this book. (See also paragraph 13.04.) However, several new categories of permitted acts have been introduced by sections 51 to 55 of the 1988 Act and these limit the scope of copyright protection in certain circumstances in the design field. These permitted acts will affect new works. Existing works are also affected, subject to transitional provisions which defer for a period the coming into operation of some of the permitted acts in relation to some existing works. The transitional provisions are dealt with in paragraph 13.12.

(a) *Design Documents and Models* (section 51)

13.08   Section 51(1) of the 1988 Act provides that:

"It is not an infringement of any copyright in a design document or model recording or embodying a design for anything other than an artistic work or a typeface to make an article to the design or to copy an article made to the design."

Furthermore, it is provided that it is not an infringement of the copyright in the design document to issue to the public, or include in a film, broadcast or cable programme service, anything, the making of which was, by virtue of section 51(1) not an infringement of that copyright. "Anything" here might be either an article made to the design or a copy (not necessarily an article) of such an article.

The meanings of "design" and "design document" are discussed fully in paragraphs 13.05 and 13.06. The overall effect of section 51 is to create a specific exclusion to copyright protection, without in any way taking away the underlying copyright in the design document, which might be protected either as a literary work or an artistic work, or the model, which might be protected as an artistic work.

The exclusion covers only the making of an article to the design and the copying of an article made to the design and the other subsequent acts described above. It would not cover other acts which infringe copyright. For example, if the design document consisted of a written description, the copyright in that literary work would be infringed by making an adaptation of the work, such as a translation, notwithstanding the provisions of section 51. If the design document consisted of data stored in a computer, this would be a literary work and the translation might easily occur when the data is converted into computer code. Once the articles are made to the design or copies are made of articles made to the design those articles and copies which are made can then be issued to the public or included in a film, broadcast or cable programme service without infringing copyright. This will also apply to articles made before the commencement of Part 1 of the 1988 Act, if they would have fallen within section 51(1), if the new copyright provisions of the 1988 Act had been in force when the articles were made. (See paragraph 14(4) of Schedule 1 to the 1988 Act.)

It is particularly worth noting that, for section 51 to apply, all that needs to be done is for the work to be recorded as a design or embodied in a design document or model. No exploitation or use of the design is required.

The exception in section 51 extends only to design documents or models recording or embodying a design for anything other than an artistic work or a typeface. If the design is for an artistic work or typeface, then section 51 will have no application, and normal copyright protection will apply, subject to the provisions of sections 52 to 55. (See paragraphs 13.09 to 13.11.)

An example of design document falling within the exception would be an industrial drawing of an exhaust pipe. An industrial drawing is a design document and an exhaust pipe is not an artistic work or typeface and so the exception applies. Similarly, a prototype exhaust pipe made without any preliminary drawings would be an example of a model recording a design for a thing (the exhaust pipe) which is not an artistic work or typeface and so the exception would apply here as well.

The industrial drawing of the exhaust pipe is a graphic work under the 1988 Act and it should therefore enjoy full copyright protection as an artistic work. The prototype exhaust pipe would not be an artistic work and no copyright protection would arise in respect of it, but, as will be seen later in this Chapter, it may be protected by the new design right. As a result of section 51, it is not an infringement of the copyright in the industrial drawing to make an article to the design or to copy an article made to the design. Thus it would not infringe the copyright in the drawing to make an exhaust pipe to the design depicted by the drawing. This will cover both direct and indirect copying, such as "reverse engineering," because it is not an infringement of copyright to copy an article made to the design, such as an authorised exhaust pipe.

The wording "to make an article to the design" is itself very wide and, given its natural meaning, would itself seem wide enough to cover indirect copying, without the addition of the words "or to copy an article made to the design."

An interesting question arises as to whether an industrial drawing is itself an "article." It may not be. The early versions of the Copyright Designs and Patents Bill contained provisions in section 51 expressly referring to copying a design document in terms that made it clear that a design document was an "article." These provisions were dropped, and it could be inferred from this that parliament did not intend a design document to be an "article." This question is not free from doubt. For example, section 228(6) of the 1988 Act provides that "infringing article" does not include a design document. This provision would only have been necessary if it was considered that a design document could be an "article."

If an industrial drawing is not an "article," then simply copying the existing industrial drawing would therefore not amount to "making an article to the design," as no article has been made. The copy industrial drawing thus made will not be an article. Nor, in a case of direct copying of the original drawing, will there have been copying of an "article" made to the design, as the original drawing is not an article. Furthermore, even if it is considered that an article has been made, it is difficult to see how duplicating a copy of a drawing of a design could be described as making an article *to the design*.

If this reasoning is correct, the copy industrial drawing will fall outside the exception in section 51 and the making of the copy drawing will be an infringement of copyright.

As will be seen, such copying may also be an infringement of design right (see paragraph 13.30) as a design document recording the design will have been made. However, section 236 (see paragraph 13.20) provides that it is not an infringement of design right to do anything which is an infringement of copyright in the relevant work.

If the copy industrial drawing is made indirectly by copying an article made to the design, the question is whether this amounts to copying the article within the meaning of section 51. The article will not be an artistic work (or section 51 would not apply), and section 17(3), dealing with two-dimensional copying of three-dimensional artistic works, will therefore not directly apply. It could be argued that, as section 17(3) does not apply, two-dimensional reproduction of the three-dimensional article does not amount to copying of the article. However, this argument is probably wrong, as the effect of the interpretation would be to make part of section 51 redundant. The words "to copy an article made to the design" would be superfluous. If only three dimensional copying of an article is covered, then this would always fall within the wording "making an article to the design".

The consequence of this interpretation would be that it is still an infringement of copyright to copy an industrial drawing, where copying is direct two dimensional reproduction, but not where reproduction is indirect. Using the infringing drawings to make articles to the design would not be an infringement of copyright. However, it would be an infringement of design right, during the term of any design right. If this interpretation is correct, it would be possible to obtain an injunction to restrain infringement by making copy drawings and all other remedies available for infringement of copyright would technically be available. This might be of significance after the design right has expired, as it would leave the door open for copyright to be used in these limited circumstances, in an attempt to maintain design right protection after it has expired.

(b) *Effect of exploitation of artistic works* (section 52)

Under the 1988 Act, where an artistic work has been exploited by or with the licence of the copyright owner by: **13.09**

(i) making by an industrial process articles falling to be treated for the purposes of Part 1 of the 1988 Act as copies of the work; and

(ii) by marketing such articles anywhere in the world

the provisions of section 52 will apply (see below).

What amounts to copying is set out in section 17 of the 1988 Act (see paragraph 5.11 onwards), and copies are construed accordingly. Somewhat similar provisions to those contained in section 52, appeared in section 10 of the 1956 Act. However, there are a number of differences. Most importantly, section 52 will, subject to certain exceptions (see below), apply to all artistic works of any kind whatsoever. Section 10 applied only to artistic works in respect of which a corresponding design could be registered under the 1949 Act. The absurd results of this anomaly are discussed in paragraph 13.02. In addition, section 51 will cut down the scope of copyright protection in some artistic works, such as some design drawings. The operation of section 52 in respect of these will, therefore, be less significant, but it will still apply to them. Sections 51 and 52 are not mutually exclusive.

The Secretary of State may, by Order, exclude from the operation of section 52, such articles of primarily literary or artistic character as he thinks fit. At the time of writing, no such Order has been made. The 1949 Act contained a somewhat similar provision in section 1(4) (now section

1(5)), which gave power for rules to be made for exclusion from registration of designs for certain articles which are "primarily literary or artistic in character." The wording is very similar and rules were made under the 1949 Act excluding from registration, designs to be applied to any of the following:

works of sculpture other than casts or models used or intended to be used as models or patterns to be multiplied by any industrial process;

wall plaques, medals and medallions;

printed matter primarily of a literary or artistic character, including bookjackets, calendars, certificates, coupons, dressmaking patterns, greetings cards, leaflets, maps, plans, postcards, stamps, trade advertisements, trade forms and cards, transfers, playing cards, labels and the like.

This may give some clue as to the sorts of item which might be included in any Order made by the Secretary of State. However, the situations are not entirely analogous.

Orders may also be made by the Secretary of State to make provision as to the circumstances in which an article, or any description of an article is to be regarded for the purposes of section 52 as made by an industrial process. The wording in the 1956 Act was "applied industrially" and in regulations made under that Act a design was taken to be "applied industrially" if it was applied to more than 50 articles, all of which did not together constitute a single set of articles, or to goods manufactured in lengths or pieces, other than handmade goods. At the time of writing, it remains to be seen what regulations will be made under the 1988 Act. They should shed some light on the meaning of "made by an industrial process" and whether it differs from "applied industrially."

"Marketing" means selling, letting for hire or offering or exposing for sale or hire. Also references to "articles" in section 52 do not include films.

The requirements of section 52 are cumulative. Articles must both be made by an industrial process and marketed before the section bites. The section expressly provides that the marketing can take place anywhere, but is silent as to where the making must take place. It could be argued from this that the making must take place in the United Kingdom. If that were not the case, additional wording could have been inserted to make the position clear, as it was in the case of marketing.

If such exploitation of an artistic work has taken place for the purposes of section 52, the effect is fairly drastic. Section 52(2) provides:

> "After the end of 25 years from the end of the calendar year in which such articles are first marketed, the work may be copied by making articles of any description, or doing anything for the purpose of making articles of any description, and anything may be done in relation to articles so made, without infringing copyright in the work."

The effect is perhaps best illustrated by an example. Suppose an animated film is made with cartoons of a fictional animal, say a teddy bear. If that teddy bear is subsequently licensed for use as a toy by way of merchandising, the toys will be copies of the cartoon drawings (section 17) and will almost certainly be made by an industrial process. Twenty-five years after the toys are first marketed, section 52 will come into operation and the following acts may be done without infringing the copyright in the work, (*i.e.* the cartoon reproduced in the form of a toy):

(i) the work may be copied by making articles (excluding films) of *any* description, (*i.e.* both two- and three-dimensional articles);

(ii) *anything* may be done for the purpose of making articles (excluding films) of *any* description; and

(iii) *anything* may be done in relation to articles (excluding films) so made.

Clearly these provisions will enable most merchandising activities to be carried out in relation to the work without copyright being infringed. If the expression "article" is wide enough to include a book (and books are not excluded by Order made by the Secretary of State), then a book could be made incorporating copies of the work. The expression "anything may be done for the purpose of making articles of any description" (in this case a book), would seem wide enough to permit reproducing the work (*i.e.* the cartoon drawing of the teddy bear) in the book and even making new revised drawings based on the work.

Section 52 will apply to all new artistic works and to existing artistic works which have not been exploited under section 10 of the 1956 Act prior to commencement of the 1988 Act. It will also apply to artistic works which have been exploited under section 10 prior to commencement, but in that case the period of 25 years in section 52 is reduced to 15 years from the date on which articles to which the design has been applied were first sold, let for hire or offered for sale or hire anywhere in the world. If the 15-year period expired before commencement of the 1988 Act, it seems that the provisions of section 52 will, in such a case, come into play immediately upon the commencement of the 1988 Act. In relation to such an artistic work any of the acts set out in section 52(2) may then be done without infringing copyright in the work. In respect of existing artistic works which have not been exploited prior to commencement under section 10, section 52 will apply, but only where articles are marketed after commencement within the meaning of section 52. Thus, even if an artistic work has been exploited before commencement, so long as section 10 did not apply, section 52(2) will only bite if marketing takes place after commencement. If it does bite, the period of 25 years will start to run from the original marketing which took place prior to commencement.

(c) *Things done in reliance of registration of design (section 53)*

Section 53 of the 1988 Act contains provisions which are roughly similar to those contained in the First Schedule to the 1956 Act. It provides a   **13.10** defence to a copyright infringement action in respect of an artistic work where a corresponding design has been registered under the 1949 Act in relation to the artistic work. The copyright in the artistic work is not infringed by anything done in pursuance of an assignment or licence made or granted by a person registered under the 1949 Act as the proprietor of a corresponding design, which is done in good faith in reliance on the registration and without notice of any proceedings for the cancellation of the registration or for rectifying the relevant entry in the register of designs. Provided these requirements are satisfied, the defence is available even if the person registered as the proprietor should not have been so registered. The defence is not available in respect of things done after notice of proceedings is received.

For these purposes, a corresponding design in relation to an artistic work means a design within the meaning of the 1949 Act, which if applied to an article, will produce something which will be treated as a copy of the artistic work, for the purposes of Part 1 of the 1988 Act. Copies are defined in section 17 of the 1988 Act. (See paragraph 5.11 onwards.)

(d) *Typefaces (sections 54 and 55)*

13.11 Special rules apply to artistic works which consist of the design of a typeface. It is not an infringement of copyright in such an artistic work: to use the typeface in the ordinary course of typing, composing text, type-setting or printing, or
to possess an article for the purpose of such use, or
to do anything in relation to material produced by such use.

This is so, notwithstanding that an article is used which is an infringing copy of the artistic work.

However, further provisions apply to persons making, importing or dealing with articles specifically designed or adapted for producing material in a particular typeface, or possessing such articles for the purpose of dealing with them. These provisions are set out in section 54(2) of the 1988 Act.

Section 55 of the 1988 Act limits the period of copyright protection in the case of artistic works consisting of the design of a typeface. This applies where articles specifically designed or adapted for producing material in that typeface have been marketed by or with the licence of the copyright owner. In this context "marketed" means sold, let for hire or offered or exposed for sale or hire, anywhere in the world. In such a case, after the period of 25 years from the end of the calendar year in which the first such articles are marketed, the artistic work may be copied by making further such articles or doing anything for the purpose of making any such articles, and anything may be done in relation to articles so made without infringing the copyright in the work. This provision is contained in section 55(2) and it is in similar, but more limited, terms to those contained in section 52(2). If such marketing took place before the commencement of the copyright provisions of the 1988 Act, the 25 year period begins to run from the end of the calendar year in which the new copyright provisions come into force. (See paragraph 14(5) of schedule 1 to the 1988 Act.)

3. Transitional provisions

The position of artistic and literary works in existence at the commencement of Part 1 of the 1988 Act is dealt with in the earlier Chapters of this book. However, special provisions apply in the field of designs, with particular reference to the new permitted acts dealt with earlier in this Chapter.   **13.12**

Until a design has been recorded or embodied in a design document or model it will often be merely an idea and enjoy no protection either under copyright or design right. If a design is recorded in another work, such as a painting, which falls outside the wide definition of "design document," then the painting will be an artistic work, protected by copyright and the design right will not be relevant at that stage.

However, if a design has been recorded or embodied in a design document or model before commencement, then the transitional provisions set out in paragraph 19 of schedule I to the 1988 Act will apply. Here, it is worth remembering the very wide definition of "design document." It could, for example, be a written description of a design or any of the other categories of design document (see paragraph 13.06). "Commencement" for the purposes of these transitional provisions means the date on which the new copyright provisions (Part I, and various other provisions, but not Part III dealing with design right) in the 1988 Act come into force.

In addition, it will not normally be possible for any new design right to arise in respect of the design, because of the provisions of section 213(7) of the 1988 Act. (See paragraph 13.19.) This provides that design right does not subsist in a design which *was recorded in a design document or to which an article has been made*, prior to the commencement of Part III of the 1988 Act. Whether this is exactly co-extensive with the wording of paragraph 19 is not quite clear. Paragraph 19 refers to a design being *recorded or embodied in a design document or model*. Clearly recording in a design document is covered in both cases. The first question is whether "embodying in a design document" goes further than "recording" in a design document. This seems improbable. The next question is whether recording or embodying a design in a model is co-extensive with "making an article to the design." It may not be. The article made to the design may not be a "model." In these circumstances the design right would be lost under the provisions of section 213(7) and the transitional provisions would not apply to defer the operation of section 51 for a period of 10 years. The effect of section 51 is to cut down copyright protection in certain design documents and models (see paragraph 13.08). Thus in these circumstances, both the design right and a substantial part of the copyright protection would be lost. Going on from there, the next question is whether recording or embodying a design in a model will always involve "making an article to the design." It is considered that it will. On this basis, the situation of both design right subsisting and paragraph 19 of the transitional provisions deferring the operation of section 51 for a period of 10 years could not apply.

It is to be hoped that the copyright provisions of the 1988 Act and Part III of the 1988 Act will have the same commencement date. If not, there could be considerable difficulty in respect of works recorded in a design document after the new copyright provisions come into force, but before the date on which Part III of the 1988 Act comes into force.

The effect of paragraph 19(1) will be that, the provisions of section 51, which cuts down copyright protection in certain design documents and models, will not apply to such a design document or model for a period of 10 years after commencement. Section 51 is dealt with at paragraph 13.08 above. The result is that, provided that the design document or model enjoys copyright protection under the 1988 Act and the unexpired term of copyright lasts for at least 10 years post commencement, the design document or model will continue to enjoy full copyright protection for 10 years after commencement, subject to the other provisions of the transitional provisions. The transitional provisions will not extend the copyright beyond its usual term.

During the 10-year period the provisions relating to design right set out in sections 237 to 239 and 247 and 248 will apply to the copyright. This means that licences of right of the copyright will be available in the same sorts of situation as in relation to design right and application can be made to the comptroller to settle the terms of such licences. These provisions are discussed in more detail in relation to the new design right. (See paragraph 13.36.) Licences of right will be available for the last five years of the 10-year period, or for so much of those last five years during which copyright subsists, but will be limited to acts which would have been permitted by section 51, if the design document or model had been made after commencement.

Where a licence of right is available by virtue of the transitional provisions, a person to whom a licence was granted before commencement may apply to the comptroller for an order adjusting the terms of that licence. Although it does not expressly say so, it is considered that it will only be possible to adjust those terms of the licence relating to acts which would have been permitted by section 51, if the design document or model had been made after commencement.

Sections 249 and 250 of the 1988 Act, dealing with appeals and rules of procedure will apply in relation to proceedings brought under or by virtue of the transitional provisions. (See paragraph 13.39.)

During the 10-year period, the right under section 100 of the 1988 Act to seize copies which infringe copyright, does not apply in relation to anything to which it would not apply if the design in question had first been recorded or embodied in a design document or model after commencement. This means that there will be no right during the 10-year period to seize infringing copies under the copyright infringement provisions, if, by reason of section 51, they would have been deemed not to infringe copyright, if the design had been so recorded or embodied after commencement. There are no provisions permitting seizure of infringing copies which infringe only the design right.

It is also provided in the transitional provisions that nothing in those provisions shall affect the operation of any rule of law preventing or restricting the enforcement of copyright in relation to a design. This wording is very wide and would certainly cover the "right to repair" restriction on the enforcement of copyright, as put forward in the *British Leyland* case. (See paragraph 13.02.) It would also cover defences of the kind discussed in the Catnics case (see paragraph 4.68) or public interest defences (see paragraph 7.126).

The transitional provisions also cover the situation where section 10 of the 1956 Act applies in relation to an artistic work at any time before the commencement. As has been indicated (see paragraph 13.02) section 10 did not apply to purely functional works. It applied only to an artistic work in respect of which a corresponding design could be registered under the 1949 Act and then only if a corresponding design of the work was applied industrially and articles to which the design has been so applied are sold, etc. In cases where there has been such exploitation, section 52 will apply, except that copyright protection will be cut down to 15 years, rather than 25 years after first exploitation. Otherwise section 52 will also apply to existing artistic works, which are marketed after the commencement of the 1988 Act. Section 52 is dealt with above in paragraph 13.09.

Paragraph 14(5) of Schedule 1 of the 1988 Act applies to defer the operation of section 55 in the case where articles covered by the section are first marketed before commencement.

Paragraph 6 of the transitional provisions in Schedule 1 contains rules governing certain artistic works which constituted registrable designs and which were made before June 1, 1957. These rules ensure that the 1988 Act does not confer copyright protection on these works. They did not enjoy copyright protection under the 1956 Act either.

4. Relationship with Design Right

Section 236 of the 1988 Act provides that where copyright subsists in a   **13.13** work which consists of or includes a design in which design right subsists, it is not an infringement of design right in the design to do anything which is an infringement of copyright in that work. This means that copyright protection takes precedence over design right protection. However, the limitations imposed on copyright protection by the new permitted acts will make it unlikely that the two rights will in practice cover the same situation. For an examination of the inter relationship of the two rights, see paragraph 13.20.

B. DESIGN RIGHT

1. The new right

The new design right is a property right which will subsist in original   **13.14** designs and it does not require registration. "Original" has a more limited meaning than the fairly wide meaning applicable to copyright (see paragraphs 1.30 onwards) and simply satisfying the "originality" test applicable to copyright works will not be sufficient. Section 213(4) provides that a design will not be treated as original, if it is commonplace in the design field in question at the time of its creation. "Commonplace" is not defined and will therefore bear its ordinary and natural meaning. It implies that a quantitative test should be used. It will be a question of fact in each case whether a particular design is commonplace in the relevant design field and evidence will have to be produced if the point arises in a particular case. If the design incorporates some new technical development, this may be relevant in deciding whether or not the design is commonplace.

(a) *What is a design?*

13.15   A "design" means the design of any aspect of the shape or configuration (whether internal or external) of the whole or any part of an article (section 213(2)). This definition is substantially the same as that contained in section 51 of the 1988 Act. (See paragraph 13.05.) This is consistent with the aim of the 1988 Act, which is to separate copyright protection from design protection. As has been discussed already, the definition is very wide indeed.

(b) *Exceptions to design right subsistence*

(i) *"Method or principle of construction"*

13.16   The first exception to design right is that it does not subsist in a method or principle of construction. This exception applies also to registered designs under the 1949 Act, both before and after amendment by the 1988 Act. In *Moody* v. *Tree* [1892] 9 R.P.C. 333 an attempt was made to register as a design a picture of a basket, which had been woven in a particular way and had thus produced what was described in the application as a "pattern." It was held that the application could not proceed because here was, in reality, simply a method of manufacture.

(ii) *"Surface decoration"*

13.17   Design right does not subsist in surface decoration. The 1949 Act, in defining a design, includes a reference to features of pattern or ornament, in addition to features of shape or configuration. No reference is made in the design right to aspects of pattern or ornament. This exception to the design right makes it clear that the new design right is not intended to cover patterns on or ornamentation to the surface of an article. It is concerned primarily with the shape or configuration of the article or any part of it. What amounts to surface decoration may give rise to debate, particularly where the surface decoration performs a function and its primary purpose is to perform that function, rather than to decorate.

(iii) *"Must fit"*

Design right does not subsist in features of shape or configuration of an 13.18
article which enable the article to be connected to, or placed in, around or
against, another article so that either article may perform its function.

The object of this exception is to deny design right protection to those
parts of an article which must be a particular shape to enable the article to
be fitted to another article in order that either article may perform its
function.

Take the example of a carburettor. Certain parts of the carburettor
must usually be a particular shape to enable it to be fitted to the rest of the
engine. If they were not that shape, it would not be possible to attach it so
that it performed its function. However, the other parts of the carburettor
could be any shape and still fit. These other parts will fall outside this
exception to the design right.

The effect of this will be that, subject to any registered design, manufacturers of carburettors will be able, without infringing design right, to
adapt their products to fit other manufacturers' engines, even if by doing
so some parts have to be incorporated from someone else's design of
carburettor in order to make the modified carburettor fit. It will not be
permissible to copy the whole carburettor, if it is protected by design
right.

This exception may also have a wider application and apply, for
example, to something like plastic connecting bricks. The wording of the
exception would seem wide enough to cover at least certain parts of such
bricks. The "must match" exception (see below) would probably cover
many of the other parts.

(iv) *"Must match"*

Design right does not subsist in features of shape or configuration of an 13.19
article which are dependent on the appearance of another article of which
the article is intended by the designer to form an integral part.

This exception has caused disquiet, particularly as it has also been
introduced as an exception to registered design right protection. The
example which has been most talked about is replacement body panels
for cars. From the debates in Parliament it is clear that these were
intended to fall within the exception. It will apply wherever an article is
made up of parts so that the whole article is intended to be a particular
shape and have a particular appearance and each part is intended by the
designer to form an integral part of the whole article.

The intention of the designer is relevant in deciding whether a particular article is intended to form an integral part of another article. How to
establish what the designer intended may present difficulties. However,
in most cases it should be fairly obvious. Areas of difficulty may possibly
arise when a part is capable of matching a wide variety of differing
articles. For example, certain panels for a range of white goods could be
made interchangeable, so that a panel for a cooker also matched and
could be used as a panel for a dishwasher, washing machine and fridge. It

could be argued that the exception did not apply here, because the article, (*i.e.* panel) is not dependent on the appearance of another article, but rather on the appearance of a number of other articles.

In similar fashion to the "must fit" exception (see above) the "must match" exception only excludes those features of shape or configuration which are dependant on the appearance of the other article. There will be features which are not so dependent and those features can still be protected, so long as one of the other exceptions does not apply. For example, in the case of a body panel for a car, there may well be some areas of the panel which do not fall within either the "must fit" or "must match" exceptions. As long as the car manufacturer ensures that there are such areas, it will be able to market spare parts which are exactly the same as the original and to prevent others from doing so. Others may produce parts which work just as well, but the original manufacturer will be able to point out the differences and claim that it is still the only source of identical spare parts.

(c) *Subsistence of design right and its relationship with copyright*

13.20   Design right does not subsist unless and until the design has been recorded in a design document or an article has been made to the design. "Design document" is defined for design right purposes in section 263(1) and has the same meaning as in section 51(3) of the 1988 Act. (See paragraph 13.06.) Further, design right does not subsist in a design which was recorded in a design document or to which an article was made before commencement of Part III of the 1988 Act. Again, "article" is not defined. (For the interrelation of these two provisions, see paragraph 13.12.)

It is worthwhile here considering again the wide definition of design document. It includes *any* record of a design, including, *inter alia*, a written description. This may produce some unexpected results as, until the 1988 Act, such a written description would have little impact on designs protected as artistic works. Under the 1988 Act, the existence of such a written description will mean that the design has been recorded in a design document. If this recording took place prior to the commencement of Part III of the 1988 Act, design right protection in the design is lost. In this connection, one should also consider patent specifications, which may contain many types of design documents. Where recording of the design takes place prior to the 1988 Act, design right protection is lost.

It would perhaps be helpful here to summarise the interrelation of copyright and design right. For these purposes, originality and all other relevant requirements for subsistence are assumed to be satisfied in respect of each work, both for the purposes of design right and copyright.

(i) The definition of design document is very wide and includes some works which are artistic works and some which are literary works. (See paragraph 13.06.) Copyright will subsist in these works.

(ii) In respect of a design recorded in a design document before commencement of Part III of the 1988 Act, there will be no design right protection. Copyright protection in the design document will be governed by Part I of the 1988 Act and the transitional provisions. (See paragraph 13.12.)

(iii) In respect of a design to which an article has been made before commencement, there will be no design right protection. If the article which is made is an artistic work, then that article will enjoy copyright protection and Part I of the 1988 Act and the transitional provisions will apply (see paragraph 13.12). If the article which is made is not an artistic work, then there will be no copyright protection in the article either. However, if a design document, such as a drawing is subsequently made recording the design of such an article, that drawing will be an artistic work and may enjoy copyright protection. However, section 51 of the 1988 Act will immediately apply to cut down the copyright protection. (See paragraph 13.08.)

(iv) In respect of a design recorded in a design document after commencement, there will be design right protection in respect of the design. There will also be copyright protection in the design document. Section 51 will apply immediately to cut down any copyright protection in the design document if the design is for anything other than an artistic work or a typeface. If the design is for an artistic work and it is exploited industrially and marketed, section 52 will apply to cut down any copyright protection, both in the design document and the artistic work. If the design is for a typeface, sections 54 and 55 will apply to cut down any copyright protection both in the design document and the typeface. (See paragraphs 13.08 to 13.11.)

(v) In respect of a design to which an article is made after commencement, there will be design right protection. If the article made is an artistic work or typeface, then that article will also enjoy copyright protection, but section 52 will, if it is exploited industrially and marketed, cut that protection down in the case of an artistic work and sections 54 and 55 will cut that protection down if the artistic work is a typeface, if the circumstances set out in these sections arise. (See paragraphs 13.09 to 13.11.)

(vi) When the design right expires, then copyright will continue to subsist in those design documents and articles in which it subsisted during the term of the design right, but such copyright will continue to be restricted by and subject to whichever provisions of sections 51 to 55, to which it was subject during the terms of the design right.

(vii) Where copyright subsists in a work which consists of or includes a design in which design right subsists, it is not an infringement of the design right in the design, to do anything which is an infringement of copyright in the work (s.236). This provision is intended to ensure that there is no duplication of remedies in respect of the same infringement. It is perhaps best illustrated by an example. Suppose there is a sculpture which is both an artistic work and an article made to a design. A copy of the sculpture is then made in infringement of copyright. The design right is also thereby, prima facie, infringed. However, by virtue of section 236, it will not be an infringement in the design right to do anything which infringes the copyright in the sculpture, and thus, in this example, the design right will effectively be deemed not to be infringed. To take another example, suppose you have a drawing of a piece of machinery. The drawing is an artistic work in which copyright subsists and a design document. The piece of machinery is not an artistic work but is an original design. It will not be an infringement of the copyright in the drawing to make a copy of the piece of machinery, because of the provisions of section 51. However, it will be an infringement of the design right and section 236 will not operate.

(d) *Qualification for design right protection*

13.21   Design right protection is conferred on a much narrower class of persons than the class of persons entitled to copyright protection. Design right subsists in a design only if the design qualifies for design right protection by reference to the designer, or the person by whom the design was commissioned or the designer employed, or the person by whom and country in which articles made to the design were first marketed. In addition, there is power to make further provision as to qualification under section 221. (See paragraph 13.25.)

The designer, in relation to a design, is the person who creates it (section 214). In the case of a computer-generated design, the designer for the purposes of Part III of the 1988 Act, is the person by whom the arrangements necessary for the creation of the design are undertaken. A computer-generated design is one generated by computer in circumstances such that there is no human designer. All these definitions are similar to the equivalent definitions in relation to copyright.

There are various further definitions (s.217) which need to be considered in order to determine the question of qualification for design right protection.

"Qualifying individual" means a citizen or subject of, or an individual habitually resident in, a qualifying country. The use of the word "habitually" is interesting, because it does not appear in the equivalent qualification provisions of Part I in relation to copyright or in Part II in relation to rights in performances. In both those cases the word "resident" is used on its own. "Habitually" is not defined and its inclusion can only have been intended to require a stronger connection than mere residence. The expression appears in Article 3(2) of the Paris Revision of the Berne Convention and this may have something to do with its inclusion. "Habitual residence" is a term used in the context of family law to decide whether English courts have jurisdiction in certain instances. It has been held (*Cruse* v. *Chittum, The Times*, March 15, 1974 that habitual residence requires a stronger connection than ordinary residence for tax purposes. In relation to the United Kingdom, a citizen or subject means a British citizen. In relation to a colony of the United Kingdom, a citizen or subject means a "British Dependent Territories citizen by connection with that colony." This is determined in accordance with the British Nationality Act 1981.

"Qualifying person" means a qualifying individual or a body having legal personality which is formed under the law of a part of the United Kingdom or another qualifying country, and has in any qualifying country a place of business at which substantial business activity is carried on. In deciding whether substantial business activity is carried on at a place of business in any country, no account is to be taken of dealings in goods which are at all material times outside that country. No mention is made of services and there is no indication of what is meant by "substantial." In addition, there is no requirement that the substantial business activity should be of any particular kind or relate in any way to any design or design right. The Crown and government of any qualifying country are also qualifying persons.

"Qualifying country" means the United Kingdom, any other Member State of the EEC, a country to which the provisions are extended by virtue of an Order made under section 255 and, to the extent that an Order made under section 256 so provides, a country designated under that section as enjoying reciprocal protection. Sections 255 and 256 are dealt with subsequently. (See paragraph 13.42.)

(i) *Qualification by reference to a designer* (section 218)

A design which is not created in pursuance of a commission or in the course of employment, qualifies for design right protection if the designer is a qualifying individual, or in the case of a computer-generated design, a qualifying person.   **13.22**

If such a design is a joint design, then it qualifies for design right protection if any one or more of the designers is a qualifying individual or, if appropriate, a qualifying person. However, in the case of such a joint design, only those designers who are qualifying individuals or qualifying persons are entitled to design right protection.

(ii) *Qualification by reference to commissioner or employer* (section 219)

A design created in pursuance of a commission from, or in the course of employment with, a qualifying person, qualifies for design right protection. Commission means a commission for money or money's worth. Employment means employment under a contract of service or of apprenticeship (see paragraph 3.68 onwards). Where such a design results from a joint commission or joint employment, it qualifies for design right protection if any of the commissioners or employers is a qualifying person. However, only those commissioners or employers who are qualifying persons will be entitled to design right protection. If none of the commissioners or employers (as the case may be) are qualifying persons then there will be no design right protection under section 219, even though the designer may be a qualifying person. The only way to get this protection would be under sections 220 or 221 (see below).   **13.23**

(iii) *Qualification by reference to first marketing* (section 220)

13.24   If a design does not qualify for design right protection by reference to the designer, commissioner, or employer, then it will qualify for design right protection if the first marketing of articles made to the design is done by a qualifying person who is exclusively authorised to put such articles on the market in the United Kingdom, and such first marketing takes place in the United Kingdom or any other Member State of the EEC or another country to which the provisions of Part III of the 1988 Act are extended under section 255. (See paragraph 13.42.) It is worth noting that not all categories of qualifying country are included for these purposes. It does not include countries designated by Order in Council under section 256 as enjoying reciprocal protection (see paragraph 13.42).

Marketing means selling or letting for hire or offering or exposing for sale or hire, in all cases, in the course of a business. Business includes a trade or profession. Marketing which is merely colourable and not intended to satisfy the reasonable requirements of the public does not count. This expression is the same as that appearing in section 49(2)(*b*) of the 1956 Act and section 175(5) of the 1988 Act in relation to publication and presumably will have the same meaning. (See paragraph 2.20.)

If the first marketing is done jointly by two or more persons, the design qualifies for design right protection if any of those persons meets the requirements outlined above. However, in such a case, only those persons who meet those requirements will be entitled to design right protection.

There are no provisions covering "simultaneous marketing" of the kind provided for in relation to copyright under section 49(2)(*d*) of the 1956 Act or section 155 of the 1988 Act. Therefore, subject to the "colourable marketing" exception, once first marketing has taken place, the opportunity for protection by this method will be lost immediately, unless the first marketing fulfils the requirements mentioned above.

For the purposes of section 220 "exclusively authorised" means authorised by the person who would have been the first owner of the design right as designer, commissioner of the design or employer of the designer if he had been a qualifying person or by a person lawfully claiming under such a person. In addition, the exclusivity must be capable of being enforced by legal proceedings in the United Kingdom. It would presumably cover an assignee of the design right or relevant part of the design right and an exclusive licensee, who has a legally enforceable exclusive licence, which is also enforceable against third parties under section 234. (See paragraph 13.32.)

(iv) *Qualification as a result of Order in Council* (section 221)

13.25   Under section 221 an Order in Council may be made providing that a design qualifies for design right protection. Such an Order may only be made with a view to fulfilling an international obligation. The Order may make different provisions for different descriptions of design or article and may make consequential modifications of the relevant ownership of design right provisions and means of qualification. This could significantly extend the number of designs qualifying for protection.

(e) *First ownership of design right* (section 215)

The designer will be the first owner of any design right in a design, unless it is created in pursuance of a commission or in the course of employment or unless the design only qualifies for protection by reference to first marketing of articles made to the design. In the case of a design created in pursuance of a commission, the person commissioning the design is the first owner of any design right in it. This differs from the provisions applying to copyright where the creator of the artistic work made in pursuance of a commission retains the copyright, but is similar to the provisions applying to registered designs under the 1949 Act, as amended by the 1988 Act. This could have a rather strange result where a design is commissioned, which is both an artistic work and a design. The commissioner will obtain the design right, but not the copyright. As can be seen from paragraph 13.20, the interrelationship of copyright and design right is far from straightforward and where the copyright is owned by one person and the design right is owned by another, complications could arise.

Where a design is created by an employee in the course of his employment and the design is not created in pursuance of a commission, his employer is the first owner of any design right in the design (s.215(39)). This presumably means that the commissioning provisions will override the employment provisions. For example, suppose a client commissions an advertising agency to create a design. That design is then created by an employee of the agency in the course of his employment. Normally, the agency as employer, would own the design right, but because this design is created in pursuance of a commission, section 215(3) does not apply and the agency is not the first owner of the design right. Nor can the employee be the first owner, because the design was created both in pursuance of a commission and in the course of employment (s.215(1)). Presumably the client is the first owner of the design right as he commissioned the design and the design was created in pursuance of that commission. An interesting question arises where the "employee" of the agency is in fact self-employed and therefore in this example, there are two commissioners, the agency and the client. Who then owns the design right is not clear. It could be either the agency or the client, as they have both "commissioned the design." Clearly in a case such as this, it would be wise to deal with the situation expressly in the contract governing the commission. However, the answer may be that, in such a case, the agency acts as agent for the client in commissioning the "employee" and thus the client is the commissioner and the design right therefore vests in the client.

Where a design qualifies for design right protection by reference to first marketing of articles made to the design, then the person by whom the articles in question are marketed is the first owner of the design right and the normal rules set out above do not apply. In such a case it would be a wise precaution for the person who would have been the first owner of the design right if he had been a qualifying person, to take an assignment of the design right from the first marketer, particularly where the exclusive authorisation granted to the first marketer is less than the period of design right protection.

(f) *Duration of design right* (section 216)

13.27   The normal rule is that design right will last until 15 years from the end of the calendar year in which the design was first recorded in the design document, or an article was first made to the design, whichever happened first. However, if, within five years from the end of that calendar year, articles made to the design are made available for sale or hire in any part of the world by or with the licence of the design right owner, then the design right will expire 10 years from the end of the calendar year in which the articles are made available for sale or hire. Thus, the period of protection could be anything between 10 and 15 years, depending on whether, and if so, when, articles made to the design are made available for sale or hire.

(g) *Dealings with design right* (sections 222 to 225)

13.28   The provisions governing dealings with the design right are set out in sections 222 to 225 of the 1988 Act. The provisions of section 222, dealing with assignments and licences, mirror similar provisions contained in section 90 relating to copyright. The provisions of section 223, dealing with prospective ownership of design right, mirror the provisions of section 91 dealing with prospective ownership of copyright. The provisions of section 225, dealing with exclusive licences, mirror the provisions of section 92 dealing with exclusive licences in relation to copyright. All of these copyright provisions have been dealt with elsewhere in this book (see paragraphs 10.20 onwards) and similar considerations apply in relation to the design right. The requirement relating to documents to be signed by companies is dealt with in section 261, which is in the same terms as section 176(1). (See paragraph 8.30.)

Section 224 covers the situation where a design consisting of a design in which design right subsists is registered under the 1949 Act and the proprietor of the registered design is also the owner of the design right. In such a case, unless a contrary intention appears, an assignment of the right in a registered design will be deemed to include an assignment of the design right as well. There is a corresponding provision in section 19(3)(B) of the 1949 Act. This provides that, in the circumstances set out above, an assignment of the design right shall be taken to be also an assignment of the right in the registered design, unless a contrary intention appears.

(h) *Rights of design right owner* (sections 226 to 228)

13.29   The owner of the design right in a design has the exclusive right to reproduce the design for commercial purposes—by making articles to that design, or by making a design document recording the design for the purpose of enabling such articles to be made.

In this context commercial purposes means "with a view to the article in question being sold or hired in the course of a business." Business includes a trade or profession (s.263). These rights are much more limited than the rights conferred by copyright.

Reproduction of a design by making articles to the design, means copying the design so as to produce articles exactly or substantially to that design. This makes it clear that copying is required for there to be infringement, which is not the case with registered designs. The wording used here setting out the similarity required before infringement takes place, differs both from the registered design provisions contained in the 1949 Act, and from the copyright provisions set out in Part I of the 1988 Act. Generally, in order to infringe a registered design, the resemblance of the infringing article has to be rather closer to the registered design than would be the case in respect of a copyright infringement. The wording chosen here seems to fall somewhere between the two, perhaps rather closer to the registered design test in view of the words "exactly or substantially to that design," which bear some similarity to the registered design wording contained in the 1949 Act: "not substantially different from the registered design."

The rights of the owner of the design right can be infringed in a number of ways.

1. Primary Infringement

There are two acts of primary infringement of design right. First, the **13.30** design right is infringed by a person who without the licence of the design right owner does, or authorises another to do, anything which is the exclusive right of the design right owner. This means that an infringer will have to reproduce the design by copying the design so as to produce articles exactly or substantially to the design with a view to the article in question being sold or hired in the course of a business. The reproduction will have to be pretty close to the design. The use of the words "making articles to" the design would seem to be wide enough to cover both direct and indirect reproduction. It is worth mentioning here that a design can include only part of an article (s.213(2)). On this basis, it is only necessary to find one part of an allegedly infringing design which is exactly or substantially to the design of the corresponding part of the original design, for there to be infringement. This differs from the situation with registered design protection, which can only cover part of an article, if that part is made and sold separately.

Where a design is contained in a design document which consists of a written description of the design, the design right will be infringed if an article is made without authority to the design from the written description. The article could be a three-dimensional object. This is an interesting extension and it is, perhaps, unlikely to happen. As has been seen (see paragraph 13.06) copyright in the design document would not be infringed by such an act, even without taking section 51 into account.

The second act of primary infringement is to reproduce the design by making a design document recording the design for the purpose of enabling articles to that design to be made and once again this must be done with a view to the articles in question being sold or hired in the course of a business. The wide meaning of design document should be borne in mind. (See paragraph 13.06.)

Reproduction may be direct or indirect and it is immaterial whether any intervening acts themselves infringe the design right. This is the same provision as is found in the copyright infringement provisions and deals with the points raised in the dissenting judgment of Lord Griffiths in the *British Leyland* case. (See paragraph 13.02.)

2. Secondary Infringement

13.31   Secondary infringement of the design right is also covered. Design right is infringed by a person who, without the licence of the design right owner:
imports into the United Kingdom for commercial purposes, or
has in his possession for commercial purposes, or
sells, lets for hire or offers or exposes for sale or hire in the course of a business,
an article which is, and which he knows or has reason to believe is, an infringing article.

Here again, "for commercial purposes" means with a view to the article in question being sold or hired in the course of a business.

The requirements are once again more onerous than in the case of secondary infringement of copyright. (See Chapter 6.)

In the case of copyright, importation of an infringing article only requires to be "otherwise than for private and domestic use." In practice it is going to be more difficult to prove the design right requirement.

In the case of copyright, possession has to be in the course of a business, whereas in the case of design right it will be necessary to prove that the infringer possesses the infringing article with a view to the article in question being sold or hired in the course of a business. It is not an infringement of the design right for a person to possess or use an infringing article in the course of a business, so long as it is not done with a view to the article in question being sold or hired.

In the case of copyright secondary infringement, it is only necessary to prove that an infringing article is sold, let for hire, offered or exposed for sale or hire and it is not necessary to prove, as it is in the case of design right, that this is done in the course of a business.

As to what is an infringing article, this is dealt with in section 228, which mirrors the provisions of section 27 dealing with infringing copies for copyright purposes. (See paragraph 6.26 onwards.) The expression "infringing article" does not include a design document, notwithstanding that its making was or would have been an infringement of design right.

It is expressly provided that all of the infringement of design right provisions are subject to the exceptions to rights of design right owners, which include licences of right, Crown use of designs and further exceptions provided by statutory instrument made under section 245. It is also subject to the provisions of section 236, which provides that copyright infringement effectively takes precedence over infringement of design right. (See paragraph 13.20.)

(i) *Remedies for infringement*

An infringement of design right is actionable by the design right owner.   **13.32**
Exactly as in a copyright action, in an action for infringement of design right, all such relief by way of damages, injunctions, accounts or otherwise is available to the plaintiff as is available in respect of the infringement of any other property right. (See Chapter 10.)

The court has a discretion to award additional damages in the case of a flagrant infringement. This provision is contained in section 229(3) which mirrors the equivalent copyright provision in section 97(2) (see paragraph 10.86 onwards). The whole of section 229 is subject to section 233, which deals with innocent infringement. Section 233(1) contains a provision which mirrors the similar copyright provision in section 97(1) (see paragraph 10.92) and deals with the case where the defendant did not know and had no reason to believe that the design right subsisted in the design to which the action relates. In the case of design right, this innocent infringement provision applies only to primary infringement, whereas in the case of copyright it applies to any infringement action.

In addition, there is a further innocent infringement provision which relates to design right and this is contained in section 233(2). This covers only secondary infringement. Where, in an action for secondary infringement of design right, a defendant shows that the infringing article was innocently acquired by him or a predecessor in title of his, the only remedy available against him in respect of the infringement is damages not exceeding a reasonable royalty in respect of the act complained of. For these purposes an article is deemed to have been innocently acquired when the person acquiring the article did not know and had no reason to believe it was an infringing article.

Section 230 contains provisions dealing with the right of a design right owner of delivery up of infringing articles. By and large these mirror the provisions contained in sections 99 and 113 of the 1988 Act dealing with the same situation in relation to copyright. (See paragraphs 10.103.) The only material difference is that in section 230 it is necessary to show that the person concerned has an infringing article in his possession, custody or control "for commercial purposes" rather than "in the course of a business." Once again, "for commercial purposes" means with a view to the article in question being sold or hired in the course of a business. For this reason, it is likely to be more difficult to obtain an order under section 230, than it is under section 99.

Section 231 relates to orders as to disposal of infringing articles and mirrors the provisions of section 114, save that section 114 also deals with the situation where articles are seized in accordance with section 100 or delivered up in criminal proceedings, in addition to the situation where infringing articles are delivered up in civil proceedings. There is no equivalent right to seize articles which infringe design right and no delivery up provisions relating to criminal proceedings. However, otherwise the provisions are largely the same. (See paragraph 10.104.)

Section 232 provides that a county court may entertain proceedings under section 230, 231 and 235(5) where the value of the infringing articles and other things in question does not exceed the county court limit for actions in tort.

Rights and remedies of exclusive licensees and provisions with respect to concurrent rights of action between design right owners and exclusive licensees are dealt with in sections 234 and 235 of the 1988 Act. These provisions mirror the provisions set out in sections 101 and 102 which relate to copyright. (See paragraph 10.20 onwards.)

There are no criminal sanctions for infringement of design right and this is a significant difference from the position regarding infringement of copyright where there are substantial criminal sanctions and related remedies.

(j) *Ownership of design right, joint ownership and joint designs* (sections 258 to 260)

13.33   Where different persons are entitled to different aspects of design right in a work, the design right owner for any particular purpose is the person who is entitled to the right in the respect relevant for that purpose. All of the provisions relating to design right in the 1988 Act have therefore to be looked at in this light.

In addition, where design right, or any aspect of design right, is owned by more than one person jointly, references to the design right owner in Part III of the 1988 Act are to all the owners, so that, in particular, any requirement of the licence of the design right owner requires the licence of all of them.

Where reference is made to the designer of a design, which is a joint design, it is to be construed in relation to that joint design as a reference to all the designers of the design. For these purposes a joint design means a design produced by the collaboration of two or more designers in which the contribution of each is not distinct from that of the other or others.

(k) *Kits* (section 260)

13.34   A kit for the purposes of Part III of the 1988 Act is a complete or substantially complete set of components intended to be assembled into an article. The provisions of Part III apply in relation to the kit as they apply in relation to the assembled article. This is not to affect the question of whether design right subsists in any aspects of the design of the components of a kit as opposed to the design of the assembled article. This means that each individual piece of the kit can be looked at separately, as well as looking at the assembled article. The intention is that kits will receive the same degree of protection as the assembled article. However, the "must fit" and "must match" exceptions result in some protection being lost for replacement parts, as would be the case for an article supplied in assembled form.

(1) *Exceptions to rights of design right owners*

(i) *Infringement of copyright* (section 236)

Where a copyright subsists in a work which consists of or includes a design **13.35** in which design right subsists, it is not an infringement of design right in the design to do anything which is an infringement of the copyright in that work. This means that the copyright owner's rights take precedence over the rights of the design right owner. (See paragraph 13.20.)

(ii) *Licences of right* (sections 237 to 239)

Any person is entitled as of right to a licence to do in the last five years of **13.36** the design right term anything which would otherwise infringe the design right. Person includes a body of persons, corporate or unincorporate.

There appears to be no scope for the licence of right to cover an infringement of copyright or an infringement of registered design and this may be particularly relevant if the copying of a design document is an infringement of copyright. (See paragraph 13.08.) It will also be necessary to carry out registered design searches to ensure that no design is registered which would be infringed by the licence of right.

The Secretary of State may by Order exclude from the operation of the licence of right provision, designs of a description specified in the Order or designs applied to articles of a description so specified. He may make the Order if it appears to him necessary in order to comply with an international obligation of the United Kingdom or to secure or maintain reciprocal protection for British designs in other countries. A British design is one which qualifies for design right protection by reason of a connection with the United Kingdom of the designer, or of the person by whom the design is commissioned or the designer is employed.

Power is given under the Fair Trading Act 1973 for licences to be made available as of right for the protection of the public interest. The provisions are contained in section 238, which mirrors the similar copyright provisions contained in section 144(1) and (2) covering the same situation in relation to copyright. (See paragraph 9.135 onwards.) Similar licences of right are now also provided for in section 11A of the 1949 Act as amended by the 1988 Act in relation to registered designs.

There is a provision in section 239 permitting a defendant to undertake to take a licence of right in infringement proceedings. These provisions mirror those set out in section 98 relating to copyright infringement. (See paragraph 9.138.) Again there are roughly similar provisions in relation to registered designs in section 11B of the 1949 Act as amended by the 1988 Act, but only in relation to public interest licences of right.

In the case of the design right, the terms of a licence of right in each case are either to be reached by agreement or, in default of agreement, to be settled by the comptroller. This applies whatever the circumstances in which the licence of right situation arose. In the case of the copyright provisions, the terms of the licence are settled by the Copyright Tribunal, rather than by the comptroller. Otherwise, the provisions are parallel. The jurisdiction of the comptroller is dealt with below. (See paragraph 13.39.)

It goes without saying that all licences of right must be non-exclusive.

Where a licence of right in the last five years of the design right term or in the public interest has been granted, the licensee is not allowed, unless he first obtains the consent of the design right owner:

to apply to goods which he is marketing, or proposes to market, in reliance on that licence a trade description indicating that he is the licensee of the design right owner; or

use any such trade description in an advertisement in relation to such goods.

For the purposes of this provision "trade description" and "advertisement" have the same meanings as those contained in the Trade Descriptions Act 1968.

The consent does not have to be in writing and may therefore be given orally or by conduct. The design right owner is entitled to take action in respect of any contravention of this provision. This provision is almost akin to a statutory passing-off remedy and will give comfort to design right owners who may fear unfair competition from licensees of right, who may seek to cash in on the goodwill of the design right owner.

(iii) *Crown use of designs* (sections 240 to 244)

13.37   It remains to be seen how important this exception to design right will be, but clearly it is going to affect some areas much more than others. The main provisions are contained in section 240. All the provisions are very one-sided in favour of the Crown.

A government department, or a person authorised in writing by a government department, may, without the licence of the design right owner:

do anything for the purpose of supplying articles for the service of the Crown; or

dispose of articles no longer required for the service of the Crown; and nothing done by virtue of this provision infringes the design right.

The powers contained in this provision are extremely wide and there is nothing that the design right owner can do to prevent such use if it falls within the provisions. However, it is only the design right which is affected by these Crown use provisions. Other rights, such as copyright and registered design would not be affected by these provisions, but might be affected by the 1949 Act, as amended, or the copyright provisions of the 1988 Act.

References to the services of the Crown are to the defence of the realm, foreign defence purposes, and health services purposes.

"The defence of the realm" is not defined and it seems unlikely that a design right owner could argue successfully against a government department in a case where the department claims that defence of the realm is involved, except in the most obvious case of abuse.

"Foreign defence purposes" means either supply for the defence of a country outside the realm in pursuance of an agreement or arrangement to which the government of that country and the government of the United Kingdom are parties, or supply for use by armed forces operating in pursuance of a resolution of the United Nations or one of its organs.

The use of the word "arrangement" is so vague as to cover almost any understanding which may be reached between the United Kingdom government and any other government.

Supply of articles for "health service purposes" means the supply for the purpose of providing pharmaceutical services, or general medical services, or general dental services of the kinds provided in Part II of the National Health Service Act 1977.

Again, the powers of the Government are enormous and it remains to be seen to what extent they will in fact be exercised. "Crown use," in relation to a design, means the doing of anything by virtue of section 240 which would otherwise be an infringement of design right in the design.

The authority of a government department in respect of Crown use of a design may be given to a person before or after the use and whether or not that person is authorised, directly or indirectly, by the design right owner to do anything in relation to the design.

A person acquiring anything sold in the exercise of power conferred by section 240, and any person claiming under him may deal with the thing in the same manner as if a design right were held on behalf of the Crown.

Section 241 contains the provisions for settlement of the terms applicable to Crown use. These will be settled by agreement or, in default of agreement, by the court. The comptroller has no jurisdiction in such a case.

The Crown is under an obligation to notify the design right owner as soon as practicable after Crown use is made of a design, and to give him such information as to the extent of the use as he may from time to time require. However, the Crown can avoid this obligation if it appears to the Government that it would be contrary to the public interest to notify the design right owner or give such information or alternatively if the identity of the design right owner cannot be ascertained on reasonable inquiry.

If the design right owner cannot be ascertained on reasonable inquiry, the government department concerned may apply to the court, which has power to order that no royalty or other sum shall be payable until the owner agrees terms with the department or refers the matter to the court for determination.

Section 242 sets out detailed provisions covering the rights of third parties, particularly licensees, in the case of Crown use. It also covers the position where a design right has been assigned by the original design right owner to a new owner. The section contains detailed provisions as to the apportionment of compensation between the respective interested parties.

Section 243 makes provision for the government department concerned to pay compensation for loss of profits to the design right owner or an exclusive licensee, for any loss resulting from the design right owner or licensee not being awarded a contract to supply articles made to the design.

Section 244 confers additional powers on the government department concerned in the case of Crown use during an emergency.

(iv) *Further exceptions*

13.38   The Secretary of State may, if it appears to him necessary in order to comply with an international obligation of the United Kingdom, or to secure or maintain reciprocal protection for British designs in other countries, by Order provide that acts of a description specified in an Order do not infringe design right.

Such an Order may make different provisions for different descriptions of design or article.

A British design, for these purposes, has the same meaning as in paragraph 13.36.

(m) *Jurisdiction of comptroller*

13.39   The 1988 Act lays down a procedure for settling disputes which may arise in relation to the design right. In the absence of a requirement of registration, there are perhaps likely to be more questions arising as to subsistence and ownership of design right than is the case for registered designs. The main provisions are set out in section 246.

If there is a dispute as to any of the following matters:
the subsistence of design right;
the term of design right;
the identity of the person in whom design right first vested;
any party to the dispute may refer it to the comptroller for his decision and that decision will be binding on the parties to the dispute. It may be difficult to say exactly when a dispute arises. For example, if the other party to a dispute refuses to answer letters or argue, it may not be clear whether or not there is a dispute. However, common sense would seem to suggest that if one party refuses to co-operate, then there is a dispute.

It is expressly provided that no other court or tribunal shall decide any of these three matters except:
on a reference or appeal from the comptroller;
in infringement or other proceedings in which the issue arises incidentally; or
in proceedings brought with the agreement of the parties, or the leave of the comptroller.

The effect of this will be that the parties to the dispute can agree to refer the matter straight to the court, or indeed either party to a dispute could seek the permission of the comptroller to refer the matter to the court, even if the other party does not agree. Appeals from the comptroller's decision on such disputes go to the High Court.

It is fairly routine in copyright proceedings for subsistence and ownership of copyright to be put in issue. There seems no reason to suppose that design right proceedings are going to be any different. There is no procedure for infringement proceedings to be taken before the comptroller and these will therefore have to be initiated in the court in the normal way. One can envisage, therefore, a dispute which falls within the jurisdiction of the comptroller, arising after proceedings have in fact been issued. The question will then arise as to whether the dispute arises incidentally to the infringement proceedings. This will depend on the circumstances of each particular case.

If experience in copyright proceedings is anything to go by, a letter before action, if it produces any response, very often produces a response questioning subsistence and ownership of copyright and may raise a number of other matters as well. A design right owner receiving such a reply will face a difficulty. He will wish to obtain an interlocutory injunction in many cases and will therefore be obliged to issue proceedings very swiftly. However, if the subsistence of design right is put in issue by the alleged infringer, it is not immediately clear whether this issue arises "incidentally" "in infringement or other proceedings," particularly if the proceedings have not in fact yet been commenced. In practice, the answer will probably be to issue proceedings and obtain an interlocutory injunction after making out a prima facie case. The main issue will then be the infringement proceedings and the subsistence issue is unlikely to be separated for decision by the comptroller.

The comptroller also has jurisdiction to decide any incidental question of fact or law arising in the course of a reference of a dispute to him. Whether this provision is sufficient to give the comptroller jurisdiction to decide a question of infringement is doubtful.

Another area where the comptroller will have considerable jurisdiction is in relation to licences of right. Application may be made to the comptroller to settle the terms of the licence. In the case of a licence available as of right in the last five years of the design right term ("a five-year licence"), or in the case of a licence available in the public interest ("a public interest licence"), application is made by the person wishing to take the licence. Application should also be made to the comptroller for a licence of right under the transitional provisions. (See paragraph 13.12.)

In the case of a five-year licence, no application may be made to the comptroller earlier than one year before the earliest date on which such a licence may take effect. Such a licence will authorise the applicant to do everything which would otherwise be an infringement of the design right in the absence of the licence. In the case of a public interest licence, the licence will authorise everything in respect of which a licence is available in the public interest.

The Secretary of State has power to make an Order setting out the factors which the comptroller must have regard to in settling the terms of a licence. At the time of writing, no such Order has been made. Some concern has been expressed over the sort of terms which the comptroller is likely to settle for licences of right. Obviously remuneration will have to be dealt with. However, of almost as much concern may be the question of quality control and it does not seem certain that the comptroller will impose terms governing quality control by the licensor. All licences of right will be non-exclusive and different terms may be considered appropriate to different types of design and product. Some guidance can perhaps be gained from the licence of right cases involving patents. These indicate that the comptroller is likely to have a wide discretion and that weight will be given to the findings of the comptroller.

Once the comptroller has settled the terms of a licence, the licence will take effect in each case from the date on which the application to the comptroller was made, except in the case of early applications for a five-year licence. In respect of an application made for such a licence before the earliest date on which the licence may take effect, the licence will take effect on that earliest date. An application for such a licence after the earliest date, will take effect on the date of application in the normal way.

There are provisions covering the situation where the applicant for a licence of right is unable on reasonable inquiry to discover the identity of a design right owner. "Reasonable inquiry" is not defined and must be given its ordinary and natural meaning. In such a case the comptroller may order that the licence shall be granted free of any obligation to pay royalties or any other payments. If the comptroller makes an order of this kind, the design right owner can apply to the comptroller to vary the terms of the licence. However, any such variation will only take effect from the date on which the design right owner makes his application. These provisions demonstrate the desirability of marking articles made to a design at least with the name of the owner of the design right. There is no legal requirement to do this, but there are obvious practical advantages.

If the comptroller settles the terms of a licence of right in these circumstances and it subsequently turns out that a licence of right was not available, the licensee is not liable for damages or an account of profits in respect of anything done before he was aware of any claim by the design right owner that a licence was not available. However, from the moment he does become so aware, the licensee is vulnerable.

Appeals from the comptroller in respect of matters relating to settlement of the terms of licences of right lie to the Appeal Tribunal constituted under section 28 of the 1949 Act. Section 28 will apply to appeals from the comptroller, but special rules may be made under that section to deal specially with design right licence of right appeals.

The Secretary of State has power to make rules regulating the procedure to be followed in connection with any proceeding before the comptroller. At the time of writing, no rules have been published. The matters likely to be covered by the rules are set out in section 250.

The comptroller has no jurisdiction in relation to matters concerning Crown use of a design.

(n) *Jurisdiction of the court* (sections 251 and 252)

The comptroller has power to refer disputes under section 246 to the High Court. He can refer the whole proceedings, or any question or issue, whether of fact or law. The comptroller is bound to refer the matter if the parties to the proceedings agree that he should do so. If the matter is referred to the court, it may exercise any powers available to the comptroller as respects the matter referred to it and after determining the issue, may refer any matter back to the comptroller. Appeals from decisions of the comptroller under section 246 go to the High Court.

13.40

The court also has considerable jurisdiction in relation to Crown use and these provisions are set out in section 252.

(o) *Threats actions* (section 253)

Section 253 contains a right for a person aggrieved by threats of proceedings for infringement of design right. There is no similar provision in relation to copyright, but section 26 of the 1949 Act contains a very similar provision in relation to registered designs, as does section 70 of the Patents Act 1977 in relation to patents.

13.41

Where a person threatens another person with proceedings for infringement of design right, a person aggrieved by the threat may bring an action against him claiming:
a declaration to the effect that the threats are unjustifiable;
an injunction against the continuance of a threat;
damages in respect of any loss which he sustained by the threats.

The plaintiff must prove that the threats were made and that he is a person aggrieved by them and he will then be entitled to the relief claimed. He does not have to show that he himself was threatened. It would, for example, cover the situation where one of his customers was threatened. However, the defendant can defeat such an action by showing that the acts in respect of which the proceedings are threatened did constitute, or if done would have constituted, an infringement of the design right concerned.

Mere notification that a design is protected by design right does not constitute a threat of proceedings. In addition, the 1988 Act has amended section 26 of the 1949 Act to introduce a new provision in relation to registered designs, which also appears in section 253 in relation to design right. This provides that proceedings may not be brought in respect of a threat to bring proceedings for an infringement which is alleged to consist of making or importing anything. This will cut down the scope of the threats action. A similar provision was introduced for the first time in relation to patents in the Patents Act 1977.

(p) *Countries to which Part III of the 1988 Act extends* (sections 255 to 257)

13.42 Provisions governing the countries to which Part III of the 1988 Act extends are set out in sections 255 and 256 of the 1988 Act.

Part III extends automatically to England and Wales, Scotland and Northern Ireland.

An Order in Council may extend Part III to any of the Channel Islands, the Isle of Man, or any colony.

Such extension may be subject to such exceptions and modifications as may be specified in the Order.

Such an Order may also extend to such countries, subject to such exceptions and modifications as may be specified in the Order, any Order in Council made under section 221 (see paragraph 13.25) or section 256 (see below).

The legislature of any country to which Part III has been extended as described above, may modify or add to the provisions of Part III, in their operation as part of the law of that country, as the legislature may consider necessary to adapt the provisions to the circumstances of that country. However, no such modification or addition may deny design right protection in a case where it would otherwise exist. This means that substantially the same minimum level of design right protection must be provided in each country to which Part III is extended.

When a colony to which Part III has been extended, ceases to be a colony, Part III will continue to be extended to that country until either an Order in Council is made under section 256 designating it as a country enjoying reciprocal protection, or an Order in Council is made declaring that it shall cease to be treated as a country to which Part III extends. The latter will only happen when the provisions of Part III as part of the law of that country have been amended or appealed.

Section 256 contains the reciprocal protection provisions. These provide that an Order in Council may designate a country which provides adequate protection for British designs, as one enjoying reciprocal protection under Part III. A British design is a design which qualifies for design right protection by reason of a connection with the United Kingdom of the designer, or the person by whom the design is commissioned or the designer is employed.

Section 256 contains provision for the situation where the country concerned provides adequate protection only for certain classes of British design, or only for designs applied to certain classes of articles. In such a case the Order designating that country must contain provisions limiting, to a corresponding extent, the protection afforded by Part III in relation to designs connected with that country.

Section 257 deals with territorial waters and the continental shelf and is in exactly similar terms to section 161 which deals with copyright. (See paragraph 5.06.) However, Part III does not apply to things done on a British ship, aircraft or hovercraft. This differs from the position of the copyright provisions, which do apply in such circumstances (s.162).

C. REGISTERED DESIGNS

1. General

Registered designs fall outside the scope of this book. However, as they **13.43** overlap to an extent both with copyright and design right, a few observations are appropriate. Registered designs are dealt with in Part IV of the 1988 Act.

The definition of "design" for registered design purposes is in some respects more, and in others less, restricted than the definition contained in either Part I or Part III of the 1988 Act. The chief differences are as follows:

(a) Registered designs must have features which appeal to and are judged by the eye. There is no such requirement for unregistered designs.

(b) Features of shape or configuration dictated solely by the function are not disqualified from unregistered design right protection.

(c) Surface decoration enjoys no unregistered design right protection, but may be registrable.

(d) The "must fit" exclusion (see paragraph 13.18) applies only to unregistered designs.

(e) A design is not registrable in respect of an article if aesthetic considerations are not normally taken into account to a material extent by persons acquiring or using articles of that description and would not be taken into account if the design were applied to the article. This is a new requirement, introduced by the 1988 Act in relation to registered designs. There is no similar provision which applies to unregistered designs.

Designs will fall into a number of categories, some of which will be registrable and others not, and some will enjoy design right protection and others not. The most important question which arises, is whether it is now worth registering a design, in cases where it is registrable. Clearly it will be, if unregistered design right protection would not be available and the only protection available is that afforded by registration. However, there will be cases in relation to the same design, where design right protection is available in addition to registered design right protection. That the two can co-exist is clearly recognised by section 224 of the 1988 Act and section 19(3)(B) of the 1949 Act as amended. (See paragraph 13.28.) The two rights will normally start off in the same ownership, as section 3(2) of the 1949 Act as amended provides that an application for a registered design will not be entertained unless it is made by the person claiming to be the design right owner. The rights could be assigned separately, but there are presumptions making this unlikely to happen accidentally. (See paragraph 13.28.)

There are considerable advantages to registered designs which may well make it worthwhile registering designs in future. The copyright protection afforded to registrable designs under the 1956 Act made the benefits of registration of a design less important. Now that the scope of copyright protection in such cases has been reduced in some circumstances, the benefits of registration seem very attractive and they will undoubtedly be used much more in future. The major benefits are:

(a) The term of new registered designs will be for up to 25 years.

(b) Licences of right and compulsory licences are only available in very limited circumstances.

(c) The registered design right is a monopoly right and it is not necessary to prove copying in infringement proceedings.

(d) Proving ownership of a registered design is easier as a result of the registration.

By comparison, the protection given by design right seems much less significant. The major shortcoming is the duration of design right, which is effectively only five years from first making available for sale or hire of articles made to the design. Thereafter licences of right are available for the next five years and then the right expires. The period of exclusivity is so short as to limit severely the value of the right.

2. Concurrent rights

13.44   If a design, which enjoys design right protection is also registered as a registered design, it seems that the protection of both rights will be available to the proprietor of the rights. Although there are some cross-references between the provisions dealing with each respective right, it is not expressly stated which takes precedence. Usually the same person will own both rights and no problem should arise. However, the question may arise in regard to licences of right of the design right.

These licences may arise in a number of circumstances, but most commonly in the last five years of the design right term. The exercise of such a licence of right would involve infringement of registered design rights if the design was registered. Which takes precedence? The wording of section 237 is very clear and states that any person is entitled as of right to a licence to do in the last five years of the design right term anything which would otherwise infringe the design right. No reference is made to registered design rights or copyright. One would have expected some provision to be made expressly to deal with potential conflicts.

In the absence of any express wording, it is thought that the registered design right and copyright must continue to exist and be exercisable and, effectively, to take precedence over the licence of right to the extent that exercise of the licence conflicts with the registered design right or copyright.

Section 2(2) of the 1949 Act envisages a situation where the right to apply a registered design to an article becomes vested "by operation of law" in a person other than the original proprietor. In such a case that person, or that person and the original proprietor jointly, are treated as the proprietor of the design. The question is whether a licence of right is a "right" which becomes vested by operation of law in the licensee of right. If it is, then one can perhaps reconcilethe conflicting provisions. It will mean that the licence of right will also apply to the registered design during the period of licence and also that the licensee will, during the term of the licence, be a joint proprietor of the registered design.

This would be a rather surprising result. It would mean that during the period of 25 years of a registered design in which design right also subsisted, licences of right would become available for a period of five years during the course of the 25-year term, depending on when licences of right first become available. At the end of that five-year period, licences of right would cease to be available and the monopoly of the registered design would be restored.

The answer is probably that a "licence" has been held not to be a "right" (see *Heap* v. *Hartley* [1889] R.P.C. 495) and therefore section 2(2) of the 1949 Act would not confer any rights on a licensee of right. That being the case, the registered design right will be unaffected by and take precedence over a licensee of right of the design right.

D. SEMI-CONDUCTORS AND TOPOGRAPHY

The Semi-Conductor Product (Protection of Topography) Regulations 1987 issued under the European Communities Act 1972 following the EEC Council Directive on the subject, introduced a new topography right in respect of designs of electronic circuitry intended to be used in semi-conductor products. Such topographical patterns might look something like a complicated London Underground map. These patterns are etched and filled into the layers of semi-conductor material which make up the semi-conductor chip. The topography right also covers the arrangement of the various layers embodying these patterns in relation to each other. **13.45**

The topography right was introduced in addition to and independent of copyright protection. Semi-conductor topographies attract copyright, but the protection offered will be subject to section 51 of the 1988 Act. (See paragraph 13.06.) However, section 51 will not apply to pre-1988 Act topographies until 10 years after the commencement of the 1988 Act and so during this period they will have full copyright protection.

Pre-1988 Act works will not have the new design right protection. However, the new design right will apply to post-1988 Act topographical design patterns and to some extent the new design right will overlap with the existing topography right. The two rights are not however identical. The topography right is subject to the peculiar exemption that it is not infringed by the creation of another original topography resulting from the analysis or evaluation of the concepts, processes, systems or techniques embodied in it. There are also differences as to qualification and duration. In addition, design right is subject to licences of right, whilst the topography right is not.

Another important distinction is that the design right can apply to computer-generated works whereas the topography right only subsists if the topography is the result of the creator's own intellectual effort.

In order to avoid these anomalies a new statutory instrument, the Design Right Semi-Conductor (Regulations) 1989 ("the 1989 Regulations") is proposed. The 1989 Regulations, if implemented, would revoke the 1987 Regulations and in its place amend Part III of the 1988 Act so that the new design right expressly applies to semi-conductor topographies, but in such a way that the design right given to semi-conductor topographies will be amended so as to be equivalent to the protection given by the topography right under the 1987 Regulations. Thus, the licence of right, duration, qualification and infringement provisions in the 1988 Act will all be amended in relation only to semi-conductor topographies to reflect what is in the 1987 Regulations.

The current drafting of the 1989 Regulations would however allow a computer-generated topography to qualify for protection.

The overall effect of the 1989 Regulations should therefore mean that the topography right itself will cease and be replaced by a new design right for semi-conductors designs, which will also supersede the design right which would otherwise exist under the 1988 Act in those designs. The relationship between this new design right and copyright will presumably be governed by section 236 of the 1988 Act, so that copyright protection will take precedence over design right protection.

14 PETER PAN

1. Introduction

Generally, copyright protection is conferred on works without discrim- **14.01**
ination. The very limited exception to this under the 1956 Act, the
perpetual university copyrights, has finally been brought to an end under
the 1988 Act. (See paragraph 4.35.) The 1988 Act however has introduced a perpetual quasi-copyright in relation to one work, the play "Peter
Pan" by Sir James Matthew Barrie. The copyright in this work was
granted and bequeathed by Barrie to the Hospital for Sick Children in
Great Ormond Street, but expired on December 31, 1987.

2. The work

The right referred to in paragraph 14.05 below arises not only in relation **14.02**
to use of the whole work, but also a substantial part (see paragraph 5.09)
of the work, and an adaptation of the work. (See paragraph 5.50.) The
right will therefore extend to a version of the play in the form of a story, or
picture book, as well as a translation.

3. Duration

No period is specified, and presumably the rights continue in perpetuity, **14.03**
subject to any subsequent legislation.

4. Ownership

The right to a royalty belongs to the special trustees appointed for the **14.04**
Hospital for Sick Children under the National Health Service Act 1977.
The right may not be assigned, and will cease if the trustees purport to
assign or charge it. It will also cease if the hospital ceases to have a
separate identity, or ceases to have purposes which include the care of
sick children.

5. The right

The trustees are entitled to a royalty in respect of any public perform- **14.05**
ance, commercial publication, broadcasting or inclusion in a cable programme service of the whole or any substantial part of the work or an
adaptation of it.
   The meaning of these provisions is the same as in the provisions
relating to copyright, and these are dealt with in paragraph 5.30 (public
performance), paragraph 4.49 (commercial publication), paragraph 5.44

(broadcasting) and paragraph 5.46 (inclusion in a cable programme service).

This right is only to claim a royalty, and not a grant of the exclusive right to do and authorise others to do the above acts. It seems to follow therefore that the trustees will have no remedy if someone refuses to pay a royalty other than to have the royalty assessed by the Copyright Tribunal (see paragraph 14.07 below), and then sue for the amount awarded. This may lead to unjust results where the party exploiting the work later becomes insolvent.

The entitlement to a royalty does not preclude the trustees agreeing to accept some other form of remuneration, such as a lump sum payment.

It is unclear whether the trustees are entitled to claim a royalty in relation to exploitation outside the United Kingdom. It is expressly stated in the copyright provisions of the 1988 Act that the copyright owner only has the exclusive right to do and authorise others to do the restricted acts in the United Kingdom. There is no similar qualification in relation to the right to a royalty for exploitation of "Peter Pan," but it seems unlikely on normal principles of construction of statutes that the Copyright Tribunal would award a royalty for exploitation abroad even where the person exploiting the work is in the United Kingdom.

5. Exceptions to the right

14.06   No royalty is payable in respect of anything which immediately before copyright in the work expired on December 31, 1987 could lawfully have been done without the licence or further licence of the trustees as copyright owners. Although the drafting of this provision is somewhat strange, the main effect of this appears to be that anything which was permitted under the 1956 Act without a licence being necessary will also be permitted under the 1988 Act without the necessity of any royalty being paid.

Furthermore, no royalty is payable in respect of anything which if copyright still subsisted in the work could by virtue of the provisions on permitted acts under the 1988 Act be done without infringing copyright. (See Chapter 7.)

Finally, no royalty is payable in respect of anything done in pursuance of arrangements made before the passing of the 1988 Act.

6. Amount of royalty

14.07   Presumably in many cases the amount of royalty will be agreed. If it is not, application may be made to the Copyright Tribunal by either party. The Tribunal has power to make such order regarding the royalty or other remuneration to be paid as it may determine to be reasonable in the circumstances. There is also power to vary orders.

APPENDIX 1

COUNTRY	ALGERIA	ANDORRA	BRITISH ANTARCTIC TERRITORY	ANTIGUA	ARGENTINA	AUSTRALIA with Norfolk Island
Nationality Status	No	No	No	Yes	No	Yes
Extended	No	No	Yes	Yes	No	No
Applied	Yes	Yes	No	No	Yes	Yes
Convention	UCC	UCC	None	None	Berne; UCC; Geneva	Berne; UCC; Geneva
Fully retroactive	No	No	Yes	Yes	Yes	Yes
Partially retroactive	Yes	Yes	N/A	N/A	N/A	N/A
Date for publication purposes	August 28, 1973	September 27, 1957	N/A	N/A	N/A	N/A
Date of commencement of 1956 Act	August 28, 1973	September 27, 1957	June 1, 1957	June 1, 1957	September 27, 1957	September 27, 1957
Application of Translation rights provisions	No	No	No	No	No	No
Limited sound recording rights	Yes	Yes	Yes	Yes	Yes	No
Vested rights clause	Yes	Yes	N/A	N/A	Yes	Yes
Sound broadcasts protected	No	No	Yes, BBC and IBA only	Yes, BBC and IBA only	No	No
Television broadcasts protected	No	No	Yes, BBC and IBA only	Yes, BBC and IBA only	No	No

481

COUNTRY	AUSTRIA	BAHAMAS	BAHRAIN	BANGLADESH	BARBADOS	BELGIUM
Nationality Status	No	Yes	Yes, from January 28, 1949 to January 1, 1975 when it was a protectorate	Yes	Yes	No
Extended	No	No	No	No	No	No
Applied	Yes	Yes	No	Yes	Yes	Yes
Convention	Berne; UCC; Rome; Geneva	Berne; UCC	None	UCC	Berne; UCC; Rome; Geneva	Berne; UCC
Fully retroactive	Yes	Yes	N/A	No	Yes	Yes
Partially retroactive	N/A	N/A	N/A	Yes	N/A	N/A
Date for publication purposes	N/A	N/A	N/A	August 5, 1975	N/A	N/A
Date of commencement of 1956 Act	September 27, 1957	June 1, 1957	N/A	August 5, 1975	June 1, 1957	September 27, 1957
Application of Translation rights provisions	Yes	No	N/A	No	No	No
Limited sound recording rights	No	Yes	N/A	Yes	No	Yes
Vested rights clause	No	Yes	N/A	Yes	Yes	Yes
Sound broadcasts protected	Yes, June 9, 1973	No	N/A	No	Yes, September 18, 1983	No
Television broadcasts protected	Yes, June 9, 1973	No	N/A	No	Yes, September 18, 1983	Yes, March 8, 1968

COUNTRY	BELIZE	BENIN	BERMUDA	BOTSWANA	BRAZIL	BRUNEI
Nationality Status	Yes	No	Yes	Yes	No	Yes
Extended	No	No	Yes	Yes	No	No
Applied	Yes	Yes	No	No	Yes	No
Convention	UCC	Berne	None	None	Berne; UCC; Rome; Geneva	None
Fully retroactive	Yes	Yes	Yes	Yes	Yes	N/A
Partially retroactive	N/A	N/A	N/A	N/A	N/A	N/A
Date for publication purposes	N/A	N/A	N/A	N/A	N/A	N/A
Date of commencement of 1956 Act	June 1, 1957	September 27, 1957	1 June, 1957	June 1, 1957	September 27, 1957	N/A
Application of Translation rights provisions	No	No	No	No	No	N/A
Limited sound recording rights	Yes	Yes	Yes	Yes	No	N/A
Vested rights clause	Yes	Yes	No	Yes	Yes	N/A
Sound broadcasts protected	No	No	Yes	Yes	Yes, September 29, 1965	N/A
Television broadcasts protected	No	No	Yes	Yes	Yes, September 29, 1965	N/A

COUNTRY	BURKINA FASO (formerly Upper Volta)	BULGARIA	BURMA	CAMEROON	CANADA	CAYMAN ISLANDS
Nationality Status	No	No	Yes, until Independence Act 1947	No	Yes	Yes
Extended	No	No	1911 Act extended up to independence in 1948	No	No	Yes
Applied	Yes	Yes	No	Yes	Yes	No
Convention	Berne; Rome; Geneva	Berne; UCC	No	Berne; UCC	Berne; UCC	None
Fully retroactive	Yes	Yes	Yes	Yes	Yes	Yes
Partially retroactive	N/A	N/A	N/A	N/A	N/A	N/A
Date for publication purposes	N/A	N/A	N/A	N/A	N/A	N/A
Date of commencement of 1956 Act	September 27, 1957	September 27, 1957	N/A	September 27, 1957	September 27, 1957	June 1, 1957
Application of Translation rights provisions	No	No	N/A	No	No	No
Limited sound recording rights	No	Yes	N/A	Yes	Yes	Yes
Vested rights clause	Yes	Yes	N/A	Yes	Yes	No
Sound broadcasts protected	Yes, January 14, 1988	No	N/A	No	No	Yes
Television broadcasts protected	Yes, January 14, 1988	No	N/A	No	No	Yes

COUNTRY	CENTRAL AFRICAN REPUBLIC	CHAD	CHANNEL ISLANDS	CHILE	COLOMBIA	CONGO
Nationality Status	No	No	Yes	No	No	No
Extended	No	No	Yes	No	No	No
Applied	Yes	Yes	No	Yes	Yes	Yes
Convention	Berne	Berne	None	Berne; UCC; Rome; Geneva	Berne; UCC; Rome	Berne; Rome
Fully retroactive	Yes	Yes	Yes	Yes	Yes	Yes
Partially retroactive	N/A	N/A	N/A	N/A	N/A	N/A
Date for publication purposes	N/A	N/A	N/A	N/A	N/A	N/A
Date of commencement of 1956 Act	September 27, 1957	September 27, 1957	June 1, 1957	September 27, 1957	September 27, 1957	September 27, 1957
Application of Translation rights provisions	No	No	No	No	No	No
Limited sound recording rights	Yes	Yes	Yes	No	No	No
Vested rights clause	Yes	Yes	N/A	Yes	Yes	Yes
Sound broadcasts protected	No	No	Yes, BBC and IBA only	Yes, September 5, 1974	Yes, September 17, 1976	Yes, May 18, 1964
Television broadcasts protected	No	No	Yes, BBC and IBA only	Yes, September 5, 1974	Yes, September 17, 1976	Yes, May 18, 1964

Appendix 1

COUNTRY	COSTA RICA	CUBA	CYPRUS	CZECHO-SLOVAKIA	DENMARK	DOMINICAN REPUBLIC
Nationality Status	No	No	Yes	No	No	No
Extended	No	No	No	No	No	No
Applied	Yes	Yes	Yes	Yes	Yes	Yes
Convention	Berne; UCC; Rome; Geneva	UCC	Berne	Berne; UCC; Rome; Geneva	Berne; UCC; Rome; Geneva	UCC; Rome
Fully retroactive	Yes	No	Yes	Yes	Yes	No
Partially retroactive	N/A	Yes	N/A	N/A	N/A	Yes
Date for publication purposes	N/A	September 27, 1957	N/A	N/A	N/A	May 8, 1983
Date of commencement of 1956 Act	September 27, 1957	September 27, 1957	June 1, 1957	September 27, 1957	September 27, 1957	May 8, 1983
Application of Translation rights provisions	No	No	No	No	Yes	No
Limited sound recording rights	No	Yes	No	No	No	No
Vested rights clause	Yes	Yes	Yes	Yes	No	Yes
Sound broadcasts protected	Yes, September 9, 1971	No	No	Yes, August 14, 1964	Yes, July 1, 1965	Yes, January 27, 1987
Television broadcasts protected	Yes, September 9, 1971	No	Yes, May 5, 1970	Yes, August 14, 1964	Yes, February 1, 1962	Yes, January 27, 1987

Appendix 1

COUNTRY	ECUADOR	EGYPT	EL SALVADOR	FALKLAND ISLANDS	FIJI	FINLAND
Nationality Status	No	No	No	Yes	Yes	No
Extended	No	No	No	Yes	No	No
Applied	Yes	Yes	Yes	No	Yes	Yes
Convention	UCC; Rome; Geneva	Berne; Geneva	UCC; Rome; Geneva	None	Berne; UCC; Rome; Geneva	Berne; UCC; Rome; Geneva
Fully retroactive	No	Yes	No	Yes	Yes	Yes
Partially retroactive	Yes	N/A	Yes	N/A	N/A	N/A
Date for publication purposes	September 27, 1957	N/A	March 29, 1979	N/A	N/A	N/A
Date of commencement of 1956 Act	September 27, 1957	September 27, 1957	March 29, 1979	June 1, 1957	June 1, 1957	September 27, 1957
Application of Translation rights provisions	No	No	No	No	No	No
Limited sound recording rights	No	Yes	No	Yes	No	No
Vested rights clause	Yes	Yes	Yes	No	Yes	No
Sound broadcasts protected	Yes, May 18, 1964	No	Yes, June 29, 1979	Yes	Yes, April 11, 1972	Yes, October 21, 1983
Television broadcasts protected	Yes, May 18, 1964	No	Yes, June 29, 1979	Yes	Yes, April 11, 1972	Yes, October 21, 1983

487

COUNTRY	FRANCE and French territories overseas	GABON	GAMBIA	GDR	GERMANY, FEDERAL REPUBLIC OF	GHANA
Nationality Status	No	No	Yes	No	No	Yes
Extended	No	No	Yes	No	No	No
Applied	Yes	Yes	No	Yes	Yes	Yes
Convention	Berne; UCC; Rome; Geneva	Berne	None	Berne; UCC	Berne; UCC; Rome; Geneva	UCC
Fully retroactive	Yes	Yes	Yes	Yes	Yes	Yes
Partially retroactive	N/A	N/A	N/A	N/A	N/A	N/A
Date for publication purposes	N/A	N/A	N/A	N/A	N/A	N/A
Date of commencement of 1956 Act	September 27, 1957	September 27, 1957	June 1, 1957	September 27, 1957	September 27, 1957	June 1, 1957
Application of Translation rights provisions	No	No	No	No	No	No
Limited sound recording rights	No	Yes	Yes	Yes	No	Yes
Vested rights clause	Yes	Yes	N/A	Yes	Yes	Yes
Sound broadcasts protected	Yes, July 3, 1987	No	Yes, BBC and IBA only	No	Yes, October 21, 1966	No
Television broadcasts protected	Yes, July 1, 1961	No	Yes, BBC and IBA only	No	Yes, October 21, 1966	No

Appendix 1

COUNTRY	GIBRALTAR	GREECE	GRENADA	GUATEMALA	GUINEA (Republic of)	GUYANA
Nationality Status	Yes	No	Yes	No	No	Yes
Extended	Yes	No	Yes	No	No	Yes
Applied	No	Yes	No	Yes	Yes	No
Convention	None	Berne; UCC	None	UCC; Rome; Geneva	UCC; Berne	None
Fully retroactive	Yes	Yes	Yes	No	Yes	Yes
Partially retroactive	N/A	N/A	N/A	Yes	N/A	N/A
Date for publication purposes	N/A	N/A	N/A	October 28, 1964	N/A	N/A
Date of commencement of 1956 Act	June 1, 1957	September 27, 1957	June 1, 1957	October 28, 1964	September 27, 1957	June 1, 1957
Application of Translation rights provisions	No	Yes	No	No	No	No
Limited sound recording rights	Yes	Yes	Yes	No	Yes	Yes
Vested rights clause	No	No	Yes	Yes	Yes	Yes
Sound broadcasts protected	Yes	No	Yes	Yes, January 14, 1977	No	Yes
Television broadcasts protected	Yes	No	Yes	Yes, January 14, 1977	No	Yes

489

Appendix 1

COUNTRY	HAITI	HONG KONG	HUNGARY	ICELAND	INDIA	BRITISH INDIAN OCEAN TERRITORY
Nationality Status	No	Yes	No	No	Yes	Yes
Extended	No	Yes	No	No	No	Yes
Applied	Yes	No	Yes	Yes	Yes	No
Convention	UCC	None	Berne; UCC; Geneva	Berne; UCC	Berne; UCC; Geneva	None
Fully retroactive	No	Yes	Yes	Yes	Yes	Yes
Partially retroactive	Yes	N/A	N/A	N/A	N/A	N/A
Date for publication purposes	September 27, 1957	N/A	N/A	N/A	N/A	N/A
Date of commencement of 1956 Act	September 27, 1957	June 1, 1957	September 27, 1957	September 27, 1957	September 27, 1957	June 1, 1957
Application of Translation rights provisions	No	No	Yes	Yes	No	No
Limited sound recording rights	Yes	Yes	Yes	Yes	No	Yes
Vested rights clause	Yes	No	No	No	Yes	No
Sound broadcasts protected	No	Yes	No	No	No	Yes
Television broadcasts protected	No	Yes	No	No	No	Yes

COUNTRY	INDONESIA	IRELAND, Republic of	ISLE OF MAN	ISRAEL	ITALY	IVORY COAST
Nationality Status	No	No	Yes	No	No	No
Extended	No	No	Yes	No	No	No
Applied	Applied as Berne country until March 19, 1960	Yes	No	Yes	Yes	Yes
Convention	None	Berne; UCC; Rome	None	Berne; UCC; Geneva	Berne; UCC; Rome; Geneva	Berne
Fully retroactive	Yes, prior to 1960	Yes	Yes	Yes	Yes	Yes
Partially retroactive	N/A	N/A	N/A	N/A	N/A	N/A
Date for publication purposes	N/A	N/A	N/A	N/A	N/A	N/A
Date of commencement of 1956 Act	September 27, 1957	September 27, 1957	June 1, 1957	September 27, 1957	September 27, 1957	September 27, 1957
Application of Translation rights provisions	Yes	Yes	No	No	Yes	No
Limited sound recording rights	No	No	Yes	No	No	Yes
Vested rights clause	Yes	Yes	No	Yes	Yes	Yes
Sound broadcasts protected	No	Yes, September 19, 1979	Yes	No	Yes, April 8, 1975	No
Television broadcasts protected	No	Yes, September 19, 1979	Yes	No	Yes, April 8, 1975	No

491

COUNTRY	JAMAICA	JAPAN	KAMPUCHEA	KENYA	KIRIBATI	KOREA
Nationality Status	Yes	No	No	Yes	Yes	No
Extended	Yes	No	No	No	Yes	No
Applied	No	Yes	Yes	Yes	No	Yes
Convention	None	Berne; UCC; Geneva	UCC	UCC; Geneva	None	UCC; Geneva
Fully retroactive	Yes	Yes	No	Yes	Yes	No
Partially retroactive	N/A	N/A	Yes	N/A	N/A	Yes
Date for publication purposes	N/A	N/A	September 27, 1957	N/A	N/A	October 1, 1987
Date of commencement of 1956 Act	June 1, 1957	September 27, 1957	September 27, 1957	June 1, 1957	June 1, 1957	October 1, 1987
Application of Translation rights provisions	No	Yes	No	No	No	No
Limited sound recording rights	Yes	Yes	Yes	Yes	Yes	Yes
Vested rights clause	N/A	No	Yes	Yes	N/A	Yes
Sound broadcasts protected	Yes, BBC and IBA only	No	No	No	Yes, BBC and IBA only	No
Television broadcasts protected	Yes, BBC and IBA only	No	No	No	Yes, BBC and IBA only	No

Appendix 1

COUNTRY	KUWAIT	LAOS	LEBANON	LESOTHO	LIBERIA	LIBYA
Nationality Status	Protectorate from January 28, 1949 to December 6, 1961	No	No	Yes	No	No
Extended	No	No	No	Yes	No	No
Applied	No	Yes	Yes	No	Yes	Yes
Convention	None	UCC	Berne; UCC	None	UCC; Berne	Berne
Fully retroactive	N/A	No	Yes	Yes	Yes	Yes
Partially retroactive	N/A	Yes	N/A	N/A	N/A	N/A
Date for publication purposes	N/A	September 27, 1957	N/A	N/A	N/A	N/A
Date of commencement of 1956 Act	N/A	September 27, 1957	September 27, 1957	June 1, 1957	September 27, 1957	September 27, 1957
Application of Translation rights provisions	N/A	No	No	No	No	No
Limited sound recording rights	N/A	Yes	Yes	Yes	Yes	Yes
Vested rights clause	N/A	Yes	No	N/A	Yes	Yes
Sound broadcasts protected	N/A	No	No	Yes, BBC and IBA only	No	No
Television broadcasts protected	N/A	No	No	Yes, BBC and IBA only	No	No

COUNTRY	LIECHTENSTEIN	LUXEMBOURG	MADAGASCAR	MALAWI	MALAYSIA (Sarawak and Sabah)	MALDIVES
Nationality Status	No	No	No	Yes	Yes	Yes
Extended	No	No	No	No	Yes	No
Applied	Yes	Yes	Yes	Yes	No	No
Convention	Berne; UCC	Berne; UCC; Rome; Geneva	Berne	UCC	None	None
Fully retroactive	Yes	Yes	Yes	Yes	Yes	N/A
Partially retroactive	N/A	N/A	N/A	N/A	N/A	N/A
Date for publication purposes	N/A	N/A	N/A	N/A	N/A	N/A
Date of commencement of 1956 Act	September 27, 1957	September 27, 1957	September 27, 1957	June 1, 1957	June 1, 1957	N/A
Application of Translation rights provisions	No	No	No	No	No	N/A
Limited sound recording rights	Yes	No	Yes	Yes	Yes	N/A
Vested rights clause	No	No	Yes	Yes	Yes	N/A
Sound broadcasts protected	No	Yes, February 25, 1976	No	No	Yes	N/A
Television broadcasts protected	No	Yes, February 25, 1976	No	No	Yes	N/A

494

Appendix 1

COUNTRY	MALI	MALTA	MAURITANIA	MAURITIUS	MEXICO	MONACO
Nationality Status	No	Yes	No	Yes	No	No
Extended	No	No	No	No	No	No
Applied	Yes	Yes	Yes	Yes	Yes	Yes
Convention	Berne	Berne; UCC	Berne	UCC	Berne; UCC; Rome; Geneva	Berne; UCC; Rome; Geneva
Fully retroactive	Yes	Yes	Yes	Yes	Yes	Yes
Partially retroactive	N/A	N/A	N/A	N/A	N/A	N/A
Date for publication purposes	N/A	N/A	N/A	N/A	N/A	N/A
Date of commencement of 1956 Act	September 27, 1957	June 1, 1957	September 27, 1957	June 1, 1957	September 27, 1957	September 27, 1957
Application of Translation rights provisions	No	No	No	No	No	No
Limited sound recording rights	Yes	Yes	Yes	Yes	No	No
Vested rights clause	Yes	Yes	Yes	Yes	Yes	No
Sound broadcasts protected	No	No	No	No	Yes, May 18, 1964	Yes, December 6, 1985
Television broadcasts protected	No	No	No	No	Yes, May 18, 1964	Yes, December 6, 1985

Appendix 1

COUNTRY	MONTSERRAT	MOROCCO	NETHERLANDS (and Netherlands Antilles)	NEW ZEALAND	NICARAGUA	NIGER
Nationality Status	Yes	No	No	Yes	No	No
Extended	Yes	No	No	No	No	No
Applied	No	Yes	Yes	Yes	Yes	Yes
Convention	None	Berne; UCC	Berne; UCC	Berne; UCC; Geneva	UCC	Berne; Rome
Fully retroactive	Yes	Yes	Yes	Yes	No	Yes
Partially retroactive	N/A	N/A	N/A	N/A	Yes	N/A
Date for publication purposes	N/A	N/A	N/A	N/A	August 16, 1961	N/A
Date of commencement of 1956 Act	June 1, 1957	September 27, 1957	September 27, 1957	September 27, 1957	August 16, 1961	September 27, 1957
Application of Translation rights provisions	No	No	Yes	No	No	No
Limited sound recording rights	Yes	Yes	Yes	No	Yes	No
Vested rights clause	No	Yes	No	Yes	Yes	Yes
Sound broadcasts protected	Yes	No	No	No	No	Yes, May 18, 1964
Television broadcasts protected	Yes	No	No	No	No	Yes, May 18, 1964

Appendix 1

COUNTRY	NIGERIA	NORWAY	PAKISTAN	PANAMA	PARAGUAY	PERU
Nationality Status	Yes	No	Yes, until September 1, 1973 when citizens ceased to be British subjects	No	No	No
Extended	No	No	No	No	No	No
Applied	Yes	Yes	Yes	Yes	Yes	Yes
Convention	UCC	Berne; UCC; Rome; Geneva	Berne; UCC	UCC; Rome; Geneva	UCC; Rome; Geneva	Berne; UCC; Rome; Geneva
Fully retroactive	Yes	Yes	Yes	No	No	Yes
Partially retroactive	N/A	N/A	N/A	Yes	Yes	N/A
Date for publication purposes	N/A	N/A	N/A	October 17, 1962	March 11, 1962	N/A
Date of commencement of 1956 Act	June 1, 1957	September 27, 1957	September 27, 1957	October 17, 1962	March 11, 1962	September 27, 1957
Application of Translation rights provisions	No	No	No	No	No	No
Limited sound recording rights	No	No	No	No	No	No
Vested rights clause	Yes	No	Yes	Yes	Yes	Yes
Sound broadcasts protected	No	Yes, July 10, 1978	No	Yes, September 2, 1983	Yes, February 26, 1970	Yes, August 7, 1985
Television broadcasts protected	No	Yes, August 10, 1968	No	Yes, September 2, 1983	Yes, February 26, 1970	Yes, August 7, 1985

497

Appendix 1

COUNTRY	PHILIPPINES	PITCAIRN ISLAND	POLAND	PORTUGAL (and its overseas territories)	QATAR	ROMANIA
Nationality Status	No	Yes	No	No	Yes, from January 28, 1949 to January 1, 1975 when it was a protectorate	No
Extended	No	Yes	No	No	No	No
Applied	Yes	No	Yes	Yes	No	Yes
Convention	Berne; Rome	None	Berne; UCC	Berne; UCC	None	Berne
Fully retroactive	Yes	Yes	Yes	Yes	N/A	Yes
Partially retroactive	N/A	N/A	N/A	N/A	N/A	N/A
Date for publication purposes	N/A	N/A	N/A	N/A	N/A	N/A
Date of commencement of 1956 Act	September 27, 1957	June 1, 1957	September 27, 1957	September 27, 1957	N/A	September 27, 1957
Application of Translation rights provisions	No	No	No	No	N/A	No
Limited sound recording rights	No	Yes	Yes	Yes	N/A	Yes
Vested rights clause	Yes	N/A	No	Portugal Yes Colonies No	N/A	No
Sound broadcasts protected	Yes, September 25, 1984	Yes, BBC and IBA only	No	No	N/A	No
Television broadcasts protected	Yes, September 25, 1984	Yes, BBC and IBA only	No	No	N/A	No

COUNTRY	RWANDA	ST. CHRISTOPHER-NEVIS	ST. HELENA (and its Dependencies)	ST. LUCIA	ST. VINCENT and the GRENADINES	SENEGAL
Nationality Status	No	Yes	Yes	Yes	Yes	No
Extended	No	Yes	Yes	Yes	No	No
Applied	Yes	No	No	No	Yes	Yes
Convention	Berne	No	No	No	UCC	Berne; UCC
Fully retroactive	Yes	Yes	Yes	Yes	Yes	Yes
Partially retroactive	N/A	N/A	N/A	N/A	N/A	N/A
Date for publication purposes	N/A	N/A	N/A	N/A	N/A	N/A
Date of commencement of 1956 Act	September 27, 1957	June 1, 1957	June 1, 1957	June 1, 1957	June 1, 1957	September 27, 1957
Application of Translation rights provisions	No	No	No	No	No	No
Limited sound recording rights	Yes	Yes	Yes	Yes	Yes	Yes
Vested rights clause	Yes	N/A	No	No	Yes	Yes
Sound broadcasts protected	No	Yes, BBC and IBA only	Yes	Yes	No	No
Television broadcasts protected	No	Yes, BBC and IBA only	Yes	Yes	No	No

COUNTRY	SEYCHELLES	SIERRA LEONE	SINGAPORE	SOLOMON ISLANDS	SOMALIA	SOUTH AFRICA (with S.W. Africa)
Nationality Status	Yes	Yes	Yes	Yes	Yes, until 1960 when it ceased to be a Protectorate	Yes, citizens were British subjects until May 31, 1962 by South Africa Act 1962
Extended	Yes	Extension lapsed in 1965	Yes	Yes	Yes	No
Applied	No	No	No	No	No	Yes
Convention	None	None	None	None	None	Berne
Fully retroactive	Yes	Yes, prior to 1965	Yes	Yes	Yes	Yes
Partially retroactive	N/A	N/A	N/A	N/A	N/A	N/A
Date for publication purposes	N/A	N/A	N/A	N/A	N/A	N/A
Date of commencement of 1956 Act	June 1, 1957	June 1, 1957	June 1, 1957	June 1, 1957	June 1, 1957	September 27, 1957
Application of Translation rights provisions	No	No	No	No	No	No
Limited sound recording rights	Yes	Yes	Yes	Yes	Yes	Yes
Vested rights clause	Yes	No	N/A	N/A	N/A	Yes
Sound broadcasts protected	Yes	Yes, BBC and IBA only, prior to 1965	Yes, BBC and IBA only	Yes, BBC and IBA only	Yes, BBC and IBA only	No
Television broadcasts protected	Yes	Yes, BBC and IBA only, prior to 1965	Yes, BBC and IBA only	Yes, BBC and IBA only	Yes, BBC and IBA only	No

COUNTRY	SOUTH GEORGIA and the SOUTH SANDWICH ISLANDS	SPAIN and Spanish Dependencies	SRI LANKA	SURINAM	SWAZILAND	SWEDEN
Nationality Status	Yes	No	Yes	No	Yes	No
Extended	Yes	No	No	No	Yes	No
Applied	No	Yes	Yes	Yes	No	Yes
Convention	None	Berne; UCC; Geneva	Berne; UCC	Berne	None	Berne; UCC; Rome; Geneva
Fully retroactive	Yes	Yes	Yes	Yes	Yes	Yes
Partially retroactive	N/A	N/A	N/A	N/A	N/A	N/A
Date for publication purposes	N/A	N/A	N/A	N/A	N/A	N/A
Date of commencement of 1956 Act	June 1, 1957	September 27, 1957	September 27, 1957	September 27, 1957	June 1, 1957	September 27, 1957
Application of Translation rights provisions	No	No	No	No	No	Yes
Limited sound recording rights	Yes	No	No	Yes	Yes	No
Vested rights clause	No	Spain Yes Depend No	Yes	Yes	N/A	No
Sound broadcasts protected	Yes	No	No	No	Yes, BBC and IBA only	Yes, May 18, 1964
Television broadcasts protected	Yes	Yes, November 19, 1971	No	No	Yes, BBC and IBA only	Yes, July 1, 1961

COUNTRY	SWITZERLAND	SYRIA	TAIWAN	TANZANIA	THAILAND	TOGO
Nationality Status	No	No	No	Yes	No	No
Extended	No	No	No	Ceased to extend upon Copyright Act 1966 (Tanzania) coming into force	No	No
Applied	Yes	Applied as Berne country until March 13, 1962	Yes	No	Yes	Yes
Convention	Berne; UCC	None	None	None	Berne	Berne
Fully retroactive	Yes	Yes, prior to 1962	No	Yes, prior to 1966	Yes	Yes
Partially retroactive	N/A	N/A	Yes	N/A	N/A	N/A
Date for publication purposes	N/A	N/A	July 10, 1985	N/A	N/A	N/A
Date of commencement of 1956 Act	September 27, 1957	September 27, 1957	July 10, 1985	June 1, 1957	September 27, 1957	September 27, 1957
Application of Translation rights provisions	No	No	No	No	Yes	No
Limited sound recording rights	No	Yes	Yes	Yes	Yes	Yes
Vested rights clause	Yes	Yes	No	Yes	No	Yes
Sound broadcasts protected	No	No	No	Yes, prior to 1966	No	No
Television broadcasts protected	No	No	No	Yes, prior to 1966	No	No

COUNTRY	TONGA	TRINIDAD and TOBAGO	TUNISIA	TURKEY	TURKS and CAICOS ISLANDS	TUVALU
Nationality Status	Yes	Yes	No	No	Yes	Yes
Extended	N/A	No	No	No	Yes	Yes
Applied	N/A	Yes	Yes	Yes	No	No
Convention	None	Berne; Geneva; UCC	Berne; UCC	Berne	None	None
Fully retroactive	N/A	Yes	Yes	Yes	Yes	Yes
Partially retroactive	N/A	N/A	N/A	N/A	N/A	N/A
Date for publication purposes	N/A	N/A	N/A	N/A	N/A	N/A
Date of commencement of 1956 Act	N/A	June 1, 1957	September 27, 1957	September 27, 1957	June 1, 1957	June 1, 1957
Application of Translation rights provisions	N/A	No	No	No	No	No
Limited sound recording rights	N/A	Yes	Yes	Yes	Yes	Yes
Vested rights clause	N/A	Yes	Yes	Yes	N/A	N/A
Sound broadcasts protected	N/A	No	No	No	Yes, BBC and IBA only	Yes, BBC and IBA only
Television broadcasts protected	N/A	No	No	No	Yes, BBC and IBA only	Yes, BBC and IBA only

Appendix 1

COUNTRY	UGANDA	USSR	UNITED ARAB EMIRATES	USA (and Guam, Panama Canal Zone, Puerto-Rico, and Virgin Islands of USA)	URUGUAY	VATICAN CITY
Nationality Status	Yes	No	Yes, from January 28, 1949 to January 1, 1975 when it was a protectorate	No	No	No
Extended	Yes	No	N/A	No	No	No
Applied	No	Yes	N/A	Yes	Yes	Yes
Convention	None	UCC	None	UCC; Geneva; Berne	Berne; Rome; Geneva	Berne; UCC
Fully retroactive	Yes	No	N/A	Yes	Yes	Yes
Partially retroactive	N/A	Yes	N/A	N/A	N/A	N/A
Date for publication purposes	N/A	May 27, 1973	N/A	N/A	N/A	N/A
Date of commencement of 1956 Act	June 1, 1957	May 27, 1973	N/A	September 27, 1957	September 27, 1957	September 27, 1957
Application of Translation rights provisions	No	No	N/A	No	No	No
Limited sound recording rights	Yes	Yes	N/A	Yes	No	Yes
Vested rights clause	Yes	Yes	N/A	Yes	Yes	Yes
Sound broadcasts protected	Yes	No	N/A	No	Yes, July 4, 1977	No
Television broadcasts protected	Yes	No	N/A	No	Yes, July 4, 1977	No

Appendix 1

COUNTRY	VENEZUELA	BRITISH VIRGIN ISLANDS	YUGOSLAVIA	ZAIRE	ZAMBIA	ZIMBABWE
Nationality Status	No	Yes	No	No	Yes	Yes
Extended	No	Yes	No	No	No	No
Applied	Yes	No	Yes	Yes	Yes	Yes
Convention	Berne; UCC; Geneva	None	Berne; UCC	Berne; Geneva	UCC	Berne
Fully retroactive	Yes	Yes	Yes	Yes	Yes	Yes
Partially retroactive	N/A	N/A	N/A	N/A	N/A	N/A
Date for publication purposes	N/A	N/A	N/A	N/A	N/A	N/A
Date of commencement of 1956 Act	September 27, 1957	June 1, 1957	September 27, 1957	September 27, 1957	June 1, 1957	June 1, 1957
Application of Translation rights provisions	No	No	Yes	No	No	No
Limited sound recording rights	Yes	Yes	Yes	Yes	Yes	Yes
Vested rights clause	Yes	No	No	Yes	Yes	Yes
Sound broadcasts protected	No	Yes	No	No	No	No
Television broadcasts protected	No	Yes	No	No	No	No

505

APPENDIX 2

A. *Broadcasters*

B. *Cable programme services*

C. *Charitable organisations*

D. *Computer Software Purchasers*

Section No.	Subject Matter	Para. No.	**A2.04**
56	Transfer of computer software	7.91	

E. *Discotheques and other places of public entertainment*

Section No.	Subject Matter	Para. No.	**A2.05**
72	Free public showing or playing of broadcast and cable programmes and sound recordings and films included in them	7.113	

F. *Educational Establishments*

Section No.	Subject Matter	Para. No.	**A2.06**
29	Fair dealing for the purposes of research or private study	7.70	
32	Acts done for the purposes of instruction or examination	7.17, 7.22, 7.28	
33	Anthologies for educational use	7.13	
34	Performing, playing or showing work in course of activities of an educational establishment	7.24	
35	Recording by educational establishments of broadcast and cable programmes	7.23	
36	Reprographic copying of passages from published works	7.18	

G. *Film and video companies*

Section No.	Subject Matter	Para. No.	**A2.07**
31	Incidental inclusion of copyright material	7.86	
57	Assumption as to expiry of copyright or death of author	7.75	
62	Artistic works on public display	7.121	

K. *Photocopying facilities*

Section No.	Subject Matter	Para. No.	**A2.11**
29	Fair dealing for the purposes of research or private study	7.70	
36	Reprographic copying of passages from unpublished works for educational establishments	7.18	
38–43	Copying for librarians (see under section dealing with librarians above)	—	

L. *Publishers*

Section No.	Subject Matter	Para. No.	**A2.12**
33	Anthologies for educational use	7.13	
57	Assumption as to expiry of copyright or death of author	7.75	
60	Abstracts of scientific or technical articles	7.102	
62	Artistic works on public display	7.121	

M. *Record companies*

Section No.	Subject Matter	Para. No.	**A2.13**
31	Incidental inclusion of copyright material	7.86	
57	Assumption as to expiry of copyright or death of author	7.75	

N. *Sound recording duplicating facilities*

	Para. No.	**A2.14**

See under film and video duplicating facilities

APPENDIX 3

NOTE:

A1.01   1. Where a provision is said to not have been re-enacted, this means it does not appear in the 1988 Act, and it no longer applies, save that it may continue to have some effect for existing works and/or acts done before commencement of the 1988 Act.

2. Where a provision otherwise has no equivalent section number against it, the effect is probably the same under the 1988 Act, but there is no precise equivalent provision. This is subject to any specific comment made.

Copyright Act 1956	Subject Matter	Copyright Designs and Patent Act 1988	Remarks
s1	Nature of Copyright		—
s.1(1)	Nature of Copyright	s.2(1) s.16(1)	—
s.1(2)	Infringement	s.16(2)	—
s.1(3)	—	—	—
s.1(4)	—	—	—
s.1(5)	Qualified Person	s.154(1)	Modified: see Paragraph 2.08
s.2	Copyright in literary, dramatic and musical works		—
s.2(1)	Qualification for unpublished literary dramatic or musical works	s.154	Modified: see paragraph 2.04
s.2(2)	Qualification for copyright in published literary, dramatic or musical works	s.154 s.155	Modified: see paragraph 2.04
s.2(3)	Duration of copyright in literary, dramatic or musical works	s.12(1)	—
s.2(3) (a)–(e)	Extended duration for unexploited works.	—	Not re-enacted but see paragraph 4.42
s.2(5):	Restricted acts in relation to copyright in literary, dramatic and musical works	s.16(1)	—
(a)	Reproduction	s.16(1)(a) s.17(1) s.17(2)	—
(b)	Publishing	—	Not re-enacted. Replaced by issuing copies to the public—see s.16(1) (b) and s.18
(c)	Performance in public	s.16(1)(c), s.19(1) s.19(2)	—
(d)	Broadcasting	s.16(1)(d) s.20(a)	—
(e)	Including in a cable programme	s.16(1)(d) s.20(a)	Now cable programme service
(f)	Making any adaptation	s.16(1)(e), s.21(1)	—
(g)	Restricted acts in relation to adaptations	s.21(2)	—
s.2(6)	Definition of adaptation	s.21(3) s.21(4) s.21(5)	New provision for computer programs
s.2	Copyright in artistic works		—

510

Copyright Act 1956	Subject Matter	Copyright Designs and Patent Act 1988	Remarks
s.3(1): (a)	Artistic works, paintings/drawings, etc.	s.4(1)(a) s.4(2)	NB: New definition "Graphic Work"
(b)	Architecture	s.4(1)(b) s.4(2)	Definition modified
(c)	Works of artistic craftsmanship	s.4(1)(c)	—
s.3(2)	Qualification for unpublished artistic works	s.154	Modified: see paragraph 2.04
s.3(3)	Qualifications for published artistic works	s.154 s.155	Modified: see paragraph 2.04
s.3(4)	Duration of copyright in artistic works	s.12(1)	—
s.3(4)(a)	Entended duration for unexploited engravings	—	Not re-enacted but see paragraph 4.42
(b)	Photographs—restricted 50 yrs from when first published	—	Not re-enacted: now normal copyright period
s.3(5)	Restricted acts in relation to artistic works:	s.16(1)	—
(a)	Reproduction	s.16(1)(a) s.17(2) s.17(3)	—
(b)	Publishing	—	Not re-enacted. Replaced by issuing to the public—see s.16(1)(b) and s.18
(c)	Including in TV Broadcast	s.16(1)(d) s.20(a)	—
(d)	Including in cable programme	s16(1)(d) s.20(a)	Now cable programme service
s.4	Ownership of copyright in literary, dramatic, musical and artistic works;		—
s.4(1)	Copyright—author	s.11(1)	NB: New definition: see paragraph 3.52
s.4(2)	Made in course of employment with newspapers	—	Not re-enacted
s.4(3)	Commissioning photograph, painting or drawing, etc.	—	Not re-enacted but note s.85 right to privacy in photographs and films
s.4(4)	In course of employment	s.11(2)	—
s.4(5)	Subject to agreement	s.11(2)	—
s.4(6)	Subject to assignment and licences	—	—
s.5	Secondary infringements;		—
s.5(1)	Infringements by importation, sale and other dealings	ss.22–26	—
s.5(2)	Importation	s.22 s.27(3)	Modified: see paragraph 6.30
s.5(3)	Selling letting for hire, etc.	s.23	Modified: see paragraph 6.30
s.5(4)	Distribution for purposes of trade	s.23(d)	—
s.5(5)	Permitting use of premises for public performance	s.25(1)	Modified: see paragraph 6.13
s.5(6)	Place of public entertainment	s.25(2)	—
s.6	Fair dealing;		—
s.6(1)	Fair dealing for purposes of research and private study	s.29	Modified see paragraph 7.70
s.6(2)	Fair dealing for purposes of criticism or review	s.30(1)	Modified: see paragraph 7.65
s.6(3)	Fair dealing for purposes of reporting current events	s.30(2) s.30(3)	Modified: see paragraph 7.66
s.6(4)	Judicial proceedings	s.45	—
s.6(5)	Recitation in public	s.59	Proviso repealed
s.6(6)	Anthology for educational use	s.33	Modified: see paragraph 7.16

Copyright Act 1956	Subject Matter	Copyright Designs and Patent Act 1988	Remarks
s.6(7)	Recordings made of literary or musical works for broadcasting (ephemeral provisions)	s.68	Extended in scope: see paragraph 7.99
s.6(8)	Adaptation	s.76	—
s.6(9)	Cable programme	s.30(2) s.30(3) s.59 s.68	
s.6(10)	Definition of sufficient acknowledgement	s.178	Modified
s.7	Exceptions as respects libraries and archives;	s.37–44	Modified: see paragraph 7.03(e)
s.7(1)	Making or supplying copies of periodical publications	s.38	Modified: see paragraph 7.41
s.7(2)(a)	Libraries non-profit making	—	Not re-enacted
(b)	Private study	s.38(2)(a)	—
(c)	Not more than one copy	s.38(2)(b)	—
(d)	Only one article	s.38(2)(b)	—
(e)	Payment	s.38(2)(c)	—
s.7(3)	Published literary, dramatic or musical works	s.39	Proviso not re-enacted
s.7(4)	Conditions applying	s.39(2) s.40	—
s.7(5)	Supply of copies of published works to other libraries	s.41	—
s.7(6)	Unpublished works over 100 years old in library	—	Not re-enacted
s.7(7)	Incorporation of old works as above in new works	—	Not re-enacted
s.7(8)	Broadcasting recording or performance of old works	—	Not re-enacted
s.7(9)	Illustrations	s.38(1) s.39(1) s.41(1)	—
s.7(10)	Definition of article	s.178	—
s.8	Records of musical works—statutory royalty	—	Not re-enacted
s.9	Exceptions from protection of artistic works;		—
s.9(1)	Fair dealing for purposes of research and private study	s.29(1)	Modified: see paragraph 7.70
s.9(2)	Fair dealing for purposes of criticism or review	s.30(1)	Modified: see paragraph 7.65
s.9(3)	Public exhibition	s.62	Modified: see paragraph 7.104
s.9(4)	Architecture	s.62	—
s.9(5)	Incidental inclusion in broadcast	s.31	New provision wider in scope: see paragraph 7.86
s.9(6)	Publication	—	Not re-enacted but similar provision for issuing to public: see s.62(3)
s.9(7)	Judicial proceedings	s.45	—
s.9(8)	Defence relating to 3 dimensional reproductions	—	Not re-enacted
s.9(9)	Subsequent artistic works by same author	s.64	—
s.9(10)	Reconstruction of building	s.65	—
s.9(11)	Cable service	s.62 s.31	—
s.10	Exceptions from protection of industrial design	—	Not re-enacted but see s.51 to s.55
s.11(1)	Anonymous and pseudonymous works	s.12(2) s.12(3)	Modified: see paragraph 4.38

Copyright Act 1956	Subject Matter	Copyright Designs and Patent Act 1988	Remarks
s.11(2)	Works of joint authorship	s.10 s.12(4)	—
s.11(3)	Definition joint authorship work	s.10(1)	—
s.12	Copyright in sound recordings;		—
s.12(1)	Qualification by maker	s.154	—
s.12(2)	Qualification by publication	s.155	—
s.12(3)	Duration of copyright	s.13	Modified: see paragraph 4.57
s.12(4)	Ownership of copyright	s.9(2)	Commissioning provision not re-enacted
s.12(5):	Restricted acts;		—
(*a*)	Making records	s.16(1)(*a*) s.17(1)	—
(*b*)	Causing to be heard in public	s.16(1)(*c*) s.19(3)	—
(*c*)	Broadcasting and including in cable programme	s.16(1)(*d*) s.20	Now cable programme service
s.12(6)	Copyright notice defence to infringement	—	Not re-enacted
s.12(7)	Non-infringement in case of hotels, clubs, etc.	s.67	Sub-clause (*a*) not re-enacted
s.12(8)	Time when made	—	Unnecessary
s.12(9)	Definition of sound recording	s.51(1)	—
s.13	Cinematograph Films;		Now just "films"
s.13(1)	Qualification by maker	s.154	—
s.13(2)	Qualification by publication	s.155	Registration provisions no longer relevant
s.13(3)	Duration of copyright	s.13	Modified: see paragraph 4.57
s.13(4)	Copyright vesting in maker	s.9(2)	—
s.13(5)	Restricted acts;		—
(*a*)	Making copies	s.16(1)(*a*) s.17(1) s.17(4)	—
(*b*)	Seen/heard in public	s.16(1)(*c*) s.19(2)(*b*) s.19(3)	—
(*c*) ⎱	Broadcasting	s.16(1)(*d*)	
(*d*) ⎰	Cable programme	s.20(*b*)	Now cable programme service
s.13(6)	Judicial proceeding	s.45	
s.13(7)	Non-infringement of underlying copyright works	—	Not re-enacted
s.13(8)	Newsreels	—	Not re-enacted
s.13(9)	Soundtrack	—	Not re-enacted— soundtrack now protected as sound recording
s.13(10)	Definition of: film	s.5(1)	
	maker	s.9(2)	
	publication	s.175	
	copy	—	Not re-enacted but see s.17(4)
s.13(11)	Film Act 1960	—	
s.14	Broadcasts;		Scope widened; see paragraph 1.50
s.14(1)	Subsistence of copyright	s.154 s.156	Not restricted to BBC/IBA see s.9(2)
s.14(2)	Duration of copyright	s.14(1)	—
s.14(3)	Repeats	s.14(2)	—
s.14(4)	Restricted acts:		—
(*a*) ⎱	Copying	s.16(1)(*a*)	—
(*b*) ⎰		s.17(1) s.17(4)	—

Copyright Act 1956	Subject Matter	Copyright Designs and Patent Act 1988	Remarks
(c)	Public performance	s.16(1)(c) s.19(3)	—
(d)	Re-broadcasting or including in cable programme	s.16(1)(d) s.20(c)	Now cable programme service
s.14(5)	Infringement by reception or use of copies	—	—
s.14(6)	Sequence of images	—	—
s.14(7)	When not for private purposes	—	See s.70 and s.71: additional exemptions for private purposes
s.14(8)	Paying audience	s.72	—
s.14(8A)	Reception and re-transmission in cable programme service	s.73	—
s.14(9)	Judicial Proceedings	s.45	—
s.14(10)	Definitions	s.6	—
s.14(11)	References to sounds	—	—
s.14A	Cable programmes	—	—
s.14A(1)	Subsistence of copyright	s.154 s.156	—
s.14A(2)	Re-transmission	s.7(6)	—
s.14A(3)	Ownership and duration of copyright	s.9(2)(a) s.14(1)	—
s.14A(4)	Repeats	s.14(2)	—
s.14A(5)	Restricted Acts;		—
(a) ⎫ (b) ⎬	Copying	s.16(1)(a) s.17(1) s.17(4)	— —
(c)	Public performance	s.16(1)(c) s.19(3)	—
(d)	Broadcasting or including in cable programme service	s.16(1)(d) s.20(c)	—
s.14A(6)	Infringement by reception or use of copies	—	—
s.14A(7)	Sequence of images	—	—
s.14A(8)	When not for private purposes	—	s.70 s.71—additional exemptions for private purposes
s.14A(9)	Paying audience	s.72	—
s.14A(10)	Judicial proceedings	s.45	—
s.14A(11)	Definition	s.7	NB: exceptions
s.14A(12)	References to sounds	—	—
s.15	Published editions;		—
s.15(1)	Subsistence of copyright	s.154 s.155	—
s.15(2)	Duration	s.15	—
s.15(3)	Restricted acts	s.16(1) s.17(5)(a)	—
s.15(4)	Exception for libraries	s.38(1) s.39(1) s.41(1) s.42(1)	—
s.16(1)	Secondary infringement for sound recordings, films, broadcasts and cable programmes	—	See generally ss.22–27
s.16(2)	Importation	s.22 s.27	Modified: see paragraph 6.30
s.16(3)	Selling and distributing	s.23	Modified: see paragraph 6.30
s.16(4)	Distribution for purposes of trade	s.23(d)	—
s.16(5) ⎫ s.16(6) ⎬ s.16(7) ⎭	Independent protection for underlying Copyrights	—	— — —

Copyright Act 1956	Subject Matter	Copyright Designs and Patent Act 1988	Remarks
s.17	Remedies;		—
s.17(1)	Types of relief	s.96(1) and (2)	—
s.17(2)	No damages from innocent infringer	s.97(1)	—
s.17(3)	Additional damages	s.97(2)	Modified: see paragraph 10.87
s.17(4)	Restriction re buildings	—	Not re-enacted
s.17(5)	Action includes counterclaim	—	—
s.17(6)	Scottish proceedings	s.177	—
s.18	Conversion	—	Not re-enacted But see s.99, s.113. s.114 right to apply to court for delivery up and s.100 – right to seize
s.19	Exclusive licensees;		—
s.19(1) and (2)	Rights of action	s.101	—
s.19(3)	Both to be party to action	s.102(1)	—
s.19(4)	Defences available	s.101(3)	—
s.19(5)	Damages not cumulative	s.102(4)(a)	—
s.19(6)	Apportionment of account of profits	s.102(4)(c)	—
s.19(7)	No damages if account of profits	s.102(4)(b)	—
s.19(8)	No liability for costs	s.102(2)	—
s.19(9)	Definition of Exclusive Licence	s.92(1)	—
s.20	Presumptions;		—
s.20(1)	Copyright presumed to exist until defendant puts it in issue	—	Not re-enacted
s.20(2)	Name of author on published literary dramatic musical or artistic works	s.104(2)	—
s.20(3)	Joint author	s.104(3)	—
s.20(4)	Publisher's name	s.104(4)	—
s.205(5)	Where author dead	s.104(5)	—
s.20(6)	Anonymous works	s.104(5)	—
s.20(7)	Sound recordings	s.105	—
s.21	Offences;		—
s.21(1) and (2)	Makes, sells, exhibits, imports and distributes for purposes of sale	s.107(1)	Extended: see paragraph 10.115
s.21(3)	Possession of plates	s.107(2)	—
s.21(4)	All copyright works	—	—
s.21(4A)	Possession of infringing sound recordings or film	s.107(1)	Extended: see paragraph 10.115
s.21(5)	Causing public performance of literary, dramatic or musical works	s.107(3)	Extended: see paragraph 10.117
s.21(6)	Acts in UK	—	—
s.21(7) and (8)	Penalties	s.107(4)	—
s.21(9)	Destruction or delivery up	s.108	—
s.21(10)	Appeal	s.108(4)	—
s.21A	Search warrants	s.109	Extended; see paragraph 10.121
s.21B	Scotland	—	—
s.22	Customs seizure;		Extended; see paragraph 10.107
s.22(1)	Notice to Customs & Excise	s.111(1)	—
s.22(2)	Application to articles made outside UK	—	Not re-enacted: now applies to any infringing copy
s.22(3)	Effect of Notice	s.111(4)	—
s.22(4) s.22(5) s.22(6)	Regulations	s.112	
s.22(7)	Limitation on penalty	s.111(4)	—

Copyright Act 1956	Subject Matter	Copyright Designs and Patent Act 1988	Remarks
s.23 to s.29	Performing Right Tribunal	s.116–149	—
s.31	Extension of Act	s.157	Proviso to s.31(3) repealed and see s.158
s.32	Application of Act	s.159	—
s.33	International Organisations	s.168	—
s.34	Application to foreign broadcasts	—	Included in s.157 and s.159
s.35	Denial of copyright protection	s.160	—
s.36	Assignments and Licences	s.90	—
s.37	Prospective ownership	s.91	Modified; see paragraph 8.14
s.38	Unpublished works passing by will	s.93	Modified; see paragraph 8.24
s.39	Crown and government Depts;		See also s.164 to s.167
s.39(1)	Qualification by making	s.163	—
s.39(2)	Qualification by publication	—	Not re-enacted
s.39(3) ⎫ s.39(4) ⎭	Duration	s.163(3)	Altered – see paragraph 4.48
s.39(5)	Sound recordings	s.163	—
s.39(6)	Subject to any agreement	—	Not re-enacted
s.39(7)	Rights applying	s.163(5)	—
s.39(8)	Crown Proceedings Act	—	—
s.39(9)	Definition of government Department	—	Unnecessary
s.40	Broadcasts of sound recordings and films		—
s.40(1) ⎫ s.40(2) ⎪	Reception of broadcasts	—	Repealed but see s.72
s.40(3) ⎪ s.40(3A) ⎬ s.40(4) ⎪ s.40(5) ⎭	Retransmission in cable programme service	s.73	— — —
s.40A	Reception of cable programmes	—	Repealed but see s.72
s.41(1) ⎫ s.41(2) ⎭	Use of material for education	s.32	Modified; see paragraph 7.29
s.41(3) ⎫ s.41(4) ⎭	Performance	s.34(1)	—
s.41(5)	Performance of recordings films and broadcasts	s.34(2)	
s.41(6)	Definition of school	s.174	Scope extended; see paragraph 7.10
s.42	Public records	s.49	—
s.43	False attribution	s.84	—
s.46	Universities copyright	—	Not re-enacted
s.47	Provisions as to Orders in Council etc.	—	—
s.48(1)	Definitions	s.178 s.174	—
s.48(2)	Broadcasts	s.6	—
s.48(3)	Cable programmes	s.7	—
s.48(3A)	Exclusion for cable service	s.7	—
s.48(3B)	Place for residing/sleeping	—	Not re-enacted
s.48(4)	Definition of reception	—	—
s.48(5)	Broadcast not to constitute performance	—	Not re-enacted
s.48(6)	Apparatus – Occupier of Premises – liability	—	Not re-enacted but see s.26
s.49	Supplementary provisions on interpretation	—	—
s.49(1)	Substantial part	s.16(3)	—
s.49(2) ⎫ s.49(3) ⎭	Publication	s.175	—
s.49(4)	Reference to when made	s.154(4)	—
s.49(5)	Different owners	s.173	—

Copyright Act 1956	Subject Matter	Copyright Designs and Patent Act 1988	Remarks
s.49(6)	Different owners for purpose of secondary infringement	—	—
s.49(7)	Right for successor to rely on grant of licence	-	Not re-enacted
s.50	Transitional provisions	s.170	—
s.51	Title and Commencement	s.306	—

INDEX

Index

523

Index

Index

Index

SUBSEQUENT OWNERSHIP—*cont.*
future assignment,
Act of 1988, 8.13
practical importance, 8–15
pre–1956 Act, 8.12
prospective owner, death of, 8.14
generally, 8.01
insolvency,
bankruptcy,
individual, effect on, 8.25
special rule for, 8.28
liquidation of company, effect of,
8.26
royalty entitlement, 8.27
reversion of rights. *See* REVERSION
OF RIGHTS
SUBSTANTIAL PART
restricted acts, 5.09
SUBSTITUTED RIGHT
reversion of. *See* REVERSION OF
RIGHTS

TABLES
protection, 1.10
TELECOMMUNICATIONS SYSTEM
meaning, 1.55
transmission by, secondary
infringement, 6.58–6.61
TELEVISION
copying broadcasts, 5.20
photographs of programmes, 7.107
public performance via, 5.34
TERMINATION OF LICENSING
AGREEMENT. *See* LICENSING
TERMS AND CONDITIONS
licensing. *See* LICENSING
TERRITORY
presumptions on title, 10.37
restricted acts, 5.04–5.06
THIRD PARTY
contempt by, 10.79
THREATS
design rights, action relating to,
13.41
letters. *See* WARNING LETTERS
TIME-SHIFTING
recording for purposes of, 7.97
TITLE
presumptions on, 10.29–10.43
successors in, 9.15–9.22

TOPOGRAPHY
design rights, 13.45
TRADE
damages for injury to, 10.82
TRANSCRIPTION
existing material, of, 1.36
TRANSLATION RIGHTS
works made before July 1, 1912,
2.82
TRANSMISSION
place of, qualification by reference
to,
broadcasts, 2.24
cable programmes, 2.25
generally, 2.23
TRIAL
injunction at, 10.73–10.76
TRIBUNAL. *See* COPYRIGHT
TRIBUNAL
TYPOGRAPHICAL ARRANGEMENTS
copying, 5.21
duration of copyright, 4.62
first ownership,
existing works, 3.49
provisions of 1988 Act, 3.65
permitted acts, 7.75–7.85
published editions, of, 1.41–1.43
qualification for protection under
1956 Act, 2.41–2.43

UNDUE INFLUENCE
avoidance of contract, 8.63–8.72,
8.78–8.85
UNEXPLOITED WORK
duration of copyright, 4.12–4.15
UNKNOWN AUTHORSHIP
duration of copyright, 4.38–4.42
UNPERFORMED WORK
made before July 1, 1912, 2.77
UNPUBLISHED WORK
archives, copying by, 7.44
libraries, copying by, 7.44
made before July 1, 1912, 2.77

WAIVER
moral rights, 11.35
WARNING LETTERS
actionable, 10.08
contractual relations, unlawful
interference with, 10.10